D1733642

The Rise of Bronze Age Society

Beginning with state formation and urbanisation in the Near East *c.*3000 BC and ending in central and northern Europe *c.*1000–500 BC, the Bronze Age marks a heroic age of travels and transformations throughout Europe. In this book, Kristian Kristiansen and Thomas Larsson reconstruct the travel and transmission of knowledge that took place between the Near East, the Mediterranean and Europe. They explore how religious, political and social conceptions of Bronze Age people were informed by long-distance connections and alliances between local elites. The book integrates the hitherto separate research fields of European and Mediterranean (classical) archaeology and provides the reader with an alternative to the traditional approach of diffusionism. Examining data from across the region, the book presents an important new interpretation of social change in the Bronze Age, making it essential reading for students of archaeology, of anthropology and of the development of early European society.

KRISTIAN KRISTIANSEN is Professor at the Department of Archaeology, University of Gothenburg. His previous publications include *Europe before History* (Cambridge, 1998) and *Social Transformation in Archaeology* (with Mike Rowlands) (London and New York, 2000). He was the co-founder and first president of the European Association of Archaeologists and is a member of the Swedish Academy of History and Letters.

THOMAS B. LARSSON is Professor of Archaeology at the Department of Archaeology and Sami Studies, University of Umeå. He is the co-editor of *Approaches to Swedish Archaeology* (with Hans Lundmark) (Oxford, 1989). He has published four monographs in Swedish and English on the Scandinavian Bronze Age, including *The Bronze Age Metalwork of Southern Sweden* (Umeå, 1986), and is a Member of the Swedish Research Council.

The Rise of
Bronze Age Society

Travels, Transmissions and Transformations

KRISTIAN KRISTIANSEN
and
THOMAS B. LARSSON

CAMBRIDGE
UNIVERSITY PRESS

CAMBRIDGE UNIVERSITY PRESS
Cambridge, New York, Melbourne, Madrid, Cape Town, Singapore, São Paulo

Cambridge University Press
The Edinburgh Building, Cambridge CB2 2RU, UK

Published in the United States of America by Cambridge University Press, New York

www.cambridge.org
Information on this title: www.cambridge.org/9780521585675

First published 2005

Printed in the United Kingdom at the University Press, Cambridge

A catalogue record for this book is available from the British Library

Library of Congress Cataloguing in Publication data
Kristiansen, Kristian, 1948–
The rise of Bronze Age society: travels, transmissions and transformations / by Kristian
Kristiansen and Thomas B. Larsson.
    p.   cm.
Includes bibliographical references and index.
ISBN 0 521 84363 4 (hardback) 0 521 60466 4 (paperback)
1. Bronze Age.   2. Prehistoric peoples.   3. Religion, prehistoric.   4. Rites and ceremonies,
prehistoric.   5. Antiquities, prehistoric.   I. Larsson, Thomas B.   II. Title.
GN777.K75   2005   930.1′5 – dc22   2004058556

ISBN 13 978 0 521 84363 8 hardback
ISBN 0 521 84363 4 hardback
ISBN 13 978 0 521 60466 6 paperback
ISBN 0 521 60466 4 paperback

Contents

List of illustrations   vi

Preface   xiii

Prologue: between Scylla and Charybdis   1

1   A theoretical strategy for studying interaction   4

2   Odysseus: a Bronze Age archetype   32

3   Rulership in the Near East and the eastern Mediterranean during
the Bronze Age   62

4   Europe in the Early Bronze Age: an archaeological background   108

5   Symbolic transmission and social transformation in Bronze
Age Europe   142

6   The cosmological structure of Bronze Age society   251

7   Among gods and mortals, animals and humans   320

8   Cosmos and culture in the Bronze Age   357

Epilogue: towards a new Culture History   369

References   373

Index   425

Illustrations

1   Chart of the dynamic relationship between hierarchy and heterarchy.   *page* 9
2   Model of intercontextual strategies of interpretation.   12
3   Model of the structured transmission of a symbolic package of objects between different cultures.   14
4   Centre–periphery structure reflecting the traditional disciplinary boundaries between archaeology and history.   21
5   Diagram showing the relationship between the period and the locality of writing down texts and their true historical origin.   23
6   Diffusion patterns through time during the period preceding the Bronze Age.   26
7   Integrated interpretative model of the transmission and transformation of material culture.   30
8   Basic archaeological categories and their interpretative relationship.   34
9   Horizontal and vertical processes of prestige goods models.   36
10   Model of interaction between two cultural systems.   38
11   Relationship between internal and external processes of hierarchisation.   41
12   Model for how an elite may link themselves to mythological origins in a Bronze Age context.   46
13   External and internal strategy for the institutionalisation of authority and chieftainship. From *Access to Origins: Affines, Ancestors and Aristocrats* by Mary W. Helms, Copyright © 1998. By permission of the author and the University of Texas Press.   47
14   Interaction-model for the selective transmission and local adaptation of new institutions in Bronze Age Europe.   49
15   Model of processes of interaction and trade.   51
16   Congruence between time and space in long-distance travels. From *Craft and the Kingly Ideal: Art, Trade, and Power* by Mary W. Helms. Copyright © 1993. By permission of the author and the University of Texas Press.   54
17   Categories of outside specialists. From *Craft and the Kingly Ideal: Art, Trade, and Power* by Mary W. Helms. Copyright © 1993. By permission of the author and the University of Texas Press.   55
18   Model showing the inside–outside cycle of the accumulation and transformation of power and energies.   56
19   Rich chiefly burial with chisel for woodworking.   59
20   Naram-Sin's victory stele.   64
21   The top of Hammurabi's 'Law Code Stele'. Detail from photo by Archives Photographiques, Louvre.   66
22   Seal showing the goddess Inanna (Ishtar). Detail from photo by the Oriental Institute, University of Chicago.   69
23   Akhenaton worshipping Aten, the solar disc. Detail from photo by the Egyptian Museum, Cairo.   74
24   Adorer on rock art from Bohuslän; Egyptian *ka* sign; Egyptian *hai* sign.   76

25 Hattian bronze stags with silver inlays from Anatolia.   77
26 Scene from the battle of Kadesh.   82
27 Seals showing Minoan rulers (or priests) with symbolic axes carried as
    sceptres, and examples of such axe sceptres from Egypt and Anatolia from
    the eighteenth and seventeenth centuries BC.   85
28 Goddess smelling lilies.   87
29 Minoan and Mycenaean rhyta, showing the high degree of diffusion and
    ritual acculturation in the Aegean Bronze Age.   89
30 The major trade routes of the city-states of the Levant and Syria during the
    early second millennium.   91
31 Model of Old Assyrian trade system.   92
32 Similarities during the early second millennium BC (nineteenth–eighteenth
    centuries) in warrior prestige axes with ribbed shaft hole and personal dress
    pins with globe-shaped, rib-shaped and disc-shaped heads from Syria and
    Anatolia to central and northwestern Europe.   94
33 Two traditions of power: mainland Mycenaean monumental elite barrows
    and fortifications versus Minoan palaces and maritime trading colonies.   97
34 Scene from Egyptian tomb showing 'Keftiu'.   100
35 The route of the Ulu Burun shipwreck.   102
36 Minoan ships from the Thera frescos.   103
37 Estimated copper production from the major mining areas during the third
    and second millennia BC and system of mining shafts in Kargaly.   110
38 Theoretical model of the relationship between commodity production and
    its economic implications for measuring and the creation of new forms of
    exchange values, its political implications for creating new social values and
    a new organisation of exchange.   113
39 Map showing the distribution of ring ingot hoards in Europe.   114
40 Mixed Unetice hoard with ring ingots, halberds and armring ingots from
    zone II. Photo: Landesamt für archäologische Denkmalpflege,
    Sachsen-Anhalt, Halle.   115
41 Chart showing the use of tin in metal-using regions in the early second
    millennium BC and the areas with tin available.   115
42 Personal contacts between central Europe and the eastern Mediterranean as
    evidenced by the distribution of so-called *Schleifennadeln*-type toggle pins
    from around 2000 BC.   119
43 Rich chiefly burials of the Wessex–Brittany Culture and amber necklace
    from the golden barrow in Upton Lowell in Wiltshire.   121
44 The tin content in Bronze Age Crete from the Pre-Palatial to the Post-Palatial
    period and the composition and origin of copper in Bronze Age Crete,
    showing the change between the Old Palace and the New Palace periods.   124
45 Map showing the cultural and political territories of the
    Hungarian–Carpathian tell cultures from the seventeenth–sixteenth
    centuries BC.   126
46 Middle Bronze Age trade routes in the Carpathians linking the major tell
    settlements and the location of some important trade goods.   129
47 Chiefly or royal swords/daggers: comparison between the gold dagger from
    Pesinara and Minoan/Mycenaean daggers; warrior swords: comparison
    between Danish, French and Mycenaean flange-hilted swords.   130

48 Differential treatment of people during the Early Bronze Age: chiefly burial from Leubingen and killed individuals in pit from Nizná Mysla.   134
49 Graph of metal depositions in Denmark 2300–1500 BC, and diagram showing the use of tin in bronzes between 2300 and 1500 BC in the Nordic region and in central Europe.   136
50 The 'Lily Prince' from Knossos.   143
51 Women picking lilies. Fresco from Thera.   144
52 The 'Captain's Cabin' fresco from Thera and central European metal forms.   146
53 Hoards from Hungary with heart-shaped and lily-shaped pendants arranged in personal sets.   147
54 Carpathian clay figurines with decorated clothing and Minoan Snake Goddess from Crete. Published by permission from The Trustees of the British Museum.   148
55 Interpretation of some Carpathian bronze pendants as bodily symbols.   151
56 Fresco from Thera showing earring, and similar earrings from Crete, Hyksos settlement and the Tufalau hoard.   152
57 International similarities in female hairstyles linked to age and social roles.   153
58 Richly decorated pendants with chariot and sun symbolism from the early Urnfield period.   154
59 Two unique, and badly executed wheel-headed pins from Mycenae (B-circle) and Bohemia (female burial), testifying to personal contacts.   155
60 Map of metal (and wooden) cups from the Middle Bronze Age in Europe.   156
61 Minoan bronze cups from Akrotiri, the Aegean and Dohnsen, northern Germany.   157
62 Shared stylistic tradition in drinking cups of the sixteenth to early fourteenth centuries BC in northwestern Europe: shale cup from Wessex, metal and wooden cups from Denmark, and northern Germany.   157
63 Early spiral band decoration from the Mycenaean and Carpathian cultures.   159
64 Spiral band decoration on the circular disc on Carpathian axes and on Minoan seals from the Old Palace period.   160
65 Wall decorations from tell settlement at Feudvar and columns and wall decorations from Aegean and Carpathian sanctuaries and houses.   163
66 Ritual hearths decorated with spirals, from the Carpathians and from the palace in Pylos.   164
67 Libation tables with circular cupmark pattern from early and late Minoan culture, Crete, and similar patterns on libation tables and rock art from Bronze Age Scandinavia. Photo Thomas B. Larsson.   165
68 Model and enlarged entrance section of complex fortified settlement with drystone architecture, in Monkodonja, Istria.   166
69 The script of the Lipari Islands.   167
70 Hittite hieroglyphs found at Hattusha.   168
71 Rock art from Oppeby and a frame-figure from Himmelstalund, Östergötland.   169
72 Ground plan structure of the fortified settlement at Arkaim, compared with the smaller ground plan structure of the fortified settlement Dimircihuyuk in Anatolia.   174
73 Reconstruction of the fortification of Arkaim, smelting activity where well and furnaces are linked by the air supply tube, and part of a house made of wood and earthen bricks.   175

74 Horses were buried along with two-wheeled chariots. Detail from chariot burial, showing the use of disc-shaped cheek pieces, and sacrifice of horse skulls. — 176

75 Selection of chariot scenes from the Andronovo Culture and related cultures from central Asia, Kazakstan, Pamir and northwestern India. — 178

76 Examples of elaborate chiefly burials in shaft graves, covered by tholos or tumulus, and surrounded by a grave circle and ditch. — 180

77 Distribution of the specialised wavy band decoration on antler, bone and ivory, as presented in Fig. 78. — 182

78 Examples of wavy band decoration (mapped in Fig. 77), here mostly on handles for whips. — 183

79 Distribution of the three major types of bits in the chariot complex in Eurasia and the east Mediterranean during the early to mid second millennium BC. — 184

80 Historical eighteenth-century drawing of the Kivik cairn and the pictorial stones, and a modern documentation of the pictorial stones. — 188

81 Kivik pictorial stone with ritual axes, pointed hat and ship and its comparative context of antithetical, heraldic compositions from Minoan Crete to Hittite royal emblems. — 190

82 Signet ring from Tiryns from the fifteenth century BC and a scene from one of the cist stones of the Kivik burial. — 192

83 Axe and spiral motives from Kivik and some parallels from Europe and Mycenaean shaft graves. — 194

84 Ritual axes with hats and knobs from Hungary, and south Scandinavia. Photo: Lennart Larsen, The National Museum, Copenhagen. — 195

85 Wheel amulets from Hungary, wheel figures from the Wismar lur and rock art figures from western Sweden. — 196

86 Horse images from Sagaholm and bronze horse from Tågaborg. — 197

87 Imitations of the twin ship motif from Kivik on cist-stones from southern Norway (Jaeren) and southern Sweden (Järrestad). — 199

88 Selection of Hittite symbols from period 1 and 2 cult axes from Scandinavia, and their Hittite and Carpathian parallels. — 201

89 Ship with central European twin axes above it from Simris and the central European prototype from Austria also found in Scania. — 202

90 The thrones from Balkåkra and Hasfalva, and the Balkåkra throne-stool reconstructed. Photo: Christer Åhlin, The National Museum of Antiquities, Stockholm. — 203

91 The distribution of personal ornaments of Hungarian type and their spread northwards to the Baltic coast. — 205

92 Shared traditions in picturing ships during 1700–1500 BC. Minoan/Aegean prototype on Late MH pottery from Aegina and early Scandinavian ship images on metalwork and rock art. — 206

93 Founder's hoard from Djursland, Denmark, with eight identical and newly cast 'Hungarian' swords of type Apa. Photo: Søren Harboe. — 207

94 The distribution of Aegean rapiers and gold crowns, central European battle axes and early solid-hilted swords, and Mycenaean/central European gold cups. — 209

95 Lifetime cycle of travelling chief, converting travel in cosmological space to travel in cosmological time upon his return, death and heroic burial. — 210

96   Summary map of the two dominant interaction zones of the earlier second
     millennium BC: the steppe corridor and the Mediterranean corridor.   211
97   The Hajdúsámson hoard.   214
98   Rare warrior burial in the Carpathian region.   215
99   Distribution map of Mycenaean type A swords and flange-hilted swords and
     lances testifying to connections between the east Mediterranean, central
     Europe and northern Europe.   216
100 Resharpened sword blades from Nordic swords and flange-hilted swords.   219
101 The chariot group lined up at Frännarp, Sweden.   221
102 Photo taken (by Ulf Erik Hagberg) at the Hungarian National Museum,
     Budapest, of two Middle Bronze Age bronze chariot wheels from Arcalia,
     Romania.   222
103 Three chariots and charioteers as rock art: rock carving in Bohuslän,
     Sweden.   223
104 Monumental Bronze Age barrows from northern Jutland. Photo: John Jedbo.   226
105 Hittite, Mycenaean and Nordic male hairstyles.   228
106 Acrobats, dancers, bull-jumpers and rope swingers. Rock art images of feats
     and a bronze figurine from the south Scandinavian Bronze Age.   230
107 Distribution of octagonally hilted swords from Montelius period 2 against
     local groups/polities and intermarriage patterns of foreign women in graves. 233
108 Tholos grave of Mycenaean type from Istria in the northern Adriatic Sea.   236
109 Reconstructions of Middle Bronze Age female costumes and headdresses.   239
110 Two illustrations of the early phase of the construction of a tumulus.   243
111 Sun symbolism in the circular layout of stone constructions found under
     Early Bronze Age barrows.   244
112 The relationship between material culture and oral, written culture.   257
113 Minoan young 'god' with staff and the 'Master Impression'.   260
114 Kneeling goddess and horned snake. Bronze figurines from Faardal,
     Denmark.   261
115 Twin goddesses riding in their chariot, from the Hagia Triada sarcophagi,
     c.1400 BC.   262
116 Examples of twin depositions from the period 1700–1400 BC.   266
117 Two of the decorated cist-stones from the Kivik burial in Scania.
     Photo: T. B. Larsson.   268
118 Hittite round cap on a king with long robe/cloak and Nordic chiefly dress of
     cloak and tunic with round cap and a scimitar.   272
119 Tall simple cap from Guldhøj and complex round cap from Trindhøj, and
     Cypriotic bronze statue from Enkomi.   273
120 Scandinavian axe with 'hat' and twin figurines with hats from the Stockhult
     hoard, hat-shaped tutuli from burials and a bronze statuette of a Levantine
     storm-god with hat found in Schernen, Poland.   274
121 Twin axe bearers in Scandinavian rock art (Simris, Scania) from Montelius
     period 1.   275
122 A double burial of 'twin rulers' from Jutland.   276
123 Chiefly farm hall with two identical living quarters and stalling for cattle in
     the central part and a farm hall of identical size and construction lying
     parallel.   277
124 The twin rulers in Scandinavia – a summary of the interpretative structure. 278
125 Large chiefly farm hall from Bruatorp, near the town of Kalmar in Sweden.   279

126 Frescos from Knossos and Pylos showing two persons sitting on campstools drinking together. 282

127 Hittite king worshipping the weather-god in his bull-shaped form. 285

128 The god of 'the open lands' standing on his stag. 287

129 Rock art showing a stag and a sun-wagon. 287

130 The 'God of War' at the King's Gate at Boghazköy. 289

131 Three rock art panels from Yazilikaya. 292

132 Hittite seals with a winged sun-cross. 293

133 The famous sun-chariot from Trundholm, Denmark. Photo: Christer Åhlin, The National Museum of Antiquities, Stockholm. 295

134 Cosmology of Bronze Age Scandinavia expressed by the find from Trundholm. 296

135 The Egtved woman's dress. Danish press photo. 299

136 The Hesselagergård woman with belt plate. 300

137 The woman from Tobøl, with a bronze wheel at her belly. 301

138 Campstool and cups from Guldhøj. 304

139 Models of the sun journey during Montelius periods 1 and 2 and during the later Bronze Age. 306

140 The sun journey and its accompanying transport animals during the Late Bronze Age. 309

141 Early Hittite bronze figurines from the seventeenth–sixteenth centuries BC and kneeling female figurine from Faardal in Denmark. 310

142 Distribution of bronze figurines from Scandinavia and northern central Europe. 311

143 The two bronze figurines from the Stockhult hoard. 312

144 Scheme for some Nordic artefacts and their counterparts in the Near East and eastern Mediterranean area. 314

145 Hittite statuette from Dövlek. 315

146 Central material attributes of the Divine Twins in the Early and Late Bronze Age compared. 318

147 Egyptian representation of the god Athum with a scarab as head. 322

148 Rock art showing a horned snake from Vitlycke. After Arkeologisk rapport från Vitlyckemuséet 1. Photo: Torsten Högberg. 323

149 Bronze statuette of stallion–human relationship from Anatolia and a Scandinavian rock art depiction of a similar relationship (photo: T. B. Larsson). 325

150 Horse pulling the sun-disc. Rock art image from Balken in Bohuslän, Sweden. 326

151 Bulls from Aspeberget and bird-man and mare from Kallsängen. Bohuslän, Sweden. 327

152 Scenes from the Sagaholm pictorial slabs depicting the myth of the birth of the Ashvinau. 327

153 Minoan ox head with horns and a double axe between the horns. Similar image from Late Bronze Age head from Fogtdarp in southern Sweden. 330

154 Rock art from Bohuslän, Sweden, showing horned divinities. 331

155 Representations of horned divinities from the Near East, Cyprus and Europe. 332

156 The location of rock art in a Swedish landscape of today. Photo: T. B. Larsson. 336

157 Plan of the Kivik area with cult buildings, and ground plans for Sandagergård and Kivik. 338

158   Rock art figure with phallus and raised arm gesture. Photo: T. B. Larsson.   340

159   Ritual axes from Viby and Bredebækgård, and decorated bottom on belt box
worn by sun priests.   341

160   The 'goddess' from Fossum – rock carving from Bohuslän, Sweden.
Photo: T. B. Larsson.   342

161   The 'sun-discs' from Fossum and Aspeberget.   343

162   Warrior depictions and a hunting scene with bow and arrow from Fossum,
Bohuslän. Photo: T. B Larsson.   345

163   *Hieros Gamos* scenes from Vitlycke and Jörlov.   346

164   Depiction of stag hunt from Massleberg.   347

165   A scene with a boar hunt from Himmelstalund.   347

166   Two antithetically arranged goats. Rock art from Himmelstalund,
Östergötland.   348

167   Cosmological model of Bronze Age landscape.   354

168   Model of overlapping cultural distributions and gender identities in Bronze
Age Europe.   362

169   Simulated socio-seismographic curve of the realisation of agency over time.   370

170   Theoretical model of the dynamic relationship between long-term tradition
and short-term transformation and their internal articulation.   370

Preface

This book wanted to be written. That is the only way to explain its birth. It emerged unexpectedly during a dinner between the two authors in late August 1998, pushed aside other publishing plans, and before the evening had come to an end we had sketched the content and agreed on a timetable. Both were to be modified several times in the course of writing, but the inspiration remained intact.

The historical background to this joint venture was based upon the convergence of our research interests during recent years. In 1997 Thomas B. Larsson published an interpretative essay about relations between the Near East and the Nordic Bronze Age (*Materiell kultur och religiösa symboler*), based upon Near Eastern/Hittite texts and material evidence from Scandinavia. At the same time Kristian Kristiansen had completed *Europe before History* (1998), where space did not allow the second millennium much room. The unfulfilled scope of both our works on this period made it obvious to join forces in a new book spanning the Bronze Age world in its entirety, from Mesopotamia to Scandinavia. We wished to approach the Bronze Age as historical epoch, going beyond a world system approach, by reconstructing the travels and the transmission of knowledge that took place between the Near East, the Mediterranean and Europe. In doing so, we are aware that western Europe has been somewhat neglected in our case studies. However, that would have demanded yet another book. We were therefore happy to realise that Richard Harrison had worked on such a manuscript, titled 'Symbols and warriors: images of the European Bronze Age' (although mainly covering the Late Bronze Age), that went to the publishers about the time we finished our manuscript.

In selecting relevant evidence and avoiding the worst academic pitfalls we have benefited from the advice of Professor Folke Josephsson (on Hittite and Vedic texts) and Professor Robin Hägg (Minoan/Mycenaean religion), both of Göteborg University. We also held an integrated research seminar in the fall of 1999 between the prehistoric and classical departments of archaeology in Göteborg. We thank all participants for lively and inspirational discussions. In March 2000 we ended the seminar with a small symposium, to which we invited a few scholars with whom we shared a yearlong academic co-operation and interest in the role of travels and trade in later prehistory. The discussions emanating from this meeting added the last touch to the manuscript and some important additional literature. Here we would like to thank Professor Mary W. Helms, North Carolina, Professor Mogens Trolle Larsen, Copenhagen, and Professor Andrew Sherratt, Oxford, in particular, for their comments and valuable contributions to the symposium discussion, but also to a later draft version of the manuscript. For productive and critical comments on the manuscript we also thank Inga Ullén, Stockholm, Volker Heyd, Bristol, and Timothy Earle, Northwestern University. Per Persson skilfully transformed many sketchy hand-drawings into beautiful figures and did most of the artwork for illustrations. The following figures have been produced by Thomas B. Larsson: 12, 14, 24a, 67d, 90b, 103, 106, 117, 125, 134, 142, 143, 144, 150, 151, 154, 155, 156, 158, 160. One of us (KK) had the opportunity to spend the fall of 2003 in Cambridge lecturing on the book, and giving lectures in other British universities and in Berlin, which helped to clarify points of uncertainty in the final editing before submitting the manuscript to the Press. Finally, we wish to thank our friends and colleagues throughout Europe and North America for maintaining an exchange network of offprints and books. Even the best library cannot compete with the personal dynamic of academic networks.

After little more than five years with our project we are now ready – and happy – to leave the final result in the hands of colleagues and students. We learned a lot in the process and hopefully readers will share some of our excitement during the Odyssey.

Prologue: between Scylla and Charybdis

In this book we set out on a risky academic Odyssey, crossing between several research cultures and theoretical paradigms, with the danger of either hitting unknown rocks and getting stranded or calling down upon us the wrath of paradigmatic rulers for being theoretically incorrect. However, we resisted the alluring temptation of settling in one of the safe paradigms and insisted stubbornly upon trying out an interdisciplinary, interpretative journey based upon the identification of social institutions in the archaeological record, and their transmission and transformation in different cultural and social environments. More precisely: in the Bronze Age. We propose that the Age of Bronze represents a historical epoch that was qualitatively different from both the preceding Neolithic and the subsequent Iron Age. Beginning with state formation and urbanisation in the Near East around 3000 BC and ending in central and northern Europe between 1000 and 500 BC, it marks the heroic age of travels, cultural transmissions and social transformations throughout the whole region. It was accompanied by the rise of new forms of cultural and social identity, but also by a new political economy (Earle 2002).

In chapters 1 and 2 we outline the theoretical and ethnohistorical background for our interpretative enterprise, and in chapters 3 and 4 we give an outline of rulership, trade and interaction in the Near East and in Europe. In chapter 5 we employ this framework in an analysis of cultural relations between the Near East, the Mediterranean world and Europe during the early and mid second millennium BC. In chapters 6 and 7 we demonstrate the organising role of religion and shared cosmologies, before drawing conclusions about the historical role of the Bronze Age in chapter 8.

When adopting such a framework it became painfully clear to us that present research cultures are unable to cope with the geographical and temporal scope of Bronze Age civilisations. With few exceptions they take on the perspective of local cultures and do not see far beyond local or regional borders (Kristiansen 2001b; Smith 2003). It is a point we wish to make that Bronze Age research is thereby missing an essential aspect of this epoch – the importance of travel and journeys, of trade and interactions. This led to a widespread transmission and transformation of social institutions with a Near Eastern/Mediterranean background in large parts of Bronze Age Europe – it is perhaps the most characteristic element of that epoch. But the influences went both ways. This makes it easier to understand why

1

and how the 'centres and peripheries' communicated, and why and how the 'peripheries' in some periods would run down or dominate the centres. They were less peripheral than we have hitherto assumed, and they shared some of the basic technological, military and ritual 'equipage' of the centre, though locally adopted and transformed.

It was Oscar Montelius who in a masterly synthesis *Die älteren Kulturperioden im Orient und in Europa* in 1903 for the first time established the typological/diffusionist context for linking the Copper and Bronze Ages in Europe with the Mediterranean and the Near East (Montelius 1903). Later Gordon Childe in several books added a social and economic explanation to this historical relationship, notably in *The Bronze Age* (Childe, 1930). However, after the Second World War Bronze Age research became increasingly regional and local in scope, with a few exceptions (Müller-Karpe 1980).

We believe these constraints in present research cultures have precluded archaeologists from grasping the otherness – or the unfamiliarity – of the Bronze Age. As one of us concluded in the book *Europe before History*: 'But the Bronze Age may also teach us about our own foreignness – the peoples of the Bronze Age lived in a world that we will never fully understand without understanding its otherness' (Kristiansen 1998a: 419).

To familiarise ourselves with the unfamiliar we applied the ethnohistorical knowledge of travels and skilled crafting and their cosmological role in premodern societies (presented in chapter 2). Here we relied especially on the pioneering works of Mary Helms (Helms 1988, 1993 and 1998). In addition we employed the contemporary written evidence from the Near East and the east Mediterranean, in order to reconstruct the full complexity of Bronze Age societies (presented in chapter 3). We further applied some of the relevant songs and epics, and we reclaim the *Iliad*, the *Odyssey* and the Irish myths and sagas as representing what is essentially a Late Bronze Age cosmology and ethos. We have reached this conclusion from an archaeological position and perspective, simply by demonstrating on archaeological grounds that this is their proper historical context. In doing so we situate the Bronze Age in protohistory (Bietti Sestieri 1996), if not in historical archaeology (Andrén 1998) or in cultural history (Morris 2000).

We were also encouraged by the innovative Aegean research environment that has developed since the 1980s, not least the many seminar and conference proceedings on such central issues as 'The Minoan Thalassocracy', 'Celebrations of Death and Divinity' or 'The Role of the Ruler', to mention but a few. In combination with a number of incredible new archaeological discoveries, such as the fully loaded Ulu Burun shipwreck from the fourteenth century BC, or the bronze disc from Nebra in Germany with sun, moon and stars, it made our task much easier (Meller 2004). We recognise that central European and north European Bronze Age research still has a long way to go in terms of interpretations. Instead we have profited from the often very systematic and well-published evidence, such as *Prähistorische Bronzefunde*, or the wonderfully illustrated catalogue on the Bronze Age by Herman Müller-Karpe in his impressive series *Handbuch der Vorgeschichte* (Müller-Karpe 1980).

The working title of our book was for several years 'The Long Journey'. It carried a double meaning. On the one hand it refers to the main theme of the book – the overarching role of travels in the Bronze Age. But it also alludes to the long journey it took archaeology, before it could approach this subject again.

Our Odyssey is of course doomed to be insufficient in numerous aspects of empirical knowledge. We are experts on neither ethnohistory, Hittite texts, Minoan rituals nor Indo-European religion. We hope, however, that our interpretations will command enough interest to make any factual omissions of less importance. And we further hope to have demonstrated the relevance of an interdisciplinary, culture-historical approach to the study of the Bronze Age. The reason being very simple and straightforward: to match the forces of history as they unfolded during the Bronze Age it is necessary to mobilise the collective forces of historical knowledge.

1 A theoretical strategy for studying interaction

Progress normally has a hidden underside, which will often not be recognised until much later. Our own time is full of such examples. The unforeseen side of industrialisation was environmental pollution. In science we may observe similar effects. The rise of a new paradigm to dominance often leads to the complete abandonment of the old, with the unforeseen effect that certain phenomena are left unexplained even in the new paradigm, which over time leads to increasing imbalances. Such was the case when processual and later postprocessual archaeology abandoned the old cultural historical framework of diffusion to account for cultural change. As a consequence explanations in archaeology have become increasingly local and historically unbalanced. The dominant paradigms have not developed the necessary theoretical and interpretative tools to deal with cultural interaction in all its variety, from travels to population movements, and the impact this may have on local and regional developments.[1]

This book attempts to remedy some of these theoretical flaws in current archaeological thinking, by proposing a new theoretical and interpretative framework for understanding cultural interaction and its effects. We like to think of the present stage in archaeology as more mature and less one-sided and paradigmatic (postparadigmatic perhaps) than earlier stages, and 'pluralism' has become a popular buzz-word to account for that. We hope that this is more than rhetoric, and that reality allows the reintroduction, not of a past, obsolete paradigm but of theoretical and interpretative concepts that account for real historical phenomena and therefore belong to the interpretative repertoire of archaeology.

1.1 Limitations in present theoretical frameworks

In this chapter we propose to develop an explicit theoretical strategy for the interpretation and explanation of interregional interaction. We consider such processes as having played a major role in later European prehistory, more precisely during the Bronze Age and Early Iron Age. 'During the

1 We note, however, that recent developments in strontium isotope analysis of teeth and bone are producing new compelling evidence of the movement of individuals in prehistory (Ezzo, Johnson and Price 1997; Grupe *et al.* 1997; Price, Grupe and Schröter 1998; Montgomery, Budd and Evans 2000; Price, Manzilla and Middleton 2000). This is now beginning to have an impact also on interpretative frameworks (e.g. Shennan 2000). So, sooner or later archaeology will have to come to grips with these new realities.

4

Bronze Age there emerged a truly international network of metal trade and exchange, making all regions dependent upon each other, despite their different cultural traditions. The question of external versus internal factors in promoting change therefore became crucial' (Kristiansen 1998a: 1). We shall exemplify this in subsequent chapters by analysing the structure and processes of interaction between the Mediterranean and central and northern Europe during the second millennium BC. Our ambition is to go beyond a macro-historical framework of centre–periphery, world system theory by dissolving specific historical processes of interregional interaction into their various symbolic, economic and social components to trace their selective, local impact in the process. As argued by John Barrett (1998), we should further situate our interpretations in the lived experience and human motivations to enter and participate in such networks, a point to be demonstrated at length in subsequent chapters.

Before we proceed, however, we need to point out briefly some constraints in present theoretical frameworks for the development of interaction studies.

The processual and postprocessual archaeologies of the last generation have one thing in common: an autonomous perspective. The local or regional unit is their favourite frame of theoretical and interpretative reference, and academic references consequently rarely transcend national or regional borders. This has led to an unintended but dangerous autonomy of learning, which is confined behind national borders and language borders (Cornell, Fahlander and Kristiansen 1998; Kristiansen 2002a). Since history is not constrained by present traditions of learning, major processes of prehistoric interaction and change are being relegated from serious study in the present archaeological frameworks of theory and interpretation. We propose that this situation needs to be changed, if theoretical and historical knowledge is to proceed.

Research traditions tend to oscillate between oppositions, like a historical pendulum (Kristiansen 1996a: Fig. 4; Sherratt 1996a: Fig. 1). In an academic context the autonomous framework of processual and postprocessual archaeology may be understood as a necessary reaction against an overt diffusionism of the first half of the twentieth century, which became obsolete after the decline and partial collapse of its interpretative and chronological framework after the Second World War. Colin Renfrew was the first to link these two processes together as a historical background for promoting a new autonomous perspective on European prehistory (Renfrew 1973 and 1984). The methodological and theoretical reorganisation of archaeology that followed has during the last generation produced a completely new historical picture of the social and economic foundations of prehistoric communities, summarised in several introductions to archaeology in recent years.

Ian Hodder and postprocessual archaeology enlarged this framework by adding to it a new understanding of symbolic meaning and the role of culture and human agency in social strategies, whether in the household or at local cultural boundaries (Hodder 1982a, 1982b, 1986) – but rarely beyond. Instead attention has been focused on the cultural construction of the surrounding landscape (Bender 1993; Tilley 1994) and its monuments (Barrett 1989 and 1994; Bradley 1993 and 2002).

If processual and postprocessual archaeology may be said to have provided archaeology with the theoretical and methodological tools for understanding prehistoric social organisation and cosmology at local and regional levels, they have failed in extending this beyond local and regional borders. Although interesting attempts have been made (Renfrew and Cherry 1986) they have not been persuasive beyond the regional polity. It was developments in social anthropology (Wolf), history (Braudel, Wallerstein) and sociology (Mann) which were integrated into a new theoretical and interpretative framework of centre–periphery and world systems by Jonathan Friedman and Mike Rowlands that provided such a perspective. This new framework was applied to archaeology to account for the interaction between local, regional and global or macro-historical changes in later prehistory (Rowlands, Larsen and Kristiansen 1987; Bintliff 1991; Sherratt 1997b; Kristiansen 1998a; Kristiansen and Rowlands 1998; Kardulias 1999; Denemark, Friedman, Gills and Modelski 2000; Chew 2001).

Limitations in this theoretical framework are rather linked to its macro-historical perspective and its general assumption of dominance (Stein 1999: ch. 2), although one of us has recently made an attempt to add to it theoretical concepts at a middle-range level of interpretation (Kristiansen 1998a: ch. 3). From this study emerged an understanding of the specific historical conditions that characterised the Bronze Age world system and made it different from the modern world system: 'What makes the Bronze Age so special is linked to the nature of centre–periphery relations that characterized the first and second millennia BC. By adopting the mastery of metallurgy, the rituals of status and the innovations of warfare from the east Mediterranean, but not the political and economic framework sustaining it, new social and economic dynamics were introduced to the societies of temperate Europe' (Kristiansen 1998a: 418). Following Edens and Kohl, the most characteristic differences between the ancient and the modern world systems are: 'the existence of multiple centres; logistical constraints impeding movements of materials, especially staples, along overland routes; the omnipresent military option to raid rather than trade; and technologies common to both peripheries and centres. These differences suggest that dependencies in the modern sense only rarely characterised centre–periphery relations in the ancient world' (Edens and Kohl 1993: 31).

We wish to explore in more detail these generalisations, and their proposed nature of interregional interaction.

What is needed, to do that, is a more explicit theoretical and interpretative strategy allowing us to trace and dissolve processes of interaction at a more fine-grained level of analysis. This was formulated quite precisely in a recent contribution to interaction studies: 'The ultimate goal of interaction research is to write "total histories" (Kohl 1987: 29) of ancient societies, histories which place local developments within the rich network of connections any one society maintained. In order to meet this objective, we need to construct a paradigm which, among other steps, identifies analytical units and the conditions under which intersocietal contacts are likely to have particular sociopolitical effects' (Shortman and Urban 1992b: 248).

We share this goal, and we consequently consider it obsolete to discuss the complexity of interaction research in traditional terms of 'falling into either an autonomist or a diffusionist trap'. Arafat and Morgan recently exemplified this problematic in a discussion of the Hallstat D residences. They argue that any investigation of material culture taking its stance in exchange and trade 'impedes understanding of local material behaviour and social development' (Arafat and Morgan 1994: 130). We do not share this standpoint, and a critique of their position has been delivered by Andrew Sherratt (1995) (see also Sherratt and Sherratt 1998).[2]

In this book we wish to abandon the whole terminology dealing with concepts of either autonomy or diffusion, and develop a new conceptual framework that accounts for the complexity of prehistoric interaction. Such studies are now beginning to appear, e.g. Stein (1999), proposing and testing two models of interaction in the early state system of Uruk: the 'distance-parity' and the 'trade-diaspora' models. It suggests that there exists a whole range of interregional relations that need to be developed, theoretically based on particular case studies. However, the theoretical traditions described above were developed in a specific academic context to address certain types of problems, and therefore to some extent were also developed in opposition to each other. It will therefore be necessary to do some critical conceptual 'cleaning' in order to redefine a new theoretical position that is neither diffusionism nor functionalism: a perspective that takes as its point of departure the interpretation and explanation of symbolic transmission and social transformation as a complex and selective process that took place and affected simultaneously both interregional and local conditions.

2 The internal/external approach was also played out in two papers by Patrice Brun and Michael Dietler in the *Journal of European Archaeology* (Brun 1995; Dietler 1995). In the debate different levels of explanation are taken to represent different theoretical approaches, leading to a polemic which tends to obscure the legitimacy of both perspectives. It reflects the need to develop a more complex theoretical framework that is able to integrate world system analysis with local and regional studies.

We propose therefore as a first step in our theoretical strategy to examine critically the concepts that in the past have been used to address such phenomena from different theoretical positions, and then to recontextualise and redefine their meaning within a new interpretative framework.

1.2 From social typology to social complexity: the role of institutionalisation

Institutionalisation and its role in the development of social complexity have become a growing concern in recent years (Stein 1998; Earle 2001; Runciman 2001). A series of conference reports and books published during the 1990s marks this research trend, which derives from the basic question: how does a minority of people achieve control over a majority of people, and how are they able to maintain their power (Price and Feinman 1995; Earle 1997)? While the answer seems simple – through institutionalisation (one of the primary criteria of power in chiefdoms and ranked societies)[3] – the process itself is poorly understood and it has become increasingly clear that even institutions themselves are complex and deserve further study. We shall take up two main areas of research relevant to our inquiry: resistance to social hierarchy and the derived concept of heterarchy.

While the nature of power was a main focus of research during the 1980s in an attempt to move beyond the social typologies of the 1970s, the interest shifted during the 1990s towards the failure of – or the difficulties in establishing – stable power relations. This can be seen as a natural outcome of the increasing knowledge of power relations acquired during the 1980s. Resistance to state formation was taken on to the research agenda in the late eighties (Patterson and Gailey 1987; Miller, Rowlands and Tilley 1989), together with a growing interest in the formation of political institutions and social complexity in non-state societies (Brumfiel and Earle 1987; Upham 1990; Earle 1991). As a result there appeared during the 1990s several major works on the evolutionary significance of resistance to state formation and colonisation in a macro- and micro-historical perspective (Dietler 1995; Kristiansen 1998a; Morris 1999b). These were followed up by studies in the processes of establishing and maintaining power in individual historical cases and in comparative contexts (Hedeager 1992; Helms 1993; Kolb 1994; Pauketat 1994 and 2000; Blanton *et al.* 1996; Earle 1997; Ruby 1999; Arnold 2000; Smith 2003). One aspect of this new research is an increasing knowledge and realisation of the complexity of the process (Feinman 1995; Hayden 1995; Morris 1999; Adams 2001) and the resulting variability in

---

3 We recognise the more universal role of institutions in the evolution and formation of social life, as demonstrated by Foley (2001) and Richerson and Boyd (2001).

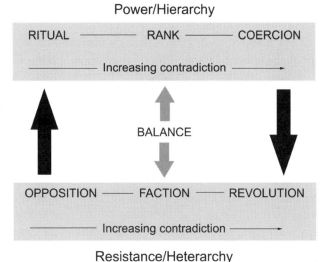

Fig. 1 Chart of the dynamic relationship between hierarchy and heterarchy.

the organisation of society (Feinman 2000; Renfrew 2001a, 2001b; Chapman 2003).

These insights have been accompanied by research into the complexity of social institutions and groupings. Especially, Elizabeth Brumfiel has drawn attention to the diversity of organisational properties in prestate societies, which are linked to different interests. Factionalism is the concept she employed to account for the constant tendency of splitting up existing groupings and institutions into competing factions (Brumfiel and Fox 1994). Carole Crumley further developed the theoretical understanding of the instability of hierarchies and the formation of alternative non-rigorous power relations by coining the concept of heterarchy, as opposed to hierarchy (Crumley 1987 and 2001; Ehrenreich, Crumley and Levy 1995). It takes as its point of departure that hierarchies are rarely fixed and one-dimensional, and stresses the flexibility of power relations and the potential for flexibility and fluctuations (Fig. 1). As stated by Crumley: 'While hierarchy undoubtedly characterizes power relations in some societies, it is equally true that coalitions, federations, and other examples of shared or counterpoised power abound. The addition of the term heterarchy to the vocabulary of power relations reminds us that forms of order exist that are not exclusively hierarchical and that interactive elements in complex systems need not be permanently ranked relative to each other' (Crumley 1995: 5). This would seem to represent an important additional property of hierarchy, with a potential for widening our understanding of the concept (McIntosh 1999). Although the basic realities of hierarchy in chiefdom societies are rarely changed (such as that between elites and commoners), they may oscillate around a number of variants (Helms 1998: ch. 9).[4]

Thus we may conclude that although institutionalisation represents an essential ingredient in the formation of more complex and ranked societies, it does not automatically lead to further institutional formalisation. Institutions are flexible and adaptive as they are integrated in networks of alliances and exchange, which are the basic instruments for gaining access to and maintaining power, to be discussed in more detail in the next chapter. Another consequence of the adaptive capacity of institutions is their long-term persistence, which will be demonstrated in chapter 5.

The implications of this brief survey are that we need to study institutions in order to build up an understanding of the organisational properties of society from the ground, so to speak. Such studies should further be culturally and historically specific. We are not proposing to revert back to a general study of institutions in chiefdoms or states. Chiefly institutions existed universally, but they cover a wide variety of organisational forms and therefore need to be dissolved into institutional properties that are historically specific, in order to understand the conditions and causes of complexity (Earle 1997; Haas 2001). How was rulership institutionalised, what institutional forms did warrior retinues or religious institutions, etc. take, and how were they interlinked vertically and horizontally? Warriors may be part of an institution of chiefly retinues (a vertical relationship), but they may also be part of an institutionalised horizontal relationship of warrior sodalities that allowed them to move geographically. It may further be sustained by kinship systems, as we shall later demonstrate in chapter 4. Such an approach has significant theoretical and methodological implications, which we shall now develop.

1.3   Towards an intercontextual archaeology: material culture and social institutions

In this section we wish to propose a new, theoretically more profitable approach to the study of institutions and interaction in the Bronze Age, and

---

4 In much recent postprocessual interpretative theorising these conditions have been described in terms of negotiations, stressing the role of human agency. We find these concepts too ideologically loaded with liberal, western connotations, as if chiefs and commoners, men and women in the Bronze Age were autonomous individuals sitting around a table negotiating, ending up signing a contract, a terminology sometimes employed (Derevenski and Sørensen 2002). While such concepts may help us to redirect and focus interest on new problems, they are in our opinion counterproductive for a deeper understanding of the nature of such processes in prehistoric societies. It demands the development of concepts based upon the study of real situations in real societies in the ethnographic past or in ancient myth and literature. We are here in agreement with Julian Thomas, that individuals are not autonomous (Thomas 2002: 38ff.)

indeed more universally. Instead of traditional random studies of the spatial distribution of cultural traits, whose significance is then evaluated within a more general historical or evolutionary model, we propose to begin by studying the transmission and transformation of social institutions – economic, political and religious – since all societies are organised around institutions. It is the institutionalised, codified behaviour of social, economic or religious actions and transactions, performed by specialists, that makes up the building blocks of society. As a first step we must therefore adopt an interpretative strategy that will allow us to identify institutions in the archaeological record. It is based upon the assumption that institutions materialise in specific and recurring ways that allow one to infer their cultural and historical formation and transmission in time and space (Renfrew 1986; De Marrais, Castillo and Earle 1996).

By this the focus is shifted from tracing and discussing random similarities in material culture to studying the transmission and possible transformation of the structured material evidence of social institutions in time and space. Meaning is attached to the role of such institutions. In this way it will be possible to evaluate the social and historical significance of former typological indications in a completely new light. It is not the typological degree of similarity in style or form that is decisive, but the adoption of a whole new set of values, their structured materialisation in iconography, ruling regalia, monuments, building, etc., to form an institution which becomes decisive and therefore the object of analysis and interpretation. We need to rediscover those lost intercontextual meanings that once unified such different material remains in an institution. In the past they would have been understood as being part of common myth and ritual events, while in the present they are separated and studied individually as archaeological categories, such as hoards, burials, settlements, etc. But as stated by Barrett: 'An understanding of the practices which took place in the context of either the enclosure or the mortuary ritual must consider how these practices referred to other, absent places from which the practitioners came and to which they may have returned' (1994: 74). To rediscover these lost intercontextual meanings demands an integrated, holistic approach, where the point of departure is the structured symbolic relationships that once defined an institutional relationship.

We call this an intercontextual archaeology, and we propose an interpretative strategy where one or several central symbols are identified and traced throughout the contexts where they appear, thereby linking them together in a cosmological or ritual field of intercontextual meaning. In the process the complexity of the symbolic and ritual messages is encircled. Secondly a relation of symbols in a specific context is analysed to understand their meaning. This adds meaning and depth to the previously encircled symbolic field at specific points of contexts. In Figure 2 we have exemplified

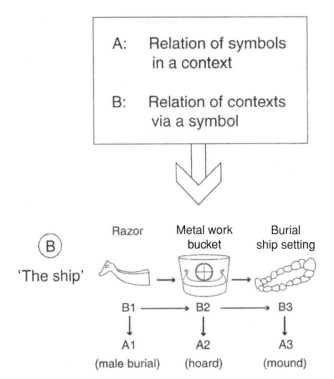

Fig. 2 Model of intercontextual strategies of interpretation.

such an interpretative strategy, and we will later apply it to concrete case studies.

Thus, an intercontextual, interpretative strategy implies, first, to trace central symbols throughout all the contexts where they appear, and second, to interpret and reconstruct the meaning and institutional structure of this new intercontextual universe in time and space. The latter, however, meets with severe difficulties, as changing material culture often makes it difficult to trace such symbols beyond their own cultural context, if traditional methods of typology are employed. We therefore need to discuss the relationship between style and symbolic structures briefly.

Style and form are linked to social and cultural conventions that produce a shared symbolic identity for social groups or communities at large. Institutional influences are thus impossible to evaluate on purely typological grounds, as most cultures have strategies for recontextualising imports and borrowing into their own cultural idioms to make them look familiar. Exceptions to this rule are periods when the input of new technologies and cultural influences are too big to be immediately assimilated, often being part of the adoption of new technologies and value systems that take time to digest. In many regions the Early Bronze Age represented such a period, characterised by a widespread flow of foreign people and goods (so-called imports or imitations) throughout Europe. It raises a whole series of questions about the formation, consolidation and dissolution/transformation of local and regional style groups. Later we shall discuss the relation between the formation of new social and religious institutions and the formation of a new material culture to symbolise and identify them. Our main concern here, however, is to suggest that what on purely typological and stylistic grounds may look like different 'cultures' may through an analysis of social and religious institutions turn out to be rather similar societies, at least in certain selective areas, characterised by mutual contacts. Such similarities, however, tend to 'disappear' through translation into the local cultural dialects. What is left may be a handful of imported prestige goods and some 'influence' or imitations in style and form.

Thus if we are able to trace a new institution and its adaptation throughout several cultures and societies in Europe, we have a new basis for evaluating the social and historical impact of interaction, which comparative typological studies can only hint at. An example of this is the diffusion of the institution of warrior aristocracies (Kristiansen 1987 and 1998a; Treherne 1995) and of religious institutions in the Bronze Age (Larsson 1997).

The problem of understanding the social and historical implications of interaction is due to a lack a theoretical categorisation of the evidence, making it suitable for historical interpretation. We suggest that archaeologically we know enough, but have not yet done the interpretative groundwork. We need to give up our archaeological terminology for a moment and translate the evidence into meaningful social, economic and cosmological categories. These should not be studied separately, since it is their selective combination that defines various types of institutions. Thus, when studying interaction, typological evidence may lead us on the way, but it may also betray us. Diffusion is the archaeological term for this phenomenon, but it does not tell us anything about the significance of the observed changes. Certain items and styles may be superficially and randomly applied, if contacts are superficial. But if they involve a recurring interaction over longer periods of time, this may lead to mutual and selective borrowing of more complex value systems and institutions, in the process transforming social organisation (Fig. 3). Thus, it is only by understanding the social, economic and religious institutions and their various forms of integration that we are able to evaluate the nature of interaction between the different societies in the east Mediterranean and central Europe.[5]

5 This approach could have significant implications for understanding not only social and cultural change, but also changes in language, if the terminology linked to new institutions follows them, as suggested recently by Colin Renfrew for Minoan language (Renfrew 1998a). This may account for widespread similarities in Indo-European vocabulary on horses and chariots, for example. Consequently questions of population movements may be evaluated in a new light, as it becomes possible to distinguish between small-scale movements of select groups of people (specialists, traders, warriors, etc.) against conquest and more massive population movements.

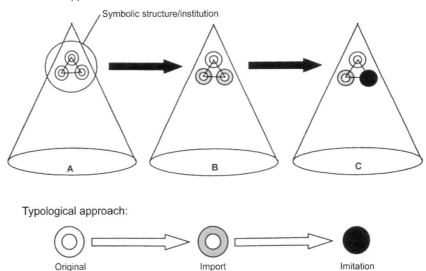

Fig. 3 Model of the structured transmission of a symbolic package of objects between different cultures, which change type or form on the way (imports into local imitations) while the structure and meaning remain intact. This is compared to a traditional typological approach.

In conclusion, institutions materialise in specific and recurring ways that allow one to infer the cultural and institutional significance of the evidence (De Marrais, Castillo and Earle 1996; Earle 1997: ch. 5). We need to decode the symbolic grammar of institutional behaviour as it materialised in the archaeological record. This has to be done for each region under study, so that we are able to compare those *recurring contextual relationships that define institutional relationships*. These may be movable, in the form of certain types of objects – or immovable, in the form of certain types of monuments, architecture, paintings, ceremonies, etc. The problem – or the challenge – is that foreign material evidence is often translated into the local cultural language, which means that only bits and pieces of the original evidence survive. It is acculturated and recontextualised. However, in this process the original meaning and message are often carried on in a selective way, leading to the adoption of new value systems, practices and eventually institutions to reinforce them. If that is the case it is only by interpreting and comparing institutions that we are able to understand, and eventually to explain, the true historical impact of social and economic interaction between societies.

In the study of institutional change we are confronted with the difficult task of analysing and understanding the dynamic relations between agency and convention, event and structure. To do that we must attempt to trace the socially and culturally determined motives and incentives for individuals to travel and to adopt new values and behaviours. And in similar ways: the motives and incentives to resist change. As such social tensions are played out by people, we need to identify those groups who had the capacity to adopt or to resist new values and behaviours. 'If we are studying peer polity interaction, it is thus of particular importance to consider circumstances in which individual members of different polities are likely to have met. Circumstances where competition and emulation could operate, and where symbolic utterances or displays could have their effect' (Renfrew 1986: 16). It is a difficult task that cannot be done by applying twentieth-century urban experience. It demands systematic studies of the rationality and motives behind travels and journeys in prestate and early state societies, a task that is carried out in chapter 2.

In doing so we share a belief in interpretation as a process – an approximation of experience, knowledge and intuition governed by a set of loosely defined rules relevant to the subject, defining meaning and accountability. In this we are in general agreement with more recent theoretical discussions on 'interpretative archaeology' (Tilley 1993; Shanks and Hodder 1995).

However, we wish to construct our *interpretative strategies* theoretically – that is: as strategies that are linked by a set of specific theoretical concepts relevant to our subject in order to define one or several interpretative directions, or routes, to stay in the language of our book. By considering interpretation as a sequence of interlinked theoretical concepts we add movement and direction, at the same time as offering choices between different interpretative routes. We are thus suggesting an interpretative practice where more theoretical labour is invested in delimiting all relevant knowledge and transforming it into more specific interpretative concepts. This may eventually lead to the formulation of a series of interpretative movements, which gradually encircles the various aspects of the subject. We believe such an approach is profitable, as it forces one to consider more than one interpretative dimension, and it forces one to step down from the general theoretical categories to develop more specific and directional concepts relevant to one's study. In opposition to earlier processual model building, which was theoretically closed and one-dimensional, our strategy is theoretically open, fluid and multi-dimensional, just as it is cumulative, adding new dimensions and concepts of theoretically digested knowledge along the way.

In the following we shall illustrate this stepwise interpretative exposition, beginning with the basic concepts needed to trace, explain and understand interaction as an archaeological phenomenon (chapter 1.4 to 1.6). From there we will move on to characterise it as a social and cosmological phenomenon, linked to agency (chapter 2.1). Finally we shall characterise the concept of institutions relevant to Bronze Age society (2.6). Before proceeding, however, it is necessary to clear some conceptual ground relating to traditional discussions about the significance of Mediterranean influences in the European Bronze Age.

1.4   The meaning of imitation in material culture studies

Imitation is at the heart of all archaeological classification. It defines cultural traditions, typology and chronology. In the history of archaeology we have witnessed debates over the archaeological construction versus the historical identity of types and cultures since the 1940s (Krieger, Rowe, Ford, Clarke, summarised in Kristiansen 1985 and Sørensen 1997). Another classic debate was over the mental template of the normative versus the functional classification of processual archaeology (Binford 1965; Renfrew 1977).[6] However, it was not until the pioneering ethnoarchaeological works of especially Ian Hodder (1982) that archaeologists began exploring the 'why'. Why do human populations in certain situations imitate and reproduce a certain material culture, whether their own or that of their neighbours or even foreigners? And how do age and gender affect the use of material culture? Hodder in his study was able to demonstrate the active role played by local material culture in reinforcing local tribal identity and gender identity among the Baringo in periods of stress and competition from neighbouring groups, which, however, did not preclude interaction across the borders. Only the major male status symbol, the spear, would remain identical across cultural borders owing to male status codes crosscutting such borders (Hodder 1982: chs. 1–4).

The reproduction of specific items of material culture through imitation (normally labelled cultural or typological similarity, forming cultures or cultural traditions in traditional archaeology) was thus governed by a set of specific social and historical causes or circumstances that gave meaning to certain material symbols and codes. Material culture was thus given back its historical role as an arena for the playing out of social, religious or political identities and strategies, which, however, had to be specified. These early results would seem to have significant consequences for a renewed study of prehistoric material culture, which, however, has been very slow to emerge in European archaeology, not least in Bronze Age research (Shennan 1989; Jones 1997). Despite the role played by these early studies in the formulation of the theoretical principles of contextual archaeology (Hodder 1986), Hodder's own studies still remain among the best examples of the application of such an interpretative strategy in European prehistory. However, the reformulation of 'style studies' may be seen as derived from the new interpretative concern of understanding the meaning and active social role of material culture (Conkey and Hastorf 1990).

---

6 While Binford retained a notion of style and cultural horizons as relevant properties of social behaviour and explanation (Binford 1965), Colin Renfrew went further in his critique. He deconstructed the notion of culture and culture groups, and wanted to replace them entirely with functional and organisational properties, so-called polities (Renfrew 1977).

Ian Hodder explored the symbolic role of material culture in the reproduction of local identity and in the playing out of social strategies in cultural border situations in Africa. The question of how and why certain items of foreign origin were adopted or imitated was not studied in the same detail in archaeological studies (but see Lemonnier 1993; Van der Leeuw and Torrence 1989). In several pioneering ethnohistorical studies, however, Mary Helms demonstrated the role of sumptuary goods and esoteric knowledge as prerequisites for the reproduction of chiefly power in prestate societies (Helms 1979, 1988 and 1993). She pointed to the universal role of travels and long-distance exchange in such societies, thereby providing the social and cultural contexts for understanding and explaining the role of diffusion and acculturation of foreign goods and knowledge. The significance of her studies for prehistory, like those of Hodder, has not been fully recognised (but see Earle 1987), and we shall make an attempt to change that situation in chapters to follow.

Thus, archaeology is today provided with a whole new ethnohistorical interpretative framework for understanding the symbolic meaning of material culture, why it is imitated and reproduced in certain situations and not in others. We shall apply and develop this framework theoretically in subsequent chapters.

However, since much controversy has been displayed over Mediterranean/Mycenaean imports and/or imitations and their impact upon the Bronze Age societies in central, western and northern Europe, we need to address this question briefly. By doing so we wish to reposition or recontextualise these earlier debates within a modern theoretical and interpretative framework.

One of the key issues for Colin Renfrew and his students during the 1960s and 1970s was first to question formerly recognised typological similarities in material culture between the east Mediterranean and Europe, and second to question their historical impact. Early calibrated C14 dates were employed as a helpful tool. While this critical endeavour was justified at the time, and certainly helped to question some of the more dubious constructions of cultural diffusion, a re-evaluation of some of its premises in the light of present knowledge makes it clear that certain principles of this methodological critique were theoretically flawed. We believe these flaws should be identified, to avoid their reappearance.[7] In an important study of Mycenaean imports in

7 In the case of chronological discrepancies between C14 datings and historical datings, the principles of the natural sciences were given automatic preference against historical interpretations of observed similarities in material culture. Since then significant adjustments in science-based C14 datings have taken place, and many of the chronological and cultural links during the Bronze Age, which were refuted by early, incorrect C14 datings, have been re-established and are supported by the revised C14 chronology and dendrochronology. This may

Bronze Age Europe, Anthony Harding (1984)[8] employed the basic principles of the Renfrew school (summarised in Renfrew 1973), which were:

1 to identify the 'real' Mycenaean imports in Europe, which were to be rather few, since criteria for 'acceptance' were strict, being limited to full formal identity;
2 to question the Mycenaean origin or impact on those items that imitated or demonstrated similarity to Mycenaean or east Mediterranean objects, a minimal definition of similarity being applied where difference counted the most.

This approach suffered from several theoretical and methodological flaws.

1 First, it deprived material culture of any symbolic role as a medium of social or ritual meaning, as a transmitter of information. It defined meaning according to strict formal criteria whose historical significance was not considered until the typological exercise had been completed.
2 The comparative critical analysis was mostly done object by object, as in traditional typological studies, thus prohibiting a contextual and holistic interpretation of the evidence. When critically scrutinised piece by piece for possible differences, little was left of the contextual framework within which imitations and imports were to be understood. Montelius' typology had been turned upside down, but the methodological strategy remained intact. That is: theory and method were treated as separate entities.
3 Consequently the social significance of imitation was rarely recognised or was simply denied. Often arguments of parallel or local development were marshalled, as in the case of the glass and faience beads widespread in certain areas of Europe that also display Mediterranean contacts. The fact that faience was possibly locally produced, in the style and technology of the east Mediterranean, or that certain swords, such as the Minoan/Mycenaean rapier, were imitated locally around the Aegean, was never seen as worthy of historical explanation. An imitation speaks perhaps even more strongly than an import about the local significance of 'foreign' prestige goods, and so does the application of foreign technological skills, as they represent foreign knowledge that is loaded with status, according to Helms (1993).

serve as a warning against letting a single methodological principle dominate over others. Dating methodologies and their interpretation should always be carefully and critically evaluated against each other.
8 Harding's book appeared at the same time as similar work by Ian Bouzek, which continued the tradition of assuming wide-ranging contacts between the Mediterranean and Europe (Bouzek 1985a; see also 1985b). The two books may be seen as paradigmatic examples of opposing research traditions, Harding providing a much needed source criticism at the time, while Bouzek attempted to add some historical interpretation to his distribution maps (also Bouzek 1969).

4 Finally, the rigorous demands of formal identity did not take into account that the representativity of metalwork of the city-states in the east Mediterranean is low, as consumption was restricted, and remelting widespread. Thus, variations found in Europe without direct parallels, but with close similarity to Mediterranean types, can very well be Mediterranean, as we do not know the full range of variation in that area. We know for sure that the quantity of metalwork and range in variation is higher in most of Europe, as conspicuous consumption was widespread among the Bronze Age chiefdoms. Today, and in the future, many such questions are resolved by trace analysis, which has already produced stunning results that we shall come back to. Generally speaking, strict formal demands of full identity between two objects in the import and export area cannot exclude the possibility that imports exist without counterparts, given the limited range of the archaeological record.

Anthony Harding's book is thus a paradigmatic example of the theoretical and methodological flaws of the Renfrew school's critique of interaction and diffusion in later European prehistory. By stripping the evidence of its context and by applying a distorted version of the typological approach that admitted structured similarity (the type) less significance than selective differences (typological elements), it became possible to construct a Bronze Age without Mycenae. The pendulum had swung to the other extreme.[9]

While European prehistory benefited from a necessary revitalisation of the social and economic frameworks of interpretation provided by the Renfrew school, interaction studies were consequently redefined to account for general anthropological categories of exchange, often quantitatively studied (Renfrew 1975; Hedeager 1978). Later Renfrew and Cherry (1986) introduced the concept of Peer Polity Interaction (PPI), an approach that applied a series of useful concepts for interaction studies, such as 'competitive emulation' and 'symbolic entrainment' which we shall discuss in a later section (Renfrew 1986). The theoretical strength of the PPI approach was the

9 In the typological method types are formed by a structured, repetitive association of typological elements. They can be documented statistically, but in the Bronze Age general types, such as type 1 and 2 flange-hilted swords, are easily recognisable, as they were in the Bronze Age. Harding's method of employing select typological elements from among the multitude of elements that define overall typological similarity between related types, which are then used to denounce the significance of similarity, is well exemplified in the discussion of the Ørskovhede sword from Denmark (Harding 1984: appendix 4; discussed by Kristiansen 1987: note 6). The point to be made is that the European type 1b sword and the Aegean type (also called *Kreutzschwerter* by Kilian-Dirlmeier 1993) are closely related. They belong to the same overall type of flange-hilted swords with straight-sided tang, and the Danish sword simply exibits more specific Aegean attributes than any other of the European type 1b swords. That does not make it Aegean, but it testifies to the historical connection in the conception of the type 1b sword. It further underlines the social and historical meaning in the construction of types in the past (Sørensen 1997).

stressing of organisational interaction (structural homology), an approach
we employ and develop. The drawback was that the diffusion of material
culture itself was relegated to the mistakes of a forgotten archaeological
past, although several of the contributions in the book relied on such studies. To defend autonomism, interaction was supposed to take place only
between regional peers, an untenable position. We shall not deny the significant results obtained within this research tradition, in which we have also
taken part (so we are providing a certain self-critique here), but we believe
that a mature archaeology should take into account all forms of social and
cultural behaviour.

In the following we shall therefore reintroduce and redefine some of these
abandoned concepts as part of a theoretical redefinition of interaction studies in archaeology. However, before doing that it is necessary to discuss the
role of textual evidence in Bronze Age studies, as this provides a supplementary historical framework.

1.5   Text and material culture: the Bronze Age as protohistory

Since the late 1990s we have witnessed a renewed interest in and discussion of material culture and text, which opens up for a new and more integrated approach (Bietti Sestieri 1996; Andrén 1998; Morris 2000). It contrasts
strongly with previous views of their relationship based upon rigid schol-
arly boundaries, that in the course of time had been formalised beyond
academic and historical reason.

Traditionally the beginnings of writing defined the borderline between
history and prehistory. This created an artificial borderline between so-called
civilised and barbarian societies, prehistory being defined as the periphery
of civilisation. Owing to this definition prehistoric societies were pushed
along the expanding frontier of textual, civilised societies (Fig. 4), creating an arbitrary interpretative and historical borderline between cultures
and societies that were historically connected, but displayed different levels
of social complexity, as in the Bronze Age. Therefore such an approach is
untenable if we wish to understand the Bronze Age as a historical epoch
beginning with state formation in the Near East in the late fourth millennium BC and its subsequent impact upon the Mediterranean and Europe
during the third and second millennia BC. This being the theme of our
book we cannot renounce employing the written evidence of the state and
palace societies of the Near East and the Mediterranean, as it provides a
necessary background to understanding political and religious institutions.
But also later historical evidence such as the writing down of old oral songs
and sagas from Greece to Ireland is considered relevant. We are thus dealing

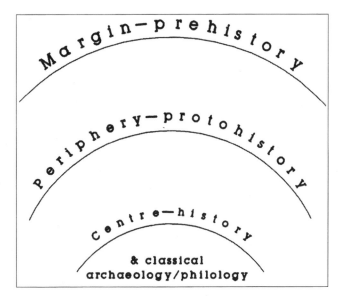

Fig. 4
Centre–periphery
structure
reflecting the
traditional
disciplinary
boundaries
between
archaeology and
history.

with different types of textual evidence that spring from different historical contexts and should be evaluated accordingly. Most fundamental is the
difference between contemporary and non-contemporary texts. Contemporary texts are of course of prime relevance, whereas texts recording much
earlier historical events preserved through oral tradition are more difficult
to interpret. It is characteristic that contemporary texts dominate in the
Near East and the east Mediterranean (administrative texts, ritual texts and
recordings of production), while non-contemporary texts recording earlier
myths and sagas dominate in Europe, as writing was introduced later.

Our approach to textual evidence is pragmatic and culture historical – we
simply employ texts along with other evidence to illuminate social, political
and religious contexts in the Near East and the Mediterranean. Textual and
material evidence in combination make it possible to define institutional
contexts that would otherwise not have been open to such precise interpretations. With this as our starting point we trace their material transmission
in space, its local adaptation and eventual transformation in the non-literate
societies of Bronze Age Europe in a number of short historical time slices.
What we cannot know is how many changes took place along the way in
institutional and political/religious meaning. However, we assume a rather
direct relationship between structures of meaning and symbolic structures
of form, as described in section 1.4 above. We are thus employing the interpretative method of correspondence, as described by Andrén (Andrén 1998:
ch. 6), by adding to it a spatial dimension of historical interaction. We further add two methodological rules:

1 Complex symbolic structures are more likely to maintain their internal meaning unchanged than simpler ones, as their transmission demands the adoption of a corresponding complex knowledge. Thus, single objects can more easily be transmitted without the accompanying information about their meaning.

2 In accordance with this the parallel transmission of two or more symbolic structures makes it increasingly likely that they maintained their internal meaning unchanged, as it testifies to a more complex and direct transmission of knowledge. We use the word 'unchanged' in a structural sense: thus names and places may change, while the overall structure of the institution or the myth has remained intact.

There exists, however, supplementary non-contemporary textual evidence, which may be employed to add probability to the above interpretations. If it can be demonstrated that corresponding or related political and religious institutions of later times have an earlier Bronze Age origin it may be taken to support and illuminate the interpretations. This raises a series of complex problems about the dating and continuity of oral tradition and its later recording as text that we cannot deal with in any detail here. Again our approach is pragmatic and culture historical – we simply evaluate the texts according to their correspondence to the archaeological evidence rather than vice versa. According to such an approach archaeological interpretations of social and political institutions may be able to contextualise a time/space framework of mythological material accumulated over a long time in oral tradition and thereby adding an independent culture-historical parameter to their dating and distribution. As an example we refer to the chapter about the sun-goddess and her twin brothers (chapter 6). Thus, it is clear from the archaeological evidence that the institution of the twin gods/rulers in Indo-European religion is primarily a Bronze Age institution that disappears or is recontextualised during the Iron Age.

According to this we maintain that in conditions of social and political continuity (or displaced continuity), oral tradition was persistent and able to transmit songs and myths over half a millennium or more without major changes, but rather adding detail from later periods to make the songs comprehensible. Oral tradition is often more persistent than literary tradition, as it puts very high demands on correctness. The success of rituals depended on the correct wording of the hymns (Cavalin 2002), and bards and druids in preliterate societies were consequently among the most learned people in history, their education taking up to twenty years (see chapter 2.5). This is in accordance with independent ethnohistorical evidence that has been archaeologically verified, as in the case of Vanuata in Oceania. Here oral

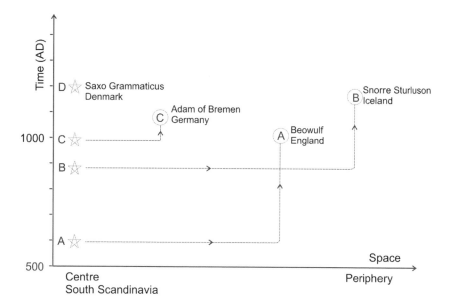

Fig. 5 Diagram showing the relationship between the period and the locality of writing down texts and their true historical origin.

tradition specified the separate burial place, burial rituals/human sacrifice and grave goods of two cultural heroes or founding chiefs, which were confirmed in detail by archaeological excavation. C14 dated the burials to the fifteenth and thirteenth centuries (Garanger 1997). We also find that certain tales and songs allowed for change while others were fixed in their form, prohibiting change, which preserved them over the centuries (Frimigacci 1997). Dynastic changes may change the relative structure of heroes and their histories, evidenced in the Nordic realm, where early versions of sagas, such as Beowulf, that survived on the Nordic periphery in England maintained heroic tales that were later marginalised in the Scandinavian centres. The same is probably true of the *Iliad* and the *Odyssey*, that were maintained not on the Greek mainland but at the courts where the fleeing elites survived (Bennet 1997).

In Scandinavia it can be testified on archaeological and iconographical grounds that the dominant mythology written down by Snorre in the thirteenth century in Iceland originated in the fifth–sixth centuries (Hedeager 1998). A similar picture is emerging from Greece, supported by mounting evidence from Linear B texts that Greek gods often have a Mycenaean/Bronze Age origin (Rystedt 1997; Thomas and Wedde 2001), as originally proposed by Martin Nilsson (1932). In Figure 5 we exemplify our observations in a diagram. According to this the Celtic sagas have a Late Bronze Age/Early Iron Age origin, the Nordic tales were formed during the later Iron Age, and in that process earlier myths and gods were recontextualised. Their Bronze Age origins are thus highly distorted. The *Iliad* and the *Odyssey* on the other hand transmit a genuine Bronze Age ethos, supported archaeologically and textually. Thus, while we accept the historical context of their writing (Morris 1986), we do not accept the far-reaching implications drawn from this about their age and origin, as it goes against the archaeology. The heroic revival of the Archaic period was replayed in many parts of Europe, from Scandinavia to Greece, and cannot alone be explained by reinvention. We would rather put it the other way round – much of the Archaic revival was orchestrated around a revitalisation of existing mythology that had been living a more peripheral life during the preceding centuries.

In conclusion, those historical relations that influenced and changed societies from the Near East to Scandinavia over a period of nearly two millennia constitute the Bronze Age as a historical epoch. The networks and the societies affected by them varied over time, and in this book we are mainly concentrating on the early to mid-second millennium BC in the western part of the known world, that is the Mediterranean and Europe. It follows from this that the Bronze Age belongs in protohistory, and can only be understood historically from such a perspective. History unfolded irrespective of present academic boundaries, and to be studied properly therefore demands an interdisciplinary approach, depending of course on the subject of investigation and its temporal and spatial dimensions. In that sense archaeology is culture history, the more precise nature of which we shall define in the following chapter, although we are in broad agreement with Morris (2000), but wish to add a stronger theoretical perspective.

Having stated this we may now turn to the theoretical task of delineating the theoretical and interpretative concepts of interaction.

1.6 Tracing, explaining and interpreting interaction

Theoretical concepts are always dynamic and relational – their interpretative meaning derives from that. It is therefore meaningless to refer to a single theoretical category, such as diffusion, as it has no interpretative power except when defined in relation to other categories. Further, theoretical concepts should always be defined in direct relation to the object of analysis and interpretation, as their external dynamic derives from that. The interpretative power of theoretical categories thus emerges from their internal relationship to each other and from their external relationship to the object of study. We wish to make the construction of theoretical concepts a flexible and dynamic ingredient in the research process, allowing theory and data to enter into a dialogue beyond deductive and inductive strategies of interpretation. In the following we shall demonstrate such an approach.

Tracing interaction: diffusion, acculturation and contextualisation

Diffusion is a descriptive, covering term for the spread of material culture and practices through time and space. To be properly understood, however, it should be linked to the theoretical concepts of acculturation and contextualisation. Only in this way can its full impact be understood. We must therefore stress diffusion as a process, not only in time, but also as a process of local integration. It is the latter process that it is important to study, and that has been missing in traditional analyses of diffusion.

While earlier research on the spatial process of diffusion in archaeology developed sophisticated analytical tools – from Mats Malmer (1962) and David Clarke (1968), to Ian Hodder (Hodder and Orton 1976) – these studies were missing the local processes of acculturation and contextualisation (examples and discussion in Hodder 1978). Although David Clarke gave some attention to this problem – but he gave attention to nearly every spatial problem – these studies never caught on, with few exceptions, such as Ian Hodder's classic works on symbols in action (Hodder 1982).

Here for the first time was a model study of the meaning and use of material culture in social processes. The focus is on an internal understanding of the dominant symbols rather than on the diffusion and acculturation of new symbols or institutions, but Hodder's symbolic and later contextual archaeology contains the major theoretical and interpretative ingredients that had been previously missing. It is indeed astonishing that archaeology did not apply Hodder's framework more generally as a platform for a new approach to interaction studies, although we could mention a handful of fine examples, such as that proposed by Sørensen (1987).

Another innovative approach to diffusion studies was Andrew Sherratt's work on the secondary products revolution and the interlinked use of alcohol and narcotics as socialising mediums (collected in Sherratt 1997b). Here the focus is on the diffusion of economic and ritual practices and their implications for local transformations during the Neolithic of Europe. These studies defined a new theoretical and interpretative framework for understanding the traditional models of migrations and cultural influences from the Near East, by focusing on technological, economic and ritual practices, going beyond the purely typological and cultural definitions.

Figure 6 gives an example of the graphic illustration of the diffusion process in time and space during the period preceding the Bronze Age. This is a classic example of the process of diffusion, with an attempt to include social and economic changes. In his later work Ian Hodder reinterpreted the process of Neolithicisation throughout Europe from a contextual perspective as a process of culturation and acculturation defining a new conceptual world

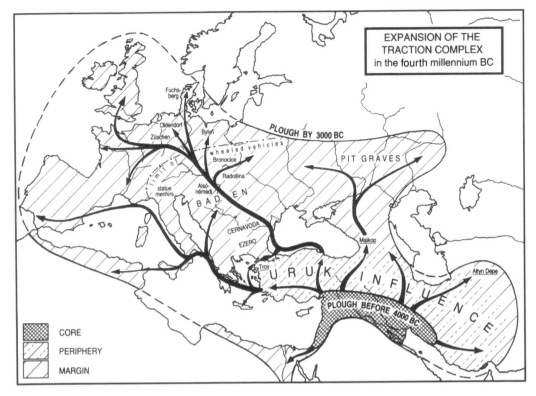

Fig. 6 Diffusion patterns through time during the period preceding the Bronze Age (after Sherratt 1997).

(Hodder 1990). This original study added a missing dimension to previous studies that is only slowly being taken up outside Neolithic studies.

What we propose to do here is to integrate parts of the theoretical framework of Ian Hodder with the interpretative framework of Andrew Sherratt, and apply it to the study of social institutions, and their diffusion, acculturation and contextualisation in Bronze Age Europe. While both Hodder and Sherratt apply general theoretical frameworks, leaving the interpretative process rather open, we prefer to be more specific, breaking up the process into a series of steps, each with a set of conceptual tools to guide us. To do so we believe it is productive to consider diffusion as but one element in a process of acculturation and contextualisation, concepts that we shall briefly define.

Acculturation is the internal or local process of assimilating foreign cultural traits as a result of diffusion between cultures. In this process the new traits are recontextualised and given meaning. The process may account for everything from technological to institutional borrowing. The concept of acculturation has been out of use in both anthropology and archaeology since the 1960s, as it was linked to the prewar paradigms of *Kulturkreislehre* in Europe and the Boas school or the normative tradition in America. Diffusion and acculturation were replaced by interaction and exchange, which focused on the formal, structural rather than the internal properties of the process (Earle and Ericsson 1977). We propose instead to redefine the traditional concepts as an interlinked interpretative strategy to account for the complexity of the process.

In sum, diffusion should not be studied in isolation, as a neutral process of cultural borrowing, because culture is never neutral, but carries meaning with it. And although this meaning may get lost, or completely redefined, the only way of knowing is to add a study of the local processes of acculturation and contextualisation. Thus, we wish to redefine diffusion as an integrated, interpretative process including diffusion – acculturation – and contextualisation (Fig. 7).

However, the process does not stop here. To grasp the full impact of the process of diffusion, another interpretative layer has to be added, one that explains the process by identifying its structural properties.

Explaining interaction: transmission, transformation and institutionalisation

The next step in our interpretative strategy is to explain the process of diffusion as defined above. For this we apply three interconnected concepts: transmission, transformation and institutionalisation. They cover the socialisation and institutionalisation of the diffusion process. While diffusion, acculturation and contextualisation set the framework for doing so, they do not automatically tell us about the impact or the structure of that process. Did it lead to significant reformulations of existing social and ritual practices, and thereby also to redefinitions of existing institutions? Were new institutions developed, and what were their place and role, or did the changes remain marginal, adding only minor adjustments in material culture and practices? This is the task we are proposing to solve by applying the interconnected concepts of transmission, transformation and institutionalisation.

Examples from the archaeological literature that can help us are few. But it could be argued that elements of the process are to be found in the already mentioned works of Sherratt and Hodder, although not explicitly formulated. More explicitly developed explanatory concepts relevant to our perspective are found in Colin Renfrew's work on Peer Polity Interaction (Renfrew 1986). Peer Polity Interaction represents a process of structural or institutional borrowing within a regional network of exchange – a regional polity. This can be a chiefdom, a state or a tribe in traditional evolutionary terms; the focus is rather on the process itself, leading to a degree of regional homogenisation or structural homology – a peer polity. Thus, the focus is on specific homologies in architecture, writing systems, symbolic systems, etc., which define the transmission of institutions rather than single, random elements of culture. By that we mean material traits, which belong functionally or symbolically together and demand complex, additional knowledge to employ them. Consequently the process of transmission is also a process of transformation, that is concluded by the institutionalisation of the new organisational traits. While diffusion, acculturation and contextualisation may be said to identify the material and cultural properties of the process, transmission, transformation and institutionalisation identify the social and political properties of the process, and they demand additional knowledge of the social and political complexity of the societies in question.

Such processes are the result of a highly organised interaction between social groups and polities. As we are speaking of the transmission of a complex package of skills, knowledge and organisational capacity, it demanded repetitive and recurring contacts at many levels, including exchange of both people and goods.

In this context it is also important to consider the role of 'security' for the individuals making the great journeys. We quote Sherratt and Sherratt (1998: 337) on this point: 'An important consideration in the development of long-distance trading-systems – which are not only cross-cultural but "trans-zonal" in that they integrate societies at different levels of development – is security, both from the point of view of foreign travellers and also their hosts: the encounter has to be controlled at a local level.' Alliances, which may take on a variety of forms from gift exchange, through trade partnerships to intermarriage, all share the same function – to ensure safe travel and the exchange of goods and people – and ancient literature is full of examples of this from Odysseus to the Nordic sagas. Guest friendships were inherited and could in the Viking period range hundreds of kilometres, and so probably also in the Bronze Age, as we shall see.

We may distinguish between two types of processes. An initial process of interaction involving the flow of people, goods and knowledge is explorative, often defining the opening of new lines of exchange between formerly autonomous polities or regional groups. At this stage, new ideas, goods and value systems are introduced. It can be followed by a process of acculturation where the new ideas and practices gain acceptance and can be recontextualised locally or regionally, and a fast process of transformation and institutionalisation follows. This was the case with the formation of the Minoan state (Cherry 1986; Schoep 1999a, 1999b), or of the Nordic Bronze Age culture around 1500 BC, a process we shall investigate later in more detail.

Interpreting interaction: meaning, message and materialisation

We have now delineated the cultural and structural properties of the processes of interaction. To interpret it we propose to apply the three interconnected concepts of meaning, message and materialisation. By doing so we simply state that material evidence contains a coded message with a meaning that should be decoded in order to understand and explain the impact of the interaction process. Our goal is to demonstrate that it is possible to become more specific about religious and cosmological meanings than normally believed through a specific theoretical strategy of interpretation.

Symbols gain meaning through context. Contextualised meanings are of many kinds, some of which are not available to archaeologists. Myth, dances and other types of performance are the primary contexts of symbolic meaning, only rarely available to archaeology. They represent the narratives, which give life to social and ritual institutions. But myth and narratives are also materialised, in paintings, decorations, luxury items, ritual structures, etc. which are often bound together through common rituals (de Marrais *et al.* 1996). In the past such different material remains would have been understood as being part of common ritual events and myths, while in archaeology they are separated and defined as different contexts, labelled burials, standing stones, rock art, votive offerings/sanctuaries. Since archaeological categories are normally the starting point for research, we are from the beginning being constrained in understanding what possible symbolic and cosmological meanings and what possible rituals and myth unified such different remains. This phenomenon of intercontextual meaning we may call symbolic permutation/emulation. It demands an integrated, holistic approach to detect and interpret permutated symbolic structures.

Any Christian recognises the cross as a basic religious symbol, with a variety of messages depending upon its context: from being a general symbol of Christianity, being worn as ornaments by women and in warfare by the crusaders, as a burial cross, as the ground plan in church architecture, as a crucifix for prayer and sacrifice, etc. The pervasive and permutative nature of the Christian cross is common to all central religious and cosmological symbols. We are suggesting that by tracing symbols through their different contexts, it will be possible to detect recurring and meaningful mythological messages and cosmological structures in the archaeological record, as demonstrated by Hodder's study of Neolithic houses and burials (Hodder 1984). If textual and mythological evidence can be added, new historical and religious meaning will suddenly emerge behind traditional archaeological typologies and classifications of art and rituals, as demonstrated by Hedeager for the Iron Age (Hedeager 1997, 2001 and 2003).

Fig. 7 Integrated
interpretative
model of the
transmission and
transformation
of material
culture.

Description: Diffusion ⟶ Acculturation ⟶ Contextualisation

Interpretation: Message ⟶ Materialisation ⟶ Meaning

Explanation: Transmission ⟶ Transformation ⟶ Institutionalisation

Thus, by adding message and materialisation to meaning, a more integrated, interpretative field is established

We have now suggested interpretative strategies for tracing, explaining and interpreting interaction. In conclusion we combine the three strategies in one chart (Fig. 7). We suggest that it is possible to enter it from all directions, both horizontally and vertically, constructing new interpretative strategies from it. With that we wish to stress the importance of conceptualising interpretation as a strategy with several layers and possible directions.

We shall exemplify these interpretative strategies in subsequent chapters. Before doing that, however, we need to address some of the hidden prejudices which constrain and misdirect current interaction studies (chapter 2.2).

1.7   Conclusion: theorising interaction and diffusion

In this chapter we have proposed that archaeology is in need of a new theoretical and interpretative framework for understanding and explaining interaction. Processual and postprocessual archaeology were seen to have neglected this field of inquiry owing to their preoccupation with autonomous development, which led to a focus on local studies. While this may have been justified at the time, a mature archaeology should be able to encompass all phenomena of historical change, including travel and population movements. This calls for a widening of the theoretical repertoire of archaeology to include diffusion and interaction.

We have presented three interconnected theoretical strategies of interpretation. *First*, we propose that institutions should be the focus of research, as they are the building blocks of society. The formation and transmission of institutions in time and space is seen to be a major area of research in interaction studies (Fig. 1). *Second*, we have designed an interpretative methodology to identify institutions in material culture. Tracing central symbols and their contexts in time and space, delineating a symbolic field of meaning (Fig. 2), does it. If it can be demonstrated that such a structural field of meaning corresponds to an institution, its history can be traced by tracing the symbolic package or structure, which defines it in time and space. It involves the employment of textual evidence when available, even if written down at a later time period (Fig. 5). Such a structural approach makes it possible to identify the symbolic transmission of institutions irrespective of cultural affiliations and periodisations (Fig. 3). It thus crosscuts cultural boundaries in both time and space. *Third*, we propose a new relational theoretical framework to trace, explain and interpret the process of interaction provided by steps one and two. This is based on the proposition that theoretical concepts should be developed to provide more accurate and integrated frameworks for interpretation as a process (Fig. 7). In doing so we have redefined earlier concepts of diffusion and acculturation and put them to work in a new theoretical framework that is relational. It thus defines new interconceptual and contextual meanings and directions allowing for a more open and dynamic process of interpretation and explanation. This interpretative strategy exemplifies a more universal theoretical need to move beyond general explanatory concepts such as power, wealth and prestige. It is rather the processes of power and prestige that need to be theoretically decoded and conceptually systematised.[10]

A theoretical framework provides an interpretative skeleton, but it needs historical flesh and blood to be added in order to create historical identity and motion. This task we therefore turn to in the next chapter.

10 This is well illustrated in an extensive and critical discussion of the explanatory frameworks for the transition from Stone to Bronze in Europe that was recently provided by Kienlin, covering the English-language literature of the last thirty years (Kienlin 1999; also Morris 1988). A theoretically informed positioning of modern Bronze Age research in Scandinavia and beyond was recently presented by Anna Gröhn (2004; also Vandkilde 2000).

2 Odysseus: a Bronze Age archetype

2.1 Mobility and immobility in prestate societies

In a recent work Zwelebil (1995) proposed that the study of European prehistory is dominated by a farming ideology. In a similar vein we wish to suggest that the study of later European prehistory, and especially the Bronze Age, has failed to make convincing progress because among other things it is dominated by a farming or peasant ideology of immobility which is derived from a more recent European past. By implicitly assuming that prehistoric farmers were as immobile as their historic counterparts, archaeologists have failed to grasp the specific historic character of the Bronze Age: they have failed to recognise its 'otherness'. These interpretative assumptions are perhaps not purely implicit. The recent revival of Fernand Braudel and his *longue durée* has enforced this unhappy transmission of a medieval historical tradition on to prehistory (Bintliff 1991). While we recognise the theoretical relevance of at least some of the Braudelian propositions, such as different 'time cycles' and a *longue durée* for certain types of social formations, it would be unwise to adopt an immobile and unchangeable medieval model of peasant societies. As we shall demonstrate, farming communities of the Bronze Age were characterised by a very different social dynamic and cosmology.

Peasants of medieval, historical time were first and foremost characterised by their obligations and economic bonds to their feudal lords. They were defined by this economic and social relationship as a dependent class, constrained in their social and economic freedom, and consequently also in their mobility. Although longer travels might be part of their duties, e.g. carrying goods and people for their lords, they were basically linked to their land. Trade was in the hands of the landed nobility and the new growing merchant classes in the towns. Marriage patterns demonstrate this immobility of the peasant class whereas the nobility had quite different marriage patterns.

The immobility of the peasant class is also reflected in a number of other ways in material culture and language. Strong local dialects in language developed, making communication difficult between certain regions. The upper class at the same time adopted international languages – Latin, and later German or English. In contrast a common Scandinavian language was used during the Late Iron Age and the Viking period, according to runic inscriptions, from rune stones to the messages of ordinary people on wooden sticks. Some hundreds of years later the development of a feudal society, with the subsequent subjection and immobilisation of the peasants, had generated dozens of local and often rather distinct dialects. The same process can be observed in the building tradition of farm-houses. From being rather homogeneous during the Late Iron Age and Viking period, although with slight regional variations, diversification dominated during the medieval and historical period leading to very distinct regional differences (Steensberg 1952 and 1973; Stoklund 1972).

This historical development may be used to demonstrate the close connection between mobility and material culture and language, a theme to which we shall return. However, our main objective in this chapter is to demonstrate that in terms of mobility the Bronze Age, and with it many prestate chiefdoms, exhibits a perception of mobility and travel completely different from historically known peasant societies. We believe that an understanding of this 'otherness' is a crucial precondition for a correct reconstruction of Bronze Age society. It comes with other characteristics, such as the integration of warrior and farming regimes and the integration of religious and social organisation, structural elements of a developed prestate society, where these functions are present in embryonic form, but have not yet been divided into separate social classes.

Before we proceed it is necessary to describe some of the basic archaeological contexts and categories, as we wish to link a new theoretical understanding and interpretative practice to the archaeological record of the Bronze Age in subsequent chapters.

2.2 Archaeological contexts and categories

Although much useful work has been done to determine the flow of goods according to provenience (typology, metal composition, etc.) in European Bronze Age research, and indeed has produced some remarkable interpretative results in recent years (Wels Weyrach 1989; Gale 1991; Jockenhövel 1991; Hansen 1995), little has been done to develop theoretical concepts relevant to the methodological level of analysis applied. At a general interpretative level there have been interesting debates over the nature of trade (Gosden 1985; Stjernqvist 1985; Wells 1989; Sherratt and Sherratt 1991; Rowlands 1993). However, they remain unresolved, perhaps owing to a lack of theoretical development at the more basic local and regional levels of analysis. It means that interpretations of Bronze Age exchange are constrained, not by lack of relevant data, but by our inability to develop relevant theoretical, and to some extent methodological concepts (Needham 1998). Theory often either is too general or is simply replaced by some sort of common-sense interpretation. Since twenty-first-century urban experience has little

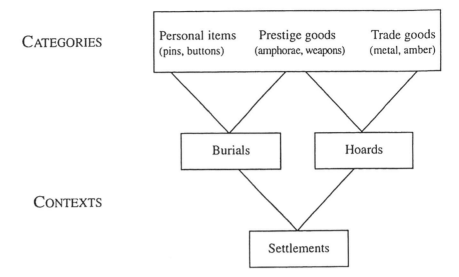

CATEGORIES

Personal items
(pins, buttons)

Prestige goods
(amphorae, weapons)

Trade goods
(metal, amber)

Burials

Hoards

CONTEXTS

Settlements

Fig. 8 Basic archaeological categories and their interpretative relationship.

in common with Bronze Age society, and since data alone cannot bridge this conceptual and historical gap, the results are often correspondingly unsatisfactory.

Instead we need to develop more specific interpretative theoretical concepts at the middle level of analysis, based on our knowledge of ranked and early state societies (for a survey of interaction studies see Shortman and Urban 1992a; Scarre and Healy 1993). With this as our starting point we shall propose an analytical and interpretative strategy for the study of exchange in a Bronze Age context.

Let us begin with the contexts and categories of the archaeological evidence itself, since they determine to large degree later analytical and interpretative results.

Normally research starts with the publication or the analysis of a settlement, a burial or a hoard. From there the analysis is then extended to questions of trade and exchange. So, traditional research strategies and methods of analysis can be classified in the following way:

1 Type studies/cultural studies: documentation and analysis of a certain type of object in time and space. This is represented by the PBF volumes, and for cultural studies by classic works such as Coffyn (1985) on the Atlantic Bronze Age or Müller-Karpe (1959) on the Urnfield Culture.

2 Localised studies: the presentation and analysis of a single find, or a group of finds. Thus a single point in space is determined in relation to the cultural and typological context of the objects found. This can be typified by the exemplary publication of the Vernant hoard (Coffyn, Gomez and Mohen 1981).

3 Contextual studies: the full presentation and analysis of all types of archaeological material within a geographical unit – local or regional. This has become a dominant publication strategy, and therefore also a dominant research strategy in recent decades, perhaps because of the multiplication of archaeologists in regional museums and heritage administration/rescue archaeology.

Of course these publication and research strategies allow certain types of analysis and interpretation and constrain others. The decontextualised study of single types in their full geographical distributions versus the holistic and contextualised analysis of all types of evidence in a small geographical area invites quite different methodological and theoretical approaches. But on the other hand the localised studies are essential to understand the distribution maps of the PBF volumes, and vice versa. The problem is that we have seen far too few analyses that combine these different types of evidence in a theoretically informed manner. Perhaps the time has now come – finally – when we have enough published evidence to define a research strategy by asking a question, by formulating historical problems to be analysed. Or put simply: letting theoretical categories instead of find contexts determine research. If this were done in just one out of ten publications (books or articles), Bronze Age research would see a tremendous interpretative development.

We can begin with simple social categories, such as *personal items*, *prestige goods and trade goods*. They can often be identified in the archaeological record of burials and hoards (e.g. Ruiz Galvez 1995; Kristiansen 1996b), and may help us to define how objects move (personal items, prestige or trade goods), by whom (male/female, high/low ranking), and how far (and by what means of transport). It is assumed that small personal items with primarily practical functions, such as pins or small fibulae, were not objects of trade or gift giving (although this may have been the case with very big, decorated pieces). When they occur outside their local context it reflects a movement of individuals. This may of course lead to imitations in the new area, but the newcomers will often make them. Of course you may during a journey break your pin and buy a new one, but in any case it reflects movements of people. We therefore propose that the numbers of personal items outside their area of production suggest the frequency of interaction and the number of people involved.

Prestige goods add another dimension to interaction. As they are defined primarily by their social value (Frankenstein and Rowlands 1978; D'Altroy and Earle 1985; Hedeager 1992: 87ff.), they are normally highly elaborate, demanding specialised craftsmanship, and can be exchanged as gifts between chiefs (peers) and between chiefs and vassals (Fig. 9).

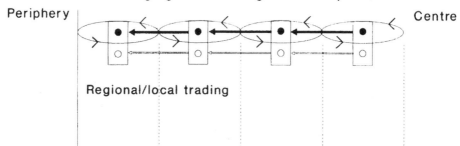

Prestige goods exchange between peers

Periphery   Centre

Regional/local trading

○   Technological, social and
    ritual information.

●   Prestige goods, locally produced.
    Centre–periphery relations are
    indirect.

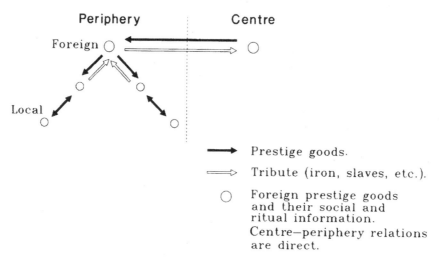

Prestige goods exchange between
centre and periphery.

Periphery   Centre

Foreign ○   ○

Local ○   ○   ○

⟶   Prestige goods.

⟹   Tribute (iron, slaves, etc.).

○   Foreign prestige goods
    and their social and
    ritual information.
    Centre–periphery relations
    are direct.

Fig. 9 Horizontal
and vertical
processes of
prestige goods
models.

Prestige goods may either be personal (ornaments, weapons) or serve special social and ritual functions (amphorae, drinking cups, musical instruments, etc.). And they may be either locally produced or imported from a
foreign cultural context. A study of prestige goods may reveal important
information about political alliances at both local and regional levels. A

study of workshops may document a local political network, and its size and its interaction with other local networks or chiefdoms. This interaction might be in the form of gifts, but sometimes an alliance would be confirmed through marriage, where either a man or a woman moved to the alliance partner. In some cases this can be documented when personal sets of prestige goods, e.g. ornaments, are found in a foreign context (Jockenhövel 1991). More often gifts were exchanged; they were often costly weapons or hammered metal vessels employed in chiefly feasting, and were thus integrated into the local context. This explains the Europe-wide distribution of certain types of swords and metal vessels, e.g. the octagonal swords that connected southern Germany and Denmark during the Middle Bronze Age (Montelius period 2). Again it can be difficult to distinguish between the movement of goods and the movement of people. One has to add other types of evidence, such as personal items or new burial rites, in order to evaluate the degree and the character of population movement within such long-distance exchange networks.

The final category, trade goods, is a difficult one. It assumes that certain goods were exchanged or traded because of their economic and practical value rather than their symbolic value. It could be amber, tin, copper, gold, bronze or other products with enough value to be traded in small quantities. Thus most metal was traded not in the form of highly worked prestige goods, but in simple forms, such as ingots and axes, or even in some periods as scrap bronze. The social value was added through craftsmanship, which could be done either locally or in foreign workshops with established positions as producers of specific high-status objects, such as metal vessels or body armour. Thousands of hoard finds give a glimpse of the complicated processes of exchange of metal in utilitarian form, and suggest that quantities were often rather small, at least in the local distribution of metal (Kristiansen 1996b; this volume, chapter 4.1). They further suggest that the production and exchange of prestige goods was a primary goal throughout the Bronze Age, as they represented the materialisation of social and political power.

Thus political power resided in the participation in political alliances that secured access not only to metal, but more importantly to social renown and status. Exchange and interaction cannot be understood as a neutral flow of material goods. They were embedded in a complicated system of social and political exchange rituals that had to do with the ways in which value, status and power were produced and reproduced. This was further a spatial phenomenon; no social entity could survive in isolation. In the following we shall attempt to dissolve these complicated processes into a number of categories – or spheres of influences – that can be subjected to empirical analysis and social interpretation. But first it is necessary to consider the meaning of cultural boundaries, the social and political implications of crossing them,

CROSSING BOUNDARIES

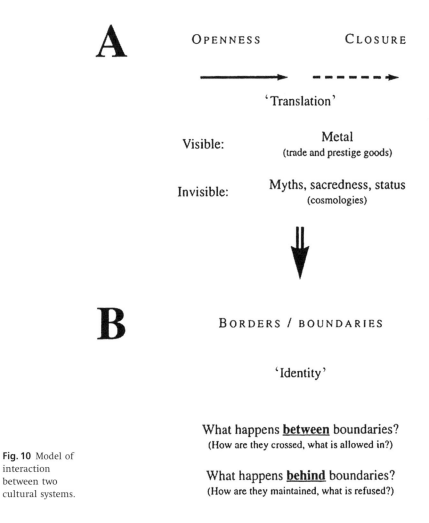

Fig. 10 Model of interaction between two cultural systems.

since it is the transfer not only of valuables but also of social and ritual value which is at the heart of interaction and exchange.

2.3 Crossing cultural boundaries: the authority of distance

Concepts of interpretation must, to be effective, grasp some of the basic characteristics of Bronze Age society. Thus, they presume a certain degree of *a priori* knowledge that is summarised to focus attention on essential areas of research. We have chosen two sets of concepts, which are openness/closure and borders/boundaries – the meaning of difference/of the other (Fig. 10).

In the Bronze Age local communities throughout Europe became dependent upon each other to maintain open lines of long-distance exchange in order to secure the distribution of metal from the few dominant source areas. In this respect Bronze Age society represents something radically new in European history. Networks would sometimes span thousands of kilometres, in opposition to the more closed regional circuits of the Neolithic. Thus, Bronze Age society was situated between two basic needs: an economic need to maintain open lines of metal exchange and information, and a cultural and social need to maintain distinct local and regional traditions. This created a new dynamic between openness and closure, between the powers of internal and external origins, Us and Other, that raises a whole series of research issues.

Cosmological origins in space and time

The first and most important thing is to understand the social and ideological meaning of distance. To achieve this we need the supplementary evidence of ethnohistorical studies, which has been summarised most coherently by Mary Helms (1988 and 1998). In her studies she has convincingly demonstrated that space and distance are never neutral, but are accorded sociological, political and especially ideological significance. 'Horizontal space and distance may be perceived in sacred or supernatural terms in much the same way that vertical space and distance from a given sacred centre is often perceived in supernatural dimensions and accorded varying degrees of cosmological significance' (Helms 1988: 4). Thus knowledge acquired from travels to such distant places may form part of a corpus of esoteric knowledge controlled by 'specialists' (chiefs, artisans, priests) as an attribute and legitimisation of their status, power and authority. Wisdom in traditional society was always expected to be linked to high office, and acquired in a variety of ways. These include artistic skills, knowledge of weather and sailing for maritime expeditions, and most importantly knowledge of traditional songs, stories and ceremonial details, not only of one's own people, but of outside people as well. Magical powers and heroic fame were gained through participating in distant travels and expeditions, where chiefs would meet and compete about their skills, mythical stories and heroic deeds, and return with new knowledge, skills and fame, and with esoteric goods to symbolise their social and ritual standing.

Travels to other chiefs in more distant places would often involve perceptions of crossing boundaries. Space in traditional society is mostly perceived in symbolic and cosmological terms (Van Gennep 1982: ch. 2), often in zones that emphasise 'Us' versus 'Others', and which may also emphasise sacred and safe (domestic) space versus the dangerous and distant. The latter may well be the home of mythical and sacred places (for pilgrimage), but to go there demands complicated rituals and preparations. Thus the ethnographic knowledge about space as being defined primarily in cultural and cosmological terms corresponds well with archaeological evidence of clearly defined cultural boundaries and boundary zones. Often travel to distant places corresponds to time travel to the origin of ancestors, making ancestors and the mythical past an ingredient of the present that can be reached through travel, and which accords to chiefs a historical and sacred status upon their return. Also linked to distance and travels are the adventures to and explorations of distant lands and foreign peoples, the ability to overcome the unknown, as in the case of Odysseus, an archetypal Bronze Age hero who travelled far and wide and returned home as a wiser and better man, a hero.

Motives for travel in the ethnographic literature vary, from achieving religious training and sacredness at ritual centres by renowned chiefs and priests, through bringing back trading goods and prestige goods, to simply conquering the unknown in search of heroism and access to new powerful exchange partners and networks. They may thus include everything from sending young sons to nearby religious centres of high chiefs to organising long-distance journeys for trade and conquest. According to Helms, 'travel and direct experience with foreign peoples and places is also a means by which an individual may gain some degree of self-realisation, escape for awhile [sic] from the limitations of village society, acquire fame, and perhaps even obtain some assurance of personal immortality' (Helms 1988: 76). Among the Trobriand Islanders: 'Men say their true personality can only be expressed in the Kula. Kula men see their ceremonial exchange activity as their best potential avenue for immortality. Ordinary men carry their names with them to the spiritual underworld after death. Famous Kula men, however, leave their names behind linked to prominent shells' (Helms 1988: 77). Similar ideologies can be found among other adventurous and travelling people, such as the ancient Greeks, the Celts and the Vikings.

The power and sacredness of geographical distance also mean that new ruling chiefs are often derived from external sources (Fig. 11). The ethnographic literature is full of descriptions that associate the arrival of strangers with chieftainship, and the introduction of new goods and techniques and the growth of foreign trade. In such situations the original homeland becomes a place of cosmological beginnings and the arrival of chiefly newcomers becomes a cosmological event rather than an intrusion. Conquest migrations, which are common in chiefdoms, are seen as resulting from the newcomers' relation with outside supernatural powers that qualify and legitimise their dominance. Similar stories are found in the European and Nordic myths and are often rejected by historians as religious clichés. However, there is much in the archaeological record to support such

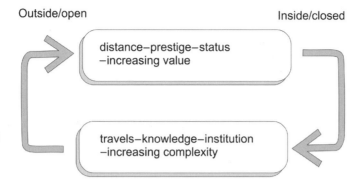

Outside/open   Inside/closed

distance–prestige–status
–increasing value

travels–knowledge–institution
–increasing complexity

Fig. 11
Relationship
between internal
and external
processes of
hierarchisation.

stories. The rise of Nordic Bronze Age culture coincides with the introduction of new long-distance exchange networks and the occurrence of foreign swords, new burial rituals and new architecture. Many similar cases of the formation of a new elite culture and the introduction of foreign exchange can be cited (Helms 1998: 157ff.). It has to do with the formation of a qualitative distinction between elites and commoners in chiefdoms, linked to the differential access to contexts of origin and to wealth, often defining a chiefly material culture differing from that of commoners. It may further be noted that crafting skills are frequently accorded special significance in the ethnographic record, as they indicate a special power, and that to work with iron, precious metals or fine textiles often involved special rituals. The artisan is a connoisseur of secrets, a magician – something we return to in a subsequent section.

Some archaeological implications and applications

With this ethnohistorical knowledge about the social and ideological meaning of space and distance as contextual baggage, we can now in a more profitable way start to analyse and interpret the archaeological evidence of geographical interaction in Bronze Age Europe and the motivations for travelling (Renfrew 1993: 10ff.). And we shall begin with a few general observations, of which the first is that basic metallurgical skills were transmitted widely throughout Europe during the Early Bronze Age, as were knowledge about warfare, warrior elites and chiefly culture. This can be inferred from the recurring appearance of the social and ritual complex of the warrior chief in burials, hoards and rock carvings throughout Europe, from the Mediterranean to Scandinavia, during the seventeenth to fifteenth centuries BC (Kristiansen 1987; Treherne 1995). Some forms, such as the flange-hilted sword, were internationally distributed, but most swords, lances and burial rituals were adapted to local and regional traditions. So while a common stock of metallurgical know-how and common social and ritual value systems accompanied the flow of bronze throughout Europe (Gomez de Soto 1993; Kristiansen 2001a), they were everywhere translated into regional and even local cultural traditions and dialects.

This raises a series of questions relating to the formation and maintenance of cultural and ethnic boundaries, and the meaning of material classification as social and/or ethnic markers (Hodder 1982). The definition of cultural boundaries and the study of how they are crossed become an essential focus of research, if we wish to understand the nature of Bronze Age interaction. This includes not only the flow of material goods (exchange), but also their social meaning and context (De Atley and Findlow 1984). What happens at borders, how are they crossed, what is refused and allowed in? What is the status of a cultural border, and did there develop special 'border cultures' in some regions? Were there certain nodal points to be used for exchange transactions, or was interaction more open? How do boundaries change, or dissolve? The potential of such studies has been demonstrated recently in northwestern France by Brun (1993).

As a starting point it may be useful to analyse the relationship between the *visible* and the *invisible* flow of goods and information. Secondly, what was the balance between *acceptance* and *refusal*, between what was accepted in its present material form as imports, and what was remelted and recontextualised into a new local form, translated into the local or regional cultural dialect? By applying these four categories we are able to define in an empirical way the balance between local and foreign, and in which forms foreign knowledge was transformed and integrated into local tradition. We may further add gender, and other interesting variations become visible (Stig Sørensen 1987 and 2000).

By employing some of the categories defined above (personal items, prestige goods, imports, etc.) and the ways in which they cross boundaries we are able to reveal in some detail how Bronze Age societies interacted with each other, and how they defined themselves against others – as different from others. This is a necessary background for understanding the significance of foreign objects and distant knowledge in a local and regional context. We may also be able to define certain regularities in the balance between openness and closure related to the historical long-term processes of the formation, maintenance and dissolution of cultural traditions. Social anthropology can stimulate our understanding of such processes, especially the actual mechanisms of barter and exchange (Gregory 1982; Humphrey and Hugh-Jones 1992). It can also help us to understand the nature of travel and the value of distant knowledge in traditional society (Helms 1988), but only archaeology can provide the long-term historical perspective that allows us to define historical regularities. However, in order to develop meaningful interpretations, we need to proceed further by classifying the evidence into more specific theoretical and interpretative categories related to the spatial organisation of exchange and its social and ritual significance as discussed above.

2.4 Geographical distance and access to origins: the sacredness of power

On the basis of ethnohistorical and archaeological evidence we have argued that Bronze Age society was obsessed with travel and esoteric knowledge brought home from outside. We shall now look more closely into the relationship between esoteric knowledge and its role in transforming local cultures. We shall consider what were the special qualifications of those who travelled, which often enabled them to achieve special status. However, first we have to discuss some more basic concepts linked to inner and outer space and the mechanisms needed to pass between them.

Cosmological centres and peripheries

The idea of boundaries between inner and outer space, nature and culture, civilised and barbarians, them and us, is rooted in every society. However, the boundaries of the world, and ways to control them, differ according to the level of social and economic complexity. What interest us here are not historical structures, but the cosmologies that governed people's behaviour in the past when certain goods and skills were needed. And we shall begin by describing the role of cosmological centres and peripheries.

Space is neither homogeneous nor neutral, except on archaeological distribution maps. It is loaded with dangers, monsters, myths and powers, it is qualitatively differentiated, and to enter it or return from it demands complex measures. The city-states of the third and second millennia BC shared with less developed prestate societies a developed mythical cosmology to describe and have direct contacts with the outer world.

It is not merely a coincidence that numerous Greek and Mesopotamian myths describe journeys made by different gods, goddesses and heroes. The famous Gilgamesh epic is a good example of the mythical king-god's journeys and adventures (Hooke 1963: 49ff.), and we have good reason to assume that this myth could have been widespread during the mid-second millennium BC (Penglase 1994: 7):

> For instance, a version of the Gilgamesh epic was found in the remains of Hattusha, the Hittite capital. In fact, extended usage of the texts and acquaintance with the stories is indicated: scribes took copies of tablets, and taught private schools of students, who learnt the texts. In addition, no doubt worshipers in the various cults concerned would have known of the stories and myths.

The story of Inanna and Dumuzi also focuses upon the goddess' journey in order to achieve power (Penglase 1994: 16). In the myth of *Inanna's Descent to the Netherworld*, the stated purpose for her journey is the acquisition of power over the netherworld, and power in the upperworld as well (Penglase 1994: 16–17). The Mesopotamian god Ninurta's journeys have the same general purpose – the acquisition of power (Penglase 1994: 71):

> The purpose of Ninurta's journeys discussed here, and of the major activities involved in them, is specifically the acquisition of power, but also its retention and demonstration. While each myth presents a different story and the question of power receives a different treatment in almost every one, this purpose is remarkably consistent. It appears, therefore, that the idea of carrying out a journey was considered to be an important ingredient in a god's acquisition of power: that is, that in these myths the god achieved his power through the performance of a journey.

Earthly men aspiring to power therefore had to do likewise, because one becomes truly a man only by conforming to the teaching of the myths, that is, by imitating the gods (Eliade 1987: 100).

Penglase argues that these and other Mesopotamian myths from the third and second millennia BC had a profound impact on later Greek myths and hymns (Penglase 1994: 128). For example, the Greek hymn to Demeter has a close parallel in the older Mesopotamian myths of Inanna and Dumuzi, not only on the level of motif, but because of the similarity in underlying ideas, religious concepts and the presentation of the gods and their activities. It suggests a fundamental structural similarity in the rise of ranked and state societies, linked to explorations and political–economic expansion and the subsequent formation of a cosmology of travelling ancestors and gods.

Thus, the notion of the outer realm, the periphery, as a land of origins links so-called superordinate centres to outlying regions in a way that differs from traditional centre–periphery analysis, which is mainly economic and political in scope. Instead it adds a sacred, cosmological element to the maintenance of contact with distant, peripheral regions, which may share identifying characteristics or their own (Helms 1993: ch. 11; Urban and Shortman 1999). The Delphic Apollo had strong northern links with the solar deity of the Baltic, from where amber came. He travelled on his white swans to the Hyperborean of the cold North during winter. This is a mythological relict of the economic role of the central and north European periphery during the Bronze Age. On numerous metal items swans carried the sun, materialising the common myth of the sun-god, which according to Herodotus (IV, 32–6) was brought to Delos by Hyperborean maidens in at least two missions (Bouzek 1997).

Heroic travels, trade and acquisitions thus integrate in complex ways that can be reduced to neither economy nor myth. The two form an integrated part of the cosmology of ancient societies. At the same time, however, the centre often maintains a moral superiority and ideological centrality that obliges it to extend its cosmos to outer territories. This in turn enhances its moral superiority and glorification. The centre normally presents to the less civilised skilfully crafted chiefly regalia, which through visiting chiefs and skilled artisans may help to instruct the receiving groups in the blessings of civilisation and elite culture. In turn the centre expects to receive exotics from the outside realm with high cosmological value in the centre (Stein 1999: 20ff. for historical examples). This ethnohistorical scenario is paralleled in the Early Bronze Age by the exchange of chiefly regalia (swords and chariots) with sacred and valued amber from Scandinavia that entered a civilising journey towards chiefly society, as we shall demonstrate later. We may envisage a web of distant cosmological centres throughout Bronze Age Europe, some of higher order than others, allowing cosmological origins to be reproduced at any given point/chiefdom by long-distance travels of cultural heroes and aristocrats to reproduce and reclaim the authenticity of cosmological origins and superiority.

In chiefly strategies 'access to origins' is crucial, and this access can, according to Helms, be achieved via the control of different media that are believed to be closely related to the Genesis: animals, ancestors, affines and other people are examples of such media (Helms 1998: 167). By relating themselves to one or more of these categories, the Bronze Age chieftains had taken the necessary first step towards the position of 'Otherness' that was needed in order to be treated as a 'real' aristocrat. We cite Helms again: 'when elites are accepted as legitimate aristocrats, it is because commoners regard and accept them as *qualitatively different types of beings* from themselves, and vice-versa' (Helms 1998: 5). We are here at the root of the process of the formation of an elite, whose historical consequences were summarised by Tim Pauketat as 'The tragedy of the commoners' (Pauketat 2000).

From studying the archaeological record in Early Bronze Age south Scandinavia we know that at least animals and ancestors can be treated as possible links to cosmos and the 'first principle origins' (Helms, manuscript). The notable focus on royal or divine attributes from distant areas, such as the Carpathian Basin and the Near East, indicates that 'Otherness' played an important role as well in the chiefly strategies (Fig. 12).

Helms points out another characteristic or rather contrast: that between polities of acquisition relating primarily to horizontal *axes mundi* and superordinate centres relating primarily to vertical *axes mundi* (Helms 1993: 199). It defines a difference between local centres or polities seeking to establish and maintain their own centredness, whereas vertically connected superordinate

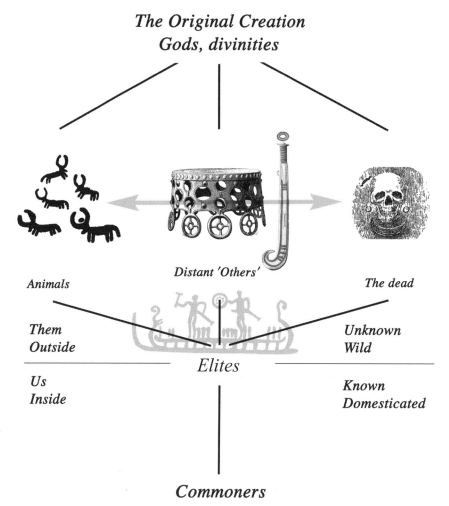

The Original Creation
Gods, divinities

Distant 'Others'

Animals   *The dead*

Them   *Unknown*
Outside   *Wild*

Us   *Known*
Inside   *Domesticated*

Elites

Commoners

Fig. 12 Model for how an elite may link themselves to mythological origins in a Bronze Age context.

centres appear to have their own political centredness more firmly structured internally, and instead seek to expand their scope of influence or range of control. It would seem to correspond to what has been termed wealth finance and stable finance (D'Altroy and Earle 1985), corporate and network societies (Feinman 2000), and it demonstrates the interlinked nature of cosmological and economic power. In her most recent book Mary Helms has expanded her study of these differences by linking them to the different status and roles accorded to affine groups (Fig. 13).

Thus affines, as coming from outside, are often those who produce skilled crafting and artistry, various forms of wealth, with a foreign or outside context linked to them, something which we shall see exemplified in a later chapter on foreign swords.

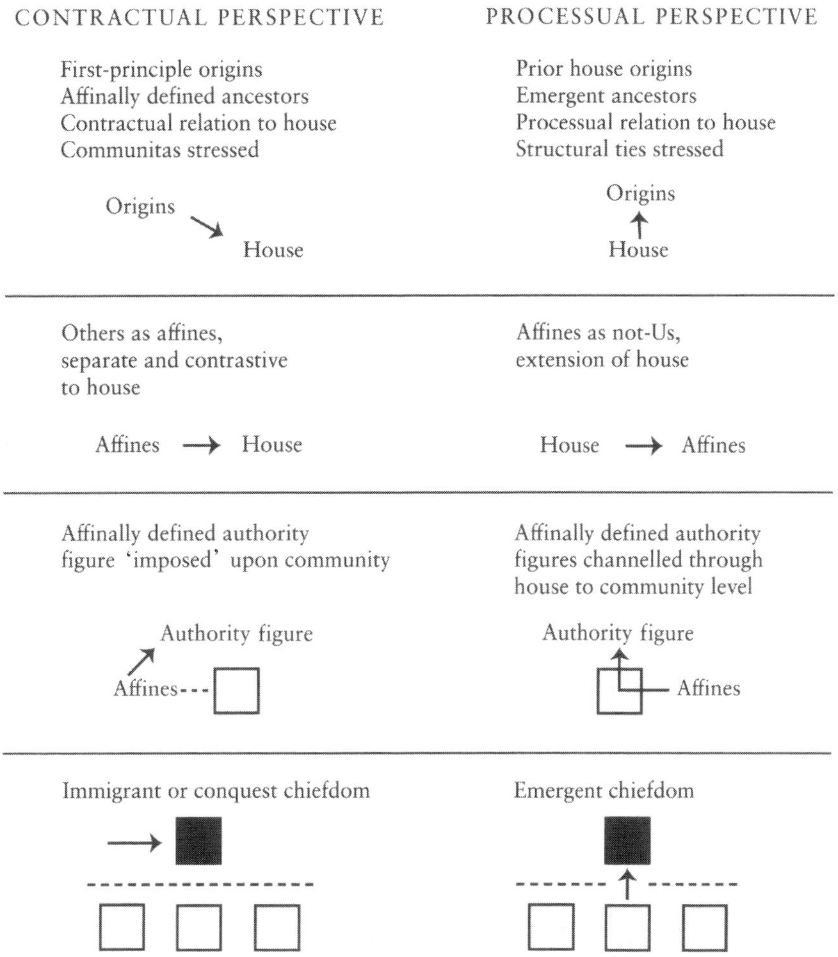

CONTRACTUAL PERSPECTIVE   PROCESSUAL PERSPECTIVE

First-principle origins   Prior house origins
Affinally defined ancestors   Emergent ancestors
Contractual relation to house   Processual relation to house
Communitas stressed   Structural ties stressed

Origins   Origins
     ↘   ↑
       House   House

Others as affines,   Affines as not-Us,
separate and contrastive   extension of house
to house

Affines ⟶ House   House ⟶ Affines

Affinally defined authority   Affinally defined authority
figure 'imposed' upon community   figures channelled through
                          house to community level

       Authority figure   Authority figure
     ↗   ↑
Affines ---□   □— Affines

Immigrant or conquest chiefdom   Emergent chiefdom

Fig. 13 External and internal strategy for the institutionalisation of authority and chieftainship (after Helms 1998: Fig. 12).

Items of tangible wealth not only associate their acquirers with categories of Others and contexts of origin, but also connect and interrelate the several origins and outside Others to each other and to the membership of the house or polity, particularly during important political-ideological ceremonies, such as mortuary rites, initiations, and political successions. (Helms 1998: 172)

If I were to further pursue the qualitative antecedents of aristocratic attributes, I would inquire more deeply into the nature of cosmological Otherness, including Masters of Animals, totemic landscapes, and the human dead, rather than into the attributes of house elders or big men per se, for I am persuaded that the concept of aristocracy is rooted in the personification and literalization of concepts about the nature of the universe rather than in differences in the individual skills or attributes of persons of the house or polity per se. (Helms 1998: 178–9)

Some archaeological implications and applications

A state society is characterised by a rather large degree of overlap between different spheres of control – military, economic and religious. Such integrated control, which entails the extraction of taxes or tribute, enables states to organise military or commercial expeditions moving far beyond their boundaries to exploit peripheral lands and resources. In a prestate social organisation (traditional society) this is not the case. As a rule the political entities were always smaller than the cultures and networks they defined. In a Bronze Age context it meant that extensive territorial control could not be exercised (as far as we know, but it should be open to debate). Consequently open networks of exchange had to be maintained in order to secure the distribution of metal. In this way Bronze Age society stands in an interesting intermediate position between the more closed regional tribal polities of the Neolithic and the territorial states of the emerging Iron Age. It defines a new organisational framework of long-distance trading networks suitable for being hooked into the more commercial enterprises from centrally organised city-states or territorial states.

Thus, in a Bronze Age context political power, as a rule, could only be practised with economic efficiency, as control of land and labour, at the local level of chiefly followers. Military power might be extended beyond that, but mostly as raiding for slaves, cattle and trade goods (the local chiefdom level of political alliances, 20–40 km). Consequently ritual power still remained the dominating integrating mechanism through which all transactions had to pass. Therefore ritual or sacred political power can play an important role in mobilising larger followings and in creating alliances far beyond the local setting (100–200 km). This may define local and regional relations of centre and periphery where goods and people are moving towards the centre in exchange for ritual services in a system of unequal exchange (Kristiansen 1987). No political control of larger areas from a single centre is possible, whereas exchange networks may be extensive. In a position intermediate to early state systems one may find confederations between chiefly centres (e.g. of Middle Bronze Age tell settlements) that control trade routes, but not the territories beyond.

We would thus envisage two types of exchange systems operating during the Bronze Age: one dominated by a 'peer polity' type of exchange between chiefs, and one dominated by a 'centre–periphery' type of unequal exchange between chiefs and vassals (Fig. 9). The latter is most often linked to an emerging commercial centre (Mycenaean, Minoan, Phoenician or Greek).

However, this only represents a 'top level' or 'top-down' level of exchange and it tells very little about the ideological and social content of exchange. Many other types of local exchanges of people and goods should be added,

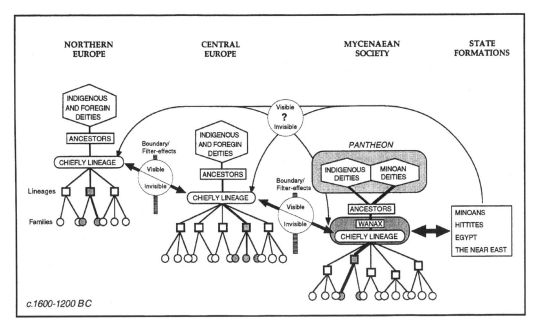

Fig. 14

Interaction-
model for the
selective
transmission and
local adaptation
of new
institutions in
Bronze Age
Europe.

defining a series of levels linked to different social and economic contexts, which can be detected archaeologically when confronted with relevant theoretical and methodological categories (e.g. Larsson 1984).

Archaeologically the different strategies often have different spatial distributions, reflecting different levels or spheres of influence. We yet have to learn how to understand the social and ritual value of objects and their place in a hierarchy of exchanges (De Marrais, Castillo and Earle 1996). As a starting point we made a crude distinction above between personal items, prestige goods and trade goods, suggesting increasing value from personal items to prestige goods (Fig. 9).

At a second level of analysis we should add the invisible values linked to travel and exchange: the bringing back of new practical and technical skills (metallurgy, warfare, architecture, etc.), of new ritual information, and the power linked to having been far away in distant, sacred lands (discussed above). This type of information has to be inferred indirectly in the employment of new rituals, new symbols, new types of warfare, etc. One outstanding example of a Nordic Bronze Age chief returning home from distant travels with all kinds of new sacred knowledge (and a chariot), securing him an extraordinary position in society and in death, is the Kivik grave in Scania, with its unique pictorial stones (Randsborg 1993).

At the final level of analysis one should consider the mechanisms of interaction (Fig. 14).

Here we suggest three different types, although with some overlap. First, there is traditional barter between local chiefs in a chain of long-distance exchanges, represented by the classic Kula ring in Melanesia, but also in a series of well-documented Bronze Age networks of interregional exchange, discussed above. Some of these networks may also have channelled warriors between centres and peripheries, that is mercenaries travelling back and forth, as known in the La Tène period and later in the Roman Iron Age. Such exchange networks might lead to the formation of closer ties of political alliances and dominance, as documented in the gradual expansion of the Nordic network south of the Baltic. More people and services would travel within such networks, and it might ultimately lead groups of people to settle, as suggested between central Sweden and Poland (the Lusatian Culture) during the Late Bronze Age (Larsson 1993; Carlsson 1995; Larsson and Hulthén 2004). Such mechanisms of exchange and interaction can be archaeologically documented in the expanding distribution of personal items and prestige goods outside their local area, leading to the subsequent formation of new local cultures. If new settlements and burial rites accompany the flow of goods and people we may talk of a more permanent settlement expansion (population movement). Thus, such studies should be followed by an attempt to characterise the organisation of travel and movements (Fig. 15), which mostly has to be inferred indirectly, although new foreign settlement types and burial rites are good indicators of a direct influx of newcomers.

The scale of trading expeditions may also be inferred from the size and content of certain types of trading hoards, some of them from sunken ship cargoes such as Ulu Burun (Bass 1991) or Huelva (Ruiz-Galvez 1995).

Movements of prestige goods and people overlapped with or were embedded in more commercial transactions. This might lead to an expansion of political and/or commercial spheres of influence, sometimes followed by settlement expansion and population movements. The balance between the various components of exchange illustrated in Figure 15 may define different types of interaction that were linked to variations in social and political organisation, and to different processes of expansion and regression in Bronze Age Europe (Sherratt and Sherratt 1991; Sherratt 1994c; Kristiansen 1994).

Thus the complexity of exchange relations in the Bronze Age should be stressed. Only by integrating the various levels and spheres of interaction in a single study is it possible to reach a full picture of the social and economic organisation of Bronze Age society. From there we may be able to extract certain recurring structures of interaction. To achieve this we badly need one or two 'model studies' which may provoke debate, such as has been the case in Early Iron Age studies of the Hallstatt princely society since the 1980s. In the following we shall attempt to provide such model studies. Before doing

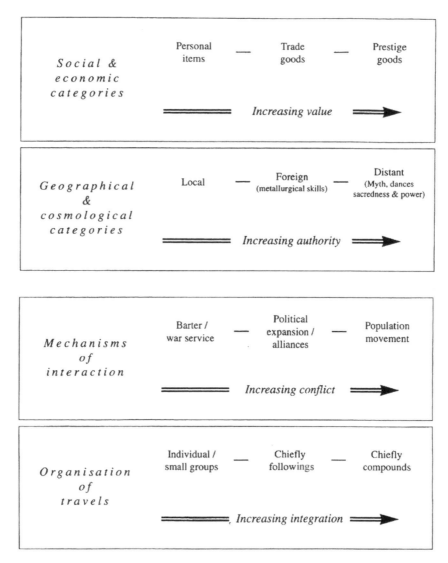

Fig. 15 Model of processes of interaction and trade.

so we shall penetrate a little deeper into the supernatural powers of skilled artisans and specialists as embodying and transmitting such cosmological virtues.

2.5 Crafts and creation: the sacred power of esoteric knowledge

In the origin myths of chiefly and state societies creator-crafters often play an important role. Their capacity to transform the world from raw material to precious goods is of the same order of magnitude as other transformative

capacities linked to gods, such as taking the shape of animals, moving
between different realms, deciding over life and death, etc. The traditional
skills linked to master artisans at chiefly courts are therefore associated with
the ancestors and with the Culture Heroes or Master Gods who originally
practised them and introduced them. The master artisan is thus connected
with sacred origins in both time and space. These qualifications are reproduced in the present by protecting access to it. Specialists – whether poets,
priests or master artisans – belong with the elite and their skills demand
years of learning and travelling.

Skilled artisans and the smith

In ranked societies chiefly aristocracies, skilled artisans and specialists
occupy a special, often sacred role as transmitters and transformers of the
power of ancestors and of the outer realm. As Mary Helms so brilliantly
demonstrates, skilled artisans and Culture Heroes are linked to the rise of
aristocracies and ancestors (Helms 1993: ch. 3), in Europe's history represented by the Bronze Age (probably also the Copper Age and the Megalithic
Age of the Neolithic, although qualitatively different).

More universally the rise of chiefdoms often corresponds to an increased
development of metallurgical skills and a whole new set of myths and gods
linked to the sacred roles of mining, smithing and rituals of transformation.
Mircea Eliade pointed to these connections and their religious-historical significance in his book *The Forge and the Crucible* (Eliade 1978). Smiths often
enjoy a privileged position linked to the role of the smith as a Culture
Hero, and the Heavenly Smith is the son, messenger and collaborator of
the Supreme God or the Creator God, and helps him to complete his work.
The transformative nature of smithing brings it into close correspondence
with other transformative rituals, from shamanism to initiation rites. Thus,
we should expect smithing to be part of other ritual and sacred functions
linked to chieftainship during the Bronze Age. Only during the later Iron
Age and in state societies would the smith begin to appear as a full-time
professional separated from these other functions. 'The Smith-Counsellor
continues and completes the work of God by making man capable of understanding mysteries. Hence the role of the smith in the initiations at puberty
and in secret societies, and his importance in religious life of the community. Even his relations with the chiefs and sovereigns, whom, in certain
regions, he overlaps, are of religious character' (Eliade 1978: 96). For these
reasons we should not expect to find the smith defined as a social category
of its own during the Bronze Age, and this will be true of other crafts as
well. They were loaded with magical-ritual functions linked to elites, and
thus rather supported primary elite function as chiefs, warriors and priests.

But this is true of other crafts as well. 'Ancestors and culture heroes (or their animal-spirit assistants) are recognised as the first dancers, first musicians, minstrels, and poets, first potters, painters, and carvers, first tattooists, first ship builders, first weavers, first jewellers and first workers in metal' (Helms 1993: 29).

The historical and magic-religious significance of the smith is his connection with the rise of new types of weapons and warriors, and consequently new types of power. The sword and lance define the beginning of the Bronze Age proper and a new age of heroic warfare, as we shall come back to in chapter 4. Here the smith occupies a central role by manufacturing the aristocratic new weapons, whose power relies on a combination of technical skills and secret magic. As master of these transformative skills, the smiths were in many cultures linked to occult sciences (magic, healing and shamanism) and to the art of song, dance and poetry. The smith-gods' weapon was the thunderbolt, being gods of thunder and lightning. This relates to another important skill of smithing: pyrotechnics and the control of fire. The rise of the smith and of metallurgy is accompanied by a new specialised knowledge of firing and pyrotechnics, which could be used for other purposes as well. They included improved firing techniques for pottery production, new skills in glass and bead production, but also new fire rituals and new traditions in cooking and chiefly cuisine.

Acquisitions and esoteric knowledge

Specialist skills and aristocratic powers do not originate locally, they are linked to distance, most clearly in the field of metalworking, which had been brought in from outside in most parts of Europe. Geographical space encompasses a sacred or supernaturally charged landscape, according to Helms, which implies that the acquisition of goods from geographically distant places is comparable in meaning and significance to the skilled crafting of goods and benefits often associated with temporal distance. Often, however, the two merge and become one: that is, when spatial and temporal distance becomes linked to cosmological origins loaded with supernatural and mythical qualities (Fig. 16). This explains why travels and trade with the outside world are essential in establishing and maintaining sacred and political power. Skilled crafting shares with travel the ability to cross boundaries and to transform things from one state to another. In the process they both become loaded with supernatural powers. The metalworker transforms the raw metal from the underworld into beautiful ornaments or weapons. This transformational process brings him into contact with supernatural powers, and adds to his technical skills a further often sacred power (Eliade 1962).

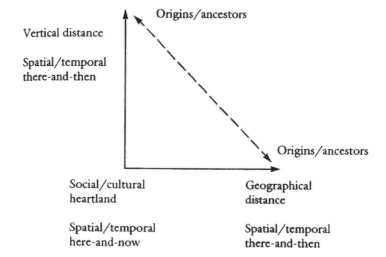

Vertical distance

Spatial/temporal
there-and-then

Origins/ancestors

Origins/ancestors

Social/cultural
heartland

Geographical
distance

Spatial/temporal
here-and-now

Spatial/temporal
there-and-then

Fig. 16
Congruence
between time
and space in
long-distance
travels (after
Helms 1993:
Fig. 3–2).

In the Bronze Age both the bronze and the new skills had to be brought in from outside. It linked from the very beginning the new metal with distant origins and supernatural centres out there. The Bronze Age is *the* age, *par excellence*, of cosmological power and distance linked to heroic travels of skilled artisans and specialists. To overcome the inherent dangers their work is often highly ritualised – whether as shipbuilders, metalworkers, hunters, poets or warriors: all typical examples of skilled craftsmen and specialists in ranked societies. Skilled craftsmen are often long-distance travellers and traders, thereby adding outside mystique and power to their craft (Fig. 17). Thus, travel as a distinctive, ritualised activity is comparable to skilled crafting. In this way trade, travel and skilled crafting become a specialist activity for certain members of the elite.

Traders, travellers and artisans may often be granted safe passage through territories that are dangerous to others, and they develop in addition professional skills of the geography of travelling and of language. Thus, the acquisition of foreign languages carries great prestige and was in Panama chiefdoms considered another form of esoteric knowledge (Helms 1979: 135). In the process they acquire personal reputation and are welcomed at the chiefly courts. But to achieve these professional skills is a long-term process. To achieve wisdom in ancient Panama chiefdoms, including chanting, rituals, myths and other chiefly skills, took years of education at a master's school. This was a prerequisite for becoming a local leader and belonging to the chiefly elite. And to become a master teacher and regional chief was an even longer process. Helms mentions an example of a regional chief and teacher who stayed as a pupil with a master for years, and after twenty-five

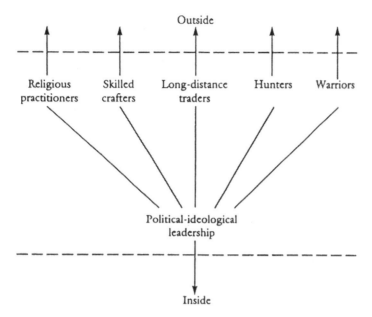

years of learning and travelling settled to become himself a regional centre of learning sought by young students and aspiring chiefs from the whole region. Thus, learning networks can often be correlated with exchange networks, and regional centres were in contact with the most distant learning and exchange centres beyond the isthmus (Helms 1979: 133 and 140).

In Celtic Europe Caesar mentions that to become a druid took twenty-one years, offering a parallel to ancient Panama. In non-literate societies the maintenance of myth, legal rules and rituals was a main occupation for specialists, who had to master the whole corpus of texts backwards and forwards. It granted enormous prestige and power to the role of the religious learned druid and bard. The quality of their craft, or wisdom, made it possible to reproduce it unaltered throughout centuries or even a millennium, as demonstrated by the religious continuity in Nordic Bronze Age rituals and iconographic narratives. The complexity of knowledge needed in ranked and chiefly societies is often underestimated, and so are their travels and prolonged studies in distant centres. Priests and poets were often highly learned, and in a world of oral wisdom master classes and centres of learning out there were part of the training and civilising process of becoming either skilled artisan, priest, poet, chief or all in one. Elite cultures of this kind therefore presume a shared ideological value system and a system of learning covering wide regions, something we consider a defining criterion of Bronze Age chiefdoms as well.

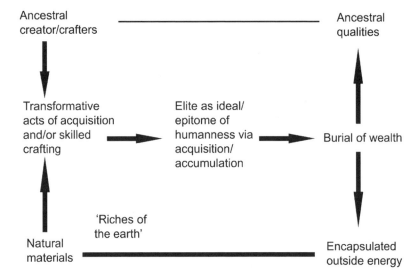

Fig. 18 Model showing the inside–outside cycle of the accumulation and transformation of power and energies (redrawn after Helms 1993: Fig. 8–3).

With this as a background we can begin to understand how and why precious (prestige) goods – often foreign acquisitions – were powerful. Power over things became power over people.

Products of skilled crafting and acquisitions from outside share a symbolic association of being transformed from nature or the realm of the outside world. They both originate in what in cosmological terms is considered the outside world and are transformed when entering the socialised world. The goods received and brought in from the outside (whether geographically or symbolically) are defined by their inalienable qualities derived from their association with specific distant and sacred places and/or the sacred value of skilled crafting. Since these are essential to the maintenance of chiefly elites and their cosmological qualifications as beings of supernatural power they organise trading expeditions and host skilled artisans to produce and bring back wealth from distant chiefdoms or ritual centres to support their prestige and their reputation. Such connections may be supported by social ties of marriage and kinship and thus develop into an extension of the external power of chiefdoms, as we shall see in a later chapter (chapter 5).

Chiefly prestige goods may also enter the sphere of burial rituals as grave goods, thus including dead chiefs and ancestors in the circuit of wealth production–circulation–consumption supporting the formation of cosmologies of origin and their transformation into local power. Burial wealth is a way to transform and sustain chiefly ideals, and may also testify to the heroic life of the deceased (Fig. 18). Here we enter dialectic between universal chiefly ideals and the individual persona, that could be expressed through small variations from that ideal. And we are able to trace the historical processes in the formation of new chiefly elites, as we shall see later. Local chiefly lineages may in this way transform origins in space to origins in time, and by constructing monumental barrows or by carving their deeds on rocks some chiefs become immortal. They will take their visible place in local mythology as dynastic founders or Culture Heroes in the tales and rituals performed in commemoration of the chiefly dynasties. Aspirations to chiefly or elite universality and heroic eternity as represented in monumental barrows or rock art may be taken as yet another defining criterion of chiefdoms. In state societies such ritual investments are instead converted into temples and monumental public buildings.

Some archaeological implications and applications

One of the expected consequences of the role of travelling chiefs and skilled artisans is the formation of a common elite culture. We should, however, expect it to be defined not in terms of identity of material culture, but rather in symbolic and cosmological terms, as we shall demonstrate later. Such an approach resolves the dichotomy between autonomous and external change, as it allows room for both to take place simultaneously.

How are we to trace the transmission of metallurgical, technological, religious and other forms of specialised knowledge if they do not materialise in a social identity, but are rather covered by other elite forms of identity, such as warrior chiefs? First, we have to test if this was also the case in the Bronze Age. As a beginning we may note the highly symbolic role skilled craft is assigned in Homer: Nestor is the tamer of horses, and for Odysseus his crafting of a special wedding bed occupies an important role in Penelope's testing of his identity. We are also in Homer presented with the skilled crafting of high-status women – that of weaving, a symbolically loaded craft sometimes performed in the great hall by the ritual hearth, as in the case of Arête. It demonstrates an important gender difference between the female domain of the home and the male domain of the external world of warfare and travels (Marinatos 1995b; Whittaker 1995). We shall see these very same gender differences repeated in the material record of the Bronze Age.

The identification of craftsmen and smiths in the archaeological record has been undertaken most consistently by Albrecht Jockenhövel (1982, 1986), and his findings were rather scarce: only now and then would the defining tools of the master artisan and smith pop up in burials. Only rarely would they alone define grave goods (Jockenhövel 1994: Fig. 29), whereas specialised settlements with metallurgical activities point to their ritualised role (Anfinset 2000; Prescott 2000).

Most commonly a special tool was added to the traditional grave goods of a chief or a member of the chiefly elite. In northern Europe the chisel for woodworking was a diagnostic tool for male chiefs, most common in the richest graves during the period 1600–1300 BC, reminding us of Odysseus and his master bed (Willroth 1985: Tables 2–4). But the elegant products of the chiefly skilled woodworking and carving are preserved in the North: campstools, decorated wooden drinking cups and woodcarvings on sword scabbards. We may assume that decorated poles in the chiefly houses were also an arena of display. New types of skilled woodworking were also manifest in chariot- and shipbuilding, which represented major new innovations in both skilled crafting and communication, although the evidence is mostly indirect, e.g. on rock art. We can thus demonstrate a correspondence between chiefly crafts in woodworking and the introduction of new prestige goods made of wood from the sixteenth century BC onwards (Fig. 19).

The Bronze Age represents a continuous process of metallurgical and related technological transfer. We have mentioned woodworking, but also linked to metallurgy was the production of glass beads, a technology that was brought along by travelling artisans and adopted in a few areas, e.g. the Wessex Culture. While the social identification of travelling smiths was incorporated or subsumed under the social identity of the chiefly elite, their tools are more often found in hoards, and as single depositions (Jockenhövel 1994; Krause 1998: Abb. 33). Hoards often represent different stages in the distribution of metal (Kristiansen 1998: 74ff.). Whereas in the Early Bronze Age this is often in the form of ingots (ring-shaped, axe-shaped, etc.), during the Middle Bronze Age diversification and specialisation develop. A single production was hoarded and preserved in a few cases, such as Smorumovre on Zealand, and this gives a glimpse of the size of central workshop production. Here were found in one hoard several hundred freshly cast axes and lances ready for local distribution. A few personal items of south German origin may testify to long-distance travels of chiefly metalsmiths, to be discussed in chapter 5.5 (Aner and Kersten 1973: Taf. 63–73).

What accompanied travelling chiefs and artisans was the transfer of new myths that contextualised and 'explained' the new skills and their social and ideological implications. We should consider the formation of a new, more complex cosmological universe as a diagnostic element in the formation of chiefdoms, and we shall later demonstrate this in a number of case studies. Their craft of oral wisdom and knowledge was preserved only indirectly in iconography and pictorial narratives, which we will trace and explain in subsequent case studies.

The overall picture of skilled artisans and smiths during the Bronze Age conforms at first glance quite well with Mary Helms' ethnohistorical findings: their skills belonged with the chiefly elites, and did not represent an established social identity, but rather were subsumed under chiefly identity or other forms of identity. We should probably also expect some

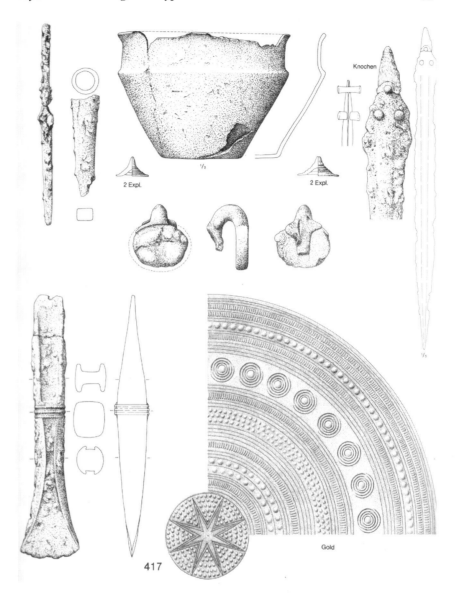

Fig. 19 Rich chiefly burial with chisel for woodworking (after Aner and Kersten 1973: No. 417).

hierarchy in the role and functions of skilled crafting. Most clear and visible – and therefore probably loaded with prestige – was the craft of woodworking. However, as we shall later demonstrate, the role of priests and bards was also highly prestigious, and their myths were materialised as part of rituals, for example in rock art, which represented the ritual narratives and symbolic manifestations of divine and chiefly endeavours. We are still a long way from the economic and social complexity of Near Eastern states and palace societies, with their organised hierarchy of artisans and divisions of labour (Laffineur and Betancourt 1997). But perhaps the distance is less than we tend to believe: also in the east Mediterranean craftsmen were rarely identified in burials, and without the written records of Linear B, for example, we would hardly dare to infer such complexity on archaeological grounds alone. Thus, we may tend to underestimate the social complexity of the non-literate Bronze Age societies in Europe outside the Near East and the east Mediterranean. What their written evidence and archaeology do testify to and confirm, however, is the high status of master artisans, and the exchange and travels of skilled craftsmen (Bloedow 1997; Gillis 1997; Shaw 1997). In that, they probably also set a model for the early European Bronze Age societies. In order to understand the transfer of Bronze Age technologies and cosmologies we need to present both sides of the interaction, and we shall begin with the Near East.

2.6   Conclusion: the Bronze Age as epoch

Based on comparative ethnohistorical evidence and historical evidence from the Near East, we propose that the rise of ranked and state societies during the Bronze Age represented the formation not only of new elites, skilled artisans and specialists, but of a new social and economic complexity (Kristiansen 1998; Harding 2000).[1] It was accompanied by a similar religious and cosmological transformation that granted the new skills and the accompanying new forms of long-distance travel an outstanding role in society. They transmitted new knowledge and skills linked to ancestral origins and powers, which over time became institutionalised and ritualised as part of local tradition. New gods were created and old ones redefined to sustain the new social and cosmological order – gods for warfare, smithing, travelling, skilled crafting, etc. 'Thus we find strong associations between creator gods and culture heroes on the one hand and human artisans and persons of influence on the other' (Helms 1993: 24), yet another indication of the eminent role of skilled artisans in ancient society. The new skills and cosmologies were quickly transmitted over vast regions by the enormous expansion of long-distance travel and exchange. We propose that these developments mark a qualitative difference between the Bronze Age and the Neolithic and

---

1 To stress the universal, and yet specific historical role of chiefdoms, Timothy Earle (2002) has recently designated them as 'Bronze Age Economics', alluding to Marshall Sahlins' *Stone Age Economics* (1972). It underscores the often noted correspondence between developments in metallurgy and the rise of states and chiefdoms. Thus, would there have been a European Bronze Age without the rise of the state and a Bronze Age economy in Mesopotamia? As we argue, the answer is no. 'Without the bronze, without the weapons there would have been no Bronze Age warrior idea' (Renfrew 2001b: 137). And these ideas originated in the first place in the Bronze Age urban societies.

Copper Ages. We do find chiefdoms in the European Later Neolithic, but of a different nature (Renfrew 1973; Sherratt 1998: Fig. 1.2).

This new heroic cosmology is echoed in the first appearance of heroic texts, such as Gilgamesh, the *Iliad* and the *Odyssey*, and the Celtic myths and sagas. Although sometimes written down at a much later time, they maintain the cultural ethos of the Bronze Age, through the continued tradition of bards and religious specialists. These people maintained the mythological heritage of Bronze Age societies, an accumulating mythological time–space continuum (see Gosden's 1994 discussion of time cycles), over centuries and even millennia, sometimes in exile, when social disaster hit as in the case of the twelfth-century collapse of the Mycenaean palaces. Such geographical (but not social) marginalisation would often tend to preserve the myths and sagas in fossilised form, as in the case with Beowulf and the *Iliad* and the *Odyssey*, as the heritage of a glorified heroic past of exiled royal and chiefly elites. To this we may add the direct historical texts of the Bronze Age, from tablets, which reveal the economic and religious complexity of the period in the east Mediterranean and the Near East. They demonstrate the economic foundations that sustained the elites and therefore never appear in heroic literature owing to its very nature.[2] In archaeological terms the Bronze Age is thus situated in protohistory. Historically it is situated in the context of the rise and subsequent spread of city-states, palace cultures and early states during the third and second millennia BC, and their impact upon and interaction with Europe and western Asia.

In this way the new Bronze Age world became interlinked in both technological and cosmological terms from the east Mediterranean and Eurasia to Scandinavia. We shall therefore begin by presenting a historical outline of rulership in the Near East and the eastern Mediterranean during the second millennium BC, followed by a presentation of Bronze Age societies in Europe during the same period, and the transformations they underwent.

---

2 It is a universal feature of elites at all times that subordinates are absent and invisible in their cultural ethos. It is therefore a mistake to use the information from Linear B bureaucracy to argue against the *Iliad* and the *Odyssey* being of Mycenaean age. The life of subordinates is only revealed if it serves a purpose to illuminate the story of the hero: in the case of Odysseus his arrival and return via the help of the swineherd, who, by the way, clearly is a high official.

Rulership in the Near East and the eastern Mediterranean during the Bronze Age

The role of the ruler in the Near East and the eastern Mediterranean has been the subject of much recent research (e.g. Buchholz 1987b; Marinatos 1993; Kuhrt 1995; Davies and Shofield 1995; Bryce 1998; Cline and Harris-Cline 1998). The purpose of this chapter is merely to point out some features related to kingship and divinity (theocratic leadership) that we believe could be of relevance for the study of social transformation in Europe during the second millennium BC.

The eastern Mediterranean and western Asia were in contact with each other during the second millennium BC (e.g. Davies and Schofield 1995; Cline and Harris-Cline 1998). Interconnections also existed between the Mediterranean and central Europe (e.g. Bouzek 1997; Kristiansen 1998a). Consequently the whole chain of contacts – from the Orient to Scandinavia – is of relevance for the present study (Larsson 1999a). We will also consider the various mechanisms of contact between states (section 3.4). Finally we shall extract from the evidence certain regularities linked to rulership and its implementation – from conquest and tribute to political alliances and trade (section 3.5).

3.1 Kingship and divinity in Mesopotamia and Egypt

Mesopotamia

In Mesopotamia, most rulers were thought to have close relations with gods and divinities, even if the kings themselves seldom were treated as divine beings during their lifetime. The traditional story tells that the rulers of the Early Dynastic periods (c.2900–2350 BC) were leaders of what have been called 'theocratic temple-states' (Kuhrt 1995: 28ff.; Wittfogel 1957), though this concept has been challenged (Diakonoff 1974). They can more neutrally be desribed as city-states. Recent research has in fact questioned the very existence of temple estates at all, and argues that the estates of the gods were the property of the king and his ruling family (Foster 1981; Tunca 1986; Kuhrt 1995: 29).

The ruler could be seen as a protector of a city in the name of the city's tutelary deity (Kuhrt 1995: 33). It was the duty of the king to build and maintain temples and his 'privileged relationship with the deity ensured divine help, blessing and plenty for the city in return for the ruler's constant attention to his (or her) needs' (Kuhrt 1995: 33). The fact that kingship and divinity were two closely related subjects is witnessed by written sources: 'After the flood had swept thereover, when kingship was lowered from heaven the kingship was in Kish' (Jacobsen 1939: 76).

At the beginning, kingship was thought to be given by certain gods ('lowered from heaven') to a profane ruler, which legitimised his social, political and religious position and that of his successors. Another inscription from the late Early Dynastic III phase (*c.*2450 BC) from Lagash describes the king Eanatum as created by the gods (Cooper 1983: 45; Kuhrt 1995: 33).

Other written documents from the city-state of Lagash show that it was not only the male ruler who possessed power and wealth. The ruler's wife and the royal children also owned and controlled large estates and the personal correspondence between queens of different cities is documented (Lambert 1953; van de Mieroop 1989).

During the period 2300–2000 BC political centralisation dominated in Mesopotamia under the two dynasties from Akkad and Ur. This led to certain changes in the ideology of rulership. Naram-Sin, the ruler of Agade *c.*2260–2223, is an interesting character because he seems to have taken the step from humanity to divinity (Kuhrt 1995: 51–2). Because of his heroic battles and great victories, he transformed (during his lifetime) from being a profane ruler to becoming a deity – the city god of Agade.

On his victory stele, Naram-Sin is depicted with a horned helmet on his head (Fig. 20), which is an exclusive divine attribute (Oates 1986: 41; see also chapter 5.6). The divinisation of a living ruler, as in the case of Naram-Sin, is a practice previously unknown in Mesopotamia, but sporadically it continued into the first half of the second millennium BC (the 'Old Babylonian' period, *c.*2004–1595 BC).

Another important role of the Mesopotamian king was as a warrior and conqueror. The ruler was the prime warrior, and war, conquest and campaigns in foreign lands were more or less 'natural' parts of kingship. For example, on the 'Vulture stele' of Eanatum of Lagash from *c.*2450 BC, the king can be seen riding his chariot and leading the army into battle.

The chariots of this period had four solid wooden wheels and were drawn by donkeys, which made them much slower and less movable than the horse-drawn war chariots with spoked wheels that emerged about 1900 BC. The text of the stele tells that after the battle the victorious king Eanatum constructed twenty burial mounds for the fallen enemy of Umma (Winter 1985).

During the Agade period, *c.*2340–2159 (Kuhrt 1995: 44), the physical wealth of the kings is pronounced in pictorial representations. He is portrayed with special cloths and with a special hairdo, often sitting on a throne, carrying royal attributes and superior weapons. Similar scenes can also be found on seal-impressions from tablets from Ur III.

Fig. 20
Naram-Sin's
victory stele
(after Kuhrt 1995:
52).

The link between the king and the divine sphere is a very close one in
Mesopotamia and the ruler has many divine aspects, even if he lacks the
most obvious divine attributes (Winter 1985). The role of the ruler during the
Ur III period is expressed by Kuhrt as: 'the king at its apex [of the bureaucratic structure] forms a bridge between the human and divine spheres'
(1995: 67).

According to royal hymns (preserved in Old Babylonian versions) the divine aspects of kingship ideology during Ur III are very clear. A sentence describing the king, such as 'You [in] your judgement, you are the son of Anu, Your commands, like the word of a god, cannot be reversed' (Falkenstein 1936), shows the divine nature of kingship. In the royal hymns, the king possesses many qualities such as physical strength and beauty. He is often a soldier, a military commander, expert in handling weapons and brave, and he is also the great hunter of dangerous animals (Hallo 1963). His great wisdom and ability to speak all languages and his knowledge of music and hymns also contributed to giving the king more or less superhuman qualities. Together with the fact that the king was thought to be divinely born, these characteristics legitimised the ruler's semi-divine role in society and secured the superior status of the royal families over generations.

In the yearly performed 'sacred marriage' festival (Kramer 1983), the king took the role of the goddess Inanna's mortal husband Dumuzi. The role of the goddess was probably played by a high priestess, and in the sexual act between the two the king entered the divine domain and thus ensured a good relation between his people and the pantheon.

Another variation on this theme, attested in Uruk already during the late Uruk period (*c*.3500–3200), has been described by Jacobsen (1987: 29ff.), and here the ruler takes the role of 'the god of the date palm', and his wife 'plays' the role of the goddess Inanna. As Jacobsen has pointed out, the sacred marriage ritual was about fertility, and during later times the focus on dates was abandoned in favour of a more general prosperity/fertility cult (*Hieros Gamos*).

The principle of divine kingship was never totally adopted in Mesopotamian religion as it was in Egyptian cosmology, where the pharaoh was believed to be a god incarnate. Though Mesopotamian rulers were treated as semi-divine and as persons with very close relations to the divinities, they were always subject to the will of the gods (Oates 1986: 41), and never treated as their equals.

Between 2000 and 1500 BC the Near East consisted of a patchwork of city-states, where individual rulers from time to time conquered larger regions. With the ruler Hammurabi, the political role of the Mesopotamian city of Babylon increased dramatically, and *c*.1755 BC Hammurabi was the paramount king of a very large territory – although shortlived – reaching from Hittite Anatolia to the Gulf coast. On the famous Hammurabi 'Law Code Stele', the king is depicted together with the sun-god Shamash who sits on a throne wearing the divine attribute in the form of a multi-horned crown (Fig. 21).

He is giving the king the two attributes of kingship, the measuring rod and coiled rope, which symbolise the king's role as a just ruler and a successful conqueror (Kuhrt 1995: 111). Again, the iconography suggests a very close

Fig. 21 The top of Hammurabi's 'Law Code Stele' (after Oates 1986: 66).

relation between kingship and divinity, but it is probably wrong to speak in terms of true divine kingship.

The Babylonian dominance over this vast region seems to have been quite stable for just over 150 years, to 1595 BC, when the Hittite king Mursili I sacked the city of Babylon (Oates 1986: 84; Bryce 1998: 103). This is a hall-mark in the history of Babylonia and the event further indicates that the Babylonian ruler Samsu-ditana's political and military control was weak. After the Hittite conquest of Aleppo, and the simultaneous fall of the king-dom of Iamhad, the way to the Euphrates – and Babylon – lay open for Mursili's army. After a march of some 800 km from Aleppo, the Hittite army was at the gates of Babylon, and the conquest of the city seems to have been quite easy.

The political or strategic purpose behind this Babylonian expedition is difficult to understand, as the Hittites withdrew immediately after sack-ing the town. The plan was surely not to make it Hittite. An alliance between the Hittites and the Kassites (the new ruling dynasty in Babylon after the Hittites left) makes an interesting scenario. According to this the conquest of Babylon increased Mursili's political power and prestige while at the same time creating the right opportunity for the Kassites in Babylon to make their move towards dynastic power (Gurney 1973: 250; Bryce 1998: 104).

The Kassite power over Babylonia lasted for more than 400 years (1595–1155 BC) and the kings' title was 'king of Babylonia', i.e. the kingship covered not only a city-state, as earlier, but a larger territorial state (Kuhrt 1995: 338).

Already during the seventeenth century the supremacy of the city-state of Babylon was being challenged by an emerging rival dynasty in southernmost Mesopotamia – the Sealand Dynasty (Kuhrt 1995: 116) – that obstructed trade networks from the Gulf to the north. This affected the lucrative Babylonian trade with copper from Oman, and the long-distance trade with the Indus valley was also hampered by the 'Sealanders' in the south. Apart from the direct economic consequences, the constriction of trade threatened royal prestige (Kuhrt 1995: 332), which, among other things, was dependent on the ruler's ability to secure a steady inflow of exotic prestige goods as well as a variety of staple products. Therefore, the obstruction of trade links to Babylon could be one possible reason why the Babylonian court and army under Samsu-ditana were not able to stop the Hittite looting of their capital.[1]

During the Kassite period, Babylonia regained control over the 'Sealand' and thus opened the trade route to the Gulf. Excavations have shown that the Kassites had a fortress and a commercial centre on Bahrain, which indicate a strong control over the trade (Kuhrt 1995: 340).

During the period 1500–1200 BC there existed an international power balance between a handful of large territorial states, known as 'the club of the Great powers' (Liverani 2001; van de Mieroop 2003: ch. 7). The diplomatic relations between Babylonians, Egyptians, Assyrians, Hittites and other states in the Near East is exceptionally well known through the 'Amarna letters', found at the site of el-Amarna in Middle Egypt (Petrie 1894; Moran 1987; Aldred 1988: 183ff.; Kuhrt 1995: 194ff.). The interrelationship between Babylonia and the eastern Mediterranean is witnessed by, for example, the large Kassite seals of lapis lazuli found in Greece (Porada 1982), and the Mycenaean oxhide ingot found at Dur Kurigalzu.

---

1 The situation discussed above exemplifies the importance of trade and prestige goods exchange as means to maintain and reproduce power and prestige within stratified social systems. A similar situation to that of Babylon might have occurred in Europe during the Early Iron Age when Celtic chiefdoms in central Europe hampered the import of copper and tin to northern Europe, causing the collapse of the Bronze Age exchange networks. This in turn caused profound social changes in south Scandinavia c.600–400 BC (Kristiansen 1998a: ch. 6).

It is clear that gift exchange (trade) between these 'superpowers' was very important, and marriage relations seem to have been frequently established between the ruling elites, for example the marriage between the Babylonian king Kadashman-Enlil's daughter and Amenophis III of Egypt during the mid-fourteenth century. Gold, precious stones, lapis lazuli, horses and specialists like sculptors, doctors and conjurors were included in this exchange network. In particular, the exchange of specialist personnel and artisans between these states, like a sculptor from Babylonia working for the Hittite king in Hattusha (Zaccagnini 1983), must have promoted transmissions of styles, forms and, in the long run, perhaps even ideologies. The importance of interaction, trade and royal gift exchange will be further elaborated in chapter 3.5.

When it comes to iconography and royal and divine attributes, we have already mentioned the horned crown or helmet as a symbol of divinity. Only in a few exceptional cases, as in the case of Naram-Sin (Fig. 20), is the horned headgear worn by mortals, and then it is the ruler who is portrayed. This attribute of divinity can either consist of a single pair of horns (Naram-Sin), or be multi-horned, as the sun-god Shamash on the famous Law Code Stele of Hammurabi (Fig. 21).

Mesopotamian goddesses were also depicted with this attribute (Fig. 22), so the horned headgear must be seen as an attribute expressing the 'divine gender', rather than relating to the traditional dichotomy: male/female, goddess/god.

Other divine (and royal?) paraphernalia of interest here are the mace, the scimitar and the bow. The first two of these attributes of divine power – mace and scimitar – are often placed in the hands of Inanna (Ishtar), as illustrated in Figure 22. She was a multi-gendered goddess with many roles in Mesopotamian cosmology: a goddess of the storehouse of dates; the power of the thunderstorms of spring; a goddess of war; the goddess of the morning and evening star (Venus); the protector of harlots (Jacobsen 1987: 21ff.). The representation of Ishtar in Figure 22 is taken from an Old Babylonian cylinder seal from Tell Asmar (after Oates 1986: 175), and here she appears in her role of war-goddess, carrying a 'lion mace' and a scimitar. We can also see that she is standing on an animal (possibly a lion), wearing a multi-horned headgear, and close to her head is the eight-pointed star of Venus, which is another of her common attributes.

Another attribute of Ishtar, and of other divinities as well – e.g. the god Ashur (Biedermann 1991: 464) – and later also heroes, is wings (Oates 1986: 130–1).

The bow is present on Akkadian seals in the hands of divinities (e.g. Oates 1986: 37), and images from the post-Kassite period show Babylonian rulers depicted with bows (1986: 106).

Fig. 22 Seal showing the goddess Inanna (Ishtar) (after Oates 1986: 175).

Egypt

In Egypt, the relationship between kingship and divinity was much more integrated than in Mesopotamia. The living pharaoh was usually titled 'Horus-king', the son of Re/Ra (the sun-god). As such he is a god incarnate, who, after his life on earth, 'ascends to the sky, joins Re on the solar bark for his voyage back and forth across the heavens' (Lesko 1987: 38). As in Mesopotamia the Egyptian rulers of the Old Kingdom (*c.*2686–2181 BC) were at the apex of the state, but the pharaoh was not only closely related to the divinities, but in fact 'the incarnation of sacred power' (Kuhrt 1995: 147). This is a major difference compared to Mesopotamia (Wengrow 1999 for a discussion of Henri Frankfort's classic works).

Of the Old Kingdom royal regalia, we can mention a special type of kilt, the sceptre, a pointed beard, a crook in his hand, and the double crown with the uraeus on his head. The royal throne on which the king sat was identified with the goddess Isis, his mother. In the Pyramid Texts, the Horus-king's parents are the sun-god Ra and the mother goddess Hathor, but, at the same time, his mother and father are also Isis and Osiris (Lesko 1987: 38).

During the First Intermediate Period (c.2180–2040 BC), when central authority was weakening, local monarchs (district or province governors) and others making claims on kingship also made claim on divinity. Further, the decentralisation of profane and ritual power affected people's relation to the divine sphere: 'commoners being associated with Thoth, great ones with Osiris, and, obviously, royalty with Re' (Lesko 1987: 40).

During the Middle Kingdom (c.2040–1730 BC), which was dominated by the twelfth dynasty, the large statues picture the kings as warrior-heroes with great strength and physical power. A text from a papyrus from the Fayum presents Sesostris I (c.1971–1926 BC) in the following way (Kuhrt 1995: 165):

> Horus: Divine in Form; the Two Ladies: Divine of Birth; Gold Horus:
> Being: the King of Upper and Lower Egypt: Khakaure; the Son of Re:
> Sesostris – he has seized the Two Lands in triumph.
> Hail to you, Khakaure, our Horus, Divine of Form!

We see that the early kings of the twelfth dynasty were still identified with Horus, symbolised by the falcon. But an identification of the king as the sun-god Re himself is also witnessed by songs in honour of the later king Sesostris III, ruling c.1878–1841 BC (Lesko 1987: 41). During the Middle Kingdom, Amun, a local god of Thebes, turned into a very important figure and he became increasingly associated/identified with Re – the most prominent divinity of all time in the Egyptian pantheon.

Egypt's trading links with other states in the region are quite well attested and it is known that the Egyptians were mining turquoise on a large scale in Sinai during the Middle Kingdom (Kuhrt 1995: 171). This period is also famous for its 'loyalist literature', through which the rulers of the twelfth dynasty represented themselves as the legitimate kings of Egypt (Posener 1956). This propaganda literature was probably a way of supporting and reproducing the dynasty's political power, which, however, ended in the late eighteenth century BC with the domination of the foreign Hyksos rulers. Their political and cultural dominance in Egypt covered a period of almost 200 years (c.1720–1550 BC), and this era was later characterised by the succeeding New Kingdom dynasties and folk-stories as both destructive and irreligious (Redford 1970; Kuhrt 1995: 173). The origin of the Hyksos rulers has been a debated subject as to the extent of their political control over Egypt (Habachi 1972; Trigger 1976; Franke 1985). In the Kamose text we can see that Kamose calls Apophis, the Hyksos ruler, 'great man of Retenu'

(Smith and Smith 1976), and, together with the fact that most Hyksos names were Semitic, it is fairly possible that they came from the Levant or Syria–Palestine. As has been pointed out by Rice, the word Hyksos is derived from '*Hikau-Khoswet*', 'rulers of foreign lands' (Rice 1997: 142).

The newly discovered Minoan wall paintings from Avaris (Tell el-Dab'a in the eastern delta) show that the Hyksos rulers were open to impulses from the eastern Mediterranean realm (Bietak 1992; Manning 1999), because the site of Avaris was the capital for the Hyksos dynasty. On one of the excavated buildings, the wall frescos show bull-leaping scenes, more or less identical with the ones in Cretan palaces, and this indicates that the Hyksos and Cretan rulers were in close contact with each other. However, it must be noted that the dating of the frescos at Avaris is not unproblematic (Manning 1999; Niemeier and Niemeier 1998: 85ff.), and the suggestions range between Late Hyksos (LM IA) and Early Dynastic XVIII (Late LM IB).

Another indication of foreign trade and interaction during the late Hyksos period may be the sudden appearance of the composite bow and the two-wheeled chariot, which were novelties in the early New Kingdom (Kuhrt 1995: 182).

The Egyptian New Kingdom comprises the eighteenth–twentieth dynasties and the dating of the period is *c.*1550–1069 BC, which makes it contemporary with the Middle and Late Bronze Age of central Europe and the Montelian periods 2–3 of the north European Bronze Age. From this perspective, it is interesting to note that the horse-drawn two-wheeled chariot seems to have been introduced simultaneously in Egypt and south Scandinavia – the chariot scene from the Kivik burial chamber in Scania and the bronze statuettes from Trundholm and Tågaborg bear witness to this. During the mid-second millennium BC, interaction and trade within and outside the eastern Mediterranean world also stimulated the transmission of symbols, concepts and ideas over vast areas, which can be identified in, among other things, some of the rock art motifs in southern Sweden (discussed in chapter 7). The chariot and the ship, which, according to the rock art, were two vital symbols for Bronze Age people in parts of south Scandinavia, are foreign elements planted in the Nordic Bronze Age context, of which the ship images may have an Egyptian origin (Olsson 1999). It should be remembered that the ship was an old motif in Egyptian iconography, but the emergence of an Egyptian navy did not occur until during the New Kingdom (Säve-Söderberg 1946). The making of figurative images on rock surfaces was a novelty in south Scandinavia during this period, and the very idea may have been introduced through interaction with other regions.

During the beginning of this 'imperial period' of Egypt's history, the Hyksos were definitely driven out of Egypt, and Egypt now took control over parts of southern Palestine. The expansionist politics of Amose was also directed towards Nubia in the south, and the many military campaigns carried out by the rulers of the early eighteenth dynasty indicate that a professional army was established (Kemp 1989; Kuhrt 1995: 190).

Dealing with kingship and divinity from a gender perspective, the reign of Hatshepsut (c.1490–1469 BC) is very interesting. 'She employed pharaonic titles, wore male royal dress, such as the ceremonial beard, used her daughter, Neferure, to act ritually as queen and was acknowledged as "king" by her officials' (Kuhrt 1995: 191). Of course, this female kingship had to be sanctioned by the priests and by the gods themselves, and therefore it was important for Hatshepsut to legitimise her divine position: 'the justification she chose to propagate was her own "divine birth." She had this recorded on the walls of her mortuary temple at Deir al-Bahri, which depicted Amun-Re in the form of her father, Thutmose I, coming to her mother Ahmose, who conceived the goddess-king, the female Horus' (Lesko 1987: 42).

Her successor, Tuthmosis III, and later official Egyptian records tried to erase or ignore the reign of Hatshepsut, which shows that female rulership was not really accepted in the Egyptian worldview. However, some scholars have suggested that the succession to royal power in ancient Egypt followed the female line (Robins 1993; Rice 1997: 146). In the pantheon, Hathor and Isis are two powerful goddesses and the role of the latter seems to have been closely related to the transfer of divine kingship: 'The act of the king seating himself on the throne at his coronation was the moment at which he was invested, not only with the Kingship, but with divinity. The throne was personified as Isis (the hieroglyph of her name actually pictured the throne) and by his contact with her lap the king became a god' (Rice 1997: 146).

During the reigns of Tuthmosis III, Amenophis II and Tuthmosis IV (c.1469–1403), the Egyptian political influence increased in the Levant owing to the intensive military campaigns in the region. The Mitanni kingdom was one of the Egyptian targets, but the Babylonians and Hittites were also disturbed by the Egyptian activities in the Levant. During Tuthmosis IV's eight-year reign, an Egypt–Mitanni agreement was signed, and to seal this pact the Egyptian ruler married the daughter of King Artatama of Mitanni (Bryan 1991; Kuhrt 1995: 194).

The Egyptian rulers of the fifteenth century were more open to foreign stimuli than earlier: 'foreign alliances, foreign wives, and foreign deities were all introduced in this period, which peaked in the reign of Amenhotep III [Amenophis III]' (Lesko 1987: 42). This ruler marks the beginning of the Amarna period – a short but very special phase in the history of ancient Egypt, more associated with his successor, Akhenaton (Amenophis IV), and his special cult of 'Aten' (Aldred 1988). He created a new cult of the sun-disc 'Aten', located to a city – Akhenaton – in the desert of el-Amarna, founded c.1360 BC. There were many open-air temples in the city devoted to Aten; because it was the sun-disc that was worshipped, the cult took place in the open. Akhenaton means 'Aten on the horizon', and during the fifth year of his reign (1359 BC) he changed his own name from Amenophis to Akhenaton, which means 'He who is beneficial to Aten' (Kuhrt 1995: 197). His wife was the famous queen Nefertiti, who also played an important role in the cult of Aten.

As we can see, the sun-disc was the prime object for worship in the 'Atenism' of Akhenaton, and the rays of the sun were likewise important; they literally connected the ruler and his family with the sun-god Re, as can be seen in many images (Fig. 23).

Further, the small hands on the rays bring the Egyptian symbol of life (ankh) to the divine royal family, and it has been argued that during the reign of Akhenaton the merging of the identity of the sun-god and the king was at its most extreme (Redford 1984).

The royal correspondence between Egypt and other states of the Near East is witnessed by the famous Amarna letters (some 350 clay slabs with Akkadian or Babylonian cuneiform signs). Letters from the ruler Burnaburiash of Babylon and from the Mitanni king Tushratta to Akhenaton are preserved, and most letters from Tushratta to Akhenaton, contain complaints about Akhenaton's failure to send the presents (gifts) which his father, Amenhotep III, had promised the Mitannian ruler.

> According to Tushratta, before his death Amenophis III had undertaken to send him additional presents, including two statues of solid gold. But when the gifts, reduced in number and value, arrived in Naharin during the first months of Akhenaton's reign, it was found that inferior statues of wood overlaid with gold had been substituted. (Aldred 1988: 193)

Akhenaton's monotheistic experiment, with the non-anthropomorphic sun-disc Aten as the sole heavenly king and himself as the god's incarnation on earth, was very short-lived. With the reign of Tutankhamen (c.1345–1335 BC) the Amun cult was restored, and he made statues of himself both as Amun and as Osiris (Lesko 1987: 43). The succeeding kings of the nineteenth and twentieth dynasties demonstrated their polytheism by building many new temples to various gods and goddesses, and eventually the remnants of the Aten cult were removed. One of the more famous pharaohs of the nineteenth dynasty was Ramesses II, who ruled for more than sixty years (c.1290–1224 BC), and the colossal statues of himself at Abu Simbel show that he was equivalent in rank with the gods.

Both Sety I (c.1305–1290 BC) and Ramesses II conducted military campaigns in Libya and in Syria in their efforts to expand the empire. One of the most famous battles of antiquity – the battle of Kadesh (c.1285 BC) – was fought in Syria between the Egyptians and the Hittites during the reign of Hattusili III and during the fifth year of Ramesses II's reign (Kuhrt 1995: 207; Bryce 1998). However, this great battle did not change the boundaries between two states in any profound way.

Fig. 23
Akhenaton
worshipping
Aten, the solar
disc (from Aldred
1988: Fig. 8).

During the first half of the early thirteenth century, the Hittites had
problems with the expanding Assyrian kingdom and the Egyptians had
serious difficulties along the western border with Libyan attacks. This may
have been one reason for the emerging friendship between Egypt and the
Hittites after the battle of Kadesh, and the bonds were further strength-
ened by the marriage between Ramesses II and Hattusili III's daughter,
*c.*1256 BC.

It was not only the king's role as an emperor and war leader that was
accentuated during the New Dynasty, but also his divine nature. The royal

ka temple in Luxor was the major construction in this cult of the divine pharaoh, and many other temples were erected in Egypt for this purpose (Kuhrt 1995: 215).

Some of the iconography of divine rulership was shared more widely. The hieroglyph *ka*, meaning soul, spirit of the creation and preservation of life (Wilkinson 1992), is depicted as two raised arms (Fig. 24b), in a fashion identical to the arm position of the 'adorers' in the Nordic rock art tradition (Fig. 24a), and as was common also in Late Mycenaean figurines.

Another Egyptian hieroglyph, which is more similar to the Nordic 'adorers' than the *ka* sign, is the sign *hai* (Fig. 24c) – a determinative used when writing 'happiness', 'joy' or 'rejoicing' (Wilkinson 1992).

In a similar way, some of the Egyptian drawings of ships show a remarkable resemblance with the rock art ships of southern Sweden (e.g. Almgren 1927; Olsson 1999). These similarities in form, and possibly even in meaning, will be further elaborated in chapter 5.6.

We may illustrate such processes by a historical example. From later Greek and Roman sources we know that parts of the Egyptian cosmology spread to Europe during the first centuries BC (Witt 1971). Michael Rice has pointed this out in his work on *Egypt's Legacy* (1997: 190):

> But the most powerful of all the images of divinity which at this time flowed out of Egypt was of the Mother holding her child on her lap. This ancient symbol of the transmission of the divine Kingship from the heiress to the Horus was transmuted into the image of Mary and her child. The Queen of Heaven and the son of Man who is also the Son of God, a divine king whose divinity is mediated through his mother's impregnation by a patriarchal divinity. The extent of Isis' cult was immense. Like that of Serapis it reached deep into western Europe, into Gaul and the basin of Danube.

3.2 Hittite rulership

The purpose of this section is to give a brief introduction to Hittite history and rulership – we are merely discussing selected aspects of very complex topics, which are more fully elaborated by authors like Akurgal (1962), Bittel (1976), Macqueen (1986), Gurney (1990), Bryce (1998), and most recently also in the illustrious book *Die Hethiter und ihr Reich* (2002).

In central Anatolia small kingdoms had already developed during the mid-third millennium, and at the site of Alaça Hüyük members of the 'royal' family were buried in richly equipped shaft graves, dated to 2300–2100 BC (Akurgal 1962: 15ff.; Bittel 1976: 30ff.; Macqueen 1986: 32; Bryce 1998: 9).

The question of the origins of the Hittites has been discussed for a long time without any real consensus being reached among scholars (Crossland

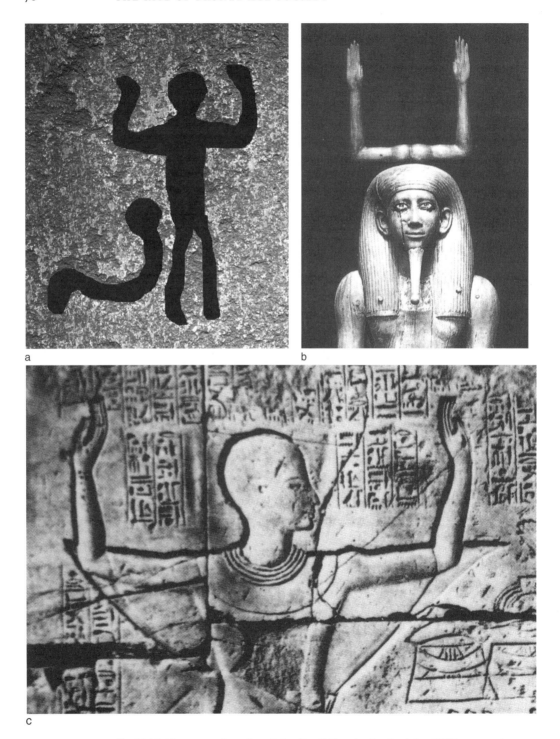

Fig. 24 (*a*) Adorer on rock art from Bohuslän; (*b*) Egyptian *ka* sign (after Wilkinson 1992); (*c*) Egyptian *hai* sign (after Wilkinson 1992).

 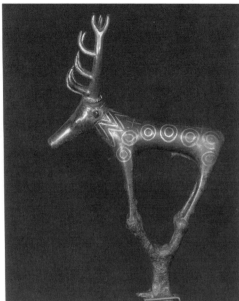

Fig. 25 Hattian bronze stags with silver inlays from Anatolia (after Özgüç 2002: Abb. 1–2).

and Birchall 1974; Steiner 1990) and the same can be said for the question of when they came.

The people inhabiting central Anatolia around 2000 BC are regarded not as Hittites, but as a people usually referred to as the Hattians – most likely an indigenous pre-Indo-European group (Güterbock 1997: 49; Bryce 1998: 11). It has been suggested that the Indo-European-speaking Hittites were immigrants from the Maikop region north of the Caucasus, arriving in Anatolia about 2200, and that the tombs at Alaça Hüyük thus belong to Hittite princes who ruled the indigenous Hattians (Yakar 1981: 94; Akurgal 1962). In fact, the artistic expressions of some of the finds from Horoztepe (Akurgal 1962: 22) show a remarkable resemblance to Caucasian decorative art (Fig. 25).

The Hittites formed their kingdom during the mid-seventeenth century, and during the following 450 years they were one of the important 'superpowers' of the Near East. As Güterbock has pointed out (1997: 52), many deities of the Hattian pantheon together with Hattian myths (e.g. the myth of the Vanished God) were accepted and adopted by the Hittite rulers, rather than being rejected or transformed. Thus, many languages were spoken – Hattic, Luwian, Palaic, Hurrian and Hittite. The latter remained the official written language of the Hittite state.

Assyrian merchants from the capitol Ashur had established trading colonies in Anatolia c.1900 BC, and these colonies had specialised in metals and textiles (to be discussed in chapter 3.4). The main imports to Anatolia were woollen textiles and *annukum*, i.e. tin (Bryce 1998: 27), and the Assyrian imports consisted mainly of gold, silver and copper (de Jesus 1978). The colonies were under the Anatolian ruler's control – *karum* = guest enclave (Trolle Larsen 1976) – and the most important node in the Assyrian colony network was situated at Nesa (*karum* Kanesh). According to the Old Assyrian texts, the Anatolian kingdoms were ruled by princes, and crown-princes, princesses and palace officials are also mentioned in the texts (Orlin 1970; Kuhrt 1995: 225). Hittite was the language in Kanesh (Nesa in Hittite), and some of the earliest Hittite inscriptions in Old Assyrian script are recorded from here. This suggests that the Assyrian merchants introduced writing to the Hittites.

In the seventeenth century, two of the earliest named Hittite rulers (Pithana and his son Anitta) formed a dynasty in the city of Kussara and the autobiography of Anitta – the Anitta text – is preserved in both the Hittite and the Akkadian languages (Kuhrt 1995: 226). The text shows that Pithana conquered the city of Nesa and this was probably a strategic move in order to come into a better military striking range of the other Anatolian kingdoms and, further, to gain control over the important Assyrian trading enclave. After a series of military campaigns Anitta established political control over a vast territory, which led to a collapse of many of the earlier kingdoms, and it seems to have put an end to the Assyrian trading activities in the region (Bryce 1998: 42).

A detail worth mentioning in relation to Anitta's conquests is related to the king of Purushanda, who surrendered and showed his inferiority by giving Anitta gifts. This is attested in the Anitta text: 'the man of Purushanda brought gifts to me; he brought to me a throne of iron and a sceptre of iron as a gift' (Bryce 1998: 41).

Obviously, the king of Purushanda gave Anitta two major symbols of supreme political power – a throne and a sceptre – which were very important royal regalia throughout the Middle East. As we will demonstrate later (chapter 4), thrones were also used by certain chieftains of central and northern Europe during the mid-second millennium. The bronze objects from Hasfalva in Hungary and Balkåkra in Sweden – often referred to as 'drums' or 'cult objects' in earlier literature (Knape and Nordström 1994) – could instead have been bronze coatings, mounted at the top of cylindrical wooden thrones.

Further, we can notice that the gifts were made of iron, and not bronze, silver or gold. At this time, in the early seventeenth century BC, ironworking was probably carried out on a very limited scale and this quite 'new' metal could have been treated as extremely valuable and prestigious (Muhly 1985). From the late third millennium we have the iron dagger from Alaça Hüyük, as mentioned above, but bronze was, without comparison, the most common metal used in Anatolia during the first half of the second millennium BC.

Of major importance for our present-day knowledge of the Hittites are the excavations of their capital at Hattusha (Boghazköy), carried out at the beginning of this century by Hugo Winkler. The German excavations, which started in 1906, produced an enormous quantity of clay tablets from the royal archive and Winkler's preliminary report from 1907 included a list of Hittite kings from the period 1380–1215 (Gurney 1990).

The Hittite period is conventionally subdivided into three phases: Old Kingdom (1650–1500 BC), Middle Kingdom (1500–1430 BC) and Empire (1430–1200 BC), but here we are adopting a division into two periods: Old Kingdom and Empire (also named New Kingdom).[2]

If we allow a minor simplification, we might argue that Hittite history really started in the seventeenth century with two kings named Labarna and Hattusili. The latter came to power *c.*1650 BC and his annals, certainly written during his lifetime, contain interesting information about his military campaigns and the booty taken:

> I went to Hahha (Elbistan/Taurus passes) and three times I brought battle into the city gates of Hahha. I destroyed Hahha, but its goods I took away and brought them to Hattusha, my city. Two complete (four-wheeled) carts were loaded with silver. One (two-wheeled) *MADNANU* (-wagon), a stag of silver, a table of gold, a table of silver, these goods of Hahha, a bull of silver, a ship whose bows were covered with silver. The Great King Tabarna, the hands of slave-women I removed from the millstones and the hands of slaves I took away from (forced) labour and freed them from forced labour and corvée, loosened their hips, and bestowed them on the sun-goddess of Arinna, my lady. This statue of gold I made, and set it up before the sun-goddess of Arinna, my lady. (Kuhrt 1995: 242)

From this passage, we can see that the Great King had a female divinity as his patroness – the sun-goddess of Arinna – and to her he dedicated much of the booty from his conquests.

The backbone of Hittite military force was the fast horse-drawn chariot (Beal 1992). It was equipped with two four-spoked bronze wheels (cf. chapter 5.6), and the Hittites were possibly among the first states in the Middle East to use this military 'innovation' on a large scale (Littauer and Crouwel 1979).

We believe that the following observation by Bryce is important, and that a similar ideology could have been practised in central and northern

2 The Hittite chronology applied in this book follows Kuhrt (1995: 230–1), and differs slightly from the list of Hittite kings given by, for example, Bryce (1998).

Europe but in a smaller scale: 'the Hittite king was the supreme military commander of his people. And the ideology of kingship demanded that he demonstrated his fitness to rule by doing great military deeds, comparable with and where possible surpassing the achievements of his predecessors. Military expansion became an ideology in its own right, a true sport of kings' (Bryce 1998: 87; also Gurney 1979: 163).

As in the case of Mesopotamia and Egypt (chapter 3.1), the Hittite ruler's position was sanctioned and supported by the supreme gods such as the weather-god and the sun-goddess of Arinna. Kingship was also dependent on the active support of the military aristocracy and the landowning elite, which together formed the *panku*: a term usually translated as 'assembly' (Kuhrt 1995: 249). The king gave the aristocracy land grants and war booty and in return he achieved loyalty oaths and troops for his army.

The Hittites campaigned in Syria and sacked Babylon in 1595 BC under the command of Mursili I, the son of Hattusili. As can be inferred from the passage below from the annals of Hantili, the successor of Mursili, the campaign (in foreign lands and against powerful opponents and cities such as Babylon and Aleppo) soon became a vital part of Hittite military history: 'For of old the Land of Hatti with the help of the Sun-Goddess of Arinna used to rage against the surrounding lands like a lion. And moreover whatever (cities such as) Aleppo and Babylon it used to destroy, the possessions of every country, the silver, the gold and the gods – they used to place them before the Sun Goddess of Arinna' (Gurney 1940: 31; also quoted by Bryce 1998: 104). The success of the campaign is obviously related to the support of the major goddess of the Hittite pantheon – the sun-goddess of Arinna – and the near relation between ruler and divinity is emphasised.

However, if Mursili's divine support in battle had a general effect of strengthening the bonds between the ruling elite and the pantheon, it did not ensure his security at home among his family. Shortly after returning to Hattusha in triumph, he was assassinated by his brother-in-law and successor Hantili (Bryce 1998: 105). Among the leading families in Hittite society, new potential rulers obviously did not waste their time contemplating Mursili's close contacts with the sun-goddess – they knew the 'rules of the game' and awaited the right opportunity to conquer the throne and the semi-divine status that followed with kingship. We will return to the Hittite rulers and divinities in greater detail in chapter 3.

The great expansion of the Hittite kingdom occurred during the Imperial Period, beginning with the reign of Tudhaliya I (*c*.1430–1410 BC). The Hittite activities in northern Syria and in the area of Isuwa, with its rich copper mines close to Mitanni, disturbed the Mitanni kings, who formed an alliance with Tuthmosis III of Egypt (Kuhrt 1995: 250). Egypt also stimulated contacts with the Arzawa kingdom in western Anatolia, and Amenophis III certainly hoped that this would prevent the Hittites from expanding further to the west.

The hostile relations between the Hittites and Egypt changed to the opposite after Suppiluliuma I's successful campaigns against the Mitanni kingdom during the mid-fourteenth century. Now, when the Hittites controlled western Mitanni and all of its vassal provinces in Syria as far as Damascus, the Egyptian king was interested in establishing friendly relations. However, this friendship did not last for long. Probably in 1335 or 1334 BC Suppiluliuma received a letter from the Egyptian queen beginning with the phrase 'My husband is dead' and continuing with a request to Suppiluliuma to send one of his sons to Egypt, to become her new husband (Bryce 1998: 193). The dead Egyptian king was no other than Tutankhamen, and his widow, looking for a Hittite prince as her husband (and, consequently, the new king of Egypt!), was Ankhesenpaaten. After serious considerations Suppiluliuma sent one of his sons, Zannanza, to Egypt, but after several weeks he got a message saying that his son had been killed on his way to Egypt. Naturally, Suppiluliuma held the Egyptians responsible for the evil deed and after this incident the friendship between the two states was definitely broken for almost eighty years. The hostilities culminated in 1286 BC[3] with the famous battle of Kadesh, in which, according to Egyptian sources, the Hittite army consisted of 47,500 men (Fig. 26). According to the same source, the Hittites brought 3500 chariots to the battleground (Beal 1992: 291ff.).

Shortly after 1200 BC the Hittites suddenly disappeared from the Middle Eastern scene, and the question of whether the collapse of their kingdom should be related to the appearance of the so-called 'Sea People' has been discussed by many scholars (e.g. Sandars 1978; Drews 1993). Earthquakes (Schaeffer 1968) or prolonged drought (Carpenter 1968) are two other explanations put forward, and a theory of systems collapse has also been discussed (Zaccagnini 1990). We believe that Bryce's cautious approach to the 'explanation' of the fall of the Hittites and other states in the eastern Mediterranean and the Near East could be adopted in the present work:

> But in attempting to find reasons for the collapse of the Hittite kingdom, we should be careful not to give undue prominence to any specific set of factors, whether internal or external. Further, its collapse did not occur in isolation. The fact that a number of centres of the Mycenaean world were destroyed in roughly the same period as the fall of Hatti and other Near Eastern kingdoms gives some credence to the view of a series of widespread upheavals and disasters, at least within the Greek and Near Eastern worlds, which led to, or helped precipitate, the downfall of the major centres in both regions. (Bryce 1998: 378)

3 An alternative date is 1274 BC (Bryce 1998: 256).

Fig. 26 Scene from the battle of Kadesh (from Müller-Karpe 1980: Taf. 61).

Recent evidence shows that the southern part of the Hittite Empire remained more or less intact (Hawkins 2002; Orthmann 2002). Thus, there existed both in Asia Minor and in some places such as Cyprus refugees from royal families after the collapse, which helps to explain why and where some of the mythology and sagas could have survived, such as the *Iliad* and the *Odyssey* (Bennet 1997).

3.3 The theocratic leaders of Crete and Mycenae

When turning to the eastern Mediterranean world, the discussion about rulers and kingship becomes more difficult than in the cases of the Near East and Egypt (for a recent debate see Rehak 1995b; Davies and Schofield 1995; Cline and Harris-Cline 1998). Because of the lack of contemporary

written documents from Crete or mainland Greece mentioning Minoan or
Mycenaean rulers, our knowledge is limited. A Minoan writing system –
Linear A – was developed on Crete during the Second Palace period (*c*.1700–
1450 BC), but this has not been deciphered yet. The later Linear B tablets
(an early form of the Greek language) contain valuable information about
the (late) Minoan and Mycenaean societies, but they are in no way as
informative as the Near Eastern or Egyptian sources. However, the latter
documents mention kings or princes from places identified as Crete and
mainland Greece. The Egyptian word 'Keftiu' has been interpreted as Crete
and the word 'Tanaja' as meaning mainland Greece, and the Hittite word
'Ahhiyawa' is likewise taken as a reference to mainland Greece (Strange
1980; Cline 1995a: 146; Mountjoy 1998 for a more narrow definition linked
to the south-east coast of Anatolia). Even Greek place names are mentioned
in Egyptian records from the fifteenth and fourteenth centuries BC, stressing their importance (Haider 2000). In the thirteenth century BC the king
of 'Ahhiyawa' is referred to in Hittite records as 'Brother', meaning equal
to the Hittite king (Bryce 1998: 60ff.; Niemeier 1999), but as early as the fifteenth century they figure as a prominent power. Thus kingship and central
polities are safely anchored in Minoan and Mycenaean society. The question
is of course what was the more precise nature of such centralised polities.

Already from the Protopalatial period, script and a single administrative
system were in use on Crete (Schoep 1999a, 2002). Palatial polities seem to
have been based upon a strong tradition of economic, political and religious
power throughout the whole period, despite sigificant changes between the
First and Second Palatial periods (Knappet and Schoep 2002). Recent discussions have introduced the concepts of heterarchy and factional competition
to suggest a less centralised polity (Hamilakis 2002). However, we wish to
warn against a simplified counterview of palatial power as being in constant and competitive flux, without stable institutions and practices. Heterarchy and factional competition are to be seen as intrinsically linked with
an institutionalised polity of power struggles (discussion in Day and Relaki
2002 and Schoep 2002). They are accompanying phenomena to already centralised polities. What need to be explored, then, are the institutionalised
practices (economic, political and religious) that constituted palatial power
and the state (Knappett and Schoep 2002; Betancourt 2002), on both Crete
and the mainland during the Bronze Age.

Minoan Crete

Since Arthur Evans' discovery of the Palace of Knossos at the beginning of the
twentieth century (Evans 1921–36), questions about the nature of Minoan
rulership and religion have been debated among archaeologists (Marinatos

1993; Rehak 1995a). Today, three more palaces are known on Crete: Malia, Zakros and Phaistos. The problem remains, though, that at Knossos we have a throne, but we still do not know who sat there. Was it a male or a female, or both (the double function). And among the many representations on frescos and seals, who among them were the rulers? In the recent conference proceedings *The Role of the Ruler* several interesting proposals are made.

Nano Marinatos proposes considering the palaces from a new perspective. While the development of these structures is often seen as an effect of economic growth and the need for redistributive centres, controlled by a social elite, she challenges this view. Instead she suggests that the primary function of the 'palaces' was not secular but ritual – one of performance. Here the rulers played out their roles as divine representatives in the annual and seasonal festivals and rituals (also Hägg and Marinatos 1987). This function was underpinned by the frescos. 'Evans's king was therefore not a secular figure, but a priest-king in a theocratic society' (Marinatos 1993: 40). According to Marinatos, the Minoans integrated the sacred and the profane dimensions of rulership into one big architectural structure, instead of building separate temples and palaces as in the Near East. Platon (1984) had earlier suggested a theocratic structure for Minoan Crete, where the ruler exercised power and authority through the control and manipulation of cosmology, religion and ritual.

This more 'peaceful' and ritual mode of kingship is supported by the iconography of the palace frescos, showing a total lack of the warrior imagery, but rather associated with rulership in Egypt, Anatolia or Mesopotamia. According to Marinatos then, a dual, divine kingship existed where the priest king and his counterpart the priestess queen were of divine descent, and had their separate roles in rituals, much as in Mesopotamia.[4] In this way we may be able to reconcile the opposition between the strong elements of female deities linked to nature sanctuaries and fertility (Mistress of Animals, Mother of the Mountain, etc.) and the male deities linked to the double axe cult and the bull cult/horns of consecration (Nilsson 1926).

Of course the many representations on frescos and seals of priests/ priestesses, deities, rulers or all three both invite discussion and research as to their identification and role (see Fig. 27). According to many leading scholars (e.g. Warren 1989: 99; Marinatos 1993: 127ff.), Minoan religion was

---

4 This implies the subordination of warrior ideology to theocratic leadership. It suggests a secularised military organisation. In recent years it has become increasingly clear that Minoan military functions were well developed, including fortifications and a system of coastal watch towers (Chryssoulaki 1999). We refer to the recent conference proceedings on Aegean warfare, in *Polemos* (Laffineur 1999).

Fig. 27 (*a*) Seals showing Minoan rulers (or priests) with symbolic axes carried as sceptres; (*b*) examples of such axe sceptres from Egypt and Anatolia from the eighteenth and seventeenth centuries BC (after Marinatos 1993: Fig. 88, Özgüç 1986: pl. 90 and Müller-Karpe 1980: Taf. 83).

dominated by female divinities related to the natural world,[5] but the male king priests are also easily recognisable in Minoan iconography, with their long robes with diagonal band (Fig. 27) of Near Eastern inspiration. They carry a club or a cestrum (Koehl 1995), another royal emblem in Egypt and the Levant (Otto 2000). It has further been debated whether Evans' Priest King (or Lily Prince) fresco really shows a Minoan king or prince, or if the painting is a representation of a young god (Bennett 1962; Niemeier 1984; Marinatos 1993; Koehl 1995). They were often portrayed on sealstones and on the famous Khania seal with a staff (Fig. 113) – the same staff that Odysseus

5 We here refer to the recent conference proceedings *Potnia: Deities and Religion in the Aegean Bronze Age* (Laffineur and Hägg 2001). Here the whole problem of female deities is covered, from archaeology, rituals and iconography to texts. It is interesting to note the mounting evidence from Linear B texts of Greek gods in the Mycenaean Age, which opens up new possibilities of understanding Minoan and especially Mycenaean religion (Gulizio, Pluta and Palaima 2001).

and other chiefs used when they spoke at the assembly of leaders in the *Iliad* (Book II, 294: 'And now Odysseus, sacker of cities, rose to speak with the staff in his hand').

Once again Nano Marinatos' interpretation solves the problem in the sense that they are both king/prince and god. She very elegantly uses the waz lily as an emblem of rulership to identify the male ruler, both in Knossos (the Prince of Lilies) and in Thera (the leader of the fleet on the fresco decorated with ivy and lily pendants), and she is also able to identify his wife. With an analogy to the seated goddess/priestess on the fresco in Akrotiri, Thera, flanked by griffin and monkey, she concludes that the Knossos throne stool, flanked by a wall fresco of a riverine landscape and griffins, symbolises the priestess queen. Thus, a specific symbolic iconography defined the priest king and the priestess queen throughout the Minoan Empire. Later we will try to demonstrate that these very same emblems and their meaning were adopted by Bronze Age societies in east central Europe during this period as a result of intense trading relations.

Contrary to Evans' suggestion, featuring the existence of one single mother goddess, modern archaeologists argue that Minoan religion was polytheistic (Warren 1989: 99), and that many female divinities co-existed (instead of one sole goddess). A mountain goddess can be positively identified, worshipped at peak sanctuaries, and a dove goddess and a goddess of childbirth are further recognised in Minoan religion, together with a 'household' goddess – symbolised by a snake (Warren 1989: 99ff.). The purely domestic function of the latter can be questioned (Marinatos 1993: 158ff.), and it is not impossible that the snake only symbolised one variant of the goddess' relation to animals.

The lilies depicted in Figure 28 are placed between the 'horns of consecration', which, in turn, are standing on an altar, and a female divinity is smelling the flowers. As pointed out by Marinatos, the fact that the woman on the seal does not bring the lilies, but smells them, suggests that she is a goddess and not a worshipper or priestess (1993: 152). The symbolism of the lily and its use in regions outside the Mediterranean we will return to in chapter 5.2.

A feature present in Minoan art, which originated in the Near East, is the antithetical structure, which can be seen in many iconographical presentations (Nilsson 1950: 383ff.). A symmetrical structure 'emphasizes monumentality' (Marinatos 1993: 154), and therefore heraldic representations are closely linked to the iconography of ruling elites in the Near East and the eastern Mediterranean (Barlay 2001).[6] It quite naturally reflects the

---

6 Such heraldic representations are very rare in Europe from the mid-second millennium, but the stone slabs of the famous Kivik burial in south Sweden (Randsborg 1993) are in fact

Fig. 28 Goddess smelling lilies (after Marinatos 1993: 123).

movement of goods, people and religious ideas following from the trading empire of the Minoans and later the Mycenaeans (Morris 2001 for a good example).

Mainland Greece: the Mycenaeans

The development of more complex societies in Greece seems to start during the final phases of the Middle Bronze Age (during the seventeenth century BC). This is witnessed, for example, in the elaboration of funerary architecture; the tholoi from Messenia, cist graves at Eleusis or the tumulus graves built at Marathon (Warren 1989: 120).

A great expansion, social, political and economic, took place in the Argolid area, where the city of Mycenae became the foremost 'power node' in mainland Greece from 1600 to 1200 BC. The two grave circles situated on the west side of the acropolis of Mycenae illustrate the extreme wealth that was in the hands of the Mycenaean ruling class during the early Prepalatial period. Schliemann excavated the A-circle in the late 1870s and the B-circle was excavated by Greek archaeologists in the 1950s. The way the A-circle was deliberately incorporated into the new architecture of the later palace further illustrates the role of ancestor heroes, and probably of the cult linked to

decorated with images arranged in a symmetrical and antithetical way. Because of these 'different' qualities, the motifs on the Kivik stones were earlier discussed as being created by foreign artisans (e.g. Nilsson 1867; Montelius 1877), even if the origins of these 'foreigners' have been debated.

them (but see Laffineur 1995 for a critical view). From this formative period of Mycenaean society little remains that can be characterised as monumental architecture, as the later palace probably destroyed it. Indeed, as we shall see, the historical role of the shaft grave kings or chiefs is best understood by their relations to the outside world, Crete and northeastern Europe. They founded those trade relations that became crucial for the rise of Mycenaean power after 1500 BC, when they took control of the Minoan maritime empire. James Wright has described this historical process as a development from chief to king through a process of secondary state formation (Wright 1995b).

According to Klaus Kilian (1988) the stratification of Mycenaean society during LH I and LH II (c.1550–1400 BC) resulted in the formation of a 'royal family' with the *wanax* at the head. A convincing argument for the existence of a royal family in Mycenae is the fact that the term *wanax* is mentioned in the Linear B texts, not to forget the existence of palace architecture (Laffineur 1995: 82). However, the term *wanax* and the palaces are primarily dated not to LH I–II, but to LH III, which makes it uncertain if Kilian's '*wanax* structure' is relevant for the shaft grave phases.

Because kingship was associated with divinity in the Minoan case (e.g. Koehl 1995; Marinatos 1995a), it is highly possible that the Mycenaean *wanax*-rulers, who were influenced by Minoan practices (Hägg 1984; Kilian 1988; Wright 1995a, 1995b), to some extent saw themselves as invested with divine power. As Hägg has pointed out (1984: 121), it is likely that the Mycenaeans used certain Minoan objects only as prestige objects, without buying into the complete religious concept associated with them (Petrovic 2003: 43ff.). However, in a recently published paper dealing with the names of deities in the Linear B tablets Hägg thinks that the impact of Minoan religion on Mycenaean society could have been 'greater than I have thought so far' (Hägg 1997a: 166). But it also remains clear that their cosmology was centred round the role of warrior kings and the warrior ethos of the hero, in some opposition to the Minoans. This difference is most clearly manifested in burial ritual (the tumulus and the tholos tomb), that remained a focus of ideological and ritual investment throughout the Mycenaean period.

The title (*wanax*) was also applied to gods, which strongly suggests that the Mycenaean rulers were treated as more or less divine (Taylor 1964: 135). However, influences from the Near Eastern civilisations, the Hittites and the Egyptian eighteenth dynasty, could have contributed a great deal to shape the Mycenaean *wanax* into a divine form, or perhaps a semi-divine one, like the Hittite rulers, who did not became gods until after their death.[7] The

---

7 The Hittite influence is of course most prominent in the palace architecture, especially the lion gate, and Atreus tholos (Frizell 1998), but is also reflected in imported prestige goods (Petrovic 2003: 56ff.) and in texts (Watkins 2002).

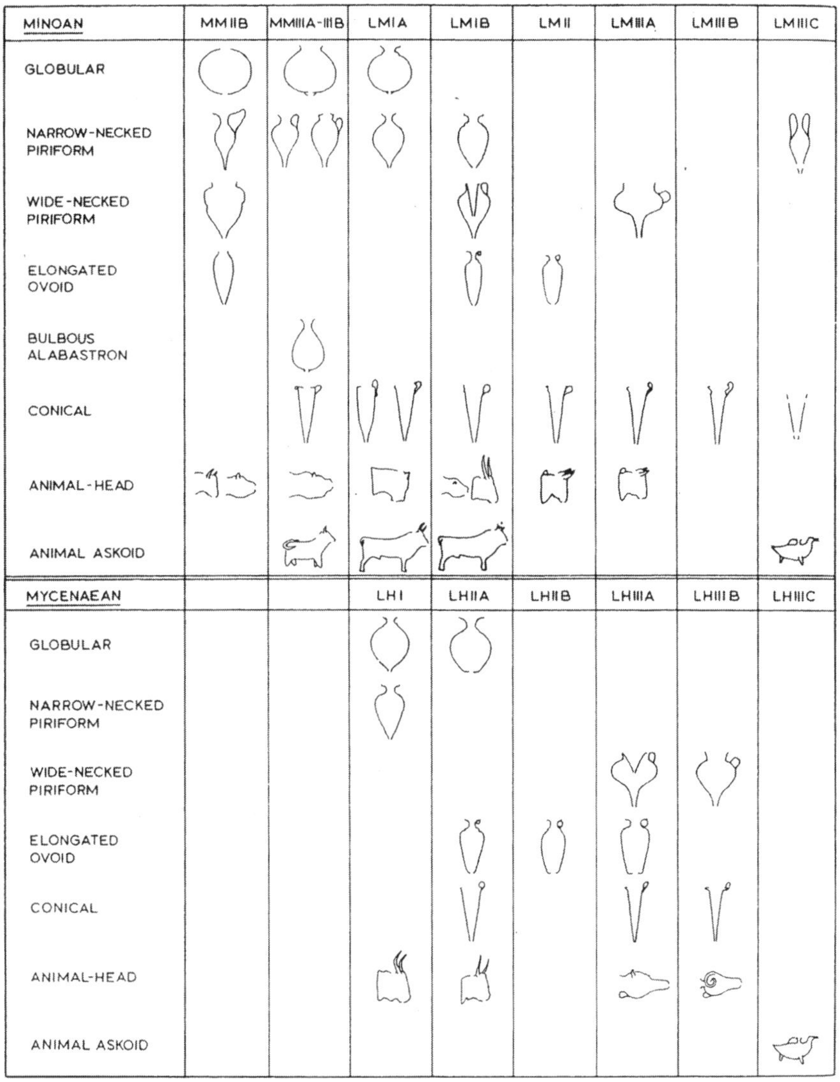

MINOAN	MM IIB	MMIIIA-IIIB	LMIA	LMIB	LMII	LMIIIA	LMIIIB	LMIIIC
GLOBULAR								
NARROW-NECKED PIRIFORM								
WIDE-NECKED PIRIFORM								
ELONGATED OVOID								
BULBOUS ALABASTRON								
CONICAL								
ANIMAL-HEAD								
ANIMAL ASKOID								
MYCENAEAN			LHI	LHIIA	LHIIB	LHIIIA	LHIIIB	LHIIIC
GLOBULAR								
NARROW-NECKED PIRIFORM								
WIDE-NECKED PIRIFORM								
ELONGATED OVOID								
CONICAL								
ANIMAL-HEAD								
ANIMAL ASKOID								

Fig. 29 Minoan and Mycenaean rhyta, showing the high degree of diffusion and ritual acculturation in the Aegean Bronze Age (after Koehl 1991: Fig. 1).

king's sacred status would further facilitate the royal trade networks and alliances with other ruling elites: 'the *wanax*-kings achieved a level of economic and political might such that they could conceive of themselves on equal terms with Near Eastern potentates and initiate (or respond to opportunities of) correspondence with the Hittite and Egyptian kings, among others' (Wright 1995b: 75).

If we summarise the later evidence from Linear B texts, frescos and material culture, it seems fairly safe to conclude that the Mycenaeans took over significant elements of political/religious symbolism (double axe cult, bull leaping, lily/ivy emblems, etc.) and some of the corresponding institutions. This, however, was a drawn-out process, already beginning during the shaft grave period, and it continued after the Mycenaean takeover of maritime power in the east Mediterranean.

3.4   Trade and transmission in the Mediterranean world

In the following we shall give an outline of the new cultural and commercial connections that characterised the Late Bronze Age (Late MH and LH I–III) in the east Mediterranean. From among the many examples we shall in subsequent chapters choose some specific cases in order to explore and explain the way these new networks were organised and the impact they had on local societies throughout Europe.

As a starting point, we can assume that already during the early second millennium many local communities throughout Europe were beginning to become dependent on each other, in order to secure the distribution of metal. Northern Europe (here meaning south Scandinavia and northern Germany/Poland) was one of the last regions to join this prehistoric 'metalwork union'. In many parts of central and southeastern Europe, the impact of bronze prestige goods on the local societies, lineages and families had, during the late third millennium BC, accelerated competition, rivalry and the process of social stratification. Indigenous deities were worshipped and the leading or chiefly families were seen as the holders of the strongest bonds to the gods and goddesses through their imagined first-hand genealogy leading back to the ancestors and deities.

Despite differences in the scale of these societies – from chiefdoms to states – their very nature as hierarchical and competitive systems made interaction, alliances and long-distance prestige exchange highly interesting for all parties (Friedman and Rowlands 1977; Kristiansen 1998a). As a prerequisite for understanding this interaction we need first to understand the nature of trade and interaction in the Mediterranean and the Near East.

The Near Eastern caravan trade

During the first century of the second millennium, the city of Ashur on the west bank of the Tigris became an important node in Middle Eastern geography, trade and politics (Fig. 30).

The Old Assyrian period, dated to c.2000–1800 BC, is particularly important in the study of early organisation of trade and interaction in the Near East (Larsen 1976 and 1987). Among other things, Ashur controlled much of the tin trade with the east and therefore it became important for the south Mesopotamian bronze industry; here it was possible both to buy tin and to

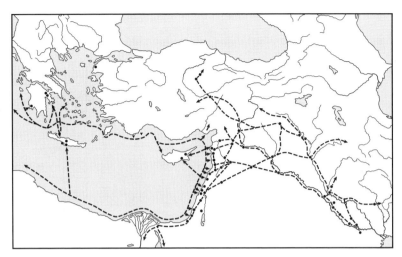

Fig. 30 The major trade routes of the city-states of the Levant and Syria during the early second millennium, including the Old Assyrian caravan trade to Kanesh and Hattusa in Anatolia (after Klengel 1990: Abb. 3).

sell their own copper. Excavations were carried out in Ashur between 1903 and 1913 by the Deutsche Orientgesellschaft, but very little of the remains from the Old Assyrian period was in fact revealed. From the royal building inscriptions in Ashur we know that the king was given a fairly simple title: iss'iak (dingir) Assur = vicegerent (or governor) of the god Ashur (Kuhrt 1995: 84). The only ruler of Ashur breaking this rule was the last king of the Old Assyrian period, Shamshi-Adad (1813–1781 BC), who was a conqueror of south Mesopotamian origin and who used the more complex royal epithets of his homeland (Grayson 1971; Larsen 1976).

Between 1900 and 1830 BC Assyrian traders settled in central Anatolia, and the site of Kanesh (about 20 km north-east of the modern town of Kayseri in Cappadocia) is the best known Assyrian *karum* – trading establishment – in Anatolia (Trolle Larsen 1976; Özgüç 1986). The two main types of Assyrian trading establishment in Anatolia – the *karum* and the *wabartum* – were not autonomous Assyrian colonies in Anatolia as argued earlier, but trading centres supervised by Anatolian rulers. Therefore, there is no reason to assume that Ashur exercised political control over Anatolia (Orlin 1970; Larsen 1976).

From the excavated clay tablets from Kanesh, we know that from Anatolia they 'exported to Assyria silver, gold and large amounts of copper, and imported tin (*annakum*) and woven material. Tin, probably obtained by the Assyrians from Azerbaijan, Elam or perhaps Afghanistan appears to have been used by the Anatolians for making bronze with the copper produced locally' (Roux 1992: 231ff.). Larsen mentions that some 13.5 tons of tin can be documented over a period of forty to fifty years, but the quantity is more likely to have been close to 80 tons. The source was probably Afghanistan, and it was brought by foreign traders to Assur who acted as

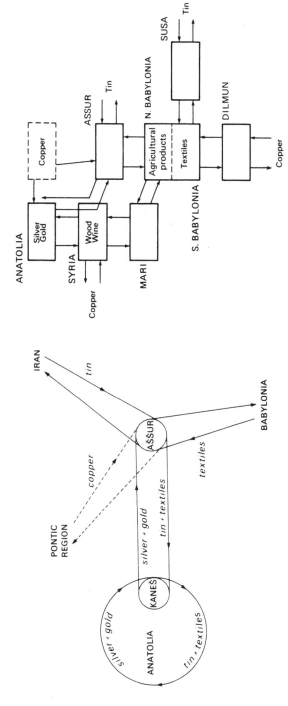

Fig. 31 Model of Old Assyrian trade system (from Larsen 1987: Figs. 5.3 and 5.2).

middlemen. Assur itself exported textiles and the available letters document 14,500 pieces of cloth imported to Kanesh over forty to fifty years. We are here dealing with highly developed systems of commercial trade, based on family companies, a model employed also in later history by trading city-states (Fig. 31). Between 1500 and 2000 men in Assur were engaged in the trade with Anatolia, which included a number of trading stations.

There is an archaeological lesson to be learnt from the Kanesh tablets: they inform us that Assyrian families lived in traditional houses and adopted much of the local culture, thus making their presence archaeologically nearly invisible. The same is true of their products of trade: the large quantities of tin, copper and textiles traded have left very little archaeological evidence. We would not even be able to hint at the highly complex caravan trade system without written sources, which suggests that even small quantities of archaeological material of foreign origin may testify to much more complex interrelations. This would have to be inferred indirectly, through the adaptation of new institutions, writing, architecture, etc., as indeed happened in Kanesh (or Nesa to use the Hittite name), where writing was adopted. However, personal items of metalwork, such as pins, pendants and axes, were brought to Kanesh, along with the Assyrian families and their metalworkers. It confirms our proposition from chapter 2.2 that there exists a direct connection between people and personal items, allowing us to infer travels and movements of groups of people by mapping such items (see also Fig. 42). In Kanesh some of the Assyrian metalwork was adopted by local rulers and brought further west along Hittite circuits of trade. This explains why we find related types of pins, pendants and axes of Near Eastern inspiration from Anatolia to the Carpathians, and even further north to Scandinavia and England (Fig. 32). They circulated through those new networks that linked the chariot-using steppe warriors with the Hittites on one hand and the copper and gold mines of the Carpathians on the other. These long-distance connections introduced new casting technology and the systematic use of tin bronze in the Carpathians, whereas gold, amber and perhaps warriors passed in the opposite direction (see chapter 5.2).

Another city-state of the early second millennium of major importance for the Near Eastern and eastern Mediterranean trade networks was Mari, situated on the Euphrates not far from the modern border between Iraq and Syria (Fig. 30). Even if the importance of the city goes way back into the third millennium, the period that has been most intensely scrutinised by archaeologists and Assyriologists ranges between 1810 and 1760 BC (Kupper 1957; Margueron 1982; Oates 1986: 63). The archives found from this phase are very rich and they throw light on the political scene in the entire Middle East (Malamat 1983). The city's strategic geographical position on important trade routes is the essential factor behind its role as a leading commercial

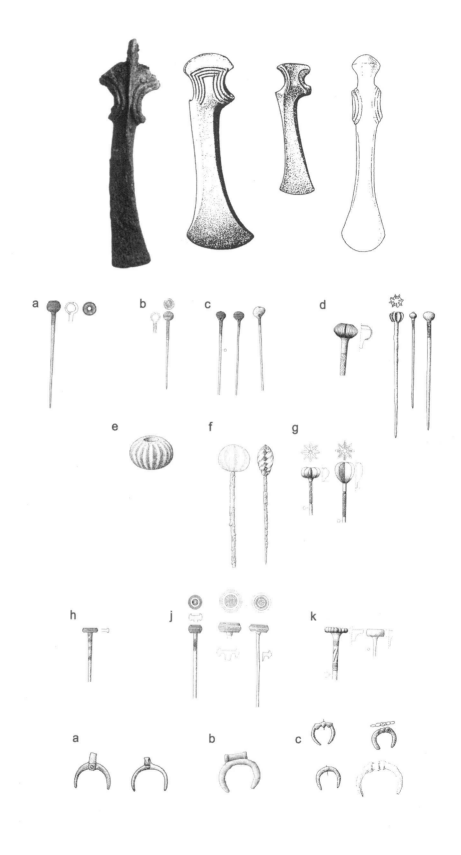

centre. The archives show that Mari was the main supplier of tin (coming from further east) for much of the Levant and the eastern Mediterranean, including Crete (Dossin 1970; Morris 1992: 102).

That tin was regarded as a very valuable metal in the Near East during this period can be illustrated by the following passage from a letter (found in the Mari archives) from the king of Qatna to Ishme-Dagan, king of Ekallate (Kuhrt 1995: 101):

> This matter is unspeakable, yet I must speak and relieve my feelings: you are a great king; you asked me for two horses, and I had them sent to you. And now you sent me (only) 20 minas (c. 10 kilos) of tin. Is it not the case that, without any quibbling and in full, you got (what you wanted) from me? And you dare to send me this paltry amount of tin! If you had sent nothing at all, by the gods of my fathers, I could not have been so angry!

The tin coming to Mari was delivered in the form of ingots of 5 kg weight, and the Mari texts further show 'that tin was usually from fifteen to eighteen times more valuable than copper' (Muhly 1995: 1509).

This letter reveals that tin was important in the trade and gift exchange between the rulers, but it also shows that horses were traded. The primary use of horses during this time was probably for drawing chariots, because the status of riding seems to have been very low among the nobles. A letter to Zimri-Lim, king of Mari (1775 BC), makes this point clear: 'may my lord not ride with horses; may my lord ride (instead) in a cart with mules and thus honour his position as king' (Kuhrt 1995: 105). Kingship and horse riding were obviously treated as two incompatible activities during the eighteenth century BC in western Mesopotamia.

Not only metals and costly gifts were exchanged among the royal potentates of the Bronze Age. New rituals, myths and religious institutions were part of the exchange, as exemplified by Walter Burkert's analysis of Greek mythology (1979). Some of the central Greek myths were derived from the Hittites, and shared a common Indo-European origin. The Hittites, in turn, would have adopted some of their gods from the Near East.

←

Fig. 32 Similarities during the early second millennium BC (nineteenth–eighteenth centuries) in warrior prestige axes with ribbed shaft hole and personal dress pins with globe-shaped, rib-shaped and disc-shaped heads from Syria and Anataolia to central and northwestern Europe. Small horn-shaped pendants show a similar distribution (after Müller-Karpe 1980; Hundt 1986; Özgüç 1986). Axes: to the left from Kültepe, Anatolia, the remainder from the Carpathians. Pins with globe-shaped head: (a) Denmark, (b) Wessex, (c) Switzerland and (d) Anatolia. With rib-shaped head: (e) from central Europe (mace head), (f) from shaft graves, Mycenae, and (g) from Anatolia. With disc-shaped heads: (h) from central Europe, (j) from northern Europe, and (k) from Anatolia. Horn-shaped pendants: (a) from Hattusa, Anatolia, (b) from Irael, and (c) from central Europe. A gold-plated piece comes from one of the Wessex burials.

The Hittite storm-god appears around 1800 BC and the influences derive most certainly from Mesopotamia, where anthropomorphic representations of this deity are known from the third millennium (Alexander 1993: 2). In Mesopotamia, he was a lesser deity, but in Anatolia and Syria he became the primary god, ruling over the mountains and providing water for agriculture. In the rock art of Yazilikaya (dated to c.1250 BC) the storm-god (Teshub, in Hurrian) is a prominent figure, together with his spouse, Hebat, the sun-goddess of Arinna (Alexander 1993: 1). Teshub is depicted standing before a calf (which is a symbolic representation of their son Sharruma), thus creating a three-dimensional relationship. This metaphor or symbolic expression came from Egypt, where it can be seen earliest in the temple of Sety I at Abydos, dated to the early thirteenth century. During this time, a peace treaty bound the Hittites and the Egyptian Empire, and many cuneiform tablets record an intense correspondence between the rulers. The close contacts in correspondence and trade between the two empires – which resulted in a marriage between a Hittite princess and Ramesses II (1256 BC) – made the transfer of an originally Egyptian expression to Anatolia possible: 'The Hittites borrowed the motif, I believe, because it provided a visual idea that could be adapted for a new Hittite purpose, the creation of the image of Sharruma as the calf of Teshub' (Alexander 1993: 5). This provides an example of how both *visible* material culture – trading goods and prestige objects – as well as *invisible* ideas, metaphors or symbolic thoughts, crossed boundaries and were adopted in new local contexts, where they took new material forms, only slightly transformed to suit their new purposes. The sequence here is as follows: original *visible form* (the pharaoh and the bull in the temple of Sety I, Egypt, c.1290 BC); transmission to *invisible form* (when the idea was taken by a certain individual and brought to Anatolia, c.1260–1250 BC); appearance of new *material form* (the making of the image of Teshub and his calf at Yazilikaya, c.1250 BC).

The east Mediterranean maritime trade

Minoan civilisation emerged during the first half of the second millennium BC as the new dominant sea power in the east Mediterranean. The character of that dominance has been debated: was it one of empire, of control of strategic ports of trade and colonies or rather of a common market? This so-called Minoan thalassocracy, meant to include the domination of the Cycladic Islands, part of the Greek mainland and the coast of Asia Minor, was the subject of a conference that still summarises the subject (Hägg and Marinatos 1984). Despite divergences of opinion, there seems to be a general agreement that the Minoans exercised a dominant position culturally and economically in the east Mediterranean during this period. It was based upon their superior naval capacities, probably a strong military

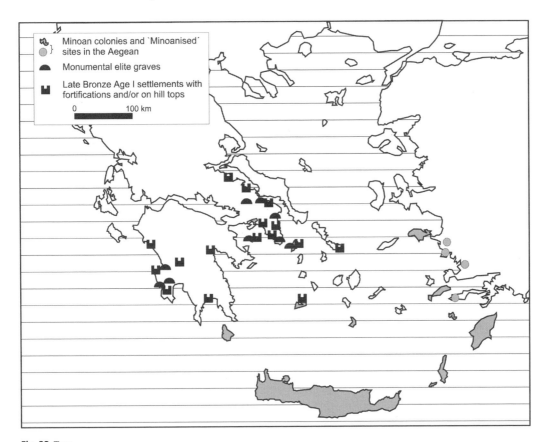

Fig. 33 Two traditions of power: mainland Mycenaean monumental elite barrows and fortifications versus Minoan palaces and maritime trading colonies (grey shading).

and a highly developed manufacture of weapons, pottery and other luxury products (Laffineur and Betancourt 1997). There is increasing evidence that Minoan towns and palaces were fortified (Schlager 1999 and 2000). We may assume centralised political control that secured internal peace, with supporting protective systems of roads and guardhouses (Chryssoulaki 1999). We are thus rather in agreement with Nano Marinatos that the Minoans controlled a maritime, commercial empire. In accordance with this there was no warrior ideology, but one of peaceful, ritual and artistic preoccupation. This has been paralleled with other maritime empires, such as the Dutch or the Venetian, that show the same lack of war scenes and ruler iconography, as first demonstrated by Weingarten (1999).

The Minoan commercial expansion began during the Old Palace period when fortified colonies were established at important strategic positions, such as Aegina, from where they expanded their activities (Kilian-Dirlmeier 1997: Abbs. 65 and 67). We should, however, not underestimate the complex nature of such expansion, including the travel and transplantation of Minoan craftsmen (see Fig. 33), linked to alliances with independent partners in an expanding trade network, and the adoption of administration and script by close partners (Owens 1999). The importation of craftsmen explains the situation best with respect to Mycenae (Bloedow 1997), which had a privileged position in the network, reflected in their access to high-quality swords and lances with spiral decoration (Kilian-Dirlmeier 1993: Tafel 64a).

A quite close relation between the palatial civilisation of Crete and the Egyptian kingdom during the sixteenth and fifteenth centuries BC (Late Hyksos/Early Dynasty XVIII) is shown by the recently made discovery of Minoan frescos in Tell el-Dab'a in Egypt (Bietak 1992, 1995; Marinatos 1995a: 37; Manning 1999).

> The Peoples from the Isles in the Midst of the Sea [Crete] not only came to Egypt but brought with them images of their religious practice, which they painted on walls while in Egypt. With no Minoan pottery associated with the paintings, the mystery of what they were doing there and why the paintings were commissioned remains unsolved. (Morgan 1995: 44)

These wall paintings in Egypt were probably made by Aegean artists during the period 1630–1580 BC and they really highlight the question of the nature of the interaction and contacts between the Aegean region and Egypt. With reference to the Old Assyrian colony in Kadesh, which on the whole adopted local culture, there is much to suggest that this was a Minoan trading colony, or they could have been painted by a master artisan, given as a gift to the Hyksos ruler in Avaris. Whatever explanation is chosen, and they may even go together, the new evidence accounts for the strong 'African' impact on Minoan fresco painting. Also Mycenaean connections with Egypt seem to have started in the shaft grave period, as is indicated by the El Tod silver treasure in Egypt (Maran 1987).

In 1990, two years before Bietak's first publication of the frescos from Avaris, Niemeier made the announcement of a site with frescos of Aegean type at Tel Kabri in Israel. Here a painted plaster floor was found *in situ*, but the wall frescos were in fragments and found as redeposit rubbish (Niemeier 1990; Manning 1999: 80). According to Manning, the frescos from Tel Kabri should be dated to 'the later MBII period' (1999: 80), i.e. *c.*1700–1675 BC, making them slightly older than the Tell el-Dab'a paintings in Egypt.

Depictions in Egyptian elite tombs at Thebes, dated from the reign of Tuthmosis III to early Amenhotep II, feature figures that are named 'Keftiu'. In clothing they look very much like Minoans and they carry objects that definitely must be of Aegean or Cretan origin (Manning 1999: 209ff., Fig. 39), indicating the role of Aegeans/Minoans as equal members of the international diplomatic community of the Near East (Panagiotopoulos 2001).

Analyses of Egyptian wooden coffins show the importance of the Egyptian timber imports, e.g. cedar, cypress or juniper (Davies 1995), and lead-isotope analyses of metals from el-Amarna indicate that Aegean and Egyptian bronzes could have been made of copper from the same deposits (Stros-Gale *et al.* 1995: 134). Further, the results of recent lead-isotope analysis have turned the old assumption that the Cretan copper came from Cyprus upside-down:

> Lead-isotope analysis has now established a distinctive 'fingerprint' for Cyprus, and all the ores, slags, and ingots found in Cyprus match this fingerprint. But the ingots from Late Minoan Crete – from sites such as Hagia Triada, Knossos, Tylissos, Gournia, and Zakros – produced a number of different fingerprints, none of which agreed with that of Cyprus. In other words, we cannot say where the copper for the Cretan ingots came from – and it might have come from as many as five different sources – but it does not seem to have come from Cyprus. (Muhly 1995: 1513)

The highly developed commercial trading system is further illuminated by the import of exotic timber on Thera, and in the Minoan world (Asouti 2003):

> the Minoan ruling class would have established regular contacts with the Hyksos dynasts, contacts which were then continued by the Egyptian 18th dynasty. We must envision not only an exchange of gifts but perhaps active alliances and trade treaties. It was to the advantage of the Minoan ruling class to project its ideology of power and to present itself as possessing exceptional skills. (Marinatos 1995a: 37ff.)

Thus the Hyksos period increasingly presents itself as one of new foreign relations, perhaps due to the origin of the Hyksos in the Levant (McGovern 2000). Cline has shown that the kings of Egypt and the Near East recognised the chieftains of the Aegean world as worthy trading partners and members of the 'brotherhood' of rulers:

> In the Egyptian tomb of Menkheperesenb, we are shown the 'Prince of Keftiu', that is the Prince of Crete, in the company of the Prince of the Hittites, the Prince of Tunip and the Prince of Kadesh. The title used to identify the figures, *wr*, meaning 'Prince' or 'Chief', is the same in each case. The *annals* of Thutmose III (42nd year) [*c*.1448 BC] similarly refer to the 'Prince of Tanaja', that is the Prince of Mainland Greece. (Cline 1995a: 146)

The above statement by Marinatos could equally be used to characterise the chiefdoms and elite societies of central and northern Europe during the early to mid-second millennium BC, as we shall see later. The chiefly lineages must have had a constant need for presenting themselves 'as possessing exceptional skills', in order to legitimise their 'first-hand' link to the

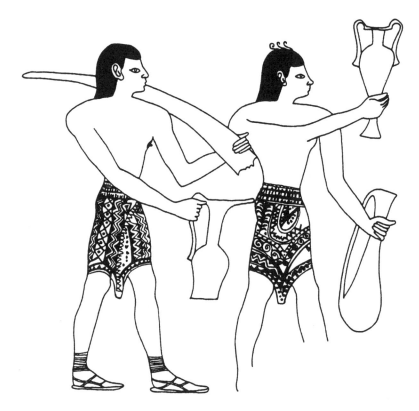

Fig. 34 Scene from Egyptian tomb showing 'Keftiu' (after Manning 1999: Fig. 39).

ancestors and to the deities. On this point we can assume strong similarities on a structural level between most Bronze Age elite lineages in Europe – the need for divine support of their supreme position – even if we at the same time can identify a differentiation in economic strategies between different communities.

This opened up new possibilities of contact beyond the east Mediterranean. Explorations for new sources of copper, gold and tin must have been a major economic incentive for the Minoans. Their attention therefore turned towards the western Mediterranean, Sardinia (copper) and Wessex/ Brittany (tin), and towards the Carpathians (gold, copper and amber traded in from the Baltic). Here we may finally be able to locate those new sources that made the Minoans capable of competing with Cyprus. Their route northward would probably have extended from colonies of trading partners on the west coast of Asia Minor, with Troy as the gate to the Black Sea and beyond (Korfmann 2001b; the most recent authoritative statement on the discussions over Troy is Easton, Hawkins, Sherratt and Sherratt 2002).

The finds from excavations in western Anatolia show that we have Minoan settlements in Asia Minor already during the LM I phase (1675–1490 BC). For example, excavations in Miletus (in the area of the Temple of Athena) have revealed storerooms for Minoan domestic pottery of local production and houses with wall frescos: 'compositions of white lilies on red background, and a winged griffin with papyrus' (Niemeier 1998: 27). A clay vessel with three signs of Minoan Linear A script – the first Linear A find from Asia Minor – has been found here and a chalice of Egyptian alabaster, illustrating that the Minoan connections with Egypt can be witnessed not only on Crete. From the following periods there is clear evidence of Mycenaean activities in Miletus, in the form of houses, clay kilns, rounded hearths and vast quantities of Mycenaean pottery, corresponding to their new domination. However, on one of the Mycenaean pottery sherds we find a representation of a Hittite pointed, conical hat with horns – a tiara – usually worn by Hittite gods and rulers (Buchholz 1974; Güterbock 1984), which indicates a certain Hittite impact on the Mycenaean community at Miletus. This is a good example of how a Hittite symbol of divinity/rulership (the horned tiara) was taken up by the local Mycenaean rulers at Miletus. At the hill of Degirmentepe, close to the Temple of Athena, eleven chamber tombs of Mycenaean type have been excavated (Fimmen 1924), a fact that further emphasises the Mycenaean presence on the west coast of Asia Minor.

Some 200 years later, about 1250 BC, a Mycenaean king is mentioned in a Hittite text as the 'King of Ahhiyawa' (in the Sausgamuwa Treaty), dating to the reign of Tudhaliya IV (Cline 1995a: 146). In this treaty, the Hittite king Tudhaliya IV writes: 'And the Kings who are my equals in rank are the King of Egypt, the King of Babylonia, the King of Assyria and the King of Ahhiyawa' (Beckman 1996: 101).

These potentates not only mentioned each other in textual documents, but were also engaged in trade with each other, perhaps disguised as gift giving (Cline 1995a: 143). There is archaeological evidence of goods going from Egypt and the Near East to Aegean rulers, as well as evidence of goods travelling in the opposite direction (Porada 1981; Cline 1991 and 1995b). The cargo of the famous shipwreck from Ulu Burun (Kas) is a perfect illustration of this trade (Bass 1986). The wreck testifies to a systematic commercial seaborne trade in the eastern Mediterranean around LH IIIA/IIIB, that is, around 1340 BC according to the Egyptian date provided by a scarab (Kilian-Dirlmeier 1995: 351ff.), or 1305 BC as suggested recently by Bass (1998). The cargo consisted mainly of copper and tin: 10 tons of copper in oxhide ingot form, and stacked along the ingots nearly 1 ton of tin. An army of 500 could have been outfitted with helmets and corselets, and equipped with

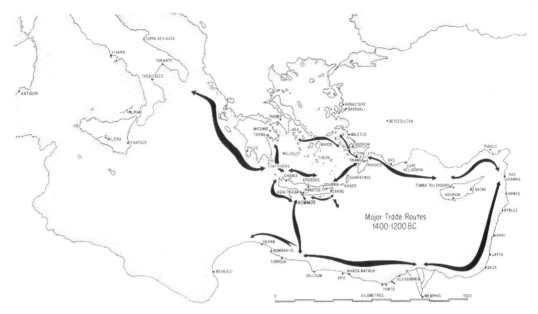

Major Trade Routes
1400-1200 BC.

Fig. 35 The route
of the Ulu Burun
shipwreck (after
Kilian-Dirlmeier
1995: Abb. 1).

5000 swords and spears.[8] Other materials in this cargo were, for example,
Canaanite jars filled with resin and glass beads, logs of ebony from Africa,
amber from the Baltic, blue glass ingots, Egyptian scarabs, Mesopotamian
cylinder seals, an Italian bronze sword, bronze weights, stone mace heads,
and ivory from both hippopotamus and elephant (Bass 1986; Pulak 1988;
Cline 1994). Kilian-Dirlmeier has reconstructed the trade route taken by this
and other merchant ships in the east Mediterranean during this period
(Figs. 35 and 36).

It corresponds rather precisely with the return journey of King Menelaus
(after the seige of Troy), who used the wealth to decorate his house.
Telemachus, son of Odysseus, spoke in awe to Menelaus when seated: 'Look
around this echoing hall, son of Nestor, friend of my heart. The whole place
gleams with bronze and gold, amber and silver and ivory. What an amazing
quantity of treasures.' Everything he mentions was found in the Ulu Burun
shipwreck, and when Menelaus answers we understand why: 'But when it
comes to men, I feel that few or none can rival me in wealth, for it took me
seven years and great hardship to amass this fortune and bring it home in

8 The Ulu Burun ingots have recently been analysed and were found to be copper of rather
  poor quality produced from raw copper, but with inclusions of slag and sulfides. It would
  have needed further purification, but was on the other hand easy to break, which was widely
  practised, as we can see from the many finds of ingot fragments (Hauptman, Madden and
  Prange 2003). Susan Sherratt has recently used the appearance of foreign swords, like the
  Italian type in Ulu Burun, to suggest increasing individual, entrepreneurial movements of
  warriors and traders towards the end of the Bronze Age (Sherratt 2000a).

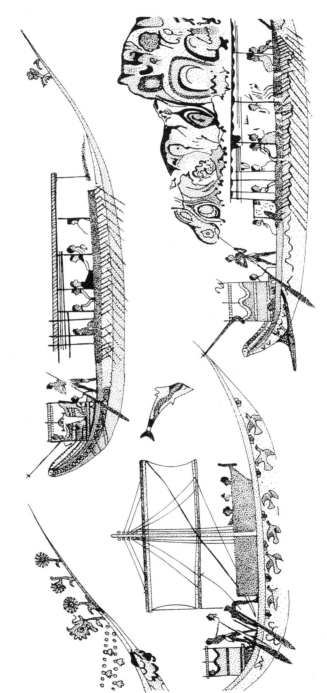

Fig. 36 Minoan ships from the Thera frescos (after Müller-Karpe 1980: Taf. 214).

my ships. My travels took me to Cyprus, to Phoenicia, and to Egypt. Ethiopians, Sidonians, Erembians, I visited them all; and I saw Libya too' (*Odyssey* IV, 70–85).

What he describes is the normal trade cycle taken by merchant ships in the east Mediterranean. From this we may deduce two things: trade was in the hands of the palaces and their kings, who might even take part in expeditions. Second, palatial wealth in the Minoan and Mycenaean age was to a large degree based upon revenues from trade and conquest, in addition to land, a fact often overlooked when discussing the later decline of the palace system (Deger-Jalkotzy 1996).[9] In the 'diplomatic' texts between rulers we see trade relations reflected in the gift exchange which operated at the top level to maintain commercial relations also. The use of words like 'brother', 'father' and 'son' in the royal letters showing the communication between these rulers does not indicate real kinship. Instead it indicates that they treated each other as belonging to equivalent social strata; the relationship could perhaps be labelled congeniality.

The trade or gift exchange between the royal palaces seems to have included objects of various types, like silver bowls, cylinder seals, horses, chariots, oil and gold objects among other things, and it is fairly clear that this exchange included objects with prestigious histories. This has been pointed out by, for example, Zaccagnini (1987: 58), and Cline has also noted this fact (1995a: 145): 'In one letter (KBo II 11 rev. 11'–14'), sent by Hattusili III to an unknown king (perhaps the king of Arzawa in south-western Anatolia), Hattusili III says: "Now then, I have taken a rhyton of silver and a rhyton of pure gold from the gift of the King of Egypt and I have sent them to you."'

Most likely this transaction took place some time between 1275 and 1245 BC and the letter suggests that the king of Arzawa was expected to be impressed by the 'glorious' biography of these rhyta. Thus prestige and power were interlinked in the royal or chiefly operation and reproduction of the political and economic systems during the second millennium BC in the east Mediterranean.

Again the archaeological evidence would not in itself be able to indicate the organised and highly complex nature of such trade relations. Eric Cline studied the Late Bronze Age commerce in the Mediterranean, and in his book, *Sailing the Wine-Dark Sea* (1994), the catalogue of imports to the Aegean area during the Late Bronze Age only covers 942 items! There are more

---

9 The collapse of complex societies can probably best be understood in a comparative historical context (Tainter 1999; Yoffee and Cowgill 1988). While ecological causes due to overexploitation and degradation have often been stressed (Chew 2001), one should not overlook the role of trade and prestige goods, as they constitute political legitimacy and, when distributed, provide loyalty from vassals and commoners (Perigrine 1999). In archaeology it is often impossible to determine which comes first: ecological crisis or decline of trade when they occur together.

imported objects, but these are the ones found in 'good LH/LM I–IIIC contexts' (Cline 1994: 9). If we make a very simple calculation and divide the 942 objects by the approximately 630 years that constitute the period LH I–III (1700–1070 BC), we get an average of 1.5 imported objects per year. This figure does not in any way mirror the real trading activity in the Aegean during this time. Instead, the 'world-wide' distribution of Mycenaean pottery in the Mediterranean during the period 1500–1200 BC illuminates the role of Mycenaean trade and its cultural and ideological impacts (Wijngaarden 1999).

The cargoes of the shipwrecks at Ulu Burun and Cape Gelidonya, together with the textual evidence from Egypt and the Near East mentioning trade, clearly show that Cline's 942 objects are only the very tip of the iceberg. Using the words of Helen Kantor, quoted by Cline (1994: 1), we believe that a similar situation also could be valid for the relations between central/ northern Europe and the Mediterranean: 'The evidence preserved to us by the passage of time constitutes but a small fraction of that which must have once existed. Each imported vessel . . . represents scores of others that have perished' (Kantor 1947: 73).

3.5 Conclusion: historical long-term trends

From the evidence on rulership, religion and trade presented above some historical regularities and long-term trends are discernible (Liverani 1990; Yoffee 1995; Baines and Yoffee 1998; see also Trigger 2003 for a comparative discussion of civilisational regularities). We observe a cyclical trend of expansion/centralisation versus fragmentation in the political landscape. City-states and their local territory remained the political/economic building blocks of society during the whole period, but in some periods they were brought under the rule of a single dominant city and its ruling family. After the Uruk expansion of urbanism during the mid to late fourth millennium BC, the Early Dynastic period of the early to mid-third millennium was a period of competing city-states, where rulership over larger territories was achieved only for short periods of time. This was followed by a period of political centralisation during the last centuries of the third millennium BC, beginning with Sargon of Akkad. The first half of the second millennium BC was again a period dominated by competing city-states, succeeded by the formation of the 'club of great powers' from 1500 to 1200 BC (Mycenae, Hatti, Assyria, Babylonia and Egypt). This international, imperial system disintegrated after 1200 BC, accompanied by migrations and a subsequent Dark Age, a major historical transformation beyond the scope of our book. We may further observe that the cyclical shifts between centralisation and fragmentation are characterised by shorter periods of crisis, leading to invasions from outside tribes and devastation of cities. Some of these, like the late third-millennium crisis around 2300 BC, have been linked to global climatic change (Dalfes, Kuklo and Weiss 1997; Matthews 2002), but reasons are probably more complex (Chew 2001). A climatic change followed by migrations was also at work around the collapse in about 3000 BC of the Uruk phenomenon and the subsequent expansion of pastoral groups in many regions from western Asia to Europe (Sherratt 1998). A similar period of major change and conquest by foreign tribes with chariots characterised the seventeenth and sixteenth centuries BC throughout the Near East and western Asia, by some scholars called a Dark Age (van de Mieroop 2003: 115). It did not lead to collapse, however, as a new era of powerful empires emerged between 1500 and 1200 BC, to be followed by a major collapse of its western part after 1200 BC (Liverani 1987). These periods of crisis and transformation or reorganisation also demarcate the major chronological transitions between Early, Middle and Late Bronze Age in the Near East and western Asia. The latest crisis around 1200 BC marks the beginning of the Iron Age.

During the whole period we witness an increasing ability to control territories and to extract tax and tribute. During the third millennium BC large tracts of uncontrolled land of pastoral herders existed outside city-states. From the late third millennium onwards the territorial state with full control of its subjects emerged. Privatisation increased during the late third millennium in Mesopotamia as well. Specialised and independently operating merchants, organised in family firms and guilds, accompanied the Near Eastern city-states from the third millennium onwards (Pettinato 1991; Postgate 2003), and we see this commercial enterprise in full operation during the early second millennium, exemplified by the caravan trade between Assur and Kanesh. Also, the balance between the temple/palace sector and private enterprise of free peasants, craftsmen and slaves changed gradually over time. Following on from this, the level of servitude increased substantially during the second millennium BC, as the old tradition of letting the state restore the balance through levelling of debts disappeared. More and more people were thus enslaved in debt, and fled to outlying regions or other states.

What remained stable throughout the period, however, was the multilingual and multi-ethnic character of states. Different language groups and ethnicities co-existed, spanning from trading colonies, over incoming ethnic groups with special skills either as craftsmen, herders or warriors, which over time might lead to their dominance or takeover in periods of decline. This is the story of the Hurrians in northern Mesopotamia and Syria (later Mittani), the Kassites in Babylonia and the Hyksos in Egypt. The important thing was not ethnicity or language but loyalty to the kingdom or the city-state. The Hittite kingdom in particular is a good example of a multi-cultural state. With the increased room for private entrepreneurs during the second millennium, movements of skilled people increased correspondingly. They were often of foreign ethnicities, which can be identified through their names in the texts, such as Indo-European charioteers and horse trainers. In this way links with regions outside the city-states and empires, sometimes from far away places, were established. This may help us to understand better some of the international connections in Bronze Age Eurasia during this period.

Another stable feature was the theocratic nature of leadership. It meant that there existed interchangeability between gods and humans. Rulers performed the rituals and sometimes the roles of the gods. Likewise gods allowed themselves to become human in the same process. Although there were variations in the character of divine rulership, it remained a defining characteristic of the Bronze Age. And as we shall demonstrate later, it was taken over by the Bronze Age societies of Eurasia.

In the following we wish to apply the concepts of travel, trade and esoteric knowledge as an integrated aspect of the reproduction of power and rulership to Bronze Age Europe. Here we have no texts, but rich archaeological evidence, which we believe is able to elucidate such aspects of Bronze Age societies, when approached with relevant theories and interpretative strategies. The comparative ethnohistoric evidence and the combined textual and archaeological evidence from the Mediterranean make it probable that related conditions prevailed in those Bronze Age societies which were in contact with the city-states and palace societies in the east Mediterranean. And they certainly had the capacity to organise long-distance trade networks, and venture upon exploratory journeys in search of metal. By the end of the third millennium, in the centuries around 2000 BC, the Bronze Age city-states turned their interest towards the barbarian peripheries in central and western Europe, and we shall therefore do the same.

Europe in the Early Bronze Age: an archaeological background

To be successful journeys must be well prepared and necessary information of importance for the journey must be collected and analysed. Therefore, before we begin our interpretative journey we shall provide a critical overview of current knowledge concerning chronology, archaeological sequences and the expansion of metallurgy in Bronze Age Europe.

4.1 The Early Bronze Age of the third millennium

The beginning of the Bronze Age coincides with the formation of early states, writing and the consolidation of urban life from around 3000 BC in Mesopotamia, that is the beginning of the Early Dynastic period (Postgate 1992: ch. 2; Yoffee 1995; van de Mieroop 2003: ch. 3). The complexity of bronze and copper technology, including mining, specialists, traders, etc., was linked to the rise of more complex social formations, writing, bureaucracy and centrally organised trade and military (Postgate 1992; Maisels 1990: 131ff.).

The early Near Eastern civilisations, from the Old Kingdom in Egypt to the Harappan and Mesopotamian civilisations, were able to transfer goods, both finished products and high-value raw materials, between these early states, to satisfy the needs of the new urban populations and the ruling elite of the palaces. Silver was employed as standard exchange value and as capital. The localised occurrence of important raw materials facilitated the development of organised trade based upon profit calculations related to scarcity and regional value differences (Kohl 1978; Marfoe 1987; Klengel 1990). In this way the early civilisations were able to level out local differences in raw materials and production and thus develop and maintain common cultural patterns of production and consumption. This is reflected in the exchange of prestige goods between the royal dynasties, which reached a high point during the later third millennium. Copper from Oman and Caucasus, tin from central Asia, textiles from Mesopotamia were traded widely to areas were they were in demand. As early as the third millennium BC this allowed the early metallurgists to mix tin and copper to make bronze, which was both harder and shinier than copper.

The source of tin during this period is still unknown, but it would have had an eastern origin (Pernicka 1998; Weeks 1999). Thus the trade routes of Early Bronze Age civilisations were looking towards the east rather than the west. It is historically significant that the isotopic composition of early bronzes from the Near East to Troy and the Aegean is similar. It implies that the bronze being used was obtained from the same source, testifying to the role of international trade, and not least the role of tin (Weeks 1999: Fig. 4 and pp. 59ff.).

In the Mediterranean, urban settlements were flourishing from Cyprus to the Cycladic islands (Renfrew 1973; Höckmann 1987; Broodbank 2000). This may even have influenced the rise of semi-urbanised settlements on the Iberian Peninsula, just as contacts were established along the Adriatic coast with the Balkans and further inland (Primas 1996; Hansen 2002).

However, from the Pontic region to the Balkans and central and northern Europe this was the period when new types of agro-pastoral economies expanded. They shared many traits in economy and burial ritual, such as the construction of tumuli over graves and the predominance of individual burials (Yamna, Corded Ware, Battle-Axe and Catacomb cultures). Recent pollen botanical evidence has made it clear that the third millennium BC represents the formation of open steppe-like environments for grazing animals from the Urals to northwestern Europe (Odgaard 1994; Andersen 1995 and 1998; Kremenetski 2003). The movable lifestyle is exemplified in the employment of mats, tents and wagons, sometimes found in burials (Ecsedy 1994). By some it has been called a 'barbarisation' or the decline of the Neolithic (Kruk and Milisauskas 1999; Rassamakin 1999: 125ff. and 154). It followed a period during the fifth–fourth millennia when stratified societies and copper metallurgy were developing in the Balkan–Carpathian region, only to collapse or be transformed during the later fourth millennium BC (Chernykh 1992: ch. 2; Sherratt 2003b). Instead the Caucasian region rose to prominence as a metallurgical centre of production, and from 3200 to 1800 BC there developed a Circum-Pontic metallurgical province, including Anatolia, that received most of its metal from the huge Caucasian mines (Chernykh 1992; Chernykh, Avilova and Orlovskay 2002). Around the centres of production and distribution there emerged a series of stratified societies, burying their dead in impressive and richly furnished kurgans. Sometimes they would contain imports not even present in the centres (see discussion in chapter 1.4), such as the famous Maikop burials from the late fourth-millennium Uruk expansion (Chernykh 1992, chs. 3–5, Figs. 17 and 31; Sherratt 1997a). From here the new social and economic organisation was adopted in the southern steppe where it proved highly dynamic (Rezepkin 2000; Trifonov 2004).

In Anatolia the use of copper goes way back to the seventh millennium BC and the use of arsenic copper from new ores started about 4200 BC. In Syria and northern Mesopotamia the corresponding dates are 6000 BC for copper and 3300 for copper alloys (Chernykh 1992). In the Balkans and the

a

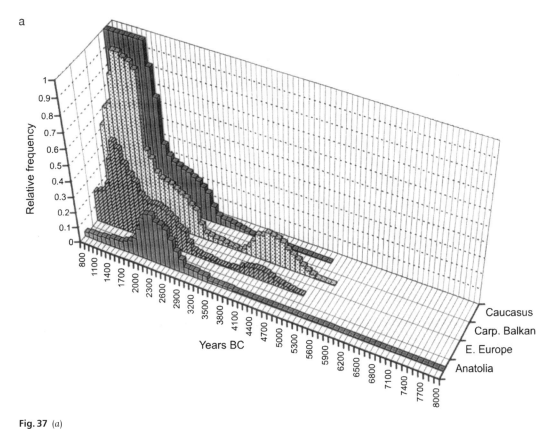

Fig. 37 (*a*)
Estimated copper
production from
the major
mining areas
during the third
and second
millennia BC
(after Chernykh
2002a); (*b*) system
of mining shafts
in Kargaly in
plan, and
photograph of an
excavated shaft
(after Chernykh
2002a).

Carpathian Basin the evidence of copper-using societies dates back to the early fourth millennium, while the metallurgical skills involving arsenic alloys came into use *c*.3300 BC in the Balkans (Fig. 37).

According to Chernykh (1992), the earliest copper and tin alloys are dated to *c*.3000 and found in Anatolia. While copper was locally available in Anatolia the tin had to be imported from other regions, and this is a major problem in archaeological studies of early Anatolian metallurgy: where were the tin mines located (Macqueen 1996: 42)? Various options have been suggested: a tin route from the British Isles, a route from Bohemia, or a long-distance connection with Afghanistan or South-East Asia. Recent excavations in central Asia have for the first time revealed prehistoric tin mines (Alimov *et al.* 1998).

Apart from the major problem with the tin sources an interesting feature that should be noted is the almost simultaneous transfer taking place over a vast geographical area when the shift from copper and/or arsenic alloys to tin bronzes occurred during a relatively short period. Between 2200 and 1700 BC metal smiths in all Europe (except the 'Stone Age' economies) and western

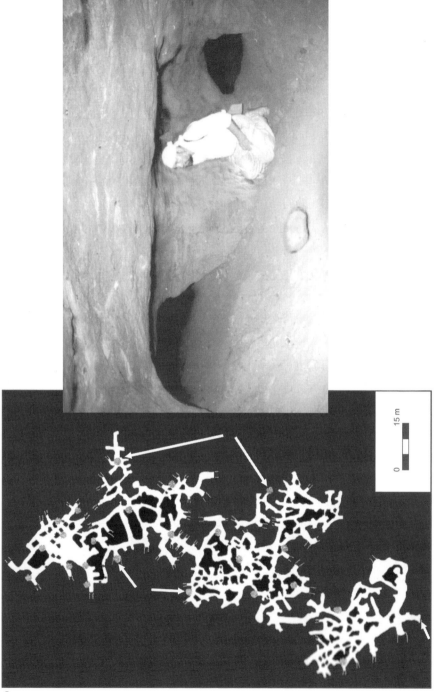

b

0   15 m

Fig. 37 (cont.)

Asia learned about and 'converted' to tin-bronze alloys in their manufacturing of ornaments, weapons and tools (Larsson 1997: 51, Fig. 11; Pare 2000: Fig. 1.14). It was a stepwise process, beginning in Wessex and Unetice around 2000 BC, from where it spread rapidly (Pare 2000). This was indeed a very fast process of technological diffusion, when we consider the enormous area that was affected almost simultaneously. It is likely that other features followed the spread of the metallurgical skills: religious beliefs, divinities, cosmologies, myths, symbols and with them also new perspectives on politics, warfare and rulership.

We here see the first historical example of the interaction between centres of civilisation with peripheries of production, which over time would also speed up the exchange of other cultural features (Hansen 2001a: Abb. 44–45). In periods of crisis in the centres the periphery might become involved, or would be tempted to take the wanted goods rather than trade them, leading to so-called barbarian invasions, which were basically a social and economic outcome of already established connections.

This was, perhaps, what happened during the later third millennium. After a widespread setback in the Near East and Anatolia and in Greece during the later third millennium where many urban settlements were burned or left, a systematic use of tin bronzes took place between 2300 and 1800 BC. At the same time we witness the first metallurgical expansion in central and western Europe of tin bronzes. After a period of experiment between 2300 and 2000 BC, a systematic use of tin bronze started around 2000 BC (Fig. 40). This marks a shift from late Corded Ware and Bell Beaker groups to the earliest Bronze Age communities of the early Aunjetitz Culture, a shift which is still badly understood, although well described and dated (Bertemes and Heyd 1996; Strahm 2002; Müller 1999: Abb. 20). It seems clear, though, that mobile Bell Beaker groups, forming specialised ethnic communities, helped to spread the new metallurgical skills in central and western Europe (Heyd 1998). This new initial Bronze Age is now often called Reinecke A0 (A zero).

Bertemes (2000), Strahm (2002) and Heyd (in press) have in recent works summarised the transformations in economy, technology and social organisation that led up to and characterise Europe after 2000 BC. The following is based on Bertemes 2000 (slightly modified):

Society: the introduction of new status and prestige goods (daggers/swords, lances, ornaments, metal cups, etc.), and the first appearance of 'princely graves'.

Religion: single graves and family groups in large cemeteries, aristocratic burials in barrows, new types of ritual depositions, new symbols and iconography.

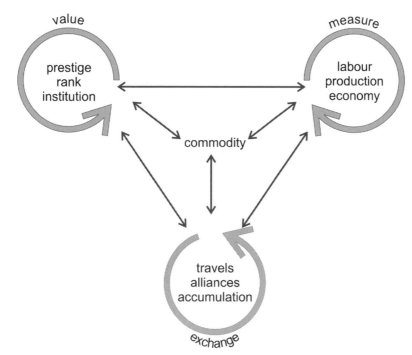

Fig. 38
Theoretical
model of the
relationship
between
commodity
production and
its economic
implications for
measuring and
the creation of
new forms of
exchange values,
its political
implications for
creating new
social values
and a new
organisation
of exchange
(developed from
Renfrew 2001a).

Settlements: open villages in the lowlands and fortified hilltop settlements. Ritual sites appear.

Economy: division of labour and specialisation, commodification of metal, weight and measuring systems, intensification of mining and long-distance trade (both finished and unfinished products).

Technology: tin bronze appears, specialised workshops, complex casting techniques, specific alloys for specific artefacts.

Everything points to the emergence of a more complex and ranked society that penetrated all spheres from technology and economy to settlement, social organisation and religion. A new aristocratic leadership had emerged on top of the traditional clan-based organisation of farmsteads and hamlets. It went hand in hand with new perceptions of wealth and commodity exchange (Fig. 38).

In the Unetice and related cultures a major expansion of production took place and ring ingots were exchanged widely (Figs. 39 and 40). And the same applies to Ireland, Scotland, Brittany and southern England (Eogan 1993; Cowie 1988; Ixer and Budd 1998; Needham 2000a and 2000b; O'Connor and Cowie 2001). These early metallurgical centres were all located close to resources of copper, and not least tin, and specific items such as halberds, daggers and pottery indicate that personal connections were maintained

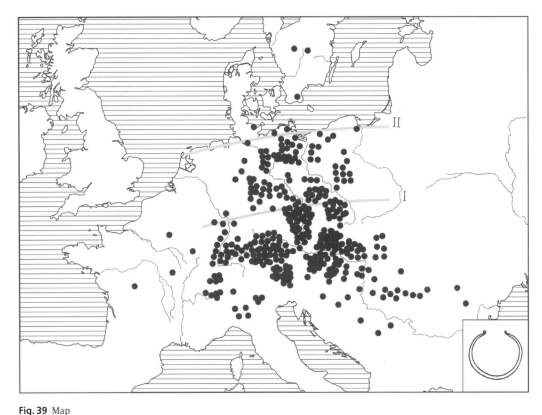

Fig. 39 Map showing the distribution of ring ingot hoards in Europe. Zone I is the production area with pure ring ingot hoards. Zone II is the distribution area where ring ingot hoards are mixed with other objects. North of zone III ring ingots are in the minority in hoards (based on Bartelheim 1998: Karte 139).

between them (Gerloff 1975: 214ff.; Schuhmacher 2002). From now on tin bronzes began to dominate and the central and western European metallurgical centres were increasingly drawn into trade relations with the palace cultures and city-states of the eastern Mediterranean and Anatolia, which reached a new flourishing after 2000 BC, when the early Minoan palaces were built (Fig. 41). The dominant trade routes were now turning westwards, in contrast to the third millennium (Fig. 30).

It seems clear that this new interest in the west was due to an increased need for tin, and in the process gold and amber were included. In this early phase we are talking about small quantities of high-value products, although quantities of tin could have been rather large. In the caravan trade between Assur and Kanesh in the early second millennium the documents mention the import of 100 tons of tin from Syria (Larsen 1987), from an unknown eastern source (but see Boroffka *et al.* 2002).

As the focus of this book is the second millennium BC, we shall describe the expansion of the metal trade during this period in a little more detail. It can be divided into three main periods: one of initial explorations and contacts from the late third millennium to around 1900/1800 BC, a second

Fig. 40 Mixed Unetice hoard with ring ingots, halberds and armring ingots from zone II. Note the two pairs of shafted halberds and ceremonial axes (after Sherratt 1994b: 257).

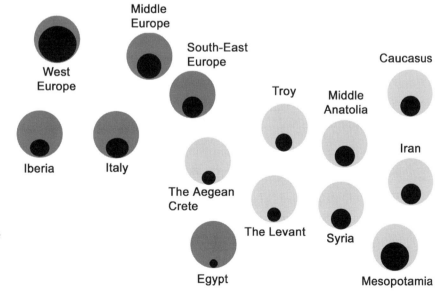

Fig. 41 Chart showing the use of tin (black shading) in metal-using regions in the early second millennium BC and the areas with tin available (darker shading) (based on Pernicka 1998: Abb. 16).

from 1900 BC to around 1600/1500 BC, and a third period from 1600/1500 to 1200 BC.

4.2   The new Bronze Age chronologies

But first a few words about chronology: as we have now a rather safe chronology based upon series of calibrated C14 dates and dendrochronological dates, the old dichotomies in dating between Wessex/central Europe and the eastern Mediterranean/shaft graves have dissolved. The cultural contacts between the Mediterranean and central and western Europe are now brought into correspondence chronologically also, with minor exceptions to be discussed. But something more than revised chronologies has changed our perception of the cultural relations between the Near East, the Mediterranean and Europe.

First of all, previous research put much too heavy an emphasis upon the shaft graves of the early Mycenaean culture, which was but one element in the wider economy of the east Mediterranean, dominated by the city-states of the Levant, Anatolia and the Minoans. This has become even more clear with the discovery of a highly organised and fortified Middle Helladic urban settlement in Aegina, at the back door of Mycenae so to speak, with a strong Minoan impact (Niemeier 1995), and rich shaft graves (MH II) (Kilian-Dirlmeier 1995 and 1997). In addition the role of the Hittites and the discoveries of highly organised Bronze Age cultures of the Steppe have widened our historical perspective, as we shall discuss later. In this new context the excavations of ancient Troy have put it back at centre stage as a major player in the Bronze Age trade (summarised in Korfmann 2001a–c; Latacz 2004).

Secondly, datings were too few and sometimes reflected a high own age of the timber, which led to severe mistakes (for up-to-date summaries we refer generally to Gerloff 1993; Randsborg 1996; Kristiansen 1998: Fig. 13). Generally speaking we now have long series of consistent datings from central Europe (Billamboz and Martinelli 1996; Voruz 1996), western Europe (Needham *et al.* 1997), northern Europe (Vandkilde, Rahbek and Rasmussen 1996), and the western Mediterranean (Mederos Martin 1997a and 1997b). We still have too few dates from eastern Europe and the eastern Mediterranean (Manning 1999; O'Shea 1991; Manning and Weninger 1992; Forenbaher 1993).

While there is general agreement to set the beginning of the Bronze Age in central Europe around 2300 BC, and the start of the Bronze Age proper (tin bronzes) around 2000 or slightly after (1900 BC), the beginning of the central European Middle Bronze Age is apparently hovering around 1600 BC. An initial phase begins around 1650 BC according to C14, while dendrochronology in Switzerland puts it in the sixteenth century, closer to 1500 BC (Krause 1996). This, however, could be due to a lack of lake dwellings from the Middle Bronze Age (Menotti 1999). Also, the beginning of the Urnfield period Br. D is now thought to start in the mid to later fourteenth century according to C14, while dendrochronology would rather say 1300 BC. At present there seems to be a slight disagreement between dendrodates and C14, the latter tending to give dates little older than the dendrodates, as also apparent in the Danish oak coffin dates (Randsborg 1996) and in Kastanas (Jung and Weninger 2002). Although some discrepancies can be due to different evaluations of the cultural sequences being dated, it seems that we should probably subtract around fifty years (sometimes more) from calibrated C14 dates, as a result of samples' own actual age, if we do not have specific information about the sample. This is exemplified by the recent analysis of the shaftwood in the Melz hoard from classical Unetice with C14 values between 2200 and 2000 BC, some 200 years too old. However, the wood for the shaft was made of old heartwood, so 100–200 years has to be subtracted, and then the date is correct (Schwenzer 2002). It underlines the need to obtain series of C14 dates with clear contextual information as a prerequisite for reaching correct dates.

The biggest changes are now taking place in the western Mediterranean, where the general trend is that dates of the later second millennium are becoming somewhat older (Mederos Martin 1996a and 1996b), especially Bronze Final I–II, corresponding to Br. D–Ha. A1/A2. Although this is also the general trend in central Europe, the discrepancy is too big for some of the Iberian dates and has to do with cultural redefinitions (Mederos Martin 1996a: Table 3). Mederos Martin redefines Bronze Final to correspond with the east Mediterranean scheme, beginning with Late Helladic/Late Minoan. In some sense this is logical. The traditional Bronze Final is then defined as BF IC, but even here the dates are too early. So here is an area of future debate and redefinition. In the British Isles we have also recently been provided with a useful update of the absolute chronology (Needham *et al.* 1997). It corresponds well with the metal groups, and suggests rather rapid shifts between periods.

The Aegean/Minoan chronology is still debating high or low – depending on the acceptance/non-acceptance of the date of the Thera eruption at 1628 BC and calibrated C14 datings. In his recent major work Sturt Manning convincingly, we think, argues for a 1628 BC date and re-evaluates the cultural and chronological relations of the Aegean and east Mediterranean in the mid-second millennium BC (Manning 1999; discussed by Macdonald 2001). New evidence and arguments for a slightly lower chronology are also marshalled (Warren 1999; Bietak 2000), now answered by new C14 datings (Manning *et al*. 2002). One of us has earlier adopted the high chronology as presented recently by Dietz (1992: Fig. 93; Kristiansen 1998a: Fig. 13), as it fits well with the central European scheme. As will be clear in subsequent chapters on the interrelations between the east Mediterranean and central Europe, there exist explicit cultural connections, where a choice sometimes has to be made between the central European chronology and the Aegean chronology. The crucial period is the Reinecke A2/A3 and B1, dating between 1700/1750 and 1500 BC. This is the first period of intense contacts between the Minoans/Mycenaeans and east central Europe and the Carpathians (as they were earlier in Romania). These far-reaching contacts were probably established during A2 (around 1750–1650 BC), intensified in A3 (end of the seventeenth century), and had their high point during the sixteenth century. As some of the cultural connections are linked to Thera in the last phase before the eruption, that is LH IB, LC I and LM IA, this phase should not be much older than 1600–1650 BC. It is clear, however, that the traditional low chronology, as employed earlier by Kilian-Dirlmeier (1993: Abb. 2) and Warren and Hankey (1989), is problematic from a central and north European perspective, in terms of both chronology and cultural relations.

In conclusion, even accepting the uncertainties of the existing absolute chronology, there are today no major discrepancies between the east Mediterranean, central Europe and northern and western Europe, either in terms of absolute dating or in terms of cultural connections. The old discussion of the 1960s and 1970s about Wessex with or without Mycenae is now obsolete. It was based upon incorrect datings and a simplistic anti-diffusionist approach, discussed in chapter 1. Instead we can approach cultural connections in Bronze Age Europe from a more productive interpretative perspective of social and historical processes. These provide a much more relevant framework for understanding the rapid transfer of goods and habits during the Bronze Age, including social and religious institutions, as we shall see.

4.3   The temporal sequence of the later third and second millennia BC

The first phase, 2300–1900 BC

Already from the later third millennium BC contacts were established between the east Mediterranean and central Europe (Gerloff 1993). So-called *Schleifennadeln* (Fig. 42) and the identical ring ingots from Moravia and city-states in the Levant bear witness to such early explorations.

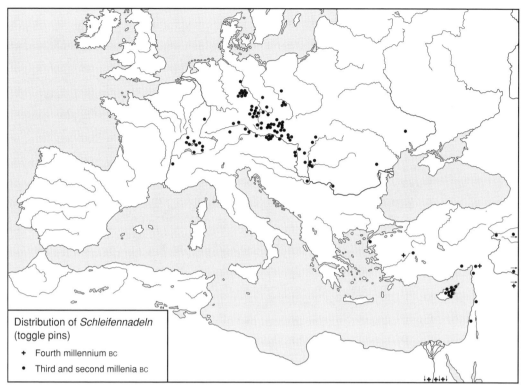

Fig. 42 Personal contacts between central Europe and the eastern Mediterranean as evidenced by the distribution of so-called *Schleifennadeln*-type toggle pins from around 2000 BC (after Gerloff 1993: Abb. 3).

Distribution of *Schleifennadeln* (toggle pins)

+ Fourth millennium BC

• Third and second millenia BC

As pins are personal dress items, the distribution suggests a rather direct contact between the east Mediterranean and central Europe, through a series of sea journeys and travels between major trade colonies and city-states, including Troy. It is characteristic of this early phase that very little exchange took place from the centre to the periphery, with the exception of a Cycladic lance (or rather a local imitation, Krause 1996), and a few other items, such as a silver ring. The line of exchange is mainly documented through local products from central Europe, and it thereby stands in some contrast to the pattern we see from the second phase onwards, where return products and influences from the centres play an important role. This may support earlier propositions that we are here seeing the results of migrating groups from central Europe, taking part in the raids in the later third millennium BC when major social and economic upheavals penetrated the Near East and Anatolia. Most of the burials and hoards from Troy to the Levant were found just over layers of destruction (Gerloff 1993). Otherwise we would have to assume that the ring ingots and the very specific pins (*Schleifennadeln*) were originally east Mediterranean and brought west by traders and adopted in the Unetice Culture. The evidence does not support this scenario. Gerloff would rather date the contact shown on Figure 42 to the late third millennium, closer to 2000 BC, and suggests it represents the opening of a more systematic trade with central Europe, which was also soon to include Wessex and Brittany. Soon after, Near Eastern metal forms found their way to central and western Europe, corresponding to the period of the *karum* trade, which seems to have had historical effects far beyond the Near East (Fig. 32). Datings of burials from the early metal cultures in central and western Europe all lie between 2300 and 1900 BC, corresponding to Troy IIg/EBA 3 (Gerloff 1993: Abb. 8). This period still defies a proper historical interpretation (for a historical scenario of Anatolia and the Pontic region, see Mallory 1998 and Tyborowski 2002).

Joseph Maran has provided a more complex explanation for some of these cultural exchanges in the Balkans. He demonstrates the existence of trade networks between late Early Helladic societies in Greece, the Adriatic and the Carpathian region from the mid-third millennium BC onwards. It was reflected in pottery forms and some prestige goods, perhaps linked to the early tin trade. With the decline of Helladic society around 2200 BC migrants from the Adriatic coast (Cetina Culture) moved south into Greece, and probably some migrants also from the Danube, as suggested by close similarities in pottery forms in the Mokrin and Nagyrev cultures (Maran 1997). One might propose to link the evidence of metal forms with the evidence of pottery and settlements. It would suggest directional movements of groups of traders and some whole communities from east central Europe and the Balkans into Greece and the east Mediterranean at the close of the third millennium BC along already established routes of contact. This formed the basis for the development of more extensive and stable contact from 2000 BC onwards.

From around 2000–1900 BC there emerged a series of richly furnished chiefly burials simultaneously in the Wessex Culture and the Unetice Culture. This represents the climax period of the early metallurgical centres and introduces the second phase.

The second phase, 1900–1600 BC

A new, more intensive exchange of goods between the Bronze Age communities of western Europe (Brittany and Wessex), central Europe (the 'classic' Aunjetitz Culture, followed by the Ottomani Culture) and the east Mediterranean now began. It seems reasonable to assume palaces in the Levant and Crete as the organisers behind these early contacts, as other evidence supports it (Kristiansen 1998a: Fig. 196).

Early metal production in most of Europe was rather small scale during the late third millennium BC, but from around 2000 BC tin was increasingly

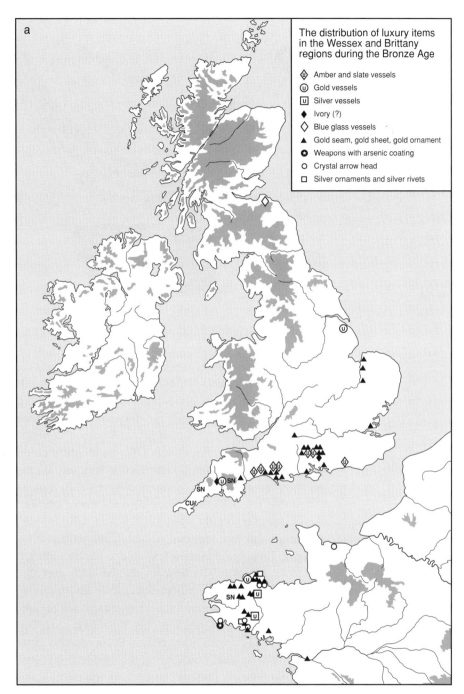

Fig. 43 (*a*) Rich chiefly burials of the Wessex–Brittany Culture and (*b*) amber necklace from the golden barrow in Upton Lowell in Wiltshire, demonstrating both regional contacts and Mediterranean contacts (after Gerloff 1975: Abb. 7 and Schauer 1984b: Abb. 20).

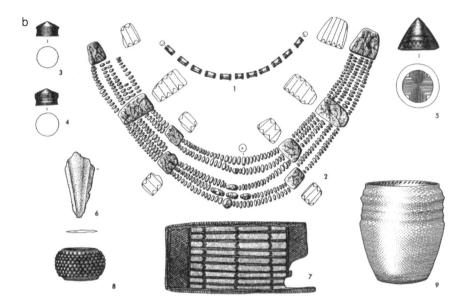

Fig. 43 *(cont.)*

employed in bronze production, earlier in England than on the continent (Pare 2000). As pointed out already by Gerloff (1975: 235), and confirmed by imported daggers and similarities in metalwork, the early centres of metal production were in contact with each other at least during the early phase. This is reflected in both pottery forms and metal forms such as halberds (Schuhmacher 2002). In the Erzgebirge in Germany production of axes, ring ingots and early metal daggers took off, and spread to neighbouring areas during Bronze A1b (1950–1750/1700 BC). The rich chiefly chamber burials of Leubingen belong here, when production in Brittany, Wessex and Ireland climaxed, as reflected in the early phase of east Mediterranean contacts. We may assume that tin, gold and amber were the major trade articles of these early connections, especially from Wessex and Brittany, which were situated at regional and interregional nodes of river communication (Sherratt 1996b). During this period Wessex was able to obtain amber from Denmark in exchange for metal in the form of English/Irish axes (Butler 1963 and 1986; Vandkilde 1996). From this period amber disappears from burials in Denmark, as it was now solely used in exchange for metal. Chiefdoms in Wessex and Brittany developed a highly organised cross-Channel network (Fig. 43a) that linked up with other central European and southern networks to the Mediterranean, that would bring tin, amber and probably gold south in exchange for foreign prestige goods and travelling specialists (Gerloff 1975; Needham 2001).

From the late eighteenth/early seventeenth centuries BC the shaft grave kings emerge, but with forerunners in Thebes and Aegina from MH II

(Kilian-Dirlmeier 1997). In the burials we find a mix of influences primarily from Crete, mostly weapons and new pottery styles, perhaps made by imported smiths and craftsmen from Crete (Bloedow 1997), and foreign exotic goods, such as amber from northern Europe and horse gear from the Carpathians/Russia. It suggests that these new rulers were able to exploit a position as middlemen in the newly opened lines of contact with central and west European societies that provided gold, copper, tin, amber and probably also horses. Figure 44 demonstrates the new economic relationship that was established between the shaft grave kings and the Minoan rulers during the New Palace period. They now received copper and tin (or tin bronze) from the Mycenaeans in exchange for weapons and prestige goods. After the Mycenaean takeover the tin content rose further, demonstrating their access to tin sources in western Europe.

As we shall see later, the shaft grave kings were part of a trade network that included the west Anatolian city-states, village-based complex societies with fortified chiefly settlements of eastern Europe and the Carpathians, and the Pontic area. All of these contacts are evidenced in the grave goods. Especially, the Pontic and east European/Carpathian contacts and influences have turned out to be significant. In the Pontic/Ural region we find highly stratified societies with burial types resembling the shaft graves rather closely, implying close connections between the two regions[1] (Licharadus and Vladar 1996).

It is characteristic also of this second phase that influences between the east Mediterranean and central and western European metallurgical centres were reciprocal, at least when we speak about the early Mycenaean culture. The Minoans, who, as we shall see, were the real organisers of these long-distance trade adventures into distant lands, were much less influenced. Here we can speak about a transmission from centre towards periphery.

New metallurgical analyses, in combination with a re-evaluation of earlier analyses, have demonstrated a close correspondence between production and distribution of metal and trade and exchange relations as evidenced in other materials, such as amber, and the distribution of prestige goods. The early Unetice phase is characterised by the wide distribution of a homogeneous metal composition from one or a few sources. In the later phases more metal types emerge, corresponding to an expansion of mining and production, especially in the Carpathians and in the Alpine region (Liversage 1994; Krause 1998; Liversage and Northover 1998; Schalk 1998).

Contacts with east central Europe and the Carpathians deepened, especially during the period 1750/1700–1600/1500 BC (Br. A2/B1 corresponding to

---

1 This evidence may find some support in the anthropological analysis of the skeletons in the B-circle, which indicated a rather large difference between males and females (Angel 1972).

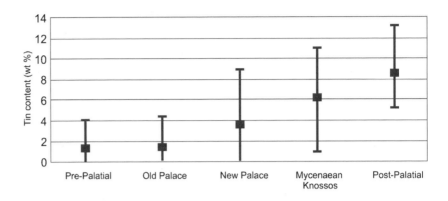

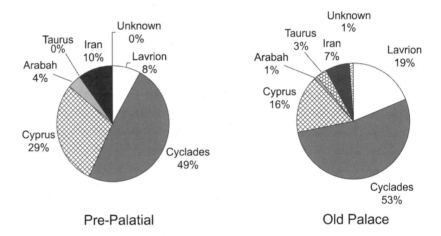

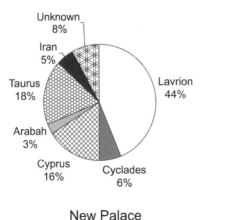

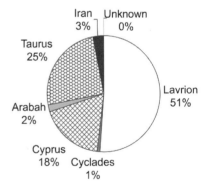

Fig. 44 *Above*: the tin content in Bronze Age Crete from the Pre-Palatial to the Post-Palatial period. *Below*: the composition and origin of copper in Bronze Age Crete, showing the change between the Old Palace and the New Palace periods, which corresponds to higher tin content.

late MH IIIAB and LH I/IIA). From the Black Sea coast trade networks extended along the Danube into the Carpathians, where highly developed Bronze Age societies emerged during the earlier second millennium BC. Their expansion corresponds to a qualitative and quantitative leap in metal production centred in the Carpathians, beginning around 1750/1700 BC. This represents an indigenous production of metalwork of high standard. A whole series of new weapon and ornament types were introduced – long swords, lances, battle-axes, arm rings, ankle rings, pendants, etc., together with new casting technologies, and a new stable tin alloying, with a slightly lower percentage of tin than in the Unetice Culture (Liversage 1994, 2000). Ornaments and weapons both were heavier and display greater variety and higher technical and artistic skills than in the preceding period, where daggers and axes mostly were small and often quite worn before finally being deposited in the cemeteries. Large-scale metal production of a scale and quality hitherto unknown in central Europe had emerged.

A stratified settlement system with fortified central settlements for production and distribution allowed an organised and widespread distribution of this new metal industry, mainly prestige goods, weapons and ornaments.

Political territories, however, were marked by differences in pottery styles, giving names to local cultures such as Wietenberg, Vatya, Veterov, Ottomani and Madarovce, reflecting political entities generally 100–200 km in diameter (Fig. 45). For convenience we employ the term Ottomani Culture for all of them. These central European societies, which were probably no less organised than mainland Greek societies at the time (palaces and urban settlements only emerging much later on the Greek mainland), established regional exchange networks that linked Scandinavia and the Black Sea coast (Kristiansen 1998a: Fig. 191).

This represented the first phase of Baltic amber reaching the east Mediterranean, as well as gold and copper from the Carpathians. Several gold hoards from central settlements, such as Spirsky and Barca, support such a proposition. Amber beads appear in burials and hoards (e.g. Barca), with types similar to those found, for example, in the A- and B-circles (Matthäus-Schumacher 1985; Mylonas 1972). Later, after 1500 BC, amber was channelled through the expanding Tumulus Culture of southern Germany, which linked Scandinavia and the central Mediterranean from the later sixteenth century onwards, while the Ottomani Culture and its international/interregional network declined (David 1998; Kristiansen 1998a: Fig. 192).

During this period contacts were still maintained with the Wessex Culture and the Armorican Culture, probably with trading stations or meeting places in southern France on the lower Rhône. Here amber and other finds point to a meeting place where goods were unloaded for river and land transport. The more indirect nature of the Wessex connection is seen in the lack of direct

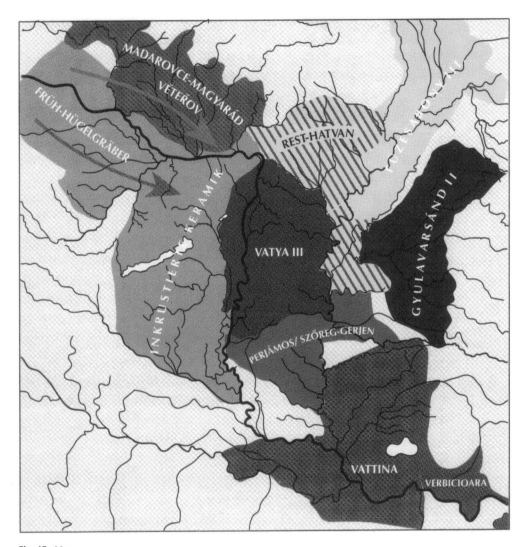

Fig. 45 Map showing the cultural and political territories of the Hungarian-Carpathian tell cultures from the seventeenth–sixteenth centuries BC (after Bona 1992b).

Minoan/Mycenaean imports, although the amber necklaces could have been produced in Greece and returned as a prestige good for exchange. Symbols of ruling elites such as sceptres, drinking cups and amber ornaments, however, point to close connections (Harding 1990: Figs. 5 and 10), not to speak of the technology of prestige goods which do demonstrate the real impact of the east Mediterranean. Crafts and knowledge rather than prestige goods were exchanged, supporting the notion of 'crafts and the kingly ideal' in Mary Helms' terminology (Helms 1993). To support their west Mediterranean trade the Mycenaeans established colonies in Sicily and southern Italy, and probably also in Sardinia (Harding 1990: Fig. 11). The colonies in Sicily and southern Italy, including the Lipari Islands with the famous evidence of writing, were probably established already from the late MH and early LH (Marazzi and Tusa 1979; Marazzi 1997; Tusa 2000).

The third phase, 1600/1500–1300 BC

Once the colonies were established the Mycenaeans expanded their trade and explored new trading partners closer at hand, such as the emerging Tumulus Culture of southwestern Europe. After 1600 (Br. B1, but especially from B2, *c*.1500 BC) this gave direct access via chiefly exchange networks to the amber of southern Scandinavia, especially Jutland, which now became a dominant region for a few hundred years (Kristiansen 1987: Fig. 4.8; Quillfeldt 1995: Taf. 112 and 113). Later trading stations or at least trading relations were established with the highly organised Terramare Culture of northern Italy, which has been extensively excavated and reanalysed (Pearce 1998), and synthesised in a monumental exhibition book (Brea, Cardarelli and Cremaschi 1997; also Cardarelli 1997). Although based on local traditions, the Terramare Culture developed close links with both Hungary and east central Europe (Primas 1997: Fig. 5) and the east Mediterranean. It is seen in the adoption of weights of Near Eastern types, and a few Mycenaean sherds (Bettelli and Vagnetti 1997; Cardarelli, Pacciarelli and Pallante 1997).

At the same time as new trade links were established with the Tumulus Culture (in its mature phase), those with eastern Europe and the Carpathians declined, as did those with Wessex and Armorica. The directional nature of the newly opened amber trade with southern Germany has recently been illuminated by finds of a wooden statue decorated with a Mycenaean gold crown and a staff, plus amber with a Linear B inscription (Gebhard 1999; Gebhard and Rieder 2003 and 2002). Wessex was now directing its interests more toward northwestern Europe (Burgess 1996: Fig. 1), also reflected in some similarities in early rapiers (Laux 1995). In the Carpathians we find a horizon of destruction of tells, sometimes linked to the expansion eastward of the Tumulus Culture, which could just as well reflect internal warfare, or a combination of both (David 1998).

However, it seems safe to conclude that a major disruption and decentralisation of settlement took place in the former tell societies, and that at least some of this disruption can be linked to conquest migrations from Tumulus chiefdoms from the west, with the conquered eventually being taken on as mercenaries. Also from the east, in the steppe, new warring groups could have added to the collapse, e.g. the formation of the Noua Culture, which represented the westward expansion of steppe economies (Sava 1998; Gershkovich 2003). At the well-excavated and analysed Tumulus period cemetery at Tape in Hungary (Trogmayer 1975), an influx of new groups can be demonstrated (Farkas and Liptak 1975), some of which of course could be a result of in-marriage from new Tumulus groups in the region. In the east Mediterranean this shift in the western trade routes corresponds to the so-called Mycenaean takeover of the Minoan maritime empire. It is tempting to see the change in trade networks as an indirect result of the rising power of the Mycenaean state and its trading empire, which had built up western connections in the Mediterranean and the Adriatic (to be discussed later).[2] Instead the Balkans, that is the closer periphery of the Mycenaean polity, now became the focus of political and economic expansion (Hänsel 1982b; Hochstetter 1982).

In conclusion: the early phase of the trade between the east Mediterranean and central Europe during the period Br. A2/MH III–LH I was in the hands of the Minoans and their partners. It took the route via the Bosporus and the Danube into the Carpathians and from the northern Adriatic into the Danube. Here the foreign traders met developed and well-organised societies that were able to meet the demands of the Minoans and their partners, including contact with the north for amber. On the Greek mainland it corresponds to the early shaft grave period (Dietz 1992: Figs. 80–82). Only in the next phase from Br. B2 onwards/LH IIIB and III did the Mycenaeans take over, perhaps as trading partners or middlemen to develop and maintain the network (A-circle). Finally, from LH III they directed their trade via their colonies in the central Mediterranean, while the Minoans and with them the eastern connection declined or failed in importance for some time to follow. The trade network could well have passed through cities such as Troy on the way. Andrew Sherratt has proposed a rather specific reconstruction of the network (Fig. 46).

Several unique finds, such as at Pesinara and Borodino (Kaiser 1997), point to the exchange of diplomatic gifts with major chiefly settlements around the Black Sea. In addition, locally produced rapiers and flange-hilted swords that imitated or were inspired by Mycenaean swords became popular in the areas affected by Mycenaean trade networks (Fig. 47).

Besides gold and copper from the Carpathians we suggest horses from the Black Sea steppe area as another item of trade for the Mediterranean chariots. The impact of these connections on the local societies can easily be read in the spread of horse-drawn chariots and weaponry – long swords and lances that will be discussed below. We should thus expect to find settlement

---

2 Manning has pointed out how this takeover was reflected in a repainting of frescos with Keftiu in Egyptian tombs of the early fifteenth century BC (see Fig. 34). The kilt was repainted in Mycenaean style (Manning 1999: Figs. 39–41). Some of the motifs on kilts and pottery, such as infilled triangles, occur on sword scabbards in Denmark from Montelius 2 in Store Kongehøj. Note also Maran's redating of the the El Tod gold hoard, which suggests an early Mycenaean/Minoan presence in Egypt (Maran 1987).

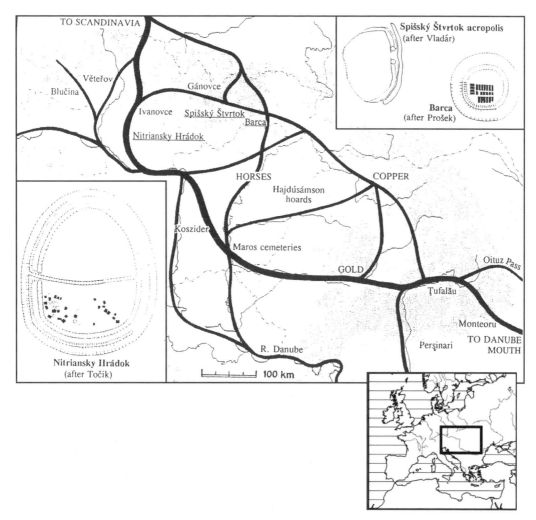

Fig. 46 Middle Bronze Age trade routes in the Carpathians linking the major tell settlements and the location of some important trade goods (based on Sherratt 1987).

evidence in the Black Sea area of Minoan trading stations, just as there is now evidence of highly developed fortified settlements with a central acropolis in the northern Adriatic from this period (Terzan, Mihovilik and Hänsel 1997; Mihovilic *et al.* 2002).

It is symptomatic that the Mycenaeans, more than the Minoans, adopted selected aspects of the Black Sea/Carpathian material culture. From the Carpathians throughout the Pontic steppe, and further south through Anatolia (the early Hittites) to Greece (the early Mycenaeans), there existed an elite material culture linked to chariots, horse harness and other chiefly regalia of chariotry (Anthony 1995; David 1997). So the process was in some ways reciprocal. Some of that borrowing may give a hint to the imports. They

a

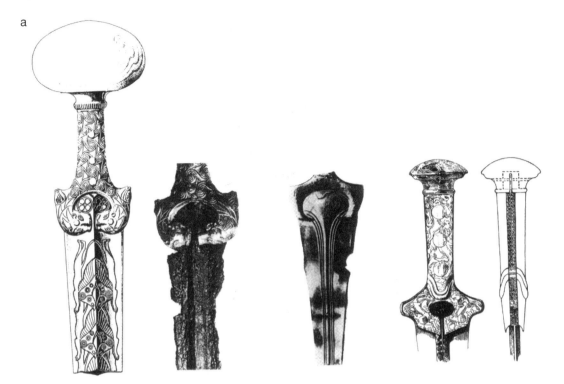

Fig. 47 (*a*) Chiefly or royal swords/daggers: comparison between the gold dagger from Pesinara and Minoan/ Mycenaean daggers (after Hänsel 1982b: Abb. 3); (*b*) warrior swords: comparison between Danish (A), French (B) and Mycenaean (C–D) flange-hilted swords (after Randsborg 1967).

are mainly linked to the area of chariotry, suggesting import of horses for the war chariots. But they also give testimony to contact with very distant regions, such as northern Europe (amber, of course, but also some imitations of north European ornaments, such as wheel-headed pins and rectangular pendants, from Wessex/Brittany).

Why the west?

Travel for gaining access to foreign prestige and wealth may explain some of the internal dynamics of Bronze Age trade and exchange. But it does not tell us why some trade networks took precedence over others through time. Here we need a larger historical perspective. Why did the civilisations of the east Mediterranean begin exploring the western Mediterranean and central Europe for metal during the earlier second millennium BC? In the process they discovered other valuables, such as amber from the remote North, or the tin of Cornwall, the gold and copper of the Carpathians and the horses of the steppe around the Black Sea. In all, their traditional networks of the early second millennium seem to have worked quite well.

If we take into account the international nature of trade connections during the Bronze Age, it must be clear that disruptions in the traditional lines

b

A B C D

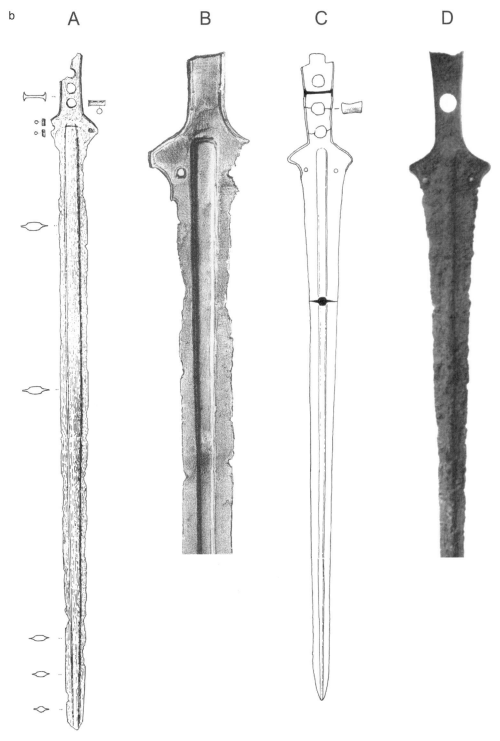

Fig. 47 *(cont.)*

of trade, such as those between Assur and the eleven colonies in Anatolia, or between Crete, the Levant and Egypt, would cause supply problems. Also the collapse of the Indus Culture, owing to the Aryan conquest, would have affected the eastern networks. Another possible factor in such large economic systems would be their inherent expansion and economic growth, giving rise to increasing demands for external supplies. Both scenarios – expansion and partial regression – might stimulate a search for new supply zones and new trade partners. And we might even expect certain world historical regularities in these patterns of expansions and regressions and social transformation. This has recently been pointed out by several scholars (Chernykh 1992: 296ff.; Frank 1993; Kristiansen 1994 and 1998a: 407ff.; Sherratt 1994a). During our period both factors were at work, and probably intermingled. During the twentieth and nineteenth centuries BC economic growth in the eastern Mediterranean and the Near East, with Crete as the new political and economic partner, would explain westward explorations (as well as the exploitation of the Caucasian metallurgical riches). These explorations, however, were never sustained until several hundred years later through colonisation. Instead the neighbouring region of the Black Sea and east central Europe were increasingly explored after the eighteenth century BC, at a time when some of the Near Eastern networks were in temporary crisis, owing to the Cassite takeover in Assur and the Hyksos conquest in Egypt. This opened up new economic and commercial possibilities for Cyprus and Crete (Crawford 1996). The new centres of production in the Carpathians, in combination with a rather well-developed system of exchange, offered an attractive alternative for a few hundred years, until the end of the sixteenth century. After this time the central Mediterranean had been colonised and offered new opportunities of direct access to central Europe and the northern amber-rich regions (Tusa 2000).

4.4   The transmission of metallurgical know-how

How much of the metallurgical know-how was transmitted from the Bronze Age states of the east Mediterranean in the process described above – and how much was local development? This question cannot be answered in any straightforward way, and there may be different answers for different periods. But certain recurring features in the process may provide a background. They are:

1 quantities – scale of mining operations and production and their implications for the organisation of society;
2 qualitative leaps – new technologies of production and their social implications.

Archaeological excavations of ancient mining areas in combination with metal analyses have made it increasingly clear that the scale of the mining operation in some places was big, and consequently also the quantities extracted (Liversage 1994; Shennan 1999; Krause 1998; Chernykh 2002a, 2002b). There is a clear trend that one or a few mining areas supplied the majority of the metal throughout a larger European and Circum-Pontic region during subsequent periods of the Bronze Age (Chernykh, Avilova and Orlovskaya 2002). The dominant metal, like *Ösenring* metal during Unetice, which provided most of the early ring and rib-shaped ingot bar bronze, must have demanded huge full-time mining operations. The unhealthy work in the mines can hardly be thought of without a highly organised and hierarchical society, employing slave labour. This is also what the archaeological evidence suggests. There is a tremendous social range, from the huge barrows with princely graves in Leubingen and Helmsdorf to the careless multiple burials in storage pits and trash pits without grave goods or ritual in the traditional settlements in the Unetice and Veterov cultures (Furmanek and Jacab 1997; Lauermann 1992; Stuchlik 2000; Veit 1997). Even in traditional cemeteries we find multiple burials, sometimes with deadly damage to the skull. Warfare and violence were daily ingredients in Bronze Age societies of east central Europe (Fig. 48), stressing their hierarchical and exploitative nature (Jacab, Olexa and Vladar 1999).[3]

Somewhat against this picture we have the local settlement evidence around the mines. It suggests working camps with little or no evidence of hierarchy (Shennan 1995; O'Brien 2000). Here the conversion of mineralised rock to metal through smelting also took place. However, we are beginning to see the emergence of fortified settlements in the vicinity of the mining areas, such as Montafon in the inner Alps (Krause 2002). This, in combination with the evidence of prestige goods in rich hoards and burials outside the mining areas, suggests the emergence of a more complex division of labour (Ottoway 2001). Political and economic control of metals was in the hands of local and regional chiefs, while the mining operations were carried out by local labour. Whether they in turn were under some central control still remains to be answered. Here the travelling trader and the craftsman enter as a possible dynamic link between mines and settlements.

3 The authors describe this horrifying killing of five individuals, some with their hands tied behind them in a pit as ritual. Again it raises the discussion about the distinction between ritual violence and other types of violence. We find the circumstances of the brutal killing in the Otomany settlement of Nizná Mysla less in accordance with prescribed rituals than with punishment through killing of either slaves or war captives. A ritualised demarcation of foreigners is evidenced in some Vatya urnfield cemeteries, where they were buried uncremated in sitting position, sometimes with a foreign pot, most often from Maros (Lörinczy and Trogmayer 1999). Thus ethnic identity and its ritual manifestations in burial rituals are evident in the tell cultures (Vicze 2000). This differs from non-formalised killing and burial of people in pits that was a widepsread practice in the western tell cultures (Hårde in press).

a

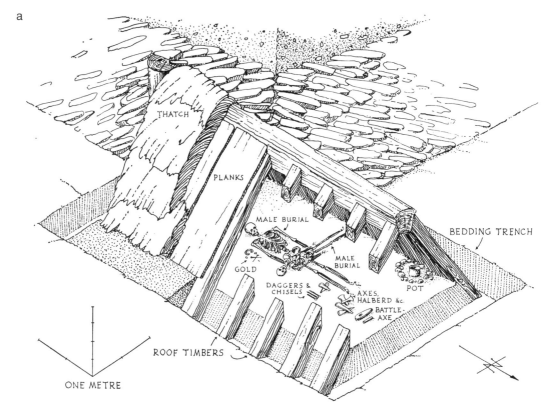

THATCH

PLANKS

MALE BURIAL

BEDDING TRENCH

GOLD

MALE
BURIAL

DAGGERS &
CHISELS

AXES,
HALBERD &c.

BATTLE
AXE

POT

ROOF TIMBERS

ONE METRE

Fig. 48
Differential
treatment of
people during
the Early Bronze
Age: (a) chiefly
burial from
Leubingen and
(b) killed
individuals in pit
from Nizná Mysla
(after Hansen
2002: Abb. 45
and Jacab, Olexa
and Vladar 1999:
Abb. 7).

From Bronze A2 the Carpathian metal takes over, again from one dominant mine and some smaller mines, supplying a large region including
southern Scandinavia. From the Middle Bronze Age onwards an Alpine
source becomes dominant, probably the Witterberg region, and this metal
seems to have supplied much of the Tumulus Culture and later the Urnfield Culture. In England/Wales we have the same picture of huge mining
operations (Dutton, Fasham and Jenkins 1994).

We do not yet know why the regional shift in metal production took
place – causes may span from internal warfare and crisis to exhaustion of
the ores. In the Caucasus, Chernykh has documented widespread ecological
degradation around the mining areas, and sees this as a major cause of
abandonment (Chernykh 1998).

We can observe a certain Europe-wide regularity in the expansion of metal
and metalwork, which deserves more detailed study (Needham 1998). The
early phase of the later third millennium may be characterised as an explorative phase when possible ore-bearing regions were settled and exploited
and output was small (Bertemes and Heyd 1996). It was only after 2000 BC
that large-scale mining and production began in a few centres, and the
large-scale distribution of ingots, now reaching more distant regions such

b

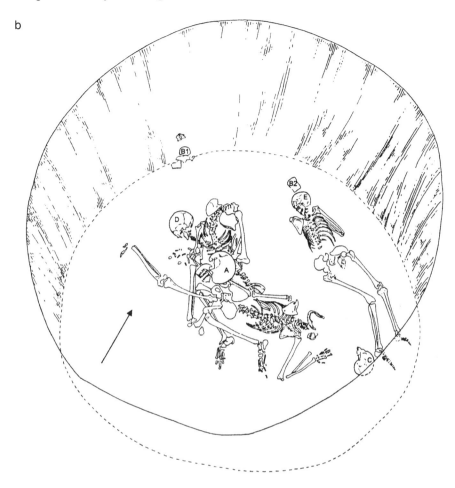

Fig. 48 (*cont.*)

as Scandinavia. From 1750/1700 BC metallurgical know-how was expanding too, as well as production, and the variety and quality of products were now reaching a high point, which was consolidated after 1600 BC. All regions in Europe were now becoming metal-using, producing their own products even if they were far away from the centres of ore production, for example Scandinavia. A graph of the metal increase in Denmark (see Fig. 49) may illustrate the above development in a region without copper or tin but with amber (Vandkilde 1996). The point to be made is that amber disappeared from graves and as personal ornaments at the same time as the metal import increased. It is now only to be found as raw amber in hoards, such as in a chiefly house in Bjerre, northwestern Jutland (Beck 2003).

It is indeed remarkable that the beginning of large-scale mining operations, demanding specialised metallurgical and organisational know-how, and the use of tin bronze begin simultaneously in Unetice and Wessex/Ireland. Margaretha Primas has recently demonstrated the enormous

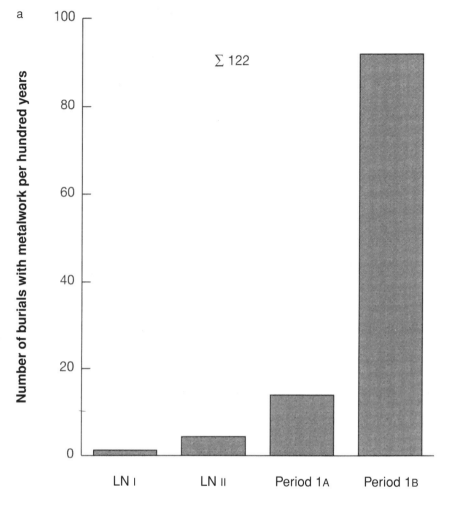

Fig. 49 (*a*) Graph of metal depositions in Denmark 2300–1500 BC, marking out the period 1B from 1600–1500 BC as a turning point (from Vandkilde 1996: Fig. 298); (*b*) diagram showing the use of tin in bronzes between 2300 and 1500 BC in the Nordic region and in central Europe. In central Europe tin is common after 1900 BC (Period Reinecke Br. A2), in the north after 1750 BC (Period Montelius 1A) (based on Pare 2000).

difference in output between the later third millennium and the Bronze Age proper after 2000 BC (Primas 1997: Fig. 3), and there is increasing consensus among researchers about the highly organised nature of production and distribution. 'In the core areas the key to the change was that copper and bronze underwent a process of commoditization – they became important as unit quantities of metal rather than as a restricted prestige item for social transactions, and may indeed have functioned in some respects as a proto-currency – as a means of exchange and store of value' (Shennan 1993: 62).

In both cases we observe a more systematic contact with the city-states of the east Mediterranean, where personal dress items such as pins and earrings suggest personal contacts and exchange of know-how: that is, the toggle pin in Unetice, the *Krückennadeln* and golden and gold-covered bronze earrings in Wessex (Schauer 1984b: Abb. 26, 28–9). But the tradition of

b

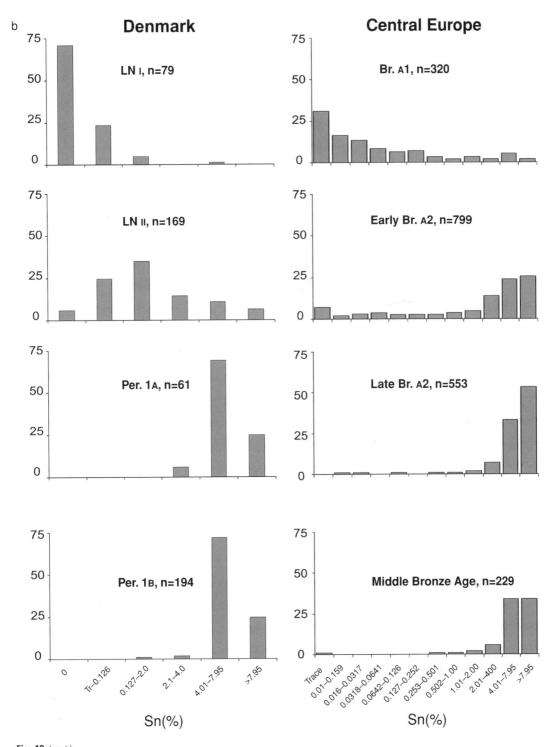

Denmark

Central Europe

Sn(%)

Sn(%)

Fig. 49 (cont.)

furnishing grave goods beyond personal needs, in the style of hoards, was also part of this early international elite culture from the Levant to western Europe (Hansen 2001b).

While the contacts with the Unetice Culture seem to have been rather sporadic after the first encounter,[4] those with Wessex were continuous. They transmitted a new technological knowledge of complex goldwork, inlaid goldwork on bronze such as the famous sword from Marais de Nantes (Schauer 1984a: Taf. 1), and production of glass beads. Certain sword types are based upon east Mediterranean prototypes, such as Arreton, or the Cypriot swords (Gerloff 1975; Burgess and Coombs 1979). There developed here a technological sophistication that is remarkable, and unthinkable without contacts and exchange of know-how with east Mediterranean specialists. But it should also be noted that influences passed in the opposite direction: amber bracelets from Wessex or certain types of spiral ornaments from Unetice found their way into the shaft graves. So, while firmly grounded locally, external connections had significant historical consequences for the course of regional history (Needham 2000b).

Thus we come to the conclusion that although the Unetice and Wessex cultures both were rooted in and developed mainly according to local and regional traditions, they received vital new knowledge from the east Mediterranean. The development of large-scale mining and production, and the systematic employment of tin and the new technological sophistication emerging from it, was triggered by direct contacts with the city-states and palaces of the east Mediterranean. They in turn were exploring new sources of tin and gold to fuel the expanding palace and urban economies. As we shall demonstrate below, the later rise of new metallurgical centres in the Carpathians, and later in the Alps, in similar ways coincided with both qualitative and quantitative developments in production and distribution, where Minoan/Mycenaean traders were also active. In these processes commercial interests were at work, as well as social and ideological ones. Therefore we need to discuss briefly the organisational capacity of Bronze Age societies.

Organisational properties

Our knowledge about the organisation of trade has changed drastically in recent years. Owing to exceptional new discoveries such as the Ulu Burun shipwreck of a trading cargo from around 1305 BC (Kilian-Dirlmeier 1995; Bass 1998), and provenience analyses of pottery and metal (Jones and Vagnetti 1991; Stros-Gale 2001), the organised and commercial nature of

---

4 More indirectly we can point to a new additional repertoire in pottery, probably inspired by metal forms (the concave convex pottery); the same types are found in El Argar in southeastern Spain, probably based upon the same east Mediterranean prototypes.

Late Bronze Age sea trade in the Mediterranean is now well established. In this the archaeological evidence has been brought into correspondence with the written evidence (Larsen 1987; Klengel 1995). Especially, the role of the east Mediterranean city-states and palaces in the Levant and Crete, and later Cyprus and the Aegean, has become apparent (Gillis 1995: 72ff.). Most of this Aegean and Cypriot involvement, however, is late, from the fifteenth–fourteenth centuries BC onwards. Sherratt and Sherratt have stressed the development in the scale of trade through time (Sherratt and Sherratt 1991; Kristiansen 1998a: 359ff.), while Gillis has stressed the interaction between local, regional and international trade (Gillis 1995). She suggests that only the latter was organised on a commercial basis (for an alternative view, Snodgrass 1991).

Likewise the directional nature of chiefly trade and exchange in the European Bronze Age communities has been established in a series of studies, although much still needs to be done. Distances of 100–150 km caused no problems for chiefly expeditions, as demonstrated by Wels-Weyrauch (1989: 117–37) and Jockenhövel (1991) for the Tumulus Culture, although normal distances were probably closer to 20–40 km, corresponding to a chiefly polity. A similar pattern can be demonstrated in east central Europe, linked to the fortified tell settlements, whose political catchment areas were of similar size, just as distribution maps of prestige goods for exchange demonstrate clusters with similar distances.

These organisational properties provide an important framework for understanding the rapid transfer of goods and habits during the Bronze Age, including social and religious institutions, as we shall see. It is now possible to envisage organised travels and trading ventures by chiefs and their retinues over long distances. Such long-distance lines of exchange would end up being linked to trading stations or colonies taking the goods back to the palaces and city-states of the east Mediterranean. While we are mainly concerned in this work with the social and political implications of such long-distance travels, their economic role remains to be explored and analysed (Shennan 1999). Amber must have had an incredible economic value, linked to its ritual and social role. Certain products and items were charged with prestige and could consequently be traded over enormous distances and still sold with profit. This was true of fine textiles from Mesopotamia, that were sold as far away as the Black Sea (Larsen 1987), much like Persian rugs today. We are thus dealing with a combination of bulk trade in metals and small-scale trade in high-value commodities, such as amber that could sustain transport costs of thousands of kilometres. We shall later illuminate this discussion in concrete case studies.

We have now delineated some of the basic chronological, technological and political components of Near Eastern and European Bronze Age societies of the third and second millennia BC. With this as a background we can proceed to analyse and interpret a number of specific historical cases of interregional interaction.

4.5 Conclusion: some historical long-term trends

When summarising the evidence for the expansion of bronze metallurgy in Europe and its social and economic impact, a certain geographical and chronological regularity can be observed: changes took place simultaneously over vast regions, suggesting that a new situation of interconnectivity and dependency in European history had emerged. This defines the Bronze Age as a world historical epoch that is qualitatively different from both the preceding Neolithic and the following Iron Age (good discussion in Pare 2000; for a global perspective, see Earle 2002). The third millennium BC formed a necessary historical prelude to this new social and economic environment, as it opened up the Eurasian continent by introducing a new extensive pastoral economy. Within a few hundred years, in some places within a few generations, it decimated the forests and created large pastures suited to a new mobile economy with a corresponding new social organisation (Yamna, Corded Ware and Single Grave cultures). By the later third millennium mining and metallurgy were added to the economy, which speeded up interaction and changes. Bell Beaker cultures and early Unetice Culture represented the first prospectors and metallurgists, who travelled and traded their skills (Brodie 2001; Price *et al.* 2004; Heyd in press). By this time Europe and the Near East had entered into a closer relationship.

The third millennium BC was a period of expanding states and urbanism in the Near East, and the concomitant employment of copper and later bronze on a large scale, not least in the agrarian sector. Trade and economy had an eastern focus, including the Indus civilisation. After the crisis in the late third millennium BC interest is increasingly turning towards the north and west for high-value metals such as tin, gold, etc. The old Assyrian caravan trade may be taken to exemplify the highly organised commercial nature of trade, where not least tin was in high demand. It should therefore come as no surprise that exploration in the western Mediterranean and through to Wessex and central Europe to the tin mines there was initiated around 2000 BC, although it is still difficult to describe the nature of these enterprises. The evidence from trace analysis points to the Mycenaeans as in command of this trade, delivering tin and copper to Crete from the New Palace period onwards.

During the third millennium BC most of Eurasia remained Neolithic, but adopted a series of technological innovations from the Near East, such as traction, sheep herding and wool production, described by Sherratt as the secondary products revolution, which now unfolded its evolutionary potential. It was a tremendously expansive period, where new colonising groups would employ ox-drawn four-wheeled wagons on their local and regional migrations, transforming the environment in the process. This new environment had a huge potential for interaction and further social ranking that was released by the first systematic use of metal in the Unetice period from the late third millennium onwards. It led to an economic process of commodification, specialisation and division of labour. Very soon the scale and highly increased frequency of interaction led to the formation of rather identical regional polities. It represented a process of social and cultural convergence that is still badly understood. Trade and travels gained new significance, including travelling metallurgists who would sometimes be recognised in burials during this initial period of metalworking (Pustovalov 1994; Heyd in press).

The Early Bronze Age societies that evolved after 2000 BC thus inherited their basic social and cosmological order from the Beaker and Battle-Axe cultures of the third millennium BC. After 2000 BC the social and economic potential of these Early Bronze Age cultures was released by the introduction of new skills in mining and bronze metallurgy and a corresponding new social and economic complexity. Metal was commodified and socialised, being employed in the sphere of power, prestige and rituals, but also in subsistence (Fig. 38). It allowed new types of value and exchange to emerge, leading to new forms of institutions. In this way bronze embodied both a new economy and a new social/religious order that gradually transformed Eurasia into an interconnected world that speeded up the transmission of people and knowledge across the continent.

In the following we shall unfold and interpret in more detail some of the historical processes that reshaped Europe after 2000 BC. In doing so we apply the interpretative strategies developed in chapters 1 and 2.

5 Symbolic transmission and social transformation in Bronze Age Europe

5.1 The material culture of ruling elites: the Minoan connection (eighteenth to sixteenth centuries BC)

Symbolic transmissions entail both hidden and open messages that create an intricate and persuasive combination. Carried by people who transmit their understanding verbally and in performance, the symbolic field entails an additional dynamic, which has been eloquently expressed by Marcus:

> it should be pointed out that visual materials have a unique role in expressions of ideology. Material culture can take on the responsibility of carrying certain messages that a culture cannot entrust to language. The ability of art and other material goods to carry messages nonverbally makes them an especially subtle and stealthy means for communicating certain potentially controversial political messages, without danger of protest, refusal or controversy. In this way they can become powerful tools of persuasion by which one group of people wins the obedience of another. (Marcus 1995: 2487)

The lily and the ivy flower: tracing the meaning of a symbol

We begin this chapter by applying the methodological strategy of tracing a single symbol through its different contexts in time and space. We hope in this way to delimit a field of intercontextual meaning, a lost institutional and symbolic framework of meaning. We have chosen the famous lily and ivy flower motif, which was employed widely in Minoan culture, on both wall paintings and pottery, but also more specifically as a religious symbol linked to high or even divine rank. Originally borrowed from Egypt, it achieved in the Minoan culture a formalised decorative form, that could also be transformed into metal forms. As such we find it symbolising the young god/goddess 'Lily Prince' from Knossos (Fig. 50), which Ellen Davis has proposed as belonging to a priestess (Davis 1995: Ia).[1]

The feather crown is decorated with what we interpret as metal lilies (of bronze or gold), and she/he(?) is wearing a bracelet of lilies, probably of metal or other precious material (Davis 1995: IIa). This proposition finds

[1] According to Kilian-Dirlmeier (1985: Abb. 3–6) the Minoan warrior graves were employing the same kind of bracelet, suggesting that the Lily Prince represents a young male god. We suggest, however, that only half of the feather crown is preserved. Originally it consisted of two 'crowns' that would bend outwards from the head, thus resembling those sometimes huge feather crowns worn by female goddesses on stamp seals and gold figurines.

Fig. 50 The 'Lily Prince' from Knossos (after Marinatos 1993: Fig. 61).

Fig. 51 Women picking lilies. Fresco from Thera (part of Marinatos 1993: Fig. 213).

support in several burial finds: from grave B-circle, close in time to the Cretan examples, we find a bronze lily of the type on the feather crown, in the form of a pair of tweezers (Mylonas 1972: Table 100). Here we must assume a male burial. Both this shape and the heart-shaped ivy flower were applied as a central decorative motif on fine pottery from the B-circle for wine drinking and on amphorae (Mylonas 1972: Plate 145). Most interestingly the heart-shaped ivy flower appears on one of the grave stelae from B-circle (Mylonas 1972: Plate 40). Later, in Dendrá and Mycenaean chamber tombs the motif is highly elaborated (Senaki-Sakellariou 1985: 305ff.), with many examples from bracelets. Thus, in chamber tomb 515 at Mycenae we find a golden bracelet of the type worn by the 'Lily Prince', and a golden strip with a different variation of the lily symbol (Wace 1932: Plate XXXII). The heart-shaped lily of the golden strip is paralleled in a separate piece from the Panagia House at Mycenae (Mylonas Shear 1987: Plate 34).

The lily dagger from Mycenae, with gold lilies on the hilt and silver lilies inlaid on the blade (Vermeule 1975: Fig. 61), clearly shows the Cretan artistic impact on the art of the shaft graves (Vermeule 1975: 46). Mycenaean jewellery also indicates the very same connection, which is very clear if we look, for example, at the necklace from Prosymna (Taylour 1964: Plate 49).

Thus, the lily and ivy symbol was used to designate high rank during several hundred years, from late MH/MM to LH IIIAB. It was apparently linked to female status and probable ritual functions in the Minoan culture, which the wall paintings on Thera may illustrate, but male functions are also suggested in Mycenaean culture. The combination of figurines and bracelets in Mycenaean tombs with lily and ivy motifs suggests some ritual functions. In her splendid little book on art and religion on old Thera, Nano Marinatos has interpreted the paintings in Room 3 as a feast or ritual of spring and of initiation (Fig. 51). Young girls, and older women to guide them, are collecting flowers, lilies and crocuses, and bringing offerings to a blood-stained altar, before presenting their flower gifts to the priestess/goddess on the throne. Lilies and crocuses are used to decorate the dresses (we suggest they were metal pendants applied to the dress), as well as the altar (Marinatos 1988: Figs. 40–49).

Here, then, we see the ritual context of the lily and ivy symbol, linked to spring rituals of fertility and initiation overseen by high-ranking women, and a female spring goddess. Only women participate. Nano Marinatos parallels the scene with the later spring festival of Demeter where only women took part.

The metal forms of the lily and ivy symbol are indirectly proved by another famous wall painting – the Captain's Cabin in the west house, Room 4, that displays a variety of metal forms from heart-shaped to lily-shaped (Fig. 52).

Again, we see the lily symbol linked to high-ranking persons – the king or the commander of the fleet. The metal forms depicted on the wall paintings are not found on Crete. We have seen contemporary examples from the Argolid, but most are later. The major distribution of the metal lily and ivy pendants is in east central Europe, in the Carpathians. Here the ivy- or heart-shaped pendant is probably the most important part of female dress accessories, together with the lily-shaped pendant. The heart-shaped pendant comes in both open and closed forms, the latter looking rather like a breast symbol (Fig. 53). The lily-shaped symbol takes on a distinctive form of its own, that is not as directly similar to the Minoan–Mycenaean prototypes as the ivy- or heart-shaped symbol.

In a study of female ornament and dress in the Carpathians Gisela Schumacher-Matthäus (1985) analysed the different ornament combinations in burials and hoards, and their distribution and chronology. They basically span the same time period as the lily symbol in Minoan/Mycenaean

Fig. 52 The 'Captain's Cabin' fresco from Thera and central European metal forms (after Furmanek 1997: Figs. 6 and 7).

culture, that is from the seventeenth to the fifteenth/fourteenth centuries BC (Reinecke A2–B2/C).[2] In the Carpathians, women occupied important positions in the stratified societies that emerged during this period: some of the richest burials belong to women. Here we find both gold and amber, but, not least, complex dress and hair styles where metal pendants and ornaments were integrated into the dress, forming a distinctive costume

2 The dating of both the heart-shaped pendants and the pottery figurines has been debated. It is clear, though, that early forms of the pendants, such as found in the Barca hoard together with amber bracelets and golden earrings, much like in Mycenaean culture, belong in Br. A2–3 (Schumacher-Matthäus 1985: Tafel 22). The recently published hoard from Satu Mare, with a combination of the early type (worn probably) and a freshly produced later type, confirms this (Kasco 1997–8; also Kovács 1986b). The early simple form is also testified in several burials, such as Kules (Bona 1975: Taf. 13–19), and is also found in Anatolia (Müller-Karpe 1980: Taf. 171). Kovács has recently dated the early figurines by comparison with metal forms to Br. A2 into B1 (Kovács 1986a; also Honti and Kiss 1999/2000 for pendants). There are no grounds for comparing these figurines with the late Mycenaean figurines, as is often done (Chicideanu-Sandaor and Chicideanu 1990: Fig. 2A), except for late forms (*ibid.*: Fig. 10). Thus the bell- or tube-shaped figures characteristic of Cirna (Dumitrescu 1961) are clearly dated by their Minoan parallels (Müller-Karpe 1980: Taf. 208; Gods and Heroes: 57, cat. no. 40) from the fourteenth century BC, continuing into the thirteenth century BC when the position with upright arms was introduced.

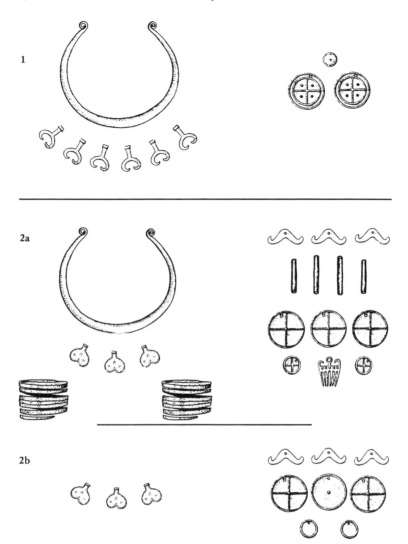

Fig. 53 Hoards from Hungary with heart-shaped and lily-shaped pendants arranged in personal sets (Schumacher-Matthäus 1985: Taf. 42).

(Sørensen 1997b). Pendants of various types, including the heart-shaped ivy flower, were applied to the dress, but could also form part of complex bracelets, or head/hair ornaments, including golden earrings (Figs. 53 and 56). Earrings of the same or related types are also depicted on fresco paintings on Thera, and were recently cited by Stuart Manning in a discussion of chronology and cultural connections to Egypt (Manning 1999: Figs. 18–19). The lavish application of pendants and bracelets all over the body shared by Minoan/Mycenaean and Carpathian women represents a rather specific correspondence not found elsewhere in Europe. But links to the western Mediterranean and beyond are equally significant, both culturally and in terms of chronology (Eogan 1990: Fig. 3). Golden earrings of Carpathian

a

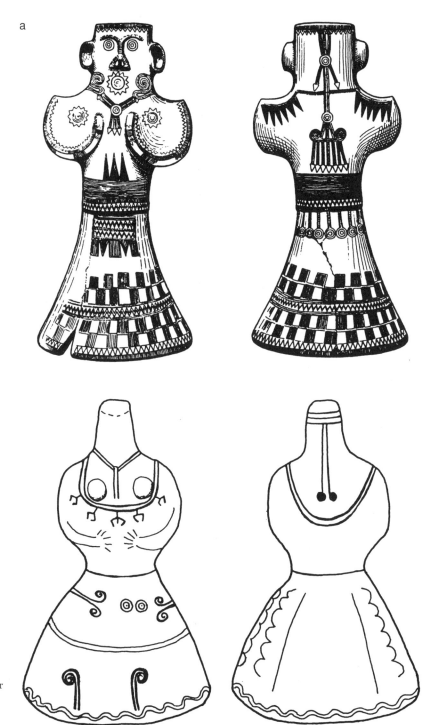

Fig. 54 (a) Carpathian clay figurines with decorated clothing (after Schumacher-Matthäus 1985: Taf. 5 and 14) and (b) Minoan Snake Goddess from Crete (after Goodison and Morris 1998: Fig. 55).

Fig. 54 (*cont.*)

type are also found in the shaft graves, together with central European spiral ornaments of Late Unetice type, once again stressing the role of international trade and communication during this period (Mylonas 1972: Plates 178–80).

In all this, the Carpathian female burials and hoards resemble the Minoan/Mycenaean dress tradition of high-ranking women/priestesses. But the parallelism goes further: in the Carpathians we find richly decorated female clay figures from the same periods, where the costumes are displayed, sometimes in great detail (Fig. 54a).

Although the costume belongs to a distinct Carpathian tradition, we also detect specific Minoan features, such as the opening of the dress to show the breasts, and the complex chessboard pattering of the long skirt (Fig. 54b). Note also that the sun symbol is employed to indicate the mouth and two breasts on the more elaborate clay figurines.

In terms of ritual functions, we can make direct comparisons with the famous Minoan terracotta figurines and the simpler, more common clay figurines employed in rituals. We may assume that the figurines of the Carpathians served similar functions. Their role was probably to take part in miniature performances of important rituals. One such example is the famous clay model from Duplje in Serbia. It shows a chariot drawn by swans, and the clay idol, representing a female goddess, was to be placed in the chariot standing on a wheel figure, representing the sun. Here the role is rather clear: it is the sun-goddess Eos who, according to myth, was riding a chariot drawn by white swans, and who is paralleled in other Indo-European myths. In the *Rig-Veda* her name is Usha. We will return to this myth and its interpretation in the chapter on Bronze Age cosmology.

Goddesses, high-ranking women and female costumes

We suggest that the similar use of the lily and ivy symbol in the Minoan culture and the Carpathian tell cultures as a female symbol of high religious and social standing suggests a closer similarity of meaning linked to the institutionalised role of high-ranking women in rituals of fertility. They represented priestesses who oversaw the rituals of fertility and took part in them as well. The lily and ivy symbols connected three related contexts: in metal forms as part of a lavishly decorated costume (both areas), in the decoration and gestures of ritual female figurines (both areas), and in burials/ hoards as personal ornaments (both areas, but not Crete). Blischke has recently pointed to the striking similarity between the heart-shaped pendant and the gesture of the arms on the clay figurines (Blischke 2002: Abb. 24). This suggests that the pendant symbolised a divine gesture, and the clay figurines represented this goddess. There existed a number of formalised ritual gestures in the Minoan/Mycenaean culture, some of which were adopted in central Europe (Hitchkock 1997: gesture 4). The heart-shaped pendants are supplemented with the breast-shaped pendants, some of them with nipples marked (Fig. 55). Together they symbolised the divine goddess with naked breasts.

The wall paintings on Thera have provided a local ritual context of the fertility ritual, which was still in use in later Greek times (the Demeter spring festival). In central Europe it was linked to the performance of rituals employing clay models and figurines. However, we wish to suggest that the

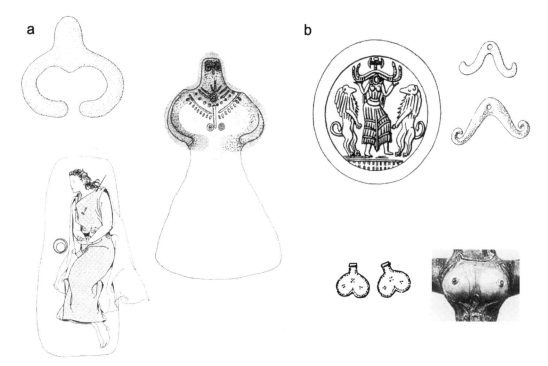

Fig. 55

Interpretation of some Carpathian bronze pendants as bodily symbols. (*a*) Heart-shaped pendant as symbolic representation of ritual gesture on clay figurines, also employed in female burials (after Blischke 2002: Abb. 24); (*b*) symbolic representation of ritual headgear and female breasts (see also Fig. 54).

priestesses of the lily and ivy pendants took part in and performed such rituals. Another similarity between the two regions is the lack or scarcity of warrior burials from the early period, before 1500 BC. We suggest that these similarities in the representation of gender reflect deeper structural and religious traditions of Near Eastern origin.

We are thus dealing with similarities of meaning, whose complexity and regularity suggest the transmission of a religious and social institution related to the role of high-ranking women and a fertility-goddess/sun-goddess (observe the sun symbol employed as mouth and eyes in Figure 54a). We are also dealing with certain formal or typological similarities, especially the heart-shaped ivy pendant, but also some more general similarities in female costume and gesture.

Although there is great variety, and a specific Carpathian tradition at play here, certain trends demonstrate familiarity with the Minoan tradition – a curved opening to show the breasts is indicated on several figurines, and the complexity of the skirt is another characteristic feature. This is demonstrated in Figure 54. The chessboard pattern of the long skirt is common to two figurines, while the exposed breasts are shared with the other figure.

In addition, the characteristic large circular earrings from the wall paintings on Thera are echoed in the golden circular earrings/hair rings from

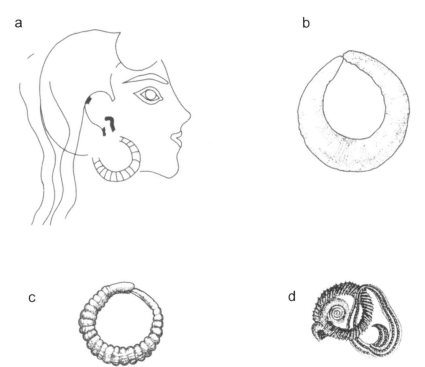

Fig. 56 (*a*) Fresco from Thera showing earring, and similar (or related) earrings from Crete (*b*), from Hyksos settlement in Palestine (*c*), and from the Tufalau hoard in Romania (*d*) (after Manning 1999: Fig. 18 and Müller-Karpe 1980: Taf. 285).

central Europe in the Tufalau hoard (Figure 56). Also, a variety of complex hairstyles were characteristic of both regions, in east central Europe (as in some Minoan frescos) supported with complex ornaments and ponytails hanging from the neck and down the back, both in burials and on figurines (Schumacher-Matthäus 1985). Again we observe that complex female hairstyles in Scandinavian oak coffins and on bronze figurines share both general and specific similarities with Minoan frescos and terracotta figurines, as shown in Figure 57.

Certain highly specific Mycenaean ornaments, such as the mussel-shaped pendant and Mediterranean shells, are also found in burials in Hungary (Bona 1975: Taf. 86–87; Pioy 1985: 307), as well as double spirals and anchor-shaped pendants (Bona 1975: Abb. 22 and plates). Furmanek has further pointed to the similarity between wheel pendants in central Europe and Aegean seals (Furmanek 1997) from the Old Palace period on Crete.

The employment of female clay figurines and of elements of dress, or rather a ceremonial dress, suggests a deeper correspondence concerning the ritual role of women in both areas. Female costumes on Crete and in east central Europe at the tell sites represented an arena for display, which reflects their importance in social and religious institutions. Combinations of symbols in a number of finds suggest that the goddess of fertility was also

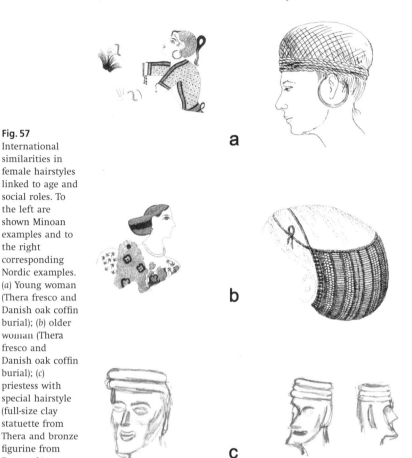

Fig. 57
International similarities in female hairstyles linked to age and social roles. To the left are shown Minoan examples and to the right corresponding Nordic examples. (*a*) Young woman (Thera fresco and Danish oak coffin burial); (*b*) older woman (Thera fresco and Danish oak coffin burial); (*c*) priestess with special hairstyle (full-size clay statuette from Thera and bronze figurine from Denmark).

a sun-goddess, riding on a chariot. The famous clay model from Dupljana confirms this role, to be discussed later. A few richly decorated pendants from the early Urnfield period of the late fourteenth to early thirteenth centuries BC (Novotna 1994) with twin wheel symbols and double axes indicate their role in the cult of the sun-maiden, riding the chariot of the sun with her brothers the Divine Twins (to be discussed in chapter 6.7). The symbol of the sun itself is also attached to the pendant (Fig. 58). As demonstrated above in Figure 53, Hungarian hoards from the earlier period entailed the same symbols, but as individual pendants: sun-wheel or heart-shaped pendants, etc. (only the axe is missing, but during this time axes were deposited separately with male objects).

On the basis of this transmission of social and religious ideas, we suggest that a Minoan connection became established with east central Europe some time during the eighteenth–seventeenth centuries BC, perhaps using the Mycenaeans as middlemen. One may point to the occurrence of several objects in the B-circle at Mycenae with a central European origin, such as

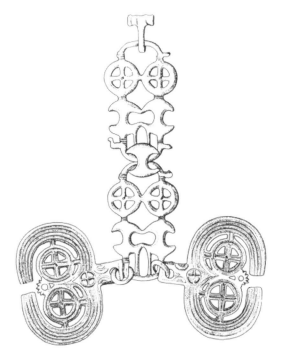

Fig. 58 Richly decorated pendants with chariot and sun symbolism from the early Urnfield period (after Furmanek 1980: Taf. 27).

a rare wheel-headed pin (Fig. 59). It belongs to a group of wheel-headed pins characteristic of the northern Tumulus Culture, among them a rather similar pin found in a burial in Bohemia. These two pins – from Bohemia and Mycenae – stand out from the rest as being crude and badly executed. They share this similarity against other wheel-headed pins, which suggests a rather personal connection between the two regions, perhaps intermarriage. As pointed out by Kilian-Dirlmeier, sets of similar flint arrowheads for hunting are found in northern tumulus burials in Lüneburg and in the shaft graves (Kilian 1995). It adds yet another small but significant detail of international connections and adaptations of elite behaviour and bodily culture (to be discussed further in chapter 5.4).

This scenario can be substantiated by other evidence for Crete's leading role in organising long-distance trade with east central Europe, and indirectly northern Europe.

Rituals of drinking: cups for cheering

Cups for drinking played a vital role in the social and religious life of the palaces. 'Antonious had just reached for his fine cup to take a draught of wine, and the golden, two-handled beaker was balanced in his hands' (*Odyssey* Book 22, 10). They represented therefore an arena for craftsmanship

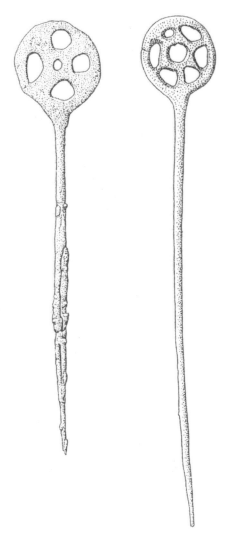

Fig. 59 Two unique, and badly executed wheel-headed pins from Mycenae (B-circle) and Bohemia (female burial), testifying to personal contacts (based on Müller-Karpe 1980).

and their status made them objects of trade and exchange between trading partners. It is therefore significant that the early distribution of metal cups and their local derivates links Crete to a central European line of exchange from the lower Danube, via the Carpathians to the Baltic and southern Scandinavia (Fig. 60). It covers the period Br. A2 to Br. B/C, corresponding to the Nordic periods I (late) and II. The development from metal imports to local metal imitations to wooden cups with tin sprags can be traced in some detail (Fig. 62). And so too can the contexts, which are always rich chiefly burials in the north. In two Scandinavian graves the content of wooden cups has been determined as mead (Koch 2003). It is interesting to note that prestigious drinking cups have three centres: Crete/Mycenae, southern Scandinavia and

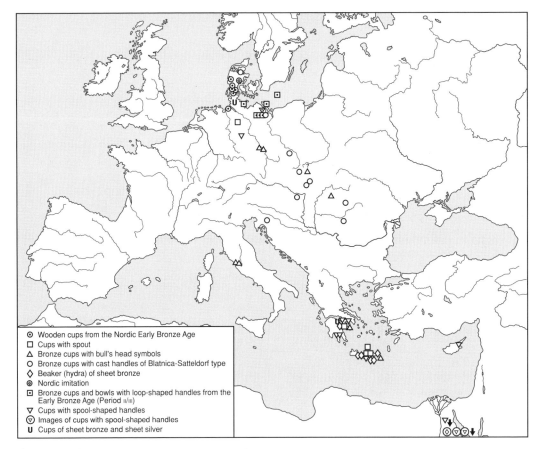

Fig. 60 Map of metal (and wooden) cups from the Middle Bronze Age in Europe (after Schauer 1985: Abb. 1).

Wessex/Armorica, and widespread similarities existed between the three regions, based upon common prototypes and local imitations.

A well-known imported Minoan *Schnabeltasse* from Dohnsen, northern Germany, represents the early phase of Minoan cups (Fig. 61). It remains unique. While the Dohnsen cup was a genuine import, later forms are rather imitations – or at least we do not know of east Mediterranean prototypes, although a cup from a Montelius period 2 burial in northern Germany could very well be an import, with its prototype in the grave A-circle (burial IV) at Mycenae (Struwe 1983).

However, the dominant type was probably based upon copying of Mycenaean pottery cups (skyphoi), though the the small axe-shaped handle on the metal cup on Figure 62 has a clear counterpart in Minoan pottery. The type materialised as 'shale cups' in Wessex, and as both cast and beaten metal cups in southern Scandinavia (fifteenth–fourteenth centuries BC) (Figure 62).

Locally the form was imitated in wood, but with tin nails to outline the decoration – horizontal bands, sometimes snake-like wavy lines, and

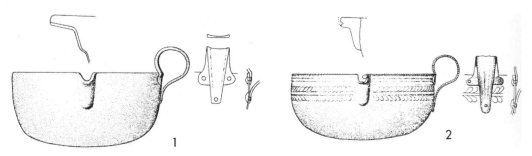

Fig. 61 Minoan bronze cups from Akrotiri, the Aegean and Dohnsen, northern Germany (after Schauer 1985: Abb. 43).

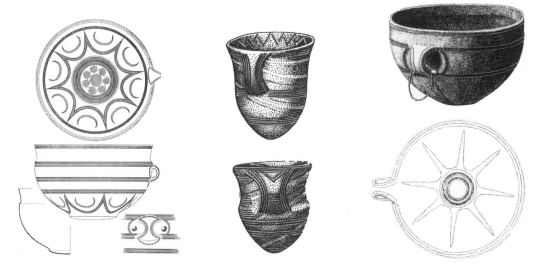

Fig. 62 Shared stylistic tradition in drinking cups of the sixteenth to early fourteenth centuries BC in northwestern Europe: shale cup from Wessex, metal and wooden cups from Denmark, and northern Germany (based on Schauer 1985: Abb. 50, 32, 51). Not to scale.

star motives at the bottom, the sun symbol. The double axe form inspires the handle. Thus there existed a shared stylistic tradition from Wessex to Scandinavia, despite differences in material and size. The origin is supposedly Mycenaean, but no suitable prototypes can be pointed out. The beaten cups may have been produced in the Carpathians, but this is pure guesswork. We may here have an example of foreign imported prototypes that were not preserved archaeologically in their place of origin, as discussed in chapter 1.4. It lends social and ritual significance to the imported hammered metal cups that the only two known pieces were found in very rich chieftains' graves: one on Bornholm from the Montelius period 2, and one in the unique Kivik burial with other indications of long-distance travels and Mycenaean/Minoan connections, to be discussed below.

Also of some historical significance is the fact that this group of drinking cups demonstrates a close connection between Wessex and southern Scandinavia. This is manifested not only in form, but also in the occurrence of imported raw tin in Jutland, and imported raw amber in Wessex, the primary trade goods of the two regions. This connection could have been direct, along the Frisian coast, or it could have been channelled through southern Germany, as we shall see later. What was circulating inside these networks? From the north came amber. Shaft grave amber was Baltic. And in southern Scandinavia, amber disappeared from burials with the advent of metal shortly after 2000 BC. We have now even documented the context of amber collecting and hoarding during the Middle Bronze Age in Jutland, as an amber hoard has been found inside a chiefly house (Kristiansen 1998c; Bech and Mikkelsen 1999: Fig. 4b). We are thus being reminded that amber was perhaps more important and costly than commonly believed in Bronze Age research. We shall take up this question below, when discussing the unique character of the Nordic Bronze Age, as it unfolds after 1500 BC.

We thus see a long-distance exchange network linking the east Mediterranean and northern Europe at work during the period of the shaft graves and beyond. It transmitted a whole series of prestige goods, only some of which we have discussed here. The drinking cups are not enough to postulate the transmission of a Mediterranean ritual; this has to be qualified by a recurring set of items that define a specific context of meaning. These other aspects of a transmission of institutions in which the drinking cups find their place (chariots, architecture) and their implications for societies in central Europe and beyond will be discussed below.

Life of the ruler: art, architecture and domestic rituals

There existed in the Early Bronze Age of the Carpathians and east central Europe a settlement tradition of villages, staying at the same place and forming a tell, from the mid to later third millennium BC (Nagyrev, Hatvan, Maros). This in itself does not imply a complex society. On the basis of burial analysis these Early Bronze Age societies have been described as autonomous communities governed by local chieftains without overarching political authority (Shennan 1978; O'Shea 1996). However, during the period Br. A2–Br. B1 (eighteenth to sixteenth centuries BC) most of the tell cultures underwent significant transformations that included both material culture and settlement organisation, some of which we have already described above (for recent summaries, see Andritoiu 1992; Bona 1992; for dating Forenbaher 1993; Bader 1998; Gogaltan 2002). It included a general application of the spiral motive in decoration of pottery and metal forms (Figs. 63 and 64), new sophisticated metal forms/casting methods, and a new type of settlement hierarchy. It centred around chiefly fortified settlements with metal workshops that functioned as centres of trade and redistribution (many hoards are buried on these sites). The sixteenth century especially was a flourishing period (Br. B1/LH I) when the products from the metal

Fig. 63 Early spiral band decoration from the Mycenaean (1–4) and Carpathian cultures (5–7) (after Hänsel 1982b: Abb. 2).

workshops were spread to both the north and the west, and when many so-called Mycenaean swords bear witness to the expansion of warrior aristocracies, which we shall discuss later. But the tell cultures continue during Br. B2, and into C, especially in the more eastern part not affected by the expansion of the Tumulus Culture.

These basic changes were already outlined in Istvan Bona's classic work on the Middle Bronze Age (Bona 1975), where they were linked to the expansion of trade with the Aegean. The evidence for this was developed in a series of works by Vladar (1973 and Vladar and Bartonek 1975), and Bouzek (1985a, 1985b). We shall now reinterpret some of this evidence, with the addition of important new excavations, especially by Bernhard Hänsel.[3]

Before proceeding, we need to address a chronological and historical problem. Earlier research was hampered in its interpretations by a short chronology that compressed historical changes and forced researchers to lump together phenomena that, with the new absolute chronology, can now be divided into temporal phases. It further implies that the central European chronology has been stretched back in time (see chapter 4.2). The interpretative implications of this have not yet been pursued, but we shall

3 For several of the classic Slovakian and Hungarian sites we are forced to rely on the earlier publications, mostly preliminary, as several of the most important tell excavations have not yet been fully published.

Fig. 64 Spiral band decoration on the circular disc on Carpathian axes (top row) and on Minoan seals from the Old Palace period (after Vulpe 1982: Abb. 4 and Sbonias 1999: Fig. 7).

make an attempt. In the following we suggest distinguishing between an early phase of Minoan influence in the eighteenth–seventeenth centuries, and a slightly later phase with increasing Mycenaean engagement from the seventeenth century BC linked to the shaft graves, which ended shortly after 1500 BC. It was resumed only from the late fourteenth century BC, with the expansion of Mycenaean influence along the Anatolian coast (the Trojan War, Iakovidis 1998) and the appearance of Aegean armour in rich central European burials around 1300 BC. This chronology is based upon a dating of the Thera eruption at 1628 BC, which implies that the use of heart-shaped and lily-shaped pendants started no later than the seventeenth century BC in the Carpathians.

We suggest that the formation of fortified tell settlements with an acropolis and the concomitant developments in metallurgy and trade had already started under the influence of Middle Minoan culture, that is the Early Palace period. We further suggest that the metalwork of this early phase was decorated with broad-banded curved linear motifs of proto-spiral type, normally linked to the Hajdúsámson group of metalwork (swords and axes). They share this decoration with Minoan seals (Fig. 64), and from the same source we find wheel-shaped pendants of various types in the early phase of the tell settlements (Sbonias 1999: Fig. 7; also Furmanek 1997: Abb. 5).

This represents the transition in time between Late Unetice and Early Middle Bronze Age (Late Reinecke A1 and A2). The period late Br. A2 and Br. B1 represents the classical tell settlements where contact with the east Mediterranean and Scandinavia was continuous and well organised, and when the spiral became a dominant decorative element on select types of material culture.

If we assign meaning to style, it follows also that we have to assign historical significance to the universal adoption in south-east Europe and Scandinavia of the spiral motif from Br. A2 onwards (*c.*1750 BC onwards). As the spiral was linked to foreign influences and high culture from Minoan Crete, we may assume that it reflected a wish to take on this civilisation's identity, often demonstrating familiarity with Minoan/Mycenaean prototypes.[4]

---

4 The pottery styles with spiral decoration during the Middle Bronze Age tell cultures reveal sometimes astonishing parallels to Minoan/Mycenaean motifs on pottery and works in bone/antler (Bouzek 1966: Fig. 7). The Suciu de Sus very clearly apply the carving technique to pottery, which sometimes has motifs of great beauty. In particular, one pot with abstract plant motifs compares directly with late Middle Minoan prototypes (compare Bader 1978: 200 with Dickinson 1994: Fig. 5.8–6 from MM IIIA). A characteristic decorative trait in the Wietenberg Culture is the use of contrasting bands of spiral ornamentation (Andritoui 1992: Plate 28, no. 9). With these two examples we wish to point out that although the pottery styles are clearly local, they demonstrate familiarity with Minoan pottery and painting. The same familiarity is demonstrated in the bone and goldwork (Vladar 1973: Fig. 53ff.). If these parallels are accepted this has chronological implications, moving back in time the spiral style on pottery in the Carpathians, including the Suciu de Sus Culture.

If that is the case we should expect it to manifest itself in other areas of lifestyle, rituals and architecture.

Since the sensational excavations in Slovakia of the fortified settlements of Barca, Spissky Stvrrtok (Vladar 1973), Nitrianski Hradok-Zamecek (Tocik 1981) and Hradisko Vesele (Tocik 1964), it has been known that the architecture on several of these sites showed imitations of Minoan/Mycenaean architecture and domestic rituals. On the wall plaster, imitations of more complex house building techniques were symbolically added (Fig. 65), and at the site of Pobedim a column with clay capital moulding was found (Bouzek 1966: Figs. 19–20).

Inside houses altars and libation tables in Minoan/Mycenaean tradition were sometimes found. We may note that the Minoan ritual tradition of libation on to a portable stone with cupmarks, beginning during the Early Palace period or even earlier, was also employed in Scandinavia. The same patterned use of cupmarks in circles can be found here, both on portable stone and on rock art (Fig. 67), hardly accidental when considered in the context of the massive influences that reached Scandinavia from the east Mediterranean during this period.

Also, the architecture on the tell settlements reveals similarities with the megaron with central hearth and altar (Fig. 66). The use of drystone construction in the building of defence works is another new architectural feature (Jockenhövel 1990), most probably derived from the south-east (Fig. 68). The recent excavation of a complex fortified settlement with acropolis at Monkodonja in Istria has exemplified this (Terzan, Mihovilic and Hänsel 1999; Mihovilic *et al.* 2002). Its beginning dates back to the eighteenth century and represented an early phase of east Mediterranean colonisation in the Adriatic region. This is demonstrated, among other things, by the importation of animals of east Mediterranean and Carpathian origin (deer and horse), as well as the stone architecture (Fig. 68). From here, influences soon penetrated northwards and eastwards, as we shall discuss later. We predict that similar settlements are to be expected in the Black Sea region around the Danube and further south.

We wish to make it clear, however, that we consider that the tell settlements originate from an autonomous tradition, and we wish to stress the strong local and regional traditions. Against this background, the application of foreign symbolic elements in architecture and domestic rituals becomes even more striking. It demonstrates a wish to signal a culture identity in pottery style, house style and architecture for an emerging elite. Even the libation rituals were adapted and brought further north to Scandinavia, which suggests that a complex ritual and cosmological knowledge accompanied these adaptations at the chiefly settlements. But contacts were to some extent reciprocal. No doubt the Mycenaean culture took on many

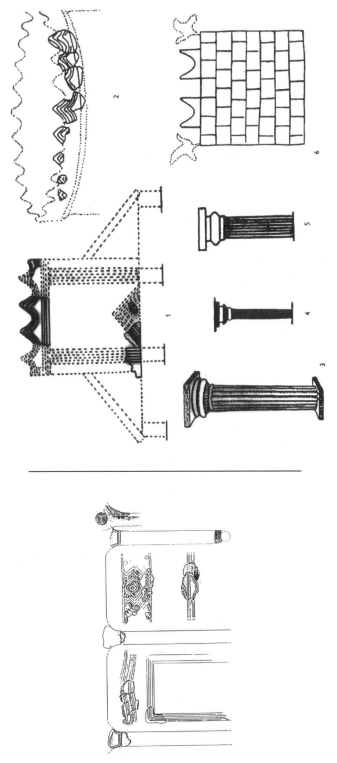

Fig. 65 Wall decorations from tell settlement at Feudvar (left) and columns and wall decorations from Aegean and Carpathian sanctuaries and houses (right). (1) Wall decoration from Trebatice, (2) Kutná Hora, (3–4) Minoan columns, (5) reconstructed column from Pobedim, (6) Piscocephalo, Crete (Feudvar after Hänsel and Medovic 1991. Others from Bouzek 1985a). Not to scale.

Fig. 66 Ritual hearths decorated with spirals. Above from the Carpathians (Wietenberg Culture), and below from the palace in Pylos (after Hänsel 1982b). Not to scale.

Crete

Scandinavia

Fig. 67 (*a–b*) Libation tables with circular cupmark pattern from early and late Minoan culture, Crete, and (*c–e*), similar patterns on libation tables and rock art from Bronze Age Scandinavia (based on Gesell 1985; Glob 1969).

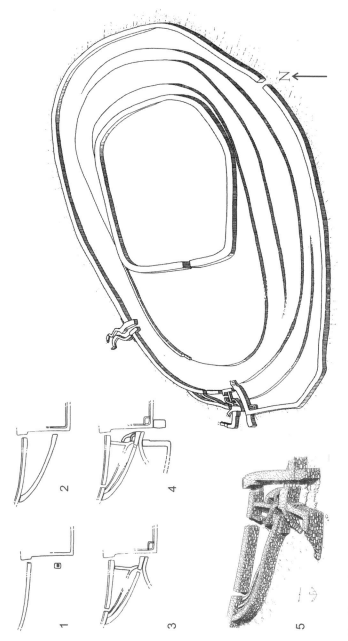

Fig. 68 Model and enlarged entrance section of complex fortified settlement with drystone architecture, in Monkodonja, Istria (after Mihovilic *et al.* 2002).

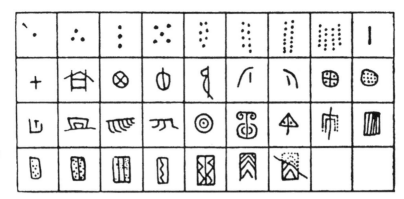

Fig. 69 The script of the Lipari Islands (after Haarmann 1996).

elements from the tell cultures, especially those linked to horse training and chariotry, but local aspects of ornaments, such as earrings, pins and bracelets were also sometimes brought back, as we have seen. In the Mycenaean context they were a testimony of successful long-distance explorations and perhaps even of marriage alliances.

This adaptation in the tell cultures of east central Europe of Minoan/ Mycenaean institutions of ritual and religion, and more superficially of architecture, further implies that they were able to transmit them further on. Visitors to the chiefly courts in the northwestern Carpathians during the seventeenth and sixteenth centuries BC would have met a shining world of painted/decorated houses in east Mediterranean imitation, chariots, new weapons and new exotic rituals of drinking and feasting which a visiting northern chief could well employ at home. That this happened we will demonstrate in the next section. But before doing that we must also delimit the limits of civilisation. The chiefly courts of the tell cultures combined a strong innovative local tradition in pottery and metalwork with exotic cultural traits from the Minoans and Mycenaeans, whom they met regularly at some of the trading points. Even script – the mysterious powerful script – did they want to adopt. Not for recording their possessions or tribute payments, as we shall see, but as a powerful, esoteric ritual.

Script and the loss of meaning: the limits of 'civilisation'

The Aegean impact on the 'outer world' is well documented in southern Italy from the time of the Mycenaeans in the form of imported pottery (von Hase 1982; Tusa 2000). From *c.*1500–1300 BC we have on the Lipari Islands (in the Tyrrhenian Sea) a locally produced pottery with engraved signs of a peculiar type (Fig. 69), showing that the islanders were in contact with written texts from the Aegean area (Haarmann 1996: 149).

Fig. 70 Hittite
hieroglyphs
found at
Hattusha (after
Buchholz 1987:
Abb. 72).

The resemblance to Linear B is weak, but comparing the signs with the non-deciphered Linear A script, some of the Lipari signs show a close similarity. As Holloway (1991: 28) has remarked: 'It may be debated whether these are distant relations of the so-called "Linear" scripts of the Aegean world: what is sure is that the islanders had come in contact with writing and now used written signs, even if in a limited way.' Buchholz (1987: 247) has pointed out the similarity between the Lipari signs and Hittite hieroglyphs (Fig. 70).

Also in the Carpathians, signs reminiscent of script were sometimes employed (Vladar and Bartonek 1977). We may consider these sporadic uses of early signs as reflecting a wish to demonstrate familiarity with and perhaps long-distance travels to the centres of civilisation in the east Mediterranean. They represented esoteric, foreign knowledge that could be manipulated locally. They remained in the sphere of magic and prestige of individuals with extraordinary long-distance connections. More recently signs of Linear A have been recorded in Bulgaria (Fol and Schmitt 2000), which if accepted would tend to confirm a Minoan presence in the region, as we have already suggested.

A limited and local use of signs coming from abroad can probably be said to be characteristic of the rock art figures from Oppeby in central Sweden as well (Fig. 71a). These carvings were discovered in 1984 (Broström and Ihrestam 1985) and what immediately became clear among Scandinavian archaeologists was the very different nature of these images in comparison with the rest of the Scandinavian rock art known today. The otherwise common motif on rock art sites, the ship, was absent here, and so were depictions of humans and animals. The only motifs in common with other rock art sites in Scandinavia are the cupmarks and the wheel-crosses. In all, more than 800 images were found at this site.

When comparing the signs shown in Figures 69 and 71, we note that many of them are quite similar. The 'closed' signs, of quadrangular or rounded shape, and the dots (cupmarks) are present in both cases. Further, the quadrangular frames are divided by lines in different conformations (straight, zigzag, V-shaped, curved) and the frames are sometimes also filled with

a

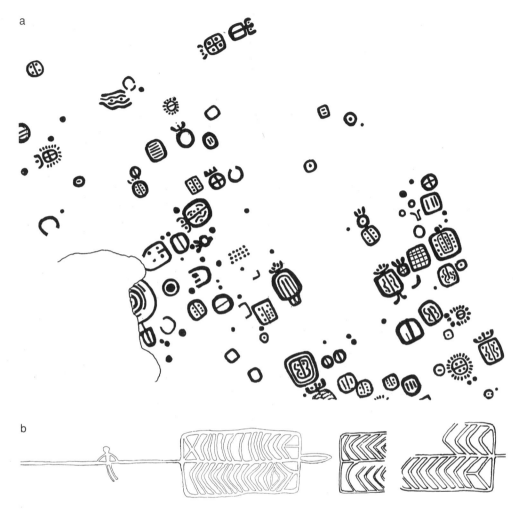

b

Fig. 71 (*a*) Rock art from Oppeby (after Wigren *et al.* 1990: Fig. 3) and (*b*) a frame-figure from Himmelstalund, Östergötland (after Nordén 1925: 187).

dots, and the rounded frames show a very similar variation of infill. This observation is valid for both the Lipari signs and the rock art from Oppeby.

A small excavation in front of the rock art panels at Oppeby was carried out shortly after the documentation, and apart from a few chopping stones (tools for making the images) charcoal was found that was C14 dated to 1800 BC. If the charcoal is contemporary with the rock art – which is highly plausible owing to the presence of chopping tools in the dated layers – these images are older than the bulk of the south Scandinavian rock art of 'traditional' type. The Oppeby rock art is contemporary with the early Minoan Palace phase, which makes it older than Linear B but more or less contemporary with the Linear A script!

The images at Oppeby are restricted to one particular spot (about 100 by 100 m) at a river-mouth. Created during the eighteenth century BC, and with no successors in the local area, they could very well have been made by foreign travellers who only once or a few times came by boat to Oppeby. If that was the case, these foreigners must have been allowed or perhaps even encouraged by the local chieftain to make their 'peculiar' signs on the rock surface. The strange, exotic touch of the signs in the eyes of commoners certainly would have increased the chief's prestige, a tangible evidence of his esoteric knowledge and connections with the worlds of distant 'Others'. But without a religious context to accompany them they remained an isolated unique event.

In Sweden the distant centre of origin for the new external impulses was the maritime chiefdoms on the east coast of southern Sweden (Kristiansen 2002a). In one of these – in Himmelstalund in Östergötland – we find a series of rich rock carvings of ships, animals and weapons (swords) from the seventeenth to fifteenth centuries BC. Spiral signs and imported swords testify to long-distance connections with the outside world in central Europe, but among the carvings, which are very rare in Sweden, we also find the geometric signs of the type discussed (Fig. 71b). It is the Linear A sign for 'cloth' with parallels in the east Mediterranean. However, in Himmelstalund this and other signs are recontextualised and incorporated into images, to transfer and transmit the magic of the signs that were otherwise unintelligible (Nordén 1925: Taf. 20 and Fig. 31).

To conclude, we propose that the signs on ceramics from the Lipari Islands in southern Italy and the rock art at Oppeby and Himmelstalund in Sweden can be seen as two border markers, indicating the northern and western limits of 'civilisation' during the mid-second millennium BC. Some faded replicas of the attributes of the 'civilised world' were present, but never used more actively in social strategies. To the north and west of this perimeter societal development took other paths, which were more independent of the legacy of the 'great civilisations'.

5.2   Horse breeders and charioteers: from the Carpathians to Sintashta, Mycenae and Hattusha

In Homer's epic *Odyssey*, the Kingly Hero Menelaus describe Argos as the place 'where the horses graze' (*Odyssey* Book 4, 95–100) and Nestor is often referred to as 'the tamer of horses' or 'the Gerenian charioteer'. The breeding of horses was a major elite activity at the palaces to ensure well-trained horses and charioteers for the war-chariots. Archaeology is now in a position to reconstruct the historical background to the role held by chariotry and war-horses in the *Iliad* and the *Odyssey*. But where did horses and chariots and the accompanying technological and horse training skills originate in the first place? Was this part of an east Mediterranean/Near Eastern military *koine*, or did part of this new military package of the early second millennium originate in the steppe region? These questions are part of an old discussion of relations between eastern/northeastern Europe and the Aegean/the Near East. To begin with we shall give an archaeological outline in brief of the problem.

The Bronze Age environments of the steppe region

Our understanding of the relationship between early Mycenaean culture and east central Europe and the steppe region has changed drastically in recent years. This is mainly due to new discoveries and research in three areas. East of the Volga, in the steppe zone of the Trans-Urals, Russian archaeologists have unearthed an impressive Bronze Age culture. Within an area some 400 km north to south and 200 km east to west twenty fortified centres have been documented, mainly by air photography, surrounded by hundreds of unfortified settlements (Zdanovich and Batanina 2002). Extensive excavations by Gening, Zdanovich and their colleagues have taken place at the sites of Arkaim and Sintashta. Burial mounds and cemeteries surround the central settlements, some with rich chariot burials. With the publication of the excavations at Sintashta in the Trans-Urals and its settlement system, we now have evidence of a highly developed warrior society – a complex chiefdom or an archaic state (Gening, Zdanovich and Gening 1992; Zdanovich 2002; Zdanovich and Zdanovich 2002). It was no less developed than its Mycenaean counterparts, with people living in heavily fortified settlements and burying their dead in shaft graves under elaborate tumuli with grave constructions like tholos tombs.[5]

---

5 The Sintashta Culture has been considered by several scholars to correspond to the descriptions in the earliest parts of the *Rig-Veda* and the *Avesta*, not least the description of the mythological 'Var' fortification, its social organisation and landscape (Medvedev 2002; Pyankov 2002). It is thus thought to represent the origin of those Indo-Iranian or Aryan people who migrated to India during the Bronze Age (Gening, Zdanovich and Gening 1992; Klejn 1999; Jones-Bley 2000a, 2000b; Kuzmina 2002). This took place probably in the first half of the second millennium BC. However, the Sintashta–Arkaim complex itself could very well have originated in Anatolian/Caucasian culture in the later third millennium BC, where similar settlement structures are known (Grigoriev 2002). Some have proposed a migration into the southern Urals from here, to explain its sudden emergence. It seems that complex societies evolved from the Urals and eastwards at nodal points of mining, trade or other economic resources (Huff 2001; Hiebert 2002). We should probably envisage the so-called Indo-Iranian culture as having emerged as a result of centre–periphery relations between the Near East/northern Iran and emerging pastoral chiefdoms during the late third and the second millennia BC (Koryakova 1996: Fig. 5; Sherratt 1998: Fig. 1.5; Sarianidi 1999). Mallory (1998) and Kuzmina (2001) have recently discussed the migrations to India/Iran. They both argue for the Andronovo Culture as a candidate for these migrations, carrying on core elements from the Sintashta Culture adapted to a mobile nomadic lifestyle. One of these migrations in the early second millennium BC could also be responsible for the isolated appearance of the Tocharian language and the Tarim mummies further to the east in the present-day Xinjiang province of China (Mallory and Mair 2000).

The second area of new research concerns the ecological and economic transformations taking place in the steppe and forest steppe regions. Here new palaeobotanical research and C14 dating of buried soils under barrows have revealed the early formation of grasslands and steppe environments, and their systematic exploitation (Anthony 1998; Shislina 2001 and 2003; Kremenetski 2003). During the third millennium BC the Yamna tribal groups (2700–2350 BC) practised small-scale pastoral herding, moving locally between summer and winter grazing, using four-wheeled vehicles. Rich grasslands and higher humidity than today secured this economic transformation and its widespread geographical adaptation, even into the Balkans and the Carpathians and Hungary, but also to the east (Ecsedy 1994; Kuzmina 1994). This was a pionering phase of expansion. Wooded areas were still preserved in the river valleys, evidenced in burials and wagons (Shislina 2001: 357ff.). The Catacomb Culture groups (2500–1900 BC) saw the further development of a pastoral economy based on sedentary settlements and long-distance herding and trade. It corresponds to the formation of a more hierarchical society, including metal production with a wide distribution (Gak 2000). Periodical ecological stress caused by overgrazing is evidenced, and some soil destruction. Seasonal migrations and herding now extended across the whole ecological zone (Shislina 2001: 259ff.). Although one can hardly generalise from these analyses in the Kalmyk steppe, they suggest a widespread development when we consider the similarity of the archaeological record throughout the steppe region.[6] It implies that by the beginning of the second millennium BC a pastoral economy was widespread in the central Eurasian zone (Anthony 1998), having acquired its final ecological boundaries (Demkin and Demkina 2002). The osteological evidence confirms that cattle were dominant (more than 50 per cent), especially big horned cattle, followed by horse and sheep. Pigs only played an insignificant role, as they need forests to roam in (Chernykh, Antipina and Lebedeva 1998: Abb. 10–11; Gayduchenko 2002; Morales Muniz and Antipina 2003: Table 22.3).

What we see is a development from localised herding/pastoralism to true pastoralism with sedentary centres of production that unfolded and reached

---

6 Based on palaeobotanical work carried out since 1990, it can now be stated that during the third millennium huge areas from the Urals to northwestern Europe were transformed into open grasslands. The transformation is very well documented in a number of case studies (Kristiansen 1989; Andersen 1995 and 1998). This massive deforestation was caused by a new economic strategy of pastoral herding with some agriculture. It thus reprented a social and economic transformation on a large interregional scale. The Yamna, Corded Ware, Beaker and Single Grave cultures all shared this new economic strategy (but with local cultural adaptations), and a similar cosmology linked to single burials, mostly under low mounds along river valleys or other ecological zones. The formation of this new open environment in northwestern Eurasia held a huge potential for large-scale interaction that was not fully exploited until the systematic introduction of metallurgy/bronze.

a climax after 2000 BC, for example in the Sintashta/Andronovo Culture and the Srubnaya/Timber Grave Culture. They further represented a new level of political organisation, led by a warrior aristocracy. Agriculture played a minor but increasing role through time as supplementary production, probably a response to increasing aridisation from 2000 BC onwards (Matveev *et al.* 2002). For recent discussions on the complex issue of economic organisation in the steppe during the early to mid-second millennium BC, see Bunyatyan 2003; Gershkovich 2003; Morales Muniz and Antipina 2003; Otrochschenko 2003; Pashkevich 2003.

The third area of new research is in the field of metallurgy and absolute chronology. Here E. N. Chernykh and his colleagues have carried out a long-term research project, which has made it possible to characterise different metallurgical provinces during the third and second millennia BC (Chernykh and Kuzminykh 1989; Chernykh 1992; Chernykh, Avilova and Orlovskaya 2000). In recent years work has been carried out in collaboration with Spanish colleagues to detail this evidence, especially the ecological impact of large-scale mining in the region (Chernykh, Antipina, Moskau and Lebedeva 1998; Vicent Garcia *et al.* 1999, 2000, n.d.). The mining area of Kargaly in the Urals produced a huge amount of copper during the Bronze Age (an estimated 150,000 tons), which was distributed to the whole steppe region. Deforestation was an immediate result, but must have been overcome by timber imports from further away, just as huge smelting and production sites in the mountains are packed with cattle bones from meat consumption. It suggests a widespread production and exchange of food and metal, that is a widespread division of labour between steppe societies and mining societies. Recent palaeobotanical research has demonstrated that the area was already completely deforested during the Bronze Age (Diaz-del-Rio *et al.* 2003). It is thus reasonable to assume that much of the copper was distributed in raw form and later remelted at centres like Sintashta.

At the beginning of the second millennium BC, from about 1800 BC, the Circum-Pontic metallurgical system expanded geographically to include the whole of Eurasia (Chernykh 1992: ch. 7; Chernykh, Avilova and Orlovskay 2002). It was based on the production and distribution from highly stratified centres such as Sintashta, with a ruling warrior elite using two-wheeled chariots and living inside heavily fortified settlements, from where they controlled the region. But it also included a widespread adoption of metallurgical know-how, and the opening of new mines. The Pontic/central Eurasian zone was thus at the beginning of the second millennium in a position to interact with the southern regions in Anatolia, Greece and the Iranian plateau on an equal basis. And there is much to suggest that these highly stratified societies had a surplus not only of metal and horses, but also of warriors.

a   Arkaim   b   Demircihuyuk

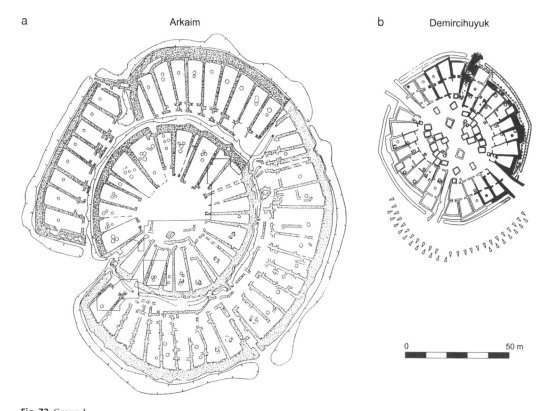

0   50 m

Fig. 72 Ground
plan structure of
(a) the fortified
settlement at
Arkaim,
compared with
(b) the smaller
ground plan
structure of the
fortified
settlement
Demircihuyuk in
Anatolia (based
on Zdanovich
and Zdanovich
2002 and
Korfmann 1983).
Same scale.

'The Country of Towns' : the formation of complex societies in the Trans-Urals and the steppe

We shall now describe the basic social, economic and religious component
of the Sintashta Culture, based on the excellent monograph presentation
in Gening, Zdanovich and Gening (1992), a useful summary in Zdanovich
(2002) and articles in Jones-Bley and Zdanovich (2002). Economically the
Sintashta/Arkaim Culture was based upon an integration of farming and
animal husbandry. This allowed a complex sedentary society to develop,
but situated in the Trans-Urals it was vulnerable to changing ecological
conditions, as we shall see. The highly organised, proto-urban settlements
(Figs. 72 and 73) demanded the production of an agrarian surplus, while
large herds of cattle and sheep were grazing the grasslands, organised from
the many smaller outlying settlements, some of them probably seasonal.
In the fortified settlements metalwork was a major concern, as was the
production of chariots, and training of horses, warriors and charioteers by
the ruling elite. The metallurgical activities demonstrate the importance of
mining and metalwork, being under the control of the fortified settlements.

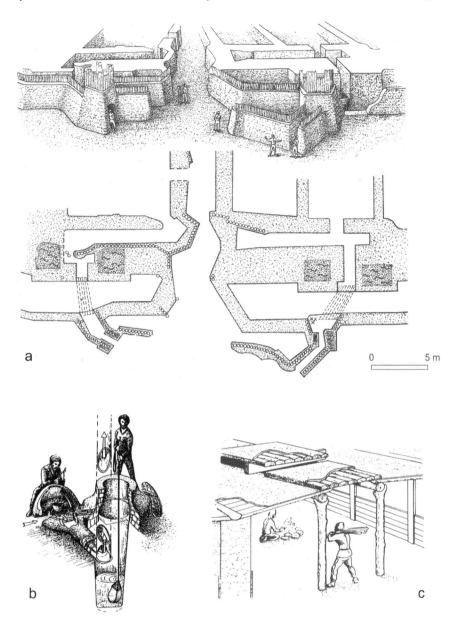

Fig. 73 Reconstruction of (*a*) the fortification of Arkaim, (*b*) smelting activity where well and furnaces are linked by the air supply tube, and (*c*) part of a house made of wood and earthen bricks. Most houses had furnaces for smelting. (After Gening, Zdanovich & Gening 1992 and popular folder.)

Fig. 74 Horses were buried along with two-wheeled chariots. *Top*: Detail from chariot burial, showing the use of disc-shaped cheek pieces; *bottom*: sacrifice of horse skulls (after Gening, Zdanovich and Gening 1992: nos. 15–16).

From here the latter were able to establish far-reaching lines of trade and exchange towards the south-west, soon followed by conquest migrations.

Conditions of preservation were exceptionally good, so wooden logs from burials and human and animal skeletons have been well preserved. This offers a unique insight into burials rituals and animal sacrifice. The latter was a dominant part of burial ritual, horses being sacrificed and buried. Many burials were plundered in antiquity, but they reveal important aspects of religion and cosmology, just as they demonstrate an elaborate system of rituals. Burial rituals and the construction of burial chambers and barrows reveal a hierarchical system, corresponding to a similar social hierarchy. Warrior chiefs were buried with chariots and horses in full horse gear (bits), ready for action in the otherworld. Sometimes only the skulls and hoofs were put down (Fig. 74). Horse sacrifice was thus an important ritual activity, and linked to the chiefly or royal strata, something we come back to in a later chapter.

The tumulus burials employed an elaborate architecture based upon the Indo-European cosmology of quadrant, open circle and vaulted dome constructed of mud bricks. The use of mud bricks and the construction of tholos-like vaulted domes suggest a southern origin, as they were ill adapted to the climate in the Trans-Urals. Southern links are also suggested by the circular architecture of the forts. As evidenced in Figure 72, rather explicit similarities are found between Anatolian architecture of the later third millennium BC, here represented by Demircihuyuk (Korfmann 1983), and the wheel-shaped settlements of the Sintashta Culture. Demircihuyuk and other similar settlements were abandoned by the late third millennium BC (Korfmann and Kromer 1993), and at the same time the Sintashta Culture appeared. The historical relation between them remains obscure, although it is well known that migrating people sometimes retain architectural features with basic cosmological meaning, while material culture may change (Collett 1987).

Material culture shows a mix of regional traditions in pottery and larger interregional cultural traits. These are mainly linked to weapons – lances, tanged knives, earrings, and not least horse gear. In this respect Sintashta was part of a shared warrior culture that stretched into the Carpathians, Anatolia and the Aegean. The tanged knives are thus also found in the shaft graves (B-circle), as are the lances (Penner 1998: Tafel 60). To the south-east this warrior/chariot complex stretched into the Caucasus, the Iranian plateau and beyond, where it is documented on pottery and in rock art (Fig. 75). It can also be documented by the distribution and expansion of the phallic and column-shaped stone sceptres from the early to mid-second millennium BC (Boroffka and Sava 1998: Abb. 32–39).

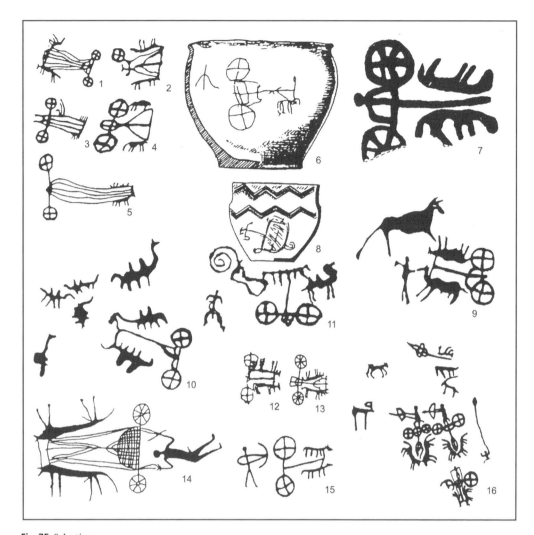

Fig. 75 Selection of chariot scenes from the Andronovo Culture and related cultures from central Asia, Kazakstan, Pamir and northwestern India (after Kuzmina 1994: Fig. 127).

Recent C14 dates going slightly beyond 2000 BC and continuing down to 1700 BC have once more raised the old discussion about the origin of the light two-wheeled war chariot (Anthony 1995; Epimachov and Korjakova 2004). The chariots in Sintashta, with complex spoked wheels and drawn by a pair of horses, now count as the oldest, although Littauer and Crouwell oppose this view and maintain that the Near East was the most probable origin of true chariotry (Anthony 1995; summary of discussion Raulwing 2000; Crouwel 2004). As the material culture of chariotry and warrior elites was shared from the Danube to Mycenae, Anatolia and the Urals, we find it likely that this formed the interaction zone of the full development and expansion of the two-wheeled chariot, during the period 1800–1600 BC. That is slightly later than Sinthashta.[7] However, as noted by Sherratt (2003), the relationship between the Near East and the steppe was a dialectical one. The steppe societies borrowed select elements from the Near East and transformed them to their social environment, which sometimes, as in the case of the lightweight two-wheeled chariot, led to a completely new construction, that gave a temporary competitive advantage. This was later re-exported to the centre, with the accompanying know-how (the Hittite Kikuli text), or in the form of conquest migrations (the Aryans, the Mitanni rulers).

The 'Country of Towns' culture has been described as 'a kind of quintessence of the Eurasian steppe world in the early Metal Ages. The "Country of Towns" is not a special archaeological culture. It is a new stage in the development of the Eurasian Steppe – a stage connected with the formation of hierarchical societies and proto-state structures' (Zdanovich and Zdanovich 2002: 253).

From *c.*1800 BC this new military structure began to expand beyond its borders towards the south-west and east, apparently owing to changing ecological conditions that gradually undermined the economy. We must envisage this expansion as one of conquest migrations in combination with the gradual movement of groups of warriors and their attached specialists and families. This historical process may account for the formation of new intensive long-distance connections between the Trans-Urals, the western steppe and the Danube and the Aegean, to be discussed next. It led to the expansion of the horse/chariot military package.

Mycenae and its northern connections

We shall now readdress the old question of the connections between Mycenae and northeastern Europe from the Carpathians to the Urals. We

---

7 Littauer and Crouwell have in several articles criticised both Drews' and Anthony's new historical scenarios (Littauer and Crouwell 1996). However, they have apparently made it a rule to criticise anyone who forwards an interpretation different from their own previously published works. Some of their critique is based upon a misunderstanding of the archaeological and ecological evidence. They propose that chariots were not functional, as they were too narrow. However, it is not possible to infer the precise construction of the Sintashta chariots directly from the burial evidence as we do not know in what condition they were laid down. Besides, the distance between wheels is bigger than they assume, and not contradictory to a use as chariots. Likewise it is not true that landscape and ecology constrained chariot driving. On the contrary: from the second millennium onwards Eurasia was dominated by open, grassed landscapes and a well-developed system of roads. It is inconceivable that a complex burial ritual of horses and chariots should be applied without chariotry playing a similarly important role in social life. Complex symbolism is meaningless without the full reality of what it symbolises. Another and probably similarly old horse bit tradition dominated in the Near East (Littauer and Crouwell 2001), and underlines that it is impossible and meaningless to determine the origin of vital technological innovations in the contexts of interacting elites in the Bronze Age. Archaeological dating methods are not accurate enough to cope with the speed of Bronze Age interaction.

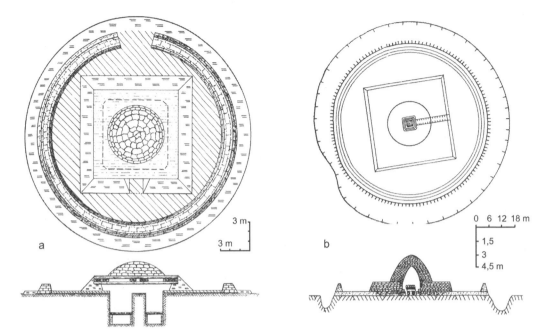

3 m

3 m

a

0 6 12 18 m

1,5
3
4,5 m

b

Fig. 76 Examples of elaborate chiefly burials in shaft graves, covered by (*a*) tholos or (*b*) tumulus, and surrounded by a grave circle and ditch (after Gening, Zdanovich and Gening 1992).

are mainly basing our interpretations on the work of Sylvia Penner (Penner 1998), David (1997, 2001 and 2002) and Boroffka *et al.* (2000). We have demonstrated that complex chiefdoms in command of a new military technology, specialists and well-trained horses were extending their social, military and commercial networks towards southeastern Europe, the Aegean and Anatolia during the eighteenth century BC, possibly even earlier. Similar expansions apparently took place to the south-east, into the Near East, northern Iran and later India, which we will not discuss (Mallory 1998; Kuzmina 2001 and 2002). This archaeological picture of expanding networks between the steppe, the Near East and the east Mediterranean is confirmed by textual evidence.

Whether or not one wishes to agree with Robert Drews about the coming of the Greeks (Drews 1988), he nonetheless points to a series of interrelated historical changes in the Near East during the eighteenth to sixteenth centuries BC. They were linked among other things to the spread and adoption of the Indo-European 'chariot package', which demanded both skilled specialists and the importation and training of horses from the steppe. This coincided with disruptions and social changes, including conquest migrations over large areas: the Kassites in Mesopotamia, the Aryans in India, the Hyksos in Egypt and a new chiefly dynasty in Mycenae (the B-circle), just as Indo-European-speaking people were emerging in Mitanni texts and other sources from the Levant and Palestine. In all cases we are dealing with rather small groups linked to the ruling elite, being warriors and specialists, sometimes rulers. 'The new rulers are in most cases a dominant minority, constituting only a tiny fragment of the population. This was especially true of the Aryan rulers in Mitanni and the Aryan and Hurrian princes in the Levant; it seems also true of the Kassites in Babylon and the Hyksos in Egypt. The Aryan speakers who took over Northwest India may have gone there en masse but were nonetheless a minority in their newly acquired domain' (Drews 1988: 63).

One can hardly overlook the interrelatedness of these major historical events, which also had far-reaching implications in central and northern Europe. In the Near East this period is considered by some scholars to be a 'Dark Age' (van de Mieroop 2004: 114ff.), just as in India (Franke-Vogt 2001) and Central Asia (Francfort 2001). Here calibrated C14 dates are pushing this transformation back into the period 1700–1500 BC or earlier. We thus find ourselves in general agreement with the historical scenario presented by Drews. In the following we shall present the archaeological evidence for the interrelations between the steppe societies, central Europe and the Aegean during the eighteenth to seventeenth centuries BC, and discuss their historical implications.

The recent works of Penner, David, Boroffka and others allow the reconstruction of a series of long-distance exchange networks between the western steppe, the Carpathians, the Aegean and Anatolia. It is characterised by the following components: a specialised package of material culture linked to horses and chariots (especially bits and handles for whips), often in bone or antler (Figs. 78 and 79); a specialised style of decoration linked to these objects, which was mostly foreign to the local style traditions (Figs. 77 and 78). This package is accompanied by new weapon types, especially lances, whose distribution extends into the east Mediterranean, and also by new burial rituals with shaft graves, sometimes covered by elaborate kurgans. The similarities between the burial ritual in Sintashta and the early Mycenaean culture cannot be overlooked. Another characteristic feature is the occurrence of identical pieces between these distant regions. It suggests far-reaching and direct personal connections.

How are we to understand these new networks linking the central Eurasian steppe with east central Europe, the Aegean and Anatolia? From a general historical perspective it represents the formation of the so-called steppe corridor linking the Altai with the Carpathians, and ultimately China with Europe. During the Iron Age and the early historical period it produced several major migrations, such as that of the Cimmerians/Scythians, the Sarmathians, the Huns, etc. Thus, the steppe corridor as an interaction zone between eastern and western Eurasia can now be demonstrated to originate 1000 years earlier, as can the social and political complexity accompanying

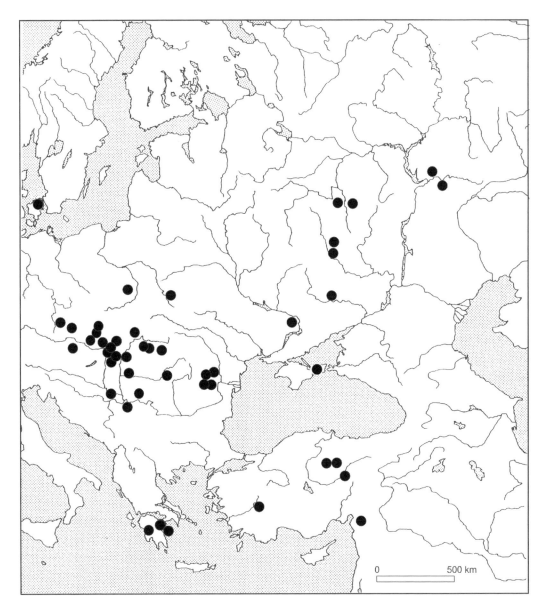

Fig. 77
Distribution of
the specialised
wavy band
decoration on
antler, bone and
ivory, as
presented in
Fig. 78.

it (Koryakova 2002). From a specific historical perpective, Sylvia Penner has
recently proposed that the archaeological distributions of the early second
millennium BC represent a conquest migration into the Aegean, leading
to the formation of the shaft grave dynasty. This interpretation is not far
from that of Robert Drews. Some evidence would seem to support Penner's
argument, including the osteological determination of the skeletons in the

Fig. 78 Examples of wavy band decoration (mapped in Fig. 77), here mostly on handles for whips (after David 1997: Taf. 7).

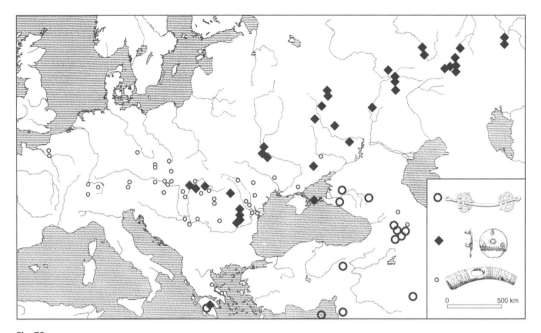

Fig. 79

Distribution of the three major types of bits in the chariot complex in Eurasia and the east Mediterranean during the early to mid second millennium BC. It demonstrates the existence of three interregional networks, which met in the Aegean and the Carpathians.

B-circle (Angel 1972), where the male population is characterised as Nordic Caucasian (robust and tall), in some opposition to the female population, which is more Mediterranean. The recently discovered shaft grave of a chiefly male warrior from Aegina from the LMH period belongs in the same group as the male chieftains of the B-circle, and he had injuries and muscle insertions on the right arm from sword fighting (Manolis and Neroutsos 1997). This evidence may show the intrusion of a new ruling segment of warriors and charioteers. They employed the specific wavy band decoration from antler, bone and ivory of the chariot complex on several of the grave stelae with horse and chariot motifs in the A- and B-circles at Mycenae (Younger 1997). Other evidence, however, points to some continuity between MH and LH, although not in the settlement system (Maran 1995).[8]

What can be inferred with some certainty is the importation of a new horse and chariot package, including steppe horses (Fig. 79). This was recently verified by an analysis of the two horse burials of paired horses from Dendra from the Late MH period, which showed they were of the larger steppe type (Payne 1990). They were well bred and out of an established breeding tradition. Thus, trade in horses, accompanied by new specialists in

8 We are aware that the anthropological evidence and the categorisations employed are subject to criticism. More recently this problem has been critically analysed by Day (2001), within a broad comparative framework of Indo-European osteological data. Even here, the shaft grave osteological material shows connections to the steppe of eastern Europe/Romania.

chariotry and horse dressage, would seem to be a necessary implication of the evidence. In addition our previous analyses of relations between the east Mediterranean and the Carpathians underpins this picture of well-organised long-distance trade connections and travels of chiefly retinues and specialists.

Concluding hypotheses: As the textual evidence of the Near East and Egypt describes conquest migrations and the influx of specialists, warriors and rulers of Aryan origin, it may seem justified to reassess some earlier interpretations of the origin of the shaft grave kings. So far the evidence is not conclusive (or our analyses are not conclusive); we therefore propose a minimal and a maximal hypothesis to inspire further research and discussion.

Hypothesis 1. Evidence: The material culture of chariotry belonged to the ruling elites, from the early Hittite kingdom in Anatolia to the chiefdoms in the Carpathians and the Aegean. It suggests elite interaction between these regions, including warriors and specialists in chariotry and horse dressage. Proposition: We thus propose that the distribution of horse gear during the shaft grave period was a result of trade in horses and craftsmanship linked to their training and breeding. It represents a systematic and institutionalised transmission of chariotry from the steppe region, originating in the highly developed fortified settlements such as Sintashta, which formed an archaic state or chiefdom during the earlier second millennium BC in the Urals. From here they controlled mining operations in the Urals, and the north–south trade to the Black Sea and further on to the shaft grave kings.

Hypothesis 2. Evidence: The material culture of chariotry in the Aegean was accompanied by new burial rituals exemplified by the shaft graves in the B- and A-circles, later followed by tholos tombs, all of which resemble the burial forms in Sintashta and the steppe region (Fig. 76). In addition the physical anthropology of the male chiefs in the B-circle showed so-called Caucasian–Nordic traits, in opposition to the women buried there. Settlement evidence further shows a break or reorganisation on the mainland during this period (Maran 1995). Also, new foreign weapon types such as lances with split socket are spread along the same lines of communication, but extend further into the east Mediterranean. Proposition: this additional evidence suggests that we are dealing with a conquest migration in the Aegean penetrating further into the east Mediterranean to Crete (the end of the Old Palace period). From here they joined forces with the Hyksos in Egypt, as originally suggested by Mylonas (1972). We consider hypothesis 1 to be verified, whereas hypothesis 2 is possible but needs more in-depth studies. Whatever interpretation one chooses, the effects of these historical processes became far reaching to both the east (not treated here) and the west. To demonstrate this we now turn our attention to northern Europe.

5.3   The iconography of ruling elites:[9] The Kivik burial and the origins of the Nordic Bronze Age

The interpretative challenge

For someone who has studied at first hand the metalwork of the second millennium in Europe for more than twenty-five years, it has become increasingly clear that the Nordic Bronze Age culture (especially its beginnings in Montelius period 2 from 1500 to 1300 BC) represents something unique. Qualitatively the artistic and technical expressions are above anything in Europe except Minoan/Mycenaean culture; quantitatively there is no region in Europe with such an accumulation of high-quality weapons and ornaments during the period 1500–1100 BC (Montelius periods 2–3), and that includes the Minoan/Mycenaean culture. One need only pick up the catalogues of Aner and Kersten and take a quick look through the first twelve or fourteen volumes, covering little more than half of the whole area, to be convinced (Aner and Kersten 1973ff.). Every gram of metal had to be imported. What was the economy behind such wealth? Tens of thousands of barrows were erected during the same period, more than in any other region in Europe of similar size, and they still crown the high points in the landscape today (in Denmark alone more than 20,000 barrows are fully preserved, most of them Bronze Age). They are big, mostly over 2 m high; several are 5–10 m high. Add to this that in the Nordic Bronze Age of period 2 one finds more east Mediterranean and Mycenaean influences in metalwork, prestige goods and cosmology than in any other region in Europe. In sum: archaeologists are here faced with a real interpretative challenge.

Why is it that the Nordic Bronze Age as a historical phenomenon is unique, and how can we explain it? We propose that part of the answer is found in a series of long-distance travels by Nordic and central European chiefs with their retinues, which over a period of 200 years from 1700 to 1500 BC connected Scandinavia to a long-distance trade network extending into the Aegean. Amber was moving south, metal and new esoteric knowledge in the opposite direction. And foreign chiefs from the south might sometimes stay in the north and vice versa. We have described this historical process in the previous chapter. However, at one point in time, around 1500 BC or slightly earlier, a person of extraordinary knowledge and creativity summarised all this into a new Nordic synthesis. Our search for

---

9 Today 'iconography' has become a term frequently used by archaeologists as well (e.g. Randsborg 1993), without any profound discussion about the relevance of using this concept when studying prehistoric images. Taking the classic works of Erwin Panofsky (e.g. 1939 and 1955) as a general point of reference, we see iconography as the study of 'the subject matter or meaning of works of art' (Panofsky 1955: 51). 'Art' (which is a concept that was born during the fifteenth century AD) is here taken to be equivalent to the notion of 'figurative representations' of different types, e.g. rock art, figurines, seals, frescos, vase paintings, etc.

the person and the location where it took place takes us to the south-east coast of Scania.

Here we shall once more discuss one of the most extraordinary Bronze Age burials in Europe, the Kivik grave. We do that as a starting point for understanding the uniqueness of the Nordic Bronze Age culture, since we believe that a set of specific triggering events have to be sought to explain what developed into a whole new social and cultural order in south Scandinavia. We are thus dealing in a historically concrete way with the relationship between structure and event and between long-term traditions and short-term transformations, between ideological/cosmological versus economic and social forces of change.

The Kivik burial confronts us with the task of understanding the unique. There is no other direct parallel to Kivik. Although it is a remarkably large cairn located at the ancient coastline and surrounded by large cult houses and a cemetery, this is not what makes it unique. Nor is it the grave goods – fragments of fibula, sword and a rare hammered, foreign metal cup. All this defines it as a ritual centre of regional importance. However, it is the eight elegantly decorated interior cist stones, with an iconography unparalleled in Bronze Age Europe, that make it unique (Fig. 80). Two possibilities are at hand: the unique is truly unique, the result of a singular event that left no other traces behind as it had no further impact, as was the case with the Oppeby rock carvings discussed earlier (Fig. 71); or – it could be a singular event that marked the beginning of a historical change and thus started a process of change. If that is the case it must be possible to trace its impact locally and regionally, and it must be possible also to trace its origin.

In the following we shall demonstrate that Kivik was indeed that singular event which represents the introduction of a new value system that was to have a tremendous effect on the formation of the specific Minoan/Mycenaean character of the Nordic Bronze Age. We shall do that first by tracing its origins outside Scandinavia, and secondly by demonstrating its lasting regional impact on the south Scandinavian Bronze Age. In our opinion it represents the port of entrance to the formation of the Nordic Bronze Age, the point of creation and transformation of foreign to local. In Kivik there started a process of local imitation because of its supernatural status as a religious and political centre, and it started – or concluded – a continued process of long-distance contacts with the outside world that supported and further accelerated the process of change. One or two generations later it led to the introduction of yet another foreign value system, this time through the south German Tumulus Culture. That represented the other major influence of what after 1500 BC, in a rapid process of regional interaction and integration, became the Nordic Bronze Age culture (described in chapter 5.4).

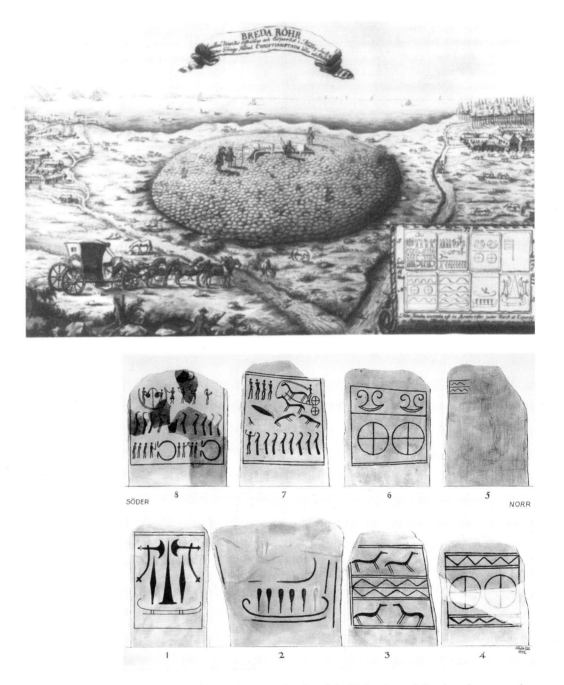

Fig. 80 Historical eighteenth-century drawing of the Kivik cairn and the pictoral stones, and below, a modern documentation of the pictoral stones (after Randsborg 1993: Fig. 3 and Malmer 1981: Fig. 6).

This interpretation of the historical role of Kivik rests on a new dating of the iconography of the stone slabs and the grave goods to the transition period between Montelius 1 and 2, Reinecke B1/B2, that is in the later sixteenth century BC. One of us has already argued for this dating (Kristiansen 1987: note 6), and we shall further substantiate it in what follows. It has to be admitted, however, that owing to its unique character, there remains room for several possible datings. Randsborg's dating to late Montelius 2/early 3 has some merits, whereas later datings can be discarded (Randsborg 1993). The dating of Kivik rests on three cornerstones: the dating of the foreign prototypes of the iconography, the local dating of the few pieces of metalwork, and the dating of those influences which locally were derived from Kivik, from single elements to imitations of the iconography. Finally we would add an additional parameter to be adopted in case of doubt: the historical context that makes most sense.

The foreign connections of Kivik and their dating

Randsborg (1993) has analysed the cultural and chronological connections of the Kivik find, and related the iconography to that of ruling elites in Anatolia, which is backed up by other evidence. This general interpretation we support and need not repeat. Instead, we shall take a closer look at the dating and the significance of the cultural connections, and their local acculturation and materialisation in southern Scandinavia.

Before doing that we need to comment briefly on Randsborg's dating of the grave goods and the pictorial stones to Montelius late period 2, or early period 3. First, from a methodological point of view, the dating of the grave goods and the pictorial stones need not be the same. As we shall demonstrate, the iconographical world of the pictorial stones must have been known and seen by many visiting chiefs during a longer period of time before their use in the burial, as their motifs were widely imitated throughout Scandinavia. Secondly, the fragmented bronzes from the plundered grave belong in our opinion in early period 2. They can only be dated with great difficulty, because of their state of preservation. The fibula and the sword pommel are early Montelius period 2 types. There remain then the fragments of an imported hammered cup with a protuding star at the bottom, which is paralleled in the Gyldensgård grave from Bornholm dated to Montelius late 2 (Randsborg 1993: Fig. 30). However, this piece could have been in circulation for a long time, being a rare prestige item. It is the prototype for the wooden cups with a protuding star or sun at the bottom, found in period 2 oak coffins from Jutland dating to the early fourteenth century BC (Fig. 62), and should therefore logically antedate them.

Fig. 81 Kivik pictoral stone with ritual axes, pointed hat and ship (*middle*) and its comparative context of antithetical, heraldic compositions from Minoan Crete (*left*) to Hittite royal emblems (*right*).

In conclusion, the grave goods should generally speaking be placed in an early part of period 2, and the iconography of the pictorial stones must logically antedate them. We will now make an attempt to reconstruct their cultural context and dating. Let us begin with stone no. 1 on Figure 80.

The antithetical, heraldic composition of the pictorial stone with two axes, a pointed hat in the middle, and two lances (?) to support the axes is paralleled in ritual royal iconography in the Hittite kingdom (Fig. 81). However the use of pairwise ritual axes, well know from ritual depositions (Fig. 84), also points towards the Aegean and the Minoan double axe stands, as they are depicted on the Hagia Triada scene, but with old traditions going back into the Middle Minoan period. The iconography thus combines Anatolian royal symbolism with a specific reference to Minoan double axe altars. This is an example of religious syncretism: a royal iconography of Hittite inspiration is recomposed and given new meaning by adding a well-known Nordic double axe symbolism with links to Mycenaean/Minoan religion. The pointed hat indicates divine status, according to Hittite tradition, and it has parallels in golden pointed hats from central Europe (Gerloff 1995). The ship that carries the composition is yet another indication of the maritime, foreign foundations of the royal, divine power expressed in this unique picture. What does the composition tell us? Its symbolic language talks about a royal person, a foreign king or chief, with divine status, coming from far away, employing Nordic cult axes in a new context of divine twin symbolism (to which we return later in chapter 6).

Thus, we have with this composition delineated the cultural background from which the Kivik king drew his inspiration – the Aegean/Anatolian world. The framing of the pictures belongs here too – being paralleled in the grave stelae of the Mycenaean shaft graves, just as the zigzag lines belong in a royal sphere during this period. Also, the carving of the male persons – with clearly delineated head, neck, body and limbs – corresponds with the shaft grave stelae. Such details are otherwise unknown in the Nordic realm, with very few exceptions, such as the grave stele in a Nordic burial from

Anderlingen in lower Saxony of a Nordic chief who died during his travels (Randsborg 1993: Fig. 41). Other motifs draw their inspiration from the Mycenaean world as well, not least no. 7 with the chariot racing, bull or horse fight, processions and four dancing males. Let us take a closer look at this picture.

The uniquenes of this composition is apparent from the three-dimensional drawing of the chariot drive. We find it replicated in two or three other examples; other Bronze Age iconography and rock art are two-dimensional: seen from the side in profile (humans, ships and animals) or from above (wagons). The chariot race or driving once again testifies to foreign inspiration, introduced from the Carpathians (Fig. 102), the steppe or the Aegean. Realistic minature (up to 20 cm wide) bronze wheels and realistic and detailed rock carvings from Fränarp of a whole army of chariots (Fig. 101) demonstrate that they were present and in use during the Bronze Age, demanding new skilled crafting, training of horses, etc. At the top, four men with swords but without arms are moving. Their broad shoulders suggest that they have their arms around each other's shoulders and are dancing. At the bottom a man with lifted arms leads a procession of eight animal- or bird-headed S-formed persons without legs – apparently in some form of long gown. They are probably women or woman-like beings, as their number corresponds to the number of males. On one rock carving a man is having intercourse with a similar being, yet on another pictorial stone a similar S-formed figure is driving a chariot. Quite evidently we are dealing with creatures of special significance, perhaps shape shifting. Finally in the middle we find bull or horse fighting, a fish and a small two-legged animal.

Nos. 7 and 8 show the rituals and feats – processions, dancing, mourning, music playing, chariot racing – performed at the funeral. On no. 8 the eight S-formed female beings stand on each side of what looks like an altar, or perhaps a coffin. Above them two lur players are active, one holding the lur down, the other holding it up. They blow towards a strange half-circle figure with two men carrying two round dishes hanging from a pole. Could these be the night and day sides of the disc of the sun, or drums? Above them, overlooking everything, is a sun or oxhead-like figure with an appendix, which appears a few times on rock art panels. At the bottom the eight males are, like the women, divided up into two groups of four, standing in front of the strange Ω-shaped circle – a grave circle? One is holding a sword. Their bodies are slightly figure-of-eight shaped: could they be carrying a figure-eight-shaped shield?

The other panels, nos. 2, 3, 4 and 6, show objects in pairs: two ships – one with lifted oars – two wheels of the chariot (twice) and two horses to draw the chariot (twice). In addition there is a figure with spiral endings. If it is an object it ought to be the box of the chariot (twice). This twin representation will be discussed later, in chapter 6.

Fig. 82 Signet ring from Tiryns from the fifteenth century BC (*top*) and a scene from one of the cist stones of the Kivik burial (*bottom*).

All scenes are skilfully orchestrated according to a well-known scheme, although never repeated. We are dealing with people with special skills: dancers, lur blowers, chariot drivers and priests, some of them specially dressed for the occasion (the eight S-shaped animal-like beings). Numbers are important – pairing, groups of four and eight persons. We shall now look more closely into some of the motifs/figures and their possible parallels.

S-shaped non-human figures are sometimes found on Mycenaean pottery from the LH period (Younger 1995: LIIi). S-shaped figures can be found on the Greek mainland as well, as on the gold signet ring from the 'treasure' of Tiryns (Fig. 82, *top*). The ring can be dated to the fifteenth century BC and the motif consists of four lion-headed demons approaching a goddess sitting on a campstool with a raised chalice in her hand. The demons are holding libation vessels and their bodies are depicted in a very accentuated S-shape, almost identical to the shape of the figures on the Kivik cist (Fig. 82, *bottom*). If we rescale one of the Kivik figures and put it on top of one of the lion-headed creatures, as is shown in Figure 82, the S-formed curve of the Kivik figure matches the shape of the Mycenaean demon perfectly. The positioning of the arms is also quite similar and it almost looks as if the figures in the Kivik procession should carry something in their hands, though nothing is depicted here. Originally, the things they may have carried could have been painted on the stone, but this is of course pure speculation.

Another similarity between the two compositions is the fact that both scenes show a row of zoomorphic creatures that approach an antithetically placed anthropomorphic figure, and, in each case, the latter figure seems to 'salute' the procession (by raising the chalice or the arms to an adorant position).

Apart from obvious iconographical differences in the way of presenting this ritual scene, the similarities between the two examples are striking when it comes to the general composition: one anthropomorphic 'saluting' figure (deity) who is facing a procession of zoomorphic S-shaped figures. All in all, this suggests that the mythology behind these images could have been related. If this comparison is relevant, a dating of the cist in the Kivik burial to early period 2 (*c.*1500 BC) must be considered.

When it comes to ritual processions we may also think of the royal Hittite rock art panels, where both gods and mortals are presented in ritual processions (see Fig. 131). Rather than looking for a specific source of similarity we should perhaps consider the complexity of the rituals with sexed processions with specially dressed participants as being of significance in relation to the Mycenaean and Hittite worlds.

However, the many specific similarities with the shaft grave stelae – from framing to motifs and pictorial style – suggest not only a historical connection of some sort, but nearness in time. These iconographic similarities place Kivik in Montelius 1, its later part, or early 2.

There are a number of motifs of unknown origin and function. To these belong the two Ω-shaped circles. They could well be interpreted either as neck rings of early Irish type (Anderson 1997) or as a special version of the ring ingots with rolled-up ends. The Irish type (dated on typological grounds to Montelius period 3) has never been found in Scandinavia, and is a less likely inspiration than central European ring ingots, which would be period 1. It should of course also be noted that they are omega-shaped, the last letter in the Greek alphabet. This provides a more likely interpretation of their meaning, but presupposes a pre-1400 BC dating of the transmission of the alphabet, as indeed argued by Bernal in an intensive comparative analysis (1987). He suggests that the origin of the omega sign was originally a double circle, before the struts were added. Their meaning still remains unclear, but they are part of a borrowing of alphabetical signs from Anatolia and the Aegean that appear in rock art, stressing their narrative reading.

The spiral curved pairwise symbols of unknown function have a number of parallels, from the Aegean to Scandinavia (Fig. 83). No two are directly similar, but they suggest a dating of the Kivik symbols within the same time frame as suggested by the shaft grave stelae – sixteenth or maybe early fifteenth century BC.

To conclude: the foreign contexts and possible parallels to Kivik's iconographic world span Montelius periods 1 and 2 (early).

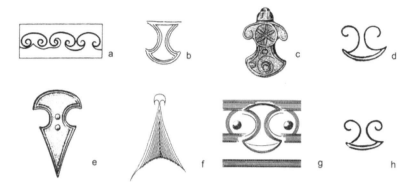

Fig. 83 Axe and spiral motives from Kivik (*d* and *h*) and some parallels from Europe and Mycenaean shaft graves: (*a*) pottery from B-circle in Mycenae, (*b* and *f*) from period 2 Nordic cult axe, (*c*) from B-circle Mycenae, (*e*) north German Unetice Culture, and (*g*) handle on cast Nordic period 2 bronze cup.

The local Nordic context and the dating of motifs

We shall now briefly consider how these results relate to a comparison with the Nordic context of the iconography. Among the few objects that can be identified with some precision are the two axes with short handles on stone no. 1. They clearly belong to the tradition of the Nordic cult axes. Their early form is a low-flanged Anglo-Irish axe with added shaft and spiral ornamentation. This is clear from an axe from Scania, which still has low horizontal ribs (Randsborg 1993). Other axes are typologically linked rather to the long slender late period 1 cult axes. Some symbolic inspiration between Nordic and Hungarian cult axes is evident (Fig. 84), both in the employment of 'hats' and in the peculiar knobs on some axes.

In time these Hungarian axes span from the Kozsider period of the sixteenth century BC (Furmanek and Marková 1996: Abb. 1 and 2) to the beginning of the Urnfield period around 1300 BC (end of Montelius period 2, early period 3). The typical Nordic cult axes originate in the transition between periods 1 and 2 around 1500 BC. The type with widely curved blade is generally later. They are cast around a clay core, and may belong in period 3, extending further down into periods 4–5 in later, more extreme forms. The Kivik axes can only be dated generally within periods 1–2. Their slenderness and the length of the blade rather suggest an early dating.

The ships are in the Nordic rock carving tradition and belong typologically to an early type linked to the Rørby ship, dated to Montelius period 1 (Malmer 1981: Figs. 2 and 3). Their upright oars are unique though.

The lurs developed during the Bronze Age into large sophisticated blowing instruments of a size and technological complexity never seen before in European prehistory (and never to be seen again). They were constructed in

a
b

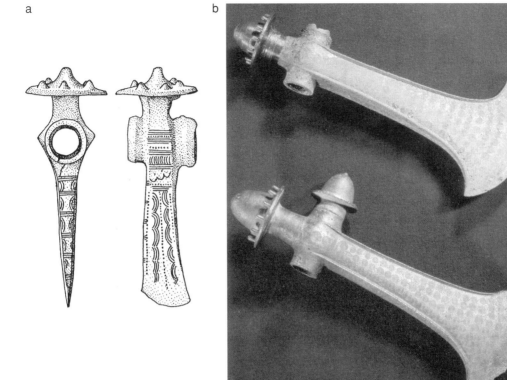

Fig. 84 Ritual
axes with hats
and knobs (*a*)
from Hungary
(after Furmanek
and Marková
1996: Abb. 1) and
(*b*) from south
Scandinavia
(after Jensen
2002: 290).

pairs, the curve of the instrument then forming two gigantic ox horns when
being played. They are synonymous with the Nordic Bronze Age. Those on
the Kivik stone clearly belong to a prototype, and are thus very early. They
are small and their blowing position is not yet standardised. They most
closely resemble the Wismar lur, or a development from that, which is
often dated to Montelius period 3. However, they could just as well, or more
likely, be dated to period 1. The ship type is early, and has the same sloping
crew lines ending with a little head or dot, as we only find at Rørby from
period 1. Also, the double symbolism found here resembles Kivik. A specific
trait is the wheel symbol with double frame, which is paralleled only in
the Carpathian tell culture from the Early Bronze Age (Bona 1975: Abb. 22).
The decoration goes well with such a dating: the U-shaped band with a
prolonged line ending in a dot is paralleled in Montelius period 1 motifs,
and in Hungarian gold rings from the same period (Kovács and Raczky 1999:
Abb. 18). We are thus inclined to redate the Wismar lur to late period 1 or
early 2 (Fig. 85). Its form and size conform well to the lurs blown on the
Kivik pictorial stone no. 8.

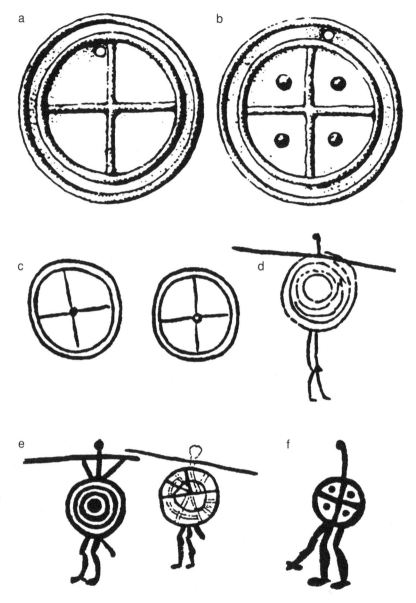

Fig. 85 Wheel amulets from Hungary (*a* and *b*), wheel figures from the Wismar lur (*c* and *d*) and rock art figures from western Sweden (*e* and *f*), all dating from Montelius late period 1.

Through a process of emulation, several of the iconographic elements from the Kivik pictorial stones spread throughout Scandinavia. They are found in contexts from Montelius periods 1 to 2. Most well known is of course the Sagaholm burial, which also has pictorial stones, although much less sophisticated. It is C14 dated to period 2 (Goldhahn 1999a). Quite

Fig. 86 Horse images from Sagaholm and bronze horse from Tågaborg.

evidently Kivik, the prototype, has to be older, not younger. The horse iconography from Kivik is paralleled in bronze figurines, most famously in the Stockhult hoard from period 2, and the Trundholm horse, which again may be defined as the bronze prototype from early period 2. As these are in a clear period 2 context, neither Sagaholm nor Kivik can be younger (Fig. 86). Finally we find a rock art panel on the coast just south of Kivik in Simris with a rich repertoire of motifs: ships, axes and ritual processions (Althin 1946). It dates to Montelius late period 1, and here we find the only other known example of the omega figure from Kivik, and a short-handled axe very similar to the Kivik axes.

In conclusion: the Nordic contexts point towards a late period 1 or early period 2 dating for the Kivik pictorial slabs.

Concluding the dating: the European and Nordic evidence spans Montelius periods 1 to 2. We are inclined to let those elements with an early dating be decisive, as they served the role of prototypes in the regional Scandinavian context, and it makes sense if we consider Kivik in a wider historical context, to which we shall now turn.[10]

The interregional context: Kivik as a centre of learning

It is possible to demonstrate how elements from the Kivik pictorial slabs were spread along the coastal zone of Scandinavia in a process of emulation (Renfrew 1986). We are talking about a coastal zone comprising several thousand kilometres that was connected by frequent maritime journeys from 1700 BC onwards. It was due to tremendous improvements in sailing technology and the need to be linked to the world of bronze. Consequently the ship became the most frequent motif on Scandinavian rock art panels, which are mostly coastal (Ling 2004). We may here talk about the emergence of maritime chiefdoms.

In a recent study by one of us (Kristiansen 2004) of ship types on rock art panels in Scandinavia it was possible to demonstrate the sea voyages behind this coastal network. Visiting chiefs would often carve a ship in their local style (which thus became a foreign ship type) to mark their visit, and by marking these 'foreign' ship types and their area of origin on a map a network of long-distance sea journeys can be reconstructed. We see here at work the expanding maritime chiefly networks, which in a few generations spread the new chiefly ideology and skilled crafts in a rapid process of social transformations throughout southern Scandinavia. It was through this very same network that the new cosmological knowledge from Kivik was spread throughout southern Scandinavia, as reflected in the repetition of the motifs from the Kivik pictorial slabs on rock art panels and cist stones at regional centres throughout southern Scandinavia (Fig. 87). We have to envisage the famous pictorial stones being preceded by a series of paintings that were employed in public rituals during a longer period until they were finally carved on the stone slabs and placed in the cist of the foreign chief and hero who created them. The content of this new cosmology was linked to the symbolic and practical role of the ship as a transmitter and transformer

---

10 An alternative dating of Kivik at the transition to period 3 would place it alongside other east central European influences, such as the rich grave at Skallerup with a wheeled cauldron, and the warrior burials in Slovakia with Greek corslets at the beginning of the Urnfield period. This is when Mycenaean influences are again spreading into east central Europe (Kristiansen 1998a: ch. 4). Shortly after, in the middle of Montelius period 3, connections to the North were cut off for one or two generations because of internal unrest and probably some conquest migrations in central Europe. There is very little in this historical scenario that makes sense, considering that Kivik contains all the basic symbolic and iconographic elements of rulership which characterised Montelius period 2. But it is only in Kivik that all the constituting elements are found together, granting it a special role as the centre of political and ritual power and complexity of a wider region, the beginning of the new Bronze Age world from which others were allowed to borrow selected elements.

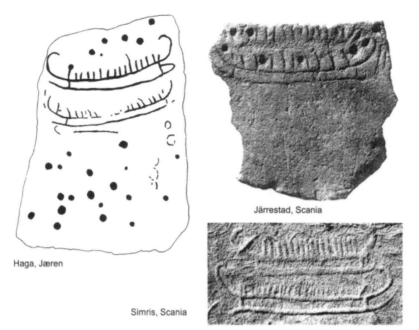

Fig. 87
Imitations of the
twin ship motif
from Kivik on
cist-stones from
southern Norway
(Jaeren) and
southern Sweden
(Järrestad). The
motif is also
common on rock
art panels, as
exemplified by
the Simris panel.

Järrestad, Scania

Haga, Jæren

Simris, Scania

of knowledge between distant realms and the role of chiefly burial rituals to reinforce the new cosmology.

We shall provide a few more examples of this fast process of emulation, which was linked to Kivik's role as a centre of learning, to be visited by all. The chariot scene and the procession are found at intervals from Östergötland on the Swedish east coast, to Bohuslän on the west coast, and further on to Trondheim, another 1000 km north on the Norwegian coast. Likewise, the pairwise wheels and horses are to be found in many of the same places. It is noteworthy that the complex scenes – procession and chariot scene – are only found in the centres of rock carvings, whereas the pairwise ships, axes, etc. can be found more frequently. We are seeing the formation of a ritual/political hierarchy in southern Scandinavia and its symbolic imprint on the landscape (Kristiansen 1996b). However, the port of entry and the centre for this new knowledge that transformed southern Scandinavia after 1500 BC is to be found in Kivik.

The international context: the transmission of royal iconography and the formation of chiefly elites

Kivik acted as a religious centre of learning for young chiefs throughout Scandinavia, together with similar centres on Zealand, where we find locally produced scimitars of Hittite inspiration, and the sun-chariot with a similar background. They were all part of a package of early Hittite and Minoan/Mycenaean influences that came to Scandinavia in a series of personal travels to and from the Carpathian tell cultures. From here there were again links directly to Hattusha in Anatolia. The Carpathian tell cultures were part of a Circum-Pontic interaction zone that had regular and systematic contacts with Anatolia and the Aegean during this period, as we described earlier (also Larsson 1999c; Engedal 2002). Other evidence of these direct chiefly expeditions between the Carpathians and southern Scandinavia are found in the early decorated solid-hilted swords of Hajdúsámson and Apa type that were introduced in Scandinavia together with the new religious and cosmological ideas. The new cosmological universe was unfolded as a demonstration piece, so to speak, in the iconography at Kivik, but it was symbolically condensed in the decoration of the ritual double axes from period 2, when it had become common knowledge. This was demonstrated by Kaul (2001) for a recently discovered axe. Here we find several of the central Hittite symbols of royalty and divinity, and it can be demonstrated that they originate on period 1 axes. New prestige goods were thus accompanied by a new symbolic language that centred round foreign value systems linked to royalty (Kivik), religious cosmology and divinity (Fig. 88).

Simris was the port of departure and the port of entry for chiefly trading expeditions across the Baltic during the sixteenth century BC, and the most famous of these foreign or returned chiefs later settled in nearby Kivik. Here we find a series of richly decorated rock art panels from period 1, the sixteenth century BC, that in ritualised form show us the trade and transmission of foreign goods, especially axes (Althin 1946). A fleet of period 1 ships suggests that maritime expeditions set out from here, and two axes of central European type were carved over one of the ships (Fig. 89) to symbolise its status and sacred role (twin rulers: see chapter 5.2).

The iconography of rock art thus helps us to contextualise the dramatic changes that took place during this period. It demonstrates, together with hoard finds with imported swords and axes (Fig. 84), that the imported metalwork was not random pieces that had lost their original context, but was part of a package of new complex knowledge, a new cosmology of ruling elites. It bears witness to the transmission of foreign chiefly ideals and lifestyles, and was backed up by new ideas of elite culture and royalty, as we shall briefly exemplify.

Apart from Kivik, we find during this initial period of the formation of a new Nordic elite ideology a few other unique items worth considering. Among them are the two identical so-called bronze drums from Balkåkra in Sweden and Hasfalva in Hungary (Fig. 90a), traditionally dated to Montelius period 1 (Knape and Nordström 1994; Larsson 1997: 80ff.). Following a recent excellent publication of the 'drums' it is possible to come up with another

A   **B**   **C**

Fig. 88 Selection of Hittite symbols from period 1 and 2 cult axes from Scandinavia (A), and their Hittite (B) and Carpathian (C) parallels.

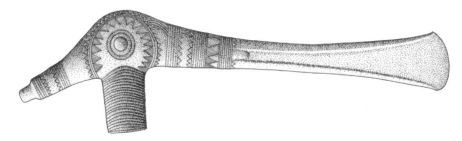

Fig. 89 Ship with central European twin axes above it from Simris (*above*). The crew-strokes are arranged in pairs. (*Below*) the central European prototype from Austria also found in Scania.

interpretation of their use. We suggest that they should be interpreted as top pieces of thrones in the form of sun-discs (Fig. 90). This interpretation is based upon two observations: the disc or seat is slightly downward curved and, most important, there remains a 3–4 cm rim that is not curved. This must reflect the inner wooden tube on which the seat was placed (see Knape and Nordström 1994: Abb. 11 and 19, Taf. I–V). We consider the depression of the central part of the disc too deep to be caused by drumming. The latter should also have left more traces of wear on the decoration in the central part of the disc. The more likely explanation is that they were used for sitting.

At least two chieftains (one in Scandinavia and the other in the Carpathian Basin) seem to have possessed bronze thrones, but the vast majority could have had wooden thrones that have now vanished. The concentric sun-ray pattern on the disc-shaped and slightly concave seating surface of the throne from Balkåkra illustrates in a symbolic way the strong bond between the

a

b

Fig. 90 (*a*) The thrones from Balkåkra and Hasfalva; (*b*) the Balkåkra throne-stool reconstructed.

chieftain and the sun – a theocratic leader supported and sanctioned by the divinities of the sun.

A close examination of the two artefacts has shown that they are so similar (except for the pattern on the disc) that the different pieces of each object were probably cast in the very same moulds (Knape and Nordström 1994). This reminds us of the importance of long-distance connections and networks in Bronze Age Europe – networks in which both artefacts and ideas could travel very far. As we shall see in the next section, they belong with a small group of foreign prestige goods from east central Europe (swords and axes) that travelled to Scandinavia during this period.

Near Eastern iconography from the second millennium BC often shows gods and rulers seated on thrones that look like chairs or stools (Oates 1986). However, on seals from the Assyrian trading colony at Kültepe, dated to *karum* Level II (*c*.1940–1840 BC Middle Chronology), we find images of rulers (divinities?) seated on low, cylindrical thrones (Teissier 1993: 604). Also, in the Minoan/Mycenaean culture we find free-standing (eventually cylindrical) throne stools, along with the campstool (Younger 1995: Plate LXIc).

We propose to consider the two bronze seats as rather unique examples from the initial period of the formation of a new royal or chiefly ideology during the seventeenth and sixteenth centuries BC. Taken together with other symbols of prestige and elite ideology from the same period, they can be seen to be part of a much more massive transfer of foreign prestige goods to Scandinavia during a period that experimented with new forms of elite expressions, including the iconography of royalty. In the next section we shall demonstrate that this transmission of foreign prestige goods was based upon a system of well-organised long-distance travels, which lasted for some generations during the seventeenth and sixteenth centuries BC.

Traders, smiths and travelling chiefs: time travels in cosmological space

It is possible to reconstruct a trade network of chiefly alliances from the Carpathians via the Oder to the Baltic and southern Scandinavia during this period (A2–3 phase, seventeenth–sixteenth centuries). It is based on the distribution of personal dress and ornaments that demonstrates the movement of people, as presented in the analysis of this period in the publication of the Bühl hoard by Rittershofer (1983).

In Figure 91 we have drawn together a group of personal ornaments which demonstrate a directional trade and exchange network between chiefly centres from the Carpathians along the Oder to the Baltic coast that was probably established in the Late Unetice (Rassman, Lutz and Pernicka

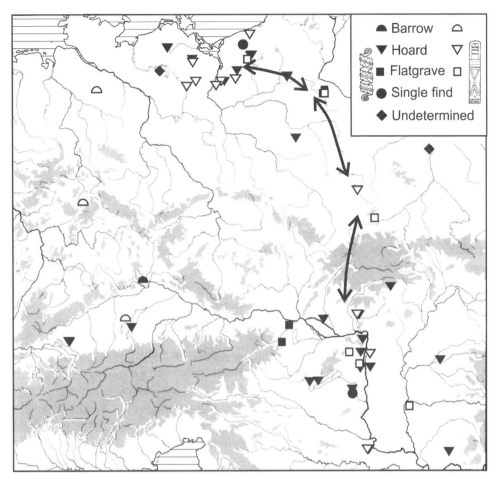

Fig. 91 The distribution of personal ornaments of Hungarian type and their spread northwards to the Baltic coast (based on Rittershofer 1983).

2001: Abb. 9). From here you can sail across the Baltic Sea to southeastern Scania where Simris and Kivik are located. In the next chapter, on warriors, we shall explain in more detail the functioning of such networks. Here it suffices to suggest that they demonstrate the movement of warrior chiefs and artisans (smiths) during the period that sees the transmission of the chiefly elite culture and its symbols (foreign swords of Hajdúsámson type, chariots, drinking cups) into southern Scandinavia along the very same route. The basis for this transmission was thus the establishment of a series of marriage alliances and trading partnerships that channelled the movement of people and goods. Some chiefs would stay in the north and become famous foreign chiefs or artisans, such as perhaps the Kivik chief; others would return with fame and amber and become local heroes at home.

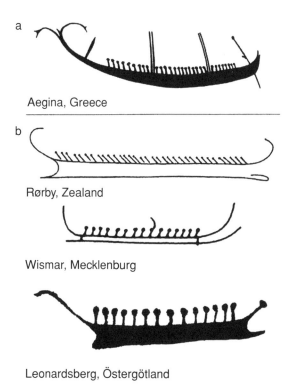

a

Aegina, Greece

b

Rørby, Zealand

Wismar, Mecklenburg

Leonardsberg, Östergötland

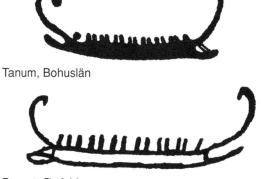

Tanum, Bohuslän

Berget, Østfold

Fig. 92 Shared traditions in picturing ships during 1700–1400 BC. (*a*) Minoan/ Aegean prototype on Late MH pottery from Aegina and (*b*) early Scandinavian ship images on metalwork and rock art.

Along the same route Scandinavian chiefly warriors would travel south and learn the new skills of metallurgy and woodworking, some of them possibly reaching Anatolia and the Aegean. A few traces of their travels are left in the archaeological record: among them the chief who died and was buried in Anderlingen not far from Berlin during Montelius 2 (fifteenth–fourteenth

Fig. 93 Founder's hoard from Djursland, Denmark, with eight identical and newly cast 'Hungarian' swords of type Apa (after Jensen 2002: 73).

centuries BC). There is also the strange rock carving of ships outside an early tholos from the Late Middle Helladic/early Late Helladic (Wachsmann 1998: Fig. 7.30–31). It represents a foreign Nordic tradition of rock carving, which suggests a Nordic chief or artisan, rather than local graffiti. Also, the famous Rørby sword and the early ship iconography in Scandinavia not only resemble the Minoan ship type, but the iconographic representation with the dotted lines is paralleled in Late Middle Helladic pottery (Fig. 92). It is impossible to understand the Rørby ship without these Mediterranean prototypes.

Since the late period 1 represents the adaptation in Scandinavia of new chiefly institutions and of new technological skills in metallurgy, house building, ship construction, etc., we have to envisage a fairly massive inflow of southern, foreign artisans and chiefs during this period. But a similar movement southwards of Scandinavian chiefs and artisans who stayed away for years to become skilled artisans and warriors was part of the operation of the network.

The existence of swords for travelling chiefs and artisans, plus Nordic finds of foreign types produced in Scandinavia, such as the newly found hoard of eight Apa swords from Djursland (Boas and Rasmussen 2001), is compelling evidence of the intensity and impact of long-distance travels (Fig. 93). If we add to this the Mycenaean and Minoan evidence so strongly manifest in the Scandinavian tradition, we are confronted with both direct and indirect evidence of a directional transmission of goods, people and knowledge. Let us illustrate this with the rise of maritime journeys and the new skills in shipbuilding.

The early Nordic Bronze Age ships are in form and construction clearly inspired by east Mediterranean ships. Ships are very complex constructions, transmitting tradition. The construction of the Nordic sea-going Bronze Age ships as depicted in rock art and an early example on the Rørby sword from the seventeenth or sixteenth century (Fig. 92) could hardly have originated in small drawings. It demanded an understanding of the craftsmanship behind the techniques of bending the wood for the high curved stems, and for the complex double construction of both keel and stem. While war chariots could be imported and then imitated, this was hardly possible with ships. It is difficult not to see the Nordic Bronze Age ship as a result of direct personal contacts, the type of contact also manifest in the unique Kivik burial. We must assume that Nordic chiefs travelled as far as the east Mediterranean, returning home with new ideas and new knowledge; or that east Mediterranean Argonauts sailed to the Baltic, which we consider less likely. Finally east Mediterranean craftsmen could have travelled north in the retinue of returning Nordic chiefs.

The distribution of east Mediterranean and Mycenaean prestige goods, such as rapiers and goldwork (Fig. 94), may give a clue, as they are seen to connect with the Carpathian–Baltic network. The spread of the Minoan/Mycenaean rapier and its imitation in east central Europe, together with other evidence described above, suggests that this region was a commercial meeting point between Minoan/Mycenaean traders and their counterparts from east central Europe (to be discussed in chapter 5.4). Here we may once again recall the finds in Bulgaria of Linear A script, as a further testimony of a Minoan influence and probable presence at the Black Sea coast, with Troy as a partner (Guzowska 2002). As we have already demonstrated (in chapter 4.3), chiefly specialists from the northern lands, the steppe and the Carpathians most probably went along in the ships to the palaces to teach their skills in horsemanship. They brought with them amber, gold and tin, which they traded for new weapons and ornaments. Some of these traders could even have come the long way from Scandinavia. The central and north European travelling chiefs and artisans entered the Mediterranean world according to the principles of gift exchange and the power of foreign skills and products. Here was an arena of shared tradition, and when to this was added the commercial interest of the east Mediterranean, the two traditions started to interact on a direct personal basis.

It was these first generations of travelling chiefs from the North who instituted new crafts and new rituals upon their return. They created the

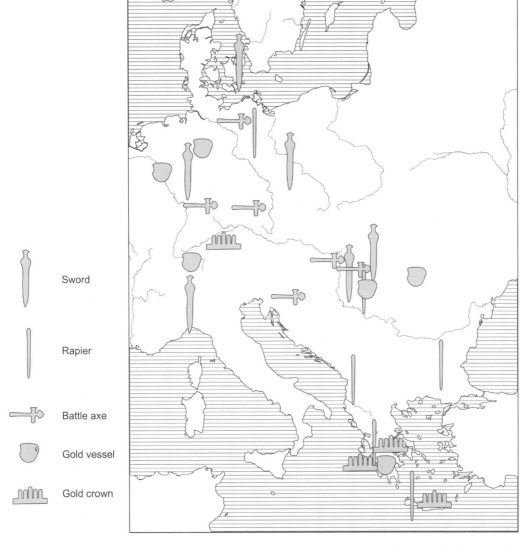

Fig. 94 The distribution of Aegean rapiers and gold crowns, central European battle axes and early solid-hilted swords, and Mycenaean/central European gold cups (after Mihovilic *et al.* 2002).

first group of mythological sagas about distant and powerful origins, and in due time they themselves became local heroes, worshipped in oral tradition as well as in rituals at their famous burials, or at the panels of rock carvings describing their journeys. In this way their travels in geographical space would be transformed into time travels in cosmological space (Fig. 95).

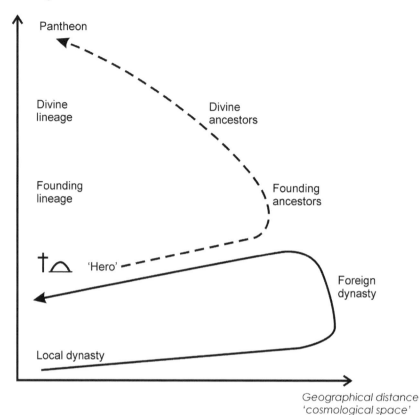

Fig. 95 Lifetime cycle of travelling chief, converting travel in cosmological space to travel in cosmological time upon his return, death and heroic burial.

Historical summary

We have demonstrated that there existed well-organised trading networks that connected southern Scandinavia with the Carpathian tell cultures during the eighteenth to sixteenth centuries BC, and from here there were similar networks to the Circum-Pontic Zone, Anatolia and the Aegean. We have further, in a series of case studies, argued that within these networks chiefs, skilled artisans, warriors and traders travelled frequently and transmitted the new cosmologies and the new skills of the rising state societies of Anatolia and the Aegean. These travels were part of a new form of long-distance trade where high-value products from the northern periphery, such as amber and horses, were exchanged for high-quality prestige goods, such as weapons and chariots. We have also suggested that the northern periphery could have taken a more active part in the historical changes in Anatolia and the east Mediterranean during this period as mercenaries or even

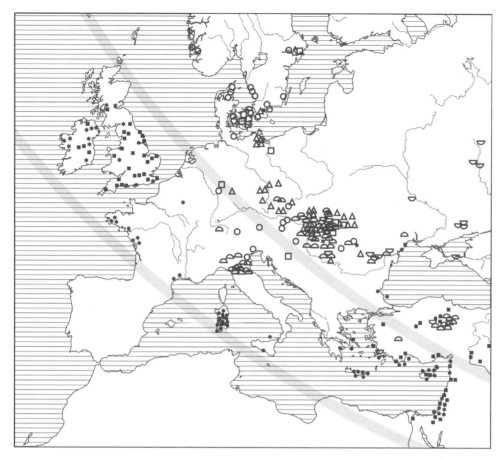

✳	Golden twisted earrings	▽	Disc cheek-pieces
•	Oxhide ingots	○	Bronze axes with curved blade
■	Arreton blades and related pieces	△	Schafthole axes of type Krtenov
⌂	Tine cheek-pieces	□	Apa swords

Fig. 96 Summary map of the two dominant interaction zones of the earlier second millennium BC: the steppe corridor and the Mediterranean corridor.

as conquest chiefs. The impact of these historical processes on social and religious institutions in central and northern Europe turned out to be profound, as we shall demonstrate in chapter 6. Here the still sceptical reader will be presented with additional evidence that supports the historical interpretation we have laid out so far. Before doing so, however, we will continue our interpretative journey in time to include the fifteenth and fourteenth centuries BC.

For reasons that are still unknown, these northeastern networks were interrupted around 1500 BC. A series of historical events that had large-scale effects happened at the same time: the tell cultures collapsed, at least in the western part of Hungary and Slovakia. To the east, in the Circum-Pontic region the more settled Noua-Sabatinovka Culture expanded to the west and eventually cut off some of the former trading networks (Sava 1998). From the west the warlike Tumulus Culture expanded eastwards, and in the process the tell cultures were transformed.

The Mycenaean takeover of the Minoan trading empire probably also had far-reaching effects, and during the next 100–200 years or so they developed their colonies and trading networks in the western Mediterranean. This led to a new period of intense interaction with the central and north European Bronze Age societies via the Tumulus Culture in southern Germany and France after 1500 BC. The Mycenaean expansion and partial colonisation in the western Mediterranean (southern Italy, the Adriatic coast) was based upon earlier explorations and trade networks between the Levant and the Wessex Culture in search of tin and gold, which we have described only briefly in chapter 4. We can summarise two interaction zones during the early and mid-second millennium BC: one that we may call the western steppe corridor, and another we may call the Mediterranean corridor (Fig. 96). They alternated in importance through time. During the early to mid-second millennium BC, summarised on Figure 96, they were both at work, but the western links to France and Wessex had declined when the steppe corridor gained importance, as described in chapter 5.2. This trend was now reversed.

5.4   The Mycenaean connection: the expansion of warrior aristocracies (fifteenth–fourteenth centuries BC)

In the following we shall demonstrate the continued transmission and transformation of social and religious institutions from the sixteenth–fifteenth centuries BC onwards: warrior aristocracies and the rituals and iconography of ruling elites. This followed in successive stages as described in chapter 4.1. While the first stage was dominated by the Minoans and Hittites, and thus represented a one-way influence from the palace cultures of the east Mediterranean to the central European Carpathian tell cultures, the second stage marks a heavier transmission of the social and ritual institutions of warrior aristocracies. It reflects increasing interaction between Mycenaean culture and central and northern Europe characterised by increased borrowing on both sides, e.g. flange-hilted swords. What is now transmitted is the whole set-up of ruling elites: encircled tumulus burials, from Greece to northern Europe, recurring international weapon combinations, ruling symbols such as folding stools, drinking sets and body culture – razor and tweezers – throughout the whole region. We further witness a homogenisation of warrior cultures and institutions in large regions of Europe, never seen before, while at the same time we witness the formation of new regional cultural identities – the Tumulus Culture and Nordic culture – being part of the process. It represents a historical regularity in the interaction between centres and peripheries, paralleled in later prehistory by the formation of Celtic and Germanic identities in material culture.

The archaeological evidence of warrior aristocracies: diffusion, acculturation and context

In temperate Europe the archaeological evidence of warrior aristocracies is consistent over 3000 years from 2000 BC to 1000 AD.[11] Shortly after 2000 BC there appear in the Wessex Culture in southern England and in the Unetice Culture in central Germany rich chiefly burials under barrows. They were furnished with new personal status items, such as dagger/short sword and axe, along with complex gold-decorated ornaments, buttons and other insignia of ruling elites such as sceptres and golden drinking cups (Gerloff 1975; Schauer 1984b; Clarke, Cowie and Foxon 1985). This reflects the first merging of Near Eastern and traditional European ruling symbols (corresponds to Br. A1b and the MH I/II period). From the late eighteenth/ seventeenth centuries BC two interlinked phenomena spread across Europe: a new weapon complex that employed long sword, lance and chariot, and accompanying it, a new social organisation of warrior aristocracies. It represented new military tactics, originating in the empires and palace cultures of the Near East and eastern Mediterranean, based upon the employment of chariots to supplement infantry. The new weapons meant heavy man-to-man fighting, and demanded new military skills and the employment of protective armour. This put new demands on the training of warriors and subsequently on their social and economic support. The professional warrior, well trained and organised, was introduced.

We can distinguish two phases in the spread of the new weapon complex: an early phase corresponding to Br. A2/A3 mainly belongs to the eighteenth and seventeenth centuries BC (the early shaft grave period, Late MH and Early LH). A later phase, corresponding to Br. B1–B2/C1, mainly belongs in the sixteenth–early fifteenth centuries BC and the later phase of the Mycenaean shaft graves and the tholos burials. The early phase is characterised by

---

11 In her most recent work Helle Vandkilde discusses the formation of warrior culture in Europe, beginning with the Corded Ware and Bell Beaker periods. She proposes that warriorhood during this period formed an important cultural and social identity for males. As warrior culture, male clubs and herding economies are often interlinked, this makes sense, and it would explain the readiness to adapt and further develop this institution after 2000 BC (Vandkilde in press). In addition it underscored a development of gender differentiation (Sofaer-Derevenski 2000) and of autonomous family groups linked by extensive patrilineal kinship systems that were well suited to the expansion of the metal trade (to be discussed below).

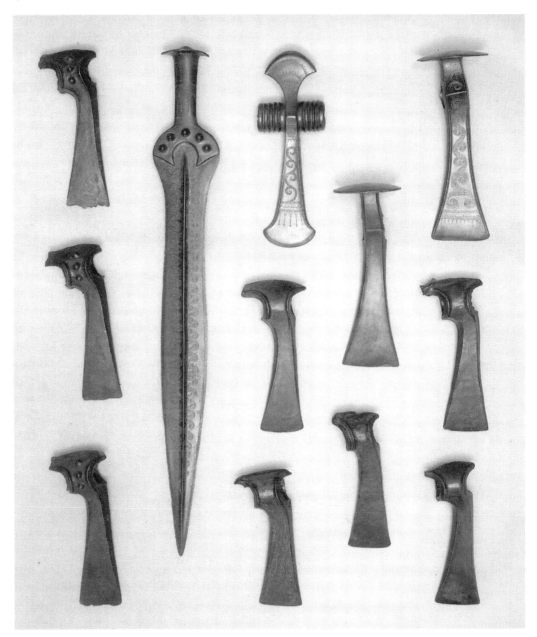

Fig. 97 The
Hajdúsámson
hoard (after Bona
1992: Abb. 22).

the first appearance of richly decorated locally produced solid-hilted swords, axes and lances in the Carpathians (Apa, Zajta horizon), early dirks and rapiers in Britain (Burgess and Gerloff 1981), and early Minoan/Mycenaean swords/daggers (Kilian-Dirlmeier 1993; compare David 2002: Taf. 247 with Mylonas 1972: Plates 55a, 122a; also Dietz 1992: Fig. 80). In the Carpathians

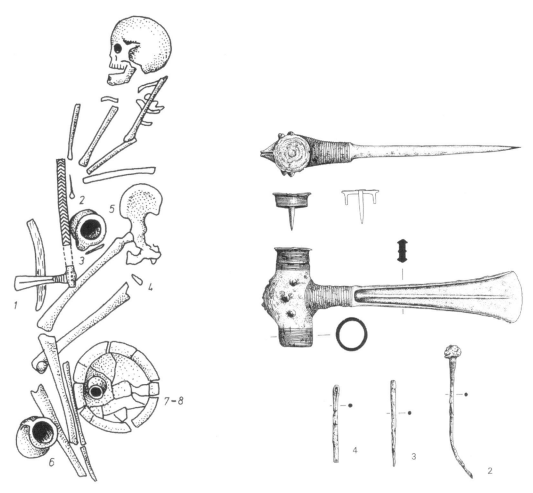

Fig. 98 Rare warrior burial in the Carpathian region (after Kovács 1995: Abb. 1–2).

the swords are mainly found in hoards accompanied by axes. Thus the Hajdúsámson hoard with its beautifully decorated sword and eleven axes could well represent a warrior chief and his retinue, sacrificing after a fight (Fig. 97). But in the later phase we find groups of warrior burials with daggers in the Carpathians (Kovács 1996b).

It should be noted that the Minoan type A swords (and related forms) are mainly found along the coastal areas of the Black Sea and the Balkans (Wanzek 1991; Kilian-Dirlmeier 1993: Taf. 60), suggesting points of entry, probably linked to Minoan/Mycenaean trading stations (Figure 99a).

The second phase (Br. B1/LH IIA) is characterised by the more extensive appearance of long swords/rapiers of so-called Mycenaean (but Minoan) origin or influence, some of which were undoubtedly made locally (Wanzek 1991). They were quickly developing into local forms, such as the central European rapiers of Sauerbrunn type (Schauer 1971: Taf. 2; Carancini 1997:

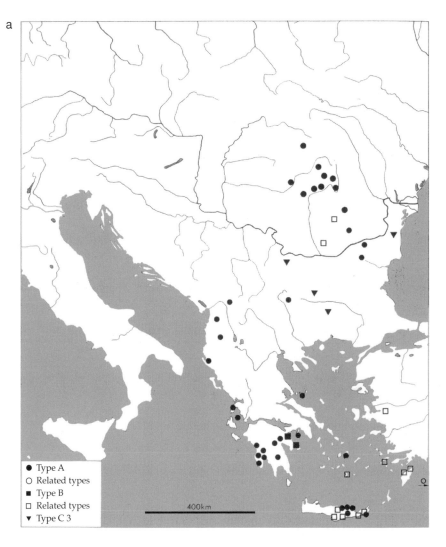

Fig. 99 (a) Distribution map of Mycenaean swords (after Bader, 1991: Taf. 62), and (b) flange-hilted swords and lances testifying to connections between the east Mediterranean, central Europe and northern Europe. The small inserted map shows the distribution of campstools and arrowheads of flint or bronze based upon Mycenaean/ Egyptian prototypes (after Schauer 1985: Abb. 25).

- ● Type A
- ○ Related types
- ■ Type B
- □ Related types
- ▼ Type C 3

400km

Fig. 223). During this phase early forms of the flange-hilted sword emerged and spread rapidly to large parts of Europe in Br. B2/C (fifteenth–fourteenth centuries BC) (Fig. 99b).

They show their origin in Crete and the early Mycenaean culture of the shaft graves, and from here the new weapon types spread through eastern Europe and the tell cultures to northern Europe and northern Italy (Terramare Culture).[12]

12 In the early Terramare burials we find warriors with rapiers, some of which are exact parallels to swords from Hungary (compare Marinis and Salzani 1997: Figs. 408 and 413 with National Museum Budapest 3.1934, Csazotaltes; also Kemenczei 1988: Taf. 11, 12 and 13).

b

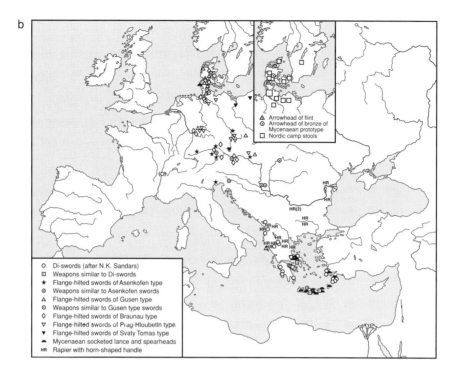

Fig. 99 (cont.)

We consider it most likely that the fully developed institution of warrior
aristocracies with retinues is reflected in the diffusion of the rapier and the
chariot mainly during the seventeenth–sixteenth centuries. An early form
of warrior aristocracy developed during the social transformations that took
place in the nineteenth–eighteenth centuries in the Carpathians and western Europe (Hajdúsámson and Wessex phase). It reflects a development from
institutional acculturation and transformation followed by consolidation. A
similar development characterised the Circum-Pontic regions, as recently
summarised by Lichardus and Vladar (1996).[13]

13 We are aware of the many unresolved chronological problems linked to this interpretation.
Earlier research tended to place Hajdúsámson in Br. A2, and Zajta later (Hänsel 1968: Beil.
2). More recent work has tended to place the Apa/Hajdúsámson horizon in Br. A3/early B1,
that is, a transition phase in the later seventeenth century BC (Vandkilde 1996: 143). However,
several of the Hajdúsámson axes are closely related to the axes in the Melz hoard, with a
calibrated C14 dating just after 2000 BC (Rassmann 1996). This corresponds with our previous
proposal for an earlier origin of the wavy band decoration in the Old Palace period (Fig. 78),
and it has most recently been supported by a new analysis of Middle Bronze Age swords
(Vogt 2004). Hajdúsámson thus rather belongs in late Br. A1 or A2, whereas Zajta is safely
anchored in A3/B1, possibly with some overlap in late A2. We notice that the decoration on
the Zajta sword (a hatched/unhatched vertical band of triangles, Hachmann 1957: Taf. 65,
no. 1) is identical to the decoration on the Bagterp lance in Denmark (Vandkilde 1996: Fig.
97F). This hoard is dated to Br. A3/B1 early (with types from both Br. A2 and Br. B1). The

In temperate Europe the new weapons were linked to the rise and expansion of a new aristocratic warrior elite, above the traditional tribal warrior who had employed bow/arrow and dagger/war axe since the third millennium BC or even earlier (Kristiansen 1987). In the archaeological record the new warrior aristocracies set themselves apart by being buried in richly furnished graves, often in a barrow with sets of weapons, which could also be deposited in hoards. From the sixteenth–fifteenth centuries BC the new warrior chiefs became a common phenomenon at both local and regional levels in temperate Europe. Warfare took on a new significance (Monk and Osgood 1998; Osgood, Monk and Toms 2000). Social and military differentiation became recognisable in different combinations of weapons in grave goods, and in different uses of weapons (Coombs 1975; Kristiansen 1984a and 1987; Schauer 1984a and 1990). A study of the use and resharpening of Danish and Hungarian sword blades for example demonstrated (points 1 and 2 below, Kristiansen 1984 and 2002b) the following.

1 Sword blades showed clear and recurring traces of resharpening and repair as a result of actual use. The pattern of resharpening could be linked to both attack and defence (Fig. 100), and edge damage in the form of notching was often visible. Similar evidence is testified on Irish Late Bronze Age swords (Bridgford 1997: 103ff.).

2 There occurred a distinctive difference in the degree of use between solid-hilted, richly ornamented swords and flange-hilted, highly functional swords. The latter always showed heavy traces of use in combat, the former only minor traces of use. This reflected a difference between chiefs and warriors that could be sustained also in grave goods. However, warriors belonged to the chiefly line as they received the same kind of chiefly burial in mounds. It may also therefore reflect a dual leadership between ritual/political leaders and war leaders.

3 A similar study of spears and lances by Schauer (1979) demonstrated the use of lances in combat. In burials they were often found pairwise, and belonged to a consistent complement of warrior equipment, as in Greece (Höckmann 1980: Abb. 74). However, lances/spears have been more often found in hoards, and seem to have been the basic weapons of the infantry,

very same decoration is found on a Carpathian axe in a hoard from Ighiel (Andritoiu 1992: Plate 69) that also contained a spiral armring of the type found in the Zajta hoard. Here we have a historical horizon linked by a specific decorative trait. Also the sword in the Trassem hoard from Br. A2, with Langquaid type axes, belongs in the Zajta sword tradition as an early prototype (Schauer 1984a: Abb. 30), and the gold pin with spirals resembles the gold spirals in B-circle shaft grave O (Mylonas 1972: Plate 179). The so-called Krtenov axe in the Apa hoard (Hachmann 1957: Taf. 63, no. 5) and a parallel piece in the Szeghalom hoard (Bona 1992: Abb. 26) are local variants of the late Unetice type, and must be parallel in time (Neugebauer 1994: Abb. 52, nos. 18–20). On the dating of the shaft graves we follow Dietz (1992), but here we are in need of C14 datings rather than debate.

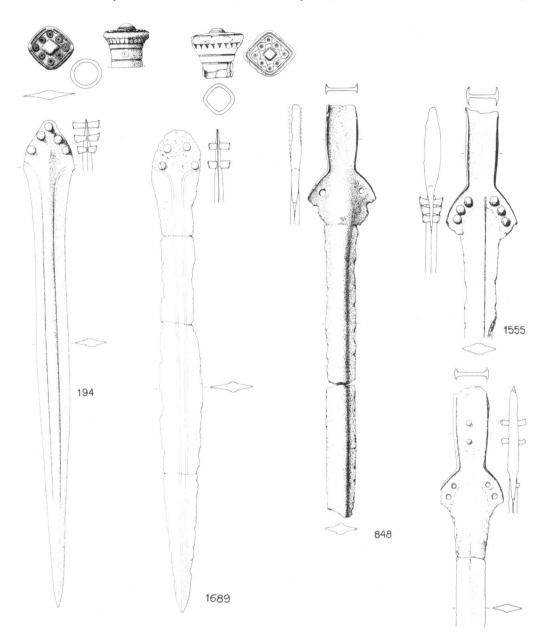

Fig. 100 Resharpened sword blades from Nordic swords and flange-hilted swords
(after Kristiansen 1983: Figs. 3 and 4).

from Greece to northern Europe. This is demonstrated both in pictorial scenes of warriors, and in the deposition of lances in single graves and in hoards (Höckmann 1980: 276ff.). The evidence suggests that the numerical relationship between spearmen/infantry and chiefly warriors/swordsmen was about 10:1 in central and northern Europe.

4 Defensive armour was already in use from the early second millennium BC, but was normally made of organic material: leather, wood and bone, as reflected in a few burials with good preservation (Makkay 1982; Schauer 1990). From the thirteenth century onwards protective armour of hammered bronze came into use, mostly for military display and status emblems of chiefly war leaders. Leather shields remained the norm (Osgood 1998: ch. III).

5 Chariots are recurrently displayed in rock art in Scandinavia (Larsson 2004), sometimes with detailed construction details (Fig. 101). Bronze wheels for models are also known, displaying great care in the detail (Kristiansen 1987: note 6; Rausing 1991), all of which points to the existence of real prototypes,[14] as in the Pontic steppe region (Piggott 1983: 91ff.).

From the late second millennium elegant full-size spoked wheels demonstrate the use of chariots in central Europe. In a recent article Stefan Winghart (1993) has convincingly demonstrated how specific constructive details like thickened spoke ends and 'double felloe' (the bronze rim frame and the added wooden felloe look like a double rim, basically on the same principle as a modern bike wheel) link the Carpathian wheels from Arcalia, Romania (Fig. 102) and Obisovce, Slovakia to Minoan and east Mediterranean types, as depicted for example on the chariots of the Hagia Triada sarcophagus. They are thus safely anchored in a (later) Middle Bronze Age context (certainly pre-Urnfield), and represent Minoan/Mycenaean influence (also Pare 1992: Figs. 23–24). As they were deposited in pairs they quite definitely represent chariots, but find circumstances are otherwise absent. The big model bronze wheel from a burial in Tobøl, Jutland, from early Montelius 2, beginning of

---

14 Willroth has surveyed rich Nordic chiefly male burials from the transition period Montelius 1/2 (c.1550/1500 BC) containing a bronze handle with a spike at the end (Willroth 1997: Abb. 7). With reference to Early Iron Age so-called *Treibstacheln* (driving stick), he interprets them as hafted on a long wooden shaft (wood is preserved in the bronze handle) to control the horses of chariots, and/or cattle (a symbolic herding staff). This is an original and important observation to explain a hitherto unexplained tool. We suggest, however, that they could also have served as handles for whips, the leather being hafted to the spike and the leather cord being wound around the midribs of the bronze handle to secure the hafting. This would explain the function of the otherwise strange midrib or midribs of the bronze handles (that were slightly enlarged with a supplementary wooden handle). They resemble the bone versions on Figure 78. Whichever interpretation is correct, the function remains basically the same, and supports the proposition that chariotry was practised in central and northern Europe from the earlier to mid-second millennium BC.

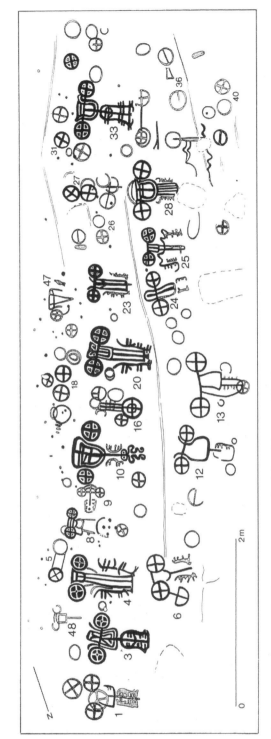

Fig. 101 The chariot group lined up at Fränarp, Sweden (after Coles 2002: Fig. 8).

Fig. 102 Photo taken at the Hungarian National Museum, Budapest of two Middle Bronze Age bronze chariot wheels from Arcalia, Romania.

the fifteenth century BC, shows decorative details that could represent the double metal/wooden felloe construction, and the joining of spoke ends and felloe is also shown (Thrane 1990: Fig. 3a–b). In Richard Beal's *The Organization of the Hittite Military* (1992), we notice that the charioteers are carefully described in the textual documents and their special clothing is also

Fig. 103 Three chariots and charioteers as rock art: rock carving at Bohuslän, Sweden.

mentioned. The Hittite charioteers wore 'a short-sleeved coat of scale armour reaching from neck to ankles' (Beal 1995: 548).

If we take a look at the Scandinavian depictions of chariots, in the form of rock art, most of the images only feature the chariot and the horses (Larsson 2004); in a few rare cases we have the charioteer portrayed (e.g. in Kivik, Fig. 80). On one site in Bohuslän, Sweden, there is a very special scene showing three chariots and their personnel (Fig. 103).

As can be seen in this illustration, we have a depiction of three chariot equipages, with two persons (driver and warrior) connected to each chariot, which exactly mirrors the crew on real-life chariots in the Hittite or Egyptian army (Littauer and Crouwel 1979; Bryce 1998). Moreover, the figures in this rock art scene are obviously dressed in a very special way – wearing long robes with a belt round the waist – making them very different from ordinary rock art representations of humans/anthropomorphic figures. This lends them special significance.

The pattern of chiefly war leaders with a retinue of lance warriors and a smaller group of chiefly warriors is seen to be consistent over wide areas from the sixteenth century onwards. Functional changes in the nature of combat and the preference in weapons occur through time and were quickly adopted from the Mediterranean to northern Europe, such as the introduction of the efficient flange-hilted warrior sword from around 1500 BC. During the early second millennium BC the lance and the short sword/dagger were dominant, to be replaced by the long sword from the seventeenth century BC. A shift from rapier/axe combinations to slashing swords/knives took place from the late fourteenth century BC, while after 1000 BC lances again gained dominance as the standard weapon of the hoplite, and also in central and northern Europe.

Numbers in battle are difficult to estimate, but they probably varied from small raiding parties, reflected in small weapon hoards, to armies numbering in the hundreds attacking the fortified settlements, as suggested by both Randsborg (1995: 44ff.) and Kristiansen (1998a).[15] In his study Randsborg suggested that Bronze Age hoards with weapons may represent ritual depositions from battle. This hypothesis can be further substantiated by the observation that the swords in weapon hoards show traces of battle and thus had not been resharpened, as is often the case in burials (Kristiansen 1984). A similar observation has been made in later studies of central European Bronze Age swords by one of us (Kristiansen 2002b). Randsborg's method of using a few distinctive weapon hoards to reconstruct war parties thus seems partly justified (selection also occurred, so hoards are not representative in a strict sense of what constitutes war equipment). It suggests variations in the scale of Bronze Age warfare from small chiefly combats to a larger military phalanx of fifty (ten commanders and forty commoners). To this we should probably add a larger group of warriors armed with slings and bows and arrows, the evidence of which can only rarely be documented archaeologically (but see Cunliffe 1986: 80; Keeley 1996: Fig. 1.1).

---

15 Robert Drews has in a recent book suggested that the military organisation of the central European Late Bronze Age infantry in combination with new heavy slashing swords was superior to east Mediterranean armies employing chariots and smaller armies of footsoldiers. The 'barbarian' armies were therefore able to overrun the more traditional organisation of the east Mediterranean armies during the turbulent thirteenth–twelfth centuries BC, changing both the balance of power and military organisation (Drews 1993). While this view has rightly been criticised for underestimating the role of infantry prior to the thirteenth century BC (Dickinson 1999), it still has the merit of making an attempt to explain the change from chariots to infantry based on military considerations. We suggest that the development of the flange-hilted sword from around 1500 BC already represented a decisive improvement in fighting technique. It could have given the Mycenaeans a military advantage in their colonial and political expansion from this time onwards.

Thus, the archaeological evidence speaks conclusively about the impact of warfare in Bronze and Early Iron Age Europe. This development was linked to the rise of so-called warrior aristocracies – a chiefly organisation of warfare whose social and cultural context we shall consider next.

The social and cultural context of warrior aristocracies: transmission, transformation and institutionalisation

The appearance of warrior aristocracies represents the formation of a new chiefly elite culture in Europe (Kristiansen 1987; Treherne 1995). It was embedded in new rituals, in new ideas of social behaviour and lifestyle (body care, clothing, etc.) and in a new architecture of housing and landscape (Kristiansen 1998a). It centred round values and rituals of heroic warfare, power and honour, and it was surrounded by a set of new ceremonies and practices. They included ritualised drinking,[16] the employment of trumpets or lurs in warfare and ritual, special dress, special stools and sometimes chariots. This meant that chiefs were both ritual leaders and leaders of war.

Thus, the new chiefly elite culture spread as a cultural package, a new social value system, rather than as separate elements. However, we can distinguish two phases – an earlier one linked to the Minoan trade with east central Europe just described, and a slightly later phase, linked to the more active involvement of the Mycenaeans, and linked to the formation of the Tumulus Culture and Nordic culture. In this latter phase all the constituting elements described below were present. We may characterise it as a new social institution of chiefly leadership. It therefore became a penetrating phenomenon, crossing cultural boundaries throughout Europe. Although it was adapted to local or regional cultural traditions, its main components are easily recognisable from the Mediterranean to northern Europe. And since appearance was an important factor, it has left rather good archaeological traces, as demonstrated above. We shall now proceed one step further, and propose to characterise the social and cultural institution of warrior aristocracies. It comprises the following interlinked elements.

1 New body culture and dress codes. Appearance and body care gain new significance, reflected in the universal employment of razor and tweezers, and in needles for tattooing (Treherne 1995; Willroth 1997: Abb. 6). Men

---

16 In a most interesting book *Lady with a Mead Cup*, Michael Enright (1996) has demonstrated continuity in the drinking rituals and social reproduction of chiefly retinues from La Tène to the Vikings, based upon literary evidence but also supported by archaeology. His findings, however, are echoed in the material culture of the preceding millennium. From the Early Bronze Age of Scandinavia we find cups with traces of mead in both male and female burials (among them the famous Egtved woman wearing a corded skirt employed in rituals, as demonstrated in female figurines, just as one figurine holds a cup). Drinking sets for several persons in bronze and gold are likewise associated with both male and female depositions during the Late Bronze Age (Kristiansen 1984: Figs. 10 and 11).

Fig. 104
Monumental
Bronze Age
barrows from
northern Jutland
(after Jensen
2002: 150).

were wearing elaborate hats and capes; women were wearing complex hair styles and elaborate ornaments which sometimes constricted their physical movements (Sørensen 1997). The chiefs were sitting on stools and drinking mead from costly metal vessels and amphorae – or more often, from imitations made of wood, but sometimes decorated with tin nails to signal status.

2 A new architecture is introduced in the form of large chiefly halls/farms that could hold the chiefly lineage and attendants, and sometimes also the cattle. In western and northern Europe the landscape is reorganised, with chiefly barrows placed on all hilltops (the holy mountain), surrounded by grazing cattle/sheep (Kristiansen 1998c) (Fig. 104). In central Europe fortified chiefly residences and villages, sometimes with an acropolis, emerge (Jockenhövel 1990). Specialist metalworkers were attached to the new residences.

3 New warrior lifestyle. The new forms of combat demanded regular training, as well as specialists to produce weapons and chariots. Thus a new warrior lifestyle became an integrated part of traditional life at every local chiefly farm. In opposition to a state society with a professional army separated from daily life, daily life was dominated by warrior values in addition to harvesting the fields and raising the cattle. Warrior ideology and lifestyle were ingredients in everyday life, and the meaning of life to

most young chiefly sons. Since every parish had its local chief, sometimes several, the influence of the chiefly warrior culture was penetrating social life.

4 New social organisation of warfare. This was reflected in the new system of clients/retinues, which was the basis for mobilising war parties for raids, trading expeditions, etc. But it was also the economic basis for the chiefs, since clientship allowed the collection of surplus to finance feasts, boats for trading expeditions, rituals and warfare. While the chiefly barrows and feasts reinforced chiefly power and generosity, the professionally trained warriors were the means to extract tribute from unwilling clients, and to enlarge tribute through raids when needed.[17]

Appearance, body culture and ethos: materialisation, message and meaning

In a recent paper Marie Louise Stig Sørensen has highlighted the role of appearance in female dress and costume (Sørensen 1997b). She points to the many overlapping categorisations that may be read from dress, depending upon social and temporal contexts (lifecycles; social identities within groups and of social groups). She proposes to take this complexity of messages and readings into account, as we shall attempt to do in the following sections.

It is remarkable to what extent the constituting elements of Bronze Age warriors, their appearance, follow similar trends from the Mediterranean to western and northern Europe. This is in some opposition to the female costume, that exhibits many local and regional characteristics, to which we return later. However, it is only in Denmark that we have preserved the full costume of the Bronze Age chief and warrior of the fourteenth century BC. It consisted of a woollen cloak, tunic and cap, supplemented with sword, axe or knife, and razor and tweezers for body care. This is the classical costume of a chiefly warrior or leader, as we recognise it in the *Iliad* and the *Odyssey*, where it is always mentioned in its role as the dress of free men/warriors (we take here costume in the sense of social identification, as proposed by Sørensen 1997b). Thus, upon arrival at the Phaeacians, where he is stranded naked, Odysseus is given a cloak and a tunic in recognition of his noble status. Later, after he has been introduced to King Alcinos, the king gives him a sword as a prestigious gift and proclaims: 'I will give him this sword which has a silver hilt and a sheet of newly carved ivory to hold it – they will be very valuable possessions' (*Odyssey* Book 8, 400–5). Now his social restitution is completed.

17 Cattle raids play a central role in Bronze Age and Indo-European myths. Motives span from warring over the most renowned bull in Ireland in the *Tain* to the divine deeds of Herakles and other gods to get the cattle herd of the Cyclops and other monster figures (Burkert 1979).

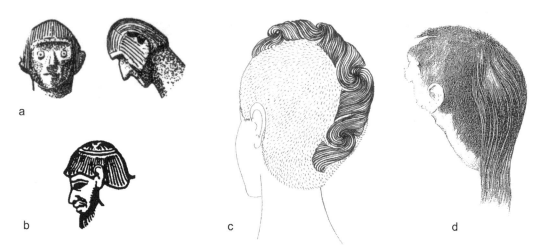

Fig. 105 Nordic, Mycenaean and Hittite male hairstyles: (*a*) two views of the handle to an Early Bronze Age razor from Denmark, (*b*) Egyptian wall painting of a Hittite, (*c*) a Mycenaean young male with partly shaved hair and (*d*) a Nordic man with partly shaved hair from a Danish oak coffin burial.

Noble warriors not only took great pride in their appearance; body culture was also a main concern (Fig. 105). Razor and tweezers symbolise that, from the Mediterranean to Scandinavia. Thus in the well-preserved oak coffin burials the hair cuts could vary from short cut with a longer tail at the back of the head (Lille Dragshøj) to uncut and curling (the young man in Borum Eshøj) (Jensen 1998: 57 and 94).

Again, in Minoan and Mycenaean frescos and other representations (seals, cups) we see similar variations. Obviously they must have had great significance, as with shaving also. Here the new warrior elites distinguished themselves by putting great daily care into their bodily appearance: by cultivating and controlling hair growth, they made it an item of display and dress (Treherne 1995 and Shanks 1999 for an extended discussion). This cultivation of the warrior ego was part of the formation of an individualised warrior ethos, grounded in social and military routines on a day to day basis, creating respect and self-respect. But heroic deeds were needed in order to be remembered, whether long journeys, successful raids or glorious combats. And heroic death was the ultimate conclusion of life. This is the most penetrating aspect of the warrior ethos of the Bronze and Iron Ages, transmitted from millennia-old oral traditions to written form, and thus surviving to this day, but also preserved in thousands of heroic burials under tumuli. Each would be known by his own heroic biography, and it was from the sum of such individual tales that were crystallised those few that became the preferred models for the warrior ethos, and that were therefore preserved and later written down. Although there are differences in social organisation and time between the Homeric tales and the Nordic and Irish myths and sagas, they share the same basic warrior ethos, and display the same aristocratic warrior culture.[18] In this they correspond to the archaeological evidence.

Games and acrobatics represented another important bodily activity in the realm of the new warrior aristocracies (Fuglestvedt 1999). They combined sports, rituals and combat technique. In Scandinavian Bronze Age rock art and bronze figurines and in Minoan and Egyptian frescos and paintings a recurring feature is the ritualised games and acrobatics. Women and men in back-bending acrobatics, young males contesting bulls in Minoan and Mycenaean frescos, men standing on horseback, or on a bull's back in Scandinavia, twin warriors leaping backwards over ships, people swinging on ropes round a high pole, dancers, runners or leapers, chariot races (Fig. 106). In all this we see integration between rituals and games, young warriors or chiefs performing contests and games according to a ritualised set of rules, perhaps to demonstrate their abilities as chiefs and young gods. Warfare as sports and sports as warfare. However, in the Iron Age these two became separated – sports were defined as an independent activity, a social institution (the Olympic Games starting 772 BC), and so was warfare. Thus the ritualised games more or less disappeared. Therefore they remain a defining characteristic of the Bronze Age. In the Irish mythology so-called feats and leaps are a basic part of both war training and games, and they are demonstrated one by one in the famous combats.

In this feature several of the Irish myths reveal their Late Bronze Age/Early Iron Age origin, whereas the Nordic mythology differs from the Irish in this

18 We consider the Homeric poems to have maintained essential aspects of their Mycenaean Bronze Age origin, this being part of their legitimacy. Opinions as to their dominant representation have ranged from Bronze Age over sub-Mycenaean to the now-prevailing Archaic period (Morris 1986, 1997). We consider the discussion about their dating obsolete. On archaeological grounds their origin is safely anchored in Mycenaean times, possibly even the shaft grave period. Over time additions and slight changes were made to make them comprehensible to contemporary audiences. They are thus the result of an acculturated heroic heritage maintained by bards at the royal courts in exile. From this heroic heritage Homer put together his two great poems. Susan Sherratt's archaeological stratigraphy of the poems clearly demonstrates acculturation (Sherratt 1990). However, the language suggests a Mycenaean age (Bennet 1997), preserved in one of the Mycenaean refuges after the collapse. The preservation of an ancient language suggests that its form fossilised at an early stage, and was preserved as cultural heritage. We further wish to accentuate the very strong conservatism of oral tradition, and its reproduction as a profession at the royal courts. It is unlikely that the numerous and structurally related descriptions of Bronze Age material culture, warfare and architecture, which basically conform to our archaeological knowledge, could have been constructed in the Archaic period. Also, those traits often considered to be late, and in opposition to a Mycenaean palace organisation, such as the swineherd or the rather simple farms described in the *Odyssey*, miss an important point. The Linear B tablets describe the world of the palace in bureaucratic terms from the centre; the *Odyssey* describes the world seen from below through an individual. Quite clearly the swineherd is an official with slaves (a Sicilian woman) and with subordinates. And the garden farm of Odysseus is just one among many estates in the family, a holiday resort. Thus when taking the perspective of the story into account there is nothing that contradicts Mycenaean conditions, either in this or in many other things thought to be Archaic in the prevailing interpretations.

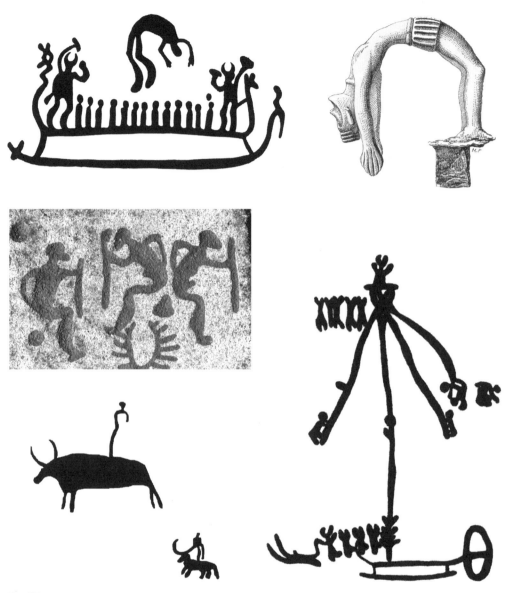

Fig. 106
Acrobats, dancers, bull-jumpers, and rope swingers. Rock art images of feats and a bronze figurine from the south Scandinavian Bronze Age.

respect, and reveals its later Iron Age context. We are not including here the many tricks and contests between giants and Asar; these are of a different nature, and may indeed have an old origin.

The gods are referred to as young in the Bronze Age texts and appear young on frescos. Therefore we see them taking part in all these acrobatics, sports and war games. And the chiefs had to prove themselves worthy to represent the gods by carrying out these feats annually at the great ritual festivals of the year, and perhaps also before and after trading and war expeditions. Thus, one of the Irish heroes dies when he fails his annual leap over a ravine. The various feats that the Irish hero Cuchulainn is taught by the woman Scathach in Alba are listed. They include the apple feat, the thunder feat, and the feat of the sword edge and the sloping shield, the feat of the javelin and the rope, the heroic salmon feat, the pole-throw, and the leap over a poisoned stake. Also the noble chariot-fighter's crouch, the spurt of speed, the feat of the chariot wheel thrown up high and several others. Most remain obscure, but leaps and runs can easily be identified: the salmon leaps appear to be acrobatic jumps from other examples, just as the pole-throw may be linked to a motif from Scandinavian rock art of people hanging or throwing themselves round a pole on ropes (Fig. 106).

The warrior aristocracies from the Aegean to Scandinavia thus shared the same basic appearance and body culture, reflected in the employment of similar dress, weapon types and combinations, similar instruments for body care – razors and tweezers – and similar rituals in burial. This demonstrates the incredible acculturating force of the new institution of warrior aristocracies, which was of course also linked to its expansionist tendencies, which we will discuss in the following section.

5.5   Life and death of the Bronze Age warrior

Mobile warriors or mobile weapons

We have now sketched some constituting factors in the expansion and consolidation of the institution of warrior aristocracies in Bronze Age Europe. It follows from this that the warrior culture created a new dynamic in warfare and social organisation, the possible consequences of which we shall now briefly discuss, as reflected in the distribution patterns of certain weapons and burial rituals.

It remains a consistent feature of the Bronze Age that (some) weapons travel long distances. In this they stand in some contrast to female ornaments, whose distributions are normally local or regional. This feature of weapons, especially swords, is normally attributed to their role among warrior chiefs as prestige goods that were exchanged and imitated widely as part of alliances between polities, as discussed earlier (chapters 2.4 and 3.4). However, certain distribution patterns are remarkable, and deserve further study: those where a specific sword type has two distributional centres separated by a rather wide area without depositions (or with very few depositions). Among them we can mention the distribution of type A rapiers in the Aegean, centred round Knossos and Mycenae and in the Carpathians (Fig. 99a), and further the octagonal-hilted swords in southern Germany and

Denmark, and the early solid-hilted swords of Hajdúsámson and Apa type, distributed in the Carpathians and Denmark, just discussed (Fig. 93, and Bader 1991: Taf. 63). And finally there are the early central European rapiers of type Boi found in tell sites in Hungary and in the Terramare settlements of the Po valley (Bader 1991: Taf. 64).

These distributions raise the question: which were moving – warriors with weapons or weapons without warriors? Were warriors seeking their fortune in foreign lands, as travelling traders and smiths, mercenaries or conquest migrants? Or did weapons move in an exchange circuit of shorter travels to allied chiefs, presented as gifts? In the latter case, we must ask why they were only deposited in the two most distant areas of the exchange circuit – at its beginning and end? Were differences in depositional rituals the main reason for their virtual non-existence in the intermediate area? In the case of Minoan Crete and the Argolid the sea is the separating factor, but even here the two concentrations are remarkable. In the other cases mentioned from mainland Europe there is nothing in the burials or hoarding ritual that separates the intermediate area from the two areas of deposition, and they are linked by regional exchange circuits (Fig. 107).

In Figure 107 we have encircled local Tumulus Culture groups or chiefly polities. The arrows indicate the origin of a 'foreign' woman buried with a set of foreign ornaments. The figure illustrates the role of interchiefly alliances supported by marriage. Wives were moving to their husbands' groups, whether between or inside local polities, we may assume. As the swords cross and unify chiefly polities their distribution must be explained differently. We suggest they represent a certain group of warriors/artisans on the move. This can be supported by a number of other observations: in the Nordic region there is a separation in burial equipment between 'Nordic' solid-hilted swords in Nordic style and 'foreign' swords without Nordic symbolism (octagonal- and flange-hilted swords). Nordic swords are distributed within the Nordic region only, while the foreign swords have a wider European distribution. Nordic sword burials have mostly razor and tweezers and other chiefly and ritual regalia, while this is not the case with the foreign swords – or rarely so.

One of us has previously proposed that these differences were related to two different institutionalised roles – that of ritual leader versus that of war leader of the retinue, a type of dual or twin leadership (Kristiansen 1987). This demonstrates that basic typological differences between sword types are meaningfully constituted in social organisation. However, here we wish to go one step further. If we accept the social and ritual significance of Nordic versus foreign identities in burial equipment, it supports the idea that professional warriors were foreign. Or at least the ideology and the material culture constructed them as foreign (in accordance with Mary Helms' ethnohistorical evidence, described in chapter 2.4). Although

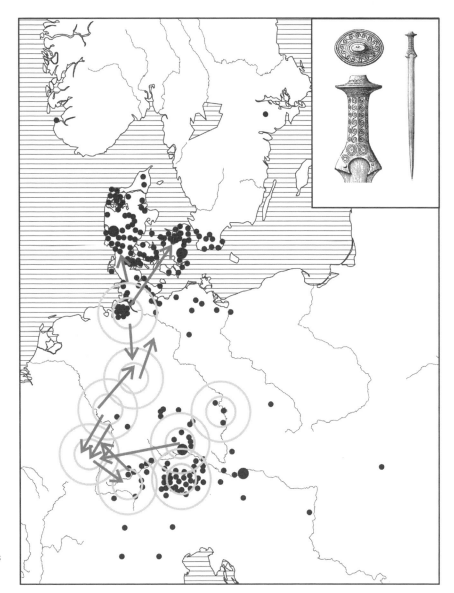

Fig. 107
Distribution of octagonally hilted swords from Montelius period 2 against local groups/polities (circles) and intermarriage patterns of foreign women in graves (arrows showing their origin).

this would not always reflect a reality, and in most cases it probably did not, it did reflect a cosmological origin of the warrior as a foreigner. Most probably it referred back to socially constructed networks allowing for travels and movements, and it probably meant that warriors in some cases could move long distances.

A closer study of the octagonal-hilted sword of Montelius period 2 carried out by Ingeborg von Quillfeldt (1995) allows a more detailed understanding of the process. Among the swords, some are distinctive by coming from the same workshop, and yet being deposited in both southern Germany and Denmark. In fact there exists such a degree of similarity between all octagonal-hilted swords that some central workshops with a kind of mass production must be assumed. This is true of most solid-hilted swords from central Europe during the Late Bronze Age in opposition to Nordic swords that are individually produced and more artistic. Some octagonal-hilted swords have been produced locally in Denmark, as they share some Nordic details in decoration and are not found in southern Germany. Here a direct personal relation, a long-distance traveller and possible smith, can be supported. Technical analyses of the octagonal-hilted swords demonstrate that their casting was different from that of Nordic solid-hilted swords, and all octagonal-hilted swords employ the same central European casting technique. This implies that foreign chiefly smiths carried out production of these foreign swords in Denmark (Quillfeldt 1995: 85ff.).

The following historical scenario can be proposed: along newly established exchange and marriage alliances chiefly traders and warriors travel to the distant north and bring with them bronze and technological know-how, and return with amber.[19] At the same time complex amber necklaces occur in female burials in southern Germany and in Mycenaean burials. The octagonal-hilted sword can be regarded as a kind of 'passport' or social identification of a certain group of chiefly traders and specialists, just as the flange-hilted sword was the social identification of the 'professional' warrior.[20] This would allow them protection among their 'brothers' along the route.

It is possible to sustain this with more detailed evidence of marriage alliances linking Denmark, especially Jutland, to chiefdoms in northern Germany (the Lüneburg region) and even further south. Here we find the beginning of the network in the late sixteenth century (Br. B1). Wheel-headed pins of Lüneburg type, which are part of female dress, show a dispersed northward distribution into Denmark (Kubach 1995). A burial from the island of Zealand contained a foreign woman with a complete female dressing outfit of Lüneburg type (Aner and Kersten 1976: No. 1264A), and a similar grave was recently excavated in southern Jutland (Zick 1993). Here we have concrete evidence of interregional marriage alliances. At the same time new swords and axes from northwestern Europe (from Brittany and Wessex) make their appearance in the same regions of Denmark, especially Jutland,

---

19 It has now been demonstrated that raw amber was collected and stored at chiefly farms in northwestern Jutland (Bech and Mikkelsen 1999: Fig. 4).

20 Travellers and traders have in all societies needed some form of identification that would secure their protection, and this could take many forms. In the passport of the United Kingdom, a former colonial and trading empire, one still reads the following text: 'Her Britannic Majesty's Secretary of State requests and requires in the Name of Her Majesty all those whom it may concern to allow the bearer to pass freely without let or hindrance, and to afford the bearer such assistance and protection as may be necessary.'

together with a new tumulus burial ritual (Laux 1995). Once established, this regional network suddenly expanded to incorporate southern Germany after 1500 BC, a change that was linked to the production and adaptation of octagonal-hilted and flange-hilted swords in west central Europe and southern Scandinavia, as we have demonstrated on Figure 107. It was followed by a rapid increase in long-distance travels of certain groups among the chiefly elite (warriors, traders and metalworkers).

The octagonal-hilted swords share their distribution with early flange-hilted swords, including a special type with parallel flanges (Struwe 1971: Table 26; also in Kristiansen 1987: Fig. 4.8). Here again a few nearly identical pieces are found in both central Europe and Denmark (Schauer 1971: Taf. 118). And of course the prototype was Mycenaean (Fig. 47 and Randsborg 1967), once again stressing the importance and the power of foreign prestige goods and their imitations. This, however, displays the height of the network in the fifteenth and fourteenth centuries BC, when Mycenaean traders settled in the western Mediterranean and established direct trading connections with southern Germany, and thus linked up with the network that reached Jutland and the amber producing areas.

Recent archaeological discoveries have completely changed our perception of Mycenaean presence in this part of Europe. Through the work of Berhard Hänsel and his colleagues, a direct Mycenaean presence in the northern Adriatic, on the southern shores of Istria, can be documented. It consists of a major fortification with stone-built walls of big cut-out stone blocks (ashlars) and an inner acropolis (Fig. 68). The complex entrance and skilled stone masonry testify to the high level of craftsmanship behind the construction (Terzan, Mihovilic and Hänsel 1999: Abb. 10 and 13). Preliminary datings of objects suggest the period eighteenth–sixteenth centuries BC. In the vicinity of the fortified settlement Hänsel has been able to reconstruct a Mycenaean tholos grave from a previously excavated grave mound (Hänsel and Terzan 2000) (Fig. 108). While local material culture dominates, the architecture is foreign and Mycenaean. However, a genuine Mycenaean find appeared in a Middle Bronze Age fortified settlement in Bavaria: a gold diadem made of gold foil of the type found in the shaft graves at Mycenae, together with some raw amber. It had been ritually destroyed by fire, but a reconstruction of the context suggests that it had been mounted on a wooden statue with a staff (some of which was preserved). A C14 dating suggests the sixteenth–fourteenth centuries BC as the possible time span (Gebhard 1999). The following year this find was supplemented by a carved piece of amber with a human face and a name written in Linear B, whose authenticity has been confirmed by several specialists (Gebhard and Rieder 2002).

Here we see the direct presence of Mycenaean traders and an exchange not only of prestige goods, amber and gold, but also of rituals and probably wider cosmological beliefs. Mycenaean and south German and even south

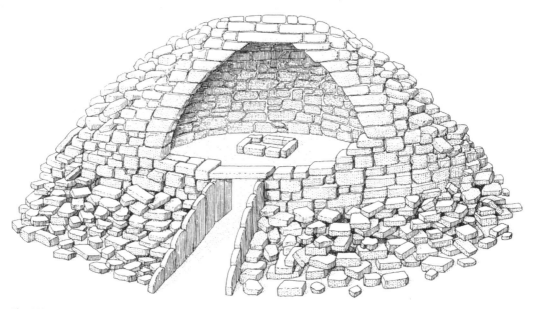

Fig. 108 Tholos grave of Mycenaean type from Istria in the northern Adriatic Sea (after Hänsel and Terzan 2000).

Scandinavian chiefs had direct personal contacts. In this new light the sudden formation and expansion of chiefly networks described above can now be linked to a direct Mycenaean intervention. Rather than use the long eastern network described in the previous chapter, a much more direct link could be established from the northern Adriatic. Whether this was a consequence of the collapse of the highly organised tell societies, or whether this collapse followed after the new trade links to southern Germany, we will probably never know. However, this stresses the incredible social and economic importance of amber in Mycenaean society and in the east Mediterranean. Moreover, it makes it easier to understand how east Mediterranean prestige goods, such as folding stools and flange-hilted swords of Mycenaean inspiration, could be transmitted so directly to southern Scandinavia. But why this region – more than other regions in Europe – adopted a Mycenaean cultural idiom as a basis for the new Nordic Bronze Age society remains yet to be explained. However, first we need to understand what social structures and mechanism made these transfers possible in the first place.

Indo-European kinship systems and the exchange of 'foreign' warriors (foster sons and brothers)

Ethnohistorical evidence of warrior cultures supports such an interpretation of warriors and traders on the move. Warriors often formed special group identities (sodalities) that linked them in a spatial network defined by rules of special behaviour and etiquette. This could be employed both for recruiting war bands, and for travelling to more distant chiefs to earn fame and foreign prestige good, as evidenced among the Maasai in Africa and among the Japanese samurai, and is a recurring feature in the literature on warriors and warfare.

Such geographically wide-ranging identities would have been supported by a kinship system where a son stays with his mother's brother, and later returns home as a 'foreign' warrior with useful knowledge and foster brother links to the mother's kin. Or he might choose to stay and form new links through marriage. In patrilineal societies, such as the Indo-European, a mother's brother will often have important duties to perform for his sister's son. Robin Fox (1967: 133) explains this by reference to the fact that relations within patrilineages are often strained, with quarrelling and competition between brothers and other agnates. Introducing the mother's brother as having a special role for his sister's son can soften this. Rowlands describes the Omaha kinship system, thought to be dominant in the Bronze Age, in this way:

> agnatic ties, particularly between male siblings, are emphasised and the household, made up of agnatically related males, their wives and offspring, is usually highly solidary and the most important political and economic unit. Households may be large and ramified descent groups, depending on the prestige of each individual member. Strong controls are exercised over the actions of group members, usually under the autocratic rule of the household head, and particularly over wives and their offspring. Residence at marriage is strictly virilocal,[21] bride wealth payments are usually high and there may be severe sanctions against divorce and adultery.

We may see a glimpse of such social controls of women in the presence of ankle rings that could be locked together, and in the use of complex ornaments which restricted movement (Fig. 109). Women were an important source of wealth as marriage partners, and had to be controlled. Such control was apparently even exercised in death. In an important study Lothar Sperber has demonstrated that sword burials in the central European early Urnfield period show an abnormally high proportion (40 per cent) of double burials with husband/wife, compared to other burials where the figure is minimal (Sperber 1999). As warrior chiefs were likely to die in combat before their wives, widow burning seems safely attested. Sperber characterises this elite group as representing nearly caste-like social divisions in burial ritual, and he is able to link this chiefly group to the existence of

---

21 Virilocal residence means that a boy has to return to his mother's village. This is linked to a marriage system where the woman moves to the man's household.

groups of farmsteads, consisting of about four families (chiefly households), with a 300-year continuity (Sperber 1999: Abb. 20 and 21).

Chiefly lineages that were successful in marrying out their daughters to (faraway) alliance partners, who then became kin, would not only receive more bridewealth than others, but also have the potential for receiving foster sons who would move to their mother's brother and become young warriors. In this way links of male solidarity were established that could be mobilised when needed, for example in conflict situations. It further opened up possibilities for warriors to travel, supported by ancient rules of guest friendship, as described in Homer. Guest friendship functioned as a counterpart to the alliance strategy, and its importance has been well described by Rowlands: 'A guest friendship between noble households was as binding as marriage and retained its strength as a bond over several generations. It is significant in this respect that guest friendship was more commonly associated with the establishment of bonds between noble elites of different kingdoms than between high-ranking and low-ranking nobles of the same kingdom' (Rowlands 1980). In a travel account from the early ninth century AD the wealthy trader Ottar from northern Norway (around Tromsø), who visited the court of King Alfred, describes his regular travels to the trade town Kaupang in the Oslo fjord, where he sold his precious skins. It was a distance of 1750 km. From there he also travelled to Haithabu in northern Germany. These extensive travels were made under the protection of some form of guest friendship or hospitality, also known from other parts of Europe (Sanchez-Moreno 2001). He also describes how he travelled north to the White Sea until he was no longer protected by guest friendship. Also, King Alfred offered him protection when he visited England. This account illuminates the role of travels in a society still organised according to ancient or prehistoric rules of guest friendship and protection, and it illustrates how far merchants or traders in such societies could travel. As stated in the the *Odyssey*: 'To any man with the slighest claim to common sense, a guest and suppliant is as close as a brother' (Book 8, 545).

The two concepts of foster sons and guest friendship supplement each other and help to explain how in the Bronze Age also it was possible to travel similar long distances, which for coastal Scandinavia can be further documented through the appearance of 'foreign ships' in local rock art panels. They cover the same distances as those described by Ottar (Kristiansen 2002a). We may note that both Icelandic and Irish sagas and myths offer many examples of the rule of sending sons to foster parents, and of the strong bonds evolving between foster brothers. Two well-known examples and their tragic fate figure prominently in the heroic literature: Achilles and Patroclus, and Cuchulainn and Ferdia. While Achilles and Patroclus fight together, as king and war leader, Cuchulainn and Ferdia meet on opposing

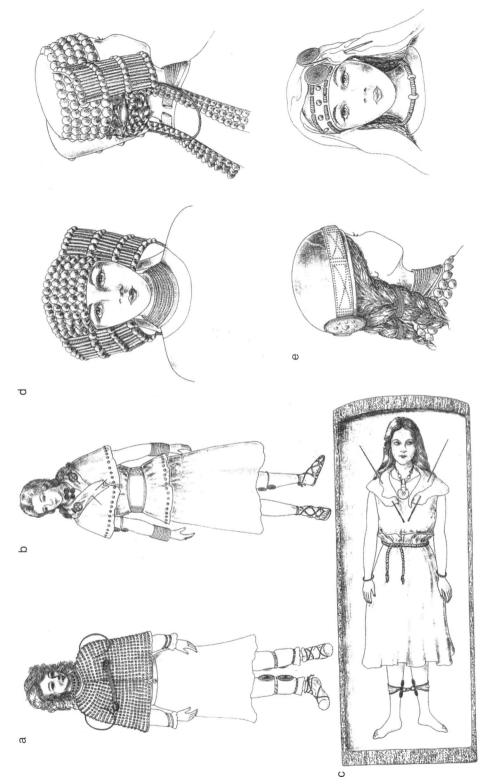

Fig. 109 Reconstructions of Middle Bronze Age female costumes: (*a*) from Mecklenburg, (*b*) from Fulda, Hessen, (*c*) from Baden-Würtenberg. Headaddresses, (*d*) from Lüneburg, (*e*) from Thüringen (from Wels-Weyrauch 1994: Abb. 56 and 57).

sides in battle and end up fighting each other in single combat. In both cases the death of the foster brother creates great despair and mourning. This institution thus had ancient roots in Indo-European societies.

Another aspect of the Indo-European Crow-Omaha kinship system was its flexibility and potential for expansion. According to Rowlands (1980), a historical feature of such Crow-Omaha kinship systems is 'that they are often highly unstable structures that have been historically incorporated into extensive trading networks that allow forms of wealth to be accumulated and that generate different kinds of demand from those which had existed previously'. This was due to the fact that their marriage strategy was opportunistic and competitive, the only rule being that you were not allowed to marry twice into the same family. Hence the marriage strategy became expansionist. As a result any one group would be linked to numerous others at any particular time. We thus have to envisage long-distance links between Bronze Age chiefdoms, such as those in Fig. 107, as constructed along lines of newly established kinship relations and guest friendships, where women and young warriors circulated, and which shared certain common values, both economic and cultural.

This scenario would seem to be a perfect description of the long-distance relations between southern Scandinavia and southern Germany in the initial period of the formation of Nordic Bronze Age society. It would account both for the movement of foreign warriors and traders in the creation of new lines of long-distance exchange and for the subsequent rapid regional formation of a new cultural identity in the decades after 1500 BC. Such a rapid transformation of a whole region demanded an incredible acceleration of local and regional interaction, which is provided by the Crow-Omaha kinship system. As a consequence of the inherent rules or logic of the system, we should expect it to develop more closed, endogamous marriage strategies over time, or to create new networks of exchange and marriage partners. This is precisely what we can observe in the rise or decline of new foreign networks throughout the Bronze Age, each of them lasting only a few generations.

The death of the warrior

Honour and death are intertwined in warrior ideology. To die in battle is the only honourable way to die. But to this belongs a proper burial. To be left on the battlefield for the birds after having been stripped of armour was the worst possible ending. We encounter this trauma in the death of both Patroclus and especially Hector. Having been killed, the dead warrior would be stripped of his weapons, as booty. In central and northern Europe such weapons, or maybe only the sword, would be sacrificed to the gods, and some would be given as prizes to the best sportsmen, as in the games after Patroclus' burial in the *Iliad*, or simply distributed to the retinue. It is probably in this light that we should see grave robbing – as stripping not only those fallen in combat of their weapons, but the buried warriors and ancestors. In Ireland heads were taken as trophies as well, as the power and the soul were thought to rest in the head.

To achieve a heroic burial was the only way to escape the worst of all fates – oblivion. Therefore the funeral rites and the burial monument promoted him to the status of hero. Bards would sing at the funeral, games would be played, and afterwards the monument became a place to honour the dead hero, who eventually over time would become semi-divine, the founder of a chiefly lineage. We are here applying Ian Morris' concept of rich warrior burials from Archaic Greece to account for the same kind of phenomenon 700 hundred years earlier (Morris 1999). It meant that much ritual energy had to be spent on the death rituals of the warrior chiefs and kings, as this represented not only a death ritual but also a memorial: most clearly so in the formation period of the warrior aristocracies, as a means of institution-alising their new social and ritual standing.

We would therefore expect the expansion of a new warrior elite to be accompanied by a complex and highly visual burial ritual, such as burial under a barrow. We would also expect this to be inspired by ritual traditions in the centres of warrior elites – the Minoan and Mycenaean palace cultures, or by the older chiefly lineages of Brittany, who were also having distant (and probably indirect) trading relations with the Minoans and the early Nordic chiefdoms.

Studies of barrow construction hold great potential for understanding the meaning of burial rituals (Goldhahn 1999a), but are unfortunately rare. The following will therefore rather serve as a heuristic guide to further, more systematic studies.

Our expectation would be that barrow construction and ritual should share widespread similarities within the area of warrior travels and alliances as described above. This would be seen to confirm the integration between travels, knowledge and the transmission of new institutions.

Secondly we would expect the burial ritual in itself to reveal significant aspects of shared myth and ritual, the barrow and the burial ritual being a paradigmatic symbol of cosmos.

On a more general level we observe that tumulus burials accompanied the spread of the new warrior aristocracy from southern Germany to southern Scandinavia. We may further observe that they share basic constructional components: a solidly built outer ring of kerbstones encircled the place of burial, and represented the first stage in the contruction. Sometimes a solid stone wall resembling the groundplan of the tholos (Fig. 110b) replaced the kerbstones. In several cases it can be demonstrated that the ringwall was open during the construction phase, and more recently it has become clear that small rectangular huts for rituals or for temporary storing of the dead were constructed in relation to the ringwall. The grave itself may have an oak coffin, or a stone cist (often later, when forests were diminishing), which was covered by a central mound either of turf or stone. Later the barrow would be completed with yet another layer of turf or sand. According to this interpretation the construction of the barrow entails several liminal phases that have to be passed (Goldhahn 1999a). In accordance with this interpretation modern excavations demonstrate that libation stones with cupmarks often occur beside graves in southern Scandinavia.[22]

On Figure 110 we show two recent reconstruction drawings from Denmark and Sweden of the construction of the first phase of the barrow. In Sagaholm, the outer ring of decorated slabs still shows a certain similarity with the grave circles at Mycenae, although of a general nature. However, highly specific construction details, such as an additional half-circle of kerbstones, link together tumulus burials from southern to northern Germany, as recently demonstrated (Görner 2002: Abb. 138; Görner and Geshwinde 2002: Abb. 1 and 4). Thus the burial rituals confirm the existence of widespread and frequent communication networks.

The uniquely well-preserved oak coffin burials from Denmark allow us to catch a glimpse not only of dress and woodworking but also of the rituals accompanying the burial. Along with the symbolic meaning of the tumulus construction just described, it makes it possible to propose the tumulus ritual as linked to a common ritual cosmology from the east European steppe through Mycenaean Greece to southern Scandinavia. In the following we summarise the cosmological components in the symbolic universe of the tumulus burial ritual. It comprises the following elements: the outer ring of kerbstones symbolises the sun-wheel, in a few cases actually constructed, but more commonly represented by one or several concentric stone rings (Fig. 111). With the tumulus added, the image of the rising sun unifying heaven and underworld is completed. The barrow rises towards the sky at the highest points in the landscape. However its construction from grass turves, the inner mound often from meadows or wetlands, also symbolises grazing lands for the chiefly herds to be carried along on the journey to the other world. A relict of that is preserved in the Hittite royal burial ritual, where a piece of turf from a meadow is given as sacrifice (as *pars pro toto*). It is accompanied by the following wording: 'Now, sun god, accept these

---

22 Cupmark stones in Early Bronze Age barrows are reported in several recent excavations, e.g. Strömberg 1977: 45; Asingh 1987: Fig. 14; Rønne 1993: Fig. 29. This indicates that they were more common than older excavations would suggest.

a

b

Fig. 110 Two illustrations of the early phase of the construction of a tumulus: (*a*) Hohøj in Jutland during construction, after the circular base was built upon which the barrow was constructed layer by layer and (*b*) Sagaholm in Sweden with the decorated stone circle before it was covered in the final phase (after Bech 2002: Fig. 128 and Goldhahn 1999a: Fig. 10.1).

meadows as correctly taken in possession, and no one shall take them or question them. And on these meadows shall for him cows, sheep, horses and mules graze' (Haas 1994a: 224). A similar ritual is found in the Irish mythology. They demonstrate the symbolic connection between grass turves and eternal meadows.

a

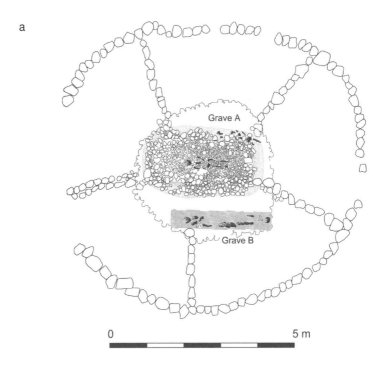

b

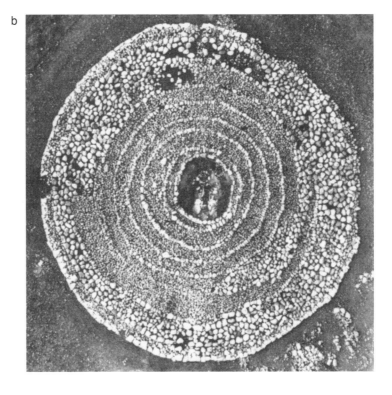

Fig. 111 Sun symbolism in the circular layout of stone constructions found under early Bronze Age barrows. (*a*) Wheel symbol from barrow in southern Jutland, and (*b*) concentric circles from barrow on the island of Gotland in Sweden (after Aner and Kersten 1981: Abb. 37 and Hallström 1971: 115).

To mobilise the eternal lifegiving forces, the dead chief is buried in an oak coffin, which consists of the central part of the tree trunk that is cleaved into two and dug out. But the trunk otherwise remains intact, this to symbolise a living tree – the life tree in Indo-European religion. In Hittite and Nordic religion the trunk symbolises the middle zone, the earth, while the roots go into the underworld and the top reaches into the heavens where the sun lives. The oak coffin thus symbolises the unification of all three realms, and ensures that the dead will be carried on to the otherworld. A recent find of a submerged well-preserved woodhenge in England had a life tree in the centre with its roots turned upward (Pryor 2002). In this it resembles Norse mythology, where some of the roots of the life tree Ydrasil grow up into heaven. It is thus clear that the perception of the life tree was shared among the Indo-European speaking people in the Temperate Zone in the Bronze Age. We are further provided with a ritual/cosmological link between woodhenges and round barrows, the life tree in the centre being replaced by an oak coffin with similar meaning. The woodhenges of the British Isles are simply a specialised version of the wooden structures of poles around barrows from central Eurasia to northern Europe from the third millennium onwards.

To ensure the divine support of the sky-god, a sacrifice of an ox is now made to his honour, before the dead is put to rest in the coffin, lying on the freshly cut out hide of the ox, which is finally wrapped around the fully clothed body. A unique find of a headdress decorated with spirals on gold foil over bronze and with golden ox horns from this period (fifteenth–fourteenth centuries BC) shows that Nordic Bronze Age religion was familiar with the Mycenaean ox sacrifice ritual (Fig. 155, No. 5). Gold foil was put around the horns to honour the sky-god when an ox was sacrificed and the head was cut off. In the *Odyssey* we find a good description of the ritual (*Odyssey* Book 3, 430ff.). 'Nestor the old charioteer gave out the gold, with which the smith gilded the heifer's horns by way of embellishment to please the goddess's eye.' Now water and barley are sprayed, prayers made, and the heifer is cut in the neck with an axe, its throat is cut and the carcass is dismembered. Then they 'cut out the thigh bones in the usual way, wrapped them in folds of fat and laid raw meat above them. The venerable King burnt these on the firewood, sprinkling red wine over the flames, while the young men gathered round with five-pronged forks in their hands.' Finally they eat the roasted meat. In northern Europe libations would have been made on the libation stone close to the burial in conclusion, before then the barrow itself was erected.

By analysing the symbolic/religious language of the tumulus burial of the Bronze Age it can be demonstrated that it encapsulates in paradigmatic form basic Indo-European religious symbols of rebirth and eternal life that are linked to the life tree and sun symbolism. It was also reflected in the orientation of the coffin that pointed towards the sunrise at the time of burial (Randsborg and Nybo 1984). This religious/cosmological symbolism of shared rituals and sacrifices spans from Eurasia and the Aegean to England and Scandinavia. Within the framework of these ritual and mythological commonalties there was still plenty of room for applying local variations in the construction of barrows and burial rituals. But to explain such variations – whether in burials rituals or in social institutions and settlement structure – we need first to understand the underlying shared similarities.

Life of the warrior

Thus, in the Bronze and Early Iron Age of central and northern Europe warfare was an integral aspect of daily life. Every local community would regularly bury their dead warriors. Farming and warfare were the two axes of male activity, military training being a main concern of the young, local chiefly males. During seasons of war local retinues were mobilised along lines of rank. Changes occurred in sword combat: during the earlier second millennium the long and narrow rapier was dominant (thrusting), while from the thirteenth century BC the wide-bladed and heavier slashing sword took over. The size of armies may have developed over time, and thereby increased the scale of combat and political control, but this is mainly based upon the size of fortifications (Kristiansen 1998a: Fig. 200), whereas the overall social organisation of warfare based on the chiefly retinue remained largely unchanged.

We do not know if the warrior function was defined by age, but we suspect this to be the case. The chosen warriors, the foster sons, would probably be initiated at puberty to their role. We may here refer to the boy troops of the hero Conchobor, starting war training at an early age (*The Tain*, ch. 4, Cuchulainn's boyhood deeds). As described earlier, the life of the warrior had its own daily routines from body care to training and hunting. Regular raids were part of the constant competition for power and honour. Those who were not your allies were potential targets of raiding to enrich your own economic base, and to establish client relations. This is a recurring scenario in all myths and sagas from the *Iliad* in Greece to the *Tain* in Ireland, and not only a legitimate behaviour, but also one of logic and necessity to feed the warriors and fuel their ethos. On such occasions barrows or cemeteries could be plundered and renowned prestige goods and weapons carried away, yet another humiliation of enemy ancestor heroes, that were thus killed twice and stripped of their weapons. This explains the recurring plundering of barrows and cemeteries in the Bronze Age, that could not have taken place without chiefly orders (Stuchlik 1990; Randsborg 1998; Batora 2000).

Highest ranked among the various types of combat was single combat. It takes up a major part of the stories in both the *Iliad* and the *Tain*, stressing its ideological loading. And we do find regular evidence of single combat in the archaeological record, when two or a few swords are deposited together in a bog (the Bronze Age sanctuary), with non-repaired scars from the fight (Kristiansen 2002b). Also Nordic rock art has many single combat scenes, although some could also represent rituals of war performed by twin chiefs (to be discussed in chapter 6.3 and 6.4) (Nordbladh 1980). This once again stresses the ideological role of single combat (Peatfield 1999). However, most combats were probably less ritualised, more cunning and cruel. We learn in passing that Odysseus on his way home from Troy sacked the town of Ismarus and destroyed its menfolk, and carried booty and women to the ships (*Odyssey* Book 9, 39–42.) The sacker of cities, Odysseus is repeatedly named. The presence of cruel death and the turmoil of battle pops up sometimes throughout heroic poetry in some painfully realistic verses, such as Patroclus' fight and death (another later example in Hanson 1999). In his recent book *Art and the Early Greek State* (1999) Michael Shanks develops and envelops the stress of warrior culture in Archaic Greece through its representations in art on painted pottery and through texts. Here we can add yet another aspect of the warrior ethos – its relation to the wild, to hunting and wild animals.

To become a member of the warrior group and the chiefly retinue demanded initiation and tests. One such initiation ritual was in all probability the boar hunt. It provided the empowered boar tusks for the warrior's helmet. Central European and Mycenaean warriors here shared a common tradition during the Early Bronze Age, and the Mycenaeans may even have adopted the ritual from east central Europe (Bartelheim 1998: Karte 165). The boar tusk helmet was highly valued and could be passed on through generations (*Iliad* Book 9, 264ff.). The description of the helmet given to Odysseus matches an early Mycenaean type, as found in the LMH shaft grave at Aegina, where the boar tusks do not provide full cover, but are added to the leather straps (Kilian-Dirlmeier 1997: Abb. 18): yet another example of the early Mycenaean roots of the *Iliad*.

The impact of warfare on Bronze Age populations has never been studied systematically, but can sometimes be demonstrated in the age statistics of cemeteries. Here we find a recurring gender variation: young women (juv./juvadult) show higher mortality than men because of the risks of giving birth, while adult men demonstrate highly increased mortality compared to women, most probably because of warfare (O'Shea 1996: Fig. 6.1; Kristiansen 1998a: Fig. 198). In some cases we also find the victims of warfare quickly buried or sometimes even thrown into mass graves, examples numbering from a handful to several dozen (Chochorowski 1993: Figs. 47 and 48; Louwe Kooijmans 1998: Abb. 12). Although medical treatment was applied for curing wounds (Arnott 1999), Mycenaean shaft grave warrior chiefs reveal low average death age at thirty-six, linked to frequent skull damage and other types of wounds, demonstrating in a concrete way the impact of warfare even in the aristocratic segment of society (Angel 1972). In that, they shared the same conditions as other Early Bronze Age warriors (Teschler-Nicola 1994: 180ff.). We shall exemplify the more cruel consequences of warfare and the subjugation and killing of captured groups by some recent research from Scandinavia and central Europe.

A 'burial pit' from Sund in western Norway contained some twenty-five to thirty individuals of both sexes and various ages, dating to the Nordic Early Bronze Age. The skeletons have been analysed for physical damage by Hilde Fyllingen (2003). They demonstrate that the whole population had been massacred using swords and lances. Cuts on arms of adult males reveal attempts to defend themselves, and several healed cuts on the right arms suggest they were warriors. There were also indications that some had been killed from behind, using a lance. All in all a rather gruesome picture of the realities of warfare in Bronze Age society.

In all this the Bronze and Early Iron Age societies of the second and first millennia BC resemble historically known chiefdoms that were characterised by systematic warfare, which involved a rather high proportion of the male population, and many casualties (data in Keeley 1996: Figs. 4.1 and 6.1, and Tables 2.1, 2.6, 3.2 and 6.2). A few ethnographic accounts may exemplify the nature of warfare as it may have taken place in Bronze Age Europe, since there are many parallels between the organisation of warfare in historically known chiefdoms and the picture we have painted above of the organisation of Bronze Age and Early Iron Age warfare.

Carneiro (1990: 195ff.) states of Fiji chiefdoms: 'hostilities are now often attended by a certain amount of protocol and ceremony'. 'The paramount chief typically leads his warriors in battle.' 'Warfare is much more likely to be fought hand to hand' (sword fighters of the Bronze and Iron Age). In battle, 'trumpet blowing and drums were beaten' (the lurs of the Bronze Age). Casualties: 'in most battles on Fiji the number of persons killed range from 20 to 200 (an estimated 1500–2000 persons per year in the nineteenth century). Skulls were taken as trophies (as also reported from the Celts). Motives: increasing the amount of tribute and slaves. This meant that success in warfare was crucial for maintaining chiefly power. Carneiro observes cycles of expansion/regression of territorial power by a single chiefdom. Thus periods of warfare alternated with periods of peace. Barbara Price notes on ranked societies: 'regular pulsation of scale among large complex ranked group: relatively brief periods of unity over wide areas alternate with longer periods of fragmentation' (Price 1984: 230).

Thus while chiefly power over larger areas is short-lived, the chiefly structure itself is long-lived. This picture of a chiefly warrior culture linked to honour and power is also what we find in the later European sagas and myths, some of them, for example Celtic, with probable Bronze Age roots (Enright 1996).[23]

5.6 Conclusion: the constitution of origins and the consolidation of hierarchy and cultural identity

We have demonstrated a historical process of travels and the transmission of new institutions between the east Mediterranean, central Europe and northern Europe. It was a two stage process. From the eighteenth century BC until the beginning of the fifteenth century BC networks were operating between the Hittites, the steppe and the Carpathians, with direct links to northern Europe. During this period basic institutions were transmitted north in exchange for amber and horses, while at the same time the institution of chariotry was transmitted south from the steppe. The processes were thus complex and European Bronze Age societies were on the whole less peripheral than often assumed. Foreign esoteric origins of high culture were adopted in religious institutions, and were reflected in architecture and in the adoption of the spiral style in pottery by tell societies of the Carpathian region in east central Europe. However, foreign origins were most consciously demonstrated in the formation of the Nordic Bronze Age Culture from 1500 BC onwards, basing itself on a Minoan/Mycenaean template. In the second stage, after 1500 BC the Mycenaean influence dominated in the west Mediterranean and new powerful links were soon established with the Tumulus Culture, which quickly assimilated the Mycenaean warrior ethos and part of its material culture. The Tumulus Culture demonstrates a ritual identity of warrior chiefs stretching from southern Germany and France to southern Scandinavia that was linked to Mycenaean perceptions of chiefly rituals and burials. But it was only in Scandinavia that religious Mycenaean symbolism was adopted, a conscious signal of powerful foreign origins transformed into a new Nordic identity.

In terms of identity it is worth noticing the sophisticated and complex use of concepts of foreign and local in material culture. Warriors were part of supra-local lines of exchange and formed a 'foreign' or international (to use

---

23 This theme and the relationship between Bronze Age and later Iron Age retinues, in archaeology and in texts, has been systematically analysed in a recent PhD by Paul Treherne. Unfortunately it has not yet been published, and we have not had access to it during the writing of this book.

a modern concept) identity among the 'regional' Nordic and Tumulus identities. Nordic identity was linked to perceptions of religious/political leadership, and its material culture was not transmitted outside its boundaries. In these ways foreign and local identities could be integrated into a dynamic relationship that allowed travel and the adoption of 'foreigners' as well as their material culture, while at the same time local and regional identity or ethnicity was maintained. This suggests a high level of cultural and ethnic consciousness that we are only beginning to understand. We may suggest, however, that the formation of distinct regional and local identities in material culture was linked to the consolidation of the new institutions of chiefly leadership. While structural and institutional similarities were widespread throughout Europe they were constantly reformulated in a complex process of identity formation linked to gender and kinship on the one hand, and political/religious power relations on the other.

This was exemplified by the travelling chiefs and their warriors/foster brothers who linked together southern Scandinavia and southern Germany in a network of exchanges of ideas and new institutions during some generations in the fifteenth and early fourteenth centuries BC. This network was further linked to Mycenaean traders who visited southern Germany from the east Mediterranean colonies in Istria. In this way we can for the first time provide a direct historical explanation for the widespread similarities between Mycenaean and Nordic Bronze Age cultures during this period. It included everything from imitation of weapons, spiral ornamentation, double axes and campstools, to the chiefly dress consisting of cloak and tunic, so often mentioned as the dress of the warrior elite in the *Iliad* and the *Odyssey*, but only preserved in Danish oak coffin burials from the fourteenth century BC.

6 The cosmological structure of Bronze Age society

6.1 The archaeological study of religion: some constituting elements

Religious traditions are long-lived and persistent. The present world religions may illustrate this point, spanning between 1000 and 3000 years, with some of the cult buildings being nearly as old (churches and monasteries). Religious traditions are further permutative and highly adaptive – they may adopt and add new elements, or take away certain elements in the process of modernisation or religious reformation. Thus Christianity has persisted and adapted to the historical process from the Roman Empire through feudalism to industrial society. These simple observations make it justifiable to consider premodern world religions from the same perspective. Permutation, acculturation and transformation form some of the constituting methodological elements in the retrospective work of tracing archaic religious structures in the pre-Christian religions, from the *Veda* to Norse mythology. The same observations apply to the spatial distribution of religions. We can thus apply the theoretical and methodological framework of chapter 1 in the study of Bronze Age religions and their institutions also.

In doing so archaeology can contribute significantly to defining religious structures and rituals, their geography and chronology, since leadership in the Bronze Age was embedded in religion and reproduced in rituals. We see this demonstrated in the Minoan palaces, which Nano Marinatos has interpreted as centres of ritual, with their pictorial stories in wall paintings of the rituals of royalty and the reproduction of society (Marinatos 1993). In the Nordic realm rock art replaced wall painting, or was added to it, and we meet the same connection between religious and political power, chiefs and warriors taking part in complex ceremonies – from the ritual wedding, through warrior processions to female acrobatics, accompanied by horn or lur blowing. For the first time since Stone Age cave art and rock art we are confronted with real pictorial stories of the myths and rituals of society. This has of course invited interpretation, but not during the last generation, which lost confidence in comparative culture-historical and religious studies.

Not since the studies of M. P. Nilsson on Minoan religion (Nilsson 1932), and Oscar Almgren (1927) and Åke Ohlmarks (summarised in a pocket book 1963) on Nordic Bronze Age religion has there been any serious attempt to interpret the religious structure of Bronze Age society on comparative grounds.[1] There existed no generally accepted theoretical or methodological frame of reference for such studies, since the new archaeology of the 1960s abolished diffusion as a historical phenomenon deserving serious study, and turned to natural science and social anthropology for interdisciplinary inspiration.[2] In this respect the study of religion can be seen to follow the general trends of theoretical and ideological shifts in interpretative frameworks in the cultural disciplines (Kristiansen 1998a: Fig. 14). It follows a cyclical pattern that changes over time according to the dominance of a Romantic/diffusionist or a Rationalistic/evolutionary framework of interpretation. Thus, the renewed interest in cosmologies and religion in prehistoric societies corresponds with the theoretical revival of a culture-historical/postprocessual framework in archaeology.

In the previous chapter we have constructed a new theoretical and methodological framework for the study of historical interaction based upon the theoretical insights and interpretative results derived from recent archaeological and ethnographical research. This has allowed us to add a new historical perspective to the history of the second millennium BC. Based upon that, we now wish tentatively to explore the consequences and possibilities of this new framework for understanding the religious structure of Bronze Age society.

To proceed successfully in this we need to shape and structure the evidence into categories that are relevant from a ritual/religious perspective, rather than from an archaeological perspective. We propose the following categories: A. Gods, B. Myths, C. Rituals and D. Institutions. This forms a logical sequence beginning with the pantheon, as far as we can know about it, and then the myths or narratives giving historical meaning to the gods, their origin and roles. Then follow the rituals performed to maintain the order of gods and humans, and the institutions created to take care of A–C.

---

1 In 1954 two remarkable studies on Bronze Age symbolism appeared. One was Georg Kossack's book on *Symbolgut der Urnenfelderzeit*, where he mapped the symbolic repertoire of the new religious beliefs, and made an attempt to interpret them in a general way. The other was Ernst Sprockhof's major article on 'Frühes Griechentum und nordisches Bronzezeit', a comparative study of religious symbolism of the Late Bronze Age and the relations between Greece, central Europe and northern Europe. These studies still stand isolated in Bronze Age research, but deserve to be followed up. Their ambition was very similar to that of this book, except that the time period was the Late Bronze Age. We shall touch briefly upon these works in our concluding perpective.

2 Efforts were instead directed towards the classification of the paintings and rock art, and towards contextual and structural studies (history summarised in Nordbladh 1995), although Peter Gelling made an interesting attempt at religious interpretation (Gelling and Davidson 1969). It means that we now have a much better empirical point of departure for renewed interpretative studies, which are already emerging (e.g. Marinatos 1993; Kaul 1998). Even in his innovative study, however, Kaul refuses to consider Nordic Bronze Age religion in a larger temporal or spatial framework. In recent years we have witnessed a remarkable theoretical and interpretative renewal of Bronze Age rock art research, bringing it back to the forefront of archaeological interpretation (Bradley 1997; Goldhahn 1999; Hauptman-Wahlgren 2002; Fredell 2003; Santos and Criado in press).

Written texts may produce evidence in all of these categories, although with great variation in time and space.

Next we shall characterise the relevant types of material evidence linked for each category (developed from Gesell 1985; see also Renfrew 1985 for a longer list of attributes):

A. Gods:
   attributes and symbols (axes, bull horns)
   shapes (humans, animals) and special gestures (lifted hands, the young god with the staff)
B. Myths:
   places of mythological importance and/or worship (Olympia, Troy)
   narrative images/performances (paintings, rock art, figurines)
C. Rituals:
   movable ritual gear/cult objects (in hoards, shrines, burials, etc.)
   fixed ritual gear: altars, libation stones
   priests/priestesses, shamans, ritual chiefs (special attributes/amulets, sealstones, wall painting, etc.)
D. Institutions:
   ritual constructions for regular use (shrines, temples, caves)
   priests/priestesses, ritual chiefs, shamans (special outfits, attributes)
   iconography/symbols of institutions (tripartite shrine amulet).

Since Minoan and Hittite culture had such apparent impact during the formative period of Mycenaean and central European societies of the earlier to mid-second millennium BC we need to consider in more depth the structure of Minoan and Hittite religion to understand its possible impact on European Bronze Age societies. As we have already discussed at some length *ritual structures*, such as altars, libation stones, etc., and *ritual tools*, such as double axes, figurines, etc. (chapter 4), we shall here rather concentrate upon the religious pantheon. We will then compare the evidence from pictorial art in Minoan/Mycenaean culture and Nordic culture, both with each other and with the most recent evidence from the comparative study of early Indo-European religion. This will be followed by a comparative analysis of the sun cult in Bronze Age religion. Finally we shall summarise the symbolic characterisation of certain gods and goddesses, adding up to a discussion about the transmission and transformation of Bronze Age religion and the changing relationship between A–D in that process. Can we speak about world religions in the Bronze Age?

We will begin our journey into Bronze Age religion with a discussion of some Proto-Indo-European (PIE) gods and their possible identification and chronology. This demands an introductory discussion about the role of oral traditions and writing in maintaining religious institutions.

6.2 Oral and religious practice: beyond the written word

The concept of memory has become the focus of a renewed interest in the active social role of remembering and forgetting in the transmission of culture (Rowlands 1993; Bradley 2002; Van Dyke and Alcock 2003). However, memory is a modern concept whose meaning in the past cannot easily be understood without reference to contextualised, comparative knowledge. We need to transform memory into meaningful interpretative concepts that are in accordance with social and cultural conditions during the historical epoch being studied.

From ethnohistory we learn that words (oral tradition) and objects (symbolically loaded objects) had a much stronger social and religious impact in society than we can imagine (Gell 1998). Consequently they were also much less subject to change, and when changes occurred it was as a result of a social or religious change of meaning. While Ian Hodder demonstrated this symbolic capacity of meaning in material culture in his book *Symbols in Action* (1982), such an approach has been slow to be taken on board in archaeological case studies. This is regrettable: only archaeology can provide historical evidence of the persistence of long-term traditions in social institutions and cosmology, as we shall demonstrate below with an example from the Nordic Bronze Age.

For premodern societies we propose the following classification that places social and religious memory in a larger cultural field of knowledge transmission:

Memory: Social framework: fluid and negotiable knowledge maintained in families. Time frame: a few generations. In traditional society memory would refer to forgetting, that is knowledge without social or religious significance, except when linked to specific objects and locales. This is what Rowlands called 'object traditions' (Rowlands 1993; also Joyce 2003). In the Bronze Age this would typically comprise heavily worn ornaments and swords with names and biographies (Kristiansen 2002b). Some of these might then be transmitted to and incorporated into the next category.

Genealogies and heroic tales: Social framework: stable and renegotiable knowledge, maintained by chiefly bards. Knowledge that constitutes an important social foundation of ranking and prestige based upon kinship genealogies and the heroic deeds of ancestors. Subject to change when leadership changes. Time frame: 500–700 years or more, as evidenced from ethnohistory and historical archaeology (Hedeager 1998). Materialised in burial monuments, iconography, feasting localities and war monuments (fortifications). From here some tales of ancestor chiefs may be transmitted to and incorporated into the final category.

Cosmology and myth: Social framework: stable and non-negotiable knowledge, maintained by priests (druids, brahmins, etc.). Subject to intentional, institutionalised change/reform in periods of religious change. Time frame: from hundreds to thousands of years (examples: Hinduism, Christianity, Buddhism). Materialised in statues, temples, sanctuaries, ritual caves and rock art localities.

Let us consider some comparative evidence with relevance for Bronze Age religion. All religious practice is based on oral performance; texts are secondary results merely documenting existing oral traditions (Graham 1987; for an alternative view Goody 1987). This is especially clear in the Vedic tradition where oral teaching techiques have been the primary method of learning up to this day. Texts are considered secondary in the context of ritual and religious practice. It is through the role of performance and recitation that the rituals achieve their desired effect, for their validity and truth. 'Knowledge or truth, especially salvific knowledge or truth, is tied to the living words of authentic persons, not authentic documents' Graham 1987: 75). As ritual and sacrifice depend on the correct wording Brahmins consequently master the hymns to a degree that is staggering to a western mind.

'Particular Brahmin caste groups still specialize in the preservation and chanting of one or another of the Vedic *samhitas*, and continue to learn and transmit their texts verbatim through the most rigorous and intricate mnemonic techniques imaginable. Specifically, the same text is normally memorized in its entirety in up to eleven different modes of recitation (*pathas*) that require complex grammatical and recitative manipulation of the base text' (Graham 1987: 72). This may serve as a reminder to those who have discredited the capacity of preliterate societies to transmit complex information unchanged through time. We have in an earlier chapter on the use of written sources referred to the role of religious specialists with a learning period of twenty years.

In a theocratic society based on the integration of religious and political power, learned religious specialists play an essential role in maintaining and performing the hymns and myths in their correct wording and under the correct circumstances. In material culture this is reflected in the recurring or repetitive nature of complex symbols and rituals over wide regions and through long periods of time, often in similar ritual contexts. To this belonged a whole set of ritual gear to be employed, such as lurs,[3]

3 'The name Lur was given to this ancient instrument by the early Scandinavian archaeologists, who also used the words "Paalstav" and "Celt" to describe two different kinds of axe. They did not properly understand the age of these ancient objects and were influenced by Romanticism when they gave them names from the Sagas. It is certain that the Lur of the Sagas had nothing whatever to do with the curved wind instrument from the Bronze Age' (Broholm 1965: 129).

rattles, special dress and masks. Religious practice and performance were thus an integrated element in daily life throughout the Bronze Age, and the power of chiefly priests and priestesses must have been immense. As we shall demonstrate, they formed their own sodality of learning, teaching and practice, controlling all major aspects of the ritual reproduction of Bronze Age society.

Thus, we should envisage the druid tradition in Gallic/Celtic society, the brahmins of India and the heroic tradition of Homer as representing the final phase of a more universal Bronze Age tradition of learned specialists – from bards to druids. In a similar way the Vedic brahmin tradition is also derived from a Bronze Age tradition, but with steppe origins. Owing to basic religious and institutional similarities between these regions, which we shall demonstrate in the following, we have to assume that brahmin or druid specialists existed during the Bronze Age, where they maintained and transmitted the huge corpus of religious songs, hymns and myths throughout centuries and even millennia. This is verified by the material culture of the Bronze Age, which documents the persistence of basic religious institutions and myths over long periods of time.

We are, however, not proposing a monumental, unchanged homogeneous Bronze Age tradition. First of all, oral tradition must be understood in its social contexts, and these varied with the complexity of Bronze Age society. Many forms of oral tradition co-existed – from heroic songs with some freedom to improvise to religious hymns with no such freedom: from chiefly priests and bards maintaining a shared oral tradition over larger regions to more local and popular singers and reciters adapting this to local tradition (Vansina 1985; Veyne 1988: ch. 2). They were part of a specialised tradition of learning and reciting, which falls beyond the scope of our book to discuss (Foley 1995). What we wish to stress is the truly performative oral basis of Bronze Age traditions in myth and religious practice. It adds an important interpretative dimension to the archaeological contexts of rituals and iconography, just as it will become apparent that it adds a new interpretative dimension to the texts – from Homer to the *Veda*.

We propose that archaeology presents an independent method to establish the chronology and spatial distribution of religious institutions and myths based upon oral tradition evidenced in later texts (Fig. 112). Homer, *Rig-Veda* and the Irish sagas embody a stock of orally preserved songs and hymns of unknown antiquity. Although complex literary and historical methods have been developed to determine their age and internal chronology, it is only through the use of archaeological methods that they can be properly dated. It demands that objects of material culture and/or specific rituals and institutions are described in the texts, which can be verified in the archaeological record. Such is often the case, as we shall demonstrate in the

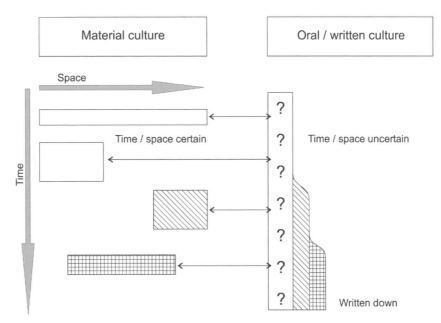

Fig. 112 The relationship between material culture and oral, written culture.

following. As epics and hymns have often been maintained and developed over long periods of time, archaeology can further establish a chronological stratigraphy for the accumulation of new traits, as demonstrated by Susan Sherratt for Homer (Sherratt 1990).[4] Where no earlier written evidence exists archaeological dating methods are primary to historical and philological methods of datings, as they are based upon contemporary evidence.

In conclusion: historical texts, such as the *Iliad*, the *Rig-Veda* and other mythological and heroic literature, preserve oral traditions that are of prime importance for understanding the nature of social and religious institutions in the Bronze Age. However, they were often written down at a later time in a specific, localised context. Consequently, their true age and geographical range remain problematic. Archaeology can here provide a complementary and independent method to determine the chronological and spatial structure of the formation of the various elements in the poems. This we shall demonstrate in the following.

4 In her important article Susan Sherratt further proposes that epic innovations took place in periods of social change, whereas epic conservatism and maintenance were characteristic of periods of social stability. This explains the 'stratigraphy'. More recently Leo Klejn has shown that the *Iliad* consists of several independent songs of different location and dating that were put together when the epic was written down. This is demonstrated empirically by applying quantititave and statistical methods to important names and synonyms (Klejn 1998). Klejn's work confirms and reveals the narrative structures behind Susan Sherratt's stratigraphy. These works effectively falsify current hypotheses of deliberate archaising by Homer to provide legitimacy. Instead we are presented with an accumulation of songs over time, composed into one epic by Homer.

6.3 The twin gods

There is one remarkable feature that links Minoan/Mycenaean and central European/Nordic Bronze Age religion, which has often been ignored or over-looked. That is the twin gods and goddesses.[5] They march hand in hand with a penetrating twin symbolism or duality in the whole religious structure and in the accompanying material culture of both societies, and may even have structured the political leadership, as we shall see demonstrated later.

Since this duality of the twin gods appears as a structuring principle both in the Aegean and in northern Europe during the early to mid-second millennium BC we should look more closely at its possible manifestation in Indo-European religion.

In a recent comprehensive study of Indo-European religion Garrett Olm-sted (1994) has made an interesting attempt to analyse the religious structure of Indo-European (IE) societies according to the same systematic methodological principles as those applied to language. He distils the original pantheon through systematic changes from a reconstructed Proto-Indo-European (PIE) pantheon, which is summarised in a series of tables of their traits. Since the earliest texts which mention gods/goddesses and rituals are going back to the second millennium BC (Hittite, Linear B, Vedic texts, some texts from the Assyrian and Mitanni empires) he has anchored certain features and names in this period.

He concludes that not only the language and institutions of many later IE cultures had their origin in PIE cultures, but also the religious structure of the pantheon of gods, many rituals and even myths. He would see this as originating in the late third millennium BC, that is Early Bronze Age cultures, as the religious structure appears already widespread during the second millennium BC. The final stage of PIE he thus dates in the period 2300–1700, that is, the formative period of the European Bronze Age. This, however, is speculative.

Here we are now able to demonstrate with some chronological precision the complex development and spread of new social and religious institutions and their local transformation throughout Europe during the early to mid-second millennium BC. Thereby it has become possible to add another explanatory parameter to the structural similarity in PIE and later IE social and religious institutions, not by assuming widespread folk migrations, but through the transmission and acculturation of institutions and their derived vocabulary and mythology. This could have been achieved by systematic travels in combination with selective conquest migrations of smaller chiefly

---

5 Sprockhoff in his classic article (1954) suggests that the twin gods of the Late Bronze Age were related to the Greek Dioskouri. Earlier researchers, such as Althin (1946), have also discussed twin gods, but have never pointed out their relationship to Minoan/Mycenaean religion.

groups, including warriors and specialists. Indeed, the Bronze Age, more than any other prehistoric period, represents the kind of long-term historical framework of interacting social systems that would account for the international spread of social/religious institutions and their mythology.

At the same time we witness a very strong regionalisation in material culture, forming Nordic, Germanic (Tumulus), Danubian and Atlantic culture groups. These regional processes of convergence in material culture were the outcome of the highly increased frequency of interaction between chiefly polities that arose with the Bronze Age, leading to the formation of new regional and local identities of shared traditions and cosmologies. With reference to historical examples of the correspondence between the frequency of interaction and language, discussed in chapter 2, we may assume that these processes were accompanied by similar processes of convergence in the formation of language and ethnicities. This would correspond to the first division of Germanic languages into Scandinavian, and west and east Germanic, and the division of Celtic into various regional groups.

Let us now return to our subject: early IE religion and its possible compatibility with Bronze Age religion of the second millennium BC. According to Olmsted's reconstruction, the prototype PIE pantheon already has the three realms, Upper, Middle and Lower, with the sky-father as the Controller of upper realms with his club or thunderbolt. This sky-father mated with the earth-mother to create the controllers of the Upper, Middle and Lower regions. The Middle Realm god used a sword, and in Ireland a 'great staff' and a sling, and both in the *Veda* and in Nordic mythology he rides a chariot. The Middle Realm gods would in some myths have taken the thunderbolt from the sky-father, reflecting competition between them over the right to use it. Gods would sometimes change names from language to language, and through time, but their functions would remain the same, as demonstrated in Olmsted's table of attributes of all gods (1994: Table 1–7). Thus in later Greek their names would be Zeus, Poseidon and Hades, all sons of Kronos. And as we now know, these names were already in use during Mycenaean times, as reflected in more and more Linear B texts. In that respect Nilsson's interpretations of continuity between Mycenaean and later Greek mythology have been proven mostly correct (Nilsson 1950).

It is not difficult to find correspondences between the attributes of the gods of the three Realms and the archaeological record and iconography of the second millennium BC. In the Minoan culture the god or the king/priest with the axe is a highly formalised and recurring figure on seals (Fig. 27), just as the young god with the staff is a well-known figure (Fig. 113). This is also the case in Nordic rock carvings, where we find the recurring giant figure with the club. The staff often has an axe at the top, but a staff with a

a

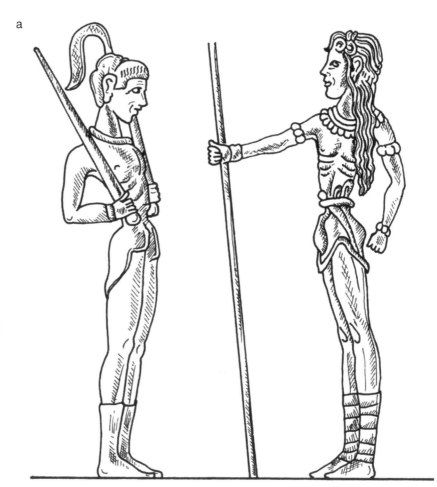

Fig. 113
(*a*) Minoan young 'god' with staff confronting a youth (after Marinatos 1993: Fig. 100),
(*b*) the 'Master Impression': young god with staff on top of a town (after Marinatos 1993: Fig. 170).

point at one end occurs in a handful of rich chiefly burials of the fifteenth century BC (Willroth 1997).

Among the PIE goddesses we find the 'Flowerful Maiden' who spends the infertile part of the year in the Underworld (Persephone). She is depicted in Minoan wall paintings, and terracotta figurines employing the lily as her attribute (chapter 5.1). Also of PIE origin is the White Cow goddess, a ceremonial cow, belonging to the lower realm. Her name, Demeter/Boand, in Greek and Irish, is associated with snakes or eels, a recurring feature of female goddesses in both Minoan and later Bronze Age cultures, including the Nordic (Fig. 114).

Irish Fergus and Scandinavian Freyr was the male controller of the Middle Realm, known for his huge sexual appetite, and huge penis often depicted on rock art and in Bronze Age art. He lost his sword trysting with a woman, and later missed it greatly in the final battle.

b

Fig. 113 (*cont.*)

Fig. 114 Kneeling goddess and horned snake. Bronze figurines from Faardal, Denmark (cf. Hittite figurine in Fig. 141) (after Broholm 1953: Figs. 316–17).

Fig. 115 Twin goddesses riding in their chariot, from the Hagia Triada sarcophagi, *c.*1400 BC (after Marinatos 1995: Figs. xvb and xvib).

We have until now made a few general comparisons between Bronze Age religious art and PIE gods, as others have done before and in more detail. Going a little further into the structure of the pantheon and their roles, however, reveals a significant and very specific PIE feature: the twin dualism of gods and their functions. The PIE Upper Realm was divided into two spheres: night (stars) and day (sun). They were controlled by two opposite, but paired, twin gods: the Mitrah and the Varunah of the *Veda* (Dumezil 1988; Belier 1995 for discussion of bipartition). Similar twin male deities are mentioned in Mitannian texts of the fourteenth century BC. So they safely belong in the second millennium BC.

From this PIE structure the pantheon expanded in several generations of marriage and internal competition. In the process, however, the polarity was preserved and extended to other god names and functions. Through this early expansion of the pantheon several of the gods are named: young, youthful or the young champion, which corresponds well to Minoan paintings of the young warrior god or the young 'Lily Prince' (Fig. 113).

Olmsted considers this dialectical twin balance a critical aspect of PIE religion, controlling dual sides of the year. Another pair of twin gods is the 'Son of Waters' and 'Nephew of Waters'. They are associated with horses, but swans or other birds also draw their chariot. They are the youngest of gods, and we shall tell their full story in the next section. However, we can easily find direct archaeological parallels to these twin gods and their chariot drawn by horses, swans or other birds, both in Minoan ritual paintings and in central European clay and bronze miniatures (Fig. 115).

Another characteristic feature of the PIE gods is their ability to take on different shapes – from bulls to swans, snakes, fishes, etc. Twin bulls thus constitute a recurring god shape (Olmsted 1994: Table 10), and Dionysus was known to appear in bull-like guise. The twin bulls were black and white, and these polar deities would fight each other in several animal guises, something we see depicted on several Bronze Age paintings, both in Scandinavia on the Kivik burial slabs, and perhaps another aspect of this ritual is seen in the Minoan bull games.

Bull heads, often twins, are of course a recurring ritual feature in the archaeological record of the early second millennium from the Near East to Crete, whereas in Scandinavia the horse is the dominant animal deity, although the bull occurs, but mostly in the first millennium BC. In IE religion the twin bulls, with golden horns, originate through several transformations from two swineherds, going through various transformations – lions, horses, fish, etc. This transformation myth belongs in PIE religion according to Olmsted (1994), and it entails many elements that would make sense in pictorial art of the Early Bronze Age. We can briefly mention the recurring use of bull horns on helmets, both in rock art and in archaeological finds. From the Early Bronze Age in Denmark we find a head application with golden horns. Also the golden horns on the bull head from Knossos and the horned helmets of the later Bronze Age belong here (to be discussed more fully in chapter 7.2; also Fig. 155).

So the gold horns as they appear from Minoan Knossos to the Nordic Bronze Age would seem to derive from and exemplify the PIE myth of the twin bulls with the golden horns in a rather concrete manner. Recurring sequences of animals are also found on pictorial art of the earlier second millennium – horses, bulls, fishes – and they conform well with this early transformation myth, to be developed and interpreted in chapter 7.

With this brief summary of the basic structure of PIE religion we wish to draw attention to some striking structural correspondences with Bronze Age gods and goddesses, especially the general concept of twin gods. In the following chapters we wish to develop this theme in order to demonstrate in concrete case studies that the dual twin structure in PIE religion is paralleled in Bronze Age gods of the second millennium from Minoan Crete to Scandinavia. Its early date is supported by the fact that the twin god structure has disappeared in much later IE religion of the Iron Age; it is not found in Nordic mythology, and Ellis Davidson could only find weak relics of this institution (Davidson 1988). In order to create a sharper interpretative focus we shall now limit ourselves to a certain pair of twins, the so-called 'Divine Twins'. Their history and functions will be presented as they appear in texts from India to the Baltic, which will then be tested archaeologically to delimit their appearance in time and space.

6.4 The Divine Twins materialised

In a special study of the 'Divine Twins' Donald Ward (1968) has defined their roles and attributes in PIE religion in some detail. The Indo-Iranian tradition, especially the *Rig-Veda*, constitutes the most detailed and important source on the Divine Twins, but the Greco-Roman and Baltic traditions also entail strong evidence. It is also clear that they are going back to the same source, as they share so many similar traits that any random or separate development can be eliminated. What interest us here, however, are the roles and attributes of the Divine Twins and their sister the sun-goddess/maiden, as they can be demonstrated archaeologically. The Divine Twins are called the Asvins in *Rig-Veda* and the Dioskouroi in the Greek traditions, in both cases sons of the sky-god. Their attributes are white horses, which draw them on a golden chariot circling the earth and the sky in a day. Sometimes winged horses draw their chariot, a direct parallel to the paintings at the Hagia Triada sarcophagus from the fourteenth century BC (Fig. 115). On sea they travel in a ship with one hundred oars, and were famed Argonauts, just as they were known as guardians of seamen. They are referred to as rescuers of sailors, and these parts from the *Veda* are in detail identical to Homer's Hymn no. 33. They are also the rescuers of the sun-goddess, to which we will return.

The Divine Twins are multi-functional gods and are also gods of light, breaking open the daylight for their sister the sun-goddess, just as they represent the Morning and Evening Star. They are known as magic healers and physicians, in Greece often depicted with snakes. Finally they appear as providers of help in battle, being themselves warriors and taking part in the battle as well. In one legend the young Dioskouroi carried white tunics, purple robes and hats, and each carried a spear.[6] In addition they were associated with the dance, and are reported to have been the inventors of the weapon dance and the flute accompanying the Spartan weapon dance.

In one aspect the Divine Twins differ from the other gods in the pantheon: although they are among the most important gods and cited in hymns more than others, they are also considered to be close to humans, having wandered among men. They frequently visited the earth in the guise of mortals. In Greece countless places have been visited by them and have participated in festivals in their honour. This quality excluded them from a place on Mount Olympus, although they had cults with priests and priestesses. But on the other hand this may explain why they are so frequently reproduced and

---

6 In Greek tradition the double hat is a shorthand reference to the Dioskouroi (Chapouthier 1934). As such hats are not common in Greece, we may here see yet another link to an earlier tradition, of the Bronze Age, where hats were used to identify gods and chiefs (see also chapter 6.5). I wish to thank Marco Garcia for this reference.

symbolised on paintings, metalwork, rock art, etc. during the Bronze Age, and why rituals with the Divine Twins were so often performed by mortal chiefs, as we shall see. Twin kings and chiefs were thought to be incarnations of the mythological Divine Twins, such as certain Spartan kings, and Nordic Bronze Age chiefs as well (Kristiansen 2001a). Finally, among their more modest attributes were two wooden poles, according to *Rig-Veda*, and this may explain why they were often depicted on rock carvings with axes on high wooden stakes or poles (Fig. 121).

In the Early Iron Age, when their role diminished, they were worshipped in the bogs of northern Europe in the form of two wooden poles with simple cuts to represent the head (Lund 2002) – a faded glory compared to the shining bronze axes a millennium earlier.

With this as a textual historical background we shall now turn to the task of contextualising archaeologically in time and space the religious/political institution of the Divine Twins in later prehistory, this meaning the Bronze Age. This will be compared with the attributes and rituals of the Divine Twins from the texts just referred to, to be considered as an independent archaeological test.

Both Ward and Olmsted make it clear that the Divine Twins originated in the early PIE period, before the eastward migrations to India, and before their spread also to the Baltic and the Greco-Roman world (whether or not this demanded migrations can clearly be discussed). Therefore we might assume that some archaeological evidence of twin rituals should be found in the Corded Ware/Battle-Axe and Yamna cultures of the third millennium BC. This would help to explain the readiness to adopt and further develop this institution during the Bronze Age, based on new foreign influences of a more complex religious and political structure. During the third millennium BC we find in the Corded Ware and Single Grave cultures of northern Europe recurring examples of double male burials, suggesting a socially and ritually embedded relationship between them as foster brothers, or twin leaders (Madsen 1970). However, there is nothing else in the material culture to suggest anything about the more precise nature and role of this twin male ritual. We therefore consider it to represent a prototype of the Divine Twins established during an early phase of PIE society.[7]

7 An analysis of twin symbolism in Eurasia during the third millennium BC would demand a separate study, certainly much needed in the light of our findings for the Bronze Age. It should be pointed out, however, that Proto-Indo-European society was most probably shaped or at least heavily influenced by its interaction with more developed urban societies of the Near East and central Asia (Sherratt 1997: ch. 18 and 1998: Figs. 1.5 and 1.6; Hansen 2001b and 2002). This may explain some of the similarities with Minoan and Near Eastern religion. It should also be noted that an archaeological determination of PIE religious institutions as belonging in the later third and earlier second millennia BC rebuts Colin Renfrew's hypothesis of a much older origin of PIE language in Anatolia, unless one separates the history of language and institutions.

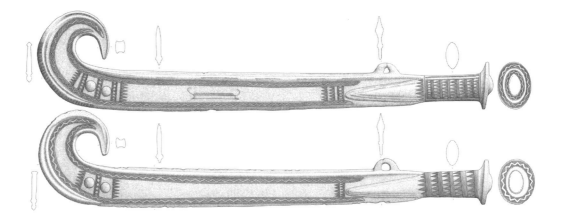

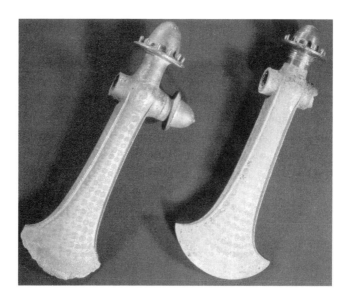

Fig. 116 Examples of twin depositions from the period 1700–1400 BC. The scimitars from Rørby in Denmark are from the sixteenth century BC and the Nordic cult axes from the fifteenth–fourteenth centuries BC (from Aner and Kersten 1976; photo as in Fig. 84).

Thus, it is only from the beginning of the Bronze Age proper after 2000 BC that the twin symbolism expands and is applied in a series of new ritual contexts. They include the double male chiefly burial at Leubingen (Hansen 2002: Fig. 1) with twin axes and daggers placed in a cross over each other like the bodies. Also from this period we see the employment of double axes on double/twin stands in Cretan rituals (Gesell 1985), and depositions of twin axes becoming increasingly common throughout Europe, especially in northern Europe (Fig. 116). The recent discovery of a bronze disc of the universe with moon, sun and stars in silver from Nebra near Halle, accompanied by twin swords and axes, is an illuminating example of the central symbols of the Divine Twins from the seventeenth–sixteenth centuries BC. It further demonstrates their relationship with the course of the sun, moon and stars. The disc clearly has Near Eastern roots, as these motifs often appear on Syrian/Mesopotamian seals, whereas the axes and daggers are produced in local central European tradition, although of outstanding quality. From this period, long-distance connections were established between the Hittites, the Minoans, the east European steppe and the Carpathians, and further on to the Baltic and southern Scandianvia, as described in chapter 5.2 (Penner 1998; David 2001; Engedal 2002). The new long-distance maritime connections were also reflected in a flourishing of ships and new ritual scenes on rock art. These distant connections between southern Scandinavia, eastern Europe and the Mediterranean and the accompanying new rituals and myths were most clearly expressed in the unique pictorial slabs on the Kivik burial from the late sixteenth century. Together with the contemporary rock art, Kivik constitutes one of those meeting places between different cultural spheres that had the potential to adopt and reshape a new value system.

Kivik: a door to Bronze Age religion

As we demonstrated in chapter 5.1, Kivik represents the port of entrance to the formation of the Nordic Bronze Age, the point of creation and transformation of foreign to local. It started a process of local imitation because of its supernatural status as a religious and political centre, and it started – or concluded – a continued process of long-distance contacts with the outside world that supported and further accelerated the process of change. One or two generations later it led to the introduction of yet another foreign value system, this time through the south German Tumulus Culture. It represented the other major influence of what after 1500 BC, in a rapid process of regional interaction, innovation and integration, became the Nordic Bronze Age culture.

In the unique pictorial slabs of the Kivik grave we find in one context all the constituent ingredients of chiefly ritualised leadership, and its religious anchoring. All of those ingredients we normally find separately, in different archaeological contexts (hoards, rock art, etc.). Kivik allows us to define the socioreligious institutional framework of ritual chiefs. Based on this, we can trace its imitation and emulation throughout Scandinavia.

Before doing that we shall illuminate some basic structural similarities between textual and symbolic meaning. Ritual texts share with symbolic iconography a level of abstraction demanding a pre-understanding

Fig. 117 Two of the decorated cist-stones from the Kivik burial in Scania.

of the religious universe behind. Bronislaw Malinowski illustrates this eloquently in his classic work *Argonauts of the Western Pacific* (1922/1983). He describes how the natives distinguish between four categories of oral tradition employed for different situations and purposes – from heroic/traditional tales through fairy tales, heroic songs and finally magical spells. Thus, their voyages are accompanied by myths and tales about the various islands, landscape formations they pass and heroic or mythical events linked to them, much as one would imagine the *Odyssey* could have originated. Heroic myth describes human origins, the origin of certain important institutions and new customs, especially linked to the Kula. These different contexts for oral performance have different structures: Malinowski illuminates this by contrasting the narrative of a famous heroic story, about a voyage leading to treacherous killing and later dramatic revenge, with the official (and very popular) song that was performed along with a dance (Malinowski 1922/1983: 292ff.). While the narrative has all the details linking the story together, the song is very condensed and subsumes the complexity of the story into short verses. We find the same contrast in much heroic/mythological singing. In the Irish myths the songs have the same condensed character presuming a pre-understanding of the wider context. This is even more true of the magical spells or ritual hymn of the *Rig-Veda*.

These increasingly abstract and condensed forms of spells and hymns corresponded to increasing ritual exclusiveness, the hymns and their rituals being the preserve of the religious specialists. We propose that the different levels of abstraction evidenced in heroic narratives, songs and ritual spells/hymns are paralleled in iconography and symbolic compositions and signs in prehistoric and Bronze Age art/rock art and decoration, most clearly expressed in the Kivik burial (Fredell 2002). They demanded the performance of corresponding rites and the singing of songs and hymns. We may even suggest that to specific signs and symbols corresponded specific spells and hyms that could vary with the composition of the symbols. Thus specific signs and symbols were intrinsically linked to performance, which again was situated in a wider world of heroic tales about chiefly and institutional origins, heroic voyages and deeds. Anders Andrén has demonstrated a similar relationship between iconography, myths and hymns for the Iron Age (Andrén 1993).

Turning to Kivik (Figs. 80 and 117) we find two compositions: one picturing performance and one picturing symbols. Performances are apparently linked to the heroic deeds of the dead chief and to the burial rituals, including the chariot race, horn blowing (music and dancing), and processions led by a priest or (twin?) chief. In addition there are some elements beyond our understanding, such as the two circular discs hanging down from a pole (the night and day sides of the sun?), held by twin priests inside a crescent, overseen at the top of the picture by the sun or the bull head.

These are the most complex and well-executed pictorial scenes in Early Bronze Age Europe outside the east Mediterranean. They share a number of specific traits with the shaft grave stelae, such as the framing, chariot driving, the gesture of the man leading the procession/the horse, bull fighting and the use of specific religious symbols. They show the institutionalisation of ritual performance linked to chieftainship and to the institution and myths of the Divine Twins. This is most clearly expressed in the twin symbolism of the slabs without scenes. Here we find the two horses twice, the two wheels of the chariots twice, two symbols with spiral ends (possibly the frame of the chariot), two ships (with lifted oars), and two ritual axes arranged on stands (of spears?) around a conical hat (a divine form in Hittite iconography). If we take the two open half-circles with the procession in front of them to represent the open circle of the tumulus (as Fig. 110), there would have been two burial mounds originally (or symbolically represented).

While one could suggest that we are here seeing the possessions of the buried chief, the double symbolism adds a specific religious meaning to them, which sets them apart from ordinary pictorial representations. These are the attributes of the Divine Twins, as we know them from the *Rig-Veda*, Greece and the Baltic. They include horses and chariot for riding around the earth, the twin ships for sailing and rescuing sailors (and their sister when she was robbed away, to be discussed in chapter 6.7). The twin axes (and spears?) represent their status as warriors and helpers in battle and the twin lur-blowers their role as master musicians. The role of twin horses and wheels we shall discuss in chapter 7.1. Thus, we propose that the twin iconography shows the ritual attributes and possessions of the Divine Twins. Ritual axes and lurs not only were symbolic representations, but were regularly employed in Bronze Age rituals and were sacrificed after use at special occasions in hoards, but never in burials (Fig. 116). This suggests they could not be in the possession of mortal chiefs but were ritual paraphernalia of the gods that demanded special ritual treatment.

What we see then in the Kivik pictorial stones is the formalisation of the myths and the accompanying symbolism of the religious institution of the Divine Twins of early Indo-European religion. While there were local religious traditions linked to twin dualism in the North they are now placed in a new and more complex religious and political setting. We further believe that this religious structure was transmitted and to some extent transformed from the Aegean to central Europe and Scandinavia during the early to mid-second millennium BC. It was part of the process of institutional transformation of European Bronze Age societies during this period, described in previous chapters. It was based upon regular movements of chiefs/craftsmen and their retinues over long distances, from south Germany to Jutland, from the Ottomani culture to the Baltic in the north and the steppe to the east, as demonstrated in previous chapters. When we consider the vast geographical extent and the temporal speed of these processes of exchange, the extraordinary similarities we observe in religious institutions become easier to understand. If we further assume that there was already a Proto-Indo-European language and religion in existence in these regions, this might explain the structural and cultural readiness to adopt and develop apparently similar gods, myths, and political and religious institutions over such vast areas. But we should not underestimate the power of the 'Great Journey' and the returning of chiefly retinues with new sacred information, technologies/foreign craft specialists and prestige goods after years abroad, as described earlier. The Kivik chief would have been either a settled foreign chief with his retinue of warriors and craftspeople from the Aegean/Balkan realm or a Nordic chief returning with his retinue from visiting some of the Mycenaean chiefly courts, where he might even have met Minoan or Hittite traders.

In the next chapter we explore in more depth how the religious structure of the Twin Gods also penetrated the social and political organisation of society, demonstrating the massive impact of foreign influences and the intertwined nature of political and religious institutions. This formed the basis of theocratic rulership, which was universally characteristic of the Bronze Age.

6.5 The twin rulers: the ritualised structure of chiefly leadership

Tracing the meaning of a symbol: the cap of the ruler and the tiara of the god

In the following we shall encircle the cosmological universe of the ruler – or rulers – by tracing a single chiefly emblem: the cap and its symbolic applications in various contexts. In doing so we employ the interpretative strategy described in chapter 1.3 and illustrated in Fig. 2.

We know from Near Eastern contexts that the pointed hat was an emblem of divinity, and the significance of hats or caps in the European Bronze Age has recently been demonstrated by Sabine Gerloff in an original interpretation of the golden caps of western Europe (Gerloff 1995). Among the Hittites it could be both tall and pointed, and rounded (Fig. 118). The extremely high, pointed hat, often with multiple horns attached, was the Hittite (and Near Eastern) symbol of divinity, only worn by gods, while the low, rounded cap was the insignia of the profane ruler, the king. Therefore, we have to distinguish carefully between these two types of headgear – the low cap and the pointed hat (tiara) – because they meant quite different things in Near Eastern iconography. The Hittite rulers were not treated as divinities during their lifetime, in contrast to the Egyptian pharaohs, and therefore the difference between the symbolic items of the divine (tiara) and the rulers (rounded cap) must be kept in mind. Following Beckman (1995: 536), when a Hittite king was installed, the officiant spoke: 'This one is now the king. [I have given] him the name of kingship. I have clothed him in [the garment] of kingship. I have put on him the cap.' The long robe and the skullcap were, together with the *kalmus*, the royal insignia and his symbols of office. The rounded cap of King Tudhaliya IV (Fig. 118) is remarkably similar in form to the caps found in some chieftain burials from Denmark. If we add the long robe, the cape and the scimitar (all found in Early Bronze Age burials/hoards in Denmark) we have a Nordic chieftain who looks extremely similar to a Hittite king.

The rounded cap is dominant in the Nordic culture of Montelius 2 (1500–1300 BC), where it has been preserved with textiles and clothing in several of the oak coffin burials (Broholm and Hald 1940). The Nordic cap comes in two versions: a complex high-quality version covered by a close pile consisting of fine, short threads ending in a knot. These are really small masterpieces and must have been time-consuming to produce. They are closely paralleled in the famous Cypriot bronze statue of the warrior god wearing a round cap covered with pile and bullhorns (also a godly symbol) (Fig. 119). Simpler versions without pile are found in some coffins, such as Trindhøj or Guldhøj (Fig. 119).

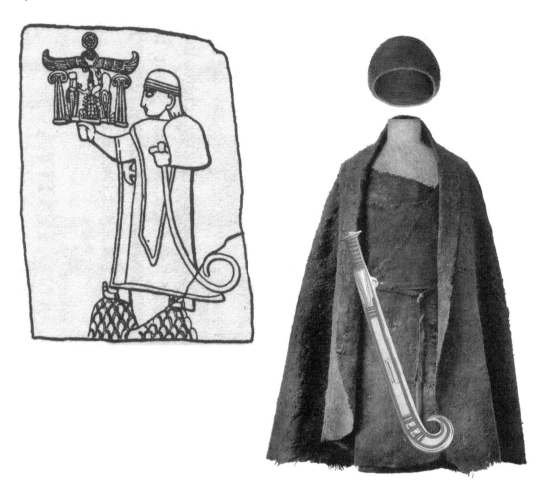

Fig. 118 Hittite round cap on a king with long robe/cloak (after Garstang 1929). Nordic chiefly dress of cloak and tunic with round cap and a scimitar (based on Broholm and Hald 1940 and Aner and Kersten 1976).

The round cap is used as a symbol in metal form in a group of rich chiefly burials, where it appears as a hat-shaped tutulus as a pair, probably used for the sword belt (Poulsen 1983). And the same symbol is applied on the richly spiral-decorated cult axes which are always found in pairs in hoards. The axes would thus symbolise two male persons (gods) with rounded caps on (Fig. 120). The shape of these axes is in fact quite similar to the Hungarian clay figurines discussed earlier (Fig. 54). If we add arms and legs to an image of a ceremonial axe we come very close to a representation of a figure with a long robe. In turn, this computer-created 'anthropomorphic axe' with its long robe shows similarities with the previously described charioteers (cf. Fig. 103).

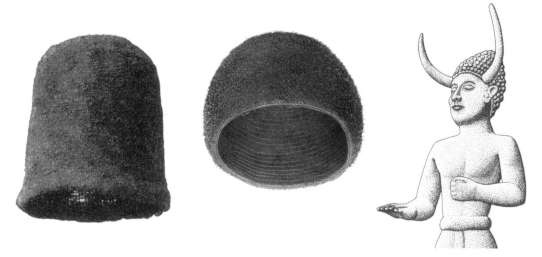

Fig. 119 Tall simple cap from Guldhøj and complex round cap from Trindhøj (after Broholm 1943: nos. 217 and 224), and Cypriotic bronze statue from Enkomi (after Müller-Karpe 1980: Taf. 188).

We meet these axes in cultic processions on rock art, often carried by two males (Fig. 121). But the twin cap bearers also materialise as bronze figurines, as in the famous hoard from Stockhult in Sweden (Fig. 120).

Here the caps are rather tall, more reminiscent of the Near Eastern tiara, but also resembling the other cap in the Trindhøj burials, which was tall (about 22 cm).[8]

In tracing the symbol of the ruler's rounded cap we have been able to encircle and define a specific institution – the chief who is also the ritual leader of axe processions in rituals. We have further got an indication that this institution consisted of twin chiefs, at least in certain ritual contexts. Would the twin leadership apply more widely, and can it be documented and defined more precisely in other contexts?

Tracing the contexts of the twin dualism

Having now surveyed the chiefly institution of the twin hat and axe bearers, we shall search for contexts that may support and add meaning to it. As we saw above, the twin axes with the round cap are found deposited pairwise in hoards, never in burials. They are represented on many rock carvings in processions, often in pairs. We may here assume a relationship in meaning

---

8 Note the loincloth of the two warrior gods, in style similar to Minoan and Hittite war-gods. Together with the (missing) movable arms – a feature unknown in Scandinavia – it most certainly indicates that these twin figurines originated in the east Mediterranean. There are two small holes on each side of the hats to add horns of organic material. Their find context – a hoard with the ornaments of the sun-priestess – indicates their mythological role in the ritual drama of the sun to be expounded in the next chapter.

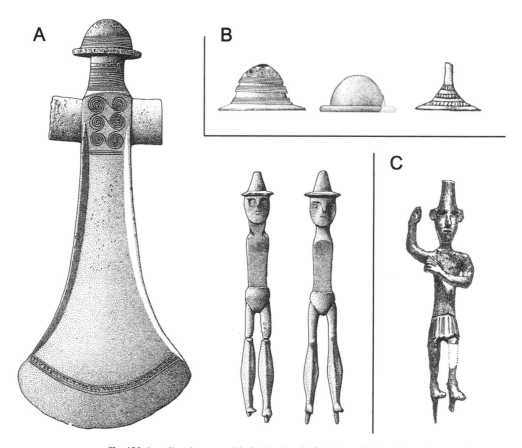

Fig. 120 Scandinavian axe with 'hat' and twin figurines with hats from the Stockhult hoard (A), hat-shaped tutuli from burials (B) and a bronze statuette of a Levantine storm-god with hat (C) found in Schernen, Poland (redrawn after Gerloff 1995: Abb. 9).

between the pairwise deposition and its employment in rituals. As they never occur in burials these axes belonged in a religious and ritual sphere, that could only be performed and taken care of by a priest or chiefly priest who would sometimes deposit the axes as a gift to the gods. Later in the Bronze Age the twin chiefs with axes appeared as miniatures, in the famous Grevensvænge find (Fig. 155: 1). Here we can observe that the ritual twin chiefs/gods are wearing a special dress, ending on the front in a flap below the belt; on the back it has rather the form of an animal tail. It probably symbolised the tail of the ox, represented by the horned helmets. This dress, however, has also been found in the context of a chiefly/priestly burial from the Early Bronze Age (Kaul 1998).

In an early Montelius period 3 burial of a Bronze Age chief with sword, razor, tweezers and knife, a piece of cloth was found in the form of a flap. This chief also had a belt purse full of amulets, and containing the

Fig. 121 Twin axe bearers in Scandinavian rock art (Simris, Scania) from Montelius period 1 (1700–1500 BC).

razor/tweezers. Furthermore the burned bones of a female suggest she had been sacrificed, a phenomenon not uncommon in the chiefly burials.

Here then we have a ritual chief and priest with special magical equipment and special dress, suggesting magical and even shamanistic functions by taking on animal guise, as we also see it on many rock carvings of ritual scenes.

The chiefly priest, however, was also a ceremonial war chief, since he normally had the solid-hilted chiefly sword and a war axe, very different from the ritual axes. But as we have seen earlier in chapter 5.4 the solid-hilted sword was not primarily for use in warfare – it was rather a ceremonial weapon, in opposition to the functional flange-hilted sword. It was artistically much more elaborated than any warrior sword, mostly decorated with spirals on the hilt, and sometimes with gold foil and amber inlays. Spirals, as we shall later see, designated priestly and ritual functions.

Thus we have now defined the joint chiefly and priestly ruler or chief. But who was the twin? It could be another similar ritual chief from a neighbouring community – or it could be within the family so to speak, as it could be the warrior chief with the flange-hilted sword, who never or rarely

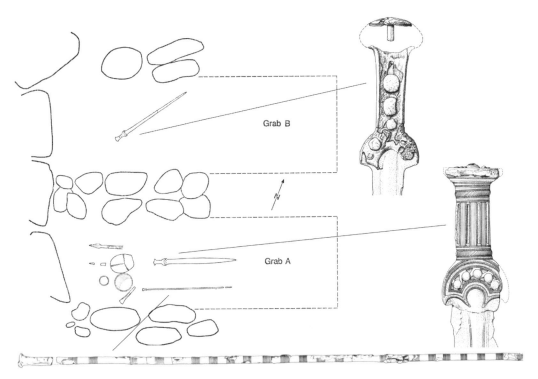

Grab B

Grab A

Fig. 122 A double burial of 'twin rulers' from Jutland (redrawn after Aner and Kersten 1978).

would be buried with items of ritual or other specialist chiefly functions. A double male burial from southern Jutland confirms that there existed a special relationship between these chiefly functions (Fig. 122).

Here we find side by side the priestly high chief with the chiefly Nordic solid-hilted sword (burial A) along with his 'twin' ruler – the warrior chief with his 'foreign' flange-hilted sword (burial B). The high chief even has a ruling staff (sceptre) of bronze, as we know them from Minoan Crete. This rather unique double burial confirms a special relationship between the ritual chief and the warrior chief – a dual political/ritual institution of leadership.[9] Normally they were buried individually, but always under a chiefly barrow. And if we again return to the chiefly cap and dress: the warrior chief also had the special rounded cap; in that, he is unified with the ritual chief, as a person of chiefly rank. Both were wearing a large cape which in later times would characterise the officers in warfare, but a cape

9 Pairwise male burials are rare. In an Early Bronze Age mound in Scania, Sweden, a pair of male twins were buried together (Håkansson 1985: 158). Both individuals were remarkably tall, almost 2 m, which makes it clear that they were biological brothers. Their height must have been regarded as something extraordinary during the Bronze Age – a particular quality of 'Otherness' that made the twins suitable for twin chieftainship. It also testifies to the healthy living conditions of the chiefly class.

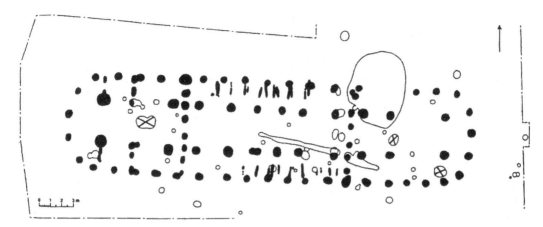

Fig. 123 Chiefly farm hall with two identical living quarters and stalling for cattle in the central part (house I). A farm hall of identical size and construction is lying parallel to this one (house II). The excavators, including one of the authors, believe that this 'twin hall' was erected after the building of the first house, since the postholes are smaller, suggesting the beginning of scarcity of wood and at least a slightly lighter construction than the rather massive timber posts in house I. But it cannot escape notice that this was built as an exact twin to house I, and placed parallel to it. (After Bech 2003: Fig. 9.)

was also worn by the war leaders in the *Iliad* and the *Odyssey*, as we have described earlier, just as we find it on the warrior bronze figurines from Sardinia.

Owing to the exceptional conditions of preservation in Danish Bronze Age oak coffin burials we can for the first time in European history define elements of a chiefly costume consisting of the cape and the cap of the ruler. We believe these two elements of dress were accompanying the introduction of the institution of warrior aristocracies in the east Mediterranean and central Europe, but can only be documented in the Nordic Bronze Age.

Having now established the dual function of rulership in the Nordic Bronze Age, we may ask how the twin chiefly functions manisfested themselves in daily life. Did there exist specific houses for these functions? The answer to that is provided by a series of remarkable settlement excavations from recent years of Bronze Age farms, and among them chiefly halls, sometimes of incredible size, 30–50 m long and 8–10 m wide. It is the typical chiefly farm hall of this period, which appears together with the new institution of warrior aristocracies and twin rulers around 1500 BC, but with similar two-aisle antecedents from 1700 BC. In these big three-aisle halls we find a bipartite architecture (Fig 123): there are two identical living quarters each with a hearth.

In the house in Figure 123 we find the central hall occupied by the most costly prestige good – stalls for the cattle. In other farm-houses there are no traces of stalls. The house has two entrances – on each side of the house

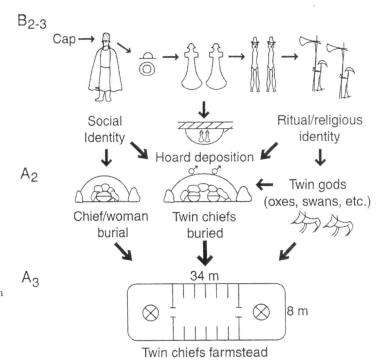

Fig. 124 The twin
rulers in
Scandinavia – a
summary of the
interpretative
structure.

close to the living quarters. So this is a farm hall for two families with their
cattle. Even then they had nearly 100 m² in the living quarters, which was
further subdivided, a truly chiefly compartment. This bipartite structure is
a recurring feature of the larger halls in the Nordic Bronze Age. We may
therefore assume that the twin chiefs were indeed as integrated into the
social and religious organisation of society as suggested by the rock art
and by the pervading twin symbolism in material culture. The farm halls
of this period range from large chiefly halls, sometimes with stalling for
cattle, to narrower and shorter farm-houses without cattle. This displays in
a concrete way the economic hierarchy indicated also by the metalwork of
the period. It was, however, a graded hierarchy within the chiefly ranks of
farm-owners, who all had the right to erect a barrow, as farms and barrows
belong together (Earle 2004).

   In Figure 124 we have summarised the interpretative strategy supporting the reconstruction of the institution of twin rulers – chief of rituals
and chief of war – but even integrated in the chiefly household, as a basic
element in chiefly social organisation.

   Another archaeological example of a house that most probably was built
for the 'twin rulers' comes from Bruatorp in Sweden (Fig. 125). It was
excavated in 2000 and it is the longest Early Bronze Age house found in
Scandinavia so far – it measures 60 by 8.5 m! It is C14-dated to 1500–1300 BC

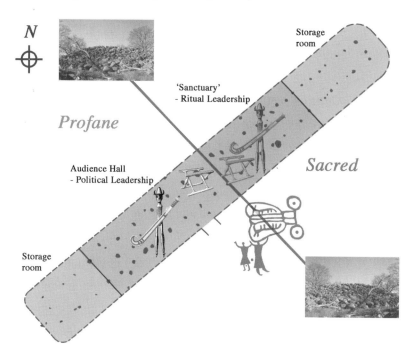

N

Storage room

'Sanctuary'
- Ritual Leadership

Profane

Audience Hall
- Political Leadership

Sacred

Storage room

Fig. 125 Large chiefly farm hall from Bruatorp, near the town of Kalmar in Sweden. A reconstructive interpretation.

(Gustafsson 2001; Lloyd-Smith 2001: 646–7). The house was built at the top of a small rise in the terrain, and around the house, at a distance of approximately 200 m, we find three stone-built cairns, most probably contemporary with the house. The structure was divided into two identical parts with two large halls and a storage facility in each end of the house. We interpret this duality in terms of the two social functions held by the twin rulers – the sacred and the profane rulership. These large houses or halls of the twin rulers represented the top of the settlement pyramid, where cattle were controlled and managed as well (Rasmussen 1999). Below we find medium-sized farms – probably for warrior chiefs – and smaller, normal-sized farms for farmers of lower chiefly rank. Finally there were very small farm-houses or labour houses (for slave labour?). The social and economic structure of society was truly hierarchical, although dominated by well-built medium-sized farms. This suggests a large and wealthy class of medium-ranked members of the chiefly lineages.

Was this a genuine Nordic tradition or was it adopted along with the new institution of warrior aristocracies? As one of us has demonstrated elsewhere, the rise of the Nordic Bronze Age, and at the same time of chiefly society, was due to a tremendous creative and organisational capacity. It transformed external influences into a genuinely new cultural and social system, with but few antecedents on home ground (Kristiansen 1987 and 1998c). By tracing structures of meaning behind symbols of rulership and through contexts – as prescribed in our theoretical chapter – it has been possible to go behind the stylistic patterns, and detect a structural pattern constituting the chiefly institution of twin rulers. We shall now briefly trace its origin.

Origins of the twin rulers

As already stated, the institution of twin rulers as it unfolded from Montelius 1 into period 2 was linked to the adaptation of the institution of warrior aristocracies during the same period. We shall now demonstrate some of the evidence supporting this proposition.

It was by the beginning of the Bronze Age proper in Scandinavia (1700 BC) that the twin symbolism was introduced, linked to the double axe symbolism. Helle Vandkilde has demonstrated the emergence by this time of a class of high-quality axes that were used not as axes, but rather in rituals and as a symbol of rank (Vandkilde 1998), and which were regularly deposited in pairs; these now also appear in rituals in rock art. From 1500 BC the institution of the twin rulers is a penetrating phenomenon, that continues down into the Late Bronze Age, where it also comes to include female depositions (double neck rings, double sets of ornaments in hoards). During the Late Bronze Age ritual paraphernalia of the twin rulers reached a high peak, and was now accompanied by bronze shields, helmets and lurs, that are often found deposited in pairs. They were used by twin chiefs/priests in the rituals, as amply demonstrated in rock art and bronze figurines, for example Grevensvænge. But during the Early Iron Age the twin symbolism disappeared. So in terms of origin one should look for evidence from the period 1700–1500 BC.

Here we can point to the Minoan/Mycenaean–Carpathian connections already discussed. The closest parallels to the twin gods and twin rulers are to be found in the Minoan and later Mycenaean culture where it was probably adopted in the later so-called *wanax* institution of the king. As Klaus Kilian has argued, the royal megaron was bipartite (Kilian 1988), and Palaima (1995) in a recent exhaustive discussion of the texts on the *wanax* has suggested that it was taken over from Crete, together with other institutions. He further makes clear that the *wanax*'s main duties were religious, although he could also have some concern for warfare. In that, he is like the Hittite king (Klengel 1996). The textual evidence makes clear, however, that there is a special chiefly or royal commander of war, named *lawagetas*, who was second in power after the *wanax*.

To this we might also add Kilian's observation that there are *two* megara on each site (Mycenae, Pylos, Tiryns) – one small, queen's megaron and the major 'king's' megaron, which are architecturally independent of each other, and Kilian took this as an indication of a dual administrative system (Kilian

1988). 'At Pylos, the duplication in both the large and small megaron of a huge central hearth along with heraldic frescoed griffins and lions on the wall, supports the idea that the two rooms are related in terms of function, though the notion that the large hall was used by the king and the smaller one by the queen has no real evidence to support it' (Rehak 1995a: 96).

What do we have here, other than the twin rulers, as we see them in the North? If Palaima is correct, then it has two implications. First, it seems reasonable to conclude that Mycenaean culture adopted Minoan religious symbols and status symbols in the shaft grave period (bull head rhytons, double axes, horns of consecration). But they also adopted the corresponding traits, such as the institution of the double axe, and the twin gods linked to them (Hägg 1984). Otherwise it is difficult to understand how the *wanax* and other Minoan institutions should appear so developed by the Palace period. It was the combination of axes in rituals, and sometimes bull horns (found on one ritual axe in Denmark), that was transmitted via the Carpathian tell cultures. Here we find a pervasive axe cult and numerous hoards with ritual axes with the pointed hat, some of them with pairs of axes and a few with bull horns. There is no clear distinction between war axes and ceremonial axes, as in Scandinavia, but in several hoards we see the combination of chiefly solid-hilted swords and richly decorated axes, as in the famous Hajdúsámson hoard.

Secondly, it implies that the *wanax* structure with its division of power between priest king and warrior king should be found on Crete. The camp-stool frieze at Knossos, with the twin gods/young males sitting face to face on campstools and lifting the cup to cheer, is the natural point of departure for understanding the institution of twin gods in Minoan culture. It is repeated in the palace of Pylos (Fig. 126). In a recent discussion Rehak (1995a) referred to a reconstruction of the Knossos frieze made by Cameron (1967) that links it to a chariot scene, with an older man in robe with diagonal band who leads a tethered bull. The female priestess or goddess on the throne is presiding over the twin males and the whole ceremony. If these additional elements are accepted we can link the ceremony to some form of initiation or ritual of young chariot warriors of high rank under the symbolic protection of the Divine Twins.

Twin gods/goddesses are also driving the chariots on the Hagia Triada sarcophagus. These scenes suggest an institutionalised structure of twin warriors/warrior gods in Minoan society, but with priestesses presiding over ceremonies and sometimes even driving the chariot (below we shall come back to the role of women in Bronze Age society). The drinking scene has much in common with the drinking ceremonies of the chiefly or royal retinue as it is known in the Iron Age of Europe, where a priestess or high-ranking woman plays a similar important role (Enright 1996). A possible

Fig. 126 Frescos from Knossos and Pylos showing two persons sitting on campstools drinking together (based on Marinatos 1993: Fig. 46 and McCallum 1987: Pl. VIIIa).

closer parallel, however, is found on the Hittite relief-vase from Inandik, dated to *c.*1600 BC, with a complete ritual sequence, including libation, bull worshipping (the weather-god), music making, dancing, *Hieros Gamos* and drinking (Özgüç 1988). Here we also find twin figures, and the final drinking scene is two seated figures, one in front of the other, one on a campstool lifting his glass (Randsborg 1993: Fig. 70; Klengel 1996: Abb. 3).

The Minoan evidence, and the textual evidence on *wanax* and *lawagetas*, adds significance to the institution of twin rulers in Scandinavia, and suggests that we are speaking of the same institution adapted to different social environments.[10] When we add the evidence of the axe god/bull-horned god, which we find from Minoan Crete through the Carpathians to Scandinavia, it seems safe to conclude that a complex transmission of religious and political institutions took place during this period. Not only chariots, but, as we shall see below, even the campstool accompanied this transmission.

6.6   Hittite religion: a selective outline

General introduction

In the previous chapters we have exemplified the potential of archaeological research to add historical meaning and time depth to ancient Indo-European

---

10 Parallel evidence from texts of a dual, divine leadership in Rome, Scandinavia and India was demonstrated as early as 1948 by Dumezil in his book *Mitra-Varuna* (1988). The evidence presented here was not at his disposal at that time. Whether the Divine Twins and the dual leadership represent one and the same or two different institutions deserves a separate study.

myths of the Bronze Age and Early Iron Age. We will therefore continue to explore this research strategy by focusing on one of the few rich contemporary literary sources of the Bronze Age – that of Hittite religion. It combines many elements from Indo-European and Near Eastern religions, and would therefore seem a good point of departure for a comparative analysis of certain mythological themes. For that purpose we will apply the rich iconographic source of Nordic Bronze Age rock art. But first a brief introduction to Hittite religion.

This chapter deals with select perspectives on Hittite religion, art and iconography, which we believe are of importance for the study of the social transmission of an elite ideology from the eastern Mediterranean to Europe during the second millennium BC.

Hittite religion was decentralised, as were many parts of Hittite life, and therefore there existed many religions in Anatolia during the period of the Hittites. We can identify local cults in various regions and the official state religion which was centred at the Hittite capital in Hattusha (Boghazköy) in central Anatolia (Bittel 1976; Gurney 1990; Macqueen 1986; Bryce 1998). The clay tablets excavated at Hattusha give detailed information about the state religion and the religious concepts forming Hittite religion.

It may be of importance to point out that for the sake of convenience we use the word 'Hittite' for the cultures occupying Anatolia during the period *c*.1700–1200 BC, which means that the Luwian-speaking people – the Hurrians – ruling at Hattusha from *c*.1400 BC are here labelled Hittites. We are clearly aware of the problems of defining what is truly Hittite, Hattian (the Hittite precursors) or Hurrian (e.g. Güterbock 1997; Hoffner 1973; Haas 1994a), but for our discussion in this book we think that 'Hittite' will do fine. Therefore, we sometimes mix Hittite and Hurrian names of divinities, for example when we speak of the sun-goddess of Arinna, Wurunsemu (Hittite) or Urunzimu, which is the Hattian name for the same goddess (Haas 1994a: 420).

The Hittite pantheon

As in Sumerian and Babylonian thinking, the Hittite worldview consisted of basic cosmological spheres such as Heaven, Earth and Netherworld, where the latter two formed one joint structure (Haas 1994a: 125). The weather-god and the sun-goddess are leading figures in Heaven and the sun-goddess is also seen as the mistress of the Netherworld, because of her nocturnal travel in the underworld from the western to the eastern horizon. Therefore, the sun-goddess has both a bright side (daytime in heaven) and a dark side (night time under the earth). In Hittite texts she is called 'sun-goddess of earth' (*Sonnengöttin der Erde*, Haas 1994a: 133) when she at night rules the

Netherworld. These two sides of the sun-goddess are indeed very interesting, and a similar dualism between bright and dark, between day and night, is illustrated by the bronze miniature from Trundholm. This magnificent piece of bronzework is one of the best existing items of 'evidence' in material culture from the mid-second millennium BC of a cosmology where the bright and dark sides of the sun are clearly expressed. This will be further elaborated in the next chapter.

A great number of divinities have been discerned by combining textual information with iconographic representations (Haas 1994a). The Hittite gods and goddesses are normally portrayed according to a repetitive scheme:

> The deities are usually distinguished:
> • by a weapon or other implement held in the right hand;
> • by a symbol carried in the left hand;
> • by wings or other adjuncts; and
> • by a sacred animal on which they frequently stand.
> (Gurney 1990: 110)

From Hittite texts we can see that kings and queens are described as 'becoming gods' when they are deceased – they are not treated as dead, they have just joined the gods and become divine themselves. During the early Hittite period, c.1700–1400 BC, the dead were usually inhumed in pits, in pithos graves or in stone cists, while cremation tended to be the dominant practice after c.1400 BC (Haas 1994a: 234). However, there seem to have existed regional variations in burial practices. For example, the excavated graveyard at Gordion, dated to c.1800–1400 BC, consisted entirely of inhumations, while a contemporary cemetery at Ilica, just 65 km away, consisted of mixed inhumations and cremations (Mellink 1956; Macqueen 1986: 134).

Springs and flowing water were important in Hittite religious belief – probably seen as links to the Netherworld – and many rock reliefs are located close to such features in the landscape:

> Traces of simple 'sacred springs' do not often survive, but a rock-monument like Eflatun Pmar, marking a perennial spring, may well be an elaborated version of a common type of open-air shrine. Other rock-monuments, such as that of Muwatallis at Sirkeli, and the much-worn 'Niobe' figure (now thought to be male) at Sipylus, are clearly positioned above flowing water, and these too may be connected with similar beliefs. A possible spring-shrine on a less pretentious scale has been discovered near Ilgin, where a spring at the foot of a hill was provided with a rectangular stone basin, whose walls were inscribed with a long hieroglyphic inscription which includes the cartouche of Tudhaliyas IV.
> (Macqueen 1986: 112)

The close connection between flowing water, shrines and rock art in the Hittite world, as pointed out in the above quotation, is extremely interesting

Fig. 127 Hittite king worshipping the weather-god in his bull-shaped form (after Garstang 1929: Fig. 12).

from a Scandinavian perspective. An overwhelming majority of the tens of thousands of rock art sites in south Scandinavia are positioned very close to water (coasts and river mouths) and in many cases the images themselves are cut on sloping rock surfaces, over which water regularly flows. The similarity at a structural level with the Hittite practice is striking, though the details, motifs, etc. differ. We will return to the south Scandinavian rock art in the next chapter.

Of special importance in the Hittite pantheon was the weather-god, Taru (Tessop in Hurrian). He is sometimes depicted in the iconography riding a cart drawn by bulls: the bull is the sacred animal of the weather-god and, as shown in Figure 127, a bull can also stand as a representation of the weather-god (Gurney 1990: 124).

Already during the fourth millennium the bull was symbolically attached to thunder and the forces of weather and the sky, and the mythological importance of the bull can be seen in the whole of the east Mediterranean and western Asia (Rice 1998).

An important religious centre in Hittite Anatolia was the town of Arinna, which is mentioned in several clay tablets but has not yet been found. According to the texts, the town of Arinna was situated one day's travel from the capital at Hattusha and the most prominent divinity here was the sun-goddess of Arinna (Hebat in Hurrian). She was: 'Queen of the Land of Hatti, Queen of Heaven and Earth, mistress of the kings and queens of the Land of Hatti, directing the government of the King and Queen of Hatti' (Gurney 1990: 115).

The weather-god, Taru, and the sun-goddess of Arinna were, together with their sons Nerik and Zippalanda, their daughter Mezzulla and their grand-daughter Zintukhi, the head figures of the Old Hittite pantheon during the period 1600–1400 BC (McMahon 1995).

An extremely powerful position in the Hittite court was that of the Tawananna – the high priestess of the land of Hatti. A female member of the ruling family exclusively held this office, and the Tawananna was mainly associated with religious rituals and ceremonies (Bryce 1998: 96). As the high priestess of the Hittite kingdom, the Tawananna was the supreme supervisor of the cult of the sun-goddess of Arinna: 'The Tawananna is the high priestess of the state and in this capacity she is also the primary supervisor for the sun-goddess of Arinna. All title holders of the Middle Kingdom founded a cult-figure of the sun-goddes of Arinna in the temple of the goddess' (translated from Haas 1994: 204).

During the Middle Kingdom, every priestess holding this office installed a 'cult-image' of the sun-goddess in the temple devoted to her, and this image was, according to the Hittite Temple and Cult Inventory Lists, a sun-disc made of gold, silver, bronze or iron (Haas 1994a: 510ff.).

In some regions of the Hittite empire we can also find a cult connected with the god Kurunta, who was the god of the countryside – 'a child of the open country' (Gurney 1990: 113). Kurunta's sacred animal was the stag and in Hittite iconography Kurunta is depicted standing on the back of a stag, holding a hooked staff and a falcon in his hands (Fig. 128).

Stag figurines have been found in burials in Alaça Hüyük, dated to the late third millennium BC, together with standards in the form of sun-discs (Akurgal 1962; Bittel 1976). The stag (like the horse) seems to have been symbolically and mythologically associated with the sun, a practice which may have been introduced in Anatolia as an effect of interaction with southern Russia/Caucasus. The famous Pazyryk mound in Altai (though later in date) contained buried horses that wore golden deer masks with antlers, which indicates that the stag was the primary carrier of the sun and that the horse could fulfil this mission if disguised as a stag (Golan 1991: 63). In this context we might further add that the stag is sometimes featured as the drawer of the sun in the iconography of the south Scandinavian rock art. One rock art scene from Backa in Brastad, in Bohuslän (Fig. 129), shows a cart with a sun-wheel and a stag standing above.

A horse god named Pirwa is known from Anatolia from the very early second millennium BC, mentioned in texts from the Old Assyrian period. This

Fig. 128 The god of 'the open lands' standing on his stag (after Garstang 1929: Fig. 15).

Fig. 129 Rock art showing a stag and a sun-wagon (after Almgren 1927).

god was portrayed in a special manner: 'In the inventory list of statuettes (figurines) of gods the statuette of the god Pirwa (from the Sippa region) is described as a man standing on a silver-plated horse' (translated from Haas 1994b: 87).

A goddess named Pirinkir can be found in the Hittite pantheon and her attributes are of specific value if we are interested in the combination of sun-discs and horses in ritual performances (the Trundholm find from Denmark):

> Pirinkir/Pirankar was originally a foreign goddess in Anatolia, whose name either is Sumerian (pirig.gal 'big lion') or may originate from the Elamite goddess Pirinkir. She is worshipped by the Hittites in the form of a sun-disc in the temple of 'the goddess of the night' in the town of Samuha (perhaps in the region south of Sivas). In the few textual remains of the ritual of Pirinkir, the horse of the goddess seems to occupy a central role in the ceremonies. (translated from Haas 1994b: 82)

From Haas' reading of Hittite texts we can see that the goddess Pirinkir was symbolised as a sun-disc and that the goddess' horse also played a crucial role in the ritual. The combination of the two (sun-disc and horse) suggests that not only rituals but also the myth of the sun-god and -goddess formed part of a wider Near Eastern and Proto-Indo-European sun cult from which the Scandinavian was derived, as we shall later demonstrate.

The sun cults in Hittite religion

If we turn our attention to the Hittite rock art from Boghazköy and Yazilikaya from the fourteenth and thirteenth centuries BC, it is possible to point out more intriguing similarities in iconography between Anatolia and south Scandinavia. For example, we might take a closer look at the famous rock relief from the King's Gate in Boghazköy (Fig. 130).

The relief possibly represents the 'God of War' (Akurgal 1962: 109), and he is portrayed in profile with a plumed helmet with horns, and cheek and neck flaps. He carries a short sword with a curved blade (or with a curved ferrule) and in his right hand he holds an axe with an extremely curved blade. He wears a short skirt fastened with a belt, and a closer look at the skirt reveals two lines with spiral decoration (Bittel 1976: 232, Fig. 268; Kohlmayer 1995: 2648). His legs are very pronounced compared with his upper limbs and the calf of his left leg is quite articulated. This anthropomorphic deity was given these attributes and features in order to present him as a divine being, thus differentiating him from depictions of mortals, such as kings or queens.

The axe, the sword and the band of spirals on his skirt are of particular interest for us, because all of these elements can be found in combination

Fig. 130 The 'God of War' at the King's Gate at Boghazköy (after Müller-Karpe 1980: Taf. 170).

in the Carpathians and south Scandinavia. Related axes with spiral-curved blade are found in hoards from the Carpathians to the Iranian plateau from the fifteenth century BC, some variations continuing into the fourteenth century BC (Müller-Karpe 1980: Taf. 282C, 366, 556A, 537A; Buchholz 1999).

The sword with the curved or hooked point has its best parallel in Europe in the six bronze scimitars from Denmark and south Sweden (Fig. 116).[11]

The northern scimitars are dated to the sixteenth century BC, making them 100–150 years older than the relief of the God of War. However, the use of the hooked sword or staff in Anatolia goes back to the late third millennium and the royal burials at Alaça Hüyük (Akurgal 1962: 112).

Finally, the two rows of spiral decoration on the god's skirt represent another striking similarity with south Scandinavia. The spiral used in this particular way – to form long chains within narrow frames – is one of

11 An important find from 1991 is the bronze sword from Boghazköy, i.e. the Hittite capital of Hattusha (Ertekin and Ediz 1993). It was found by chance during road repair work outside the ancient town, some 750 m from the famous Lion Gate. The sword represents the first real Hittite sword found in Turkey, though swords are mentioned in textual documents. It is 79 cm long and the blade is very narrow and pointed, with a raised rib from the point towards the handle (Ertekin and Ediz 1993: 719). The long and narrow blade with its ribs and grooves indicates that it must have been used as a thrust-weapon. On one side of the blade there is an inscription made by a chisel, bearing the characteristics of the Middle Hittite Period, saying that the sword was dedicated to the storm-god by Tudhaliya II after a victory (Ertekin and Ediz 1993: 721). Following the Hittite chronology (e.g. Kuhrt 1995: 230), the Middle Kingdom is dated to the period 1500–1430 (1420) BC, while the reign of Tudhaliya II is set to 1400–1390 (alt. 1390–1370). According to analyses of the patina, it is likely that the inscription was made soon after the manufacturing of the blade (Ertekin and Ediz 1993: 721; Bryce 1998: 136). The offering of the sword to the storm-god was probably executed by the king around 1400 BC or shortly after. It reminds us of the hundreds of similar sword depositions in the European Bronze Age.

Among other Hittite objects with inscriptions, we can mention the spearhead from a burnt monumental structure at Kültepe. This inscription reads: É GAL A-ni-ta ru-ba-im ([the property of] the Palace of Anitta, the King), and the building may have been the palace of Anitta, one of the first Hittite kings, c.1750 BC (Macqueen 1986: 21; Bryce 1998: 38).

Another sword with an inscription, dated to an earlier period (c.1800 BC) and with lion figurines on the hilt, is shown by Bittel (1976: Fig. 255). The inscription on this sword reads: 'To the Lord of H., his lord, has Liluanium, son of Azizum, for his own Life and the Life of his sons dedicated a sword of 12 minas "weight"' (Ertekin and Ediz 1993: 721).

A possible Scandinavian parallel to these Anatolian inscriptions on swords and spearheads is the image of a ship on the Rørby sword from Denmark (Fig. 116).

Instead of a written language, many of the rock art symbols in Scandinavia could have had a pictographic purpose, similar to hieroglyphs, where the ship image had a specific meaning. The ship symbol could have had a range of meanings depending on context, and the combination of many different symbols could have produced quite complex narratives (as the sequence of images on the stone slabs in the Kivik and Sagaholm burials shows). The image of a ship in isolation, as on the blade of the Rørby scimitar, probably had a more restricted meaning than ship images combined with other signs, as on many of the Scandinavian rock art panels (Fig. 152).

The ship on the Danish scimitar could have been 'read' by Bronze Age people as one single word, like 'divine', 'chieftain', 'sacred', 'travel', etc. Combined with the object itself – a sword of an unusually exotic form – the contextual meaning of the ship image could have formed a far more complex reading, like 'property of the chief who made a great journey', 'I sailed and learned the secret skills of foreign lands', or 'the sword of the sun-god, sailing his barque'. Of course, this is pure speculation because we do not know the meaning of a symbol such as the ship, or if the Nordic Bronze Age symbols should be given a linguistic meaning at all (Nordbladh 1978), but the fact that the sole ship image on a sword known in Scandinavia is placed on the blade of a sword of an extreme type – a scimitar – is surely no coincidence. The scimitar is known in the Near East, and depicted in the hands of divinities on seals, but in Europe the only examples (six) are found in south Scandinavia, and most likely they were all manufactured there (Gräslund 1967; Vandkilde 1996; Engedal 2002).

the most typical iconographic features of the period 1500–1300 in south Scandinavia, and it is also used in the Aegean region during the second millennium.

The rock sanctuary at Yazilikaya, situated just a kilometre from the capital of Hattusha, is the most important Hittite religious structure that is known today. This rock sanctuary is located at a spot where spring water once flowed (Macqueen 1986: 123), and according to excavations the building activities started around 1500 BC. Apart from the temple buildings, which block the entrance to the open-air rock sanctuary, most impressive at this site are the images carved on the walls of the rock. Processions of male and female divinities are shown (Fig. 131), and many of the figures have been identified as certain gods or goddesses; a king, Tudhaliya IV, is also portrayed together with the god Sharruma (Bittel 1976).

The gods are depicted with a pointed, conical hat with horns on their heads, which is an official symbol of divinity, while the king carries a rounded cap. The more horns depicted on the god's hat, the higher position he had in the pantheon (Haas 1994a: 633). Linguistic studies of the texts accompanying the rock-cut images at Yazilikaya have revealed that the language is Luwian, and the names of the divinities are the Hurrian ones.

Another prominent Hurrian divinity was the goddess Shaushka (the Semitic Ishtar), who is depicted with wings, standing on a lion. She was worshipped mainly in the Taurus region and the ruler Hattusili III made her his special goddess of protection, as can be seen from his autobiography that was written down sometime around 1260 BC: 'I tell the divine power of Ishtar; let all men hear it, and in the future may the reverence of me, the Sun, of my son, of my son's son, and of my Majesty's seed be given to Ishtar among the gods' (Gurney 1990: 145). The passage 'me, the Sun' shows that the ruler saw himself as 'the sun'. The use of this phrase, instead of the earlier epithet 'me, the king' (*tabarna*), was introduced among Hittite rulers by Mursili II (1335–1310 BC), and it represented a new way of expressing royalty in a semi-divine way, which was probably taken from the Mitanni rulers or the Egyptians. Together with this new expression – the ruler as the 'sun' – was also introduced the image of a winged sun-disc (with or without radiant spokes), which became the royal monogram (Fig. 132). However, some scholars question the Egyptian connection behind this expression:

> the appearance of the designation already in the Hittite Old Kingdom, before significant contacts with Egypt had been established, as well as the total absence of other Egyptian elements among Hittite conceptions of kingship, make it unlikely. Rather, it seems that the expression – really a respectful salutation – was taken over from northern Syria, where already in the Mari period a ruler could be so addressed. (Beckman 1995: 532)

Fig. 131 Three rock art panels from Yazilikaya (after Müller-Karpe 1980: Taf. 174).

Fig. 132 Hittite seals with a winged sun-cross (after Müller-Karpe 1980: Taf. 172).

Another sign of the semi-divine status of the king Mursili II can be inferred from his annals, where we can see that he treated the sun goddess of Arinna, at least symbolically, as his lady:

> When I, the Sun, seated myself upon my father's throne, before I moved against any of the hostile countries which had declared war upon me, I attended to the recurrent festivals of the Sun-goddess of Arinna, my lady, and celebrated them, and to the Sun-goddess of Arinna, my lady, I raised my hand and spoke . . . (Gurney 1990)

The king was the sun and his lady was the sun-goddess of Arinna; this is a striking example of how to manifest and reproduce political power by giving a leading individual in society divine status. In this perspective the choice of a female deity as a mate is logical, because the profane rulers were mostly of male sex. Here the traditional marriage ritual between different sexes, as it was known to the ordinary Hittite population, was extended to a ritual marriage between the king (sun) and the sun-goddess. Profane political power was thus secured and legitimised.

The sun-goddess was represented on earth by sun-discs made of gold, silver, bronze, copper or iron, which were kept in temples devoted to different gods and goddess (Haas 1994a: 510ff.): 'The sun-discs were mostly made of gold, but other metals, such as iron, silver, bronze and copper, were also employed. The discs were worshipped in temples of different gods and goddesses; but mostly in the name of the sun-goddess of Arinna and her daughter Mezulla' (translated from Haas 1994a: 510).

Here follows another passage concerning the sun-discs, taken from Haas' impressive work on the history of Hittite religion (1994a: 424), where the priest speaks: 'From the fathers of our fathers we inherited a sun goddess of Arinna (in the form) of a sun disc; they worshipped her through cults. The gold, however, is the property of the goddess'.

These Hittite texts provide a striking historical context for understanding the Trundholm chariot with its gold disc drawn by a horse, the bronze disc carried by four-spoked wheels from Balkåkra in south Sweden or the disc-formed belt plates found exclusively in rich female burials from the Early Bronze Age. The latter are often found together with bronze necklaces of a type similar to the large Egyptian *menyet* necklace, yet another link with the Near East (Larsson 1997: 87). In the following chapter we shall demonstrate that the religious institution of the sun-goddess and its mythology accompanied this transmission of material symbolism from Anatolia and the east Mediterranean.

6.7 The sun cult in Nordic Bronze Age religion

The sun and the horse

The famous sun chariot from Denmark (Fig. 133) was found by chance in 1902 in Trundholm's bog on northwestern Zealand in connection with earthworks (Aner and Kersten 1976). This unique bronze sculpture, dated to the second Montelian period (*c.*1500–1300 BC), shows a horse pulling a sun-disc, both mounted on a rod that is carried by three pairs of four-spoked wheels.

It can hardly symbolise anything other than the sun pulled by a horse. The disc is made up of two convex, circular halves joined together, where both halves are made of bronze, but only one is covered with a thin layer of sheet gold. This difference produces one golden 'front' side and a darker 'back' side, which symbolically may have represented the sun deities of the day and the ones related to the night and the Earth/Netherworld. The golden side of the disc is seen when the item is rolled from left to right (like the movement of the sun during daytime). The non-golden side of the disc will face the spectators when it is moved in the opposite direction (illustrating

Fig. 133 The
famous
sun-chariot from
Trundholm,
Denmark.

the sun's nocturnal travel in the Netherworld from west to east). The movable wheels suggest that this statuette was made to be used: probably a
miniature representation of the horse-drawn sun-disc to be used at ceremonies and religious performances related to the sun-god or sun-goddess.
The difference between the two sides of the disc can be linked to the duality
of the 'sun of the day' (a male sun- or weather-god) and the 'night sun' (a
female sun-goddess) as in Hittite cosmology.

In fact, the Trundholm equipage may have served as a 'pedagogic model' of
the cosmology related to the sun for Bronze Age people in south Scandinavia.
The schematic illustration presented in Figure 134 shows the disc from above
and the various features related to each side.

The golden side, as seen when moving the chariot clockwise, is associated
with daytime, light and the sky and its sun or weather-god. When pulled in
the opposite direction it is night and the horse is pulling the bronze disc
through the dark Netherworld, where the sun-goddess is the mistress. The
two points of liminality in this model are sunrise and sunset – the times of
day when the sun crosses the horizon: when light becomes dark, when gold
is replaced by bronze, when the powers of the sun/weather-god of heaven
are turned over to the sun-goddess of earth and Netherworld.[12]

12 The horse from Trundholm deserves some attention as to its origin. It remains unique also
in a Nordic context, both in terms of technological mastership and in terms of its style and
decoration. Especially its head and neck decoration is strange, and can most reasonably be

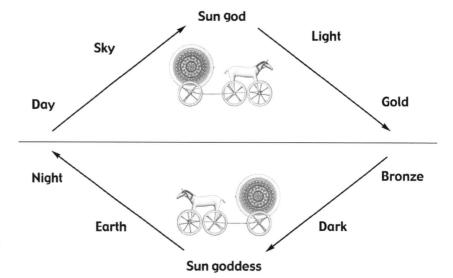

Fig. 134
Cosmology of
Bronze Age
Scandinavia
expressed by the
find from
Trundholm.

It is clear that the symbolism expressed by the Trundholm statuette could be nicely fitted into Hittite religious belief about the divine couple: the weather-god and the sun-goddess of Arinna.

But it is also clear that their ritual representations (priests and priestesses) among the chiefly elite can be identified in the burial record of the Nordic Bronze Age during Montelius period 2 (1500–1300 BC). Here we find a select group of women buried with the night side of the sun – the bronze sun-disc. In addition we find a very small group of male chiefs buried with a gold sun-disc (Fig. 19), the day side of the sun. We shall elaborate more on the meaning of these and other findings in the next sections.

explained as representing the chamfrein of a Near Eastern warhorse, as suggested by Ashbee (1989). Even if that may be questioned, the trappings of a Near Eastern chariot horse are clearly depicted in the decoration. The implications of this have not yet been considered: that the horse was either an imported piece, or cast by a foreign craftsman with an intimate knowledge of the east Mediterranean, probably the Hittite world. It shares this foreign origin with the two young twin gods or warriors from the Tågaborg hoard in Scania, found together with two simple, locally produced horses. They clearly imitate the Trundholm horse, and according to find descriptions there should have been a sun-disc in the Scanian hoard as well, but it could equally well have been a chariot. Here we may have had in a single context the complete set-up of sun-chariot, horses and divine charioters. These two finds are interlinked, both containing a mix of foreign imports and local products and imitations. This interpretation situates the sun cult and the Trundholm find in an international context of travelling artisans and chiefs, and a subsequent exchange of new religous and technological knowledge and practices. The external origin of the Trundholm master artisan is further supported by the construction of spiral decoration. This represents a special early version where the spirals are pairwise, encircled by a hatched band, and on the one side it appears in a special version where the pairwise bands are staggered, creating a shifting overlap. This structure has no parallels in the North, but is commonly found in the Mycenaean shaft grave period, e.g. on swords and pottery (Müller-Karpe 1980: Taf. 123, 1).

The sun-goddess and her twin brothers

Among the many ancient Indo-European myths about the sun-god Britt-Mari Näsström has pointed out one that has a similar narrative in the Old Indian *Veda* and in Greek mythology, but with different (although related) names for the gods. The sun-goddess drives the sun over the sky in a chariot drawn by white horses, or she can be represented by a sun-disc as well. At dawn the sun-goddess is captured and held prisoner, but her twin brothers come to her rescue so the sun can rise again in the morning. The name of the sun-goddess in Old Indian is Usha, in Greek mythology it is Eos (in Roman Aurora), and her twin brothers are in Indian the Ashvins (Ashvinau), in Greek the Dioskouroi (sons of Zeus). The myth reappears in several other contexts of captured women (Helena, originally a goddess of Sparta) saved by her twin brothers (Castor and Polydeukes). White swans also play an important role in some versions: Zeus appeared as a white swan, and white swans draw the Indian goddess Usha's chariot, just as for the Ashvins' chariot. Mostly the twin brothers are symbolised through white horses (Ashvins/Ashvinau comes from asvah, meaning horse: Olmsted 1994: 236), but their chariot can also be drawn by white swans. We can summarise the actors in the myth in a table (after Näsström 2001).

Name	relation	extra name	attribute	sister/mother
Ashvins	twins	rescuer	white horses/swans	Usha
Dioskouroi	twins	rescuer	white horses/swans	Helena

We propose that the archaeological record of the Bronze Age presents a historical context for understanding this myth and its development through time. First we shall identify the representatives of the sun-goddess and her brothers.[13]

---

13 It is remarkable that this central Bronze Age myth should not be preserved in Old Norse mythology. Once again it demonstrates that Norse or Nordic religion was reshaped during the Iron Age, most probably by the introduction of the æsir gods in the Migration Period. However, some highly significant remnants of the Bronze Age sun myth that correpond to the Vedic and Greek myth are preserved. The sun-goddess 'Sol' is pulled in a chariot drawn by two horses named Arvak and Alsvin (early-awake and very-swift). The name Alsvin is remarkably similar to the Old Vedic Ashvin. The sun-goddess is running very fast, being frightend by two wolves chasing her to take her. Their names are Sköll and Hati. The last name has no Nordic parallels (could it be derived from the Hatti in Anatolia?). In the North also the sun-goddess is being chased. But the story is never completed, it remains a relict, told to explain why the sun appears and disappears (Lindow 2001: entries Arvak and Alsvin, Sol and Sköll). The Caucasian sagas also preserve in relict form the story about the Sun Maiden and her twin brothers, riding a golden horse and a black horse (day and night) (Colarusso 2002: 351). Here

Sun-discs and women: the sun-priestess personified

Given that there was a sun-goddess, and that her activities were seasonally performed in rituals, we need to define her female priestess, which is not difficult at all. A select group of chiefly elite women during the period 1500–1300 BC carried the symbol of the sun, identical to the Trundholm sun-chariot, on their bellies as an ornament that symbolised their chosen role. These women were also wearing the short corded skirt, and we see the very same (young) priestesses in the female figurines from the ritual miniatures, to be discussed shortly.

The disc-shaped bronze belt plates associated with rich female burials in Denmark from 1500 to 1300 BC (Fig. 136) are most certainly 'akin' to the solar disc from Trundholm: the Trundholm disc is in fact made up of two belt plates put together (Fig. 133). So, this special female garment must have been related to the sun and could only be worn by priestesses devoted to the cult of the sun and its divinities. The women buried in the big earthen mounds at Egtved, Hesselagergård and Ølby in Denmark are good examples of such sun-priestesses (Fig. 135). The round plates are always placed on the belly and, as can be seen in the burial from Hesselagergård, the woman's hands are placed in her lap, forming a cross over the belt plate (Fig. 136).

This symbolism is interesting because it resembles the form of the wheel-cross, which is a symbol regarded as highly associated with the sun (e.g. Gelling and Davidson 1969; Goodison 1989; Biederman 1991; Golan 1991; Kaul 1998). The four-spoked wheels of the Trundholm equipage, along with numerous other examples of the use of the wheel-cross symbol in Bronze Age Europe (rock art, bronze pendants, pins, etc.), make a good case for a connection between this symbol and the sun.

In fact, we have an elucidating example of the intimate metaphorical relation between the spoked wheel and the sun-disc in the female burial from Tobøl in Jutland, Denmark (Fig. 137: Tobøl; Aner and Kersten 1986: 65ff.). It belongs in a very early phase of period 2, before the institutionalising of the spiral-decorated belt as sun symbol. In an oak coffin underneath a huge mound (36 m in diameter and 6 m high, suggesting an outstanding person) a woman was buried with a bronze wheel placed on her belly, in the very same position as the belt plates in other burials. Among other things, she had a necklace of amber beads around her neck, a spiral ring of gold close to her head and a dagger at the hip. Here, the spoked bronze wheel replaced the belt plate as a symbol of the sun, thus demonstrating the

---

there is also an old Vedic name for the father of the Divine Twins. His name *Tw-atr, meaning two-star, goes back to PIE language and Tocharian, and attests an old origin in the Caucasus for this myth (Colarusso 2002: 240ff.).

Fig. 135 The Egtved woman's dress.

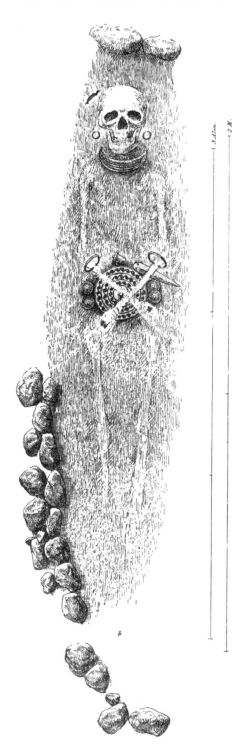

Fig. 136 The Hesselagergård woman with belt plate (Aner and Kersten 1977: 160).

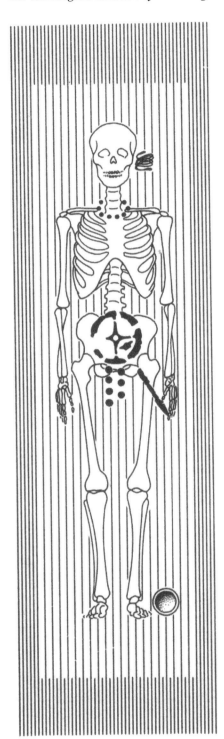

Fig. 137 The woman from Tobøl, with a bronze wheel at her belly (after Aner and Kersten 1986: Abb. 41).

interchangeability between spoked wheel and disc as metaphors of the sun and its divinities.

Without anticipating the study of symbols in the next section, we might anyhow point out the formal similarity between the dead with their discs or wheels placed against their bellies, and the rock art figures that are depicted with a wheel- or disc-shaped belly (cf. Fig. 137). It is the very same symbolism and metaphor that we meet in these rock art images – the divinities of the sun and their officiates on earth with their attributes.[14]

Women of the later Unetice Culture would sometimes wear a sun-disc with protruding star ornament, and bronze tubes suggest that some of them may also have been wearing a corded skirt, although such bronze tubes were widely used in female dress for other purposes as well. Thus the transmission of the sun cult to northern Europe could very well have taken place during

14 In Mycenaean culture there seems to have existed a similar use of sun-discs in certain female burials. In her study of *Death, Women and the Sun* Lucy Goodison has focused on, among other things, the relationship between the sun and death in Mycenaean time (1989: 84). The *mirrors* in Goodison's text, translated into the 'language' spoken in the Scandinavian context, should be read as bronze *belt plates*, as becomes clear when reading the passages that we have chosen to italicise and place within brackets. Also note that the figure numbers refer to Goodison's work, and not this book.

> Nor are the mirrors created by the rivets on the ivory mirror-handle from the tholos 'Tomb of Clytemnestra' at Mycenae shown in use for self-adornment; rather they are being [*placed against the belly*] by the two women holding them (Fig. 188a).'
>
> Persson has commented of the 'Goddess with mirror' scene shown on a gold signet ring from Mycenae (Fig. 188b) that the mirror may sometimes represent [*a solar symbol*], used in magic rites to make the sun shine (1942, 89); he bases this idea on Syro-Hittite reliefs.
>
> On the plaque from the mirror-handle shown in Fig. 188d, circular objects created by the rivet ends are again pointedly [*placed at the belly*], rather than being used for self-adornment, and the presence of birds in the women's hands would again seem to suggest that we are looking at a cult or ritual representation rather than a scene from daily life or involving toilet preparation. One might conclude that one use at least of mirrors [*or shiny circular objects*] pertained to ritual or religious beliefs. An association with the sun is possible.
>
> The [*placing of the (usually shiny) disc at the belly in the Pylos burial*] and in Fig. 188a and d provides an extremely interesting parallel to the sun motifs placed on the belly of the 'frying-pans' of the earlier periods. An emphasis on the significance of the belly seems again to be indicated by the placing of one or both of the dead person's hands in their lap for burial in Mycenaean tombs (Wace 1932, 139). (Goodison 1989: 87)

If we have a closer look at the signet ring from Mycenae it is obvious that the seated holder of the sun-disc (or mirror) is female, a sun-goddess, and the figures on the ivory mirror-handle from the tholos 'Tomb of Clytemnestra' at Mycenae are definitely also interpreted as women (Goodison 1989: 87). This iconography seems to anchor the use of sun-discs and mirrors to the female sex. However, as a bronze mirror was found as part of a funeral offering at the 'Chieftain's Grave' at Zafer Papoura (Evans 1906), this means that sun-mirrors and discs were not only used by high-ranking females in Mycenaean society – priestesses in service of the divinities of the sun. The mirror from Clytemnestra's tholos tomb and the mirror or disc shown on the signet ring from Mycenae have their parallels not only in rock art images from Scandinavia, showing sun-crosses and discs with handles, but also in a sun-disc of amber mounted in a bronze handle found in Denmark (Kaul 1998: 24–5). When looking at the sun through the amber disc, a wheel-cross, otherwise hard to see, becomes clearly visible (Müller 1920: 128; Kaul 1998: 25).

period 1 of the Bronze Age. However, if we consider the spiral to be a symbol of the sun, and grant it high symbolic value, we may link the adoption of the spiral style as an identifying symbol of the Nordic Bronze Age between 1500 and 1300 BC, to the adoption of a new sun cult. This interpretation is supported by the similar employment of the sun-disc as a cult symbol both in the Trundholm sun-chariot and in a select group of Nordic female burials. Likewise the spiral was employed on the solid-hilted sword of the Nordic chieftain, and on the ritual cult axes from the same period. We may thus consider the use of the spiral in chiefly burials and on ritual gear as identification not only of a Nordic identity of Mycenaean origin, but more specifically of a group of high-ranking priests and priestesses. This we shall elaborate on in the next section.

The chiefly priest with the campstool

We have already identified the twin rulers of the North. However, we wish to add a few characteristics that add meaning to their functions and roles.

In July 1891 a damaged tumulus in Vamdrup parish on Jutland, Denmark, was excavated. The local name of the mound was 'Guldhøj' (Gold Mound), and it was situated in arable land and therefore was severely damaged by ploughing. It contained four burials dated to the Early Bronze Age; three of these were placed in oak coffins (Aner and Kersten 1986: no. 3820). The largest of the coffins (Burial A) contained the remains of a Bronze Age chieftain. He was equipped with a cape, two hats, shoes, a woven belt, a finger ring of bronze, a bronze fibula, a shafted bronze axe, a Nordic bronze dagger, a folding stool, two wooden drinking cups, a spoon of antler and a wooden box (Aner and Kersten 1986: 31). It is dendrodated to 1401 BC, calibrated to a felling year of 1381 BC (Randsborg 1996: Fig. 3). All oak coffin burials in the barrow date to that same year.

The two cups are decorated with small tin nails (Fig. 138). They should be associated with the spoon, thus forming a drinking service. The tin nails on the cups indicate the wealth and high social position of the buried chief, because tin was much more scarce than copper in Scandinavia and it was probably regarded as more valuable than gold during the Bronze Age. The nails form a protuding star under the bottom of the cups, to be seen when lifted for drinking, and indicate their association with the sun cult.

During the eighteenth dynasty the folding stool (or campstool) became: 'A common piece of upper-class furniture; it was a status symbol throughout much of the ancient world and may even have served as a gift of royal favour in Egypt. It is composed of three basic elements: seat, legs and floor runners' (der Manuelian 1995: 1631).

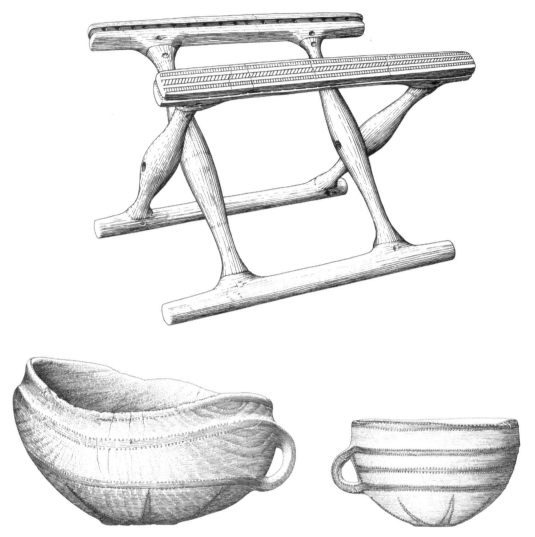

Fig. 138
Campstool and
cups from
Guldhøj (after
Aner and Kersten
1986: Taf. 16, 17
and 19).

Looking closely at the campstool from Guldhøj (Aner and Kersten 1986: Taf. 19), it is clear that this stool is manufactured in the very same way: (1) the seat (made of otter skin); (2) the legs (almost in the shape of human calves); (3) the floor runners. As on the Egyptian folding stools, the joints are between these three pieces, making the Guldhøj stool very similar to the Egyptian ones in construction principle, as demonstrated by Wanscher in precise drawings (Wanscher 1980).

From a study of Bronze Age burials from period 2 (1500–1300 BC) in northwestern Germany (Schleswig-Holstein) and parts of Denmark (southern Jutland), it can be seen that campstools are highly correlated with the presence of drinking cups, swords/daggers, axes, fibulae and (in one case) a gold disc (Willroth 1989: 93). This outfit represents the 'royal' (and perhaps 'divine') insignia of the high-ranking Bronze Age chieftains of south Scandinavia.

Folding stools are known from other places as well, and the so-called 'Campstool Fresco' from Knossos shows several pairs of males, seated on folding chairs (campstools) opposite each other and drinking from chalices (Fig. 126). It illustrates a toasting ceremony, not unlike depictions from the Near East (Ur), from Anatolia or from Pylos on the Mycenaean mainland (Frankfort 1954; Lang 1969: Plates 125–6), but of particular interest here are the 'twin syndrome', the campstools and the chalices (drinking cups).

The connection between campstools and a drinking ceremony, as shown on the fresco from Knossos and from Hittite iconography, is thus paralleled in south Scandinavian chiefly burials, where the chieftains from Guldhøj and from other places were equipped with the same combination of items: drinking cup and campstool.

The relationship between the chiefly priest leaders and the priestess with the sun-disc is illuminated by the fact that the priestess often wears a solid-hilted dagger in Nordic spiral style. She thus had some functions related to warfare and/or sacrifice in addition to or as part of her role as sun-priestess. Whether this is an early Athena goddess we here see reflected remains to be studied.

We can now propose a reconstruction not only of the ritual play of the sun's journey during the Early Bronze Age, but of the performers overseeing and acting in the ceremonies.

We are now able to reconstruct the ritual of the sun (the sun-chariot) and the myth of its journey during the day. It was performed by the sun-goddess and her twin brothers, represented by the group of female and male chiefly burials that contain the symbols of the sun-goddess: the sun-disc, and the symbols of Nordic twin rulers – rounded hats/caps, campstool, tweezers and razor with horsehead. The latter symbolises the white horses, thus indicating a divine person. They are all connected by the use of spiral decoration. The few rich male burials with a gold sun-disc are thought to represent a male sun-god (the day side according to some PPI myths), and this suggests that mythological variations and interchanging roles are also to be taken into account during this period.

We thus propose that among the Nordic chiefly elite this chiefly group represented the leaders of rituals, where they performed the roles in the mythological drama of the sun-goddess and her twin brothers coming to her rescue. The twin rulers can in this way be linked to the mythological universe of the Bronze Age. We may assume that the numerous scenes on rock art where the twins perform – either with axes as their symbols, or as

a

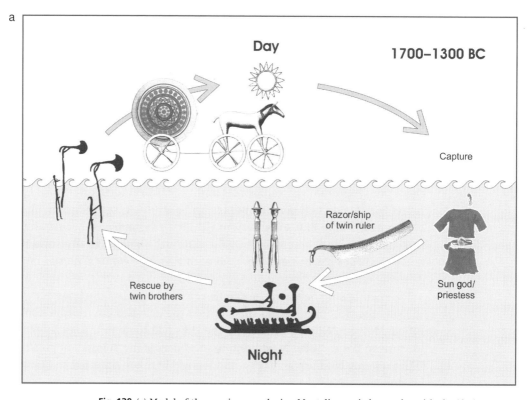

Fig. 139 (*a*) Model of the sun journey during Montelius periods 1 and 2 with the (day) sun-horse from Trundholm, twin chiefs and priestess with sun disc. Night ship with the sun and two axes of the twin brothers is represented from rock art panel in Simris from Montelius period 1. The twins rise in the morning and accompany the sun now drawn by the horse. (*b*) Model of the sun journey during the later Bronze Age with the day sun chariot from Duplje drawn by swans, priestess with drinking cup, and twin chiefs from Grevensvænge to make the sun rise. The swan-headed night ship with the sun is represented from bronze buckets with a pan-European distribution.

musicians blowing lurs – are replays of this and other Proto-Indo-European myths about the twin brothers and their deeds. This lasted during most of the Bronze Age – at least down to 750 BC and perhaps longer. Likewise we can now personify the appearance of the sun-goddess/priestess during the same period, and we may assume that the corded skirt and the belt orna-ments of later periods continued to symbolise the same role throughout the Nordic Bronze Age. They appear in numerous ritual depositions, sometimes in combination with golden drinking cups and amphorae. Pairwise lurs and ritual axes were also deposited. Thus items of the ritual paraphernalia of the sun cult, as shown in Figure 139, were regularly deposited in the natural sanctuaries of bogs during the Bronze Age.

In Figure 139 we have added the archaeological evidence just discussed in a model of the myth of the sun's journey, as it can be exemplified during the period 1700–1300 BC. During the day a horse drew the sun, but during

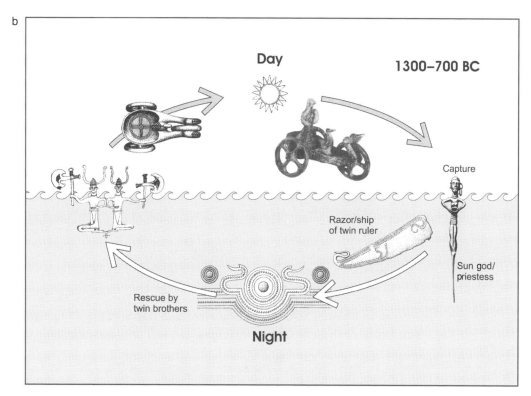

Fig. 139 *(cont.)*

the night it was carried on a ship. However, it is the strength of archaeology that it can add historical depth and dating to the early mythology. Thus the use of swans in some stories and white horses in others can be explained by the archaeological record to represent a historical change, that took place during the thirteenth–twelfth centuries BC and lasted until the end of the Bronze Age. Swan heads replace horse heads as the dominant animal on sun ships, and the journey of the sun increases in complexity. We have concrete evidence of this transformation – or variation – in the myth of the sun-goddess and her twin brothers, in a clay model of a chariot drawn by swans, together with a female clay figurine to be placed on the chariot. This famous clay model from Duplje in Serbia (Fig. 139b) represents a regional east central European variation of the horse-drawn chariot from Trundholm, except here we also have the sun-goddess added. She does not differ from other clay idols of the period, and this suggests that these were representations of goddesses and symbolised priestly roles for the women who had them in their graves. The chariot had on its platform a four-spoked wheel as a representation of the sun. Thus we have all the elements of the myth represented. Although Duplje is probably contemporary with Trundholm in the North we may take it to represent the change from horses to swans that took place in central and northern Europe in the subsequent period with the expansion of the new Urnfield burial practice and rituals. We have therefore used the model and other archaeological evidence to reconstruct the participants of the Later Bronze Age in the myth about the sun-goddess and her brothers.

During the Late Bronze Age, sequences from this myth became a dominant theme on razors from chiefly burials (another indication of the chief's role as priest), and this suggests the dominant position the sun cult still had. Fleming Kaul has reconstructed the journey of the sun in the Nordic Late Bronze Age, presenting a fascinating and complex picture of the myth, now including horse, fish, swans/birds and chariots and ships as carriers of the sun (Fig. 140). It demonstrates a characteristic feature of most religions – their capacity to assimilate new elements in a cumulative historical process.

The bronze figurines

Another relevant field of investigation concerns the Hattian plastic art, i.e. the bronze statuettes from Alaça, Horoztepe and Hasanoglan (Akurgal 1962: 25 ff.; Bittel 1976: 44ff.). These small figurines and idols are all female and they are portrayed with big ears and eyes, and marked brows, noses, thick lips and small button-shaped breasts. The position of the arms and hands placed under the breasts is also typical of the Hittite sculptures of the seventeenth century BC.

Some of the figurines from Alaça and Horoztepe have: 'identical protruding buttocks. In both cases this part of the body is so prominent that when seen in profile they give the impression of seated figures' (Akurgal 1962: 26). The eye sockets on many figurines were fitted with eyeballs of semi-precious stones or metal. The big ears have in many cases holes for ear-rings and one of the figurines from Horoztepe has a ring in her right ear (also in the left?) (Bittel 1976: Fig. 27). A female figurine (from Alaça) carries a vessel in her hands – a Hattian princess offering libation to a goddess (Akurgal 1962: 26) – while another figurine from Horoztepe is holding a child (Bittel 1976: Figs. 29 and 32).

Many characteristic features of Hattian and early Hittite female figurines are rather similar to a group of Nordic bronze figurines (Figs. 141 and 142), generally dated to the Nordic Late Bronze Age: Montelius periods 5–6, c.900–500 BC (e.g. Arne 1909; Broholm 1949: 263 ff.; Thrane 1990: 72–4; Malmer 1993).

The eleven Nordic figurines of this type come from Sweden (7), Denmark (3) and Pomerania (1), and they are portrayed with marked noses and eyebrows and button-shaped breasts, and some have big ears with earrings. Further, they have their arms and hands placed under their breasts,

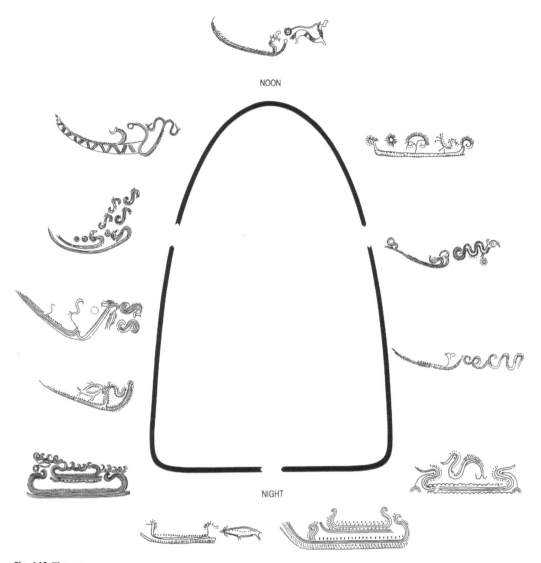

NOON

NIGHT

Fig. 140 The sun journey and its accompanying transport animals during the late Bronze Age (from Kaul 1998: Fig. 170).

in a position very similar to that of the Hattian/Hittite sculptures, and some have slightly curved legs – almost giving the impression of being seated.

Eight of the female deities are wearing what look like twisted neck rings; three figures have two to three rings around their necks (which look more like ribbed neck collars instead of rings). It is the presence of the twisted neck ring that has led archaeologists to date these female figurines to the Late Bronze Age (Montelius 1917; Stenberger 1969: 159). This was done with analogy to the full-size twisted neck rings found in hoards, often in pairs

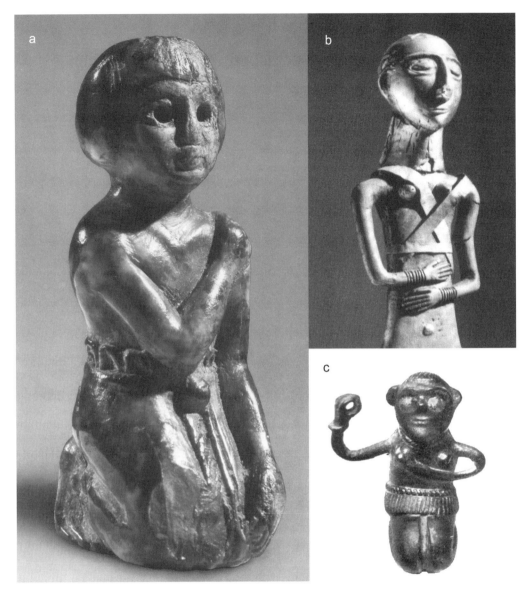

Fig. 141 (*a* and *b*) Early Hittite bronze figurines from the seventeenth–sixteenth centuries BC (after Bittel 1976: Abb. 30 and 46), and (c) kneeling female figurine from Faardal in Denmark, also with gold inlaid eyes (after Broholm 1953: no. 317).

(Baudou 1960: 56ff.; Larsson 1986: 59ff.). However, none of the figurines has been found together with other objects or in a datable context.

The neck decorations of the Bavarian Bronze Age tradition (*c.*2000–1700 BC) consisted of many rings of slightly different size put together,

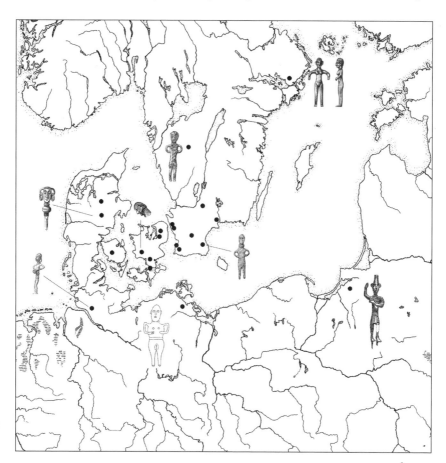

Fig. 142
Distribution of
bronze figurines
from Scandinavia
and northern
central Europe.

forming a collar-like ornament, and we have one find of this type in northern Jutland, dated to *c.*1700 BC (Vandkilde 1996: 216). This ring-ornament has been regarded as the prototype of the later Nordic ribbed neck collars (Montelius 1917), dated at the earliest to late period 1, *c.*1600–1500 BC (Broholm 1952: no. 50).

According to our present dating of the Hattian and Nordic figurines, the difference in time between the two 'schools' of artistic expression is about 500 to 1200 years, which is a quite remarkable time-gap. This difference in time might indicate that the two traditions of making figurines should be seen as totally separated, or that the Nordic tradition should be redated to the Early Bronze Age.

The earliest example in south Scandinavia of figurative plastic art (featuring a human head) is dated to 1500–1300 BC (Fig. 105). The head is sculpted at the terminal of the handle of a bronze razor, found in an Early Bronze

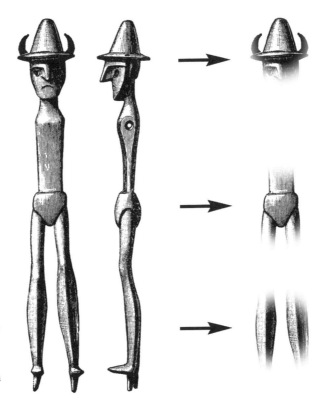

Fig. 143 The two bronze figurines from the Stockhult hoard. Here shown with added horns.

Age barrow (Tinghøj) in Denmark, together with a pair of tweezers, three long needles and a sword (Aner and Kersten 1972: no. 473).

The male figurines from the hoard from Stockhult, Scania are further examples of early figurative plastic art in south Scandinavia, dated to 1500–1300 BC. The two bronze figurines have conical hats and accentuated noses, and their calves are slightly exaggerated, in a similar way to many of the rock art representations from southern Sweden (Fig. 143) – a feature that can also be seen on the Hittite sculptures from the period 1500–1300 (Akurgal 1962: Plates 50–51).

There are (at least) three features that make these bronze figurines of particular interest for the general theme of this book: (1) the pointed hat (tiara), (2) the short loincloth, and (3) the very accentuated calf of the legs (Fig. 143). As was noted when the hoard was found, the brims of the hats had two holes just above the ears, which indicate that something had been mounted here – most probably horns.

Horns in combination with a pointed hat make a markedly divine combination if we turn to Anatolia or the Near East during the second millennium

BC (see chapter 3), so the figurines from Stockhult in Sweden bear clear evidence of long-distance symbolic interrelations. The pointed hat and horns put together is definitely not a Nordic 'creation', but a combination of divine attributes that is typical of the Near East at least from the third millennium BC.

From the 'royal' burial at Dendrá (Persson 1928: 120) there is one find of a pair of miniature horns made of lead, with fittings that resemble the kind of fitting that the horns of the Stockhult figurines must have had.

The tight and very short loincloth of the figurines is the second trait that leads us to the south – but this time to the Minoans in the first instance. A naked body, only covered by a minimal loincloth, is found in many anthropomorphic figures on Minoan frescos and seals, particularly on the figures performing acrobatics, such as the 'bull-leapers' (Marinatos 1993).

The third feature of particular interest with these bronze figurines is the way that the calf is depicted. Enlarged calves can be seen on figures on Mycenaean pottery – a fact that again links these figurines with the east Mediterranean – but this is also a feature typical of many rock art renderings. The dating of the figurines from Stockhult to period 2 (1500–1300 BC) makes a dating of the rock art figures with similar calves to the fifteenth or fourteenth century BC highly possible. For example, the 'goddess' from Fossum (Fig. 160) with her very articulated lower legs, or the 'warriors' with axes from the same site (Fig. 162), could have been depicted as early as the fifteenth century BC, if we allow ourselves a comparison with the Stockhult figurines. Therefore, we do not agree with scholars dating the majority of the south Scandinavian rock art images to the Late Bronze Age. On the contrary, the twins from Stockhult are outstanding examples of the fact that anthropomorphic representations with exaggerated calves *are* present in south Scandinavian iconography during the second Montelian Bronze Age period, as is the ideological concept of the pointed hat (with horns).

A very peculiar thing is the obvious lack of similar bronze figurines from this period in central and southeastern Europe; according to our knowledge plastic art of this type is totally unknown in this broad geographical area.

It is possible, then, that the Nordic female figurines with their characteristic positioning of the arms and hands under the breasts, traditionally dated to the Late Bronze Age (periods 5 and 6), could have been produced as early as the Early Bronze Age. This would have been an effect of long-distance impulses from Anatolia or the Aegean world during this period (Fig. 144). A similar long-distance scenario could be the relevant context for the manufacturing of the Scandinavian scimitars, taking place during the sixteenth century BC (Vandkilde 1996).

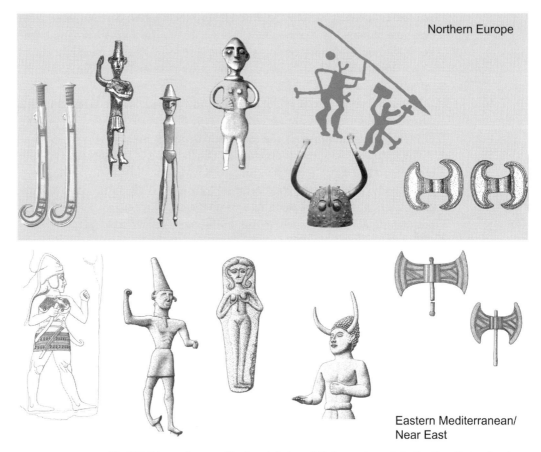

Fig. 144 Scheme for some Nordic artefacts and their counterparts in the Near East and eastern Mediterranean area. According to this scheme, the Nordic female figurines could belong to the second millennium BC.

Much more detailed faces can be found on bronze knives from period 5 (900–700 BC), and on a kneeling female figurine in a hoard from Fangel, Funen, dated to the same period, but heavily worn (Broholm 1953; Thrane 1990).

One of the bronze figurines, found in Scheren in northeastern Poland (Bouzek 1972), is definitely an imported item from Anatolia/Syria (Fig. 142), indicating long-distance interaction during the sixteenth–fifteenth centuries BC.

Most likely, this figurine represents a male deity, wearing a pointed hat (tiara) of a type well known from Anatolia (Akurgal 1962; Bittel 1976; Macqueen 1986; Gurney 1990). The tiara was the major attribute of gods and goddesses – never worn by mortals, not even the semi-divine kings or other

Fig. 145 Hittite statuette from Dövlek (after Müller-Karpe 1980: Taf. 176).

members of the royal family. Bronze figurines very similar to the one found in Poland, with respect to both the positioning of the arms and the form of the pointed hat, have been found in Anatolia. The figurine from Dövlek is dated to the fourteenth–thirteenth centuries BC by Bittel (1976: 148) but to the sixteenth century by Akurgal (1962: Plate 44).

Almost identical hats can also be found on bronze figurines from Ugarit, dated to the fourteenth century BC (Bittel 1976: 166) and figurines representing divinities exclusively wear tiaras. Apart from the tiara, the divinity from Tokat has horns on the side of the head and very accentuated calves on the legs. These two features are as interesting as the tiara, because they too are typical of the Scandinavian Bronze Age iconography. Here we find horns on bronze helmets (Fig. 155), on rock art figures (Fig. 154), and on the bronze figurine from Fogtdarp (Fig. 153). The accentuated calves can further be found on many rock art representations of anthropomorphic figures (Fig. 154).

We suggest therefore that the tradition of producing and using bronze figurines in rituals originated in the Near East/Anatolia, and was adopted in Scandinavia as part of the transmission of new political and religious institutions described earlier. The figurines add important detail to our understanding of the nature of ritual, as we have already demonstrated (see also section 7.5). They illuminate furthermore a difference between static, divine symbolism of anthropomorphic goddesses and actively performing priests/priestesses taking part in rituals, between symbol (divinity) and action (priest). The Nordic Bronze Age thus employed the whole religious and ritual repertoire of the east Mediterranean, but adapted to a different social and economic environment (see also section 7.4).

6.8   Conclusion: institutional and cosmological *longue durée*

Common to all societies is the recognition of origin, a beginning, which refers to a cosmological point of origin, such as the birth of Christ or Mohammed. This underscores a perception of cosmological continuity, a shared heritage, which may be broken only by exceptional circumstances of major historical disruptions and social transformations. In early state societies genealogical lists of kings and ancestors would constitute a time frame that linked mortals and gods together, supported by myth, such as the story of Gilgamesh, an early king of Uruk from the mid-third millennium BC. His adventures (with his 'twin' brother Enkidu) evolved into a heroic and mythological prototype about the relation between humans and gods, the meaning of life and how to become heroic and wise. It was translated and preserved for more than 2000 years throughout the Near East, as part of a common cultural heritage. It thus transcended its original cultural context and became part of a larger cosmological context that was shared by the societies of the Near East and the east Mediterranean during the Bronze Age and the Early Iron Age, who in turn incorporated part of it into their local myths and tales. It thereby exemplifies how shared traditions and local cultures co-existed during the Bronze Age, being part of what we have called the Bronze Age world system.

A concrete example of that was the shared religious and political institution of the Sun Maiden and her Divine brothers, which would be incorporated and renamed time and time again during the Bronze Age. It appeared in the written texts from India to the Baltic and Greece over a period of more than 1000 years, changing only the names, but not the basic structure of the myth and its institution. This persistence in the written record can be verified by independent archaeological means, as we shall demonstrate.

The beginning of a new cosmological time in the North was marked by a major social transformation around 1500 BC. Within one or two generations there emerged a new shared Nordic tradition in metalwork, a new chiefly culture that reshaped landscape and settlements, and a building programme of monumental barrows for the local chiefly elites (Kristiansen 1998). Within a brief period of 200 years it resulted in the construction of tens of thousands of barrows, which even today dominate the landscape in many regions in southern Scandinavia. The adoption of the spiral motif was a conscious choice to signal that the ancestors of the Nordic culture originated in Minoan and Mycenaean culture, whose institutions they had selectively adopted and recontextualised during the preceding generations. By 1500 BC, in an explosion of creativity, the new social order was materialised into a new cultural order that persisted for nearly 1000 years in unbroken tradition, yet incorporating new rituals and symbols along the way. Central among these was the institution of the Sun Maiden and her twin brothers, linked to and supporting the institution of twin rulers.

In the Nordic Bronze Age where oral traditions constituted the medium for preserving cosmological and mythical tradition, material culture helped to preserve memory. The barrows were gradually developing into mounds of chiefly ancestors, where selected members of the lineage would be buried in secondary burials, sometimes with a continuity throughout the whole Bronze Age. Likewise farms and chiefly hamlets remained in the same locations throughout hundreds of years, often from the fifteenth to the sixth century BC, leaving behind dozens of farmsteads that had superseded each other in time. In the bogs or sanctuaries sacrifices and depositions of prestige goods and ritual gear took place from time to time, and the rock art of Sweden and Norway gave eternal life to myth and stories, accompanied by sacrifice and rituals.

Thus there emerged a thoroughly ritualised, cosmological landscape of memory, where lineages and chiefly genealogies could be maintained and linked to specific barrows, where myth and rituals were retold and re-enacted in front of rock art panels and other means of memorising and preserving the old Nordic heritage. 'People, houses, landscapes and portable objects all lived parallel lives and each of them would have provided a medium for human memory. Oral traditions were vitally important, but it was through an interplay between those accounts and the biographies of things that people without written documents were able to trace their histories' (Bradley 2002: 81). And, of no less importance, the highly sophisticated art and wisdom of bards and priests. They would transmit between the generations the hymns, songs and chiefly genealogies, maintaining them as unchanged as their material world, but adding to them the specific flavours

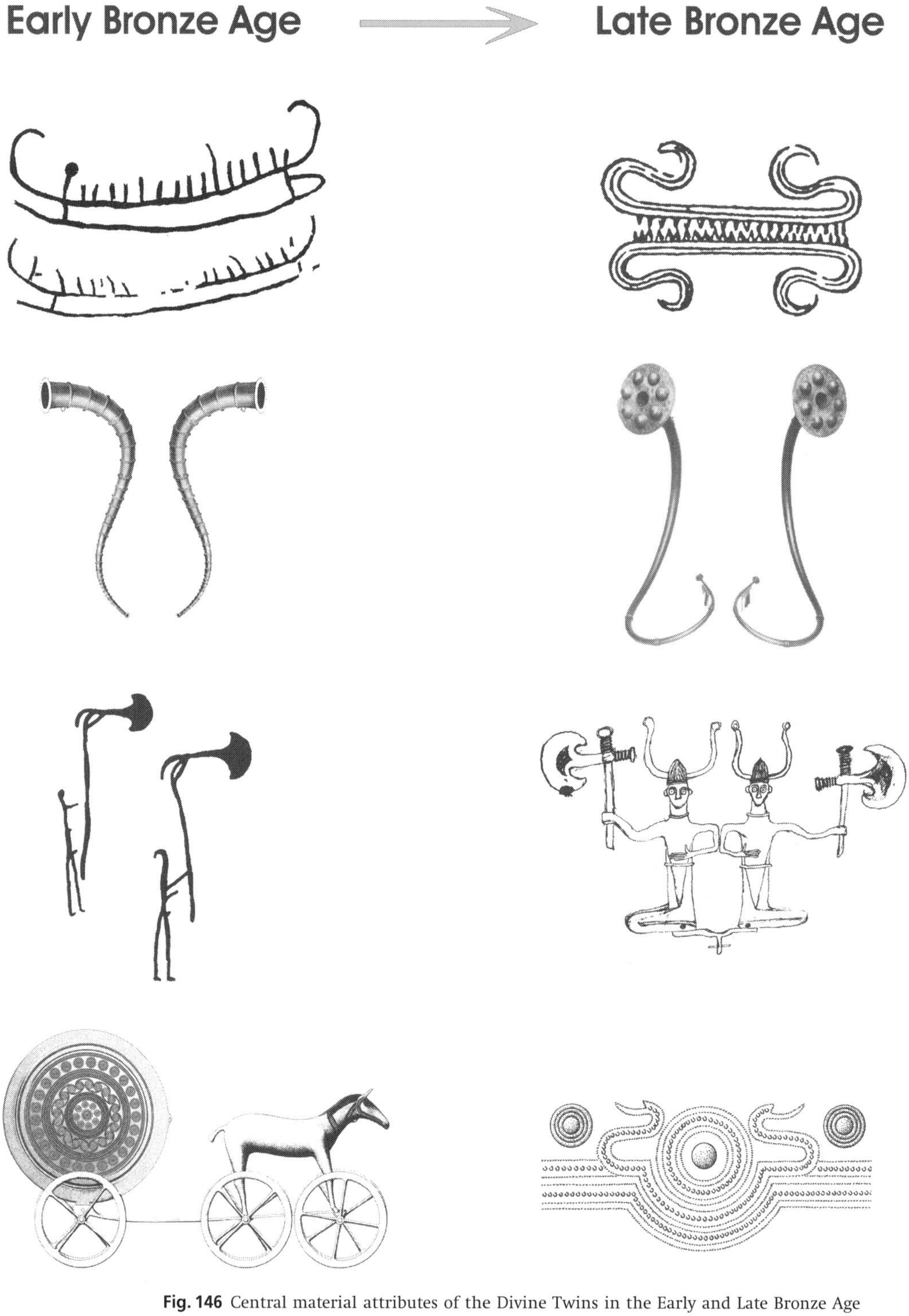

Early Bronze Age → Late Bronze Age

Fig. 146 Central material attributes of the Divine Twins in the Early and Late Bronze Age compared.

and colours of local deeds, and the new names and symbols arriving from the outer world from their travels.

In such a social and cultural environment, with its emphasis on tradition, new rituals, myths and symbols were recontextualised and incorporated into the existing repertoire, as shown on Figure 146. It demonstrates how the institution of the Divine Twins and the Sun Maiden remained a central religious political institution during the whole of the Bronze Age, especially in the North, where its ritual and material manifestations increase in size and technological mastery. In that process it integrated new symbols and forms, but the basic attributes remained intact, constituting an institutional *longue durée* from *c.*1600 to 600 BC, perhaps even longer. It is reinforced by settlement continuity and ritual continuity in the continuous use of Early Bronze Age barrows for secondary burials. The myths are further eternalised in rock art. This combination of continuity and visualisation had a strong stabilising effect, and made it easier to sustain heroic and religious memory as it was evidenced in the landscape.

During the ninth and eighth centuries BC a revival of old Bronze Age traditions swept through Europe, from the east Mediterranean to the Atlantic façade, from Italy to Scandinavia. Here we witness the final flourishing of the myth of the Divine Twins and its institutions in Bronze Age Europe. The social and economic disruptions in central and northern Europe during the subsequent centuries and the beginning of urbanisation in the Mediterranean led to the fall of the Heroic Age of Bronze and its institutions. They continued but were recontextualised, and therefore they are still preserved in the later texts of the Romans, the Celts and the Baltic region. However, a cosmological and institutional *longue durée* of more than 1000 years – an epoch – had come to its end.

7 Among gods and mortals, animals and humans

7.1 The role of animals in Egyptian, Near Eastern and Nordic religion

Animals, humans and gods

In this chapter we wish to demonstrate the important role (and use) of animals in the religion and ritual of ruling elites in Egypt, the Near East and the North during the second millennium BC. As we have demonstrated, many of the specific similarities that can be noted between the different areas are a result of interaction and symbolic transmission on a large scale. But we should also be aware that on a general level Bronze Age religions shared a perception of a unified cosmos, where animals and humans, gods and mortals, nature and culture were intertwined, much of which lived on in later Celtic and Nordic mythology (Green 1992). In this respect Bronze and Iron Age religions were basically different from a modern perception of cosmos, and therefore they represent an interpretative obstacle that needs to be recognised. One might say that Bronze Age religions maintained a unified perception of cosmos derived from a Stone Age past. It was later transformed and partly abandoned with the advent of the Iron Age, Greek philosophy and the new world religions emerging in the wake of these changes in the Near East and the Mediterranean. During the Bronze Age, however, this unified perception of cosmos reached a high point of complexity when it was linked to the rise of state formation and complex societies throughout the Near East and Europe.

To overcome the conceptual and interpretative obstacles inherent in Bronze Age religion we need to identify the most basic differences between a modern and a premodern perception of cosmos. In the modern perception of animals and nature they are subordinated to Man and represent a separate and indivisible entity. They are in the service of Man: if not always practically (wild animals and wild nature) then in a moral sense. In the premodern perception of cosmos animals and nature are powerful and equal to Man. Animals and nature took part in the creation of the universe, and the difference between them is constantly fluid. Animals become humans and vice versa. Gods take animal shape to achieve their special powers and abilities, or animals take over part of the human soul. Animals and nature are spirited.

Much of this is of course common knowledge in social anthropology, and
Lévi-Strauss has in several studies illuminated the role of animals in primitive myth (Lévi-Strauss 1962). However, it is the social anthropologist Tim
Ingold who, in a series of pioneering works, has exposed the fundamental
philosophical and theoretical implications of this basic difference between a
premodern and a modern perception of nature and of cosmos (Ingold 2000:
chs. 4 and 6). Animals can have a variety of roles, each of them defined by a
specific ritual and/or social context and activities linked to it. Hunting the
lion or the wild boar thus takes on a new dimension – it becomes more than
an elite activity, or a heroic test of skills and manhood. The hunter and the
warrior need the power of the animal, and they can transfer that power in a
number of ways: from drinking the blood and eating the flesh in a sacrifice
to employing the tusks of the wild boar in the construction of the warrior's
helmet (Hedeager 2004). The Mistress of Animals commands the strength
and power of animals; she communicates with them, shares their world
and takes their shape when needed. Animals can travel between realms and
between life and death, a vital ingredient in shamanism. Gods and humans
therefore have animal counterparts, Dionysus the bull, the Divine Twins,
the horse, etc. In the same vein nature is empowered, the gods live on a
mountain, peak sanctuaries or ritual caves are made, to communicate with
the gods on the mountain.

The snake and other animals in Egyptian and Nordic mythology

Animal symbolism played an important role in Egyptian cosmology and religion from the Predynastic period until the end of antiquity. The Egyptians
did not worship animals *per se*; instead, 'Attributes admired or feared in
the animal kingdom were thought to be directly linked with the divine'
(Houlihan 1996: 2) – the animals acted as symbols of the gods and goddesses. Already during the first dynasty some divinities were manifested in
the form of animals (Houlihan 1996; Rice 1997: 54), for example the jackal
Anubis, the great bull Apis, Hathor the cow and Horus the falcon. From
the beginning of the second dynasty (*c*.2890 BC), the divinities were often
portrayed with animal heads and human bodies and this way of presenting
the gods was also in use during the New Kingdom (Fig. 147).

The same species of animal could be associated with different divinities
in various parts of Egypt and a geographical variation has also been noted
in the use of certain animals as divine creatures (Houlihan 1996: 2).

It can be noted that the animal images in the south Scandinavian Bronze
Age rock art also show a geographical variation: cattle in western Sweden;
snakes in western and southernmost Sweden; horses in Denmark and south

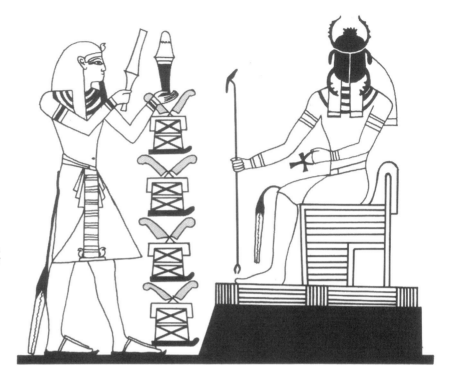

Fig. 147 Egyptian representation of the god Athum with a scarab as head. Ramesses I's grave at Thebes, nineteenth dynasty (after Wilkinson 1992).

Sweden; swine in central Sweden; birds almost exclusively in west Sweden (Malmer 1989: 21).

Originally, the Egyptian belief was that a divinity manifested itself in a sole chosen animal of the right species. These animals were carefully selected and held in temples devoted to the divinity the animal represented; the cult of the Apis-bull in Memphis, connected with the gods Osiris and Ptah, is a good example of this. During the eighteenth dynasty, many animals of the same species were treated as representatives of a particular divinity. The animal cult increased dramatically in popularity among the Egyptian people during the Late Dynastic period (Houlihan 1996: 7).

As in many states of the Near East, the horse was 'seen as a noble creature of eminent rank, worthy of royal praise and affection' (Houlihan 1996: 33), but in Egypt the horse does not seem to be introduced until the mid-seventeenth century BC.[1]

1 In written documents, horses are first mentioned during the seventeenth dynasty, and during the eighteenth dynasty horses are often depicted together with chariots in Egyptian art. As in Mesopotamia or Hittite Anatolia, the art of horseback riding is not well attested in Egyptian sources from the mid-second millennium. However, an inscription on the war-chariot of Tuthmosis IV (c.1412–1403), found in the Valley of the Kings, tells that the king is 'valiant on horseback like Astarte' (Houlihan 1996: 34). Astarte was a foreign (Semitic) goddess introduced into Egypt during the eighteenth dynasty, who was often depicted riding naked on a horse.

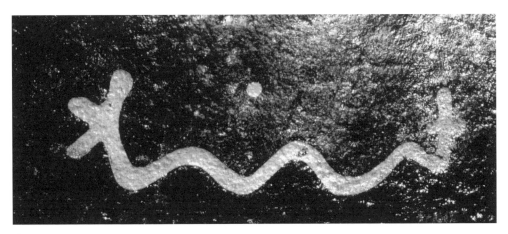

Fig. 148 Rock art showing a horned snake from Vitlycke.

The deadly horned viper is a snake used as an Egyptian hieroglyphic sign (*f*), but not so much in Egyptian art after the Late Predynastic period. The horned vipers of the desert have a long spiky horn above each eye (Houlihan 1996: 169) and this gives them a very special appearance and makes them easy to distinguish from other snakes.

This characteristic feature – horns – is not typical of any European species of snake, which makes Bronze Age images and statuettes of horned snakes in south Scandinavia rather intriguing (Fig. 148). Egypt is the only other region that we know of in Europe or the Near East where horned snakes were systematically depicted during the second and first millennia BC.

The Danish miniature snake-statuette of bronze from Faardal is one example of the horned snake (Fig. 114), and about twenty horned snakes can be found as rock art images in western Sweden (Lindgren 1997: 45) (Fig. 148).

The horned helmets or big axes were perhaps worn by chieftains in certain rituals, but the horned figures and axes cut in the rock or rendered on bronzes could in any case have represented images of divinities and divine attributes – there is no contradiction in this. The elite founded and reproduced their supremacy and power in society by controlling the unknown and by positioning themselves in a divine context. The ritual gear of the semi-divine ruler must therefore be a copy of the outfit and attributes used by the leading divinities in the Bronze Age pantheon.

If we look at images produced by literate societies contemporary with Nordic Bronze Age society, such as the Hittites or the Babylonians, the vast majority of the representations relate to myths and divinities. The figures on seals, rock-cut images and plastic art from these regions can, in many cases, be deciphered by using textual evidence, and here it is quite clear that it is mythical heroes and deities that dominate the scene. In the case of the Hittite rock reliefs from Yazilikaya, gods and goddesses are the main motifs; in a single case a king – Tudhaliya IV – is portrayed together with a divinity (Akurgal 1962).

In the next two sections we shall exemplify the divine man–animal relationship of the horse, some of its mythology and its iconographic representations.

Royalty and horse sacrifice/copulation (hierogamy)[2]

Man–animal relations can be seen as important parts of rituals and myths during the second millennium, and the horse had a prominent position in certain regions, certainly in Hittite and Vedic society and in the Nordic Bronze Age. Owing to this central role, horse rituals were linked closely to royalty during the earlier to mid-second millennium BC.

> The Indo-European pattern of theriomorphic hierogamy was clearly King and Mare, the Near Eastern and Mediterranean one Queen and Beast (e.g., Europa, Pasiphae, and the wife of Archon Basileus copulating with bulls; the Roman women ordered to cohabit with Faunus's he-goat) . . . That in Indo-European tradition the basic myth-sanctioned pattern was rather Man and Mare is made likely also by the Hittite Law Code. Unlike the sweeping injunction against bestiality in sources such as Lev. 20:15, the Hittite code expressly exempts from punishment men having intercourse with (presumably female) horses or mules, after sternly meting out capital punishment for such behaviour with cattle, sheep, and swine. The only reservation is that the perpetrator 'does not become priest', which seems to anchor the practice squarely in the warrior class, that is, among potential candidates for kingship. (Puhvel 1988: 276)

The similarity to the man–stallion relationship, as expressed by the two scenes in Figure 149, is obvious. Even if there are formal differences between the two compositions – man and horse embracing each other and man and horse greeting each other – the main purpose with both representations must have been to put emphasis on the bonds and unification between man and horse (stallion). Bronze Age Scandinavia and Anatolia shared parts of a mythological or religious context, where man–horse relations were important. Within the framework of an almost pan-European emergence of social stratification and the development of elites and warrior aristocracies during

2 In the *Dictionary of Northern Mythology* by Rudolf Simek, *hieros gamos* is defined as 'the wedding between the god of heaven and the mother goddess of earth, whose union results in the revival of nature's fertility' (Simek 1993: 146). *Hieros gamos* was ritually enacted in public, as evidenced in many rock art scenes, but also in the later written sources of Adam of Bremen and Saxo, where they express their disgust at the orgiastic scenes that took place at the temple at Uppsala. Also Tacitus alludes to *hieros gamos* in the cult of Nerthus. The tradition continued up into early modern times in the springtime tradition of folklore in which sexual intercourse took place in the fields to secure fertility (Simek 1993: 146 for further references).

Fig. 149 Bronze statuette of stallion–human relationship from Anatolia (after Bittel 1976) and a Scandinavian rock art depiction of a similar relationship (photo: Thomas B. Larsson).

the second millennium, the symbolic and ideological importance of the 'horse–chariot–warrior–ruler' complex was immense. In all probability, it was also linked to a cosmology populated by divinities such as sun-gods and -goddesses (Larsson 1997; Kaul 1998).

The two representations of man–stallion interaction as shown in Figure 149 may both have been related to a ritual with the purpose of

Fig. 150 Horse pulling the sun-disc. Rock art image from Balken in Bohuslän, Sweden.

reproducing the supreme status of a horse-using aristocracy. However, simultaneously, these images could also have represented the mythological connection between the ruler (chief or king) and a zoomorphic divinity, or the horse that pulls the sun-god (or goddess) over the sky (Fig. 150). Performance and myth are thus brought into an indissoluble conjunction, and the two spheres form an integrated part of a Bronze Age ideology aiming at reproducing and legitimising elite power and social inequality. The medium that linked the paramount powers of the sun-god and -goddess with the profane rulers on earth was the horse.

The Vedic texts describe in some detail the annual horse sacrifice the king and his wife had to carry out (Polomé 1994). After many preparations a selected white stallion is scarified. The king's wives walk around the horse nine times to symbolise the beginnings of the universe. The horse is then covered with a piece of cloth and the queen crawls under the cloth and performs a sexual act with the horse's organ. During this copulation she carries out an obscene dialogue with the priests and the other wives. Finally the horse is cut up in pieces, the king eats some of its meat and the renewal of the year, the universe and his royal power is completed. In Irish mythology intercourse with a selected white mare was part of the initiation ritual for a new king, a ritual shown on several Scandinavian rock carvings (Figs. 151 and 152). The Christian Irish text describes this initiation ritual as a symbolic sexual act, which it truly was not originally. When the act is accomplished the mare is sacrificed and the meat cooked. The King then

Fig. 151 Bulls from Aspeberget and bird-man and mare from Kallsängen. Bohuslän, Sweden.

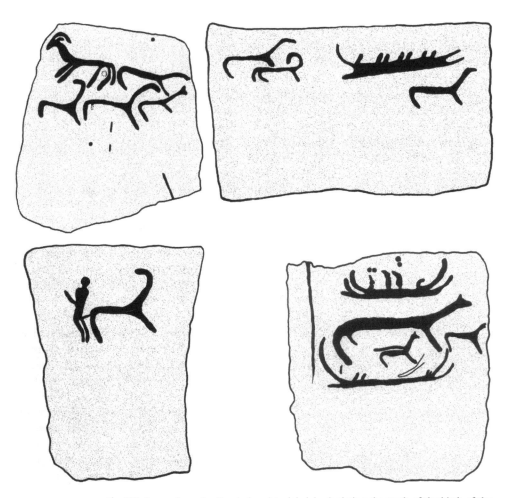

Fig. 152 Scenes from the Sagaholm pictorial slabs depicting the myth of the birth of the Ashvinau (after Goldhahn 1999a).

sits in the cauldron, eats the flesh and drinks the broth to gain the power of the divine horse goddess, probably Macha (Green 1992: 187; also Anderson 1999a).

As noted by Puhvel (1988: 276), the Hittite Law Code does not specify a mare – therefore man–stallion intercourse is also a highly possible scenario. Further, it is of vital importance for our discussion about social strategies and elite ideologies to emphasise the close link between horses and warriors (potential kings) in Anatolia (Puhvel 1988).[3]

Many of the horse images are representations of stallions, i.e. depicted with an exaggerated male sexual organ as in Figure 149. Other animals have no clear sexual marking, and in some cases the presence of a round cupmark close to the animal may be interpreted as a feminine determinative. The cupmark as a gender determinative can also be used to separate bulls and cows on the rock art panels (Lindgren 1997). In some cases (a few bull/cow images from Aspeberget, Sweden) the creatures have both a male organ and a cupmark behind the tail – a possible third gender among the bovines (Fig. 151)?

Animal symbolism is a key feature in both Hattian and Hittite iconography and plastic art from the early and mid-second millennium BC (e.g. Akurgal 1962; Bittel 1976). We also notice that animals played an important role in Nordic Bronze Age rock art, as well as in Celtic mythology (Green 1992). The Kivik and Sagaholm monuments from Sweden both have many representations of horses on the cist stones (Randsborg 1993; Goldhahn 1999a) to which we shall now turn our attention.

---

3 In his study of Hittite military texts, Beal has shown that chariotry was of major importance in Hittite warfare (Beal 1992: 141ff.). From the Anitta text, dated to the beginning of the Hittite Old Kingdom, chariotry was meant when using the term 'teams (SIMDU) of horses', and the Hittite texts show the great number of chariots that occasionally were in use; in some texts 600 chariots and 10.000 infantry troops are mentioned (Beal 1992: 146). A close relation between kingship and chariots can be inferred from these texts:

> The king frequently rode in chariots. One of the major disasters that might befall the king, according to one text, was for his chariot driver to flee from the chariot. Even worse, the other men in the chariot could easily turn on the king and assassinate him. Finally, special care was taken to use only ritually pure leather in constructing the king's chariot.

> Chariots (or models of chariots) could be given as symbolic gifts. Hattusili I, after his victory over Zalpa, presented three chariots to the Sungoddess of Arinna. (Beal 1992: 147)

The evidence for horse riding or the existence of a Hittite cavalry is more difficult to infer from the textual documents. The texts mentioning the king mounting or dismounting horses should perhaps be read 'mounting [a chariot pulled by] horses' (Beal 1992: 191). However, neighbours of the Hittites such as the Egyptians (already during the twelfth dynasty) and the Mycenaeans practised horse riding and had small-scale cavalry, and from Mesopotamia we know that the ruler of Mari, Zimri-Lim (c.1775 BC), rode horses (Beal 1992: 193). This means that riding was known and practised in Near Eastern and Mediterranean contexts during the Bronze Age, but it was not considered noble.

Hippomorphic gods: the birth of the Divine Twins

In the old Vedic tradition we find this myth about the birth of the Divine
Twins (Polomé 1994, trans.):

> *Saranyu*, the wife of the sun god *Surya*, flees from her husband in the shape
> of a mare, but leaves a copy of herself, *Savarna*, with the husband. After some
> time he recognises what has happened and starts to search for his real wife.
> In the shape of a stallion he takes to the meadow (under the name of *Vivasvat*
> 'the lightning') where his wife is grazing (under the name of *Asvini* 'mare').
> From their horny copulation came the Divine Twins (*Asvinau*).[4]

We propose that this charming story is being narrated on the pictorial
slabs of the Sagaholm barrow. It is dominated by horses and ships (the representations of the Divine Twins) and a group of images, seen on Figure 152,
corresponds well to the myth. From left to right we see first, in no. 31, the
queen grazing in the meadow with other mares, looking back and detect-
ing her husband (the looking back position signals sexual arousal). There is
also a horned goat, whose role is unclear. On slab B (not depicted) the stallion (Vivasvat), runs after his wife (Asvini), who looks back, ready for copulation. Three slabs show the copulation: no. 26 shows stallion and mare,
whereas on no. 30 the god in his human shape copulates with the mare.
This may also allude to an initiation rite for a new chief/king. On no. 23
(not depicted) both the stallion and the man seem to copulate. Finally no. 6
shows the father with the two newborn *asvinau*, their small size alluding
to foals. Alternatively it could show the birth situation, with a line linking
the mother horse and the foal, partly broken on the slab. The two ships also
symbolise the role of the Divine Twins as rescuers of ships and sailors. On
nos. 4 and 8 (not depicted) we probably see the mother and her twins, now
grown up (the twins shown with all four legs, the mother only with one).
Then follow several slabs where the Divine Twins are depicted on their own
(on no. 32 with a ship).

The closed contexts of the pictorial slabs at Sagaholm and Kivik, or the
bronze horn from Wismar, offer an opportunity to study the full, original
context of an iconographic world that we have attempted to decode. It shows
the potential of interpretative strategies based upon the knowledge derived
from oral tradition in the old Indic, Hittite and Irish texts. The iconography
of the Nordic Bronze Age correspondingly provides an independent archaeological confirmation of the temporal and spatial distribution of the myths.

---

4 In Greek mythology this story is preserved as a relic. Here it is about the begetting of the
first horse, called Arion. 'Poseidon sired this horse, turning himself into a stallion, when the
goddess fled from him and turned into a mare to escape' (Burkert 1979: 127). The offspring
from this horse adventure of Demeter and Poseidon were twins.

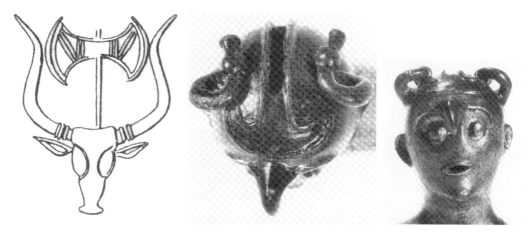

Fig. 153 Minoan ox head with horns and a double axe between the horns. Similar image from Late Bronze Age head from Fogtdarp in Southern Sweden (photo after L. Larsson 1974).

In the following we shall go one step further and compare the structure of east Mediterranean religion with the Nordic evidence (section 7.4).

7.2   Horns and horned gods

Before doing that, we will briefly summarise the evidence from representations of the horned bull – in Greece sometimes depicted with the attribute of Zeus between the horns: the double axe. Zeus himself appeared in the shape of a bull in the myth about Minos and the labyrinth – another hierogamy. When the double axe is placed as an attribute to the bull horns we should perhaps rather see this as an additional function linked to the thunder-god, who also appears as the Divine Twins. Thus throughout the Bronze Age ox horns and double axes remained divine symbols of the thunder-god and the master of the gods. In Scandinavia, as in Minoan Crete they were often associated in ritual and iconography (Fig. 153).

Representations of horns and horned gods are known in many parts of the Near East and on the islands of Crete and Cyprus. The Minoan horns of consecration are perhaps the most famous and the horns relate to the bull cult practised on Crete. In iconography it is exemplified on the Minoan gold cups found in a tomb at Vapheio dated to *c.*1500 BC. An example of a horned deity produced by a Minoan artisan can be seen on a sealstone from Knossos, showing the Mistress of Animals goddess (Warren 1989: 97). This sealstone is dated to the sixteenth–fifteenth centuries BC.

The examples of horn-bearing anthropomorphic images, helmets and statuettes shown in Figure 155 are merely a few representatives of this 'genre'. The oldest in this selective collection of horned divinities (no. 2)

Fig. 154 Rock art from Bohuslän, Sweden, showing horned divinities.

is the Mesopotamian picture on the victory stele of King Naram-Sin (*c.*2260–2223 BC), showing the king wearing a horned helmet, an attribute normally worn only by gods (Kuhrt 1995: 51). The reason for the divinisation of Naram-Sin during his lifetime can be found in an inscription on a copper statue from northern Iraq:

> Naram-Sin, the mighty king of Agade: when the four corners of the world opposed him with hostility, he remained victorious in nine battles because of the love of Ishtar and even took the king who had campaigned against him prisoner. Because he succeeded when heavily pressed in maintaining his city in strength, his city [i.e. its inhabitants] implored Ishtar of Eanna, Enlil of Nippur, Dagan of Tuttul [near confluence of Balikh and Euphrates], Ninhursanga of Kesh, Enki of Eridu, Sin of Ur, Shamash of Sippar, Nergal of Kutha to have him [Naram-Sin] as the god of their city Agade and they built him a temple in the midst of Agade. (Farber 1983)

Fig. 155 Representations of horned divinities from the Near East, Cyprus and Europe.
(1) Bronze figurines from Grevensvænge, Denmark, (2) image from victory stele of Naram-
Sin, Mesopotamia, (3) Neo-Hittite representation of two bull-men with winged sun, (4)
horned helmet from Viksø, Denmark (Late Bronze Age), (5) gold-plated horned headpiece
from Bregninge, Denmark (Early Bronze Age), (6) bronze figurine from Enkomi, Cyprus,
(7) rock art representation of horned helmets (Late Bronze Age).

Because of his heroic strength and great victories in nine battles (due to his love of the goddess Ishtar) the gods decided to make him the city-god of Agade, and therefore he was allowed to carry the divine attribute: the horned helmet. The wars and victorious battles were the result of the king's extensive campaigns, reaching from Syria to Iran, and the great campaigns (journeys) to foreign lands gave Naram-Sin increased power of both profane and divine nature.

The Neo-Hittite example (no. 3) is a rock-cut relief featuring two bull-men holding an emblem of the winged sun, and dated to about the same period (*c.*1000–900 BC) are the figurines from Grevensvænge in Denmark (no. 1, Broholm 1953), of which only one is preserved today.

The bronze figurine from Enkomi, Cyprus (no. 6), also wears a horned helmet and the conical top of the helmet is quite similar in style to that of both Naram-Sin and the twin gods of Grevensvænge (see Fig. 155). The shape of the horns from the Grevensvænge find differ from the other examples presented in Figure 155 because they are S-shaped, resembling the big lurs. A similar shape of the horns is characteristic also of the two full-size bronze helmets found at Viksø in Denmark (one shown in Fig. 155, no. 4), dated to *c.*1000 BC. When the two horn-bearing chiefs played the lurs, as seen on several rock carvings, the lurs imitated two gigantic ox horns. This once again stresses the powerful symbolism of the horned gods. An even older Danish example of similar ritual requisites, dated to *c.*1500–1300 BC, has been found in a bog in Bregninge on Zeeland (Aner and Kersten 1976: no. 9701). A thin gold sheet covers the spiral-decorated plate between the horns, and this pair of horns was most certainly a very prestigious cult object (Fig. 155: no. 5). The gold-plated horns indicate familiarity with the similar Mycenaean ritual tradition, as described earlier. They could have been employed on a horse, turning it into a goat-like horse, as in Figure 115 from Hagia Triada. This could be a relic of an old Indo-European tradition of goats drawing the chariot, as preserved in Norse mythology.

The Bronze Age rock art of western Sweden shows many examples of anthropomorphic images with horns (no. 7). The horns often tend to replace the head, instead of being placed on top of it, and the beings usually carry swords, spears and axes.

It is obvious that in the eastern Mediterranean, Asia Minor and the Near East horned anthropomorphic beings or those with horned helmets represented divinities. The divinities were very close to the ruling elite families and sometimes, as in the case of Naram-Sin, the horns symbolised a divine ruler. The relationship between divinity and leadership in south Scandinavia may also have been a close one – the presence of horned helmets and other 'imported' or 'copied' royal paraphernalia of Mediterranean or Oriental origin favours such an interpretation. This conclusion leads on to a broader comparison between Scandinavian rock art/ritual and east Mediterranean/Near Eastern ritual practice.

7.3 South Scandinavian rock art and ritual: the propagation of an elite ideology

In an elaborate analysis of Minoan religion (1993), Nano Marinatos has shown that both ritual performances (by an elite) and divinities were depicted in Minoan iconography. The famous wall painting of the 'Priest-King' or 'Lily Prince' from Knossos, restored by Evans, may well represent images of deities, as suggested recently by Niemeier (1987). It is not always easy to distinguish between renderings of 'real' mythological deities and renderings of god/goddess impersonation ceremonies. According to Marinatos, impersonation ceremonies were commonly practised on Crete during the Palace period, and these ritual performances made cult statues (which were the principal foci of the cult in the Orient) unnecessary in Minoan religion (Marinatos 1993: 243). Despite this difference, Marinatos recognises many similarities between the Minoan and Egyptian/Near Eastern religious iconography (Marinatos 1993: 242):

1 the emphasis on death and regeneration
2 the concept of a fertility goddess and the young hunter/warrior god
3 sacred marriage of a divine pair
4 the use of nature imagery as a framework for cyclical regeneration
5 ritual hunting and animal-based metaphors

On the social level, Marinatos points out another important similarity: 'The use of monumental visual art (mostly wall paintings in the case of Crete) for the propagation of official ideology' (1993: 242). She uses these general similarities as a way of placing Minoan Crete in its east Mediterranean religious context. Even if the similarities in iconography between the Near East, Egypt and Crete are of a general nature, as stressed by Marinatos (1993: 242), they anyhow suggest some form of interaction, making a transfer of certain general religious ideas (or iconographical concepts) possible.

We go one step further and propose that Marinatos' five themes may be applied more widely to characterise a Bronze Age religious structure that shared these basic elements from the Mediterranean to northern Europe. During the Bronze Age it would undergo changes over time and develop regional and local variations. Despite that, it is believed that behind such variation it is still possible to trace the underlying or basic religious manifestations. They are general enough to be identifiable across various local gods and rituals, and yet specific enough to mark them out as different from later Iron Age and earlier Neolithic religions. An illustration of this was recently provided by Marinatos in her analysis of the religious institution/goddess 'Mistress of Animals' (Marinatos 2000).

In the following, we shall take Marinatos' five religious characteristics listed above and see if they are applicable to the south Scandinavian rock art images and ritual practices from the second and early first millennia BC. We have chosen Scandinavia because of its rich iconographic evidence, and we will supply further examples covering the whole Bronze Age, because of its institutional continuity in Scandinavia (chapter 6.8).

A similarity between the eastern Mediterranean and the south Scandinavian social contexts that can immediately be noted is 'the use of monumental visual art' (Marinatos 1993: 242). Nowhere in Europe during the second millennium is this tradition as strong as in parts of south Scandinavia, where the rock art images of southern Sweden are of particular significance (Nordbladh 1980; Malmer 1981; Bertilsson 1987; Coles 1995, 2000). Together with some rock carving areas in northern Italy (Sansoni 1987; Anati 1993) and on the Iberian Peninsula (Clestino 2001; Pena and Rey 2001), the images from south Sweden constitute the closest parallels to the Mediterranean tradition of large-scale visual monumental art from the second millennium BC. The large panels of rock-cut images in the provinces of Bohuslän, Scania and Östergötland in Sweden are the closest we can get in monumental scale to the Minoan wall paintings or Hittite rock reliefs during this period. And they are richer in both numbers and themes. As we have noted earlier, the hierarchical social structure of most south Scandinavian Bronze Age societies favours an interpretation of these renderings in terms of official religious-ideological expressions. Therefore, the comparison with images from the Bronze Age Aegean, Egypt or the Near East can be contextually relevant, even if there are great differences in scale – from chiefdoms to states – between the northern and Mediterranean social formations.

The monumentality of the Nordic rock art can in fact be more profound than, for example, the Minoan frescos, because the northern pictures were cut in the rock in open terrain, and not placed on the interior walls of temples, sanctuaries or palaces. If the Swedish rock art panels were meant to be accessible (at least visible) for a broader public, the monumentality and ideological significance of sites such as Vitlycke in Bohuslän, Himmelstalund in Östergötland, or Oppeby in Södermanland (Fig. 156) must have been immense. Here, thousands of people could simultaneously have watched the religious performances being carried out by priests or chieftains, or worshipped the deities depicted on the rock.

It is difficult to evaluate whether the rock art panels were 'open' and accessible to the public during the Bronze Age or if they were closed areas.

Fig. 156 The location of rock art in a Swedish landscape of today. Oppeby.

Excavations in front of rock art panels in south-eastern Norway (Johansen 1979) have in one case revealed a line of stones that delimited the area of the rock where the images were placed. A large number of potsherds were found inside this 'fence', indicating that certain human activities had taken place there. The line of stones indicates that some kind of wall probably surrounded the rock art images during the Bronze Age, which means that this site could have been 'closed to the public'. Fire-cracked rocks and charcoal close to other excavated rock art panels in Norway and Sweden show that fires were used in the rituals in front of the images (Hygen and Bengtsson 1999: 156).[5]

The Minoan, Egyptian, Hittite or Near Eastern buildings with wall paintings/rock reliefs showing deities or ritual ceremonies were probably not accessible to anyone other than kings, queens, priests, priestesses, nobles or other elite persons, though they were often open-air temples. At the Hittite rock sanctuary at Yazilikaya, the images of divinities (and a few kings) were

5 Recent excavations around and in front of rock art panels in Bohuslän have documented these obsevations of various rituals in front of the panels as a regular feature (Bengtsson 2004). In addition environmental analyses demonstrate that the rock art panels were situated in liminal areas some distance from settlements and fields, often close to low-lying wetlands or the seashore. These observations are part of the Tanum project, a collaborative project between the departments in Gothenburg, Umeå and Santiago de Compostela. It includes similar work in Galicia and in eastern Sweden.

cut in the rock surface in the open. The whole area was then 'fenced off' by temple buildings, making the images of the divinities accessible only for authorised personnel: the priesthood and the royal family. Possibly, the situation was similar with the Aten cult in el-Amarna (Akhenaton), where the temples devoted to the sun-disc, Aten, were open to the sky and the divine sun rays (see chapter 3.1).

However, the existence of 'open' Hittite rock art sites indicates that rock reliefs were also made for a more public purpose, and these sites are probably more comparable with Scandinavian rock art. Robert L. Alexander writes about the Hittite rock art: 'The rock reliefs, on the other hand, were large, stationary, and unique. Placed along travel routes, they served as guides, signalling the passage from one region to another' (Alexander 1993: 10).

It is likely that the geographical positioning of the rock art sites in, for example, the province of Östergötland in Sweden was connected to a major east–west travel route (Larsson 1986 and 1995; for a local contextual interpretation Hauptman 2002). It thus served a similar purpose to the 'open' Hittite rock reliefs, and the same is true of coastal rock art sites in relation to sea journeys (Ling 2004).

When it comes to the very uniform style of Scandinavian rock art in different provinces, we might add another observation by Alexander concerning the Hittites that may be of relevance: 'Nevertheless, all of these examples of artistic influence required fairly intimate knowledge of the original at Yazilikaya. Drawings and verbal descriptions are not sufficient; the transfer of style and modelling implies movement of the artists themselves' (Alexander 1993: 11).

This is a model that could be applied to the making of rock art in Scandinavia as well. At a general level, it is safe to say that the south Scandinavian rock art images are made after the very same 'blueprints' in the entire area; the different ship types that exist (Malmer 1981) can be found in Norway, Denmark and Sweden. This holds true for other motifs as well. At a more detailed level, we can find regional differences in style and in the choice of motifs (Bertilsson 1987: 39), and this may indicate movement of individual artists within defined regions – perhaps one or two artists at a time moving around and 'managing' the rock art sites in each regional polity.

It is not impossible that the Nordic open-air rock art panels were hidden behind fences or palisades, making access prohibited for anyone other than authorised personnel. If this was the case, the images were perhaps made for the divinities of heaven to see, and the theocratic chieftains and their families. In addition, we do not know if ritual buildings in Bronze Age Scandinavia had painted walls with motifs similar to those of the rock art; therefore, the pictures on the rock surfaces are the only images we can work with at the present.

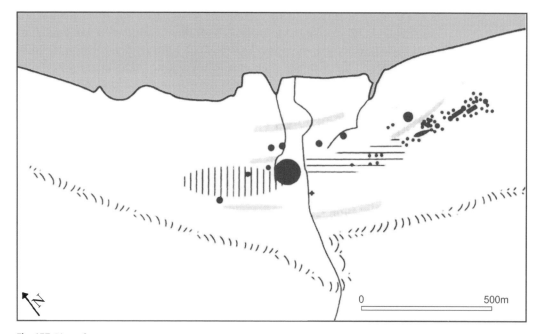

Fig. 157 Plan of
the Kivik area
with cult
buildings, and
ground plans for
(a) Sandagergård
and (b) Kivik
(after Victor
2002: Figs. 23
and 40).

Let us now return to Marinatos' five points, and briefly see if these aspects can be inferred when looking at the south Scandinavian rock art iconography or religious practices.

(i) An emphasis on death and regeneration can immediately be witnessed if we turn our attention to the Early Bronze Age burial practice in south Scandinavia. The thousands of tumuli that were erected in Denmark and south Sweden, 1500–1000 BC, reflect a society where the concern about death and regeneration must have played a crucial part in everyday life. The ancestors and their burial mounds certainly dominated the physical landscape around the Early Bronze Age settlements in many parts of Denmark and southernmost Sweden (Fig. 104); people were actually living among their ancestors.

In some cases stones with rock carvings have been found inside burial mounds, as in the case of Kivik and Sagaholm in Sweden (Goldhahn 1999a; Randsborg 1993), which further indicates a relationship between burial rituals and the making of rock art.

Long, rectangular stone-walled cult buildings appear regularly in connection with large barrows, forming local centres of death rituals. This probably also included the deposition of hoards in bog sanctuaries (Victor 2002: Figs. 59 and 60). Some of the largest cult houses, more than 30 m long, were found at the Kivik cemetry (Fig. 157). At one of the well-excavated examples from northern Zealand (Kaul 1987), four pictorial stone slabs were found

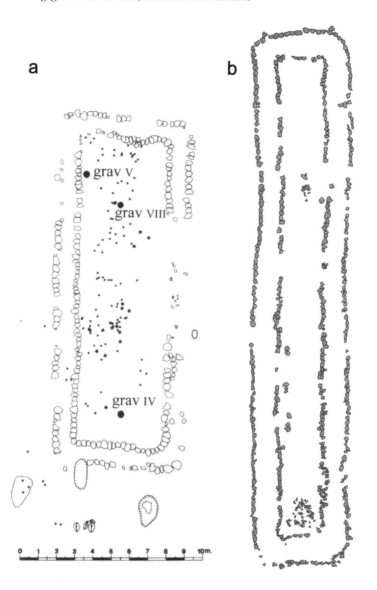

a

b

grav V.

grav VIII

grav IV

0 1 2 3 4 5 6 7 8 9 10m.

Fig. 157 *(cont.)*

with carved hand signs, as well as a few urns. More recently the cult houses at the huge 'Håga' barrow with a rich period 4 grave, have been excavated (Victor 2002: ch. 7). The evidence, including smashing of pots and burning of bones (roasting of meat?), clearly indicates that rituals took place inside the walls. The rituals have some similarity to those found to have taken place in front of many rock carvings. Thus, death rituals, and possibly rituals for ancestors, occupied a prominent place throughout the Bronze Age in Scandinavia, having their own ritual houses/temples.

Fig. 158 Rock art figure with phallus and raised arm gesture. This may symbolise the horns of the ox god.

When studying the actual rock art iconography and what is depicted, it is not at all clear that the images themselves should be directly associated with death or funeral rites. On the contrary the many potent figures with their phalluses are quite easily associated with fertility and regeneration, so here we can state an iconographic similarity with the east Mediterranean and Near East according to Marinatos' first point.

The ploughing scenes that we know of in the south Scandinavian rock art record are also commonly interpreted as scenes related to fertility and regeneration, particularly when the oxen are driven by a man with an accentuated phallus and a tree branch in his hand. Images of trees are quite rare in rock art and they may be associated with regeneration and life (Hygen and Bengtsson 1999: 118). In many European and Asian myths a 'sacred tree' forms a link between the sky and the netherworld.

The snake goddess represents the netherworld of death. She appears as a figurine with a snake (Figs. 54b and 114), and on many rock carvings. Snakes also appear on their own, both in rock art and in metalwork, throughout the Bronze Age, sometimes antithetically arranged, at other times following the

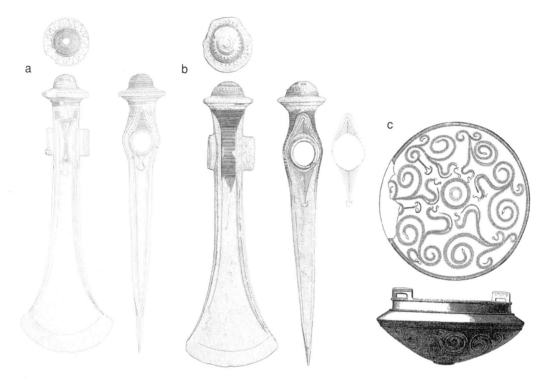

Fig. 159 Ritual axes from the Early Bronze Age, Montelius period 2: (*a*) from Viby and (*b*) from Bredebækgård; (*c*) decorated bottom on belt box worn by sun priests on their back from the Late Bronze Age, Montelius period 5 (after Kaul 2001: Figs. 1–3).

goddess, and sometimes encircling the universe. This corresponds well with similar uses of the snake in the east Mediterranean and in Indo-European religion. The netherworld of death and night is thus well represented in Nordic iconography and ritual.

In more abstract form the cosmogony of the universe is sometimes symbolically woven into the decoration on metalwork (exemplified from the Early and Late Bronze Age in Figure 159). On the ritual axe from the fifteenth–early fourteenth centuries BC we see the upper and lower realms, represented by the heavenly axe at the top, with the netherworld encircled by the snake at the bottom (Fig. 159a). For this reading, the axe should be turned around with the blade upward. The well-known Hittite symbol from royal seals connects the two realms. On another ritual axe (Fig. 159b) the heavenly axe symbol is placed on top of a raised triangle, as on Hittite royal seals, symbolising perhaps the tree of life with heaven at its top. On a belt box from the tenth/ninth century BC (Fig. 159c) we see the horse-drawn day sun with the heavenly axe symbol and the night sun with the snakehead symbolising night/netherworld. Here the whole cosmogony of the sun is unified in a single symbolic form. These examples demonstrate once again that style carries meaning far beyond what we are normally inclined to imagine. But

Fig. 160 The 'goddess' from Fossum – rock carving from Bohuslän, Sweden.

perhaps even as important: meaning was also linked to the ritual and social role of the objects.

(ii) The second point of proposed similarity that we will check is whether '*the concept of a fertility goddess and the young hunter/warrior god*' existed in Bronze Age Scandinavia. Here, the rock art iconography is of particular value. There are numerous images of male figures engaged in both hunting and warfare and there are also many images of females that may fit the description of a fertility goddess.

The rock art site at Fossum in Bohuslän, Sweden, can serve as a good example of a rock panel with many representations of presumed hunter/warrior gods and what could well be an image of a fertility goddess (Fig. 160).

The goddess is depicted with her hair in a ponytail and a cupmark between her legs as a symbol of femininity as well as fertility. The extremely accentuated calves of her legs are rather typical of many rock art representations

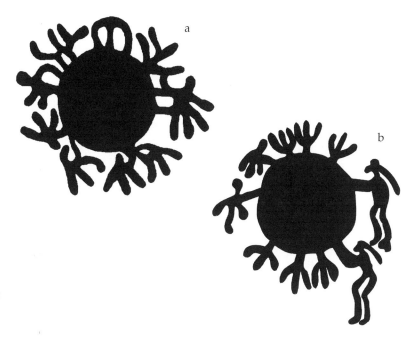

Fig. 161 The 'sun-discs' from (*a*) Fossum and (*b*) Aspeberget (after Larsson 1997).

of anthropomorphic figures in south Scandinavia – an artistic trait that we also can find in Mediterranean paintings from the late second and early first millennia BC. Representations like this are extremely rare, and underneath the goddess we can see a special sign or symbol in the form of a circle divided by a vertical line, which is also a very rare motif in Scandinavia. It may be a mere coincidence, but the divided circle is actually the Hittite hieroglyph meaning 'divine' (Macqueen 1986: 23), and placed under an image of a female figure it automatically creates the word 'goddess'.

This symbol of 'divinity' appears once more on the panel at Fossum (Fig. 161a), but now associated with a representation of what may be a sun-disc. It is placed on top of the disc and it differs clearly in shape from the other 'protuberances' of the sun.

If the sign means 'divine' and it is placed on top of a sun-disc, the reading of this image must be 'the divine sun' or 'sun-god/goddess'. We can make this case stronger by adding another image to this scenario, a motif from a nearby site named Aspeberget (Fig. 161b).

Here we have a similar sun-disc, but with three 'protuberances' of a well-known type on each side – the divine gesture with upright arms. Two female goddesses with ponytails at the right perimeter are holding the sun, together with two male gods to the left, although not as clearly marked. We suggest that male and female Divine Twins are holding the sun, giving birth to triple divinities with upright arms. Soon they will leave the sun-disc, probably as swans, as seen in other examples of the scene.

In Scandinavia the concept of female fertility is most clearly linked to the life-giving role of the sun-goddess and her female servants/priests. Despite a Canaanite figurine from Solna in Sweden (see Fig. 142) of the naked goddess, there is no evidence of the 'Mistress of Animals' from Crete and the Near East (Marinatos 2000). It is not until the end of the Bronze Age and the Early Iron Age that the goddess Artemis with stag and warriors appears regulary in metalwork, for example the Strettweg cult wagon, and in rock art. However, from the Carpathians to Scandinavia we find the priestess of the sun-goddess, as described earlier in chapter 6.7. We can also identify her as a warrior priestess with a dagger, perhaps defining a ritual role linked to the well-being of the young warriors.

In Figure 162 we can identify both warriors with their axes and swords, together with hunters with spears and bows and arrows. War and hunting scenes are very common in south Scandinavian rock art, so there is no problem in finding suitable hunter/warrior gods in this iconography. However, it would take a more systematic study to understand the meaning of these scenes. At present we cannot sustain a specific institution of the young hunter/warrior god and a fertility goddess, although we can point to several indications.

(iii) Scenes showing a '*sacred marriage of a divine pair*' are present in the rock art iconography from Bronze Age Scandinavia, as in Minoan, Hittite and Near Eastern iconography.

In the first case (Fig. 163 (left)) there is no problem defining the female (goddess) and male (god) actors in this *Hieros Gamos* if we use the ponytail as an indicator of femininity as in the above examples. The god is carrying a sword and, apart from the 'natural' physical connection through the sexual organ, the divine couple is further unified by a line connecting their upper calves. Perhaps this connection is a symbolic way of emphasising the strong bonds between the divinities; they are physically and mythologically tied close together.

The second picture shows a similar scene (Fig. 163 (right)), but made in a more simplified manner. The god is probably the figure to the right, but there are no obvious gender attributes in this composition.

We can also note that in these two scenes a cupmark is depicted close to the couple – in both cases closer to the god than the goddess – which could have had a meaning in Bronze Age people's reading of this 'text'. In analysing south Scandinavian rock art in detail, it is clear that the use of the cupmark is so wide that it becomes almost impossible to give this simple sign a single meaning (Almgren 1927; Malmer 1981; Lindgren 1999; Coles 2000: 31; Hygen and Bengtsson 1999: 121). 'Sites may have none or only a few cupmarks, others have a scatter amidst other images, some have cupmarks grouped apart from other images, some have many cupmarks and no figures,

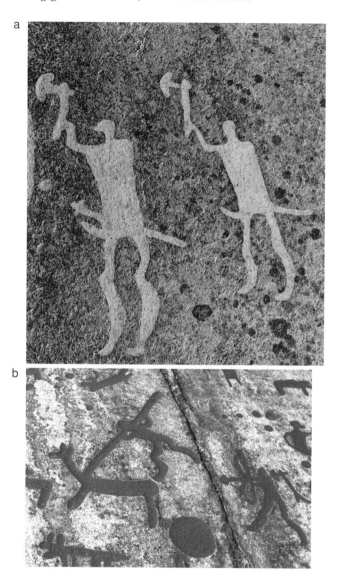

Fig. 162 (*a*)
Warrior
depictions and
(*b*) a hunting
scene with spear
and bow and
arrow from
Fossum,
Bohuslän.

and their organisation often appears to be, to our eyes, quite haphazard; it
was probably just the opposite' (Coles 2000: 31).

(iv) The fourth of Marinatos' points, '*the use of nature imagery as a frame-*
work for cyclical regeneration', can be found in the form of rock art depictions
of trees, as mentioned under (i) above. However, nature imagery is otherwise absent in Nordic Bronze Age iconography. The reason is probably quite
simple: nature itself was the scene for rituals, rock art and sanctuaries and
need not be depicted.

a

b

Fig. 163 *Hieros Gamos* scenes from (*a*) Vitlycke and (*b*) Jörlov.

(v) *Ritual hunting and animal-based metaphors* constitute our fifth and final point for comparison. As mentioned in relation to (ii) above, hunting scenes and depictions of animals are quite common in Scandinavian rock art (Malmer 1981; Lindgren 1997). We have chosen two images that show ritual hunting scenes and one that could represent an animal-based metaphor.

Beginning with the stag hunt from Massleberg in west Sweden (Fig. 164), we can identify a big stag that is surrounded by seven dogs and a hunter. The image of the hunter is interesting, because he has been depicted with a circular body shape, which is a rather unusual way of presenting anthropomorphic figures. On other figures with a circular body we find two lines inside the circle, making up a sun-cross, which is an indication that we are dealing with images of divinities. He is apparently wearing an animal mask, a bird head. So, the circular form could very well indicate that this is an animated divinity who is out hunting with his dogs, which makes the whole composition a ritual hunting scene. Again, we can note the cupmarks, here placed above and under the stag, and the Hittite symbol of divinity appears in front of the stag, defining it as divine. The scene is thus mythological.

Hunting with dogs is common in Hittite iconography as well as in the Near East and Egypt (Gurney 1990: 174; Houlihan 1996). Here it is only divinities,

Fig. 164
Depiction of stag
hunt from
Massleberg.

Fig. 165 A scene
with a boar hunt
from
Himmelstalund
(after Larsson
1997).

heroes or rulers who are the hunters; hunting stags, boars, bulls or lions
was an exclusive prerogative of the elites and the gods (Kilian 1995). As some
wild animals were considered divine and empowered, such as the stag, the
hunt served a religious purpose, a repetition of a mythical story leading to
the sacrifice of the divine animal, transmitting its power to the hunter, and
at the same time restarting the lifecycle.

From the large rock art site at Himmelstalund in Östergötland, Sweden,
comes another hunting scene (Fig. 165). In this 'narrative' it is a huge
boar that is the hunters' target and, as in the previous scene, dogs have

Fig. 166 Two antithetically arranged goats. Rock art from Himmelstalund, Östergötland (after Larsson).

surrounded the prey. The monstrous boar is very accurately depicted, with a raised, forked tail, standing shag and clearly marked tusks.

The forked tail, shag and marked tusks are also accentuated on a Hittite boar hunting scene in the form of an orthostatic relief from the city walls of Alaça Hüyük dated to the thirteenth century BC (Müller-Karpe 1980: Taf. 176; Larsson 1997: Fig. 32). It shows that the details signifying a boar in iconographic representations were the same in south Scandinavia and in Anatolia during the second millennium BC. Maybe these details are so typical of a furious boar that they are almost universally known, but to our knowledge iconographic representations of boars with these particular traits marked are extremely rare in the European Bronze Age imagery (if they exist at all?), apart from in the south Scandinavian rock art.

The two hunters with spears may be another reflection of the 'twin syndrome', as discussed many times in this book; the boar is hunted by two gods or brave rulers, making the scene ritual in its nature at the same time as it may express an animal-based metaphor. The wild boar could have been a metaphor of the things that the gods and/or rulers had to fight, like evil, chaos or enemy tribes, and by defeating these threats society could live on. The gesture of holding the spear with upright arms, the divine symbol, is also one we find in Greece, for example on a scene from the *Odyssey* on an Archaic pot (*Gods and Heroes* 1998: 182).

Our final animal image (Fig. 166) shows two goats with long, slightly curved horns, that are depicted in a truly antithetical position, resembling pictures of goats that can be seen on Babylonian cylinder seals (Oates 1986). On a stone rhyton from the Minoan palace of Zakros on Crete there is a depiction of a peak sanctuary with two antithetically placed mountain goats with long horns (Marinatos 1993: 120), that also resembles the goats from Himmelstalund.

Two isolated animals in this position are quite rare among the rock art motifs and goats with long, curved horns are also uncommon in the Scandinavian rock art tradition, whereas they were highly popular in the Near East and in Minoan culture (Bloedow 2003). A single example comes from the Sagaholm pictorial slabs discussed earlier, from the Early Bronze Age. The antithetical and almost heraldic structure of the image suggests a metaphorical meaning linked to the twin dualism. Two foreign bronze goats with similar long horns were found in a hoard with female ornaments in Norway from the Late Bronze Age/Early Iron Age. The age of the imported goats, however, could be much older.

If we take Nano Marinatos' five characteristics to represent a thematic religious structure, it is on the whole represented in the Scandinavian Bronze Age, with the exception of nature images. Nature was the scene of rituals. Even if there are major differences in artistic quality, expression and style between the two areas, this does not change the basic fact that the iconographic elements of the eastern Mediterranean religious images are also present in south Scandinavia. They were accompanied by a selection of the mythological and ritual universe of the very same regions, mixed into a specific Nordic religious cosmology, whose origin can still be detected and decoded, as we have demonstrated. Bronze Age religion was not a world religion; it was rather a gigantic syncretic melting pot with a shared cosmology. This is further confirmed by the archaeological identification of basic myths and religious institutions from the Old Indic *Veda* and Greek religion in the Bronze Age societies of central and northern Europe. These general similarities also apply to oppositions between social and religious behaviour, which we shall discuss next.

7.4 Enculturing the body: the dialectic of social and religious behaviour

Consider the famous Iceman, dated to about 3000 BC (Egg and Spindler 1993), recovered from the Alps, with his functionally elaborate but primitive dress of natural materials. Consider the similarly well-preserved bodies and sophisticated woollen garments and instruments of bodily care of the Danish Bronze Age *c.*1400 BC (Broholm and Hald 1940; Jensen 1998). They are worlds apart, not only in time, but also in body culture and dress. What happened during the intervening period? To put it briefly, after 2000 BC the elites of temperate Europe became bodily encultured and engendered by the east Mediterranean palace cultures and states. Dress and bodily appearance reached a new level of sophistication, as did gender roles and social identities (Treherne 1995; Sørensen 1997b). From Egypt through the Aegean to central and northern Europe we can trace this new package of bodily

culture and care: razors, tweezers, combs, mirrors and colours for make up.
For the dress, a complex package of pins, buttons and dress fasteners (fibulae), combined with a whole new repertoire of bracelets, earrings, arm and ankle rings, pendants, tubes and much more. As stated by Lyn Meskell for Egypt: 'The sheer popularity of these items of grooming suggests that bodily maintenance was a time consuming and culturally necessary requirement that transcended any gender boundaries' (Meskell and Joyce 2003: 58).

While the encultured and engendered body of the Bronze Age would demand, and indeed deserves, a book of its own, we shall focus upon some aspects of gender and sexuality. Nordic and European Bronze Age culture shared with the Egyptian Bronze Age a religious sexuality and a phallic culture (Meskell and Joyce 2003: ch. 6) that transgresses any western or Judaeo-Christian notion of sexuality and religion. This goes hand in hand with rigid social definitions of gender roles. It can thus hardly escape notice that there existed a highly visible opposition between social and ritual behaviour during the Bronze Age, at least in a number of popular rituals and games. Especially, the figurines demonstrate this difference, but rock art also displays ritualised drinking, sex, and sports and games where the participants are showing their torso naked. This seems to be a general rule from Minoan Crete to southern Scandinavia.

It is of course nothing new that certain rites and religious festivals, such as midsummer or the Dionysian games, were but a thin cover for people to feast and do many of the things that were otherwise prohibited. Likewise temples acted in some periods as centres of prostitution. Some might object and suggest that what we are seeing are representations: the *Hieros Gamos* did not imply public intercourse; female breasts did not imply erotic games. Greek vases, however, leave nothing to the imagination when they portray ritualised drinking and sexual excesses, and Celtic, Hittite and some Greek texts are also at times quite sexually explicit, just as in the Egyptian phallus culture. We should probably adopt a different perception of sexuality in Bronze Age religion and accept this as an arena for sexual behaviour (Marinatos 2000). The same observation for Bronze Age Egypt led Meskell to the following conclusion of its otherness compared to the Christian tradition: 'That the sexual and religious could exist harmoniously in Pharaonic Egypt suggests that we are witnessing real cultural difference' (Meskell 2000: 255). In the Old Babylonian period of the early second millennium BC a similar integration of rituals and sexual services is documented in texts. Here so-called 'kezertu' women of low status served the goddess Isthar by providing sexual services as part of a ritual ceremony that was officially paid for by high-ranking males and their wives (Yoffee 1998). Rather than term this prostitution, we should probably understand it as being part of a different cultural perception of religion and sexuality (Yoffee 1998). Be this as it may, it is the contrast between the social and the ritual dress that appears so striking.

Women's costume in the Bronze Age was one of physical constriction. Excessive ornaments impeded certain movements. Wear studies carried out by one of us (Kristiansen 1974 and unpublished) have demonstrated that even the most grotesque ornaments were used on a daily basis. Furthermore a large overdress was often worn which covered most of the body, including the inner dress and the ornaments. This can be inferred from the widespread surface wear observable on all types of ornaments. Complex hairstyles and headgear added to social prestige, but also further constrained certain types of activities. Chiefly women of the Bronze Age were thus enclosed in their costume, at least during long periods of the year. This they shared with Mycenaean and Minoan women (Lee 2000: 119).

In stark opposition to this, the ritual dress is free of all constriction, at least during certain rituals and games. It is sexually inviting by showing the body naked except for the short corded skirt. In a society where women most of the time were enclosed in their costume, this must have been experienced as erotic behaviour. Acrobatics and dances were part of the ritual repertoire, and from figurines (Grevensvænge) and rock art we learn that the male priest would also appear in a special dress, imitating animal hide, and parade a huge penis (whether artificial or real we do not know) during certain rituals. Again, the opposition to the social costume is apparent, with its cloak, tunic and cap, although much less constraining than the women's costume. In the east Mediterranean the young gods/chiefs wore only a short loincloth, ready for games and feats, some of them highly sexual as described earlier. The same is true of divine/priestly women (German 2000).

Thus rituals inhabited a free space for carrying out a whole number of activities that were otherwise prohibited by social etiquette and dress. As we have stated earlier, chiefly women were probably highly controlled as an important source of wealth. The role of priestess may therefore have represented another arena for female and male activities during a certain period of life that counterbalanced the rigid social divisions prevailing in Bronze Age society. It may also have empowered women in a number of ways we can also guess at so far. Quite clearly their role in rituals and as priestesses increased during the Bronze Age. We may thus consider the apparent contradiction between ritual and social behaviour as part of a constant playing out of the inherent tensions in society, but also an arena for testing new roles and rituals, and thus potentially challenging social order.

7.5   Conclusion: religion and ritual performance

Performance, whether oral or through acting, was at centre stage for social and religious institutions in the Bronze Age, as in most traditional societies. But in the Bronze Age, social and religious life was enriched with a new complexity, new mythologies and rituals. Knowledge about their correct performance was therefore in the hands of religious specialists and leaders with a lifelong education behind them (Olmsted 1994: 18ff.). These were the doctors and professors of Bronze Age society. Some of the most outstanding would become long-remembered heroes, and would have the capacity to change and renew tradition under conditions of social change. But a performer has an audience who watch and judge; the bard or the priest was never free to change at will. Like the actor he had to stick to his text. Variation had to fall within the known repertoire of stories, in opposition to the scribe in early medieval times, who had much more freedom to add to and change the manuscripts of the written versions of oral tradition, once it had been removed from its social context. That is when change was introduced. In the Nordic Bronze Age, however, we can observe how the performance of the central rites was maintained unchanged throughout a millennium. The material culture of the rituals might change or develop, horses were sometimes replaced by swans to draw the sun, and new gods or religious symbols could be added. But the core remained unchanged.

The heritage of Bronze Age social and religious institutions makes it clear that in conditions of no major social disruptions rituals and religion and the corresponding mythology, we must assume, could remain essentially unchanged not only for centuries but for a millennium or more. Even in the Aegean, struck by a Dark Age, the basic gods and goddesses of the Mycenaean Age were preserved into the Archaic and Classical periods and revived. To reproduce this complexity throughout such a long period demonstrates a capacity and strength of oral tradition highly unfamiliar to our own culture. While historians have made often successful attempts to discredit this capacity of their ancient colleagues, the archaeological evidence of the Bronze Age makes it clear that social and religious institutions can be preserved and transmitted down through the millennia in nearly unchanged form, precisely because of their performative nature. And when small changes are introduced they are often cumulative. Only periods of major social transformation would open up opportunities for reinvention and for the introduction of new heroes and mythologies, as happened in Scandinavia in the Iron Age. But even then, relics of the former pantheon are preserved, or rearranged within the new order of things.

Living in a culture of ritualised performance implied that the people of the Bronze Age had a visual memory and knowledge that could be employed in iconography. Such iconography – whether painted on the palace walls in the Aegean or carved on the rock in Scandinavia – helped to maintain memory, not only for the elite, but perhaps more importantly for the commoners, like the wall paintings in a medieval church. The performative nature of Bronze Age religion is also evidenced in figurines and models – whether of bronze or clay – that were employed in rituals. Thus, the combined evidence of Bronze Age epics and texts, pictorial art, figurines and the paraphernalia of rituals establishes the Bronze Age as the great period of ritual and social performance, from ritual processions to feats, dances and war games. Another characteristic is the linkage between nature and ritual, from Minoan peak sanctuaries to Nordic rock carvings or bog sanctuaries. Although cult houses or temples were in use throughout Europe, mainly linked to the local ritual centres and cemeteries, the association with nature is essential.

Some scholars have doubted whether the images of the Bronze Age rock art reflect real rituals and knowledge of their mythology. Mats Malmer suggested that rock art was a substitute for the real thing in more marginal areas of Scandinavia. Only south Scandinavia was able to carry through the whole repertoire of the rituals and the subsequent depositions of ritual gear and the construction of rich burials (Malmer 1970). This proposition rests on several false premises: rock art is not marginal, it belongs to the central areas of Bronze Age Scandinavia, but rocks are rare in southern Scandinavia. And just as there can be no swords without the reality they symbolise, so there can be no images without the mythological reality they display. As we are talking about systematic and recurring motifs in time and space, they were linked to a common Nordic ritual and religious knowledge.

Other researchers have doubted whether there existed a divine pantheon in the Bronze Age, that is gods and goddesses. Flemming Kaul in his important work on Bronze Age ship iconography has put forward such a proposition (1998). Since chiefs and priest were enacting the rituals of fertility, the ritual ploughing, *hieros gamos*, etc., they were unable to envisage abstract gods and goddesses. This proposition also rests on several false premises: it assumes that European and Nordic Bronze Age societies were too primitive to adopt and maintain an advanced religious system, and it implicitly assumes an obsolete evolutionary perspective on European Bronze Age societies and on religion. As we have demonstrated to the contrary, European societies of the Early Bronze Age underwent a social and religious transformation in the process of adopting new social and religious institutions. In that process they quite naturally dressed and named them to local needs. However, the basic pantheon of gods and goddesses can be identified in the Nordic Bronze Age, as we have demonstrated, just as with the mythology linked to them. Finally, we should recognise the theocratic nature of the

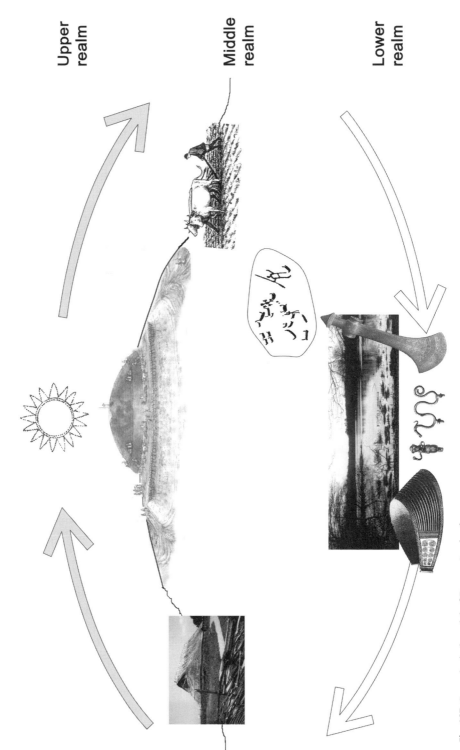

Upper realm

Middle realm

Lower realm

Fig. 167 Cosmological model of Bronze Age landscape.

Bronze Age: chiefs and priests/priestesses enacted and personified gods and goddesses in the annual and seasonal rituals. And again: there can be no personification without knowledge of the mythological and divine reality of your performance. This takes us to our next major characteristic of Bronze Age religion: the relationship between landscape and cosmological order.

The linking with nature and the open probably has to do with another important characteristic of Bronze Age ritual performance – participation in and the ritualisation of landscape. Thus the landscape was constructed according to a mythological or divine order (Kristiansen 1998c; Johansen 1992; Goldhahn 1999b). Closest to the upper realm are the barrows. The bog and lake sanctuaries represent the lower realm (for hoarding). The living stay in the middle realm and have to conform to and consolidate the gods and spirits of the dead in liminal areas, demanding taboos, specific actions, rituals to cross, etc.

We know from Minoan and Mycenaean religion that landscape was ritually empowered and had its gods and sanctuaries, which are preserved on sealstones, in frescos and not least in the archaeological evidence of their construction and function. In the Nordic Bonze Age we can only hint at such regularities: we can state with some certainty that different activities seem to have been located to certain, selected areas (Fig. 167).

If we are to describe a 'typical' south Scandinavian Bronze Age landscape, with its features, such as barrows, settlements, rock art and hoards, we might start with the burials – the earthen barrows (or stone-built cairns) of the ancestors. As mentioned above, barrows (and cairns) are often located on high ground or hillocks in the terrain; it is clear that the topographical position closest to the sky (heaven) was preferred when building graves of this type. Apart from the fact that hilltops represent natural, liminal positions between earth and heaven, which could be read as a metaphor for the relationship between the living and the dead (and the divine), this geographical position also enhanced the monumentality of the burial constructions. At the same time their visibility and intervisibility, sometimes 5–10 km between those at the highest points, created a monumental landscape of horizontal interaction.

Settlements and rock art sites are often situated a little bit lower in the terrain – on the slopes below the barrows or cairns. The rock art can be separated into two broad categories: figurative images and cupmarks, the latter being much more widespread. The patterning and spatial relations between settlements and the two types of rock art differ from region to region in south Scandinavia, whereas their internal patterning in the landscape conforms to a more generalised structure. For example, in the provinces of Östergötland and Södermanland in Sweden the cupmark sites are widely distributed in the terrain, and they seem to be spatially correlated with

Bronze Age settlements, while the figurative images are located to three major centres with no indications of settlements close by (Larsson 1986). This suggests a separation between common and exclusive rituals, which prevails in most of Scandinavia. In Bohuslän, though, the figurative images are not so intensively centred on just a few spots, although the most central ritual themes are spatially distributed in a few locations (Bertilsson 1987).

Hoards (or ritual depositions of bronze objects) represent the link to the netherworld; they are commonly found in wet environments such as bogs, streams and lakes (Larsson 1986: 158), and their deposition was likewise accompanied by ritual and common rules of deposition (Kristiansen 1996b).

Thus, the spatial separation vertically and horizontally between different areas of different social, economic and ritual activities suggests that cosmological principles governed the use of the landscape, empowering it with divine forces that determined their accessability and use. Liminal areas were often defined by special ritual activities, such as rock art (Bradley 1997), which was a stage for performance and sacrifice (Schauer 1996 and Branigan 1998 for comparative evidence in Europe and the Aegean). When applying such an approach we can more profitably begin to understand the landscape as a structured cosmos.

8   Cosmos and culture in the Bronze Age

Cosmos and chaos form the two opposing poles of the world. Man takes possession of land by transforming chaos into cosmos, and he does so according to the rules of the gods. Every inhabited territory therefore is an attempt to conform to cosmos, since it was originally the work of the gods: 'to organize space is to repeat the paradigmatic work of the gods' (Eliade 1987: 32). This means that landscape was sacred, but different places and locations would occupy different roles in cosmos and display different degrees of sacredness. Settlements, the placing of barrows or cemeteries, and ritual places are interlinked to reproduce in each local settlement the sacred order of the cosmos, and when these are radically changed we may assume the introduction of a new cosmological order. This lends new significance to the study of the organisation of landscape, settlements, burial places, etc. as an indication of the nature of cosmos (Pauketat and Alt 2003; Van Dyke and Alcock 2003). We may therefore use a comparative study in time and space of settlement organisation as a means to discover important changes and differences in cosmological and religious organisation. We shall exemplify this briefly and then carry out a comparison between centred and decentred Bronze Age cosmologies.

In the Near East a sacred mountain is considered the centre of the world. We find this conception especially developed in Minoan religion, with its peak sanctuaries and the goddess of the mountain, Mistress of Animals. The mountain represented the *axis mundi* that connected heaven and earth. This was later transferred to the temple, the sanctuary and other ritual sites, which in local territories would achieve the same role. Thus we find here from the beginning the notion of religious centres and their local replicas. We have demonstrated this paradigmatic principle in the spread of iconographic scenes from the Kivik burial in southern Sweden to large areas in southern Scandinavia. A similar process explains the tumulus burials and their location on high points in the landscape from southern Germany to Denmark as representing a new cosmological order linked to chiefly elites. Likewise we may consider the Minoan and later Mycenaean palaces as paradigmatic cosmological centres of the world, where the rituals of the gods were performed to maintain this order.

Turning to central and northern Europe we note a major change of settlement and barrows at the beginning of the Bronze Age proper, especially during the period 1700–1500 BC, first in central Europe, and later in northern

357

Europe. As we have demonstrated in chapter 5 these changes were linked to the introduction of new social and religious institutions and we could demonstrate that they were materialised also in a new cosmological order of landscape and settlement. While in east central Europe these changes were added to already existing traditions of agglomerated tell settlements, in northern Europe they represented a complete break with previous tradition. A new cosmology was imposed upon the landscape (Kristiansen 1998c). However it is worth noting the basic difference in cosmological thinking in the tell societies of east central Europe and the tumulus societies of northwestern Europe. We suggest that they correspond to two different cosmological principles – that of centredness and that of decentredness. What do we mean by that?

8.1 Centred and decentred cosmologies

In the centred cosmology the world is considered in vertical terms where everything is unified in the civilised centre of the village or urban settlement. Here we find the acropolis, the ritual areas or temples and the cemetery close by. The outer zone is made up of fields and further away the wild, uncivilised world (forests, mountains.) These were areas for mining, hunting and other dangerous activities, and the home of the gods in the mountains. The dichotomy between civilised and uncivilised, nature and culture, is consequently a major theme in the centred cosmology, reflected in religion. The Mistress of Animals controls the powers of the wild and employs their strength. Humans may achieve the same strength through rituals, hunting and sacrifice, e.g. the many lion hunting scenes in Minoan and Mycenaean iconography. Community, government and settled 'urban' life in villages are defining characteristics of a centred cosmology. And their perceptions of death and burial are similarly linked to community: cemeteries are large and collective, urbanised one might say, and they belong with the settlement. Societies out there are often perceived of in the same terms of opposition between culture and nature: they are dangerous, uncivilised, and have to be taught the virtues of culture through civilising ventures – for example, explorations and trade expeditions. Outside the borders of civilisation one can meet dangerous godlike figures, not yet drawn into the realm of the cosmological centre, as experienced and explored by Odysseus. They represent the supernatural counterparts to the foreign lands of the uncivilised people.

In the decentred cosmology the world is considered in horizontal terms, implying that there is no centrality. The landscape is divided into parallel blocks: the barrow landscape of grazing cattle and sheep of the upper realm, the settled landscape of the middle realm centred around the chiefly hall, and the ritual lakes and bogs – the sanctuaries of the lower realm.

There is no strong dichotomy between a civilised and uncivilised Nature, except in the usual way at the borders of the world, where dangers are waiting. There are no central urban or large village settlements; individual farms and hamlets form a continuum in the cultural landscape. Death and the perception of burials are correspondingly individual and family based, linked to the farm or hamlet. This means that the cosmological, paradigmatic model of the world is constantly being repeated by adding yet another parallel settlement with its barrows, etc. The barrows often stress this geographical continuum by being constructed in lines, and at high points, forming a communicative system. The world is thus ordered horizontally, and social communication is horizontal. Cosmos is everywhere, not in the single central settlements, although some of course may be granted a higher order of sacredness and power. It further implies that the dichotomy between culture and nature takes on different forms, and is of less importance than in centred cosmologies. Decentred cosmologies invite movement and travel, and the incorporation of others by symbolic addition, e.g. through intermarriage, foster sons, etc., alternating with raiding, whereas centred cosmologies are more inclined to stress their own identity, approaching others from the outside as foreigners. Contracts, client relationships rather than marriage and incorporation, are the probable means of contact and communication. Conquest rather than raiding is their alternative.

We suggest that these differences ought to be visible in many other aspects of ritual and religion, and that they must have had quite significant historical implications, not least in terms of the nature of interaction between the two (Kristiansen 1998c: Figs. 224 and 225). It was perhaps such cosmological and social differences that were decisive for the differential selection and adoption of east Mediterranean and Near Eastern influences during the earlier second millennium BC in central and northern Europe. In the Mediterranean, Minoan and Mycenaean culture may be said originally to represent the two cosmologies; later they integrated. In Europe they are represented by the tell cultures versus the tumulus cultures, which were later integrated in the formation of the so-called Urnfield Culture. Although the process of integration is an important object of study, we have focused on the early period of the interaction between Minoan (Mycenaean) culture and the tell cultures, and the Mycenaean culture and the tumulus cultures. We consider it no coincidence that connections were established between precisely these cultures, as they shared basic cosmological similarities that facilitated their interaction. One might further suggest that decentred cosmologies were mainly linked to societies speaking Indo-European languages, while centred cosmologies were mainly of Near Eastern origin. However, it is their constant competition and interaction that creates the dynamic of the Bronze Age, and to some extent also the Iron Age.

8.2 The formation and consolidation of cultural identity and ethnicity

We have previously pointed to cosmologies as being institutionally embedded. In this way they were able to transcend cultural boundaries in material culture, creating widespread structural and cosmological similarities throughout Europe, despite the plethora of local and regional cultural identities. In addition we have shown that style had meaning, as in the case of the formation of the Nordic culture. Here a correspondence was demonstrated between cosmology and style, as the spiral was linked to the sun cult. But the so-called Nordic style also created a boundary with other cultures, that did not exist during the preceding period. Similar boundaries, however, were already present during the late third millennium BC, during the so-called Dagger period, but they had been more or less erased during the early centuries of the second millennium BC when a new era of travels introduced metallurgy to southern Scandinavia.

This suggests that material culture as identity played different roles during periods of social change and periods of social consolidation.

In periods of social change former cultural boundaries in material culture are erased, at least when it comes to certain types of objects, notably those linked to social and religious organisation. Foreign objects are accepted, representing the introduction of new value systems and, in the long run, new institutions. Sometimes this is followed up by small-scale population movements. There is a flow of people and ideas between former local and regional identities and ethnicities.

After a period of innovation and acculturation the conditions for forming and enforcing a new social order are being realised, leading to highly intensified regional interaction and the formation of a new regional identity in material culture. Cultural boundaries are re-established and social rules are established for the interaction across regional cultural boundaries, as described in chapter 5.4. The acceptence of new influences in material culture is thus socially regulated, often linked to the male sphere. A stable social order has been established, with a similar stable cultural indenty in material culture.

These historical regularities suggest that material culture is associated with the role and meaning of social and religious institutions, including their origin. The formation of strong regional boundaries with long-term continuity further suggests that social and religious identity were closely linked to a shared mythology of origins and cosmos. This corresponds to ethnohistorical definitions of ethnicity (Jones 1997). Language was but one element in these processes. Our study has further demonstrated that although myths of origin are highly dynamic and need not reflect direct historical events, they nonetheless share a core of historical truth transformed into the language of myth. We may further suggest that these myths of origin typically originate in the historical periods where new institutions are being formed in a context of long-distance contacts and travels, epitomised by the Kivik burial. They are later formalised and mythologised during a period of cultural consolidation and the formation of ethnic identity in material culture.

We are here encountering the relationship between the formation of the self through a social identity and its dialectical relationship with collective identities (from social groups/classes to polities/ethnicity). While ethnicity undoubtedly plays a central role in all human societies as part of a common origin and shared historical identity (tradition), its material expressions have been an underdeveloped field of study, since Hodder's seminal work (1982). It occupies a domain of cultural regularities of a non-evolutionary nature, and it has become increasingly clear that material culture forms part of complex and sometimes overlapping social and ethnic identities, as our study has demonstrated (Fig. 168).

In the Carpathian tell cultures from the Bronze Age, strong traditions in pottery production distinguish different groups or polities from each other, but several of these ethnic groups, as it were, share a common tradition in metalwork and in the social tradition of tell settlements. How are we to interpret this complexity? It may refer to different levels of political and ethnic identities that can only be properly understood by a complete analysis and interpretation of the societies in their particular historical and cosmological setting. A similar pattern is found in the so-called Tumulus Culture from the Bronze Age in central and northern Europe. Here local identities are expressed in female ornaments, while such local groups share a common burial ritual of burials under a barrow, just as certain types of male weapons display the same interregional distribution. Again we are faced with a complex picture of different types of shared and non-shared identities and traditions that also display different gender roles and traditions. Various types of interactions rooted in kinship and alliance systems may account for some part of the variation, while other parts are to be found in an understanding of shared symbolic meanings and a shared cosmological tradition, yet others in technological traditions and their role.

In many ways these findings correspond to the recent study by Jonathan Hall on the formation of certain Greek ethnic identities (Hall 1997), or whether we reserve that for all Greeks as suggested by Renfrew (1998a). We may also note the universal role of dress and ornaments in demarcating ethnic boundaries in complex societies (Eicher 1995). In the Bronze Age this ethnic identification was most clearly linked to high-status women and ritual chiefs, whereas chiefly warriors signalled their participation in

Tell cultures

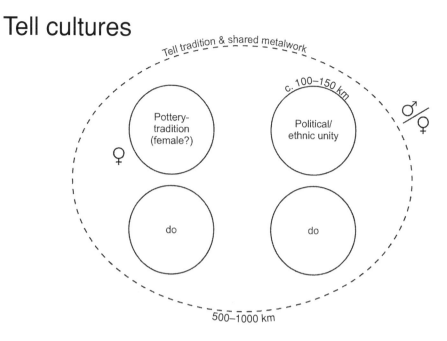

Tumulus cultures

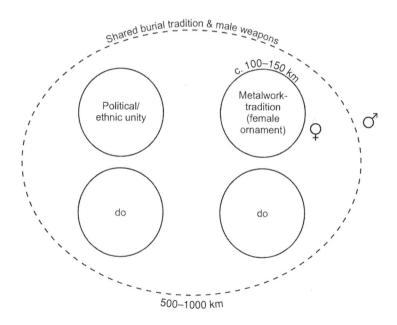

Fig. 168 Model of overlapping cultural distributions and gender identities in Bronze Age Europe: (*top*) the Carpathian tell cultures; (*bottom*) the central and north European tumulus cultures.

supra-regional identities and travels through a shared material culture linked to armour and weaponry. In this way Bronze Age societies were simultaneously able to maintain ethnic boundaries and traditions, while interacting across such borders in an organised way, linked to specific social groups. Gil Stein has convincingly demonstrated the interplay of different ethnic groups (foreign and local) in the Uruk expansion, which he relates to the formation of a trade diaspora originating in Mesopotamia but beyond their immediate control. In this way new local dynamics ermerged that led to the formation of new social frameworks (Stein 1999: chs. 4 and 8). In Europe we are perhaps seeing the effects of these new social and economic dynamics adapted to a non-state social organisation.

These observations help to solve the old problem of identifying population movements with a homogeneous material culture, and linking this to an ethnic identity. As we have demonstrated, it is precisely in periods of foreign influence and eventually some population movements that material culture appears non-homogeneous and disparate. And it is only after a longer period of acculturation and integration that a new synthesis may emerge in the form of a more homogeneous material culture. This simply reflects internal reorganisation based upon an agreed symbolic language in material culture to demonstrate this new social and cosmological unity. And even here there are opportunities and rules for adopting 'foreigners' and their culture. This is the way complex societies operate to handle internal and external relations in an organised way, and in the process they generate an accordingly complex material culture. Thus, we can never subsume variations in material culture under a single interpretative or methodological system without violating its underlying social and historical complexity.[1]

With these tentative propositions we are merely suggesting that there is much more to be learned from an integrated and interdisciplinary study of

1 The analysis and interpretation of material culture is today the focus of theoretical and interpretative controversies. Evolutionary archaeology has adopted a Darwinian theoretical framework of inheritance, transmission and selection to explain behavioural regularities, in the tradition of David Clarke (Shennan 2002). It treats culture as a behavioural product with an own identity, whose meaning is only interpreted after the analysis. Culture is thus given a predefined meaning according to the theoretical framework employed (critical discussion in Clark 2000). It further raises the possibility of creating arbitrary and constructed continuities with the potential of ideological and political exploitation in the present. In opposition to this socially and historically decontextualised approach, a majority of archaeologists wish to begin with a contextualised historical interpretation of variations in material culture in order to understand their proper social and symbolic meaning. These observations may serve as a warning against applying uniform theoretical and methodological frameworks, such as evolutionary theory (O'Brien and Leman 2003), to describe and explain variations in material culture. The evolutionary approach is an attempt to revitalise an obsolete theoretical and methodological framework in archaeology that falsely assumes material culture can be treated as a living organism. It reduces all variation to a single set of explanatory parameters divorced from social and historical interpretation. This brand of evolutionary archaeology should thus be approached critically, as the results produced have little or no bearing upon social and historical changes.

myth, social institutions and their use of material culture in the formation of ethnic and other forms of identity.

8.3 Periphery and centre dynamics in the Bronze Age

The late third and the earlier second millennia BC were a formative period in European history. For the first time there developed direct and dynamic links between centres of civilisation in the Near East/east Mediterranean (states, palaces and city-states) and Europe/Eurasia; from Wessex and Brittany in the west through central and east central Europe to the Urals. They were initially based upon explorations from the centres in search of minerals and other valuable products. However, very quickly the periphery adopted some of the social institutions and technological mastery from the centres, and by the early to mid-second millennium BC it began to exploit and influence the centres as well. This is the great period of international long-distance travels and trade that would eventually lead to a transfer of warriors, chariots and specialists from the periphery to the centre (in addition to minerals).

From the Aegean to Anatolia, Mesopotamia, Egypt and India warriors and specialists on the move would bring in their skills, and well-trained horses and chariots, sometimes peacefully, sometimes by conquest. The intertwined nature of warriors and specialist craftsmen during this period has been stressed in several recent studies (Moorey 2001). This explains in part why we find such compelling correspondences in social and religious institutions between India and Scandinavia during this period. The maritime aspects of the Divine Twins in the *Rig-Veda* point to a shared history (whatever its nature) between these cultures that would have to be located in a not-too-distant past, considering the detailed level of correspondences. The historical implication of these findings invites further interdisciplinary research, where we hope to have contributed some of the historical framework.[2]

---

2 Our historical findings imply the following. (1) The Proto-Indo-European period belongs with the rise of ranked societies, most probably of the third millennium BC, unless one wishes to separate the spread of language and the spread of institutions. The Yamna, Corded Ware and other related cultures most probably represent this phase archaeologically in temperate Eurasia. The early centuries of the second millennium might thus be considered to represent either the final PIE or an early period of the formation of more complex Indo-European societies and institutions. (2) The weak and marginalised appearance of the Divine Twins and the Sun Maiden in later Nordic mythology implies that it was heavily transformed during the Iron Age, especially during the Migration Period, by influences from the steppe (the Huns). Nordic Bronze Age religion is much closer to Vedic religion than to later Nordic religion. This demands some revision of the comparative work of Dumezil and his followers, as already suggested (Belier 1995). On the other hand, it creates a historical framework for understanding much of Dumezil's comparative work in IE mythology. In *The Stakes of the Warrior* the same connections between India, Greece and Scandinavia as for the Divine Twins are demonstrated in the very specific, structurally similar but transformed mythological tales of the sins of the warrior (Dumezil 1983).

The dynamic responses from the peripheries during this period of the Bronze Age did not lead to the downfall of the centres, but rather created a new basis for further developments and empire formation, in opposition to the rather similar historical events some hundreds of years later. As the Bronze Age societies on the peripheries had selectively adopted institutions and know-how from the centres, so did the centres in much the same way assimilate and adopt the new military skills and know-how into its institutional framework. In the process they also borrowed some of the cosmological and religious knowledge linked to the new skills and institutions. In the case of conquest migrations, such as India, the whole political and religious framework was adopted and soon after written down in a civilising process, as it is known from many later historical cases. Here the demand for cosmological purity was probably much higher, and therefore we have preserved in the *Rig-Veda* a unique door to Bronze Age society and cosmos. This was shared by the many early Indo-European societies, owing to the tremendous interaction from Scandinavia to the Carpathians and beyond and from the Eurasian steppe to the Carpathians during this period.

Although we have been mainly concerned with tracing and explaining the transmission and transformation of political and religious institutions there can be little doubt that economics were operating in tandem with ideology and politics. The periphery provided goods highly valued in the centres, mainly horses, precious materials such as amber, gold and tin, and specialist craftsmen and warriors. The centres in turn provided highly valued exotic knowledge and prestige goods to the periphery. While we have demonstrated the political/ideological impact on the periphery in this process, the reverse process and its political and economic impact in the centres deserves to be studied in more depth.

By adding historical flesh and blood to the study of centres and peripheries, but without losing sight of the larger historical framework, we believe it is possible to add new perspectives and understandings to the general processes of centre–periphery dynamics.

8.4 The end of the Bronze Age

So far we have demonstrated that worldwide institutional and cosmological correspondences emerged during the Bronze Age. This materialised in numerous local and regional cultural variations, but Bronze Age people would still be able to feel at home when travelling to other groups because of this structural homology. The theocratic nature of Bronze Age societies meant that leadership and divine power were interlinked and interchangeable. People of the Bronze Age lived in a divine, hierarchical order that must have seemed unquestionable and unchangeable. The later caste system in India demonstrates its potential for formalising this social and religious order into a rigid class system in a state regime. It is difficult, if not impossible, to question the divine order when chiefs and kings are considered semi-divine. However, towards the end of the Bronze Age new conditions emerged in Europe, and indeed worldwide, which tended to undermine the cosmological authority of the old order. The Age of Iron gradually changed the economic necessity for travels, as iron was available locally in many places, and thus the whole cosmological order linked to distant ancestors and powers (although they would soon be reconstructed and linked to Roman values).

Two phenomena emerged from this new global situation: the rise of world religions and the concomitant call for a new, less hierarchical order which in many places led to social uprising and revolution. The two phenomena were of course inseparable. The new world religions of the Iron Age – from Buddhism to Christianity – shared a concern with the individual: salvation was to be achieved through personal deeds rather than through the intervention of the divine leadership that often commanded excessive sacrifices to achieve its worldly objectives. Gods were relegated from human intervention by becoming truly divine, and humans became mortals and were separated from the gods. The cosmological transformation and separation is most clearly expressed by the Greeks, who started to distinguish between gods and heroes, the heroic generation belonging to the Bronze Age and the time before and during the Trojan War. 'Criticism of the heroic generations consisted in transforming heroes into simple men and giving them a past that matched that of what were called the human generations, that is history since the Trojan War. The first step of this criticism was to remove the intervention of the gods from history' (Veyne 1988: 41). Thus, the ritual dramas of the Bronze Age gradually turned into theatre, the ritual games and feats into sports and the Olympic games. Cosmos and cosmology became an arena for philosophical reflection, astronomy and mathematics, and atheism became possible (Wright 1995). A new perception of humans, animals and nature followed from this, much closer to that of our own time. After all, we still live in the aftermath of the world religions of the Iron Age.

Responses to these new historical conditions varied – from democracy in Greece to new community-based collectives in northern Europe. One of us has in a previous work demonstrated that there existed a cyclical tendency between egalitarian and hierarchical cosmologies in later prehistory:

> There remained always throughout history a memory – sometimes preserved in myths, sometimes in philosophy – of democratic rights, enforcing a check upon tyranny and exploitation. One of the insights derived from this study is the apparent world-historical pulse in the changes between elite culture and popular movements. Such a case is represented by the 5th century BC, characterised by the fall of 'tyranny' from Greece to central and northern Europe.

> Was the call for democracy running as a silent whisper throughout Europe, preceding social and economic changes? Or were these events simply structurally interlinked, forming world-historical patterns of economic expansions and recessions? Both explanations are probably true. (Kristiansen 1998a: 433, note 15)

One of the insights derived from the present study is the interlocked nature of power and religion during the Bronze Age. Once a separation between the two could be accomplished, if only to a modest degree, it paved the way for a new dynamic between leadership and subordinates, between hierarchy and heterarchy. It enabled commoners and 'dissidents' to voice their opinion against leaders without condemning the gods and the divine order. This opened the way for a new historical dynamic that gradually separated European history from its Bronze Age past, caught in poetry by Hesiod when he described the fall of men from the gods, beginning with a golden race of mortal men, followed by a silver race and a bronze race, ending with the fourth last generation before our own: 'A godlike race of heroes, who are called the demi gods – the race before our own.' These were the Homeric heroes, but now we live in the fifth race of iron: 'I wish I were not of this race, that I had died before, or had not yet been born. This is the race of iron. Now, by day, Men work and grieve unceasingly; by night they waste away and die. The Gods will give harsh burdens, but will mingle in some good' (Hesiod 'Works and Days': 178–82).

8.5   Contemplating the unfamiliar

We started our interpretative journey by claiming that archaeologists have so far not been able to grasp the distinctive historical character – the otherness – of the Bronze Age. We blamed this in part on flaws in present archaeological theorising, having neglected to develop knowledge and concepts for interpreting travels and population movements. We also blamed an implicit back projection of a medieval notion of stable, immovable peasant societies onto later prehistory. While this may hold true for the later Iron Age, the Bronze Age occupies a position between prehistory and history, which has left it without interpretative identity. The Stone Age, and especially the Neolithic, has been accepted as belonging in an unfamiliar prehistory, which opened up new avenues of interpretation (Bradley 1993; Tilley 1996; Thomas 1999). The Iron Age, on the other hand, was anchored in historical time, which provided it with an interpretative identity as well. The Bronze Age fell between two stools, without historical identity. We have identified a number of factors constraining our understanding of the historical nature of the Bronze Age in the past. They include:

1 a theoretical unwillingness to deal with interaction in concrete social terms, in the form of travels and population movements of various kinds

2 an unconscious or implicit bias towards projecting back onto the Bronze Age a medieval/Iron Age feudal model of stable, immovable peasant societies

3 an interpretative or 'cosmological' unwillingness to understand the otherness of the Bronze Age in terms of its embedding of gods, humans, animals and nature

4 an interdisciplinary unwillingness to consider philological, religious and historical sources of the Bronze Age as relevant evidence.

We contend that the otherness of the Bronze Age can only be grasped by taking all these different forms of evidence into consideration. Indeed, we hope to have demonstrated that any broader historical study of religious and social institutions that does not put textual and archaeological/material evidence on an equal footing is doomed to remain historically unbalanced. Our book is an attempt to provide such a new interdisciplinary, interpretative framework and to provide the Bronze Age with a historical identity of its own. It is one that carried along the ritual and cosmological embeddedness of a Neolithic past, while at the same time it took over in a selective way new social and political institutions and dynamics of the Early Bronze Age states and city-states, which continued into the Iron Age. Here they were finally integrated also with new economic dynamics, and a corresponding new cosmological framework. An epoch had come to its end.

Epilogue: towards a new Culture History

Having completed our interpretative journey, we now wish to return to our point of departure in the prologue. To remain in the metaphor of the journey, we propose that archaeologists should leave the safe harbours and homesteads of local processual and contextual studies and enter the roads and seaways that were travelled numerous times during the Bronze Age and beyond. Participation in these networks, some of which we have reconstructed and reinterpreted, was a simple necessity for every local community, from Scandinavia to the Mediterranean and from Ireland to beyond the Urals. Such a framework represents the historical and cosmological context for the social reproduction of local communities throughout the Bronze Age. Consequently we contend that a balanced interpretative strategy is one that engages in the dialectic between openness and closure, between local tradition and foreign influence, and attempts to contextualise and identify those social groups and institutions that undertook travels versus those that stayed home. Only then are we able to understand the social conditions and the motivations for individuals and groups either to travel or to stay at home. This has further theoretical implications.

Since the 1990s archaeological theorising has been characterised by borrowing of theoretical and philosophical concepts and positions from philosophy (time and being), sociology (agency and structuration) and psychology (self and the body), to name a few. While initially this opened up new doors to interpretation it has in the long run tended to constrain rather than promote our understanding of the past. The reason is that such concepts are highly demanding in terms of both their theoretical and their empirical application. Therefore they cannot be generally employed as interpretative tools. The popular notion of agency may exemplify this. We are in agreement with Henrietta Moore when, in a recent book on agency, she characterises concepts linked to understanding self and person, agency and agents, as domain terms, disciplinary shorthand to indicate essential areas of human life (Moore 2000: 262). Their role is to create spaces, and to open things up for analysis, as further stated by Moore. It implies that, to move on from there, they need to be historically contextualised to establish interpretative meaning and direction. Or to stay in the metaphor: once the door is opened the room is empty and needs to be furnished. Agency without social and institutional frameworks is abstract and creates agents without motivation and direction – with the unwarranted effect of leaving too much scope for

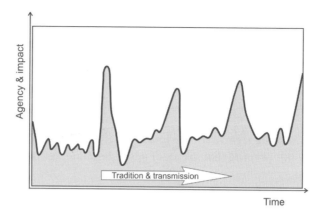

Fig. 169
Simulated socio-seismographic curve of the realisation of agency over time.

Fig. 170
Theoretical model of the dynamic relationship between long-term tradition (A) and short-term transformation (B) and their internal articulation.

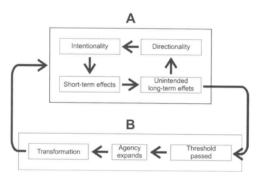

creative interpretations to fill the gaps. Self and social identity, agency and innovation, can only be properly understood against a background of tradition and the socialising role of institutions. Or as succinctly summarised by Sassaman: 'normative structures are long-term derivatives of agency' (Sassaman 2000: 149).

Consequently there is no need for a general theory of agency, as its role emerges from specific historical contexts when properly theorised and contextualised. This is exemplified in Alfred Gell's book *Art and Agency* (1998). He defines agency as being social and relational. That also includes material objects and art, which are ascribed agency (or secondary agency in Gell's terminology) once they are immersed into social relationships. This is exemplified by case studies on religious idols and style. Animation, divinity and power can thus be ascribed to specific objects that have undergone special rituals and/or are decorated in a certain way. The observed practice of interchangeability of agency and power between humans, animals and objects in ethnohistorical contexts can only be meaningfully understood by applying a particular, contextualised definition of agency. In this way Gell turns an abstract western concept of agency into a useful theoretical tool in a specific interpretative context. The same holds true of the related concepts of self, and lived and embodied experience. Only when applied in historical settings with rich and multifaceted evidence on social and institutional conditions do they emerge as meaningful (Meskell and Joyce 2003 for a good example).

Our book may be considered to illustrate such a strategy. It provides historical and institutional frameworks for understanding the social dynamics and motivations linked to travels and interaction. We rarely mention agency, as its meaning is dependent upon a culture-historical and theoretical framework specific to our problematic. The first chapters are devoted to this task, representing a precondition for contextualising the conditions for understanding the formation of the self and the conditions for individuals to act. Such intellectual labour is rarely undertaken in current studies of agency. The preoccupation with agency, knowledgeable agents, embodied experience, rather bears witness to a narcissistic self-centredness of the present academic discourse. Apparently we cannot imagine or accept other conditions in the past than those prevailing in our own lives in the present. But the wish to find comfort or confirmation in the past rarely enlarges our understanding of the otherness of the past. The truly historical contribution from past histories lies in our ability to learn something new and unexpected from their otherness. This may ultimately change and enrich our perspectives on the present.

During the Bronze Age, realisation of the self for certain groups of male chiefly individuals was to be achieved by travelling. If we consider the potential for agency in a time/space framework one might say that there was little room for acting out individual ambitions at the local level. Other mechanisms were available to channel human creativity and social stress, exemplified by the role of religious women in rituals (chapter 5.1) and warriors on the move (chapter 5.2). By accumulating wisdom and knowledge from distant places, there was more room for employing this new prestige upon returning to the local community. However, such acting out was constrained by tradition. In periods of change new room for outstanding individuals – whether male or female – emerged, as exemplified by the Kivik burial (chapter 5.3), but such periods were few and far between. Normally agency remained a controlled, vibrant quality that helped to promote gradual change or to resist change. In Figure 169 we have exemplified this difference between temporal and spatial axes of agency in the Bronze Age.[3] In Figure 170 we provide the theoretical model to account for the dynamic

---

3 In addition our study proposes that the creation of large-scale historical interactions during the Early Bronze Age left a lasting impact on the history of Eurasia. Knut Odner has taken over the concept of Great Traditions from social anthropology to account for the emergence of such traditions, such as Bantu or Indo-European – traditions that share certain fundamentals and yet are divided in numerous ways by local adaptations and deviations, so-called Little Traditions (Odner 2000; Rowlands 2003). However, we are less concerned with discussing the historical end-product than with reconstructing and understanding the concrete historical processes taking place. We must know what historically constituted the formation of Great Traditions – if they ever existed – before we can start discussing them. In the process we learn

relationship between social change and agency under conditions of continuity (case A) and their development over the long term into a social transformation (case B). In this way we summarise the theoretical implications of our study for the role and conditions of human agency/intentionality in social change.

What we are proposing and exemplifying in our book is a return to a truly holistic cultural historical framework. Moving forward towards archaeology as history demands a return to Culture History and a contextualised search for historical and evolutionary regularities in the formation of particular histories. It represents the only authentic framework for archaeological theorising, as it is rooted in the historical realities of past lived experiences, their accumulated effect and their historical materialisation in time and space. Consequently the theoretical and interpretative repertoire of archaeology should be derived from the general field of culture-historical studies – history, social anthropology, ethnology and history of religion to name a few. We thus propose a return to a comparative, contextualised Culture History for constructing relevant theoretical and interpretative concepts at a particular level of historical reconstruction and explanation. From here we see a rich field of enquiry that combines local, regional and interregional studies at all levels. Local studies gain new significance when understood in their proper historical contexts, just as interregional studies of travels and trade may probe deeper into the dynamics between foreign and local in the formation of (or resistance to) new social institutions and cultural cosmologies. Such an approach takes material culture studies far beyond agency and other ideological symptoms of the present poverty of theory. Instead it situates archaeology and culture history at the centre stage for a powerful revival of a new Culture History that is both particular and generally comparative. History has happened, and it should be unfolded in all its variety irrespective of disciplinary boundaries. This demands a reorientation at many levels of academic training and research. Our book is a contribution towards such goals.

that political-religious institutions (theocratic leadership) were transmitted and transformed widely throughout Eurasia during the Bronze Age, and to understand them demands the development of a comparative, interdisciplinary culture-historical approach. Thus, the Bronze Age was the major historical epoch of theocratic leadership, only to decline with the advent of the Iron Age and the formation of world religions. But even in the Bronze Age we find at least two opposing and competing traditions of leadership and gender roles: one where warriors and warfare were heroic and ritualised in burials (the Indo-European tradition), and one where this was not the case (the Near Eastern tradition), but women instead played a major role in religion. These two traditions were represented by Mycenaean and Minoan society, but they are replayed in central and northern Europe, where they finally merge. They represent two potentially different lines of historical trajectory and one might see them unfolded historically in Buddhism and Christianity/Islam.

References

Acheson, P. 1999 The role of force in the development of early Mycenaean polities. In Laffineur 1999: 97–104.

Adams, R. McC. 2001 Complexity in archaic states. *Journal of Field Archaeology* 20: 345–60.

Akurgal, E. 1962 *The Art of the Hittites*. London.

Alberti, B. 2002 Gender and the figurative art of Late Bronze Age Knossos. In Hamilakis 2002b: 74–98.

Aldred, C. 1988 *Akhenaten: King of Egypt*. London.

Alexander, R. L. 1993 The storm-god at Yazilikaya: sources and influences. In *Aspects of Art and Iconography: Anatolia and Its Neighbors. Studies in Honor of Nimet Özgüç*, ed. A. J. Mellinik, E. Porada and T. Özgüç, pp. 1–13. Ankara.

Algaze, G. 1989 The Uruk expansion. Cross-cultural exchange in early Mesopotamian Civilization. *Current Anthropology* 30, no. 5: 571–608.

Alimov, K. *et al.* 1998 Prähistorischer Zinnbergbau in Mittelasien. Vorbericht der Kampagne 1997. *Eurasia Antiqua* 4: 137–99.

Almgren, O. 1927 *Hällristningar och kultbruk*. Stockholm.

Alp, S. 1988 Einige weitere Bemerkungen zum Hirschrhyton der Norbert Schimmel-Sammlung. In *Studi di storia e di filologia anatolica dedicato a Giovanni Pugliese Carratelli*, ed. F. Imparati, pp. 17–23. Florence.

Althin, C.-A. 1946 *Studien zu den bronzezeitlichen Felszeichnungen von Skåne*. Lund.

Anati, E. 1993 *World Rock Art: The Primordial Language*. Capo di Ponte.

Andersen, S. T. 1995 History of vegetation and agriculture at Hassing House Mose, Thy, Northwest Denmark. *Journal of Danish Archaeology* 1992–3: 39–57.

1998 Pollen analytical investigations of barrows from the Funnel Beaker and Single Grave cultures in the Vroue area, West Jutland, Denmark. *Journal of Danish Archaeology* 1994–5: 107–33.

Anderson, E. R. 1999 Horse-sacrifice and kingship in the secret history of the Mongols and Indo-European culture. *Journal of Indo-European Studies* 27, no. 3–4: 379–95.

Anderson Ambrosiani, P. 1997 Avbildningar av guldhalsringar i Kiviksgraven. In *Till Gunborg: arkeologiska samtal*, ed. A. Åkerlund, pp. 463–70. Stockholm.

Andrén, A. 1993 Doors to other worlds: Scandinavian death rituals in Gotlandic perspectives. *Journal of European Archaeology* 1: 33–56.

1998 *Between Artefacts and Texts: Historical Archaeology in Global Perspective*. New York.

2000 Re-reading embodied texts – an interpretation of rune-stones. *Current Swedish Archaeology* 8: 7–32.

Andritoiu, I. 1992 *Civilizatia Tracilor din Sud: Vestul Transilvaniei Epoca Bronzului*. Bibliotheca Thracologica 2. Bucarest.

Aner, E. and Kersten, K. 1973 *Die Funde der älteren Bronzezeit des nordischen Kreises in Dänemark, Schleswig-Holstein und Niedersachsen*, vol. I. Copenhagen.

1976 *Die Funde der älteren Bronzezeit des nordischen Kreises in Dänemark, Schleswig-Holstein und Niedersachsen*, vol. II. Copenhagen.

1977 *Die Funde der älteren Bronzezeit des nordischen Kreises in Dänemark, Schleswig-Holstein und Niedersachsen*, vol. III. Copenhagen.

1978 *Die Funde der älteren Bronzezeit des nordischen Kreises in Dänemark, Schleswig-Holstein und Niedersachsen*, vol. IV. Copenhagen.

1981 *Die Funde der älteren Bronzezeit des nordischen Kreises in Dänemark, Schleswig-Holstein und Niedersachsen*, vol. VII. Neumünster.

1986 *Die Funde der älteren Bronzezeit des nordischen Kreises in Dänemark, Schleswig-Holstein und Niedersachsen*, vol. VIII. Copenhagen.

Anfinset, N. 2000 Copper technology in contemporary western Nepal. A discussion of its form, function and context. In Olausson and Vandkilde 2000: 203–12.

Angel, J. L. 1972 Human skeletons from grave circles at Mycenae. In Mylonas 1972: 141–9.

Anretter, P., Bartosiewicz, L., Jerem, E. and Meid, W. (eds.) 1998 *Man and the Animal World: Studies in Archaeozoology, Archaeology, Anthropology and Palaeolinguistics in memoriam Sandor Bökönyi*. Budapest.

Anthony, D. W. 1986 The 'Kurgan Culture', Indo-European origins, and the domestication of the horse: a reconsideration. *Current Anthropology* 27, no. 4: 291–313.

1995 Horse, wagon and chariot: Indo-European languages and archaeology. *Antiquity* 69: 554–65.

1998 The opening of the Eurasian steppe at 2000 BCE. In *The Bronze Age and Early Iron Age Peoples of Eastern Central Asia*, ed. V. Mair, vol. I, pp. 94–113. Philadelphia.

Antonova, I., Tolstikov, V. and Treister, M. 1996 *The Gold of Troy: Searching for Homer's Fabled City*. London.

Arafat, K. and Morgan, C. 1994 Athens, Etruria and the Heuneburg: mutual misconceptions in the study of Greek–barbarian relations. In *Classical Greece: Ancient Histories and Modern Archaeologies*, ed. I. Morris. Cambridge.

Arnold, J. E. 2000 Power, labor rights, and kinship. Archaeology and social theory. In Schiffer 2000: 14–30.

Arnott, R. 2002 (ed.) *The Archaeology of Medicine*. British Archaeological Reports. International Series 1046. Oxford.

Ashbee, P. 1989 The Trundholm horse's trappings: a chamfrein. *Antiquity* 63: 539–46.

Ashing, P. 1987 Diverhøj. The excavation of a complex burial mound and a Neolithic settlement. With a contribution by Lise Beder Jørgensen. *Journal of Danish Archaeology* 6: 130–54.

Asouti, E. 2003 Wood charcoal from Santorini (Thera): new evidence for climate, vegetation and timber imports in the Aegean Bronze Age. *Antiquity* 77: 471–84.

Åström, P. 1977 *The Cuirass Tomb and Other Finds at Dendra*. Göteborg.

Atley, S. and Findlow, F. (eds.) 1984 *Exploring the Limits: Frontiers and Boundaries in Prehistory*. Oxford.

Bader, T. 1978 *Epoca Bronzului in nord-vestul Transilvaniei*. Bucharest.

1990 Bemerkungen über die ägäischen Einflüsse auf die alt- und mittelbronzezeitliche Entwicklung im Donau-Karpatenraum. In *Orientalisch-ägäische Einflüsse in der europäischen Bronzezeit: Ergebnisse eines Kolloquiums*, ed. T. Bader, pp. 7–31. Römisch-Germanisches Zentralmuseum 15. Bonn.

1991 *Die Schwerter in Rumänien*. Prähistorische Bronzefunde 4, 8. Stuttgart.

1996 Neue Bronzefunde in Nordwestrumänien. In *Studien zur Metallindustrie im Karpatenbecken und den benachbarten Regionen*, ed. T. Kovács, pp. 265–301. Budapest.

1998 Bemerkungen zur Bronzezeit im Karpatenbecken Otomani/Füzesabony-Komplex. Überblick und Fragestellung. *Jahreschrift für Mitteldeutsche Vorgeschichte* 80: 43–108.

Baillie, M. 1998 Evidence for climatic deterioration in the 12th and 17th centuries BC. In B. Hänsel 1998a: 49–56.

Baines, J. and Yoffee, N. 1998 Order, legitimacy, and wealth in ancient Egypt and Mesopotamia. In Feinman and Marcus 1998: 199–260.

Bamforth, D. G. 1994 Indigenous people, indigenous violence: precontact warfare on the North American Great Plains. *Man* (N.S.) 29: 95–115.

Barfield, L. 1991 Wessex with and without Mycenae: new evidence from Switzerland. *Antiquity* 65: 102–7.

1994 The Bronze Age of northern Italy: recent work and social interpretation. In Mathers and Stoddart 1994: 129–44.

Barlay, A. 2001 The Potnia of Theron: adaptation of a Near Eastern image. In Laffineur and Hägg 2001: 374–86.

Barrett, J. 1989 Time and tradition: the rituals of everyday life. In Nordström and Knape 1989: 113–27.

1994 *Fragments from Antiquity*. Oxford.

1998 The politics of scale and the experience of distance: the Bronze Age world system. *KVHAA Konferencer* 40: 13–25. Stockholm.

Bartelheim, M. 1998 *Studien zur böhmischen Aunjetitzer Kultur: Chronologische und chorologische Untersuchungen*. Universitätsforschungen zur prähistorischen Archäologie 46. Bonn.

2002 Metallurgie und Gesellschaft der Frühbronzezeit Mitteleuropas. In *Vom Endneolithicum zur Frühbronzezeit: Muster sozialen Wandels?*, ed. J. Müller, pp. 29–45. Bonn.

Bartelheim, M., Pernicka, E. and Krause, R. (eds.) 2002 *Die Anfänge der Metallurgie in der alten Welt*. Forschungen zur Archäometrie und Altertumswissenschaft 1. Rahnen, Westfalen, and Leidorf.

Bass, G. 1986 A Bronze Age shipwreck at Ulu Burun (Kas), 1984 campaign. *American Journal of Archaeology* 90: 269–96.

1991 Evidence of trade from Bronze Age shipwrecks. In *Bronze Age Trade in the Mediterranean*, ed. N. H. Gale. Studies in Mediterranean Archaeology, pp. 69–83. Jonsered.

1997 Prolegomena to a study of maritime traffic in raw materials to the Aegean during the fourteenth and thirteenth centuries BC. In Laffineur and Betancourt 1997: 153–71.

1998 Sailing between the Aegean and the Orient in the second millennium BC. In *The Aegean and the Orient in the Second Millennium*, ed. E. H. Cline and D. Harris-Cline, pp. 183–91. Liège.

Batora, J. 1995 Fayence und Bernstein im nördlichen Karpatenraum während der Frühbronzezeit. In Hänsel 1995: 187–96.

2000 *Das Gräberfeld von Jelsovce/Slowakei: ein Beitrag zur Frühbronzezeit im nordwestlichen Karpatenbecken*, vols. I–II. Prähistorische Archäologie in Südosteuropa 16. Kiel.

Baudou, E. 1960 *Die regionale und chronologische Einteilung der jungeren Bronzezeit im nordische Kreis.* Stockholm.

Beal, R. 1992 *The Organization of the Hittite Military.* Heidelberg.

   1995 Hittite military organization. In *Civilizations of the Ancient Near East*, ed. J. M. Sasson, vol. I, pp. 545–54. New York.

Bech, J. 2002 *Fra fortidsminder til kulturmiljø.* Copenhagen.

Bech, J. H. 2003 The Thy Archaeological Project – results and reflections from a multi-national archaeological project. In Thrane 2003: 45–61.

Bech, J. H. and Mikkelsen, M. 1999 Landscapes, settlement and subsistence in Bronze Age Thy, NW Denmark. In Fabech and Ringtved 1999: 69–77.

Becker, C. *et al.* (eds.) 1997 *Studia honoraria: Festschrift für Bernhard Hänsel.* Internationale Archäologie 1. Espelkamp.

Beckman, G. 1995 Royal ideology and state administration in Hittite Anatolia. In *Civilizations of the Ancient Near East*, ed. J. M. Sasson, vol. I, pp. 529–43. New York.

   1996 *Hittite Diplomatic Texts.* Atlanta.

Behre, K.-E. 1998 Landwirtschaftliche Entwicklungslinien und die Veränderung der Kulturlandschaft in der Bronzezeit Europas. In Hänsel 1982a: 91–109.

Belier, W. 1995 The first function: a critical analysis. In *Indo-European Religion after Dumezil*, ed. E. Polome. Journal of Indo-European Studies Monograph Series 16, pp. 13–37.

Bender, B. (ed.) 1993 *Landscape: Politics and Perspectives.* London.

Benecke, N. 1998 Haustierhaltung, Jagd und Kult mit Tieren im bronzezeitlichen Mitteleuropa. In Hänsel 1998a: 61–75.

Bengtsson, L. 2004 *Bilder vid vatten.* (English summary). Gotarc Serie C, 51. Gothenburg University.

Bennet, J. 1997 Homer and the Bronze Age. In *A New Companion to Homer*, eds. I. Morris and B. Powell, pp. 511–34. Mnemosyne, Biblioteca Classica Batava. Brill, Leiden, New York and Cologne.

Bennett, E. L. 1962 On the use and misuse of the term 'priest-king'. *KretChron* 15–16: 327–35.

Berggreen, B. and Marinatos, N. (eds.) 1995 *Greece and Gender.* Papers from the Norwegian Institute at Athens 2. Bergen.

Bernal, M. 1987 On the transmission of the alphabet to the Aegean before 1400 BC *BASOR* 267: 1–19.

Bertemes, F. 2000 Zur Entstehung der danubischen Frühbronzezeit in Mitteleuropa. In Memoriam Jan Rulf. *Pamatky Archeologické, Supplementum* 13: 25–37.

Bertemes, F. and Heyd, V. 1996 Definition et origine de l'Age du Bronze ancien en Europe centrale. In Mordant and Gaiffe 1996: 13–37.

   2002 Der Übergang Kupferzeit/Frühbronzezeit am Nordwestrand des Karpatenbeckens – kulturgeschichtliche und paläometallurgische Betrachtungen. In Bartelheim, Pernicka and Krause 2002: 185–229.

Bertilsson, U. 1987 *The Rock Carvings of Northern Bohuslän.* Stockholm.

Betancourt, P. 2002 Who was in charge of the palaces? In Driessen, Schoep and Laffineur 2002: 207–13.

Betancourt, P., Karageorghis, V., Laffineur, R. and Niemeier, W.-D. (eds.) 1999 *Meletemata: Studies in Aegean Archaeology Presented to Malcolm H. Wiener as He Enters His 65th Year.* Aegaeum 20. Liège.

Bettelli, M. and Vagnetti, L. 1997 Aspetti delle relazioni fra l'area egeo-micenea e l'Italia settentrionale. In Brea, Cardarelli and Cremaschi 1997: 614–20.

Biedermann, H. 1993 *Symbollexikonet*. Borås.

Bietak, M. 1992 Minoan wall-paintings unearthed at ancient Avaris. *Egyptian Archaeology* 2: 26–8.

1995 Connections between Egypt and the Minoan world: new results from Tell el-Dab'a/Avaris. In *Egypt, the Aegean and the Levant: Interconnections in the Second Millennium BC*, ed. W. V. Davies and L. Schofield, pp. 19–28. London.

2000 Rich beyond the dreams of Avaris: Tell el-Dab'a and the Aegean world – a guide for the perplexed: a response to Eric Cline. *Annual of the British School of Athens* 95: 185–205.

Bietti-Sestieri, A. M. 1992 *The Iron Age Community of Osteria dell'Osa: A Study of Socio-Political Development in Central Tyrrhenian Italy*. Cambridge.

Billamboz, A. and Martinelli, A. 1996 La recherche dendrochronologique en Europe pour l'Age du Bronze ancien. In Mordant and Gaiffe 1996: 85–97.

Binford, L. R. 1962 Archaeology as anthropology. *American Antiquity* 28: 217–25.

1965 Archaeological systematics and the study of culture process. *American Antiquity*, 31(2): 203–210.

(ed.) 1991 *The Annales School and Archaeology*. Leicester.

Bittel, K. 1976 *Die Hethiter*. Berlin.

Blankholmer, F. (ed.) 2000 *Österreichische Forschungen zur ägäischen Bronzezeit 1998*. Akten der Tagung am Institut für klassische Archäologie der Universität Wien 2.3. Mai 1998. Vienna.

Blanton, R. E., Feinman, G. M., Kowalevski, S. A. and Peregrine, P. N. 1996 A dual-processual theory for the evolution of Mesoamerican civilisation. *Current Anthropology* 37: 1–14.

Blench, R. and Spriggs, M. (eds.) 1997 *Archaeology and Language I. Theoretical and Methodological Orientations*. One World Archaeology 27. London.

Blischke, J. 2002 *Gräberfelder als Spiegel der historischen Entwicklung während der mittleren Bronzezeit im mittleren Donaugebiet*. Universitätsforschungen zur prähistorischen Archäologie 8, 80. Bonn.

Bloch, M. 1977 The disconnection between power and rank as a process: an outline of the development of kingdoms in central Madagascar. In *The Evolution of Social Systems*, eds. J. Friedman and M. Rowlands. London.

Bloedow, E. F. 1997 Itinerant craftsmen and trade in the Aegean Bronze Age. In Laffineur and Betancourt 1997: 439–49.

2003 The significance of the goat in Minoan culture. *Praehistorische Zeitschrift* 78: 1–59.

Boas, N. A. and Rasmussen, L. W. 2001 Dystrup. *Journal of Danish Archaeology* 14 (in press).

Bohannan, P. (ed.) 1967 *Law and Warfare: Studies in the Anthropology of Conflict*. American Museum Sourcebooks in Anthropology. New York.

Bona, I. 1975 *Die mittelere Bronzezeit Ungarns und ihre südöstlichen Beziehungen*. Budapest.

1992a Bronzeguss und Metallbearbeitung bis zum Ende der mittleren Bronzezeit. In Bona 1992b: 48–65.

(ed.) 1992b *Bronzezeit in Ungarn: Forschungen in Tell-Siedlungen an Donau und Theiss*. Frankfurt-am-Main.

Born, H. and Hansen, S. 2001 *Helme und Waffen Alteuropas*, vol. IX. Mainz.

Boroffka, N. 1998 Bronze- und früheisenzeitlichen Geweihtrensenknebel aus Rumänien und ihre Beziehungen. In *Eurasia Antiqua*, pp. 81–135. Zeitschrift für Archäologie Eurasiens 4. Mainz.

Boroffka, N. and Sava, E. 1998 Zu den steinernen 'Zeptern/Stössel-Zeptern', 'Miniatursäulen' und 'Phalli' der Bronzezeit Eurasiens. *Archäologische Mittellungen aus Iran und Turan* 30: 17–113. Berlin.

Boroffka, N. *et al.* 2002 Bronze Age tin from Central Asia. In Boyle, Renfrew and Levine 2002: 135–59.

Bouzek, J. 1966 The Aegean and Central Europe, an introduction to the study of cultural interrelations 1600–1300 BC. *Pamatky Archeologické* 57, 1: 242–77.

1969 *Homerisches Griechenland*. Prague.

1972 Syrian and Anatolian Bronze Age figurines in Europe. *Proceedings of the Prehistoric Society* 38: 156–64.

1985a *The Aegean, Anatolia and Europe: Cultural Interrelations in the Second Millennium B.C.* Studies in Mediterranean Archaeology 29. Göteborg.

1985b *Relations between Barbarian Europe and the Aegean Civilizations. Advances in World Archaeology* 4. New York.

1996a European Bronze Age hoards and their Mediterranean parallels. In *Studien zur Metallindustrie im Karpatenbecken und den benachbarten Regionen*, ed. T. Kovács, pp. 421–2. Budapest.

1996b The problem of migration in Mycenaean Greece. In De Miro, Godart and Sacconi 1996: 685–92.

1997 *Greece, Anatolia and Europe: Cultural Interrelations during the Early Iron Age*. Studies in Mediterranean Archaeology 122. Jonsered.

2001 Apollon Hyperboréen, le héro solaire et l'âme humaine. *Bulletin de Correspondence Hellénique. Supplement 38. Myth et Cultes*: 57–62.

Boye, W. 1896 *Fund af Egekister fra Bronzealderen i Danmark*. Copenhagen (reprinted 1986, Aarhus).

Boyle, K., Renfrew, C. and Levine, M. (eds.) 2002 *Ancient Interactions: East and West in Eurasia*. Cambridge.

Boymel, N. (ed.) 1996 *Sexuality into Ancient Art: Near East, Egypt, Greece and Italy*. Cambridge.

Bradley, R. 1993 *Altering the Earth*. Society of Antiquaries of Scotland. Monograph Series 8. Edinburgh.

1997 *Rock Art and the Prehistory of Atlantic Europe*. New York and London.

2002 *The Past in Prehistoric Societies*. New York and London.

Branigan, K. 1984 Minoan community colonies in the Aegean? In Hägg and Marinatos 1984: 49–53.

1998 The nearness of you: proximity and distances in Early Minoan funerary landscapes. In *Cemetery and Society in the Aegean Bronze Age*, ed. K. Branigan, pp. 13–26. Sheffield Studies in Aegean Archaeology. Sheffield.

Braudel, F. 1972 *The Mediterranean in the Age of Philip II*. London.

Bravik, J. 1997 Horses and ships in Vedic and Old Greek material. *Journal of Indo-European Studies* 25, no. 3–4: 345–51.

Brea, M. B., Cardarelli, A. and Cremaschi, M. (eds.) 1997 *Le Terramare*. LaPiu Antica Civiltà Padana Milan.

Bridgford, S. D. 1997 Mightier than the pen? (An edgewise look at Irish Bronze Age swords). In Carman 1997: 95–116.

Brodie, N. 1997 New perspectives on the Bell-Beaker Culture. *Oxford Journal of Archaeology* 16, no. 3: 297–314.

2001 Technological frontiers and the emergence of the Beaker culture. In *Bell Beakers Today*. Riva del Garda, 11–16 May 1998 – Trento, pp. 487–96. Trento.

Broholm, H.-C. 1943 *Danmarks Bronzealder*, vol. I. Copenhagen.

1944 *Danmarks Bronzealder*, vol. II. Copenhagen.

1949 *Danmarks Bronzealder*, vol. IV. Copenhagen.

1952 *Danske oldsager: Ældre Bronzealder*. Copenhagen.

1953 *Danske oldsager: Yngre Bronzealder*. Copenhagen.

1965 *Lurfundene fra bronzealderen* (Resumé: The Lurs of the Bronze Age in Denmark). Copenhagen.

Broholm, H.-C. and Hald, M. 1940 *Costumes of the Bronze Age in Denmark*. Copenhagen.

Broodbank, C. 2000 *An Island Archaeology of the Early Cyclades*. Cambridge.

Brück, J. 1999 Ritual and rationality: some problems of interpretation in European archaeology. *European Journal of Archaeology* 2, no. 3: 313–44.

2000 Settlement, landscape and social identity: the Early–Middle Bronze Age transition in Wessex, Sussex and the Thames Valley. *Oxford Journal of Archaeology* 19, no. 3: 273–300.

Brumfiel, E. and Fox, J. (eds.) 1994 *Factional Competition and Political Development in the New World*. Cambridge.

Brumfiel, E. M. and Earle, T. K. 1987 Specialization, exchange and complex societies: an introduction. In *Specialization, Exchange and Complex Societies*, ed. E. M. Brumfiel and T. K. Earle, pp. 1–9. Cambridge.

Brun, P. 1993 East–west relations in the Paris Basin during the Late Bronze Age. In *Trade and Exchange in Prehistoric Europe*, ed. C. Scarre and F. Healy, pp. 171–82. Oxford.

1995 Contacts entre colons et indigènes au milieu du Ier millénaire av. J.-C. en Europe. *Journal of European Archaeology* 3, no. 2: 113–23.

Bryan, B. 1991 *The Reign of Thutmose IV*. Baltimore.

Bryce, T. 1998 *The Kingdom of the Hittites*. Oxford.

Buchholz, H.-G. 1974 *Archaeologia Homerica: die Denkmäler und das frühgriechische Epos*. Göttingen.

1987a Spätbronzezeitliche Beziehungen der Ägäis zum Westen. In *Ägäische Bronzezeit*, vols. I–II. Darmstadt.

(ed.) 1987b *Ägäische Bronzezeit*, vols. I–II. Darmstadt.

1999 Ein aussergewöhnlichen Steinzepter im östlichen Mittelmeer. *Praehistorische Zeitschrift* 74, no. 1: 68–78.

Bunyatyan, K. P. 2003 Correlations between agriculture and pastoralism in the northern Pontic Steppe area during the Bronze Age. In Levine, Renfrew and Boyle (2003): 269–87.

Burenhult, G. 1980 *The Rock Carvings of Götaland*. Stockholm.

Burgess, C. 1996 'Urns', culture du Wessex et la transition bronze ancien–bronze moyen en Grande-Bretagne. In Mordant and Gaiffe 1996: 605–23.

Burgess, C. and Coombs, D. 1979 *Bronze Age Hoards: Some Finds Old and New*. BAR British Series 67. Oxford.

Burgess, C. and Gerloff, S. 1981 *The Dirks and Rapiers of Great Britain and Ireland*. Prähistorische Bronzefunde 4, 7. Stuttgart.

Burkert, W. 1979 *Structure and History in Greek Mythology and Ritual*. Sather Classical Lectures 47. Berkeley.

Butler, J. J. 1963 *Bronze Age Connections across the North Sea: A Study in Prehistoric Trade and Industrial Relations between the British Islers, The Netherlands, North Germany and Scandinavia c.1700–700 B.C.* Palaeohistoria 9. Groningen.

 1986 *Drouwen: end of a 'Nordic' Rainbow?* Palaeohistoria 28. Groningen.

Cameron, M. A. S. 1967 Unpublished fresco fragment of a chariot composition from Knossos. *Archäologischer Anzeiger*: 330–44.

Carancini, G. L. 1997 La produzione metallurgica delle terramare nel quadro dell'Italia protostorica. In Brea, Cardarelli and Cremaschi 1997: 379–405.

Cardarelli, A. 1997 The evolution of settlement and demography in the Terramare Culture. In Rittershofer 1997b: 230–8.

Cardarelli, A., Pacciarelli, M. and Pallante, P. 1997 Pesida bilancia dell'età del bronzo? In Brea, Cardarelli and Cremaschi 1997: 629–43.

 (ed.) 1997 *Material Harm: Archaeological Studies of War and Violence*. Glasgow.

Carman, J. (ed.) 1997 *Material Harm. Archaeological Studies of War and Violence*. Glasgow.

Carneiro, R. L. 1970 A theory of the origin of the state. *Science* 169: 733–8.

 1990 Chiefdom-level warfare as exemplified in Fiji and the Cauca Valley. In Haas 1990: 733–8.

Carpenter, R. 1968 *Discontinuity in Greek Civilization*. New York.

Cavalin, C. 2002 *The Efficacy of Sacrifice: Correspondences in the Rigvedic Hrahmanas*. Göteborg.

Cavruk, V. 1998 Once more about the Ponto-Caspian factor in the formation of the Noua Culture. *Thraco-Dacica* 19, nos. 1–2: 93–111.

Celestino Perez, S. 2001 *Estelas de guerrero y estelas diademadas: la precolonizacion y formacion del mundo tartesico*. Barcelona.

Chapman, R. 2003 *Archaeologies of Complexity*. London and New York.

Chapoutier, F. 1934 *Les Discoures au service de la Déese: étude d'iconographie religieuse*. Paris.

Chernykh, E. N. 1998 Ancient mining and metallurgy in Eastern Europe: ecological problems. In Hänsel 1998b: 129–33.

 1992 *Ancient Metallurgy in the USSR*. Cambridge.

 2002a Ancient mining and metallurgic production on the border between Europe and Asia: the Kargaly center. *Archaeology, Ethnology and Anthropology of Eurasia* 3, no. 11: 88–106.

 (ed.) 2002b *Kargaly Volume I: Geological and Geographical Characteristiscs. Histories of Discoveries, Exploitation and Investigations. Archaeological Sites*. Moscow.

 (ed.) 2002c *Kargaly Volume II: Gorny – the Late Bronze Age Settlement. Topography, Lithology, Stratigraphy. Household, Manufacturing and Sacral Structures. Relative and Absolute Chronology*. Moscow.

Chernykh, E. N., Antipina, E. E. and Lebedeva, E. J. 1998 Produktionsformen der Urgesellschaft in den Steppen Osteuropas (Ackerbau, Viehzucht, Erzgewinnung undverhüttung). In Hänsel and Machnik 1998: 233–53.

Chernykh, E. N., Avilova, L. I. and Orlovskaya, L. B. 2000 *Metallurgical Provinces and Radiocarbon Chronology*. Moscow (English abstract).

2002 Metallurgy of the Circumpontic Area: from unity to disintegration. *Der Anschnitt. Zeitschrift für Kunst und Kultur im Bergbau* 15: 83–100. Anatolian Metal II.

Chernykh, E. N. and Kuzminykh, S. V. 1989 *Ancient Metallurgy in the Northern Eurasia (Seyma-Turbino Phenomenon)*. Moscow (English Summary).

Cherry, J. F. 1986 Polities and palaces: some problems in Minoan state formation. In Renfrew and Cherry 1986: 19–47.

Chew, S. C. 2001 *World Ecological Degradation: Accumulation, Urbanization, and Deforestation 3000 B.C.–A.D. 2000*. Walnut Creek.

2002 Globalisation, ecological crisis, and Dark Ages. *Global Society* 16, no. 4: 334–56.

Chicideanu-Sandor, M. and Chicideanu, I. 1990 Contributions to the study of the Girla Mare anthropomorphic statuettes. *Dacia* N.S. 34: 53–75.

Childe, V. G. 1930 *The Bronze Age*. Cambridge.

Chochorowski, I. 1993 *Ekspansja kimmeryska na tereny europy srodkowej* (Zusammenfassung: die kimmerische Expansion in das mitteleuropäsiche Gebiet). Krakow.

Chryssoulaki, S. 1999 Minoan roads and guard houses: war regained. In Laffineur 1999: 75–86.

Clark, J. E. 2000 Towards a better explanation of hereditary inequality: a critical assessment of natural and historical agents. In Dobres and Robb 2000: 92–113.

Clarke, D. L. 1968 *Analytical Archaeology*. London. Methuen.

Clarke, D. V., Cowie, T. G. and Foxon, A. 1985 *Symbols of Power: At the Time of Stonehenge*. Edinburgh.

Cline, E. H. 1991 Hittite objects in the Bronze Age Aegean. *Anatolian Studies* 41: 133–43.

1994 *Sailing the Wine-Dark Sea*. BAR International Series 591. Oxford.

1995a 'My brother, my son': rulership and trade between the Late Bronze Age Aegean, Egypt and the Near East. In *The Role of the Ruler in the Prehistoric Agaean*, ed. P. Rehak, pp. 143–50. Aegaeum 11. Liège.

1995b Egyptian and Near Eastern imports at Late Bronze Age Mycenae. In *Egypt, the Aegean and the Levant: Interconnections in the Second Millennium BC*, ed. W. Vivian Davies and L. Schofield, pp. 91–115. London.

Cline, E. H. and Harris-Cline, D. 1998 (eds.) *The Aegean and the Orient in the Second Millennium*. Aegaeum 18. Liège.

Coffyn, A. 1985 *Le Bronze final atlantique dans la péninsule ibérique*. Paris.

Coffyn, A., Gomez, J. and Mohen, J.-P. 1981 *L'Apogée du bronze atlantique*. L'âge du bronze en France 1. Paris.

Colarusso, J. 2002 *Nart Sagas from the Caucasus*. Princeton.

Coles, J. 1995 *Bilder från forntiden*. Uddevalla.

2000 *Patterns in a Rocky Land*. AUN 27. University of Uppsala.

2002 Chariots of the Gods? Landscape and imagery at Frännarp, Sweden. *Proceedings of the Prehistoric Society* 68: 215–46.

2003 And on they went. Processions in Scandinavian Bronze Age rock carvings. *Acta Archaeologica* 74: 211–50.

Collett, D. 1987 A contribution to the study of migrations in the archaeological record: the Ngoni and Kololo migrations as a case study. In *Archaeology as Long-Term History*, ed. I. Hodder, pp. 105–17. Cambridge.

Conkey, M. and Hastorf, C. (eds.) 1990 *The Uses of Style in Archaeology*. Cambridge.

Coombs, D. 1975 *Bronze Age Weapon Hoards in Britain*. Archaeologia Atlantica 1. Bonn.

Cooper, J. S. 1983 *The Curse of Agad*. Baltimore.

Cornell, P., Fahlander, F. and Kristiansen, K. 1998 *Arkeologiska texter. Trendanalyser av Nordisk Periodica*. GOTARC Series C, 21. Gothenburg.

Cowie, T. 1988 *Magic Metal: Early Metalworkers in the North-East*. Aberdeen.

Crawford, H. 1996 Dilmun, victim of world recession. *Proceedings of the Seminar for Arabian Studies* 26: 13–22.

Crielaard, J. P. 2000 Homeric and Mycenaean long-distance contacts: discrepancies in the evidence. *BaBesh* 75: 51–65. Leiden.

Crossland, R. A. and Birchall, A. (eds.) 1974 *Bronze Age Migrations in the Aegean: Archaeological and Linguistic Problems in Greek Prehistory*. Princeton.

Crouwel, J. 2004 Der alte Orient und seine Rolle in der Entwicklung von Fahrzeugen. In Fansa and Burrmeister 2004: 67–86.

Crumley, C. 1987 A dialectical critique of hierarchy. In *Power Relations and State Formation*, ed. T. Patterson and C. Gailey, pp. 155–68. Washington, DC.

   1995 Heterarchy and the analysis of complex socities. In *Heterarchy and the Analysis of Complex Societies*, ed. R. M. Ehrenreich, C. M. Crumley and J. E. Levy, pp. 1–5, Archaeological Papers of the American Anthropological Association 6. Washington, DC.

   2001 Communication, holism, and the evolution of sociopolitical complexity. In *From Leaders to Rulers*, ed. J. Haas, pp. 19–37. New York.

Cunliffe, B. 1986 *Danebury: Anatomy of an Iron Age Hillfort*. London.

D'Altroy, T. N. and Earle, T. K. 1985 Staple finance, wealth finance and storage in the Inka political economy. *Current Anthropology* 26, no. 2: 187–206.

Dabney, M. K. and Wright, J. C. 1990 Mortuary customs, palatial society and state formation in the Aegean area: a comparative study. In Hägg and Nordquist 1990, pp. 45–53.

Dalfes, H. Nüzhet, Kukla, G. and Weiss, H. (eds.) 1997 *Third Millennium BC Climatic Change and Old World Collapse*. Berlin.

Damell, D. 1989 Södermanland. In *Hällristningar och hällmålningar i Sverige*, ed. S. Janson, E. B. Lundberg and U. Bertilsson, pp. 166–72. Helsinborg.

David, W. 1997 Altbronzezeitliche Beinobjekte des Karpatenbeckens mit Spiralwirbel- oder Wellenbandornamnet und ihre Parallellen auf der Peloponnes und in Anatolien in frühmykenischer Zeit. In Roman 1997: 247–305.

   1998 Zum Ende der bronzezeitlichen Tellsiedlungen im Karpatenbecken. In *Archaeologische Forschungen in urgeschichtlichen Siedlungslandscahften: Festschrift für Georg Kossack zum 75. Geburtstag*, ed. H. J. Küster, A. Lang and P. Schauer, pp. 231–67. Regensburg.

   2001 Zu den Beziehungen zwischen Donau-Karpatenraum, osteuropäischen Steppengebieten und ägäisch-anatolischen Raum zur Zeit der mykenischen Schachtgräber unter Berücksichtigung neuerer Funde aus Südbayern. *Anados. Studies of Ancient World* 1: 51–80.

   2002 *Studien zu Ornamentik und Datierung der bronzezeitlichen Depotfundgruppe Hajdusamson–Apa–Ighiel–Zajta*, vols. I and II. Alba Julia.

Davidson, H. E. 1988 *Myths and Symbols in Pagan Europe*. Early Scandinavian and Celtic Religions. Manchester.

   1998 *Roles of the Northern Goddess*. London.

Davies, W. V. 1995 Ancient Egyptian timber imports: an analysis of wooden coffins in the British Museum. In Davies and Schofield 1995: 146–56. London.

Davies, W. V. and Friedman, R. 1998 *Egypt*. London.

Davies, W. V. and Schofield, L. (eds.) 1995 *Egypt, the Aegean and the Levant: Interconnections in the Second Millennium BC*. London.

Davis, E. N. 1995 Art and politics in the Aegean: the missing ruler. In *The Role of the Ruler in the Prehistoric Agaean*, ed. P. Rehak, pp. 11–20. Aegaeum 11. Liège.

Davis, J. L. and Bennet, J. 1999 Making Mycenaeans: warfare, territorial expansion, and representations of the Other in the Pylian kingdom. In Laffineur 1999: 105–20.

Davis-Kimball, J., Murphy, E., Koryakova, L. and Yablonsky, L. (eds.) 2000 *Kurgans, Ritual Sites, and Settlements: Eurasian Bronze and Iron Age*. BAR International Series 890. Oxford.

Day, J. V. 2001 *Indo-European Origins: The Anthropological Evidence*. Washington, DC.

Day, P. M. and Relaki, M. 2002 Past factions and present fictions: palaces in the study of Minoan Crete. In Driessen, Schoep and Laffineur 2002: 217–35.

Day, P. M. and Wilson, D. 2002 Landscapes of memory, craft and power in Prepalatial and Protopalatial Knossos. In Hamilakis 2002b: 143–66.

De Jesus 1978 Metal resources in ancient Anatolia. *Anatolian Studies* 28: 97–102.

De Marinis, R. C. and Salzani, L. 1997 La necropole del Bronzo Medio e Recente nella Lombardia orientale e nel Veneto occidentale. In Brea, Candarelli and Cremaschi 1997: 703–19.

De Martino, S. 1995 Music, dance, and processions in Hittite Anatolia. In *Civilizations of the Ancient Near East*, ed. J. M. Sasson, vol. IV, pp. 2661–9. New York.

De Miro, E., Godart, L. and Sacconi, A. (eds.) 1996 *Atti e memorie del secondo congresso internazionale di micenologia*. Roma–Napoli, 14–20 ottobre 1991. Rome.

Deger-Jalkotzy, S. 1996 On the negative aspects of the Mycenaean palace system. In De Miro, Godart and Sacconi 1996: 715–28.

    1999 Military prowess and social status in Mycenaean Greece. In Laffineur 1999: 121–31.

DeMarrais, E., Castillo, L. J. and Earle, T. 1996 Ideology, materialization, and power strategies. *Current Anthropology* 37, no. 1: 15–31.

Demkin, V. A. and Demkina, T. S. 2002 Paleoecological crises and optima in the Eurasian Steppes in ancient times and the middle ages. In Jones-Bley and Zdanovich 2002: 389–99.

Denemark, R. A., Friedman, J., Gills, B. K. and Modelski, G. (eds.) 2000 *World System History: The Social Science of Long-Term Change*. London.

Der Manuelian, P. 1995 Furniture in ancient Egypt. In *Civilizations of the Ancient Near East*, ed. J. M. Sasson, vol. I, pp. 1623–34. New York.

Derevenski, J. S. and Sørensen, M. L. S. 2002 Becoming cultural: society and the incorporation of bronze. In Ottoway and Wager 2002: 117–21.

Dergachev, V. 2002 Two studies in defense of the migration concept. In Boyle, Renfrew and Levine 2002: 93–112.

Diakonoff, I. M. 1974 Slaves, harlots and serfs in early antiquity. *Acta Antiqua Academiae Scientiarium Hungaricae* 22: 45–78.

Diakonoff, I. M. (ed.) and Kohl, P. (project ed.) 1991 *Early Antiquity*. Chicago.

Diaz-Andreu, M. 1998 Ethnicity and Iberians: the archaeological crossroads between perception and material culture. *European Journal of Archaeology* 1, no. 2: 199–218.

Diaz-del-Rio, P., López-Garcia, P., López-Saez, Martinez-Navarette, M., Rovira-Llorens, S. and Vicent-Garcia, J. M. 2003 Understanding the productive economy during the Bronze Age through archaeometallurgical and palaeoenvironmental research at Kagarly (southern Urals, Orenburg, Russia). Paper presented at the European Association of Archaeologists 9th Annual Conference in St Petersburg, 2003.

Dickinson, O. 1994a Comments on a popular model of Minoan religion. *Oxford Journal of Archaeology* 13, no. 2: 173–84.

  1994b *The Aegean Bronze Age*. Cambridge.

  1999 Robert Drews' theories about the nature of warfare in the Late Bronze Age. In Laffineur 1999: 21–7.

Die Hethiter und ihr Reich: Das Volk der 1000 Götter 2002 Exhibition catalogue. Stuttgart.

Dietler, M. 1995 The cup of Gyptis: rethinking the colonial encounter in early-Iron Age western Europe and the relevance of world-systems models. *Journal of European Archaeology* 3, no. 2: 89–111.

Dietz, S. 1992 *The Argolid at the Transition to the Mycenaean Age: Studies in the Chronology and Cultural Development in the the Shaft Grave Period*. Copenhagen.

Dobres, M.-A. and Robb, J. (eds.) 2000 *Agency in Archaeology*. London and New York.

Doonan, O. 2001 Domestic architecture and settlement planning in Early and Middle Bronze Age Sicily: thoughts on innovation and social process. *Journal of Mediteranean Archaeology* 14, no. 2: 159–88.

Dossin, G. 1970. La route de l'étain en Mésopotamie au temps de Zimrilim. *Revue d'Assyriologie* 64: 97–106.

Drews, R. 1988 *The Coming of the Greeks*: Indo-European Conquests in the Aegean and the Near East. Princeton.

  1993 *The End of the Bronze Age: Changes in Warfare and the Catastrophe ca. 1200 B.C.* Princeton.

Driessen, I., Schoep, I. and Laffineur, R. (eds.) 2002 *Monuments of Minos: Rethinking the Minoan Palaces*. Aegaeum 23. Liège and Austin, Texas.

Du Gardin, C. 1996 L'ambre en France au Bronze ancien: données nouvelles. In Mordant and Gaiffe 1996: 189–95.

  2003 Amber spacer beads in the Neolithic and Bronze Ages in Europe. In *Amber in Archaeology. Proceedings of the Fourth International Conference on Amber in Archaeology, Talsi 2001*, ed. C. W. Beck, I. B. Loze and J. M. Todd. Riga.

Dumezil, G. 1958 *L'Idéologie tripartie des Indo-Européens*. Brussels.

  1969 *De nordiske Guder*. Copenhagen. (Translation of *Les Dieux des Germaines: essai sur la formation de la religion scandinave*. Paris, 1959.)

  1970 *The Destiny of the Warrior*. Chicago.

  1983 *The Stakes of the Warrior*. Berkeley.

  1988 *Mitra-Varuna*. New York. (Originally published in France, 1948.)

Dumitrescu, V. 1961 *Necropola de incineratie din opoca Bronzului de la Cirna*. Bucharest.

Dutton, A., Fasham, P. and Jenkins, D. 1994 Prehistoric copper mining on the Great Orme, Llandudno, Gwynedd. *Proceedings of the Prehistoric Society* 60: 245–86.

Earle, T. 1978 *Economic and Social Organisaton of a Compex Chiefdom: The Halelea District, Kaua'i, Hawaii*. Anthropological Papers, Museum of Anthropology, University of Michigan, 63. Ann Arbor.

  1987 Chiefdoms in archaeological and ethnohistorical perspective. *Annual Review of Anthropology* 16.

1991 Property rights and the evolution of chiefdoms. In *Chiefdoms: Power, Economy and Ideology*, ed. T. Earle, pp. 71–99. Cambridge.

1997 *How Chiefs Come to Power: The Political Economy in Prehistory*. Stanford.

2001 Institutionalization in chiefdoms. Why landscapes are built. In Haas 2001: 105–24.

2002 *Bronze Age Economics: The Beginnings of Political Economies*. Boulder, Colorado.

2004 Culture matters in the Neolithic transition and emergence of hierarchy in Thy, Denmark: distinguished lecture. *American Anthropologist* 106, no. 1: 111–25.

Earle, T. and Ericsson, J. E. 1977 *Exchange Systems in Prehistory*. New York.

Easton, D. F., Hawkins, J. D., Sherratt, A. G. and Sherratt, E. S. 2002 Troy in recent perspective. *Anatolian Studies* 52: 75–109.

Ecsedy, I. 1994 Camps for eternal rest. Some aspects of the burials of the earliest nomads of the Steppe. In Genito 1994: 167–77.

Edens, C. M. and Kohl, P. 1993 Trade and world systems in Early Bronze Age western Asia. In *Trade and Exchange in Prehistoric Europe*, ed. C. Scarre and F. Healy, pp. 17–34. Oxbow Monographs 33. Oxford.

Egg, M. and Spindler, K. 1993 Die Gletschermumie vom Ende der Steinzeit aus den Ötztaler Alpen. Vorbericht. *Jahrbuch des Römisch-Germanischen Zentralmuseums* 39: 1–128.

Ehrenreich, R., Crumley, C. and Levy, J. (eds.) 1995 *Heterarchy and the Analysis of Complex Societies*. Archaeological Papers of the American Anthropological Association 6. Washington, DC.

Eicher, J. B. (ed.) 1995 *Dress and Ethnicity*. Oxford and Washington, DC.

Eichmann, R. and Parzinger, H. (eds.) 2001 *Migrationen und Kulturtransfer: Der Wandel vorder- und zentralasiatischer Kulturen im Umbruch vom 2. zum 1. vorchristlichen Jahrtausend. Akten des Internationalen Kolloquiums 23.-26. November Berlin*. Römisch-Germanische Kommission, Frankfurt a.M. Eurasien-Abteilung, Berlin. Koll. zur Vor- und Frühgeschichte 6. Bonn.

Eliade, M. 1978 [1962] *The Forge and the Crucible*. Chicago and London.

1987 [1957] *The Sacred and the Profane: The Nature of Religion*. San Diego, New York and London.

Eliten der Bronzezeit 1999 Ergebnisse zweier Kolloquien in Mainz und Athen. Römisch-Germanisches Zentralmuseum, Forschungsinstitut für Vor- und Frühgeschichte. Bonn.

Emre, K. and Çinaroglu, A. 1993 A group of metal Hittite vessels from Kinik-Kastamonu. In *Aspects of Art and Iconography: Anatolia and Its Neighbors. Studies in Honor of Nimet Özgüç*, ed. A. J. Mellinik, E. Porada and T. Özgüç, pp. 675–703. Ankara.

Engedal, Ø. 2002 *The Nordic Scimitar: External Relations and the Creation of Elite Ideology*. BAR International Series 1050. Oxford.

Enright, M. J. 1996 *Lady with a Mead Cup: Ritual, Prophecy and Lordship in the European Warband from La Tène to the Viking Age*. Dublin.

Eogan, G. 1990 Possible connections between Britain and Ireland and the east Mediterranean region during the Bronze Age. In *Orientalisch-Agäische Einflüsse in der europäischen Bronzezeit*, pp. 155–65. Römisch-Germanisches Zentralmuseum (Mainz), Monographien. Mainz.

1993 Aspects of metal production and manufacturing systems during the Irish Bronze Age. *Acta Praehistorica et Archaeologica* 25: 87–110.

Epimachov, A. and Korjakova, L. 2004 Streitwagen der eurasischen Steppe in der Bronzezeit: Das Wolga-Uralgebiet und Kasachstan. In Fansa and Burmeister 2004: 221–36.

Ertekin, A. and Ediz, I. 1993 The unique sword from Bogazköy/Hattusa. In *Aspects of Art and Iconography: Anatolia and Its Neighbors. Studies in Honor of Nimet Özgüç*, ed. A. J. Mellink, E. Porada and T. Özgüç, pp. 719–25. Ankara.

Evans, A. 1906 *The Prehistoric Tombs of Knossos*. London.

    1921–36 *The Palace of Minos at Knossos*, vols. I–IV. London.

Evans, C. 2004 Material and oral records: a shamans' meeting in Pokhara. In *Material Engagements: Studies in Honour of Colin Renfrew*, ed. N. Brodie and C. Hills, pp. 165–80. McDonald Institute Monographs. Cambridge.

Evely, D. 1996 The Neo-Palatial Minoan warrior: fact or fiction? In *Minotaur and Centaur: Studies in the Archaeology of Crete and Euboa Presented to Mervyn Popham*, ed. D. Evely, I. S. Lemos and S. Sherratt. BAR International Series 638. Oxford.

Ezzo, J., Johnson, C. M. and Price, T. D. 1997 Analytical perspectives on prehistoric migration: a case study from east-central Arizona. *Journal of Archaeological Science* 24: 447–66.

Fabech, C. and Ringtved, J. (eds.) 1999 *Settlement and Landscape: Proceedings of a Conference in Århus, Denmark, May 4–7 1998*. Jutland Archaeological Society. Århus.

Falk, H. 1994 Das Reitpferd im Vedischen Indien. In Hänsel and Zimmer 1994: 91–101.

Falkenstein, A. 1936 Archaische Texte aus Uruk 1. *Archaische Texte aus Uruk* (ADFU). Berlin.

Fansa, M. and Burmeister, S. (eds.) 2004 *Rad und Wagen: Der Ursprung einer Innovation. Wagen im vorderen Orient und Europa*. Mainz am Rhein.

Farber, W. 1983 Die Vergöttlichung Naram-Sins. *Orientalia* 62: 67–72.

Farkas, G. and Liptak, P. 1975 Anthropologische Auswertung der bronzezeitlichen Gräberfelds beu Tapé. In Trogmayer 1975: 229–35.

Feinman, G. 1995 The emergence of inequality. A focus on strategies and processes. In Price and Feinman 1995: 255–75.

    2000 Corporate/network: new perspectives on models of political action and the Puebloan Southwest. In Schiffer 2000: 31–52.

Feinman, G. M. and Marcus, J. (eds.) 1998 *Archaic States*. Santa Fe.

Ferguson, B. R. (ed.) 1984 *Warfare, Culture and Environment*. New York.

Fimmen, D. 1924 *Die Kretisch-Mykenishe Kultur*. Leipzig.

Fischer, C. 1996 Aspects of social stratification based on Middle Bronze Age burials. In Peroni *et al.* 1996: 89–97.

Fol, A. and Schmitt, R. 2000 A Linear A text on a clay reel from Drama, south-east Bulgaria? *Prähistorische Zeitschrift* 75: 56–62.

Foley, J. M. 1995 *The Singer of Tales in Performance*. Bloomington.

Foley, R. A. 2001 Evolutionary perspectives on the origins of human social institutions. In Runciman 2001: 171–97.

Forenbaher, S. 1993 Radiocarbon dates and absolute chronology of the central European Early Bronze Age. *Antiquity* 67, no. 255: 218–57.

Foster, B. R. 1981 A new look at the Sumerian temple state. *Journal of the Economic and Social History of the Orient* 24: 225–41.

Fox, R. 1967 *Kinship and Marriage*. Harmondsworth.

Francfort, H.-P. 2001 The cultures with painted ceramics of south Central Asia and their relations with the northeastern steppe zone (late 2nd–early 1st millennium BC). In Eichmann and Parzinger 2001: 221–35.

Frank, G. 1993 The Bronze Age world system and its cycles. *Current Anthropology* 34, no. 4: 431–46.

Franke, D. 1985. An important family from Abydos of the seventeenth dynasty. *Journal of Egyptian Archaeology* 71: 175–6.

Franke-Vogt, U. 2001 The southern Indus Valley during the later 2nd and 1st millennium BC. The Dark Age. In Eichmann and Parzinger 2001: 247–91.

Frankenstein, S. and Rowlands, M. 1978 The internal structure and regional context of Early Iron Age society in south-western Germany. *Bulletin of the Institute of Archaeology* 15: 73–112.

Frankfort, H. 1954 *The Art and Architecture of the Ancient Orient*. London.

Fredell, Å. 2002 Hällbilden som förskriftligt fenomen – en ansats inför nya tolkningar. In *Bilder av bronsålder*, ed. J. Goldhahn, pp. 243–60. Lund.

    2003 *Bildbroar: figurativ bildkommunikation av ideologi och kosmologi under sydskandinavisk bronsålder och forromersk jernålder* (*Bridging Images: Pictorial Communication of Ideology and Cosmology in the Southern Scandinavian Bronze Age and the Pre-Roman Iron Age*). English summary. Gotarc Serie B, Gothenburg Archaeological Theses. 25. Gothenburg.

Friedman, J. and Rowlands, M. 1977 Notes towards an epigenetic model of the evolution of 'civilisation'. In *The Evolution of Social Systems*, ed. J. Friedman and M. Rowlands, pp. 201–76. Duckworth.

Frimigacci, D. 1997 Puhi, the mythical paramount chief of Uvea and ancient links between Uvea and Tonga. In Blench and Spriggs 1997: 331ff.

Frizell, B. S. 1998 Giants or geniuses? Monumental building at Mycenae. *Current Swedish Archaeology* 6: 167–85.

Fuglestvedt, I. 1999 Adorants, voltigeurs and other mortals – an essay on rock art and the human body. In Goldhahn 1999b: 25–40.

Furmanek, V. 1980 *Die Anhänger in der Slowakei*. Prähistorische Bronzefunde 11, Band 3. Munich.

    1982 Das Gebiet der Slowakei zwischen den Jahren 1600 und 1000 v. u. Z. In *Südosteuropa zwischen 1600 und 1000 v. Chr.*, ed. B. Hänsel, pp. 371–85. Prähistorische Archäologie in Südosteuropa 1. Berlin.

    1997 Bronzeanhänger als Belege für Kontakte des Karpatenbeckens mit dem östlichen Mittelmeerraum. In Becker *et al.* 1997: 313–24.

Furmanek, V. and Jacab, J. 1997 Menschliche Skelettreste aus bronzezeitlichen Siedlungen in der Slowakei. In Rittershofer 1997a: 14–24.

Furmanek, V. and Marková, K. 1996. Ein zweiter Bronzehortfund aus Včelince. In *Studien zur Metallindustrie im Karpaterbecken und den benachbarten Regionen*, ed. T. Kovács, pp. 137–46. Budapest.

Fyllingen, H. 2003 Society and violence in the Early Bronze Age: an analysis of human skeletons from Nord-Trøndelag, Norway. *Norwegian Archaeological Review* 36, no. 1: 27–43.

Gale, N. H. 1991 Copper oxhide ingots: their origin and their place in the Bronze Age metals trade in the Mediterranean. In *Bronze Age Trade in the Mediterranean*, ed. N. H. Gale, pp. 197–240. Studies in Mediterranean Archaeology 90. Jonsered.

2001 Archaeology, science based archaeology and the Mediterranean Bronze Age metals. *European Journal of Archaeology* 4, no. 1: 113–30.

Gale, N. H. and Gale, A. Z. 1999 Copper oxhide ingots and the Aegean metals trade. New perspectives. In Betancourt *et al.* 1999: 267–79.

Gamlekrelidze, T. V. 1994 PIE 'horse' and 'cart' in the light of the hypothesis of Asiatic homeland of the Indo-Europeans: Indo-European–Caucasian aspects. In Hänsel and Zimmer 1994: 37–42.

Garanger, J. 1997 Oral traditions and archaeology: two cases from Vanuatu. In Blench and Spriggs 1997: 321–30.

Garcia, L. Sanjuan 1999 Expressions of inequality: settlement patterns, economy and social organisation in the southwest Iberian Bronze Age (*c.*1700–1100 BC). *Antiquity* 73: 337–51.

Garstang, J. 1910 *The Land of the Hittites*. London.

1929 *The Hittite Empire*. London.

Gayduchenko, L. L. 2002 The biological remains from the fortified settlements of the Country of Towns of the south Trans-Urals. In Jones-Bley and Zdanovich 2002: 400–16.

Gebhard, R. 1999 Der Goldfund von Bernstorf – Zubehör eines Kultbildes der älteren Bronzezeit. *Das archäologische Jahr in Bayern 1999*: 22–4. Stuttgart.

Gebhard, R. and Rieder, K. H. 2002 Zwei bronzezeitliche Bernsteinobjekte mit Bild- und Schriftzeichen aus Bernstorf (Lkr. Freising). *Germania* 80: 115–33.

Gedl, M. 1996 Jungbronzezeitliche bronzene Trinkhörner aus Nordpolen. In *Studien zur Metallindustrie im Karpatenbecken und den benachbarten Regionen*, ed. T. Kovács, pp. 379–95. Budapest.

Gell, A. 1998 *Art and Agency: An Anthropological Theory*. Oxford.

Gelling, P. and Davidson, H. E. 1969 *The Chariot of the Sun and Other Rites and Symbols of the Northern Bronze Age*. London.

Gening, V. F., Zdanovich, G. B. and Gening, V. V. 1992 *Sintashta: Archaeological Sites of Aryan Tribes of the Ural-Kazakh Steppes*. Chelyabinsk.

Genito, B. (ed.) 1994 *The Archaeology of the Steppes: Methods and Strategies*. Papers from an International Symposium held in Naples 9–12 November 1992. Naples.

Gerloff, S. 1975 *The Early Bronze Age Daggers in Great Britain and a Reconsideration of the Wessex Culture*. Prähistorische Bronzefunde, VI, 2. Munich.

1993 Zu Fragen mittelmeerländischer Kontakte und absoluter Chronologie der Frühbronzezeit in Mittel- und Westgebirge. *Praehistorische Zeitschrift* 68: 58–102.

1995 Bronzezeitliche Goldblechkronen aus Westeuropa. Betrachtungen zur Funk- tion der Goldblechkegel vom Typ Schifferstadt und der atlantischen 'Gold- schalen' der Form Devil's Bit und Atroxi. In Jockenhövel 1995: 153–95.

1996 Wessex, Mycenae and related matters: the chrononlogy of the British Bronze Age in its European setting. In Peroni *et al.* 1996: 11–21.

German, S. C. 2000 The human form in the Late Bronze Age Aegean. In Rautman 2000: 95–111.

Gershkovich, Y. P. 2003 Farmers and pastoralists in the Pontic Lowland during the Late Bronze Age. In Levine, Renfrew and Boyle 2003: 307–18.

Gesell, G. 1985 *Town, Palace and House Cult in Minoan Crete*. SIMA 67. Gothenburg.

Gillis, C. 1995 Trade in the Late Bronze Age. In *Trade and Production in Premonetary Greece 3*, ed. C. Risberg and B. Sjöberg. *Studies in Mediterranean Archaeology and Literature* 134: 61–86.

1997 The smith in the Late Bronze Age – state employee, independent artisan, or both? In Laffineur and Betancourt 1997: 505–13.

Gillis, C., Risberg, C. and Sjöberg, B. (eds.) 1997 *Trade and Production in Premonetary Greece*. Production and the Craftsman. Proceedings of the 4th and 5th International Workshops, Athens 1994 and 1995. Jonsered.

Gilman, A. 1995 Prehistoric European chiefdoms. Rethinking 'Germanic' societies. In Price and Feinman 1995: 235–51.

Glob, P. V. 1944 Studier over den jyske Enkeltgravskultur. *Aarbøger for nordisk Oldkyndighed og Historie*. Det kgl. nordiske Oldskirftsselskab, pp. 1–283. Copenhagen.

1969 *Helleristninger i Danmark*. Jysk Arkeologisk Selskabs Skrifter 7. Copenhagen.

1970 *The Mound People*. Copenhagen.

Gods and Heroes 1999 *Gods and Heroes of the Bronze Age: Europe at the Time of Ulysses*. 25th Council of Europe Art Exhibition. Strasbourg.

Gogaltan, F. 2002 Die Tells der Bronzezeit im Karpatenbecken, terminologische Fragen. In Rustoiu and Ursutiu 2002: 11–45.

Golan, A. 1991 *Myth and Symbol*. Jerusalem.

Goldhahn, J. 1999a *Sagaholm-hällristningar och gravritual*. Studia Archaeologica Universitatis Umensis 11. Umeå.

(ed.) 1999b *Rock Art as Social Representation*. BAR International Series 797. Oxford.

1999c Rock art and the materialisation of a cosmology – the case of the Sagaholm barrow. In Goldhahn 1999b: 77–100.

Goodison, L. 1989 *Death, Women and The Sun: Symbolism of Regeneration in Early Aegean Religion*. London.

Goodison, L. and Morris, C. 1998 Beyond the 'Great Mother'. The sacred world of the Minoans. In *Ancient Goddesses: The Myths and the Evidence*, ed. L. Goodison and C. Morris, pp. 113–32. London.

Goodnick Westenholz, J. 1998 Goddesses of the ancient Near East 3000–1000 BC. In *Ancient Goddesses: The Myths and the Evidence*, ed. L. Goodison and C. Morris, pp. 63–82. London.

Goody, J. 1987 *The Interface between the Written and the Oral*. Cambridge.

Goody, J. and Tambiah, J. 1973 *Bridewealth and Dowry*. Cambridge.

Görner, I. 2002 *Bestattungssitten der Hügelgräberbronzezeit in Nord- und Osthessen*. Marburger Studien zur Vor- und Frühgeschichte 20. Rahden-Westfalen.

Görner, I. and Geshwinde, M. 2002 Ripdorf und Queck. Komplexe Grabhügelbefunde der lüneburger und der osthessisichen Gruppe der Hügelgräberkultur. *Archäologisches Korrespondenzblatt* 32: 197–206.

Gosden, C. 1994 *Social Being and Time*. Oxford.

1985 Gifts and kin in Early Iron Age Europe. *Man* 20.

Graf, F. (ed.) 1998 *Ansichten griechisher Rituale: Geburtstag-Symposium für Walter Burkert*. Stuttgart und Leipzig.

Graham, W. A. 1987 *Beyond the Written Word: Oral Aspects of Scripture in the History of Religion*. Cambridge.

Gräslund, B. 1967 *Hethitische Schwerter mit Krummscheiden*. Opuscula Atheniensia 7. Lund.

Grayson, A. K. 1971 The early development of the Assyrian monarchy. *Ugarit Forschungen* 3: 311–19.

Green, M. 1992 *Animals in Celtic Life and Myth*. London.

1998 Some Gallo-British goddesses. In *Ancient Goddesses: The Myths and the Evidence*, ed. L. Goodison and C. Morris, pp. 180–95. London.

2001 Cosmovision and metaphor: monsters and shamans in Gallo-British cult-expression. *European Journal of Archaeology* 4, no. 2: 203–32.

Gregersen, M. L. B. 1997 Craftsmen in the Linear B archives. In Gillis, Risberg and Sjöberg 1997: 43–51.

Gregoriev, G. I. 1982 Die Erforschung der Bronzezeit in Nordwestbulgarien. In *Südosteuropa zwischen 1600 und 1000 v. Chr.*, ed. B. Hänsel, pp. 187–202. Prähistorische Archäologie in Südosteuropa 1. Berlin.

Gregory, C. A. 1982 *Gifts and Commodities: Studies in Political Economy*. London.

Grigoriev, S. A. 2000 Investigation of Bronze Age metallurgical slag. In Davis-Kimball *et al.* 2000: 141–9.

2002 *Ancient Indo-Europeans*. Eurasian Ancient History, 1. Russian Academy of Sciences, Ural Branch. Chelyabinsk.

Gröhn, A. 2004 *Positioning the Bronze Age in Social Theory and Research Context*. Acta Archaeologica Lundensia Series in 8, 47. Lund.

Grupe, G. *et al.* 1997 Mobility of Bell Beaker people revealed by strontium isotope ratios of tooth and bone: a study of southern Bavarian skeletal remains. *Applied Geochemistry* 12: 517–25.

Gulizio, J., Pluta, F. and Palaima, T. G. 2001 *Potnia: Deities and Religion in the Aegean Bronze Age. Proceedings of the 8th International Aegean Conference, Göteborg University, 12-15 April 2000*. Aegaeum 22: xx. Liège.

Gurney, O. R. 1940 *The Hittite Prayers of Mursili II*. Liverpool Annals of Archaeology and Anthropology 27. Liverpool.

1973 Anatolia *c.* 1750–1600 B.C. In *Cambridge Ancient History*, vol. II, 1, pp. 228–55. Cambridge.

1977 *Some Aspects of Hittite Religion*. Oxford.

1979. The Hittite Empire. In *Power and Propaganda*, ed. M. T. Larsen, pp. 151–65. Mesopotamia 7. Copenhagen.

1990 *The Hittites*. London.

Gustafsson, M. 2001 Från största hus till minsta hydda. In *Möre historien om ett småland*, ed. G. Magnusson, pp. 587–610. Kalmar.

Güterbock, H. G. 1954 The Hurrian element in the Hittite Empire. *Journal of World History* 2: 383–94.

1984 Hittites and Akhaeans: a new look. *Proceedings of the American Philosophical Society* 128: 114–22.

1997 *Perspectives on Hittite Civilization: Selected Writings of Hans Gustav Güterbock*, ed. H. A. Hoffner Jr. Assyriological Studies 26. Chicago.

Guzowska, M. 2002 The Trojan Connection or Mycenaeans, Penteconters, and the Black Sea. In Jones-Bley and Zdanovich 2002: 504–18.

Haarmann, H. 1996 *Early Civilization and Literacy in Europe: An Inquiry into Cultural Continuity in the Mediterranean World*. Approaches to Semiotics 124. Berlin.

Haas, J. (ed.) 1990 *The Anthropology of War*. Cambridge.

(ed.) 2001 *From Leaders to Rulers*. New York.

Haas, J. and Creamer, W. 1993 *Stress and Warfare among the Kayenta Anasazi of the Thirteenth Century A.D.* Fieldiana: Anthropology, New Series 21, Publication 1450. Chicago.

Haas, J.-N., Giesecke, T. and Karg, S. 2002 Die mitteleuropäische Subsistenzwirtschaft des 3. Bis. 2. Jahrtausends v. Chr. aus paläoökologischer Sicht. In *Vom Endneolithicum zur Frühbronzezeit: Muster sozialen Wandels?*, ed. J. Müller, pp. 21–9. Bonn.

Haas, V. 1994a *Geschichte der Hethitischen Religion*. Leiden.

   1994b Das Pferd in der hethitischen religiösen Überlieferung. In Hänsel and Zimmer 1994: 77–90.

Habachi, L. 1972 *The Second Stela of Kamose and His Struggle against the Hyksos Ruler and His Capital*. Glückstadt.

Hachmann, R. 1957 *Die frühe Bronzezeit im westlichen Ostseegebiet und ihre mittel- und südosteuropäischen Beziehungen: Chronologische Untersuchungen*. Hamburg.

Hagberg, U.-E. 1988 The bronze shields from Fröslunda near Lake Vänern, West Sweden. In *Trade and Exchange in Prehistory*, ed. B. Hårdh *et al.* Acta Archaeologigica Lundensia 16, pp. 119–26. Lund.

Haider, P. W. 2000 Die Peloponnes in ägyptischen Quellen des 15. und 14. Jhs. v. Chr. In Blankholmer 2000: 149–59.

Hall, J. 1997 *Ethnic Identity in Greek Antiquity*. Cambridge.

Hallo, W. W. 1963 Royal hymns and Mesopotamian unity. *JCS* 17: 112–18.

Hallström, A. 1971 Boplats och gravar på Nygårdsrum i Vallstena. *Gotländskt Arkiv* 43: 114–15.

Hamilakis, Y. 2002a Too Many chiefs? Factional competition in Neopalatial Crete. In Driessen, Schoep and Laffineur 2002: 179–99.

   (ed.) 2002b *Labyrinth Revisited: Rethinking 'Minoan' Archaeology*. Oxford.

Hamilakis, Y., Pluciennik, M. and Tarlow, S. (eds.) 2002 *Thinking through the Body: Archaeologies of Corporeality*. New York.

Hansen, S. 1995 Aspekte des Gabentauschs und Handel während der Urnenfelderzeit in Mittel- und Nordeuropa im Lichte der Fundüberlieferung. In Hänsel 1995: 181–202.

   2001a Helme und Waffen der Bronzezeit in der Sammlung Axel Guttmann. In Born and Hansen 2001: 11–166.

   2001b Vom Tigris und die Lahn. Eine mesopotamische Statuette in Hessen. In *Archäologie in Hessen: Festschrift F.-R. Herrmann*, ed. S. Hansen and V. Pingel, pp. 47–53. Berlin.

   2002 'Überausstattuttungen' in Gräbern und Horten der Frühbronzezeit. In *Vom Endneolithikum zur Frühbronzezeit: Muster sozialen Wandels?*, ed. J. Müller, pp. 151–73. Bonn.

Hanson, V. D. 1999 Hoplite obliteration: the case of the town of Thespiae. In *Ancient Warfare: Archaeological Perspectives*, ed. J. Carman and A. F. Harding, pp. 203–19. Sutton.

Harding, A. 1984 *The Mycenaeans and Europe*. New York.

   1990 The Wessex connection: developments and perspectives. In *Orientalische-ägäische Einflüsse in der europäischen Bronzezeit: Ergebnisse eines Kolloquiums*, ed. T. Bader, pp. 139–55. Römisch-Germanisches Zentralmuseum 15. Bonn.

   1997 Wie gross waren die Gruppenverbände der bronzezeitlichen Welt. In *Studia Honoraria: Beiträge zur prähistorischen Archäologie zwischen Nord- und Südeuropa. Festschrift für Bernhard Hänsel*, ed. C. Becker *et al.*, pp. 443–53. Espelkamp.

   2000 *European Societies in the Bronze Age*. Cambridge.

Harrisson, R. 1994a The Bronze Age in northern and northeastern Spain 2000–800 BC. In Mathers and Stoddart 1994: 73–97.

1994b La cultura dei Vasi Campaniformi: 2600–1900 a. C. In *Storia d'Europa*, vol. II. *Prehistoria e antichità*. Turin.

Harrisson, R. and Mederos, A. 2000 Patronage and clientship: a model for the Atlantic Final Bronze Age in the Iberian Peninsula. In Pare 2000: 133–52.

Hase, F. W. von 1982 Mykenische Keramik in Italien. In *Das mykenische Knossos und das Alter von Linear B*. Kleine Schriften aus dem Vorgeschichtlichen Seminar Marburg 11. Marburg.

Hassan, F. A. 1998 The earliest goddesses of Egypt. In *Ancient Goddesses: The Myths and the Evidence*, ed. L. Goodison and C. Morris, pp. 98–112. London.

Hauptman, S., Madden, R. and Prange, M. 2003 On the structure and composition of copper and tin ingots excavated from the shipwreck of Uluburun. *Bulletin of the American School of Oriental Research* 328: 1–30.

Hauptman Wahlgren, K. 1998 Encultured rocks. Encounter with a ritual world of the Bronze Age. *Current Swedish Archaeology*: 85–97.

2002 *Bilder av betydelse: hällristningar och bronsålderslandskap i nordöstra Östergötland* (*Images of Significance: Rock-Carvings and Bronze Age Landscape in North-eastern Östergötland*) English summary. Stockholm.

Hawkins, J. D. 2002 Die Erben des Grossreiches II. In *Die Hethiter und ihr Reich*, pp. 264–74. Exhibition catalogue. Bonn.

Hayden, B. 1995 Pathways to power. Principles for creating socioeconomic inequalities. In Price and Feinman 1995: 15–86.

Hayward, L. G. 1990 The origin of the raw elephant ivory used in Greece and the Aegean during the Late Bronze Age. *Antiquity* 64: 103–9.

Hedeager, L. 1978 A quantitative analysis of Roman imports in Europe north of the Limes (0–400 AD), and the question of Roman–German exchange, in *New Directions in Scandinavian Archaeology*, ed. K. Kristiansen and C. Paludan-Müller, pp. 158–91. Copenhagen.

1992 *Iron-Age Societies: From Tribe to State in Northern Europe 500 BC to AD 700*. Oxford.

1997 *Skygger af en anden virkelighed: Oldnordiske myter*. Copenhagen. (Published in Swedish 1998.)

1998 Cosmological endurance: pagan identities in early Christian Europe. *Journal of European Archaeology* 3: 383–97.

2001 *Asgard* reconstructed? Gudme – a 'central place' in the north. In *Topographies of Power in the Early Middle Ages*, ed. M. de Jong, F. Theuws and C. van Rhijn, pp. 467–507. Leiden, Boston, and Cologne.

2003 Beyond mortality – Scandinavian animal style AD 400–1200. In *Sea Change: Orkney and Northern Europe in the Later Iron Age AD 300–800*, ed. J. Downes and A. Ritchie pp. 127–36. Balgavies, Angus.

2004 Dyr og andre mennesker – mennesker og andre dyr. Dyreornamentikkens transcendentale realitet. In *Ordning mot kaos: studier av nordisk förkristen kosmologi*, ed. A. Andrén, K. Jennbert and C. Raudvere. Lund.

Helms, M. 1979 *Ancient Panama: Chiefs in Search of Power*. Austin, Texas.

1988 *Ulysses' Sail: An Ethnographic Odyssey of Power, Knowledge, and Geographical Distance*. Princeton.

1993 *Craft and the Kingly Ideal: Art, Trade, and Power*. Austin, Texas.

1998 *Access to Origins: Affines, Ancestors and Aristocrats*. Austin, Texas.

2000 Tangible durability: thoughts on aristocrats and the wider world, paper presented in Gothenburg 9 March 2000.

Hermann-Müller, H. 1994 Pferde der Bronzezeit in Mitteleuropa. *Zeitschrift für Archäologie* 27: 131–50.

Herrmann, J. 1982 Militärische Demokratie und die übergangsperiode zur Klassengesellschaft. *Etnographisch-Archäologische Zeitschrift* 23: 11–31.

Hesiod and Theognis 1973 *Hesiod: Theogony, Works and Days. Theognis: Elegies*, trans. and with introduction by Dorothea Wender. Harmondsworth.

Heyd, V. 1998 Die Glockenbeckerkultur in Süddeutschland – Zum Stand der Forschung einer Regionalprovinz entlang der Donau. In *Some New Approaches to the Bell Beaker 'Phenomenon': Proceedings of the 2nd Meeting of the 'Association Archaeologie et Gobelets' Fledber (Germany), 18th–20th April 1997*, ed. M. Benz and S. van Willingen, pp. 87–106. BAR International Series 690. Oxford.

2001 On the earliest Bell Beakers along the Danube. In *Bell Beakers Today: Pottery, People, Culture and Symbols in Prehistoric Europe*, ed. F. Nicolis, pp. 387–409. International Colloquium Riva del Garda (Trento Italy), 11–16 May 1998. Trento.

In press Families, goodies, warriors and complex societies: Beaker Groups and the 3rd millennium BC along the Upper Danube. *Proceedings of the Prehistoric Society.*

Hiebert, F. 2002 Bronze Age interaction between Eurasian Steppe and Central Asia. In Boyle, Renfrew and Levine 2002: 237–48.

Hielte-Stavropoulou, M. 2001 The horseshoe-shaped and other structures and installations for performing rituals in funeral contexts in Middle Helladic and Early Mycenaean times. In Laffineur and Hägg 2001: 153–66.

In press The 'Middle Helladic People' in southern Balkan in the late 3rd millennium and the first half of the 2nd millennium: sedentary versus nomadic lifestyles. *Acta Archaeologica.*

Hiller, S. 1984 Pax Minoica versus Minoan thalassocracy. Military aspects of Minoan culture. In Hägg and Marinatos 1984: 27–31.

Hing, A. E. de 2000 *Food Production and Food Procurement in the Bronze Age and Early Iron Age (2000–500 BC)*. Leiden.

Hitchkock, L. A. 1997 Engendering domination: a structural and contextuual analysis of Minoan Neopalatial bronze figurines. In Moere and Scott 1997: 113–30.

Hochstetter, A. 1982 Spätbronzezeitliches und früheisenzeitliches Formengut in Makedonien und im Balkanraum. In *Südosteuropa zwischen 1600 und 1000 v. Chr.*, ed. B. Hänsel, pp. 99–118. Prähistorische Archäologie in Südosteuropa 1. Berlin.

Hodder, I. (ed.) 1978. *The Spatial Organisation of Culture*. London.

1982a *Symbols in Action*. Cambridge.

1984 Burials, houses, women and men in the European Neolithic. In *Ideology, Power and Prehistory*, ed. D. Miller and C. Tilley, pp. 51–68. Cambridge.

(ed.) 1987 *The Archaeology of Contextual Meanings*. Cambridge.

1990 *The Domestication of Europe*. Oxford.

(ed.) 2001 *Archaeological Theory Today*. Cambridge.

Hodder, I. and Orton, C. 1976 *Spatial Analysis in Archaeology*. Cambridge.

Hoffner, H. A. 1973 The Hittites and Hurrians. In *Peoples of the Old Testament Times*, ed. D. J. Wiseman, pp. 197–228. Oxford.

2002 The treatment and long-term use of persons captured in battle according to the Masat texts. In Yener and Hoffner 2002: 61–72.

Holloway, R. R. 1991 *The Archaeology of Ancient Sicily*. London.

Homer 1991 *The Odyssey*. Translated by E. V. Rieu 1946. Revised by C. H. Rieu in consultation with Peter V. Jones. Harmondsworth.

    1991 *The Iliad*. Translated by E. V. Rieu 1949. Revised by C. H. Rieu in consultation with Peter V. Jones. Harmondsworth.

Honti, S. and Kiss, V. 1999/2000 Neure Angaben zur Bewertung der Hortfunde vom Typ Tolnanémedi. *Acta Archaeologica Academiae Scientiarum Hungaricae* 51: 71–109.

Hooke, S. H. 1963 *Middle Eastern Mythology*. Harmondsworth.

Houlihan, P. F. 1996 *The Animal World of the Pharaohs*. London.

Huff, D. 2001 Bronzezeitliche Monumentalarchitektur in Zentralasien. In Eichmann and Parzinger 2001: 181–99.

Hughes-Brock, H. 1999 Mycenaean beads: gender and social contexts. *Oxford Journal of Archaeology* 18, no. 3: 277–97.

Hultkrantz, Å. 1986 Rock drawings as evidence of religion: some principal points of view. In *Words and Objects*, ed. G. Steinsland, pp. 43–66. Oslo.

    1989 Hällristningsreligion. In *Hällristningar och hällmålningar i Sverige*, ed. S. Janson, E. B. Lundberg and U. Bertilsson, pp. 43–58. Helsingborg.

Humphrey, G. and Hugh-Jones, S. (eds.) 1992 *Barter, Exchange and Value: An Anthropological Approach*. Cambridge.

Hundt, H.-J. 1986 Zu einigen vorderasiatischen Schaftlochäxten und ihrem Einfluss auf den Donauländischen Guss von Bronzeäxten. *Jahresbericht Römisch-Germanischen Zentralmuseums Mainz* 33, no. 1: 131–57.

Hygen, A.-S. and Bengtsson, L. 1999 *Hällristningar i gränsbygd*. Borås.

Hägg, R. 1984 Degrees and character of the Minoan influence on the mainland. In *The Aegean and the Levant: Interconnections in the Second Millennium BC*, ed. W. V. Davies and L. Schofield, pp. 29–53. London.

    1985 Mycenaean religion: the Helladic and the Minoan components. In *Linear B: A 1984 Survey*, ed. D. Morpurgo Davies and Y. Duhoux, pp. 203–25. Louvain-la-Neuve.

    1992 The palaces of Minoan Crete/architecture and function in a comparative perspective. In *Haus und Palast im alten Ägypten*. Internationales Symposium 8. Bis 11. April 1992 in Kairo, pp. 81–4. Vienna.

    1995 State and religion in Mycenaean Greece. In Laffineur and Niemeier 1995: 387–91.

    1997a Religious syncretism at Knossos and in post-palatial Crete. In *La Crète mycénienne*, ed. J. Driessen and A. Farnoux, pp. 162–8. Bulletine de Correspondance Hellenique Suppl. 30. Athens.

    1997b Did the Middle Helladic people have any religion? *Kernos: Revue Internationale et Pluridisciplinaire de Religion Grecque Antique* 10: 13–18. Liège.

    1998 Ritual in Mycenaean Greece. In Graf 1998: 99–113.

Hägg, R. and Marinatos, N. (eds.) 1984 *The Minoan Thalassocracy: Myth and Reality*. Proceedings of the Third International Symposium at the Swedish Institute in Athens, 31 May–5 June 1982. Skrifer utgivna av det svenska institutet i Athen 4, 32. Stockholm.

    (eds.) 1987 *The Function of the Minoan Palaces: Proceedings of the Fourth International Symposium at the Swedish Institute in Athens*. Gothenburg.

Hägg, R. and Nordquist, C. (eds.) 1990 *Celebrations of Death and Divinity in the Bronze Age Argolid*. Skrifter utgivna av svenska institutet i Athen 4, 40. Stockholm.

Håkansson, I. 1985 *Skånes gravfynd från äldre bronsålder som källa till studiet av social struktur*. Malmö.

Hänsel, B. 1968 *Beiträge zur Chronologie der mitteleren Bronzezeit im Karpatenbecken* 1–2. Bonn.

(ed.) 1982a *Südosteuropa zwischen 1600 und 1000 v. Chr.* Prähistorische Archäologie in Südosteuropa 1. Berlin.

1982b Südosteuropa zwischen 1600 und 1000 v. In Hänsel 1982a: 1–38.

(ed.) 1995 *Handel, Tausch und Verkehr im Bronze und Früheisenzeitlichen Südosteuropa*. Prähistorische Archäologie in Südosteuropa 11. Munich and Berlin.

1996 Bronzezeitliche Siedlungssysteme und Gesellschaftsformen in Südosteuropa: vorstädtische Entwicklungen und Ansätze zur Stadtwerdung. In Peroni *et al.* 1996: 241–53.

(ed.) 1998a *Mensch und Umwelt in der Bronzezeit Europas*. Kiel.

1998b Die Steppe und das Karpatenbecken im Spannungsfelt zwischen nomadischen und sesshaften Lebensformen – Eine Einführung in das Thema. In Hänsel and Machnik 1998: 9–19.

2002 Zusammenfassende Bemerkungen zum Siedlungsverlauf in Kastanas – Kontinuität und Bevölkerungswandel. In *Kastanas. Die Drehscheibenkeramik der Schichten 19 bis 11*, vol. I, ed. R. Jung, pp. 12–27. Kiel.

Hänsel, B. and Machnik, J. (eds.) 1998 *Das Karpatenbecken und die Osteuropäische Steppe: Nomadenbewegungen und Kulturaustausch in den vorchristlichen Metallzeiten (4000–500 v. Chr.)*. Südosteuropa Schriften 20. Munich.

Hänsel, B. and Medovic, P. 1991 *Vorbericht über die jugoslawisch-deutschen Ausgrabungen in der Siedlung von Feudvar bei Mosorin von 1986–1990*. Bericht der Römisch-Germanischen Kommission 72. Mainz.

Hänsel, B. and Terzan, B. 2000 Ein bronzezeitliches Kuppelgrab in Norden der Adria. *Prähistorische Zeitschrift* 75: 62–183.

Hänsel, B. and Zimmer, S. (eds.) 1994 *Die Indogermanen und das Pferd*. Budapest.

Hårde, A. in press Ritual killing and warfare: the context of violence in the early Bronze Age. In *War and Society, in a Cross-disciplinary Focus: Current Anthropological and Archaeological Focuses in the Field of War, Violence and Identity*, ed. T. Otto, H. Thrane and H. Vandkilde. Århus.

Höckmann, O. 1980 Lanze und Speer. In *Archaeologia Homerica: Kriegwesen*, vol. II, pp. 275–319. Göttingen.

1987 *Frühbronzeitliche Kulturbeziehungen im Mittelmeergebiet unter besondere Berücksichtigung der Kykladen*, ed. H.-G. Buchholz. Ägäische bronzezeit I–II. Darmstadt.

Hüttel, H.-G. 1982 Zur abkunft des Danubischen Pferd-Wagen-Komplexes der altbronzeit. In *Südosteuropa zwischen 1600 und 1000 v. Chr.*, ed. B. Hänsel, pp. 39–63. Prähistorische Archäologie in Südosteuropa 1. Berlin.

Iakovidis, S. 1999 Homer, Troy and the Trojan War. In Gods and Heroes 1999: 203–6.

Ingold, T. 2000 *The Perception of the Environment: Essays in Livelihood, Dwelling and Skill*. London and New York.

Ixer, R. A. and Budd, P. 1998 The mineralogy of Bronze Age copper ores from the British Isles: implications for the composition of early metalwork. *Oxford Journal of Archaeology* 17, no. 1: 15–43.

Jacab, J., Olexa, L. and Vladar, J. 1999 Otomani-Kultur in Nizna Mysla. *Slovenska Archeologia* 47, no. 1: 91–127.

Jacobsen, T. 1939 *The Sumerian King List*. Chicago.

1987 Mesopotamian religions. In *Religions of Antiquity*, ed. R. M. Seltzer, pp. 3–33. New York.

Jankovits, K. 1996 Beiträge zu der Situla und Bronzepfanne mit Handgriff in Nordostitalien in der Spätbronzezeit. In *Studien zur Metallindustrie im Karpatenbecken und den benachbarten Regionen*, ed. T. Kovács, pp. 303–22. Budapest.

Jensen, J. 1998 *Manden i kisten: hvad bronzealderens gravhøje gemte*. Copenhagen.

2002 *Danmarks Oldtid*. Bronzealder. Copenhagen.

Jensen, M. Skafte 2000 The writing of the Iliad and the Odyssey. In *Textualization of Oral Epics*, ed. L. Honko, pp. 67–81. Trends in Linguistics, Studies and Monographs 128. Berlin and New York.

Jetmar, K. 1996 Sintasta – ein gemeinsames Heiligtum der Indo-Iranier? *Eurasia Antiqua* 2: 215–22.

Jockenhövel, A. 1982 Zeugnisse der primären Metallurgie in Gräbern der Bronze- und Alteisenzeit Mitteleuropas. *Archeologia Polski* 27: 293–301.

1986 Struktur und Organisation der Metallverarbeitung in urnenfelderzeitlichen Siedlungen Süddeutschlands. In *Siedlung, Wirtschaft und Gesellschaft während der jüngeren Bronze- und Hallstattzeit in Mitteleuropa*, ed. D.-W. Buck and B. Gramsch, pp. 213–34. Veröffentlichungen des Museums für Ur- und Frühgeschichte Potsdam 20. Berlin.

1990 Bronzezeitliche Burgenbau in Mitteleuropa. Untersuchungen zur Struktur frühmetallzeitlicher Gesellschaften. In *Orientalisch-ägäische Einflüsse in der europäischen Bronzezeit*, pp. 209–28. Römisch-Germanisches Zentralmuseum, Monographien 15. Bonn.

1991 Räumliche Mobilität von Personen in der mittleren Bronzezeit des westlichen Mitteleuropa. *Germania* 69: 49–62.

1994 Arbeiten an Ofen und Tiegel- frühe Metallurgen und Künstler. In *Bronzezeit in Deutschland*, ed. A. Jockenhövel and W. Kubach, pp. 36–40. Archäologie in Deutschland 1994. Stuttgart.

(ed.) 1995 *Festschrift für Hermann Müller-Karpe zum 70. Geburtstag*. Bonn.

Johansen, B. 1992 Människan och rummet. Rumsliga strukturer i Södermanland under bronsålder. In *Forntid i Förändring: Aktuell arkeologi III*, ed. P. Anderson, Å. Hyenstrand and A. Tomasdotter Jacobsson, pp. 57–69. Stockholm Archaeological Reports 25. Stockholm.

Johansen, Ø. 1979 New results in the investigation of the Bronze Age rock carvings. *Norwegian Archaeological Review* 12: 108–12.

1993 *Norske depotfund fra bronsealderen*. Universitetets Oldsaksamlings Skrifter, ny rekke 13. Oslo.

Johnson, A. W. and Earle, T. 1987 *The Evolution of Human Societies: From Foraging Group to Agrarian State*. Stanford.

Jones, R. E. and Vagnetti, L. 1991 Traders and craftsmen in the central Mediterranean: archaeological evidence and archeometric research. In *Bronze Age Trade in the Mediterranean*, ed. N. H. Gale, pp. 197–239. Studies in Mediterranean Archaeology 90. Jonsered.

Jones, S. 1997 *The Archaeology of Ethnicity: Constructing Identities in the Past and the Present*. London and New York.

Jones-Bley, K. 2000a Sintashta burials and their western European counterparts. In Davis-Kimball *et al.* 2000: 126–33.

2000b The Sintashta 'chariots'. In Davis-Kimball *et al.* 2000: 135–40.

Jones-Bley, K. and Zdanovich, D. G. (eds.) 2002 *Complex Societies of Central Eurasia from the 3rd to the 1st Millennium* BC: *Regional Specifics in the Light of Global Model*, vols. I–II. Journal of Indo-European Studies Monograph Series 46. Washington, DC.

Jonsson, M. and Lögdqvist, A. 1998 Religiösa symboler och föreställningar. Seminar Paper, University of Umeå.

Jung, R. and Weninger, B. 2002 Appendix: Zur Realität der Diskrepanz zwischen den kalibrierten C14-Daten und der historisch-archäologischen Datierung in Kastanas. In R. Jung, *Kastanas: Ausgrabungen in einem Siedlungshügel der Bronze- und Eisenzeit Makdeoniens 1975–1979: die Dreshscheibenkeramik der Schichten 19 bis 11. Von Reinhard Jung: mit Beiträge von Bernhard Hänsel und Bernhard Weninger*, pp. 281–98. Kiel.

Junk, M., Krause, R. and Pernicka, E. 2001 Ösenringbarren and the classical Ösenring copper. In *Patina: Essays Presented to Jay Jordan Butler on the Occasion of His 80th Birthday*, ed. W. H. Metz, B. L. van Beek and H. Steegstra, pp. 353–66. Groningen.

Kadrow, S. 1994 Social structures and social evolution among Early-Bronze-Age communities in south-eastern Poland. *Journal of European Archaeology* 2, no. 2: 229–48.

Kaiser, E. 1997 *Der Hort von Borodino: kritische Anmerkungen zu einem berühmten bronzezeitliche Schatsfund aus dem nordwestlichen Schwarzmeergebiet*. Universitätsforschungen zur prähistorischen Archäologie 44. Bonn.

Kaliff, A. 1998 Grave structures and altars: archaeological traces of Bronze Age eschatological conceptions. *European Journal of Archaeology* 1, no. 2: 177–98.

Kantor, E. 1947 The Aegean and the Orient in the second millennium BC. *American Journal of Archaeology* 51: 1–103.

Kardulias, P. N. (ed.) 1999 *World-Systems Theory in Practice: Leadership, Production and Exchange*. Oxford.

Kasco, C. 1997–98 Das Depot von Satu Mare. *JAMÉ* 39–40: 25. Nyiregyháza.

Kaul, F. 1987 *Sandagergård: A Late Bronze Age Cultic Building with Rock Engravings and Menhirs from Northern Zealand, Denmark*. Acta Archaeologica 56: 31–54. Copenhagen.

1995 Ships on bronzes. In *The Ship as a Symbol in Prehistoric and Medieval Scandinavia*, ed. O. Crumlin-Pedersen and B. Munch Thye, pp. 59–70. Copenhagen.

1998 *Ships on Bronzes: A Study in Bronze Age Religion and Iconography*. Publications from the National Museum Studies in Archaeology and History 3.1 and 3.2. Copenhagen.

2001 En sjælden kultøkse fra bronzealderen. *Nationalmuseets Arbejdsmark* 2001: 50–69. Copenhagen.

Keeley, L. H. 1996 *War before Civilization: The Myth of the Peaceful Savage*. Oxford.

Kemenczei, T. 1982 Nordostungarn in der Spätbronzezeit. In *Südosteuropa zwischen 1600 und 1000 v. Chr.*, ed. B. Hänsel, pp. 305–20. Prähistorische Archäologie in Südosteuropa 1. Berlin.

1988 *Die Schwerter in Ungarn*, vol. I. *PBF*. Munich.

Kemp, B. J. 1989 *Ancient Egypt: Anatomy of a Civilization*. London.

Kessler, H. L. and Simpson, M. S. (eds.) 1985 *Pictorial Narrative in Antiquity and the Middle Ages*. Studies in the History of Art 16. Washington, DC.

Kienlin, T. L. 1999 *Vom Stein zur Bronze: Zur soziokulturellen Deutung früher Metallurgie in der englishcen Theoriediskussion*. Tübinger Texten 2. Rahden/Westf.

Kilian, K. 1988 The emergence of wanax ideology in the Mycenaean Palace. *Oxford Journal of Archaeology* 7, no. 3: 291–302.

Kilian-Dirlmeier, I. 1985 Noch Einmal zu den 'Kriegergräbern' von Knossos. *Jahresbericht des Romisch-Germ.-Zentralmuseums Mainz* 32: 196–214.

1993 *Die Schwerter in Griechenland (ausserhalb Peloponnes), Bulgarien und Albanien.* Prähistorische Bronzefunde 4, 12. Stuttgart.

1995a Steinerne Pfeilspitzen in bronzezeitlichen Gräbern. In Jockenhövel 1995: 35–42.

1995b Überlegungen zum spätbronzezeitlichen Schiffswrack von Ulu Burun (Kas). *Jahrbuch des Römisch-Germanischen Zentralmuseums Mainz* 40, no. 1: 31–48.

1997 *Das Mittelbronzezeitliche Schachtgrab von Ägina.* Römisch-Germanisches Zentralmuseum Forschungsinstitut für Vor- und Frühgeschichte. Kataloge Vor- und Frühgeschichtliche Altertümer 27. Alt Ägina 4, 3. Mainz.

2000 Thera and warfare. In *The Wall Paintings of Thera: Proceedings of the First International Symposium 30 August – 4 September 1997*, ed. S. Sherratt, pp. 119–46. Athens.

Kirch, P. 1984 *The Evolution of the Polynesian Chiefdoms.* Cambridge.

1991 Chiefship and competitive involution: the Marquesas Islands of eastern Polynesia. In *Chiefdoms: Power, Economy and Ideology*, ed. T. Earle, pp. 825–30. Cambridge.

Klejn, L. 1998 Anatomy of Iliad. Lecture read in Aarhus, Denmark, 1998. Summary of two books in Russian.

1999 The early evolution of dice between the Danube and the Indus. *Acta Archaeologica* 70: 113–35.

Klengel, H. 1990 Bronzezeitlicher Handel im vorderen Orient: Ebla und Ugarit. In *Orientalisch-Ägäische Einflüsse in der europäischen Bronzezeit: Ergebnisse eines Kolloquiums*, ed. T. Bader, pp. 7–31. Römisch-Germanisches Zentralmuseum 15. Bonn.

1995 Handel und Tausch in den Schriftquellen des alten Orient. In Hänsel 1995: 39–49.

1996 Kultgeschehen und Symbolgut im Textzeugnis der Hethiter. In Schauer 1996: 557–81.

Knape, A. and Nordström, H.-Å. 1994 *Der Kultgegenstand von Balkåkra.* Swedish National Museum of Antiquities. Stockholm.

Knapp, A. B. 1990 Ethnicity, entrepreneurship, and exchange: Mediterranean inter-island relationships in the Late Bronze Age. *Annual of the British School of Archaeology at Athens* 85: 115–53.

2000 Archaeology, science-based archaeology and the Mediterranean Bronze Age metals trade. *European Journal of Archaeology* 3, no. 1: 31–56.

Knappet, C. and Schoep, I. 2002 Continuity and change in Minoan palatial power. *Antiquity* 74: 365–71.

Kobylinski, Z. (ed.) 2001 *Quo vadis archaeologia? Whither European Archaeology in the 21st Century?* European Science Foundation. Warsaw.

Koch, E. 2003 Mead, chiefs and feasts in later prehistoric Europe. In *Food, Culture and Identity in the Neolithic and Early Bronze Age*, ed. M. Parker Pearson. BAR International Series 1117, pp. 125–43. Oxford.

Koehl, R. 1981. The function of Aegean Bronze Age rhyta. In *Sanctuaries and Cults in the Aegean Bronze Age*, ed. R. Hägg and N. Marinatos, pp. 179–87. Acta Instituti Atheniensis Regni Sueciae 28. Athens.

1995 The nature of Minoan kingship. In *The Role of the Ruler in the Prehistoric Aegean*, ed. P. Rehak, pp. 23–6. Aegaeum 11. Liège.

2001 The sacred marriage in Minoan religion and ritual. In Laffineur and Hägg 2001: 237–44.

Kohl, P. 1978 The balance of trade in southwestern Asia in the third millennium BC. *Current Anthropology* 19: 462–92.

1987 The ancient economy, transferable technologies and the Bronze Age world system: a view from the northeastern frontier of the ancient Near East. In *Centre and Periphery in the Ancient World*, ed. M. Rowlands *et al.* Cambridge.

Kohlmeyer, K. 1995 Anatolian architectural decorations, statuary and stelae. In *Civilizations of the Ancient Near East*, ed. J. M. Sasson, vol. IV, pp. 2639–60. New York.

Kolb, M. 1994 Monumental grandeur and the rise of religious authority in precontact Hawaii. *Current Anthropology* 34: 1–38.

Kopaka, K. 2001 A day in Potnia's life. Aspects of Potnia and reflected 'mistress' activities in the Aegean Bronze Age. In Laffineur and Hägg 2001: 15–31.

Korfmann, M. 1983 *Demirchihüyük, B and I. Architektur, Stratigraphie und Befunde.* Berlin.

2001a Der prähistorische Siedlungshügel Hisarlik. Die 'zehn Städte Troias' – von unten nach oben. In *Troia: Traum und Wirklichkeit*, pp. 346–54. Stuttgart.

2001b Troia als Drehscheibe des Handels im 2. und 3. vorchristlichen Jahrtausend. In *Troia: Traum und Wirklichkeit*, pp. 355–68. Stuttgart.

2001c Die Troianische Hochkultur (Troia VI and VIIa). In *Troia: Traum und Wirklichkeit*, pp. 395–406. Stuttgart.

Korfmann, M. and Kromer, B. 1993 Demircihüyük, Besik-Tepe, Troia – eine Zwischenbilanz zur Chronologie dreier Orte in Westanatolien. *Studia Troica* 3: 133–71. Mainz am Rhein.

Koryakova, L. 1996 Social trends in temperate Eurasia during the second and first millennia BC. *Journal of European Archaeology* 4: 243–80.

2002 Social landscapes of central Eurasia in the Bronze and Iron Ages: tendencies, factors, and limits of transformation. In Jones-Bley and Zdanovich 2002: 97–117.

Kossack, G. 1954 *Studien zur Symbolgut der Urnefelder- und Hallstattzeits Mitteleuropas.* Römisch-Germanische Forschungen. Mainz.

1996 Flügelperlen: Bemerkungen zu spätbronzezeitlichen Goldschätzen den Karpaterländern. In *Studien zur Metallindustrie im Karpatenbecken und den benachbarten Regionen*, ed. T. Kovács, pp. 339–60. Budapest.

Kovács, T. 1982 Einige neue Angaben zur Ausbildung und inneren Gliederung der Füzeabony-Kultur. In Hänsel 1982a: 287–304.

1986a Ein Beitrag zur Untersuchung der bronzezeitlichen Verbindungen zwischen Südtransdanubien und der unteren Donaugebiet. *Folia Archaeologica* 37: 93–113.

1986b Zsqadany-Orosi Puszta: ein alter Hortfund (Grabfund?) nach der Restaurierung. *Communicates Archaeologicae Hungaricae*: 27–48.

1995 Auf Mitteleuropa weisende Beziehungen eininger Waffenfunde aus dem östlichen Karpatenbechen. In Hänsel 1995: 173–85.

1996a. Halberds in Hungary and adjacent territories. In *Studien zur Metallindustrie im Karpatenbecken und den benachbarten Regionen*, ed. T. Kovács, pp. 89–101. Budapest.

1996b The Tumulus Culture in the Middle Danube region and the Carpathian Basin: burials of the warrior elite. In Peroni *et al.* 1996: 113–27.

Kovács, T. and Raczky, P. (eds.) 1999 *Prähistorische Goldschatze aus dem ungarischen Nationalmuseum.* Budapest.

Kovács, T. and Stanczik, I. (eds.) 1988 *Bronze Age Tell Settlements on the Great Hungarian Plain.* Inventaria Praehistoria Hungariae. Budapest.

Kramer, S. N. 1983 *Le Mariage sacré*. Paris.

Krattenmaker, K. 1995 Palace, peak and sceptre: the iconography of legitimacy. In *The Role of the Ruler in the Prehistoric Aegean*, ed. P. Rehak, pp. 49–61. Aegaeum 11. Liège.

Krause, R. 1996 Zur Chronologie der frühen und mittleren Bronzezeit Süddeutschlands, der Schweiz und Österreichs. *Acta Archaeologica* 67: 73–86.

1998 Zur Entwicklung der frühbronzezeitlichen Metallurgie nördlich der Alpen. In Hänsel 1998a: 163–92.

2002 Sozialstrukturen und Hierachien – Überlegungen zur Frühbronzezeit im süddeutschen Alpenvorland. In *Vom Endneolithicum zur Frühbronzezeit: Muster sozialen Wandels?*, ed. J. Müller, pp. 45–59. Bonn.

Kremenetski, K. 2003 Steppe and forest steppe belt of Eurasia: Holocene environmental history. In Levine, Renfrew and Boyle 2003: 11–29.

Kristiansen, K. 1974 Glerupfundet. Et depotfund med kvindesmykker fra bronzealderens femte periode. *Hikuin* 1: 7–38.

1983 Kriger og høvding I Danmarks Bronzealder. Et bidrag til bronzealdersvaerdets kulturhistorie. In *Struktur och förändring I bronsålders samhälle*, ed. B. Stjernquist, pp. 63–87. Report Series 17. Lund.

1984 Krieger und Häuptlinge in der Bronzezeit Dänemarks. Ein Beitrag zur Geschichte des bronzezeitlichen Schwertes. *Jahrbuch des Römisch-Germanisches Zentralmuseums* 31: 187–208. Mainz.

1985 The place of chronological studies in archaeology. A view from the Old World. *Oxford Journal of Archaeology* 4, no. 3: 251–67.

1987 From stone to bronze: the evolution of social complexity in northern Europe 2300–1200 BC. In *Specialization, Exchange, and Complex Societies*, ed. E. M. Brumfiel and T. Earle, pp. 30–52. Cambridge. Reprinted in Kristiansen and Rowlands 1998: 106–42.

1989 Prehistoric migrations – the case of the Single Grave and Corded Ware Cultures. *Journal of Danish Archaeology* 8: 211–25.

1991 Chiefdoms, states and systems of social evolution. In *Chiefdoms: Power, Economy and Ideology*, ed. T. Earle, pp. 16–44. Cambridge. Reprinted in Kristiansen and Rowlands 1998: 243–68.

1994 The emergence of the European world system in the Bronze Age: divergence, convergence and social evolution during the first and second millennia BC in Europe. In *Europe in the First Millennium B.C.*, ed. K. Kristiansen and J. Jensen, pp. 7–34. Sheffield Archaeological Monographs 6. Sheffield.

1996a Old boundaries and new frontiers. Reflections on the identity of archaeology. *Current Swedish Archaeology* 4: 103–22.

1996b Die Hortfunden der jüngeren Bronzezeit Dänemarks. Fundumstände, Funktion und historische Entwicklung. In Schauer 1996: 255–71.

1998a *Europe before History*. Cambridge.

1998b A theoretical strategy for the interpretation of exchange and interaction in a Bronze Age context. In *L'Atelier du bronzier en Europe du XXe au VIIIe siècle avant notre ère: Actes du colloque international 'Bronze 96' Neuchâtel et Dijon, 1996. Tome III (session de Dijon) Production, circulation et consommation du bronze*, ed. C. Mordant, M. Pernot and V. Rychner, pp. 333–43. Paris.

1998c The construction of a Bronze Age landscape. Cosmology, economy and social organisation in Thy, Northwest Jutland. In Hänsel 1998a: 281–93.

2001a Rulers and warriors: symbolic transmission and social transformation in Bronze Age Europe. In *From Leaders to Rulers*, ed. J. Haas, pp. 85–105. New York.

2001b Borders of ignorance: research communities and language. In Kobylinski 2001: 38–44.

2002 The tale of the sword – swords and swordfighters in Bronze Age Europe. *Oxford Journal of Archaeology* 21, no. 4: 319–32.

2004 Sea faring voyages and rock art ships. In *The Dover Bronze Age Boat in Context: Society and Water Transport in Prehistoric Europe*, ed. P. Clark, pp. 111–22. Oxford.

Kristiansen, K. and Rowlands, M. 1998 *Social Transformations in Archaeology: Global and Local Perspectives*. London and New York.

Kruk, J. and Milisauskas, S. 1999 *Rozkwit i upadek spolecze'nstw rolniczych neolitu* (*The Rise and Fall of Neolithic Societies*). Krakow.

Kubach, W. 1995 Zweiseitig gerippte Radnadeln im westlichen Ostseegebiet. In Jockenhövel 1995: 250–73.

Kuhrt, A. 1995 *The Ancient Near East*, vols. I–II. London and New York.

Kupper, J.-R. 1957 *Les nomades en Mésopotamie au temps des rois de Mari*. Paris.

Kuzmina, E. E. 1994 Stages of development of stock-breeding husbandry and ecology of the Steppes in the light of the archaeological and palaeoecological data (4th millennium BC – 8th century BC). In Genito 1994: 17–31.

2000 The Eurasian Steppes. The transition from early urbanism to nomadism. In Davis-Kimball *et al.* 2000: 118–25.

2001 The first migration wave of Indo-Iranians to the south. *Journal of Indo-European Studies* 29, no. 1: 1–40.

2002 Ethnic and cultural interconnections between Iran and Turan in the 2nd millennium BC. In Jones-Bley and Zdanovich 2002: 21–36.

Laffineur, R. 1995 Aspects of rulership at Mycenae in the shaft grave period. In *The Role of the Ruler in the Prehistoric Aegean*, ed. P. Rehak, pp. 81–94. Aegaeum 11. Liège.

(ed.) 1999 *Polemos. Le contexte guerrier en Egée à l'Age du Bronze. Actes de la 7e Rencontre égéenne internationale, Université de Liège, 14–17 avril 1998*. Aegaeum 19. Liège.

Laffineur, R. and Betancourt, P. (eds.) 1997 *Techne: Craftsmen, Craftswomen and Craftsmanship in the Aegean Bronze Age*. Aegaeum 16. Liège.

Laffineur, R. and Hägg, R. (eds.) 2001 *Potnia: Deities and Religion in the Aegean Bronze Age. Proceedings of the 8th International Aegean Conference, Göteborg University, 12–15 April 2000*. Aegaeum 22. Liège.

Laffineur, R. and Niemeier, W. D. (eds.) 1995 *Politeia: Society and State in the Aegean Bronze Age. Proceedings of the 5th International Aegean Conference/University of Heidelberg 10–13 April 1994*. Aegaeum 12. Liège.

Lambert, M. 1953 Textes commerciaux de Lagash. *Revue d'Assyriologie* 47: 57–69.

Lang, M. L. 1969. *The Palace of Nestor at Pylos in Western Messenia*. Princeton, NJ.

Larsen, M. T. 1976 *The Old Assyrian City-State and Its Colonies*. Mesopotamia 4. Copenhagen.

1987 Commercial networks in the ancient Near East. In Rowlands, Larsen and Kristiansen 1987: 47–57.

Larsson, L. 1974 The Fogdarp find. A hoard from the Late Bronze Age. *Meddelanden från Lunds universitets historiska museum. 1973–74*: 169–238. Lund.

Larsson, T. B. 1984 Multi-level exchange and cultural interaction in late Scandinavian Bronze Age. In *Settlement and Economy in Later Scandinavian Bronze Age*, ed. K. Kristiansen, pp. 63–83. BAR International Series 211. Oxford.

1986 *The Bronze Age Metalwork in Southern Sweden: Aspects on Social and Spatial Organization 1800–500 BC*. Archaeology and Environment 6. Umeå.

1993 *Vistad: kring en befäst gård i Östergötland och östersjökontakter under yngre bronsålder*. Studia Archaeologica Universitatis Umensis 4. Umeå.

1995 Maktstrukturer och alliansystem i östgötsk bronsålder. In *Samhällsstruktur och förändring under bronsåldern*, ed. M. Larsson and A. Toll, pp. 8–15. Riksantikvarieämbetet 11. Norrköping.

1997 *Materiell kultur och religiösa symboler: Mesopotamien, Anatolien och Skandinavien under det andra förkristna årtusendet*. Arkeologiska Studier vid Umeå Universitet 4. Umeå.

1999a Symbols, divinities and the reproduction of social inequality. In *Marxistiska perspektiv inom skandinavisk arkeologi*, ed. J. Goldhahn and P. Nordqvist, pp. 47–84. Arkeologiska Studier vid Umeå Universitet 5. Umeå.

1999b Kontext, form och mening: att läsa bronsålderns symboler. In *Spiralens öga*, ed. M. Olausson, pp. 347–63. Stockholm.

1999c The transmission of an élite ideology – Europe and the Near East in the second millennium BC. In *Rock Art as Social Representations*, ed. J. Goldhahn, pp. 49–64. BAR International Series 794. Oxford.

2004. Streitwagen, Karren und Wagen in der bronzezeitlichen Felskunst Skandinaviens. In *Rad und Wagen: Der Ursprung einer Innovation Wagen im vorderen Orient und Europa*, ed. M. Fansa and S. Burmeister, pp. 381–98. Mainz.

Larsson, T. B. and Hulthén, B. 2004. *Vistad '88 Revisited: Ceramological Analyses and Lusatian Connections*. Archaeology and Environment 17. Umeå.

Latacz, J. 2004. *Troy and Homer: Towards a Solution of an Old Mystery*. Oxford.

Lauermann, E. 1992 Sonderbstattungen der frühen Bronzezeit im Weinviertel Niederösterreichs. *Praehistorische Zeitschrift* 67: 183–200.

Laux, F. 1995 Westeuropas Bedeutung für die Bronzezeit Niedersachsens zum Übergang von der Sögel-Wohlde-Zeitstufe zur älteren Bronzezeit. In Jockenhövel 1995: 85–102.

Lee, M. M. 2000 Deciphering gender in Minoan dress. In Rautman 2000: 111–24.

Lemonnier, P. (ed.) 1993 *Technological Choices: Transformation in Material Cultures since the Neolithic*. London and New York.

Lesko, L. H. 1987 Egyptian religion. In *Religions of Antiquity*, ed. R. M. Seltzer, pp. 34–61. New York.

(ed.) 1989 *Women's Earliest Records from Ancient Egypt and Western Asia*. Brown Judaic Studies 166. Atlanta, Georgia.

Lévi-Strauss, C. 1962 *La pensée sauvage*. Paris.

Levine, M., Renfrew, C. and Boyle, K. (eds.) 2003 *Prehistoric Steppe Adaptations and the Horse*. Cambridge.

Licharadus, J. and Vladar, J. 1996 Karpatenbecken–Sintasta–Mykeene. Ein Beitrag zur Definition der Bronzezeit als historische Epoke. *Slovenska Archeologia* 44, no. 1: 25–93.

Lincoln, B. 1991 *Death, War and Sacrifice*. Chicago.

Lindgren, B. 1997 Djuren på stenhällarna. Seminar paper, Univerity of Umeå.

1999 Rock art and gender – the case of the cup-marks. In *Rock Art as Social Representations*, ed. J. Goldhahn, pp. 41–7. BAR International Series 794. Oxford.

Lindow, J. 2001 *Norse Mythology: A Guide to the Gods, Heroes, Rituals, and Beliefs.* Oxford.

Ling, J. 2004 Beyond transgressive lands and forgotten seas. Towards a maritime understanding of rock art in Bohuslän. *Current Swedish Archaeology* 12: 121–40.

Littauer, M. A. and Crouwel, J. H. 1979 *Wheeled Vehicles and Ridden Animals in the Ancient Near East.* Leiden.

1996 Robert Drews and the role of chariotry in Bronze Age Greece. *Oxford Journal of Archaeology* 15, no. 3: 297–305.

2001 The earliest evidence for metal bridle bits. *Oxford Journal of Archaeology* 20: 329–38.

Liverani, M. 1987 The collapse of the Near Eastern regional system at the end of the Bronze Age: the case of Syria. In Rowlands, Larsen and Kristiansen 1987: 66–74.

2001 *International Relations in the Ancient Near East, 1600–1100 BC.* New York.

1990 *Prestige and Interest: International Relations in the Near East ca. 1600–1100 BC.* History of the Ancient Near East/Studies 1. Padua.

Liversage, D. 1994 Interpreting composition patterns in ancient bronze: the Carpathian Basin. *Acta Archaeologica* 65: 57–134.

2000 *Interpreting Impurity Patterns in Ancient Bronze: Denmark.* Copenhagen.

Liversage, D. and Northover, J. P. 1998 Prehistoric trade monopolies and bronze supply in northern Europa. In Mordant, Pernot and Rychner 1998: 137–53.

Lloyd-Smith, L. 2001 293 Radiocarbon dates from South Möre. In *Möre: historien om ett småland*, ed. G. Magnusson, pp. 625–56. Kalmar.

Lomborg, E. 1960 Donauländische Kulturbeziehungen und die relativen Chronologie der frühen norsischen Bronzezeit. *Acta Archaeologica* 30 (1959): 51–146.

Lörinczy, G. and Trogmayer, O. 1999 Über eine eigenartige bronzezeitliche Bestatungssitte im mittleren Theissgebiet. *Studia Archaeologica* 5: 191–5. Szeged.

Louwe Kooijmans, L. P. 1998 Bronzezeitlichen Bauern in und um die niederländische Delta-Niederung. In Hänsel 1998a: 327–41.

Lund, J. 2002 Foerlev Nymølle. En offerplads fra yngre førromersk jernalder. *Kuml* 2002: 143–195. Århus.

McCallum, L. 1987 *The Decorative Program in the Mycenaean Palace of Pylos: The Megaron Frescoes.* Philadelphia.

Macdonald, C. F. 2001 Chronologies and the Thera eruption. Review article. *American Journal of Archaeology* 105: 527–32.

McGovern, P. E. 2000 *The Foreign Relations of the 'Hyksos': A Neutron Activation Study of Middle Bronze Age Pottery from the Eastern Mediterranean.* BAR International Series 888. Oxford.

McIntosh, S. 1999 Pathways to complexity: an African perspective. In *Beyond Chiefdoms: Pathways to Complexity in Africa*, ed. S. Keech McIntosh, pp. 1–16. Cambridge.

McMahon, G. 1995 Theology, priests and worship in Hittite Anatolia. In *Civilizations of the Ancient Near East*, ed. J. M. Sasson, vol. III, pp. 1981–95. New York.

Macqueen, J. G. 1986 *The Hittites and Their Contemporaries in Asia Minor*, 2nd edn. London.

Madsen, H. J. 1970 To dobbeltgrave fra jysk enkletgravskultur (Two double graves from the Jutland Battle-Axe Culture). *Kuml* 1970: 249–61.

Mair, V. H. (ed.) 1998 *The Bronze and Early Iron Age Peoples of Eastern Central Asia*, Vols. I–II. Washington, DC.

Maisels, C. K. 1990 *The Emergence of Civilization: From Hunting and Gathering to Agriculture, Cities and the State in the Near East.* London.

Makkay, J. 1982 The earliest use of helmets in south east Europe. *Acta Archaeologica Hungarica* 34: 3–22.

Malamat, A. 1983 Silver, gold and precious stones from Hazor in a new Mari document. *Biblical Archaeology* 46: 169–74.

Malinowski, B. 1922/1983 *Argonouts of the Western Pacific: An Account of Native Enterprise in the Archipelagos of Melanesian New Guinea.* London and New York.

Mallory, J. P. 1989 *In Search of the Indo-Europeans: Language, Archaeology and Myth.* London.

 1998 A European pespective on Indo-Europeans in Asia. In Mair 1998: 175–201.

Mallory, J. P. and Mair, V. H. 2000 *The Tarim Mummies: Ancient China and the Mystery of the Earliest Peoples from the West.* London.

Malmer, M. P. 1962 *Jungneolitische Studien.* Acta Archaeologica Lundensia 8 (2). Lund.

 1970 Bronsristningar (Bronze engravings) *Kuml* 1970: 189–211.

 1981 *A Chorological Study of North European Rock Art.* Antikvariska Serien 32. Stockholm.

 1989 Bergkonstens mening och innehåll. In *Hällristningar och hällmålningar i Sverige*, ed. S. Janson, E. B. Lundberg and U. Bertilsson, pp. 9–28. Helsingborg.

 1993 Bronsåldershandelns struktur och sociala funktion. In *Ekonomi och näringsformer i nordisk bronsålder*, ed. L. Forsberg and T. B. Larsson, pp. 117–25. Studia Archaeologica Universitatis Umensis 3. Umeå.

Mann, M. 1986 *The Sources of Social Power*, vol. I. *A History of Power from the Beginning to A.D. 1960.* Cambridge.

Manning, S. 1996 Dating the Aegean Bronze Age: without, with and beyond, radiocarbon. *Acta Archaeologica* 67: 15–37.

 1999 *A Test of Time.* Oxford.

Manning, S. W., Ramsey, C. B., Doumas, C., Marketou, T., Cadogan, G. and Pearson, C. L. 2002 New evidence for an early date for the Aegean Late Bronze Age and the Thera eruption. *Antiquity* 76: 733–44.

Manning, S. and Weninger, B. 1992 A light in the dark: archaeological wiggle matching and the absolute chronology of the close of the Aegean Late Bronze Age. *Antiquity* 62: 636–63.

Manolis, S. K. and Neroutsos, A. A. 1997 The Middle Bronze Age burial of Kolona at Aegina Island, Greece: study of the human skeletal remains. In Kilian-Dirlmeier 1997: 169–75.

Maran, J. 1987 Die Silbergefässe von el-Tod und die Schachtgräberzeit auf dem griechisen Festland. *Praehistorische Zeitschrift* 62: 221–7.

 1995 Structural changes in the pattern of settlement during the shaft grave period on the Greek mainland. In Laffineur and Neimeier 1995: 67–72.

 1997 Neue Ansätze für die Beurteilung der Balkanisch-Ägäischen Beziehungen im 3. Jahrtausend v. Chr. In Roman 1997: 171–92.

 1998 *Kulturwandel auf dem griechishen Festland und den Kykladen im späten 3. Jahrtausend v. Kr.* Universitätsforschungen zur prähistorischen Archäologie 53. Bonn.

Marazzi, M. 1997 I contatti transmarini nella preistoria Siciliana. In *Prima Sicilia, alle origini della società siciliana*, ed. S. Tusa, pp. 365–74. Palermo.

Marazzi, M. and Tusa, S. 1979 Die mykenische Penetration im westlichen Mittelmeerraum. *KLIO* 61, 2: 309–51.

Marcus, M. I. 1995 Art and ideology in ancient Western Asia. In *Civilizations of the Ancient Near East*, ed. J. M. Sasson, vol. IV, pp. 2487–2505. New York.

Marfoe, L. 1987 Cedar forest to silver mountain: social change and the development of long-distance trade in early Near Eastern societies. In Rowlands, Larsen and Kristiansen 1987: 25–36.

Margueron, J. L. 1982 *Recherches sur les palais mésopotamiens de l'Age du Bronze*. Paris.

Marinatos, N. 1988 The fresco from Room 31 at Mycenae: problems of method and interpretation. In *Problems in Greek Prehistory*, ed. E. B. French and K. A. Wardle, pp. 245–8. Bristol.

  1993 *Minoan Religion*. Columbia, SC.

  1994 The 'export' significance of Minoan bull-hunting and bull-leaping scenes. *Ägypten und Levante* 4: 89–93.

  1995a Divine kingship in Minoan Crete. In *The Role of the Ruler in the Prehistoric Aegean*, ed. P. Rehak, pp. 37–48. Aegaeum 11. Liège.

  1995b Battle and harmony. The women in the Odyssey. In Berggreen and Marinatos 1995: 1–28.

  2000 *The Goddess and the Warrior: The Naked Goddess and Mistress of Animals in Early Greek Religion*. London and New York.

Marinatos, S. and Hirmer, M. 1960 *Crete and Mycenae*. London.

  1974 *Kreta, Thera und das mykenische Hellas*. Munich.

Markova, K., Tirpakova, A. and Karkechova, D. 2003 The social ranking of graves with amber during the Early Bronze Age in south-west Slovakia. In C. W. Beck, I. B. Loze and J. M. Todd (eds.), *Amber in Archaeology*, pp. 198–203. Riga.

Máthe, M. S. 1996 The 'missing' axe of the Hajdúsámson treasure. In *Studien zur Metallindustrie im Karpatenbecken und den benachbarten Regionen*, ed. T. Kovács, pp. 125–8. Budapest.

Mathers, C. and Stoddart, S. (eds.) 1994 *Development and Decline in the Mediterranean Bronze Age*. Sheffield.

Mathiassen, T. 1953 Et krumsværd fra bronzealdern. *Aarbøger* 1952: 229–34.

  1958 Endnu et kumsværd. *Aarbøger* 1957: 38–55.

Matthews, R. 2002 Zebu: harbingers of doom in Bronze Age western Asia. *Antiquity* 76: 438–46.

Matveev, A. V., Ryabogina, N. E., Semochkina, T. G. and Larin, S. I. 2002 Materials on the palaeogeographic description of the Andronovo age in the Trans-Urals Forest Steppe. In Jones-Bley and Zdanovich 2002: 443–53.

Mederos Martin, A. 1997 Nuevo chronologia del Bronce Final en el Occidente de Europa. *Complutum* 8: 73–96.

Medvedev, A. P. 2002 Avestan 'Yima's Town' in historical and archaeological perspective. In Jones-Bley and Zdanovich 2002: 53–68.

Mellaart, J. 1999 Anatolia 2300–1750 BC. In *Cambridge Ancient History*, vol. I, part 2, pp. 681–722. Cambridge.

Meller, H. (ed.) 2004 *Der geschmiedete Himmel: Die weite Welt im Herzen Europas vor 3600 Jahren*. Stuttgart.

Mellinek, A. J., Porada, E. and Özgüç, T. (eds.) 1993 *Aspects of Art and Iconography: Anatolia and its Neighbors. Studies in Honor of Nimet Özgüç*. Ankara.

Mellink, M. J. 1956 *A Hittite Cemetery at Gordion*. Philadelphia.

Menke, M. 1996 Mühlhabing. Ein Neufund des Typs Spatzenhausen aus dem bayerischen Oberland. *Studien zur Metallindustrie im Karpatenbecken und den benachbarten Regionen*, ed. T. Kovács, pp. 147–58. Budapest.

Menotti, F. 1999 The abandonment of the ZH-Mozartstrasse Early Bronze Age lake-settlement. GIS computer simulations of the lake-level fluctuation hypothesis. *Oxford Journal of Archaeology* 18, no. 2: 143–57.

Meskell, L. 2000 Re-em(bed)ding sex: domesticity, sexuality, and ritual in New Kingdom Egypt. In Schmidt and Voss 2000: 253–62.

Meskell, L. and Joyce, R. 2003 *Embodied Lives: Figuring Ancient Maya and Egyptian Experience*. London and New York.

Meyer, M. (ed.) 2001 *Trans albim fluvium*: Leidorf. *Festschrift für Achim Leube*.

Mihovilic, K., Terzan, B., Hänsel, B., Matosevic, D. and Becker, C. 2002 *Rovinj vor den Römern*. Kiel.

Miller, D., Rowlands, M., and Tilley, C. (eds.) 1989 *Domination and Resistance*. One World Archaeology. London.

Milstreu, G. 1987 Rapport fra Museets arbejdsmark. In *Adoranten*, pp. 3–8. Yearbook of the Scandinavian Society for Prehistoric Art. Underslös.

Moere, J. and Scott, E. (eds.) 1997 *Invisible People and Processes: Writing Gender and Childhood into European Archaeology*. Leicester.

Monk, S. and Osgood, R. with Toms, J. 2000 *Bronze Age Warfare*. Sutton.

Montelius, O. 1877 *Sveriges hednatid, samt medeltid, förra skedet, från år 1060 till år 1350*. Stockholm.

  1903 *Die älteren Kulturperioden im Orient und Europa*. Stockholm.

  1917 *Minnen från vår forntid*. Stockholm.

Montgomery, J., Budd, P. and Evans, J. 2000 Reconstructing the lifetime movements of ancient people: a Neolithic case study from southern England. *European Journal of Archaeology* 3, no. 3: 370–85.

Moore, H. L. 2000 Ethics and ontology: why agents and agency matter. In Dobres and Robb 2000: 259–64.

Moorey, P. R. S. 2001 The mobility of artisans and opportunities for technology transfer between western Asia and Egypt in the Late Bronze Age. In Shortland 2001: 1–14.

Morales, A. and Antipina, E. 2003 Srubnaya faunas and beyond: a critical assessment of the archaeozoological information from the east European Steppe. In Levine, Renfrew and Boyle 2003: 329–51.

Moran, W 1987 *Les Lettres d'el Amarna*. LAPO 13. Paris.

Mordant, C. and Gaiffe, O. (eds.) 1996 *Cultures et sociétés du Bronze ancien en Europe*. Paris.

Mordant, C., Pernot, M. and Rychner, V. (eds.) 1998 *L'Atelier du bronzier en Europe du XXe au VIIIe siècle avant notre ère. Actes du colloque international 'Bronze 96' Neuchâtel et Dijon, 1996*. Tome I (session de Neuchâtel): *Les analyses de composition du metal, leur apport a l'archéologie de l'âge du bronze*; tome III (session de Dijon) *Production, circulation et consommation du bronze*. Paris.

Morgan, L. 1995 Minoan painting and Egypt: the case of Tell el-Dab'a. In *Egypt, the Aegean and the Levant: Interconnections in the Second Millennium BC*, ed. W. V. Davies and L. Schofield, pp. 29–53. London.

Morres, C. 1990 In pursuit of the white tusked boar: aspects of hunting in Mycenaean society. In Hägg and Nordquist 1990: 149–61.

Morris, I. 1986 The use and abuse of Homer. *Classical Antiquity* 6: 81–138. Reprinted in D. Cairns (ed.), *Oxford Readings in Homer's Iliad*. Oxford.

    1997 Homer and the Iron Age. In *A New Companion to Homer*, ed. I. Morris and B. Powell, pp. 535–59. Leiden.

    1999a Iron Age Greece and the meaning of 'princely tombs'. In Ruby 1999: 57–80.

    1999b Negotiated peripherality in Iron Age Greece: accepting and resisting the East. In Kardulias 1999: 63–85.

    2000 *Archaeology as Cultural History*. Oxford.

Morris, M. 1988 Changing perceptions of the past. The Bronze Age: a case study. In Bintliff 1988: 69–86.

Morris, S. P. 1992 *Daidalos and the Origins of Greek Civilization*. Princetown.

    2001 Potnia Aswiya: Anatolian contributions to Greek Religion. In Laffineur and Hägg 2001: 423–34.

Mountjoy, P. A. 1998 The East Aegean Anatolian interface in the Late Bronze Age: Mycenaeans and the Kingdom of Ahhiyawa. *Anatolian Studies* 48: 33–67.

Mozsolics, A. 1967 *Bronzefunde des Karpatenbeckens: Depotfundhorizonte von Hajdúsámson und Koziderpadlás*. Budapest.

Muhly, J. D. 1985 End of the Bronze Age. In *Ebla to Damascus: Art and Archaeology of Ancient Syria*, ed. H. Weiss. Washington, DC.

    1995 Metalwork in ancient western Asia. In *Civilizations of the Ancient Near East*, ed. J. M. Sasson, vol. III, pp. 1501–21. New York.

Müller, J. 1999 Radiokarbonchronologie – Keramiktechnologie – Osteologie – Anthropologie – Raumanalysen. Beiträge zum Neolithicum und zur Frühbronzezeit im Mittelelbe–Saale–Gebiet. *Bericht der Römisch-Germanischen Kommission* 80: 28–51.

    2002 Modelle zur Einführung der Zinnbronzetechnologie und zur sozialen Differenzierung der mitteleuropäischen Frühbronzezeit. In *Vom Endneolithicum zur Frühbronzezeit: Muster sozialen Wandels?*, ed. J. Müller, pp. 267–91. Bonn.

Müller, S. 1920 *Billed- og Fremstillningskunst i Bronzealdern*. Aarbøger 1920. Copenhagen.

Müller-Karpe, H. 1959 *Beiträge zur Chronologie der Urnenfelderzeit nördlich und südlich der Alpen*. Römisch-Germanische Forschungen 22. Berlin.

    1980 *Handbuch der Vorgeschichte: Die Bronzezeit*, vol. IV. Munich.

Mylonas, G. E. 1972 *Ho taphikos kyklos B ton Mykenon*. Athens.

Needham, S. 1998 Modelling the flow of metal in the Bronze Age. In Mordant, Pernot and Rychner 1998: 285–307.

    2000a Power pulses across a cultural divide: cosmologically driven acquisition between Armorica and Wessex. *Proceedings of the Prehistoric Society* 66: 151–207.

    2000b The development of embossed goldwork in Bronze Age Europe. *The Antiquaries Journal* 80: 27–65.

    2001 When expediency broaches ritual intention: the flow of metal between systemic and buried domains. *Journal of the Royal Anthropological Institute* (N.S.) 7: 275–98.

Needham, S. *et al.* 1997 An independent chronology for British Bronze Age metalwork: the results of the Oxford Radiocarbon Accelerator Programme. *The Archaeological Journal* 154: 55–107.

Neugebauer, J.-W. 1994 *Bronzezeit in Ostösterreich*. St Pölten and Vienna.

Neustupny, E. (ed.) 1998 *Space in Prehistoric Bohemia*. Prague.

Niemeier, W.-D. 1984 The end of the Minoan thalassocracy. In Hägg and Marinatos 1984: 205–15.

1987 Das Stuckrelief des 'Prinzen mit der Federkrone' aus Knossos und minoische Götterdarstellungen. *AM* 102: 65–98.

1990 Area D: The painted plaster floor in room 611. Technical, stylistic, iconographic and chronological implications. In *Excavations at Kabri 5: Preliminary Report of 1989 Season*, ed. A. Kempinski and W.-D. Niemeier. Tel Aviv.

1995 Aegina – first 'Aegean' state outside of Crete. In Laffineur and Niemeier 1995: 73–81.

1998 The Mycenaeans in western Anatolia and the problem of the origins of the Sea Peoples. In *Mediterranean Peoples in Transition: Thirteenth to Early Tenth Centuries BCE*, ed. S. Gitin, A. Mazar and E. Stern. Jerusalem.

1999 Mycenaeans and Hittites at war in western Asia Minor. In Laffineur 1999: 141–56.

Niemeier, W.-D. and Niemeier, B. 1998 Minoan frescoes in the Eastern Mediterranean. In *The Aegean and the Orient in the Second Millennium*, ed. E. H. Cline and D. Harris-Cline, pp. 69–97. Aegaeum 18. Liège.

Nilsson, M. P. 1926. *Orientens forntid.* Stockholm.

1932/1972 *The Mycenaean Origin of Greek Mythology.* With a New Introduction and bibliography by Emily Vermeule. Sather Classical Lectures 8. Berkeley, Los Angeles and London.

1950 *The Minoan–Mycenaean Religion and Its Survival into Greek Religion*, 2nd edn. Lund.

Nilsson, S. 1867 *Skandinaviska nordens ur-innevånare.* Lund.

Nocete, F. 2001 *Tercer milenio antes de nuestra era: relaciones y contradicciones centro/periferia en el Valle del Guadalquivir.* Barcelona.

Nordbladh, J. 1978 Images as messages in society. Prolegomena to the study of Scandinavian petroglyphs and semiotics. In *New Directions in Scandinavian Archaeology*, ed. K. Kristiansen and C. Paludan-Müller, pp. 63–78. Copenhagen.

1980 *Glyfer och rum kring hällristningara i Kville.* Göteborg.

1995 The history of Scandinavian rock art research as a corpus of knowledge and practice. In *Perceiving Rock Art: Social and Political Perspectives*, ed. K. Helskog and B. Olsen, pp. 23–34. ACRA: The Alta Conference on Rock Art. Oslo.

Nordén, A. 1925 *Östergötlands bronsålder.* Linköping.

Nordström, H.-Å. and Knape, A. (eds.) 1989 *Bronze Age Studies: Transactions of the British–Scandinavian Colloquium in Stockholm, May 10–11, 1985.* The Museum of National Antiquities, Stockholm, Studies 6. Stockholm.

Novotna, M. 1994 A rare find of a pendant from the Bronze Age. In *Bronze Age in Slovakia*, pp. 24–5. *Pamatky Muzea*, Special issue. Bratislava.

1998 Zur Chronologie der Bronzezeit im Karpatenbecken. In *Tradition und Innovation: Festschrift Strahm*, pp. 349–69. Studie honoria 3. Espelkamp.

Näsström, B.-M. 2001 Soljunfruns öde. Från myt til historia. In *Kontinuitäten und Brücke in der Religionsgeschichte: Festschrift für Andes Hultfård zu seinem 65. Geburtstag am 23.12.2001*, ed. M. Stausberg, pp. 492–502. Berlin and New York.

In press Svanhild och hennes bröder. En reflex av den dioskuriska traditionen?

O'Brien, M. J. and Leman, R. L. 2003 Resolving phylogeny: evolutionary archaeology's fundamental issue. In *Essential Tensions in Archaeological Method and Theory*, ed. T. L. VanPool and C. S. VanPool, pp. 115–37. Salt Lake City.

O'Brien, W. 2000 *Ross Island and the Mining Heritage of Killarney.* Galway.

O'Connor, B. and Cowie, B. 2001 Scottish connections: some recent finds of Early Bronze Age decorated axes from Scotland. In *Patina: Essays Presented to Jay Jordan*

Butler on the Occasion of his 80th birthday, ed. W. H. Metz, B. L. van Beek and H. Steegstra, pp. 207–30. Groningen.

O'Shea, J. M. 1991. A radio-carbon-based chronology for the Maros Group of south-eastern Hungary. *Antiquity* 65: 97–102.

1996 *Villagers of the Maros: A Portrait of an Early Bronze Age Society*. New York and London.

Oates. J. 1986 *Babylon*, revised edn. London.

Odgaard, B. V. 1994 *The Holocene Vegetation History of Northern West Jutland, Denmark*. Opera Botanica 123. Copenhagen.

Odner, K. 2000 *Tradition and Transmission: Bantu, Indo-European and Circumpolar Great Traditions*. Bergen.

Oestigaard, T. 1999 Cremations as transformations: when the dual cultural hypothesis was cremated and carried away in urns. *European Journal of Archaeology* 2, no. 3: 345–64.

Ohlmarks, Å. 1963 *Hällristningarnas Gudar: en sammenställning och ett förklaringsförsök*. Stockholm.

Olausson, D. 1993 The Bronze Age barrow as symbol. In Larsson 1993b: 91–113.

Olausson, D. and Vandkilde, H. (eds.) 2000 *Form, Functions and Context: Material Culture Studies in Scandinavian Archaeology*. Acta Archaeologica Lundensia, Series in 8, 31. Lund.

Olmsted, G. S. 1994 *The Gods of the Celts and the Indo-Europeans*. Budapest.

Olsson, L. 1999 Mediterranean symbols in Late Bronze Age rock art in southern Scandinavia. In *ARKEOS – perspectivas em diálogo*, ed. A. R. Cruz and L. Oosterbeek, vol. VI, pp. 133–75. Tomar.

Orientalisch-Ägäische Einflüsse in der europäischen Bronzezeit 1990 Ergebnisse eines Kolloquiums. Römisch-Gemanisches Zentralmuseum, Monographien 15. Bonn.

Orlin, L. L. 1970 *Assyrian Colonies in Cappadocia*. The Hague.

Orthmann, W. 2002 Kontinuität und neue Einflüsse. Die Entwicklung der späthethitischen Kunst zwischen 1200–700 v. Chr. In *Die Hethiter und ihr Reich* 2002: 274–82.

Osgood, R. 1998 *Warfare in the Late Bronze Age of North Europe*. BAR International Series 694. Oxford.

Osgood, R., Monk, S. and Toms, J. 2000 *Bronze Age Warfare*. Stroud.

Østmo, E. 1997 Horses, Indo-Europeans and the importance of ships. *Journal of Indo-European Studies* 25: 285–326.

Otrochschenko, V. 2003 The economic peculiarities of the Srubnaya cultural-historical entity. In Levine, Renfrew and Boyle 2003: 319–28.

Otterbein, K. F. 1967a An analysis of Iroquois military tactics. In Bohannan 1967: 345–51.

1967b The evolution of Zulu warfare. In Bohannan 1967: 351–9.

Otto, B. 2000 Hoheitszeichen in der altkretischen Kunst. In Blankholmer 2000: 83–9.

Ottoway, B. S. 2001 Innovation, production and specialization in early prehistoric copper metallurgy. *European Journal of Archaeology* 4, no. 1: 87–112.

Ottoway, B. and Wager, E. C. (eds.) 2002 *Metals and Society*. BAR International Series 1061. Oxford.

Owens, G. 1999 Linear A in the Aegean: the further travels of the Minoan script. A study of the 30+ extra-Cretan Minoan inscriptions. In Betancourt *et al.* 1999: 574–83.

Özgüç, N. 1988. Anatolian cylinder seals and impressions from Kültepe and Acemhöyük in the second millennium BC. In *Essays on Anatolian Studies in the Second Millennium BC*, ed. P. T. Mikasa, pp. 22–34. Wiesbaden.

Özgüç, T. 1986. *Kültepe-Kanis II: New Reseaches in the Trading Centre of the Ancient Near East*. Ankara.

1993. Studies on Hittite relief vases, seals, figurines and rock-carvings. In *Aspects of Art and Iconography: Anatolia and Its Neighbors. Studies in honor of Nimet Özgüç*, ed. A. J. Mellinik, E. Porada and T. Özgüç, pp. 497–506.

2002 Frühe Bronzezeit. Die Kultur der Hattier als Quelle der hethitischen Kultur. In *Die Hethiter und ihr Reich*, pp. 37–41. Exhibition Catalogue. Stuttgart.

Palaima, T. G. 1995 The nature of the Mycenaean wanax: non-Indo-European origins and priestly functions. In *The Role of the Ruler in the Prehistoric Aegean*, ed. P. Rehak, pp. 119–38. Aegaeum 11. Liège.

1997 Potter and fuller: the royal craftsmen. In Laffineur and Betancourt 1997: 407-13.

Panagiotopoulos, D. 2001 Keftiu in context: Theban tomb-paintings as historical source. *Oxford Journal of Archaeology* 20, no. 3: 63–85.

Panofsky, E. 1939 *Studies in Iconology*. Oxford.

1955 *Meaning in the Visual Arts*. Harmondsworth.

Pare, C. 1992 *Wagons and Wagon-Graves of the Early Iron Age in Central Europe*. Oxford University Committee for Archaeology Monograph 35. oxford.

(ed.) 2000 *Metals Make the World Go Round: The Supply and Circulation of Metals in Bronze Age Europe*. Oxford.

Parker Pearson, M. 2003 *Food, Culture and Identity in the Neolithic and Early Bronze Age*. BAR International Series 1117. Oxford.

Parzinger, H. and Boroffka, N. 2002 Zur bronzezeitlichen Zinngewinnung in Eurasien. Die Bergarbeitersiedlung bie Karnnab, Uzbekistan. *Godisnjak Jahrbuch. Zentrum für Balkanforschung* 30: 161–78. Sarajevo and Frankfurt am Main.

Pashkevich, G. 2003 Palaeoethnobotanical evidence of agriculture in the Steppe and the Forest-Steppe of east Europe in the Late Neolithic and Bronze Age. In Levine, Renfrew and Boyle 2003: 287–97.

Patay, P. 1996 Einige Worte über Bronzegefäe der Bronzezeit. In *Studien zur Metallindustrie im Karpatenbecken und den benachbarten Regionen*, ed. T. Kovács, pp. 403–19. Budapest.

Patterson, T. and Gailey, C. W. (eds.) 1987 *Power Relations and State Formation*. Washington, DC.

Pauketat, T. R. 1994 *The Ascent of Chiefs: Cahokia and Mississippian Politics in Native North America*. Tuscaloosa and London.

2000 The tragedy of the commoners. In Dobres and Robb 2000: 113–30.

Pauketat, T. R. and Alt, S. M. 2003 Mounds, memory, and contested Mississippian history. In Van Dyke and Alcock 2003: 151–80.

Payne, S. 1990 Field report on the Dendra horses. Appendix to E. Protonotariou-Deilaki: The tumuli of Mycenae and Dendra. In Hägg and Nordquist 1990: 85–106.

Pearce, M. 1998 New research on the *terramare* of northern Italy. *Antiquity* 72: 743–6.

Peatfield, A. 1999 The paradox of violence: weaponry and martial art in Minoan Crete. In Laffineur 1999: 68–73.

Pena Santos, A. de la and Rey Garcia, J. M. 2001 *Petroglifos de Galicia*. Coruña.

Pendi, F. 1982 Die Bronzezeit und der Beginn der Eisenzeit in Albanien. In *Südosteuropa zwischen 1600 und 1000 v. Chr.*, ed. B. Hänsel, pp. 203–33. Prähistorische Archäologie in Südosteuropa 1. Berlin.

Penglase, C. 1994 *Greek Myths and Mesopotamia: Parallels and Influence in the Homeric Hymns and Hesiod*. London and New York.

Penner, S. 1998 *Schliemanns Schachtgräberrund und der europäische Nordosten: Studien zur Herkunft der Mykenischen Streitwagenausstattung*. Saarbrücker Beitrage zur Altertumskunde 60. Bonn.

Perigrine, P. N. 1999 Legitimation crises in prehistoric worlds. In Kardulias 1999: 37–53.

Pernicka, E. 1998 Die Ausbreitung der Zinnbronzen im 3. Jahrtausend. In Hänsel, 1998a: 135–47.

Peroni, R. et al. (eds.) 1996 *The Bronze Age in Europe and the Mediterranean. Colloquium 10–12. XIII International Congress of Prehistoric and Protohistoric Sciences Forli-Italia 8/14 September 1996.* Forli.

Persson, A. W. 1928 *Kungagraven i Dendrá: guldfynd och andra fynd från utgrävningarna 1926 och 1927.* Stockholm.

Peter, H. 1998 I gudarnas sällskap. Hettitiskt gudabruk och polyteismbegreppet. In *Röster: religionshistoriska perspektiv*, ed. C. Raudvere and L. Stenberg, pp. 40–65. Stockholm.

Peters, F. 2000 Two traditions of Bronze Age burial in the Stonehenge landscape. *Oxford Journal of Archaeology* 19, no. 4: 343–58.

Petrie, W. M. F. 1894 *Tell el-Amarna*. London.

Petrovic, N. 2003 *Beliefs from Far Away: Context and Function of Foreign Cult Objects in the Late Bronze Age Aegean*. Göteborg.

Pettinato, G. 1991 *Ebla: A New Look at History*. Boston.

Piggott, S. 1983 *The Earliest Wheeled Transport: From the Atlantic Coast to the Caspian Sea*. London.

Pingel, V. 1982 Zum Schatzfund von Valcitran in Nordbulgarien. In *Südosteuropa zwischen 1600 und 1000 v. Chr.*, ed. B. Hänsel, pp. 173–86. Prähistorische Archäologie in Südosteuropa 1. Berlin.

Platon, N. 1984 The Minoan thalassocracy and the golden ring of Minos. In Hägg and Marinatos 1984: 65–9.

Politis, T. 2001 Gold and granulation: exploring the social implications of a prestige technology in the Bronze Age Mediterranean. In Shortland 2001: 161–94.

Polomé, E. 1994 Das Pferd in der Religion der eurasichen Völker. In Hänsel and Zimmer 1994: 93–112.

  (ed.) 1995 *Indo-European Religion after Dumezil*. Journal of Indo-European Studies Monograph Series 16. Washington, DC.

Porada, E. 1981 The cylinder seals found at Thebes in Boeotia. *Archiv für Orientforschung* 28: 68–77.

  1982 Remarks on the Tôd treasure from Egypt. In *Societies and Languages of the Ancient Near East: Studies in Honour of I. M. Diakonoff*, ed. M. Dadamaev et al., pp. 285–303. Warminster.

Posener, G. 1956 *Littérature et Politique dans l'Egypte de la XIIe dynastie*. Paris.

Postgate, J. N. 1992 *Early Mesopotamia: Society and Economy at the Dawn of History*. London and New York.

2003 Learning the lesson of the future: trade in prehistory through a historian's lens. *Bibliotheca Orientalis* 40, no. 1.2: 5–26.

Poulsen, J. 1983 Nogle reflektioner omkring Vognserup Enge-fundet. In *Struktur och förändring i bronsålderns samhälle. Rapport från det tredje nordiska symposiet för bronsåldersforskning i Lund 23–25 april 1982*, ed. B. Stjernquist, pp. 121–9. University of Lund, Institute of Archaeology, Report Series 17. Lund.

Prescott, C. 2000 Symbolic metallurgy – assessing early metallurgic processes in a periphery. In Olausson and Vandkilde 2000: 213–25.

Prescott, C. and Walderhaug, E. 1995 The last frontier? Processes of Indo-Europeanization in northern Europe: the Norwegian case. *The Journal of Indo-European Studies* 23, nos. 3–4: 257–78.

Price, B. 1984 Competition, productive intensification, and ranked society: speculations from evolutionary theory. In Ferguson 1984: 209–37.

Price, T. D. and Feinman, G. (eds.) 1995 *Foundations of Social Inequality*. New York.

Price, T. D., Grupe, G. and Schröter, P. 1998 Migration in the Bell Beaker period of central Europe. *Antiquity* 72: 405–11.

Price, T. D., Knipper, C., Grupe, G. and Smrcka, V. 2004 Strontium isotopes and prehistoric human migration: the Bell Beaker period in central Europe. *European Journal of Archaeology* 7, no. 1: 9–40.

Price, T. D., Manzanilla, L. and Middleton, W. D. 2000 Immigration and the ancient city of Teotihuacan in Mexico: a study using strontium isotope ratios in human bone and teeth. *Journal of Archaeological Science* 27: 903–13.

Primas, M. 1996 *Velika Gruda I: Hügelgräber des frühen 3. Jahrtausends v. Chr. im Adriagebiet – Velika Gruda, Mala Gruda und ihr Kontext*. Bonn.

1997 Bronze Age economy and ideology: central Europe in focus. *Journal of European Archaeology* 5: 115–30.

Pryor, F. 2002 *Seahenge: A Quest for Life and Death in Bronze Age Britain*. London.

Puhvel, J. 1988 *Comparative Mythology*. London.

Pulak, C. 1988 The Bronze Age shipwreck at Ulu Burun, Turkey, 1985 campaign. *American Journal of Archaeology* 92: 1–37.

1991 *Homer and Hittite*. Innsbruck.

Pustovalov, S. Z. 1994 Economy and social organisation of northern Pontic Steppe – forest steppe pastoral populations: 2700–2000 BC (Catacomb Culture). *Baltic-Pontic Studies* 2: 86–134.

Pyankov, I. V. 2002 Arkaim and the Indo-Iranian Var. In Jones-Bley and Zdanovich 2002: 36–42.

Quillfeldt, I. von 1995 *Die Vollgriffschwerter in Süddeutschland*. Prähistorische Bronzefunde 4, 11. Stuttgart.

Randsborg, K. 1967 'Aegean' bronzes in a grave in Jutland. *Acta Archaeologica* 38: 1–27.

1993 *Kivik: Archaeology and iconography*. Acta Archaeologica 64, 1. Copenhagen.

1995 *Hjortspring: Warfare and Sacrifice in Early Europe*. Aarhus.

1996a The Nordic Bronze Age: chronological dimensions. In *Absolute Chronology: Archaeological Europe 2500–500 BC*, pp. 61–73. Acta Archaeologica 67. Copenhagen.

(ed.) 1996b *Absolute Chronology: Archaeological Europe 2500–500 BC*. Acta Archaeologica 67. Copenhagen.

1998 Plundered Bronze Age graves. Archaeological and social implications. *Acta Archaeologica* 69: 113–38.

Randsborg, K. and Nybo, C. 1984 The coffin and the sun. Demography and ideology in Scandinavian prehistory. *Acta Archaeologica* 55: 161–84.

Rasmussen, M. 1999 Livestock without bones. The long-house as contributor to the interpretation of livestock management in the southern Scandinavian Bronze Age. In Fabech and Ringtved 1999: 281–90.

Rassamakin, Y. 1999 The Eneolithic of the Black Sea steppe: dynamics of cultural and economic development 4500–2300 BC. In *Late Prehistoric Exploitation of the Eurasian Steppe*, ed. M. Levin, Y. Rassamakin, A. Kislenko and N. Tatarintseva, pp. 59–143. Cambridge.

Rassmann, K. 1996 Zum Forschungstand der absoluten Chronologie der frühen Bronzezeit in Mitteleuropa auf Grundlage von Radiocarbondaten. *Acta Archaeologica* 67: 199–211.

Rassman, K., Lutz, J. and Pernicka, E. 2001 Frühbronzezeitliche Vollgriffsdolche vom Malchiner Typ – 'Importe' oder erste Zeugnisse nordischen Bronzehandweks? In Meyer 2001: 87–100.

Raulwing, P. 2000 *Horses, Chariots and Indo-Europeans: Foundations and Methods of Chariotry Research from the Viewpoint of Comparative Indo-European Linguistics.* Archaeolingua, Series Minor. Budapest.

Rausing, G. 1991 The chariots of the petroglyphs. In *Regions and Reflections: In Honour of Märta Strömberg*, ed. K. Jennbert, L. Larsson, R. Petré and B. Wyszomirska-Werbart, pp. 153–62. Acta Archaeologica Lundensia, Series in 8, 20. Lund.

Rautman, A. (ed.) 2000 *Reading the Body: Representations and Remains in the Archaeological Record.* Philadelphia.

Redford, D. B. 1970 The Hyksos invasion in history and tradition. *Orientalia* 39: 1–51.
  1984 *Akhenaten: The Heretic King.* Princeton, NJ.

Rehak, P. 1995a Enthroned figures in Aegean art and the function of the Mycenaean megaron. In Rehak 1995b: 95–117.
  (ed.) 1995b *The Role of the Ruler in the Prehistoric Aegean.* Aegaeum 11. Liège.

Rehak, P. and Younger, J. G. 1998 Review of Aegean prehistory VII: Neopalatial, Final Palatial, and Post palatial Crete. *American Journal of Archaeology* 102: 91–173.

Renfrew, C. 1972 *The Emergence of Civilization: The Cyclades and the Aegean in the Third Millennium B.C.* London.
  1973 *Before Civilization: The Radiocarbon Revolution and Prehistoric Europe.* London.
  1975 Trade as action at a distance: questions of integration and communication. In *Ancient Civilizations and Trade*, ed. J. Sabloff and C. C. Lamberg-Karlovsky. Albuquerque.
  1977 Space, time and polity. In *The Evolution of Social Systems*, ed. J. Friedman and M. Rowlands, pp. 89–111. London.
  1984 *Approaches to Social Archaeology.* Edinburgh.
  1985 *The Archaeology of Cult: The Sanctuary at Phylakopi.* British School of Archaeology at Athens Suppl. Vol. 18. London.
  1986 Introduction: peer polity interaction and socio-political change. In *Peer Polity Interaction and Socio-political Change*, ed. C. Renfrew and J. Cherry, pp. 1–18. Cambridge.
  1987 *Archaeology and Language: The Puzzle of Indo-European Origins.* London.
  1993 Trade beyond the material. In Scarre and Healy 1993: 5–17.

1998a From here to ethnicity. In review feature: *Ethnic Identity in Greek Antiquity*, by Jonathan Hall. *Cambridge Archaeological Journal* 8, no. 2: 275–7.

1998b Word of Minos: the Minoan contribution to Mycenaean Greek and the linguistic geography of the Bronze Age Aegean. *Cambridge Archaeological Journal* 8, no. 2: 239–64.

1999 Time depth, convergence theory, and innovation in Proto-Indo-European: 'Old Europe' as a PIE linguistic area. *The Journal of Indo-European Studies* 27, nos. 3–4: 257–93.

2001a Commodification and institution in group-oriented and individualizing societies. In Runciman 2001: 93–119.

2001b Symbol before concept. Material engagement and the early development of society. In Hodder 2001: 123–40.

Renfrew, C. and Cherry, J. F. (eds.) 1986 *Peer-Polity Interaction and Socio-economic Change*. Cambridge.

Rezepkin, A. 2000 *Das frühbronzezeitliche Gräberfelt von Klady und die Majkop-Kultur in Nordwestkaukasien*. Archäologie in Euroasien 10. Rahden/Westfalia.

Rice, M. 1997 *Egypt's Legacy*. London and New York.

1998 *The Power of the Bull*. London and New York.

Richerson, P. J. and Boyd, R. 2001 Institutional evolution in the Holocene: the rise of complex societies. In Runciman 2001: 197–235.

Rittershofer, K.-F. 1983 Der Hortfund von Bühl und seine Beziehungen. *Bericht der Römisch-Germanischen Kommission* 64: 141–402.

(ed.) 1997a *Demographie der Bronzezeit: Paläodemographie – Möglichkeiten und Grenzen*. Internationale Archäologie 36. Espelkamp.

(ed.) 1997b *Sonderbestattungen in der Bronzezeit im östlichen Mitteleuropa*. Espelkamp.

Robb, J. 2001 Island identities: ritual, travel and the creation of difference in Neolithic Malta. *European Journal of Archaeology* 4, no. 2: 175–202.

Robins, G. 1993 *Women in Ancient Egypt*. London.

Roman, P. (ed.) 1997 *The Thracian World at the Crossroads of Civilizations*, vol. I. *Proceedings of the Seventh International Congress of Thracology, Constanta–Mangalia–Tulcea 20–26 May 1996*. Bucarest.

Romano, J. F. 1995 Jewelry and personal arts in ancient Egypt. In *Civilizations of the Ancient Near East*, ed. J. M. Sasson, vol. III, pp. 1605–21. New York.

Rønne, P. 1993 Kongens Høje. En gruppe gravhøje fra ældre bronzealder på Ringsted Mark, Midtsjælland. In Larsson 1993: 9–46.

Rousioti, D. 2001 Did the Mycenaeans believe in theriomorphic divinities? In Laffineur and Hägg 2001:

Roux, G. 1992 *Ancient Iraq*. Harmondsworth.

Rowlands, M. 1980 Kinship, alliance and exchange in the European Bronze Age. In *Settlement and Society in the British Later Bronze Age*, ed. J. Barrett and R. Bradley, pp. 15–55. BAR British Series 83. Oxford. Reprinted in Kristiansen and Rowlands 1998.

1993 The role of memory in the transmission of culture. *World Archaeology* 25: 141–51.

2003 The unity of Africa. In *Ancient Egypt in Africa*, ed. D. B. O'Connor and A. Reid, pp. 39–54. London.

Rowlands, M., Larsen, M. T. and Kristiansen, K. (eds.) 1987 *Centre and Periphery in the Ancient World*. Cambridge.

Ruby, P. (ed.) 1999 *Les Princes de la protohistoire et l'émergence de l'état*. Naples and Rome.

Ruiz Galvez, M. (ed.) 1995 *Ritos de paso y puntos de paso: la Ria de Huelva en el mundo del Bronce Final Europeo*. Complutum-Extra 5. Madrid.

Runciman, W. G. (ed.) 2001 *The Origin of Human Social Institutions*. Oxford.

Rustoiu, A. and Ursutiu, A. (eds.) 2002 *Interregionale und kulturalle Beziehungen im Karpatenraum (2. Jahrtausend v. Chr. – 1 Jahrtausend n. CHr.)*. Cluj-Napoca.

Rystedt, E. 1997 Approaching the question of Bronze-to-Iron Age continuity in ancient Greece. *Current Swedish Archaeology* 5: 147–54.

Sahlins, M. 1972 *Stone Age Economics*. Chicago.

Sanchez-Moreno, E. 2001 Cross-cultural links in ancient Iberia: socio-economic anatomy of hospitality. *Oxford Journal of Archaeology* 20, no. 4: 391–414.

Sandars, N. 1978 *The Sea Peoples: Warriors of the Ancient Mediterranean*. London.

Sansoni, U. 1987 *L'arte rupestre di Sellero*. Capo di Ponte.

Santos, M. E. and Criado, F. B. in press Deconstructing rock art spatial grammar in the Galician Bronze Age.

Sarianidi, V. 1999 Near Eastern Aryans in Central Asia. *The Journal of Indo-European Studies* 27, nos. 3–4: 295–327.

Sassaman, K. E. 2000 Agents of change in hunter-gatherer technology. In Dobres and Robb 2000: 148–69.

Sava, E. 1998 Die Rolle der 'östlichen' und 'westlichen' Elemente bei der Genese des Kulturkomplexes Noua-Sabatinovka. In Hänsel and Machnik 1998: 267–313.

Säve-Söderbergh, T. 1946. *The Navy of the Eighteenth Egyptian Dynasty*. Uppsala.

Sbonias, K. 1999 Inter-settlement relations and symbolic representation in Prepalatial Crete. In *Eliten der Bronzezeit*: 1–19.

Scarre, C. and Healy, F. (eds.) 1993 *Trade and Exchange in Prehistoric Europe*. Oxbow Monographs 33. Oxford.

Schaeffer, C. F.-A. 1968 *Nouveaux texts accadiens, hourrites et ugaritiques*. Ugaritica 5. Paris.

Schalk, E. 1998 *Die Entwicklung der prähistorischen metallurgie im nördlichen Karpatenbecken: eine typologische und metallanalytische Untersuchung*. Internationale Archäologie, Naturwissenschaft und Technologie, 1. Rahden and Wesfalen.

Schauer, P. 1971 *Die Schwerter in Süddeutschland, Österreich und der Schweiz 1*. Prähistorische Bronzefunde 2. Munich.

1979 Eine urnenfelderzietliche Kampfweise. *Archäologishe Korrespondenzblatt* 9: 69–80.

1984a Überregionale Gemeinsamkeiten bei Waffengräbern der ausgehenden Bronzezeit und ältgeren Urnenfelderzeit des Voralpenraumes. *Jahrbuch des Römisch-Germanischen Zentralmuseums* 31: 209–35. Mainz.

1984b Spuren Minoisch-Mykenischen und orientalischen Einflusses im atlantischen Westeuropa. *Jahrbuch des Römisch-Germanischen Zentralmuseums* 31: 137–86.

1985 Spuren orientalischen und ägäischen Einflusses im bronzezeitlichen Nordischen Kreis. *Jahrbuch des Römisch-Germanischen Zentralmuseums* 32: 123–95.

1990 Schutz- und Angriffswaffen bronzezeitlicher Krieger im Spiegel ausgewählter Grabfunde Mitteleuropas. In Furmanek, V. and Horst, F. (eds.): pp. 381–410.

(ed.) 1996 *Archäologische Forshungen zum Kultgeschehen in der jüngeren Bronzezeit und frühen Eisenzeit Alteuropas*. Regensburg.

Schiffer, M. (ed.) 2000 *Social Theory in Archaeology: Foundations of Archaeological Inquiry.* Salt Lake City.

Schjødt, J. P. 1995 Archaeology, language and comparative mythology. In Polome 1995: 184–96.

Schlager, N. 1999 'A Town of Castles': an MM/LM fortified site at Aspro Nero in the far east of Crete. In Laffineur 1999: 171–9.

2000 Hogarath's Zakro sealing no. 130: Phantasiegebilde oder realistische Stadtdarstellung? In Blankholmer 2000: 69–83.

Schmidt, R. and Voss, B. L. (eds.) 2000 *Archaeologies of Sexuality.* London.

Schoep, I. 1999a The origins of writing and administration on Crete. *Oxford Journal of Archaeology* 18, no. 3: 265–77.

1999b Tablets and territories? Reconstructing Late Minoan IB political geography through undeciphered documents. *American Journal of Archaeology* 103: 201–21.

2002 The state of the Minoan palaces or the Minoan palace state? In Driessen, Schoep and Laffineur 2002: 15–35.

Schubart, H. 1972 *Die Funde der älteren Bronzezeit in Mecklenburg.* Offa 26. Neumünster.

Schuhmacher, T. X. 2002 Some remarks on the origin and chronology of halberds in Europe. *Oxford Journal of Archaeology* 21, no. 3: 263–88.

Schumacher-Matthäus, G. 1985 *Studien zu Bronzezeitlichen Schmucktrachten im Karpatenbecken.* Mainz.

Schwabe, C. W. 1994 Animals in the ancient world. In *Animals and Human Society: Changing Perspectives,* ed. A. Manning and J. Serpell, pp. 36–58. London and New York.

Schwantes, G. 1939 *Arbeitsweise und einige Ergebnisse der vorgeschichtlichen Sinnbildforschung.* Offa 4. Neumünster.

Schwenzer, S. 2002 Zur Frage der Datierung der Meltzer-Stabdolche. *Praehistorische Zeitschrift* 77, no. 1: 76–83.

Seidel, U. 1995 *Bronzezeit.* Sammlungen des Würtembergischen Landesmuseums Stuttgart 2. Stuttgart.

Senaki-Sakellariou, A. 1985 *Les Tombes à chambre de Mycènes: fouilles de Chr. Tsountas (1887–1898).* Paris.

Service, E. 1971 *Primitive Social Organization: An Evolutionary Perspective.* New York.

Sestieri, A. M. Bietti 1996 *Protostoria: teoria e practica.* Rome.

Shanks, M. 1992 Style and the design of a perfume jar from an Archaic Greek city state. *Journal of European Archaeology* 1: 77–107.

1999 *Art and the Early Greek State: An Interpretative Archaeology.* Cambridge.

Shanks, M. and Hodder, I. 1995 Processual, postprocessual and interpretive archaeologies. In *Interpreting Archaeology,* ed. I. Hodder *et al.,* pp. 3–29. London and New York.

Shanks, M. and Tilley, C. 1987 *Social Theory and Archaeology.* Cambridge.

Shaw, M. C. 1997 Aegean sponsors and artists: reflections on their roles in the patterns of distribution of themes and representational conventions in the murals. In Laffineur and Betancourt 1997: 481–505.

Shear, I. M. 1987 *The Panagia House at Mycenae.* Philadelphia.

Shennan, S. 1978 Archaeological 'cultures': an empirical investigation. In Hodder 1978: 113–41.

(ed.) 1989 *Archaeological Approaches to Cultural Identity*. London.

1993 Commodities, transactions and growth in the Central European Early Bronze Age. *Journal of European Archaeology* 1, no. 2: 59–72.

1995 *Bronze Age Copper Producers of the Eastern Alps*. Universitätsforschungen zur prähistorischen Archäologie 27. Bonn.

1999 Cost, benefit and value in the organisation of early European copper production. *Antiquity* 73: 352–63.

2000 Population, culture history, and the dynamics of culture change. *Current Anthropology* 41: 811–36.

2002 *Genes, Memes and Human History: Darwinian Archaeology and Cultural Evolution*. London.

Sherratt, A. 1987 Warriors and traders: Bronze Age chiefdoms in central Europe. In *Origins: The Roots of European Civilization*, ed. B. Cunliffe, pp. 54–66. London.

1994a Core, periphery and margin: perspectives on the Bronze Age. In Mathers and Stoddart 1994: 335–45.

1994b The emergence of élites: earlier Bronze Age Europe, 2500–1300 BC. In *The Oxford Illustrated Prehistory of Europe*, ed. B. Cunliffe, pp. 244–76. Oxford.

1994c What would a Bronze Age world system look like? Relations between temperate Europe and the Mediterranean in later prehistory. *Journal of European Archaeology* 1, no. 2: 1–59.

1995 Fata Morgana: illusion and reality in Greek–barbarian relations. *Cambridge Archaeological Journal* 5, no. 1: 139–56.

1996a 'Settlement patterns' or landscape studies. Reconciling reason and romance. *Archaeological Dialogues* 3, no. 2: 140–59.

1996b Why Wessex? The Avon route and river transport in later British prehistory. *Oxford Journal of Archaeology* 15, no. 2: 211–35.

1997a Troy, Maikop, Altyn Depe: Early Bronze Age urbanism and its periphery. In Sherratt 1997b: ch. 18.

1997b *Economy and Society in Prehistoric Europe: Changing Perspectives*. Edinburgh.

1998 The human geography of Europe: a prehistoric perspective. In *An Historical Geography of Europe*, ed. R. A. Butlin and R. A. Dodgshon, pp. 1–25. Oxford.

2003a The horse and the wheel: the dialectics of change in the Circum Pontic region and adjacent areas, 4500–1500 BC. In Levine, Renfrew and Boyle 2003: 223–53.

2003b The Baden (Pécel) culture and Anatolia: perspectives on a cultural transformation. In *Morgenrot der Kulturen. Frühe Etappen der Menschheitsgeschichte in Mittel- und Südosteuropa: Festschrift für Nándor Kalicz zum 75. Geburtstag*, ed. E. Jerem and P. Raczky, pp. 415–31. Budapest.

Sherratt, A. and Sherratt, S. 1991 From luxuries to commodities: the nature of Mediterranean Bronze Age trading systems. In *Bronze Age Trade in the Mediterranean*, ed. N. H. Gale. Studies in Mediterranean Archaeology 90. Jonsered.

1998 Small worlds: interaction and identity in the ancient Mediterranean. In Cline and Harris-Cline 1998: 329–42.

Sherratt, S. 1990 'Reading the texts': archaeology and the Homeric question. *Antiquity* 64: 807–24.

2000a Circulation of metals and the end of the Bronze Age in the eastern Mediterannean. In Pare 2000: 82–99.

(ed.) 2000b *The Wall Paintings of Thera: Proceedings of the First International Symposium 30 August–4 September 1997*. Athens.

2003 The Mediterranean economy: 'globalisation' at the end of the second millennium B.C.E. In *Symbiosis, Symbolism, and the Power of the Past: Canaan, Ancient Israel, and Their Neighbours from the Late Bronze Age through Roman Palaestina*, ed. W. G Denver and S. Gitin, pp. 23–35. Winona Lake.

Shislina, N. I. 1997 The bow and arrow of the Eurasian steppe Bronze Age nomads. *Journal of European Archaeology* 5, no. 2: 53–66.

(ed.) 2000 *Seasonality Studies of the Bronze Age Northwest Caspian Steppe* (English summaries). Papers of the State Historical Museum 120. Moscow.

2001 The seasonal cycle of grassland use in the Caspian Sea steppe during the Bronze Age: a new approach to an old problem. *European Journal of Archaeology* 4: 323–46.

2003 Yamna Culture pastoral exploitation: a local sequence. In Levine, Renfrew and Boyle 2003: 353–67.

Shishlina, N. I., Alexandrovsky, A. L., Chichagova, O. A. and Plicht, J. van der 2000 Radiocarbon chronology of the Kalmykia Catacomb Culture of the west Eurasian steppe. *Antiquity* 74: 793–9.

Shislina, N. and Hiebert, T. H. 1998 The steppe and the sown: interaction between Bronze Age Eurasian nomads and agriculturalists. In Mair 1998: 222–37.

Shortland, A. J. (ed.) 2001 *The Social Context of Technological Change: Egypt and the Near East, 1650–1550 BC*. Oxford.

Shortman, E. M. and Urban, P. A. 1992a Current trends in interaction research. In Shortman and Urban 1992b: 235–55.

(eds.) 1992b *Resources, Power and Interregional Interaction*. New York.

Simek, R. 1993 *Dictionary of Northern Mythology*. Cambridge.

Sicherl, B. 2002 Der 'Sweinskopf' bei Tecklenburg-Brochterbeck, Kr. Steinfurt. Eine altbronzezeitliche Befestigung in Nordwestdeutschland. *Archäologische Mitteilungen aus Nordwestdeutschland* 25: 45–81.

Smith, A. T. 2003 *The Political Landscape: Constellations of Authority in Early Complex Polities*. Berkeley.

Smith, H. S. and Smith, A. 1976 A reconsideration of the Kamose text. *Zeitschrift für Ägyptische Sprache und Altertumskunde* 103: 48–76.

Snodgrass, A. M. 1991 Bronze Age exchange: a minimalist position. In *Bronze Age Trade in the Mediterranean*, ed. N. H. Gale, pp. 15–20. Studies in Mediterranean Archaeology. Jonsered.

Sofaer-Derevenski, J. 2000 Rings of life: the role of early metalwork in mediating gendered life course. *World Archaeology* 31, no. 3: 389–406.

Soles, J. S. 1995 The functions of a cosmological center: Knossos in Palatial Crete. In Laffineur and Niemeier 1995: 405–15.

1997 A community of craftsmen at Mochlos. In Laffineur and Betancourt 1997: 425–33.

Sørensen, M. L. S. 1987 Material order and cultural classification: the role of bronze objects in the transitition from Bronze Age to Iron Age in Scandinavia. In Hodder 1987: 90–101.

1997a Material culture and typology. *Current Swedish Archaeology* 5: 179–92.

1997b Reading dress: the construction of social categories and identitites in Bronze Age Europe. *Journal of European Archaeology* 5, no. 1: 93–114.

2000 *Gender Archaeology.* Cambridge.

Sperber, L. 1999 Zu den Schwertgräbern im westlichen Kreis der Urnenfelderkultur: profane und religiöse Aspekte. In *Eliten der Bronzezeit:* 605–60.

Sprockhoff, E. 1954 Nordische Bronzezeit und frühes Griechentum. *Jahrbuch des Römisch-Germanischen Zentralmuseums:* 28–110. Mainz.

Stavrianopoulou, E. 1995 Die Verflechtung des Politischen mit dem Religiösen im mykenischen Pylos. In Laffineur and Niemeier 1995: 423–35.

Steensberg, A. 1952 *Bondehuse og vandmøller i Danmark gennem 2000 år* Copenhagen.

1973 *Den danske landsby gennem 6000 år.* Copenhagen.

Stein, G. J. 1998 Heterogenity, power, and political economy: some current research issues in the archaeology of Old World complex societies. *Journal of Archaeological Research* 6, no. 1: 1–44.

1999 *Rethinking World-Systems: Diasporas, Colonies, and Interaction in Uruk Mesopotamia.* Tuscon, Arizona.

Steiner, G. 1990 The immigration of the first Indo-Europeans into Anatolia reconsidered. *Journal of Indo-European Studies* 18: 185–214.

Stenberger, M. 1969 *Sten, brons, järn.* Stockholm.

Stjernquist, B. 1985 Methodische Überlegungen zum Nachweis von Handel aufgrund archäologischer Quellen. In *Untersuchungen zu Handel und Verkehr der vor- und frühgeschichtlichen Zeit in Mittel- und Nordeuropa,* ed. K. Düwel and A. Lundström, vol. I, pp. 56–83. Göttingen.

1990 A couple from Stockhult, Scania. In *Oldtidens ansigt,* ed. P. Kjaerum and R. A. Olsen, pp. 54–5. Århus.

Stoklund, B. 1972 *Bondegård og byggeskik før 1850.* Copenhagen.

Strahm, C. 2002 Tradition und Wandel der sozialen Strukturen vom 3. Zum 2. Vorchristlichen Jahrtausend. In *Vom Endneolithicum zur Frühbronzezeit: Muster sozialen Wandels?,* ed. J. Müller, pp. 175–95. Bonn.

Strange, J. 1980 *Caphtor: A New Investigation.* Leiden.

Stros-Gale, Z. 2001 Minoan foreign relations and copper metallurgy in Protopalatial and Neopalatial Crete. In Shortland 2001: 195–210.

Stros-Gale, Z., Gale, N. and Houghton, J. 1995 The origin of Egyptian copper: lead isotope analysis of metals from El-Amarna. In *Egypt, the Aegean and the Levant: Interconnections in the Second Millennium BC,* ed. W. V. Davies and L. Schofield, pp. 127–35. London.

Struwe, K. V. 1971 *Geschichte Schleswig-Holsteins. Die Bronzezeit Periode I–III.* Neumünster.

1983 *Zwei getriebene Bronzetassen der älteren Bronzezeit aus Schleswig-Holstein.* Offa-Zeitschrift 40. Kiel.

Strömberg, M. 1977 *Bondesamhällen under Ingelstorps forntid.* Ystad.

Stuchlik, S. 1990 Die sekundären Eingriffe in den Gräbern der Uneticer Kultur. *Antropologie* 28, nos. 2–3: 159–67.

Szathmári, I. 1996 Bronze wire and sheet ornaments of the Vatya Culture. In *Studien zur Metallindustrie im Karpatenbecken und den benachbarten Regionen,* ed. T. Kovács, pp. 75–87. Budapest.

Tainter, J. 1999 *The Collapse of Complex Societies.* Cambridge.

Tasic, N. 1998 Elemente der Viehzuchtbewegungen in der Bronzezeit im Raum Donaubecken – Nordgriechenland. In Anretter *et al.* 1998: 531–8.

Taylour, Lord William 1964 *The Mycenaeans*. London.

Teissier, B. 1993 The ruler with the peaked cap and other Syrian iconography on glyptic from Kültepe in the Early Second Millennium B.C. In *Aspects of Art and Iconography: Anatolia and Its Neighbors. Studies in honor of Nimet Özgüç*, ed. A. J. Mellink, E. Porada and T. Özgüç, pp. 601–9. Ankara.

Terzan, B., Mihovilic, K. and Hänsel, B. 1999 *Eine protourbane Siedlung der älteren Bronzezeit im istrischen Karst*. Prähistorische Zeitschrift 74. Berlin.

Teschler-Nicola, M. 1994 Bevölkerungsbiologische Aspekte der frühen und mittleren Bronzezeit. In *Bronzezeit in Österreich*, ed. J. W. Neugebauer, pp. 167–82. Wissenschaftliche Schriftenreihe Niederösterreich. St Pölten and Vienna.

Thomas, C. and Wedde, M. 2001 Desperately seeking Potnia. In Laffineur and Hägg 2001: 3–15.

Thomas, J. 1999 *Understanding the Neolithic*, revised 2nd edn of *Rethinking the Neolithic*. London.

2002 Archaeology's humanism and the materiality of the body. In Hamilakis, Pluciennik and Tarlow 2002: 29–45.

Thrane, H. 1990 The Mycenaean fascination: a northerner's view. In *Orientalisch-ägäische Einflüsse in der europäischen Bronzezeit*. Römisch-Germanisches Zentralmuseum, Monographien 15. Bonn.

(ed.) 2003 *Diachronic Settlement Studies in the Metal Ages: Report on the ESF Workshop at Moesgård, Denmark, 14–18 October 2000*. Jutland Archaeological Society Publications 45. Århus.

Tilley, C. (ed.) 1993 *Interpretative Archaeology*. Oxford.

1994 *A Phenomenology of Landscape: Places, Paths and Monuments*. Oxford.

1996 *An Ethnography of the Neolithic*. Cambridge.

Tocik, A. 1964 *Opevnená osada z doby bronzovej vo Veselom (Befestigte bronzezeitliche Ansiedlung in Vesele)*. Archaeologica Slovaca Fontes 5 Bratislava.

1981 *Nitriansky Hrádok-Zámecek: bronzezeitliche befestigte Ansiedlung der Madarovce-Kultur*. Materialia Archaeologica Slovaca 1 and 2. Nitra.

Tournavitou, I. 1997 The social and economic position of artisans in the Mycenaean world. In Gillis, Risberg and Sjöberg 1997: 29–43.

Treherne, P. 1995 The warrior's beauty: the masculine body and self-identity in Bronze Age Europe. *Journal of European Archaeology* 3, no. 1: 105–45.

Treister, M. 1996 The Trojan treasures. Description, chronology, historical context. In Antonova, Tolstikov and Treister 1996: 197–234.

Trifonov, V. 2004 Die Majkop Kultur und die ersten Wagen in der südrussischen Steppe. In Fansa and Burmeister 2004: 167–77.

Trigger, B. 1976 *Nubia under the Pharaohs*. London.

2003 *Understanding Early Civilizations*. Cambridge.

Trogmayer, O. 1975 *Das Bronzezeitliche Gräberfeld bei Tápé*. Budapest.

Tunca, Ö. 1986 Le problème des archives dans l'architecture religieuse proto-dynastique. In *Cuneiform Archives and Libraries*, ed. K. Veenhof. Leiden.

Turney-High, H. 1949 *Primitive War: Its Practice and Concepts*. Reissue with new preface and afterword. Colombia, South Carolina, 1971.

Tusa, S. 2000 La società siciliana e il 'contatto' con il mediterraneo centro-orientale dal II millennio a.C. agli inizi del primo millennio a.C. *Sicilia Archeologica* 33: 10–39.

Tyborowski, W. 2002. fluted maces in the system of long-distance exchange trails of the Bronze Age: 2350–800 BC. *Mesopotamia, Anatolia and the Circumpontic Region in the Early Bronze Age. Baltic Pontic Studies* 11: 82–98.

Upham, S. (ed.) 1990 *The Evolution of Political Systems: Sociopolitics in Small-Scale Sedentary Societies*. Cambridge.

Urban, P. A. and Shortman, E. M. 1999 Thoughts on the periphery. The ideological consequences of core/periphery relations. In Kardulias 1999: 125–53.

van de Mieroop, M. 1989 Women in the economy of Sumer. In *Women's Earliest Records from Ancient Egypt and Western Asia*, ed. B. S. Lesko, pp. 53–66. Brown Judaic Studies 166. Atlanta.

2004 *A History of the Ancient Near East, ca. 3000–323 BC*. Blackwell History of the Ancient World 1. Oxford.

Van der Leeuw, S. E. and Torrence, R. (eds.) 1989 *What's New? A Closer Look at the Process of Innovation*. London.

Van Dyke, R. M. and Alcock, S. (eds.) 2003 *Archaeologies of Memory*. Oxford.

Van Gennep, A. 1982 *The Rites of Passage*. London.

Vandkilde, H. 1996 *From Stone to Bronze: The Metalwork of the Late Neolithic and Earliest Bronze Age in Denmark*. Jutland Archaeological Society Publications 32. Aarhus.

1998 Denmark and Europe: typochronology, metal composition and socio-economic change in the Early Bronze Age. In Mordant, Pernot and Rychner 1998: 119–37.

1999 Social distinction and ethnic reconstruction in the earliest Danish Bronze Age. In *Eliten der Bronzezeit*: 245–76.

2000 Material culture and Scandinavian archaeology: a review of the concepts of form, function and context. In Olausson and Vandkilde 2000: 3–51.

In press Warriors and warrior institutions in Copper Age Europe. In *Warfare in Archaeological and Social Anthropological Perspective*, ed. T. Otto, H. Thrane and H. Vandkilde. Aarhus.

Vandkilde, H., Rahbek, U. and Rasmussen, K. L. 1996 Radiocarbon dating and the chronology of Bronze Age southern Scandinavia. *Acta Archaeologica* 67: 183–99.

Vansina, J. 1985 *Oral Tradition as History*. London.

Veit, U. 1997 Skelettfunde in Siedlungen der Bronzezeit – Ein Beitrag zur Paläodemographie? In Rittershofer 1997b: 14–22.

Vencl, S. 1984 War and warfare in archaeology. *Journal of Anthropological Archaeology* 3: 116–32.

Vermeule, E. T. 1975 *The Art of the Shaft Graves of Mycenae*. Norman, OK.

Veyne, P. 1988 *Did the Greeks Believe in Their Myths? An Essay on the Constitutive Imagination*. Chicago.

Vicent Garcia, J. M., Rodriquez, A., Lopez, J., de Zavala, J., Lopez, P. and Martinez, M. 1999 Una propuesta metodologica para el estudio de la metalurgia prehistorica: el caso de Gorny en la region de Kargaly (Orenburg, Rusia). *Trabajos de Prehistoria* 56, no. 2: 85–113.

2000 Catastrofes eologicas en la estepa? Arqueologia del paisaje en el complejo minro-metalurgico de Kargaly (region Orenburg, Rusia). *Trabajos de Prehistoria* 57, no. 1: 29–74.

n.d. Landscape, subsistence and metallurgical production during the Bronze Age in the mining and metallurgical complex of Kargaly (southern Urals, Orenburg, Russia). Paper delivered at the 7th annual meeting of the European Association of Archaeologists in Esslingen, session *European Steppe of Bronze Age*. Organisers: P. Kouznetsow and O. Motchalov.

Victor, H. 2002 *Med graven som granne: om bronålderns kulthus* (Summary: The Grave as a Neighbour. On Bronze Age Ritual Houses). AUN 30. Uppsala.

Vicze, M. 2000 The symbolic meaning of Urn 715. *Komárom-eszterergom Megyei Muzeumok Közleményei* 7: 119–31.

Vladar, J. 1973 Osteuropäische und mediterrane Einflüsse im Gebiet der Slowakei während der Bronzezeit. *Slovenska Archaeologia* 21, no. 2: 253–357.

Vladar, J. and Bartonek, A. 1977 Zu den Beziehungen des ägäischen, balkanischen under karpatischen Raumes in der mittleren Bronzezeit und die kulturelle Ausstrahlung der ägäsichen Schriften in die nachbarländeri. *Slovenska Archaeologia* 25, no. 2: 371–432.

Vogt, I. 2004 *Der Ubergang von der frühen zur mittleren Bronzezeit in Mittel- und Nordeuropa under Berücksichtigung der Griffplattenklingen*. Saarbrücker Beiträge zur Altertumskunde 79. Bonn.

Voruz, J.-L. 1996 La chronologie absolue de l'Age du Bronze ancien. In Mordant and Gaiffe 1996: 97–165

Vulpe, A. 1982 Beitrag zu den bronzezeitlichen Kulturbeziehungen zwischen Rumänien und Griechenland. In *Südosteuropa zwischen 1600 und 1000 v. Chr.*, ed. B. Hänsel, pp. 321–8. Prähistorische Archäologie in Südosteuropa 1. Berlin.

Wace, A. J. B. 1932 *Chamber Tombs at Mycenae*. Archaeologica 82. Oxford.

Wachsmann, S. 1998 *Seagoing Ships and Seamanship in the Bronze Age Levant*. London.

Wallerstein, I. 1974 *The Modern World System: Capitalist Agriculture and the Origins of the European World-Economy in the Sixteenth Century*. New York.

Wanscher, O. 1980 *Sella, Curulis, the Folding Stool, an Ancient Symbol of Dignity*. Copenhagen.

Wanzek, B. 1991 Ein Gussmodel für einen Dolch mykenischen Typs von der unteren Donau. *Zeitschrift für Archäologie* 25: 1–28.

Ward, D. 1968 *The Divine Twins: An Indo-European Myth in Germanic Tradition*. Folklore Studies 19. Berkeley and Los Angeles.

Warren, P. M. 1989 *The Aegean Civilizations from Ancient Crete to Mycenae*, 2nd edn. Oxford.
    1999 LM IA Knossos, Thera, Gournia. In Betancourt *et al.* 1999: 893–902.

Warren, P. M. and Hankey, V. 1989 *Aegean Bronze Age Chronology*. Bristol.

Watkins, C. 2002 Homer and Hittite Revisited II. In Yener and Hoffner 2002: 167–76.

Weeks, L. 1999 Lead isotope analyses from Tell Abraq, United Arab Emirates: new data regarding the 'tin' problem in western Asia. *Antiquity* 73: 49–64.

Weingarten, J. 1999 War scenes and ruler iconography in a Golden Age: some lessons on missing Minoan themes from the United Provinces (17th century AD). In Laffineur 1999: 341–7.

Wells, P. S. 1989 Intensification, entrepeneurship, and cognitive change in the Bronze-Iron Age transition. In *The Bronze Age–Iron Age Transition in Europe* ed. M. L. S. Sørensen and R. Thomas, pp. 73–92. BAR International Series 483. Oxford.

Wels-Weyrauch, U. 1989 Mittelbronzezeitliche Frauentrachten in Süddeutschland (Beziehungen zur Hagenauer Gruppierung). In *Dynamique du bronze moyen en Europe occidentale*, pp. 119–33. Paris.
    1994 Im Grab erhalten, im Leben getragen – Tracht und Schmuck der Frau. In *Bronzezeit in Deutschland* ed. A. Jockenhövel and W. Kubach, pp. 59–64. Archäologie in Deutschland, Sonderheft 1994. Theiss.

Wengrow, D. 1999 The intellectual adventure of Henri Frankfort: a missing chapter in the history of archaeological thought. *American Journal of Archaeology* 103: 597–613.

Whittaker, H. 1995 Gender roles in the Odyssey. In Berggreen and Marinatos 1995: 29–41.

Wigren, S., Broström, S.-G., Ihrestam, K. and Eriksson, B. 1990 *Hällristningarna i Släbroparken, Nyköping.* Nyköping.

Wijngaarden, G.-J. van 1999 An archaeological approach to the concept of value. Mycenaean pottery at Ugarit (Syrie). Discussion. *Archaeological Dialogues* 6, no. 1: 2–46.

Wilkinson, R. H. 1992 *Reading Egyptian Art.* London.

Williams-Forte, E. 1993 Symbols of rain, lightning, and thunder in the art of Anatolia and Syria. In Mellinik, Porada and Özgüç 1993: 185–90.

Willroth, K.-H. 1985 Zu den Meisseln der älteren nordischen Bronzezeit. *Offa* 42: 393–430.

1989 Nogle betragtninger over de regionale forhold i Slesvig og Holsten i bronzealderns periode II. In *Regionale forhold i nordisk Bronzealder*, ed. J. Poulsen, pp. 89–100. Aarhus.

1997 Prunkbeil oder Stosswaffe, Pfriem oder Tätowierstift, Tüllengerät oder Treibstachel? Anmerkungen zu einigen Metallobjekten der älteren nordischen Bronzezeit. In Becker *et al.* 1997: 469–95.

2001 Haus, Acker und Grabhügel. Variable Konstanten im Siedlungsgefüge der älteren nordischen Bronzezeit. In Meyer 2001: 113–24.

Winghart, S. 1993 Überlegungen zur Bauweise hölzerner Speichenräder der Bronze- und Urnenfelderzeit. *Acta Praehistorica et Archaeologica* 25: 153–67.

2002 Die Eliten der mittleren und späteren Bronzezeit. Grundlagen, Enststehung und Vorstellungswelt. In *Menschen – Zeiten – Räume: Archäologie in Deutschland*, pp. 174–85 Stuttgart.

Winter, I. J. 1985 After the battle is over: the stele of the vultures and the beginning of pictorial narrative in the art of the ancient Near East. In Kessler and Simpson 1985: 11–32.

1996 Sex, rhetoric, and the public monument. In Boymel 1996: 11–26.

Witt, R. E. 1971 *Isis in the Ancient World.* Boston.

Wittfogel, K. A. 1957 *Oriental Despotism: A Comparative Study of Total Power.* New Haven.

Wolf, E. R. 1982 *Europe and the People without History.* Berkeley.

Wright, J. C. 1995a The archaeological correlates of religion: case studies in the Aegean. In Laffineur and Niemeier 1995: 341–9.

1995b. From chief to king in Mycenaean society. In Rehak 1995b: 63–80.

Wright, M. R. 1995 *Cosmology in Antiquity.* London and New York.

Xenaki-Sakellariou, A. 1985 *Tombes à chambre de Mycènes: les fouilles de Chr. Tsountas (1887–1998).* Paris.

Yakar, J. 1981 The Indo-Europeans and their impact on Anatolian cultural development. *Journal of Indo-European Studies* 9: 94–112.

Yates, D. T. 1999 Bronze Age field systems in the Thames Valley. *Oxford Journal of Archaeology* 18, no. 2: 157–70.

Yener, K. A. and Hoffner, H. A. (eds.) 2002 *Recent Developments in Hittite Archaeology and History: Papers in Memory of Hans G. Güterbock.* Eisenbrauns.

Yoffee, N. 1995 Political economy in early Mesopotamian states. *Annual Revue of Anthropology* 24: 281–311.

1998 The economics of ritual at Late Old Babylonian Kish. *JESHO* 41, no. 3: 312–43.

Yoffee, N. and Cowgill, G. L. (eds.) 1988 *The Collapse of Ancient States and Civilizations.* Tucson, Arizona.

Younger, J. G. 1995 The iconography of rulership in the Aegean: a conceptus. In Rehak 1995b: 151–211.

1997 The stelai of Mycenae Grave Circles A and B. In Laffineur and Betancourt 1997: 229–39, and tables.

Zaccagnini, C. 1983 On gift exchange in the Old Babylonian period. In *Studi Orientalistici in Ricordo di Franco Pintore*, ed. O. Carruba *et al.*, pp. 198–253. Studia Mediterranea 4. Pavia.

1987 Aspects of ceremonial gift exchange in the Near East during the late second millennium B.C. In Rowlands, Larsen and Kristiansen 1987: 57–66.

1990 The transition from bronze to iron in the Near East and in the Levant: marginal notes. *Journal of the American Oriental Society* 110: 496–7.

Zdanovich, D. G. 2002 Introduction. In Jones-Bley and Zdanovich 2002: xix–xxxviii.

Zdanovich, G. B. and Batanina, I. M. 2002 Planography of the fortified centers of the Middle Bronze Age in the southern Trans-Urals according to aerial photography data. In Jones-Bley and Zdanovich 2002: 119–47.

Zdanovich, G. B. and Zdanovich, G. 2002 The 'Country of Towns' of southern Trans-Urals and some aspects of steppe assimilations in the Bronze Age. In Boyle, Renfrew and Levine 2002: 249–63.

Zick, B. 1993 Eine Frauenbestattung der Ilmenau-Kultur aus Flintbek. Zur Frage von Handels und Personenkontakte in der Älteren Bronzezeit. In *Archäologie in Schleswig/arkæologi i Slesvig* 1992: 185–91.

Zimmer, S. 1994 Die Indogermanen und das Pferd-Befunde und Probleme. In Hänsel and Zimmer 1994: 29–35.

Zwelebil, M. 1995 Indo-European origins and the agricultural transition in Europe. *Journal of European Archaeology* 3, no. 1: 33–71.

Index

Note: Page numbers for figures appear in italics.

abstraction, in oral traditions and rock art, 269
Abydos temple, 96
acculturation, 25, 26–7, *30*, 363
acrobats/acrobatics, *230*, 229–31, 351
affines, 45, 46
agency
  socio-seismographic curve of, *370*
  theory of, 370–72
agro-pastoral economies, 109
Akhenaton, 72–3, *74*
Akkad dynasties, 63
Akkadian languages, 78
Akurgal, E., 315
Alaça Hüyük site, Anatolia, 75, 78, 308, 348
Alcinos, 227
Aldred, C., 73
Alexander, R. L., 96, 337
Alfred, 238
alliances
  confirmed through marriage, 37, 205, 232, 234, 240
    Egyptian, 68, 72, 74
  guest friendships, 28, 238–40
  power and, 37, 74, 80
  travel and, 204–9
Almgren, O., 251
Die älteren Kulturperioden im Orient und in Europa (Montelius), 2
Amarna letters, 67, 73
amber
  in hoards, 135, 158
  with Linear B inscriptions, 127, 235
  necklaces, 234
  sun-discs, 302n.14
  as a trade item, 122, 125, 127, 186
  value of, 139, 236

Amenhotep III, 72, 73, 80
Amenophis II, 72
Amenophis III, *see* Amenhotep III
Amenophis IV, *see* Akhenaton
Amun, 70
Anatolia
  Alaça Hüyük site, 75, 78, 308, 348
  Demircihuyuk site, *174*
  Hasanoglan site, 308
  Hattusha site, 79, 200
  Horoztepe site, 77, 308
  Miletus site, 101
  rulers, 75–7, *85*
  trade networks, 77, 91–3, 181–5
  use of metal, *77*, 109
  see also Boghazköy rock art; Hittites
ancestors, 45, *54, 56, 210*
Anderlingen burial, 191, 206
Andrén, A., 21–2, 269
Andronovo Culture, 171n.5, *176*, 173–9
Aner, E., 186
animals, 45, *309*, 348
  as burial sacrifices, *176*, 177, 245
  Mistress of Animals, 358, 344
  role in religion, 320–4
  used for sun journey transport, *309*
  see also specific animals
Anitta, 78
ankh, 73
Ankhesenpaaten, 81
Apophis, 70
appearance, 227–31, 349–50; *see also* costumes; hairstyles
Arafat, K., 7
archaeological record
  confirmation of ethnohistorical evidence, 22, 259, 329
  contexts and categories, *34*, 33–8

archaeological record (*cont.*)
 correspondence with written texts,
  139
 trade goods and, *34*, 93
archaeology
 disciplinary boundaries, *21*
 study of religion and, 251–3
architecture
 chieftain halls, 226, *277*, 279, 277–80
 columns, *163*
 cult buildings, 338
 fortifications, 133, 226, 235
 funerary, *see* burial practices
 houses, 7, 29, 33
 Minoan/Mycenaean imitations, 162
 similarities between cultures, 177
 tell settlements, 162
Arête, 57
Argonauts of the Western Pacific
  (Malinowski), 268
Arkaim site, 171, *174*, *175*; *see also*
  Sintashta culture
Armorican culture, 125
armour, 220, 223
arrowheads, distribution patterns, *216*
Art and Agency (Gell), 370
Art and the Early Greek State (Shanks), 247
artefacts, chronology, *314*
artisans
 in the archaeological record, 57–60
 supernatural powers of, 51–4
 travel and, 68, 97, 133, 141, 234, 337,
  364
Aryans, 171n.5, 180
Arzawa kingdom, 80
Ashur, 90–3
Ashvinau, 297, *327*
Aspeberget rock art, *327*, 343
assassinations, 80
Assyria, 67
Aten, 72–3, *74*
Aunjetitz Culture, 112, 120
authority, institutionalisation of, *47*, *49*
autonomous framework, 5–6
axes, ritual, *95*, *201*, *275*, *281*, *306*, *341*
 in antithetical compositions, 190, *190*
 dating, 218n.13

distribution, *209*, 288–91
in double burials, 266
with hats, *195*, *274*
between horns, *330*
Nordic, 194, 200, *266*
production, 122
with ships, *202*
with spiral decorations, *160*, *194*, *272*
symbolism of, *85*, 280, *330*, 341
Unetice hoard, *115*
axes, war, 218, 281
axes mundi, 357

Babylon, 65–7
Backa, Brastad rock art, 286
Bagterp lance, 217n.13
Balkåkra, Sweden, throne, *203*, 294
Balkan-Carpathian region, metallurgy,
  109
Baltic Sea, 204
Barca site, Slovakia, *129*, 162
bards, 55, 59
Barret, J., 5, 11
barrows
 construction, 241, 242
 Gotland, *244*
 grave goods, 213
 Håga, 339
 Jutland, *226*, *244*
 placement, 226, 355
 Sagaholm, 196, 242, *243*, 328, 329, 349
 Tinghøj, 312
 Upton Lowell, *121*
Battle-Axe Culture, 109
Bavaria, 235
beads, 18, 58, 138
Beal, R., 328n.3
 The Organization of the Hittite Military,
  222
Beckman, G., 271, 291
behaviour, social
 control of women, 237
 dress codes, 225
 vs. ritual, 349–51
Bell Beaker Culture, 112, 140
belt boxes, *341*
belt plates, 294, *300*, 306

Beowulf, 23
Bernal, M., 193
Bertemes, F., 112
bestiality, 324–8
Bietak, M., 98
bits, distribution of, *184*
Bittel, K., 315
Bjerre, Denmark, 135
Black Sea trade networks, 125
Blischke, J., 150
Boand, 260
boars
    hunting, 247, *347*, 348
    tusks, 247
Boas school, 27
Boghazköy rock art, 288, *289*
Bohuslän rock art, 335, 336n.5, 356
    chariot motifs, 223, *223*
    Fossum, *342, 343,* 342–3, *345*
    horned divinities, *331*
    raised arm gesture, *76*
    sun-disc pulled by horse, *326*
Bona, I., 159
Bornholm, Gyldensgård burial, 157, 189
Borodino find, 128
Boroffka, N., 181
boundaries, *38*, 38–43, 361
bows
    arrows and, 218, *345*
    composite, 71
    as symbols of divinity, 68
Braudel, F., 32
breasts, naked, *148*, 150, *151*
Bregninge, Denmark, *332*
Brittany, *121*, 122
bronze
    commoditisation of, 136
    composition of, 99, 109, *124*, *136*
    expansion of technology, 140–1
    see also specific artefacts
Bronze Age
    end of, 365–7
    as protohistory, 1, 20–4
    trends, 140–1
    see also European Bronze Age culture;
        Nordic Bronze Age culture
The Bronze Age (Childe), 2

brotherhood of rulers, 83, 99, 101, 104
Bruatorp, Sweden, *279*
Brumfiel, E., 9
Brun, P., 7n.2, 42
Bryce, T., 81
Buchholz, H.-G., 168
Bühl hoard, 204
bull jumpers, 71, *230*
bulls, *327*
    cult of, 330
    Divine Twins as, 263
    horns, 281, 330
    weather god's sacred animal, *285*,
        285–6
burial practices, 284
    barrows, 213, 226, 241, 242, *244*, 355
        Håga, 339
        Jutland, *226*, *244*
        Sagaholm, 196, 242, 328, 329, 349
        Tinghøj, 312
        Upton Lowell, *121*
    burial pits, 248
    cemeteries, 127, 133n.3, 246, 284
    chamber tombs, 144
    chariot burials, *176*
    funerary architecture, 87
    grave circles, 87, 144, 154, 156
    kurgans, 109
    mass graves, 248
    oak coffins, 152, 242, 245
    pit graves, *134*
    shaft graves, 75, 88, 122–3, 128, 145,
        180, 181–4
    tholos graves, 235, *236*, 241
    tumuli, 109, 171, 177, 235, 241,
        338
burial rituals
    animal sacrifices, *176*, 177, 245
    social hierarchy in, 177
    weapons and, 231–6
    widow burning, 237, 274
burials
    Anderlingen, 191
    chief/priest, 274
    Clytemnestra, Tomb of, 302n.14
    dating of, 120
    Dendrá, 144, 313

burials (*cont.*)
  double burials, 237, 265, 266, 276,
    276n.9, *276*
  Egtved woman, 225n.16, 298, *299*
  of foreign women, 234
  Guldhøj, 303, 304
  Gyldensgård, 157, 189
  Hagia Triada, 220, *262*, 264
  Helmsdorf, 133
  Hesselagergård woman, 298, *300*
  Ilica cemetery, 284
  Kivik, Scania, 49, 71, 86n.6, 157, *188*,
    187–9, 267–70
    cist-stones, 187, *188*, *190*, *192*, 267,
      268, 269–70, 328
    context; interregional, 198–9; local,
      194–8
    dating, 189–93, 197, 198n.10
    grave goods, 187, 189–90
    plan view, *338*
  Leubingen, 122, 133, *134*, 266
  Maikop, 109
  Montelius, 156
  Neolithic, 29
  Nizná Mysla, *134*
  Ølby woman, 298
  single burials, 172n.6
  Tape cemetery, 127
  Terramare, 216n.12
  Tobøl woman, 220, 298, *301*
  travelling metallurgist, 141
  Unetice Culture, 120
  Vapheio, 330
  Vatya cemeteries, 133n.3
  warriors, 151, *215*, 218, 231–6, 240–6
  Wessex Culture, 120
  Zafer Papoura, 302n.14
Burkert, W., 95
Burnaburiash, 73

calves of legs, exaggerated, 312–13, 315,
  342
Cameron, M., 281
campstools, *216*, 281, *282*, *304*, 303–8
Cape Gelidonya shipwreck, 105
caps, *see* headgear
Carneiro, R. L., 248

Carpathian tell cultures
  adaptation of Minoan/Mycenaean
    institutions, 158–67
  architecture, 162, *163*
  collapse of, 127, 211, 236
  cosmology, 359
  female costumes, 145, 150–4
  iconography, 145, *164*, 200
  metal production, 134
  model of, *362*
  polities, 361
  territories, 17–16th c. BC, *126*
  trade networks, *129*, 179–85
  use of early signs, 168
Castor, 297
Catacomb Culture, 109, 172
cattle, 172
Caucasian region, 109, 134
Celtic sagas, 23
cemeteries, 127, 133n.3, 246, 284,
  358
centralisation vs. fragmentation, 105,
  359
centres
  cosmological centres, 357
  peripheries and, 5, 6, *21*, 43–7
    interaction among, 48, 112, 119,
      364–5
ceremonies, drinking, 281, *282*
cestrums, 85
chariots
  buried with horses, *176*
  charioteers and, 223, *223*
  groups of, *176*, *221*
  military use of, 180–1, 184, *184*, 191
  origins, 185
  symbols of, *154*
  twin gods/goddesses and, 262, *262*,
    281
  wheels
    bronze, 220
    two-wheeled, 71, 178
    wooden, 63
  see also sun-disc; sun-chariot
Chernykh, E. N., 110, 134
Cherry, J., 19
chiefdoms

characteristics, 40, *47*, 52, 55–7, 58
Fijian, 248
maritime, 198
Panamanian, 54
see also elite culture
chieftain halls, 226, *277*, *279*, 277–80
chieftains
  costumes, 264n.6, *272*, 277, 351
  from external sources, 40
  grave goods, 56, 58, *59*, *121*, 271, 303,
    305
  as priests, 303–8
  reproduction of power, 17
  as the sun, 291
  swords, *130*
  travel and alliances, 204–9, *210*, 234
  travel by, 39–40, 371
  see also elites; warrior aristocracies
Childe, C. G., *The Bronze Age*, 2
chisels, woodworking, diagnostic of
    male chieftains, 58, *59*
chronologies
  of artefacts, 313, *314*
  Bronze Age, 116–17
    in central Europe, 159
    first phase (2300–1900 BC), 118–20
    Reinecke, 112, 118
    second phase (1900–1600 BC), 120–7
    third phase (1600/1500–1300 BC),
      127–30
  Egypt
    Amarna period, 72
    First Intermediate period
      (2180–2040 BC), 70
    Hyksos period (1720–1550 BC), 70–1
    Middle Kingdom (2040–1730 BC), 70
    New Kingdom (1550–1069 BC), 71–5
    nineteenth and twentieth
      dynasties, 73
    Old Kingdom (2686–2181 BC), 69
  of figurines, 313
  Hungary
    Kozsider period, 194
  Mesopotamia
    Agade period (2340–2159 BC), 63
    Akkad and Ur dynasties (2300–
      2000 BC), 63

Early Dynastic periods (2900–
      2350 BC), 62–3, 108
    Kassite period (1595–1155 BC), 67
    Old Babylonian period (2004–
      1595 BC), 63
    Uruk period (3500–3200 BC), 65
  Minoan Crete
    Second Palace period (1700–1450
      BC), 83
  of religious institutions, 256
Circum-Pontic Metallurgical System, 173
cist-stones
  Kivik burial, 187, *188*, *190*, *192*, 267,
    268, 269–70, 328
    dating, 189–93
  Sagaholm barrow, *327*, 328, 329,
    349
Clarke, D., 25–6, 363n.1
classes, social, 32
classification, normative vs. functional,
    16
clientship, 227
climate change, 106
Cline, E. H., 99, 104
  Sailing the Wine-Dark Sea, 104
closure/openness, 38, *38*
club of the great powers, 67, 105
Clytemnestra, Tomb of, 302n.14
coffins
  oak, 152, 242, 245
  wooden, 99
columns, *163*
commoditisation of copper and bronze,
    136
commodity production, model of
    economic and political
    implications of, *113*
competitive emulation, 19
compositions
  antithetical, 86, 190, *190*, *348*
  three-dimensional, 191
Conchobor, 246
conquest migrations, 179, 180, 182, 185,
    365
construction methods
  drystone, 162
  mud bricks, 177

contextualisation, 25, 26–7, *30*

copper
    alloys, 110, 112, *124*
    commoditisation of, 136
    Kargaly mines, *110*, 173
    mine production, *110*
    sources, 99, 100, *124*
    as a trade item, 67, 78, 108, 125
    in Ulu Burun shipwreck, 101, 102n.8

Corded Ware Culture, 109, 112, 140, 265

correspondence (interpretative method), 21–2, 152–3, 154, 157

correspondence (letters)
    Amarna letters, 67, 73
    between queens, 63
    between rulers, 73, 95, 96

cosmological categories
    gods/goddesses, 252–3
    institutions, 252–3
    myths, 252–3, 254
    rituals, 242, 252–3

cosmological nature of power, 46–7, 48, *54*, 55–7, 367

cosmological order
    culture and, 357–8
    nature and, 355–6

cosmological origins, 40, 45–7, 316–19, 360

cosmological space, 209

cosmologies
    Bronze Age, 259–63, *296*, *306*, 341, *354*, 355
    centred, 358–9
    decentred, 358–9
    Egyptian, 321–4
    modern perception of, 320–1
    premodern perception of, 320–1

costumes
    definition, 227
    dress codes, 225
    female, 145, 227, *239*, *299*, 351
    figurines with short loincloths, *274*, *312*, 312–13, *314*
    male, 227–31
        chieftains, 264n.6, *272*, 277, 351
    ritual dress, 274–7

crafting skills, 41, 57–60

craftsmen, *see* artisans

crocus, 145

Crouwell, J. H., 178, 179n.7

crowns, *see* headgear

Crow-Omaha kinship system, 237, 240

Crumley, C., 9

Cuchulainn, 231, 246

cult buildings, 338

cultural systems, model of interaction between, *38*

culture-historical theoretical framework, 4, 24, 369–72

cuneiform signs, 73

cupmarks, 168, 344, 346
    as female symbols, 328, 342
    on libation stones, 162, *165*, 242, 242n.22
    vs. figurative images, 355

cups, *156*, *157*, *304*
    gold, 330
    ritual, *89*, 154–8, 303
    see also ceremonies, drinking

currency, 136

Cycladic lance, 119

Cyprus, Enkomi figurines, *272*, *332*, *333*

daggers, 78, 122, *130*, 145, 218, 305

Dark Ages, 105, 181

dating
    of burials, 120
    C14 dates, 17n.7, 116–17
    dendrochronological dates, 116–17
    Kivik burial, 189–93, 197, 198n.10

David, W., 181

Davidson, E., 263

death, 341

Death, Women and the Sun (Goodison), 302n.14

deforestation, 172n.6

Delphic Apollo, 44

Demeter, 260

Demircihuyuk site, Anatolia, *174*, 177

democracy, 366

Dendrá burials, 144, 313

dendrochronological dates, 116–17

Denmark
  Bjerre, 135
  Bregninge, *332*
  Djursland hoard, *207*
  Faardal figurines, *261*, *310*, 323
  Grevensvænge figurines, 274, *332*,
      333
  metal imports, 135, *136*
  Rørby
      paired scimitars, *266*
      sword, 207, 208, 290n.11
  Tinghøj barrow, 312
  Trundholm sun-disc/chariot, 197,
      295n.12, *295*, *296*, 294–6,
      306
  Viksø horned helmets, *332*, 333
  see also Jutland
Deutsche Orientgesellschaft, 91
dichotomies, 358, 359
Dietler, M., 7n.2
Dietz, S., 118
diffusion, 4, 13, *30*, 25–30, 252
diffusion patterns, before Bronze Age,
    26
Dioskouroi, 264, 297
distance
  esoteric knowledge and, 53–4
  ideological meaning of, 39–43
distance-parity model, 7
Divine Twins, *see* Twins, Divine
divinity
  Hittite hieroglyph for, 343
  symbols of
      bows, 68
      maces, 68
      naked breasts, *148*, 150, *151*
      scimitars, 68
      wheel-cross, 195, 298–302, 346
      wings, 68, *293*, *332*; *see also*
          symbolism of headgear
  see also leadership, theocratic
Djursland, Denmark, *207*
Dohnsen, Germany, 156
Dövlek figurine, 315, *315*
dress codes, 225
Drews, R., 180, 181, 182, 224n.15
Druids, 55

dualism, 273–80
Dumezil, G., 364n.2
Dumuzi, 65
Duplje, Serbia, figurines, 150, 307

Eanatum, 63
Earle, T., 60n.1
earrings, 136, 147, 151, *152*
east Mediterranean trade networks, 90,
    102, 96–105, 123, 128
economies
  agro-pastoral, 109
  pastoral, 172, 172n.6
Edens, C. M., 6
egalitarianism, 366
Egtved woman's burial, 225n.16, 298,
    299
Egypt
  alliances, 67, 72, 74, 98
  chronology
      Amarna period, 72
      First Intermediate period
          (2180–2040 BC), 70
      Hyksos period (1720–1550 BC), 70–1
      Middle Kingdom (2040–1730 BC), 70
      New Kingdom (1550–1069 BC), 71–5
      nineteenth and twentieth
          dynasties, 73
      Old Kingdom (2686–2181 BC), 69
  cosmology, 321–4
  hieroglyphs, 75, *76*
  ka temple, Luxor, 75
  leadership, 69–75, *85*
  tombs, Minoan figures on, *100*
  trade networks, 70
Egypt's Legacy (Rice), 75
Eliade, M., 44, 357
  The Forge and the Crucible, 52
elite culture, 55, 129, 212, 225–7, 283
  crafting skills' role in, 57–60
  domestic rituals, 158–67
  iconography, 126, 142–50, 199–204
  power, control of, 323
  symbolic transmissions via material
      culture, 142, 167–70, 254, 255
  treatment of subordinates, 61n.2
  see also warrior aristocracies

elites
  as immortal, 57
  mythological origins, *46*
  otherness of, 45, 170
  see also chieftains
El Tod silver treasure, 98
emulation, *see* symbolic permutation
England, 134
Enkomi, Cyprus, figurines, *272, 332,*
      333
Enright, M., *Lady with a Mead Cup,*
      225n.16
Erzgebirge, Germany, 122
esoteric knowledge, 17, 39, 43, 186
  distance and, 53–7
  languages as, 54
  written signs, 168, 170
ethnic groups, 106, 133n.3, 259; *see also*
      identity
ethnohistorical evidence,
      archaeologically verified, 22, 259,
      329
European Bronze Age culture, 108–16
  contact with Mediterranean cultures,
      17–19, 118–27, 136, 138, 249–50
Europe before History (Kristiansen), 2, 6
Evans, A., 83, 334
exchange, *see* trade
exchange categories
  personal items, *34, 35, 136, 147,*
      205
  prestige goods, 35–7, 112, *121,* 139,
      208, 235
    horizontal and vertical exchange
      models, *36*
    trade goods, 35–8
      archaeological record and, *34,* 93

Faardal, Denmark, figurines, *261, 310,*
      323
Falkenstein, A., 65
families, royal, 88
Fangel, Funen hoard, 314
farming, mobility and, 32
feather crowns, 142, 142n.1, *143*
females, *see* women
Fergus, 260

fertility
  goddesses, 342–4
  rituals, 145, 150
figurative images vs. cupmarks, 355
figures, S-shaped, 192
figurines
  bronze, 152, *311,* 308–16
  chronology of, 313
  clay, *148, 151,* 152
  Dövlek, 315, *315*
  Duplje, Serbia, 150, 307
  Enkomi, Cyprus, *272, 332,* 333
  Faardal, Denmark, *261, 310,* 323
  Grevensvænge, Denmark, 274, *332,*
      333
  Hattian, 308–16
  Hittite, *310, 315,* 308–16
  lack of in central and southeastern
      Europe, 313
  Nordic, 308–16
  Scheren, Poland, *274,* 314
  with short loincloths, *274, 312,*
      312–13, *314*
  Stockhult hoard, *274, 312*
  Ugarit, 315
  used in rituals, 150, 353
Fiji chiefdoms, 248
fire, control of, 53
Flowerful Maiden, 260
Fogtdarp, Sweden, double axes with
      horns, *330*
The Forge and the Crucible (Eliade), 52
fortified settlements, 133, *166, 174*
Fossum rock art, *342, 343,* 342–3, *345*
foster sons, exchange of, 236–40
Fox, R., 237
fragmentation vs. centralisation, 105
Fränarp rock art, 191, *221*
frescos
  Hagia Triada, 281
  Knossos, 281, *282,* 305
  Minoan, 71, 84, 98, 101
  Pylos, *282*
  Tel Kabri, Israel, 98
  Thera, 86, *103, 144,* 145, *147,* 150, *152*
Freyr, 260
Friedman, J., 6

'Frühes Griechentum und nordisches
  Bronzezeit' (Sprockhofs), 252n.1
Fyllingen, H., 248

games, 229–31
Gell, A., *Art and Agency*, 370
Gelling, P., 252n.2
gender identities, 349–50, *362*; *see also*
  men; women
genealogies, 254
Gening, V. F., 171, 174
Gening, V. V., 174
Gerloff, S., 119, 122, 271
Germany
  Dohnsen, 156
  Erzgebirge, 122
  Nebra bronze disc, 2
gestures, ritual, 150, *151*
  raised arms, *76*, 343
    phallus and, *340*
gift exchanges, 67, 95, 104, 128
Gilgamesh epic, 43, 316
Gillis, C., 139
goats, *348*, 348–9
goddesses
  animals as symbols of, 321–4
  with corded skirts, *261*
  as a cosmological category, 252–3
  of fertility, 342–4
  Flowerful Maiden, 260
  Fossum rock art, *342*
  Greek, 23
  hippomorphic, 329–30
  Mistress of Animals, 344
  smelling lilies, *87*
  snake-goddess, *148*, 340
  sun-goddess, 264
    of Arinna, 79, 80, 96, 283, 285, 293
    in chariot drawn by swans, 150,
      153, *306*
    divine twins and, 153, 297
    names of, 150, 297
    priestess of, 286, 344
    ritual marriage with king, 293
    symbols of
  twins riding in a chariot, 262, *262*,
    281

White Cow goddess, 260
  see also gods/goddesses
gods
  animals as symbols of, 321–4
  Athum, *322*
  attributes of, 259
  as a cosmological category, 252–3
  Divine Twins, 22, 258–63, 264–7, 319
    attributes of, *318*
    birth myth, 329–30
    as bulls, 263
  God of War, 288, *289*
  Greek, 23
  hippomorphic, 329–30
  horned, *331*, *332*, 330–4
  Kurunta, standing on a stag, 286, *287*
  Prince with the Feather Crown, 142–4
  ritual dress, 274–7
  storm-god, *274*
  sun-goddess and, 153, 297
  symbolism of, 190, 264n.6, 269–70
  twins riding in a chariot, 262, *262*,
    281
  weather-god, 283, *285*, 285–6
  young hunter/warrior, *260*, 342–4
  see also gods/goddesses
gods/goddesses
  Bronze Age pantheon, 353–5
  human separation from, 366
  Proto-Indo-European (PIE) pantheon,
    258–9, 265, 364n.2
    realms, 259–63, 341, 358
    shape shifting, 263, 264
gold
  Carpathian, 125
  crowns, 127, *209*
  cups, 330
  diadems, 235
  earrings, 136, 147
  exploration for new sources, 100
  inlaid, 138, *310*
  staff, 127
  as a trade item, 78, 122
Goodison, L., *Death, Women and the Sun*,
  302n.14
Gordion graveyard, 284
Gotland, Sweden, barrows, *244*

grass turves, symbolic of eternal
   meadows, 242
grave goods
   in barrows, 213
   beyond personal needs, 138
   of chieftains, 56, 58, *121*, 271, 303,
      305
   Kivik burial, 187, 189–90
   of metal, *136*
Greece, 87–90
   gods/goddesses, 23
   mythology, 44, 95, 259
   see also Mycenae, Greece
Greek language, 83; *see also* Linear B
Grevensvænge, Denmark, figurines, 274,
   332, 333, 351
griffins, as symbols of Priestess Queens,
   86
guest friendships, 28, 238–40
Guldhøj, Jutland
   artefacts, *304*
   burials, 303, *304*
Gurney, O. R., 286, 291, 293
Güterbock, H. G., 77
Gyldensgård burial, Bornholm, 157,
   189

Haas, V., 286, 294
Håga barrow, 339
Hägg, R., 88
Hagia Triada
   sarcophagus, 220, *262*, 264, 281
hair styles, *153*
   female, 152, 351
   male, 228, *228*
Hajdúsámson hoard, 161, *214*, 215,
   217n.13, 281
halberds, *115*, 122
Hall, J., 361
Hallstat D residences, 7
Hammurabi
   Law Code Stele, 65, *66*
Handbuch der Vorgeschichte (Müller-Karpe),
   3
Hankey, V., 118
Hantili, annals of, 80
Harding, A., 18, 19

Hasanoglan site, Anatolia, 308
Hasfalva, Hungary, throne, 200, *203*
Hathor (mother goddess), 70
hats, *see* headgear
Hatshepsut, 72
Hattians, 77, 283
   figurines, 308–16
   see also Hittites
Hattusha site, Anatolia, 79, 200; *see also*
   Boghazköy rock art
Hattusili, 79
Hattusili III, 73, 291
headgear
   female, *151*, 239
   symbolism of, 351
      caps (ruler), 227, 265, 272, 351
      crowns: feather (divine), 142,
         142n.1, *143*; gold, 127, *209*;
         horned (divine), 68, 101, 247, 323,
         332, 333
      hats: axes with, *274*; double, of gods
         and chieftains, 264n.6; pointed
         (divine), 101, *190*, 281, 291,
         312–13, 314–16; storm-god with,
         274; twins figurines with, *274*
      helmets: horned (divine), 68, 101,
         247, 323, *332*, 333
hearths, with spiral decorations, *164*
Hector, 240
Hedeager, L., 29
Helena, 297
helmets, *see* headgear
Helms, M.
   on access to origins, 45–7
   on esoteric knowledge, 17, 54
   on imitation, 18
   on skilled artisans and culture
      heroes, 2, 52–3, 58, 60, 126
   on space and distance, 39, 40,
      53
Helmsdorf burials, 133
Herodotus, 44
heroes, *210*, 228, 254
   separation from the gods, 366
Hesiod, 367
Hesselagergård woman's burial, 298,
   300

heterarchy, 8, 9, 83
  relationship with hierarchy, *9*
Die Hethiter und ihr Reich, 75
Heyd, 112–14
hierarchy, 8, 279, 365, 366
  processes of hierarchisation, *41*
  relationship with heterarchy, *9*
hierogamy, 324–8
hieroglyphs
  Egyptian, 75, *76*
  Hittite, 168, *168*, 343
Hieros Gamos, 344, *346*, 350
Himmelstalund rock art, *169*, 170, 335,
    347, *348*, 347–8
history, disciplinary boundaries, *21*
Hittites
  alliances, 66, 67, 74
  chronology
    Imperial period (1430–1200 BC), 79,
        80
    Middle Kingdom (1500–1430 BC),
        79
    Old Kingdom (1650–1500 BC), 79
  definition, 283
  fall of, 81–2
  figurines, *310*, *315*, 308–16
  hieroglyphs, 168, *168*, 343
  iconography, 190, *190*, 193, 200, 271,
      284
  Inandik relief-vase, 282
  languages, 77
  Law Code, 328
  leadership, 271, *285*
    theocratic, 75–82
  military texts, 328n.3
  religion, 96, 253, 282–8
    sun cults, 288–94
  seals, *293*
  see also Anatolia; Hattians
hoards, 50, 273
  amber in, 135, 158
  Bühl, 204
  deposited in bogs, 338
  Djursland, Denmark, *207*
  Fangel, Funen, 314
  Hajdúsámson, 161, *214*, 215, 217n.13,
      281

Hungarian, *147*
  linked to the Netherworld, 356
  ritual axes in, *115*
  as ritual depositions from battle, 224
  Stockhult, 197, 273, *274*, *312*, 312–13
  Tågaborg, 296n.12
  tools in, 58
  Tufalau, 152
Hodder, I., 6, 16, 25–6, 29
  Symbols in Action, 254, 361
Holloway, R. R., 168
Homer, 57–60, 104, 170, 229n.18,
      256
  Hymn No. 33, 264
  Iliad, 23, 170, 227, 240, 246–7
  Odyssey, 23, 170, 227, 245
horned crowns or helmets, *see* headgear
horned gods, *331*, *332*, 330–4
horned vipers, *261*, *323*, 323
horns
  anthropomorphic images with, 333
  bull, 281, 330
  on crowns or helmets, 68, 101, 247,
      323, *332*, 333
  ox, 330, *330*
horns of consecration, 330
Horoztepe site, Anatolia, 77, 308
horses, 172, 197, 322
  breeding of, 184
  buried with chariots, *176*
  with deer masks, 286
  human–horse relationships, *325*, *327*,
      324–8
  military horse and chariot package,
      180–1, 184
  pulling sun-disc/chariot, 128–30, 170,
      264, 288, 297, *326*
    Trundholm, 197, 295n.12, *295*, *296*,
        294–6, *306*
    Sagaholm rock art, *197*
    Tågaborg hoard, *197*
    as trade items, 95, 128
    in written texts, 322n.1
Hradisko Vesele site, Slovakia, 162
Hungary
  Hasfalva throne, 200, *203*
  hoards, *147*

Hungary (*cont.*)
   Kozsider period, 194
   swords, *207*
   Tape cemetery, 127
hunting
   boars, 247, *347*
   with bow and arrow, 218, *345*
   rituals, 321, 346–9
   stags, *347*, 346–7
Hurrians, 283
Hyksos dynasty, 99, 180

Icelandic sagas, 23, 238
iconography
   definition, 186n.9
   elite culture, 126, 142–50
   on Kivik cist-stones, 187, 189–93
   royalty, 190, *190*, 193, 199–204, 271,
      284
   S-shaped figures, 192
   visual memory and, 353
   see also spiral ornaments/
      ornamentation; symbols
identity, 249, 259, 349, 360–4; *see also*
      appearance; gender identities
Ighiel hoard, 218n.13
Iliad (Homer), 23, 170, 227, 240, 246–7
Ilica cemetery, 284
imagery of mother and child, 75
imitation
   in material culture, 16–20, 155, 156,
      162, 198–9, 235
   of value systems, 187
immobility, peasant societies and,
      32–3
imports, *14*, 17–19, 135, 155, 156,
      186
Inandik relief-vase, 282
Inanna, 65, 68, *69*; *see also* Ishtar
Inanna's Descent to the Netherworld, 44
individuals, as autonomous, 10n.4
Indo-European languages, 180, 359
Indo-European religion, 258–9
Indo-Iranian people, 171n.5, 180
Indus civilisation, 140
Ingold, T., 321
initiation rituals, 145

inscriptions, 290n.11, 322n.1
institutionalisation, 8–10, 27–8, *30*
   of authority, *47*, *49*
institutions
   as a cosmological category, 252–3
   identified in the archaeological
      record, 10–11
   religious, 256, 259, 270
   transmission of, 13–15, 249–50, 364
   wanax institution, 88, 280–2
   warrior aristocracies, 80, 277–80
interaction, 24, 25–30
   among centres and peripheries, 48,
      112, 119
   models of, 7, *38*, *49*, *51*
   peer polities, 15, 19, 27–8, 48
   types of, 49–51
interaction zones
   Circum-Pontic, 200
   Mediterranean corridor, *211*, 212
   western steppe corridor, 179–85, *211*,
      212
intercontextual archaeology, 4–5, *12*,
      10–15, 16, 24, 25–30, 368
intermarriage, *see* alliances
interpretative archaeology, 12, 15,
      368–72
interpretative model of material
      culture, *30*
Ireland, 122
Irish sagas, 238, 246–7, 256, 326
iron
   dagger, 78
   sceptre, 78
   throne, 78–9
Iron Age, 29, 106, 366–7
Ishtar, 291; *see also* Inanna
Isis, 70
Ismarus, sacked by Odysseus, 247
Israel, Tel Kabri frescos, 98
Istria, 235
   Monkodonja, 162, *166*
ivy, lilies and, *144*, *147*, 142–50

Jacobsen, T., 63, 65
Jockenhövel, A., 57
Jones-Bley, K., 174

Jörlov rock art, *346*
Jutland
  barrows, *226*, *244*
  double burial, *276*
  Guldhøj burials, 303, 304, *304*
  Hohøj tumulus burial, *243*
  Tobøl woman's burial, 220, 298, *301*

Kadesh, battle of, 73, 81, *82*
Kanesh, 78, 91–3
Kantor, H., 105
Kargaly mines, *110*, 173
Kassites, 66, 67, 180
ka temple, Luxor, 75
Kaul, F., 200, 252n.2, 308, 353
Keftiu, *see* Minoan Crete
Kersten, K., 186
Khania seal, 85
Kilian, K., 88, 280–2
Kilian-Dirlmeier, I., 102, 118, 154
kingship, 79–81, 84, 284
  lilies as symbols of, 86, *144*
  warrior kings, 88, 177
  see also leadership, theocratic; regalia,
    royal
kinship systems
  Crow-Omaha, 237, 240
  exchange of foster sons and, 236–40
  male solidarity and, 238
  patrilineal societies, 237
Kivik, Scania
  burial, 49, 71, 86n.6, 157, *188*, 187–9,
    267–70
    cist-stones, 187, *188*, *190*, *192*, 267,
      268, 269–70, 328
    context: interregional, 198–9; local,
      194–8
    dating, 189–93, 197, 198n.10
    grave goods, 187, 189–90
    origins, 189–93
    plan view, *338*
  as a religious centre of learning,
    199
Klejn, L., 257n.4
knives, tanged, 177
Knossos, palace of, 83, 281
  frescos, 281, *282*, 305

Prince of the Lilies, *143*
  seal, 330
knowledge, systems of learning, 55
Kohl, P., 6, 7
Kossack, G., *Symbolgut der Urnenfelderzeit*,
  252n.1
Kristiansen, K., 5, 224, 367
  Europe before History, 2, 6
Krtenov axe, 218n.13
Krückennadeln, 136
Kuhrt, A., 64, 72, 79
Kültepe, 204
  spearhead, 290n.11
Kulturkreislehre, 27
Kurunta, 286

Labarna, 79
labour, division of, 173
Lady with a Mead Cup (Enright), 225n.16
Lagash (city-state), 63
lances, 53, 119, 177, 181, 217n.13
languages
  Akkadian, 78
  as esoteric knowledge, 54
  Greek, 83
  of the Hittites, 77
  Indo-European, 180, 359
  international, 32
  local, 32, 259
  Luwain, 291
  Minoan, 13n.5
  multi-lingual states, 106
  in pre-state societies, 33
  Scandinavian, 32
  see also writing systems
Larsson, T., *Materiell kultur och religiösa
  symboler*, 13, 112, 200, 294
Lawagetas, 280
Law Code Stele of Hammurabi, 65, *66*
leadership, theocratic, 62, 107, 365
  Egyptian, 69–75
  Hittite, 75–82
  legitimation of lineages, 99
  Mesopotamian, 62–8
  Minoan Crete, 82, 83–7
  Mycenaean, 82, 87–90
  Old Assyrian period (2000–1800 BC), 90

leadership, theocratic (*cont.*)
  ritual/political leaders and war
      leaders, 218, 225, 232, 255–6, 267,
      355
  Scandinavian, 204, 333
lead-isotope analyses of bronze, 99
Lesko, L. H., 69–70, 72
Leubingen burials, 122, 133, *134*, 266
Lévi-Strauss, C., 321
libation stones, 162
  with cupmarks, 162, *165*, 242, 242n.22
lilies
  goddess smelling, *87*
  ivy flowers and, *144*, *147*, 142–50
  as symbols of kingship, 86, *144*
Linear A, 83, 101, 168, 170, 208
Linear B, 83, 168
  inscriptions on amber, 127, 235
  names of gods, 259
Lipari Islands
  pottery, 167, 169
  script, *167*
Littauer, M. A., 178, 179n.7
longue durée, 32
lurs, 195, *196*
Luwain language, 291
Luxor, *ka* temple, 75

maces, 68
McGovern, P. E., 99
Macqueen, J. G., 284
Maderovce Culture, 125
Maikop burials, 109
males, *see* men
Malinowski, B., *Argonauts of the Western
    Pacific*, 268
Malmer, M., 25, 353
Manning, S., 98, 117, 147
Maran, J., 120
Marcus, M. I., 75
Mari (city-state), 93–5
Marinatos, N., 84–6, 97, 99, 145, 334–5
marriage
  alliances confirmed through, 37, 205,
      232, 234, 240
    Egyptian, 68, 72, 74
  intermarriage patterns, 32, *233*

ritual between king and sun-goddess,
    293
  sacred, 65, 44–5
  virilocal residence, 237, 237n.21
Massleberg rock art, *347*, 346–7
material culture, 363n.1
  as identity, 360–1
  relationship to oral/written culture,
      257
materialisation, *30*, 29–30
Materiell kultur och religiösa symboler
    (Larsson), 13, 112, 200, 294
matrilineal succession to power, 72
mead, 155
meaning, contextualised, *30*, 29–30
Mederos Martin, A., 117
Mediterranean corridor, *211*, 212
Mediterranean cultures
  city-states, 62, 105
  contact with Europe, 17–19, 118–27,
      136, 138, 249–50
megara, dual, 280–2
Melz hoard, 217n.13
memory, social and religious, 254
men
  costumes, 227–31
    chieftains, 264n.6, *272*, 277, 351
  kinship systems and male solidarity,
      238
  roles, 85, 145
  woodworking chisels diagnostic for
      chieftains, 58
Menelaus, 102, 170
merchants, 77, 106
Meskell, L., 350
Mesopotamia
  chronology
    Agade period (2340–2159 BC), 63
    Akkad and Ur dynasties (2300–
        2000 BC), 63
    Early Dynastic periods (2900–
        2350 BC), 62–3, 108
    Kassite period (1595–1155 BC), 67
    Old Babylonian period (2004–
        1595 BC), 63
    Uruk period (3500–3200 BC), 65
  leadership, theocratic, 62–8

message, *30*, 29–30
metal
    production, 120, 125, 134
    as a trade item, 39, 77, 108–12, 186
metallurgist's burial, 141
metallurgy
    in Balkan-Carpathian region, 109
    Circum-Pontic Metallurgical System,
        173
    composition of alloys, 99, 109, 110,
        124, 133, *136*
    expansion of bronze technology, 41,
        58, 123, 132–8, 140–1
    research in, 173
    smelting, *175*
metalwork, 19
    Hajdúsámson group, 161
    in Sintashta culture, 174
methodology
    analytical units, 7
    archaeological record, contexts and
        categories, *34*, 33–8
    C14 dates, 17n.7, 116–17
    correspondence (interpretative
        method), 21–2, 152–3, 154, 157
    rules for symbolic structures, 21
    traditional research strategies, 34–5
    typologies, 19n.9
    see also cosmological categories;
        exchange categories; theoretical
        framework
Middle Helladic pottery, 207
Miletus site, Anatolia, 101
military organisation, 224, 224n.15
military technology, horse and chariot
        package, 79–81, 180–1, 184
mining, 133–6, 138, 173
    copper production, *110*
Minoan Crete
    cosmology, 359
    frescoes, 71, 84, 98, 101
    hair styles, *153*
    iconography, 200
    leadership, *85*
        power tradition, *97*
        theocratic, 82, 83–7
    Linear A, 83

Minoan figures on Egyptian tombs,
        100
    religion, 253
    rhyta, *89*
    settlements in Asia Minor, 101
    ships, *103*
    state formation, 28
    swords, 215
    symbolic transmissions via elite
        material culture, 142, 154–8,
        167–70
        lily and ivy flowers, *144*, *147*, 142–50
    tin content in bronze, *124*
    trade networks, 98, 128
Minoan language, 13n.5
Minoan thalassocracy, 96–9
Mitanni kingdom, 72, 80
    texts, 180
mobility in prestate societies, 32–3
models
    distance-parity, 7
    economic and political implications
        of commodity production, *113*
    exchange of prestige goods,
        horizontal and vertical, *36*
    of interaction, 7, *38*, *49*, *51*
    of material culture, *30*
    of symbolic transmissions via elite
        material culture, *14*
    of tradition and transformation, *370*
monkeys, as symbols of Priestess
        Queens, 86
Monkodonja, Istria, 162, *166*
monotheism, 73
Montafon, 133
Montelius, O., *Die älteren Kulturperioden
        im Orient und in Europa*, 2
Montelius burial 2, 156
Montelius typology, 18
Moore, H., 369
Morgan, C., 7
Morgan, L., 98
Morris, I., 24, 241
Muhly, J. D., 99
Müller-Karpe, H., *Handbuch der
        Vorgeschichte*, 3
Mursili I, 66, 80

Mursili II, 291–3
Mycenae, Greece
  adoption of
    Black Sea/Carpathian material
      culture, 129
    Minoan symbols, 281
  alliances, 98
  chamber tombs, 144
  conquest migrations, 180
  cosmology, 359
  grave circles, 87, 144, 154, 156, 184
  iconography, 200
  imitations of, 162
  leadership, theocratic, 82, 87–90
  myths, 259
  networks, 98
    northern, 179–85, 235–6
  Panagia House, 144
  pottery, 105
  power tradition, *97*
  rhyta, *89*
  swords, 128, 159, 215, 235
  trade, maritime, 123, 128
  trade colonies, 126
  traders, 235
Mylonas, G. E., 185
myths
  Achilles and Patroclus, 238
  archaeological confirmation of, 329
  as a cosmological category, 252–3,
    254
  Cuchulainn and Ferdia, 238
  Divine Twins' birth, 329–30
  of elites' origins, *46*
  Gilgamesh epic, 43, 316
  Greek, 44, 95, 259
  Inanna and Dumuzi story, 44
  of journeys, 43, 305–8
  Mesopotamian, 44
  Mycenaean, 259
  transfer of, 58–60
  of transformation, 263
  in written texts, 323
  see also sagas; tales

Naram-Sin, 63, 331–3
  victory stele, *64, 332*

Nässtrom, B.-M., 297
nature
  cosmological order and, 355–6
  imagery, 345
Near Eastern trade networks, *91*, 90–6,
    108
Nebra, Germany, bronze disc, 2
neck rings, 309
Nefertiti, 73
negotiation, 10n.4
Neolithic of Europe, 25, 30
Nesa, 78, 91–3
Nestor, 57–60, 170
Netherworld, hoards linked to, 356
Niemeier, W.-D., 98, 101
night, 341
Nilsson, M., 23, 251, 259
Ninurtha, 44
Nitrianski Hradok-Zamecek site,
    Slovakia, *129*, 162
Nizná Mysla burial, 133n.3, *134*
Nordic Bronze Age culture
  elite culture, 200
  figurines, 308–16
  hairstyles, *153*
  identity, 250
  interaction and trade, 71
  Montelius periods, 186, 189–90, 197,
    271
  origins of, 41, 186–9
  religion, 55, 294–6
  ritual axes, 194, 200, *266*
  see also Kivik, Scania
Nordic Iron Age culture, 297n.13
Nordic tales, 23, 321–4
Noua Culture, 127

object traditions, 254
Odysseus, 40, 57, 61n.2, 85, 227, 247,
    358
Odyssey (Homer), 23, 170, 245
Ohlmarks, Å., 251
Ølby woman's burial, 298
Old Assyrian period (2000–1800 BC)
  Anitta text, 78
  leadership, theocratic, 90
  trade networks, *92*

Old Babylonian period (2004–1595 BC), 63
Olmsted, G., 258, 259, 262, 263, 265
Olympic Games, 229, 366
omega symbols, 193, 197
openness/closure, 38, *38*
Oppeby rock art, *169*, 168–70, 335, *336*
oral traditions, 22–4, 228, 229n.18, 254–7, 352
  abstraction in, 269
  categories of, 268
  relationship to material culture, *257*
The Organisation of the Hittite Military (Beal), 222
origins, 39, *54*
  cosmological, 40, 45–7, 316–19, 360
Ørskovhede sword, 19n.9
Osiris, 70
Östergötland, Sweden, 335, 337, 355; *see also* Bohuslän rock art; Himmelstalund rock art
otherness, 2, 39, 47
  of elites, 45, 170
Ottar, 238–40
Ottomani culture, 125; *see also* Nizná Mysla burial
ox horns, 330, *330*

Panagia House, 144
Panama chiefdoms, 54
panku, 80
Panofsky, E., 186n.9
pantheons, *see under* gods/goddesses
partnerships, *see* alliances
pastoral economy, 172, 172n.6
patrilineal societies, 237
Patroclus, 240, 247
Pauketat, T., 45
Pazyryk mound, 286
peasant societies, immobility and, 32–3
Peer Polity Interaction, 15, 19, 27–8, 48
pendants, *95*, *147*, *151*, *154*
Penelope, 57
Penglase, C., 43–4
Penner, S., 181, 182
peripheries, *see* centres

Persephone, 260
personal items, *34*, 35, 136, *147*, *205*
Pesinara find, 128
phallic cultures, 350
phallus, raised arm gesture and, *340*
PIE (Proto-Indo-European) pantheon, 258–9, 265, 364n.2
  realms, 259–63, 341, 358
  shape shifting, 263, 264
  see also Twins, Divine
pigs, 172
pins
  Schleifennadeln, *119*, 118–19
  similarities among, *95*
  toggle pins, 136
  wheel-headed pins, 154, *155*, 234
Pirinkir, 288
Pirwa, 286
Pithana, 78
Platon, N., 84
plunder of cemeteries, 246
Pobedim site, Slovakia, 162
Poland, Scheren figurines, *274*, 314
political territories, pottery styles marking, 125
polities, 361
Polydeukes, 297
polytheism, 73, 86
pony-tails as female symbols, 342, 343, 344
population movements, 13n.5, 120, 363
pottery, 125, 161n.4
  Lipari Islands, 169
  Middle Helladic, 207
  Mycenaean, 105
power
  alliances and, 37, 74, 80
  chieftains' reproduction of, 17
  club of the great powers, 67, 105
  cosmological nature of, 46–7, 48, *54*, 55–7, 367
  elites' control of, 323
  matrilineal succession to, 72
  Minoan/Mycenaean tradition, *97*
  nature of, 8–10
  via journeys, 17, 44, 270

prestate societies, *see* societies, traditional
prestige goods, 35–7, 112, *121*, 139, 208, 235
  horizontal and vertical exchange models, *36*
Price, B., 248
priests/priestesses, 59
  chieftain priests, 303–8
  Priest King, 86
  Priestess Queen, 86
  sodality of, 256
Primas, M., 135
Prince of the Lilies, *143*, 334
Prince with the Feather Crown, 142–4
privatisation, 106
processual and postprocessual archaeology, 4, 5–6, 16, 252
Prosymna, 145
proto-currency, 136
Proto-Indo-European (PIE) pantheon, 258–9, 265, 364n.2
  realms, 259–63, 341, 358
  shape shifting, 263, 264
  see also twins, divine
Puhvel, J., 328
Pylos, palace of, *164*, 281, *282*

queens
  becoming divine, 284
  correspondence between, 63
  Priestess Queen, 86
  as the sun-goddess of Arinna, 293
Quillfeldt, I. von, 233

radiocarbon dates, 17n.7, 116–17
raised arm gesture, *76*, 343
  phallus and, *340*
Ramesses I, *322*
Ramesses II, 73
Randsborg, K., 189, 224
rapiers, 127, *209*, 215, 231, 232
razor, tweezers and, 228
Re/Ra, 69, 70
regalia, royal, 85, 126
  mace, scimitar and bow, 68

measuring rod and coiled rope, 65
Old Kingdom (Egypt), 70
staffs, 85
Rehak, P., 281
religion
  analysis and interpretation of, 251–3
  archaeological study of, 251–3
  Hittite, 96, 253, 282–8
    sun cults, 288–94
  Indo-European, 258–9
  Minoan Crete, 253
  Nordic
    Bronze Age, 55, 294–6
    Iron Age, 297n.13
  rituals and, 334–5, 352–6
  role of animals, 320–4
  world religions, 366–7
  see also cosmological categories; cosmologies
religious behaviour, 349–51
religious institutions, 256, 259, 270
religious specialists, 255–6, 268, 352
religious themes, shared, 342–4, 346–9
  death and regeneration, 338–42
  nature imagery, 345
  sacred marriage, 65, 344–5
Renfrew, C., 5, 13n.5, 15, 17, 19, 27–8, 361
Renfrew School, 18–19
rhyta, *89*
Rice, M., 72
  Egypt's Legacy, 75
Rig-Veda, 256, 264, 364, 365
ring ingots, 113, *114*, *115*, 118–19, 122
Rittershofer, K.-F., 204
ritual behaviour, 349–51
ritual depositions, *see* hoards
ritual paraphernalia, 255
  cups, *89*, 154–8, 303
  figurines, 150, 353
  sun cult, 306
  see also axes, ritual
ritual/political leaders and war leaders, 218, 225, 232, 255–6, 267, 355
ritual sites, 357
rituals

animal sacrifices, *176*, 177, 245
  weapons and, 231–6
ceremonies, drinking, 281,
    282
as a cosmological category, 252–3
domestic, 158–67
fertility, 145, 150
in front of rock art, 336n.5
gestures, 150, *151*
  raised arms, *76*, *340*, 343
horse sacrifice/copulation, 324–8
hunting, 321, 346–9
initiation, 145
marriage
  of king and sun-goddess, 293
  sacred, 65, 344–5
religion and, 334–5, 352–6
roles of women, 152
sun-disc/chariot, 305
see also hoards
rock art
  abstraction in, 269
  chronology, 313
  processions, 291
  rituals in front of, 336n.5
  see also specific locations; specific motifs
Rørby, Denmark
  paired scimitars, *266*
  sword, 207, *208*, 290n.11
Roux, G., 91
Rowlands, M., 6, 238, 254

Sagaholm, Sweden
  barrow, 196, 242, *243*
  cist-stones, *327*, 328, 329, 349
  rock art, *197*
sagas
  Celtic, 23
  Icelandic, 23, 238
  Irish, 238, 246–7, 256, 326
  see also myths; tales
Sahlins, M., 60n.1
Sailing the Wine-Dark Sea (Cline), 104
Samsu-ditana, 66
Sandagergård site, *338*
sarcophagi
  Hagia Triada, 220, *262*, 264

Sargon of Akkad, 105
Scandinavia
  leadership, theocratic, 204, 333
  monumental visual art, 334–7
  shared religious themes, 338–42
  trade networks, 125, 186
Scandinavian languages, 32
sceptres
  iron, 78
  stone, 177
Schauer, P., 218
Scheren, Poland, figurines, *274*, 314
Schleifennadeln pins, *119*, 118–19
Schnabeltasse, 156
Schumacher-Matthäus, G., 145
scimitars, 199, *272*, 290, 313
  in pairs, *266*
  as symbols of divinity, 68
Sealand Dynasty, 67
seals
  Hittite, *293*
  Minoan, 161
  with spiral band decorations, *160*
secondary products revolution, 141
security while travelling, 28
Serbia, Duplje figurines, 150, 307
Sesostris I, 70
Sesostris III, 70
settlement patterns, 125, 133, 158, 357
Sety I, 73, 96
sexuality, 350–1
Shamash, 65
Shamshi-Adad, 91
Shanks, M., *Art and the Early Greek State*,
    247
Shaushka, 291
sheep, 172
Sherratt, A., 7, 25–6, 28, 128, 139
Sherratt, S., 28, 139, 179, 257, 257n.4
shields, 220
shipbuilding, 208
ships
  on cist-stones, *190*
  double, *199*
  foreign, 238
  of night, *306*
  Nordic, 194, 207

ships (*cont.*)
  with ritual axes, *202*
  Rørby ship, 194, *208*
  similarities among, 75, *206*
  on swords, 290n.11
  symbolism of, 71, 198–9
  Thera frescos, *103*
shipwrecks
  Cape Gelidonya, 105
  Ulu Burun, 2, 102, 105, 138
    cargo, 101, 102n.8
    route, *102*
signet rings, 192, *192*, 302n.14
silver, 78, 98, 108
Simris rock art, 197, 200
Single Grave Culture, 140, 265
Sintashta Culture, 171, 171n.5, 173–9
skeletal analysis, Caucasian-Nordic
    traits, 184, 185
skirts, corded, *261*, 298, 302, 306
slavery, 106, 133
Slovakia
  Barca site, *129*, 162
  Hradisko Vesele site, 162
  Nitrianski Hradok-Zamecek site, *129*,
    162
  Pobedim site, 162
  Spissky Stvrrtok site, *129*, 162
smelting, *175*
smiths, *see* artisans
snake-goddess, *148*, 340
snakes, 340
  horned vipers, *261*, *323*, 323
Snorre Sturluson, 23
social behaviour, *see* behaviour, social
societies, traditional, 33, 48
society, ranked, 112–14, 174–9
sodalities, 236, 256
Södermanland, Sweden, 355
sons, symbolised by calves, 96
Sørensen M. L. S., 227
space, 43
  cosmological, 209
  ideological meaning of, 39–43
spearheads, inscribed, 290n.11
spears, 16
specialists

  as outsiders, *55*
  religious, 255–6, 268, 352
Sperber, L., 237
spiral ornaments/ornamentation, 149,
    194, 218n.13, 288–91, 296n.12
  band decorations, *159*
  hearths, *164*
  paired, 193
  on pottery, 158, 161n.4
  proto-spirals, 161
  as sun symbols, 303
Spissky Stvrrtok site, Slovakia, *129*,
    162
sports, 229, 366
springs, 284, 291
Sprockhofs, E., 'Frühes Griechentum
    und nordisches Bronzezeit,'
    252n.1
Srubnaya culture, 173
staffs, 85, 127
stags
  bronze, 77
  hunting, *347*, 346–7
  Kurunta's sacred animal, 286, *287*
  sun-wagon and, *287*
state societies, 48
states
  early formation of, 108
  multi-lingual and multi-ethnic, 106
  territorial, 106
statuettes, *see* figurines
status symbols, 16, 18
Stein, G. J., 7, 363
stelae
  Hammurabi's Law Code, 65, *66*
  Naram Sin's victory, *64*, 332
  Vulture, 63
steppe corridor, western, 179–85, *211*,
    212
steppe cultures, 171–9, 181–5
Stockhult hoard, 197, 273, *274*, *312*,
    312–13
strontium isotope analysis, 4n.1
Suciu de Sus culture, 161n.4
sun
  cults, 72–3, *74*, 288–94, 337
    ritual paraphernalia, 306

duality of, 295
journey
    Bronze Age cosmology of, *296*, *306*, 341, *354*
    transport animals, *309*
symbolism, *154*, *244*, 246
winged, 291, *293*, *332*
sun-disc/chariot, 297n.13
    drawn by horses, 170, 264, 288, 297, *326*
        Trundholm, 197, 295n.12, *295*, *296*, 294–6, *306*
    drawn by stags, *287*
    drawn by swans, 150, 153, *306*
    ritual, 305
sun-discs, 286, 294, *299*, 302n.14, 298–303, 343, *343*; *see also* Aten
sun-goddess, 264, 283
    of Arinna, 79, 80, 96, 283, 285
        queens as, 293
    in chariot drawn by swans, 150, 153, *306*
    Divine Twins and, 153, 297
    names of, 150, 297
    priestess of, 286, 344
    ritual marriage with king, 293
Sun Maiden, 319
sun-priestess, 298–303
Sund, Norway, burial pits, 248
Suppululiuma I, 81
swans, 44, 297, *306*
Sweden
    Balkåkra, *203*, 294
    Bohuslän rock art, 335, 336n.5, 356
        chariot motifs, 223, *223*
        Fossum, *342*, *343*, 342–3, *345*
        horned divinities, *331*
        raised arm gesture, *76*
        sun-disc pulled by horse, *326*
    Bruatorp, *279*
    Fogtdarp double axes with horns, *330*
    Gotland barrows, *244*
    Himmelstalund rock art, *169*, 170, 335, *347*, *348*, 347–8
    Kivik, Scania

    as a religious centre of learning, 199
    Kivik, Scania, burial, 49, 71, 86n.6, 157, *188*, 187–9, 267–70
        cist-stones, 187, *188*, *190*, *192*, 267, *268*, 269–70, 328
        dating, 189–93, 197, 198n.10
        grave goods, 187, 189–90
        origins, 189–93
        plan view, *338*
    Östergötland, 335, 337, 355
    Sagaholm
        barrow, 196, 242, *243*
        cist-stones, *327*, 328, 329, 349
        rock art, *197*
    Södermanland, 355
swords
    Apa type, 200, 207, 217n.13
    Bogazköy, 290n.11
    as Bronze Age weapons, 53
    chiefly, *130*
    with curved points, 288–91
    distribution patterns, *216*, 231–2
    foreign, 46
    Hajdúsámson type, 200
    hilts
        flanged, *130*, 216, 234
        octagonal, 231, *233*, 233–5
        solid, *209*, 214, 218, *233*, 275
    Hungarian type, *207*
    Marais de Nantes, 138
    Minoan type A, 215
    Mycenaean, 128, 159, 215, 235
    Ørskovhede, 19n.9
    resharpened, 218, *219*
    Rørby, Denmark, 207, 208, 290n.11
Symbolgut der Urnenfelderzeit (Kossack), 252n.1
symbolic entrainment, 19
symbolic permutation, 29
symbolic structures, rules for, 21
symbolism of headgear
    caps (ruler), 227, 265, *272*, 351
    feather crowns (divine), 142, 142n.1, *143*
    horned crowns or helmets (divine), 68, 101, 247, 323, *332*, 333

symbolism of headgear (*cont.*)
   pointed hat (divine), 101, *190*, 281,
      291, 312–13, 314–16
symbols
   of chariots, *154*
   contextualised meanings, 29
   cupmarks for females, 328, 342
   of divinity, 348
      bows, 68
      maces, 68
      naked breasts, *148*, 150, *151*
      scimitars, 68
      wheel-cross, 195, 298–302,
         346
      wings, 68, *293*, *332*
      see also symbolism of headgear
   Minoan adopted by Mycenaeans, 281
   style and form, 11–13
Symbols in Action (Hodder), 254, 361
Szeghalom hoard, 218n.13

Tågaborg hoard, 296n.12
   bronze horse, *197*
tales
   heroic, 61, 228–31, 254
   Nordic, 23, 321–4
   see also myths; sagas
Tanum project, 336n.5
Tape, Hungary, cemetery, 127
Taru, 285, 286
Tawananna, 286
Telemachus, 102
Tel Kabri, Israel, frescos, 98
tell cultures, *see* Carpathian tell cultures
terminology, redefinition of, 7, 13
Terramare culture, 127, 216n.12
Teshub, 96
textiles, 77, 108, 139
texts
   archaeological record's
      correspondence with, 139
   as evidence, 20–4
      clay tablets, 283
      contemporary vs.
         non-contemporary, 21
   historical origins, *23*
   Hittite military texts, 328n.3

horses mentioned in, 322n.1
Mitanni kingdom, 180
of myths, 323
Old Assyrian Anitta text, 78
relationship to material culture,
   257
as secondary, 255
see also writing systems
theocratic leadership, *see* leadership,
   theocratic
theoretical framework, 4, 5–8, 24
   culture-historical approach, 4, 24
   intercontextual archaeology, 4–5, *12*,
      10–15, 16, 24, 25–30, 368
   interpretative strategies, 30, 368–72
   limitations of, 4–8
   of processual and postprocessual
      archaeology, 4, 5–6, 16, 252
   see also methodology; Renfrew School
Thera eruption (1628 BC), 117, 161
Thera frescos, *103*, *144*, 145, 147, 150,
   152
tholos burials, *180*, *236*
thrones, 70
   Balkåkra, Sweden, *203*, 200–4
   Hasfalva, Hungary, 200, *203*
   of iron, 78–9
Timber Grave Culture, 173
tin, 78, 90, 108, 114, *115*, 122
   in bronze production, 120, 123, *124*,
      136
   sources, 100, 110
   in Ulu Burun shipwreck, 101
   value of, 95
Tinghøj, Denmark, barrow, 312
Tiryns signet ring, *192*
Tobøl woman's burial, 220, 298, *301*
toggle pins, 136
Traction Complex, *26*
trade
   analysis and interpretation of, 17,
      33–9, 364
   control of, 67
   directional nature of, 139
   exchange systems, 48–51
   model of interactions, 7, *51*
   secondary products revolution, 141

trade centres, 158
trade colonies, 126, 129
trade goods, 35–8
  archaeological record and, *34*, 93
trade networks/routes
  Anatolian, 77, 91–3, 181–5
  Black Sea, 125
  Carpathian, *129*, 179–85
  development of, 130–2, 138–40, 158,
    204–9
  east Mediterranean, 90, *102*, 96–105,
    123, 128
  Egyptian, 70
  maritime, 267
  Minoan Crete, 98, 128
  Mycenaean, 98, 179–85, 235–6
  Near Eastern, *91*, 90–6, 108
  Old Assyrian, *92*
  open, 48
  population movements along, 120
  Scandinavian, 125, 186
  shift in, 128
  Sintashta culture, 177
  Tumulus Culture, 127–8, 139, 212
  western, 114
  see also interaction zones
traders
  Mycenaean, 235
  travel by, 235
transformation, 27–8, 53
  model of, *30*
  tradition and, model of, *370*
transmission
  of institutions, 13–15, 249–50, 364
  model of, *30*
  of social and religious ideas, 27–8, 153
  see also transmissions, symbolic
transmissions, symbolic
  via elite material culture, 142, 154–8,
    167–70, 254, 255
    domestic rituals, 158–67
    female costumes, 145, 150–4, 227
    lily and ivy flowers, *144*, *147*, 142–50
    model of, *14*
    ritual cups, *89*, 154–8
Trans-Urals, 171–9
Trassem hoard, 218n.13

travel, 17, 43, 364
  chiefly alliances and, 204–9, *210*, 234
  by chieftains, 39–40, 371
  congruence between time and space
    and, *54*
  linked to value systems, 53
  by traders, 235
  by warriors and artisans, 232, 235
  see also distance
Trebatice wall decorations, *163*
tree
  of life, 245, 246
  sacred, 340
Treibstacheln, 220n.14
tribute, 227
Trobriand Islanders, 40
Troy, 100, 116
Trundholm, Denmark, sun-disc/chariot,
  197, 295n.12, *295*, *296*, 294–6,
  306
Tudhaliya I, 80
Tudhaliya II, 290n.11
Tudhaliya IV, 101, 271, 324
Tufalau hoard, 152
tumulus burials, 177, *180*, 242, *243*
Tumulus Culture, 125, 134, 187, *362*
  alliances supported by marriage,
    232
  cosmology, 359
  polities, 361
  trade networks, 127–8, 139, 212
  wheel-headed pins, 154
Tushratta, 73
Tutankhamen, 73, 81
Tuthmosis III, 72, 80
Tuthmosis IV, 72, 322n.1
tutuli, *274*
tweezers, razor and, 228
twins
  brothers, *306*
  Divine Twins, 22, 258–63, 264–7, 319
    attributes of, *318*
    birth myth, 329–30
    as bulls, 263
    ritual dress, 274–7
    sun-goddess and, 153, 297
    symbolism of, 190, 269–70

twins (*cont.*)
    gods/goddesses, riding in chariots,
        262, 281
    rulers, *276*, *278*, 280–2, 303, 305

Ugarit figurines, 315
Ulu Burun shipwreck, 2, 102, 105, 138
    cargo, 101, 102n.8
    route, *102*
Ulysses, *see* Odysseus
Unetice Culture, 113, *115*, 120, 138, 140,
        302
universe, bronze disc of, 266
Upton Lowell barrow, *121*
Ur dynasties, 63
Urals, 173, 179–85
Urnfield Culture, 117, 134, 153, *154*, 194,
        237
    cosmology, 359
Uruk
    state system, 7, 105
Uruk Culture, 363

value systems, 13–14, 53, 187, 225
    warrior ethos, 88, 228, 246–7
Vandkilde, H., 213n.11, 280
Vanuata in Oceania, 22
Vapheio burial, 330
Vatya Culture, 125, 133n.3
Vedic traditions, 255, 326, 329–30
vehicles, wheeled, 172; *see also* chariots
Venus, 68
Veterow Culture, 125, 133
Viby ritual axes, *341*
Viksø, Denmark, horned helmets, *332*,
        333
violence
    death by, 133
    ritual, 133n.3
Vitlycke rock art, *346*
Vulture stele, 63

Wales, 134
wall decorations, *163*
wanax institution, 88, 280–2
Wanscher, O., 304
Ward, D., 264, 265

warfare, 229, 247–8
    social organisation of, 227
Warren, P. M., 118
warrior aristocracies, 171, 173, 177–9,
        212
    appearance, 227–31
    archaeological evidence of, 159,
        213–25
    institution of, 80, 277–80
    kinship systems, 236–40
    social and cultural context, 225–7
    see also chiefdoms
warrior ethos, 88, 228, 246–7
warriors
    burials, 151, *215*, 218, 231–6, 240–6
    lifestyle, 246–9
    professional, 213, 232, 234
    on rock art, *345*
    traditional, 218
    travel and, 232, 235, 364
wavy band decoration, *182*, *183*, 184
weapons, 53, 125, 218, 231–6; *see also*
        specific weapons
weapons complexes, 213
    early phase (18th and 17th c. BC),
        213
    late phase (16th and 15th c. BC),
        213–20
weather-god, 283
    bull as the sacred animal of, *285*,
        285–6
Weingarten, J., 97
Wessex Culture, *121*, 122, 125, 127,
        138
    burials, 120
    prestige goods, *121*
    Scandinavia and, 157
wheel-crosses, 168, 195, *244*, 298–302,
        346
wheel figures, *196*
wheel-headed pins, 154, *155*, 234
wheels
    bronze, 220, *222*
    spoked, 220
    wooden, 63
whips, *183*
White Cow goddess, 260

Wietenberg culture, 125
Winghart, S., 220
wings, as symbols of divinity, 68, *293*, *332*
Winkler, H., 79
Wismar lur, 195, *196*
women
    costumes, 145, 150–4, 227, *239*, 351
      Egtved woman, *299*
    deities, 84–6
    foreign, 234
    hair styles, 152, 351
    picking lilies, *144*
    as rulers, 72
    social control of, 237
    status and functions, 145, 152
    symbols, 328, 342, 343, 344
woodworking, 59, *59*
world religions, 366–7
world systems, 6, 316
Wright, J., 88
writing systems, 167–70
    cuneiform signs, 73

Egyptian hieroglyphs, 75, *76*
Hittite hieroglyphs, 168, *168*, 343
Linear A, 83, 100, 168, 170, 208
Linear B, 83, 168
Lipari Islands script, *167*
signs as esoteric knowledge, 168, 170
transmission of alphabets, 193
use of early signs, 168
see also languages; texts

Yamna Culture, 109, 140, 172
Yazilikaya rock art, 96, 288, 291, *292*, 324, 336–7

Zafer Papoura burial, 302n.14
Zajta, 217n.13
Zakros palace, Crete, 348
Zannanza, 81
Zdanovich, G. B., 171, 174
Zeus, 297, 330
Zimri-Lim, 95
Zwelebil, M., 32